Al-Maqrīzī's *al-Ḫabar ʿan al-bašar*

Volume v, Section 4

Bibliotheca Maqriziana

OPERA MAIORA

Edited by

Frédéric Bauden (*Université de Liège*)

VOLUME 9

The titles published in this series are listed at *brill.com/bima*

Al-Maqrīzī's
al-Ḫabar ʿan al-bašar

Volume V, Section 4:
Persia and Its Kings, Part II

Edited and translated by

Jaakko Hämeen-Anttila

With assistance from

Marwa Mouazen

TUTA SUB AEGIDE PALLAS · 1683 ·

BRILL

LEIDEN | BOSTON

Library of Congress Cataloging-in-Publication Data

Names: Maqrīzī, Aḥmad ibn ʿAlī, 1364-1442, author. | Hämeen-Anttila, Jaakko
Khabar ʻan al-bashar fī ansāb al-ʻArab wa-nasab Sayyid al-Bashar. Selections. |
Hämeen-Anttila, Jaakko, editor, translator.
Title: Al-Maqrīzī's al-Ḫabar ʻan al-bašar Vol. V, section 4: Persia and its kings, part II
/ edited and translated by Jaakko Hämeen-Anttila.
Other titles: Khabar ʻan al-bashar fī ansāb al-ʻArab wa-nasab Sayyid al-Bashar.
Selections. English
Description: Leiden : Boston : Brill, [2022] | Series: Bibliotheca maqriziana, 2211-
6737 ; 9 | Includes bibliographical references and index. | In English and
Arabic.
Identifiers: LCCN 2022045584 (print) | LCCN 2022045585 (ebook) | ISBN
9789004528758 (hardback) | ISBN 9789004528765 (ebook)
Subjects: LCSH: Sassanids–Early works to 1800. | Iran–History–To 640. | Iran–
History–640-1256. | Arabs–Genealogy–Early works to 1800. |
Iranians–Genealogy–Early works to 1800.
Classification: LCC CS1549.5 .M368213 2022 (print) | LCC CS1549.5 (ebook) | DDC
202/.18–dc23/eng/20220921
LC record available at https://lccn.loc.gov/2022045584
LC ebook record available at https://lccn.loc.gov/2022045585

Typeface for the Latin, Greek, and Cyrillic scripts: "Brill". See and download: brill.com/brill-typeface.

ISSN 2211-6737
ISBN 978-90-04-52875-8 (hardback)
ISBN 978-90-04-52876-5 (e-book)

This book is printed on acid-free paper and produced in a sustainable manner.

Contents

Preface VII
List of Plates IX
Abbreviations X

Introduction 1
1 al-Maqrīzī and the *Ḫabar* 1
2 Sources 1
3 Quoting 11
4 Mistakes 12
5 Description of the Manuscripts 16
6 The Copying of Manuscript A-2926/5 (MS T) 16
7 Sasanian Kings and Queens according to al-Maqrīzī 18
8 Translation and Transliteration of Names 20

Plates 23

Abbreviations and Symbols 31

Critical Edition and Translation of al-Maqrīzī's* al-Ḫabar ʿan al-bašar*, Vol. V, Section 4: Persia and Its Kings, Part II

The Fourth Class of Persian Kings, the Sasanians 35

Chapter concerning the Religion and Rites of the Persians and the Traces of Their Empire and the Advantages of Their Government 384

Bibliography 391
List of Quoted Manuscripts 399
Index of Qurʾānic Verses 400
Index of Verses 401
Index of Names (People and Places) 402
Index of Quoted Titles in *al-Ḫabar ʿan al-bašar* 411
Index of Sources in *al-Ḫabar ʿan al-bašar* 412
Index of Glosses 413
Index of Technical Terms 414

Preface

This volume continues and completes my edition and translation of the Persian section of al-Maqrīzī's *Kitāb al-Ḫabar ʿan al-bašar*, the first part of which (Volume V, Section 4: Persia and Its Kings, Part 1) was published in 2018.

The second part of volume V, section 4 of al-Maqrīzī's *Ḫabar* relates the history of the Sasanian dynasty of Persia. It depends heavily on al-Ṭabarī's *Taʾrīḫ*, partly directly, but more importantly through Miskawayh's *Taǧārib*, a work that is itself largely, in this section, based on al-Ṭabarī. Hence, I have been in the luxurious situation of building on the work of two outstanding predecessors, Theodor Nöldeke and C.E. Bosworth. Nöldeke published his German translation of this section of al-Ṭabarī's *Taʾrīḫ* under the title *Geschichte der Perser und Araber zur Zeit der Sasaniden* in 1879. The book is still eminently useful, and it is telling that it was considered important enough to be reprinted in 1973, almost a century after its first publication.

Bosworth's learned English translation appeared in 1999, titled *The Sāsānids, the Byzantines, the Lakhmids, and Yemen*, as the fifth volume of the *Bibliotheca Persica* translation of *The History of al-Ṭabarī*. Both translations are remarkably accurate and contain ample notes and commentaries, which are extremely helpful in understanding al-Ṭabarī. As especially Bosworth's work is easily available, I have seen no reason to duplicate all his notes, partly already overlapping with those of Nöldeke.

Miskawayh's work, on the contrary, has not, to my knowledge, been translated into any Western language, but several long excerpts of its Sasanian section, or of texts parallel to it and quoted by al-Maqrīzī, have been translated into French by Mario Grignaschi in his long article "Quelques spécimens de la littérature sassanide conservés dans les bibliothèques d'Istanbul," *Journal Asiatique* 1966: 1–142. Grignaschi's notes are extremely useful, although his translations are not always completely satisfactory.

The third major source of al-Maqrīzī for this volume, is Ḥamzah al-Iṣfahānī's *Taʾrīḫ*, which is now partially translated by Robert G. Hoyland in his *The 'History of the Kings of the Persians' in Three Arabic Chronicles. The Transmission of the Iranian Past from Late Antiquity to Early Islam* (2018), which has also been helpful. J.M.E. Gottwaldt's old Latin translation *Hamzae Ispahanensis annalium libri X* (1848) is still useful for other parts of Ḥamzah's book, not included by Hoyland in his translation, but its Sasanian part is now superseded by Hoyland's book.

In the Introduction, some short passages, such as the description of the manuscripts have been here reprinted from the first part of this section with few changes, to allow for independent use of this volume. The same goes for a small number of footnotes to the translation, e.g., those that identify characters already identified in the first volume.

As with the first part of this work, my warmest thanks go to Dr Frédéric Bauden, Professor of Arabic and Islamic Studies at the University of Liège and the editor-in-chief of the series *Bibliotheca Maqriziana*, who invited me to edit this part of the *Ḫabar*, provided me with copies of the relevant parts of the manuscripts, and helped in preparing the final manuscript for print. He also kindly provided me with copies of some of his relevant articles, both published and unpublished. My dear colleague, Marwa Mouazen (Edinburgh), kindly went with me through some difficult passages and helped me to prepare the Arabic text for print.

Jaakko Hämeen-Anttila
Edinburgh, 31 March 2022

Plates

1 Istanbul/ Süleymaniye Kütüphanesi, MS Ayasofya 3365, p. 437 25
2 Istanbul/ Süleymaniye Kütüphanesi, MS Ayasofya 3365, p. 527 26
3 Istanbul/ Topkapı Sarayı Müzesi Kütüphanesi, MS A 2926/5, fol. 70a 27
4 Istanbul/ Topkapı Sarayı Müzesi Kütüphanesi, MS A 2926/5, fol. 124b 28
5 Algiers/ Bibliothèque nationale, MS 1589, fol. 92b 29
6 Algiers/ Bibliothèque nationale, MS 1589, fol. 145a 30

Abbreviations

EI[2]	*The Encyclopaedia of Islam. New Edition*, ed. C.E. Bosworth et al. (Leiden: Brill, 1960–2007), 11 vols.
EI[3]	*The Encyclopaedia of Islam—Three*, ed. Kate Fleet et al. (Leiden: Brill, 2007 ff.).
EIr	*Encyclopaedia Iranica*. Online at http://www.iranicaonline.org.
GAL	Carl Brockelmann, *Geschichte der arabischen Literatur* (Leiden: Brill, 1936–1944), 2 vols. and 3 supplementary vols.
GAS	Fuat Sezgin, *Geschichte des arabischen Schrifttums* (Leiden: Brill, 1967–1984), 9 vols.
JA	*Journal Asiatique*.
JAOS	*Journal of the American Oriental Society*.
JRAS	*Journal of the Royal Asiatic Society*.
JSAI	*Jerusalem Studies in Arabic and Islam*.

Introduction

1 al-Maqrīzī and the *Ḫabar*

The Egyptian historian Taqī al-Dīn Aḥmad b. ʿAlī al-Maqrīzī (766–845/1364–1442) wrote his last work, *al-Ḫabar ʿan al-bašar*, towards the end of his life to complete his historiographical *oeuvre* by adding to it this history of the world in pre-Islamic times.[1] The six-volume[2] work was begun in 836/1433 and the third volume was completed in 844/1441.[3] It seems, though, that before the completion of the third volume, al-Maqrīzī had collected materials for the remaining parts, too, and may partly have written them before finalising the third volume.

The whole text will be edited in parts in the *Bibliotheca Maqriziana*.[4] This volume covers the history of the Sāsānian kings. The earlier history of pre-Islamic Iran from the Creation to and including the Ašġānians has been published in 2018.[5]

2 Sources

For this part of the *Ḫabar*, al-Maqrīzī has used three main sources, as well as half a dozen additional ones. When quoting them, al-Maqrīzī only names his source occasionally, mostly just appropriating the text without mentioning its provenance. He also brings together information from several sources without indicating these. In this second part, Miskawayh is mentioned, as Ibn Miskawayh, 13 times (§§ 23, 91, 102, 104, 119, 120, 161, 250, 254, 255, 257, 258, 260), al-Ṭabarī 8 times (§§ 12, 61, 65, 91, 102, 104, 120, 295), and Ḥamzah 9 times (§§ 4, 18, 67, 101, 102, 103, 120, 257, 259). Al-Hamdānī (§§ 21, 22), al-Āmidī (§ 60), al-Marzubānī (§ 60), al-Suhaylī (§§ 60, 62, 63), Ibn Hišām/Ibn

1 For a detailed discussion of al-Maqrīzī and the *Ḫabar*, see Bauden (2014) and (forthcoming).
2 Five of the volumes are extant as al-Maqrīzī's holographs, see Bauden (forthcoming).
3 Bauden (2014): 197.
4 After the plan of editing this work in the *Biblioteca Maqriziana* had been conceived by Frédéric Bauden and the editorial work for this and the preceding volume had begun, a very deficient edition by Ḫālid Aḥmad al-Mullā l-Suwaydī and ʿĀrif ʿAbd al-Ġanī (2013) appeared. The edition leaves much to be desired, especially in its sixth volume, which, in addition to being ridden with other mistakes, leaves blank a large number of Persian and other names which the editors were unable to read. Volume 6, pages 130–229, of their edition covers the same ground as the present volume.
5 Hämeen-Anttila (2018a).

 | DOI:10.1163/9789004528765_002

Isḥāq (§§62, 63, 64), Orosius (§29), and Abū Nuʿaym (§§235, 236, 237) are each named a few times. In addition, there are the indirect sources, like Hišām b. Muḥammad al-Kalbī (§§60, 61, 78, 103), mainly quoted through al-Ṭabarī. Not all the used sources, however, have been indicated. Thus, Ibn al-Nadīm's *Fihrist* is the source for much of the information on Mani (§§72–77), but it is nowhere indicated as a source,[6] and the same goes for al-Bīrūnī's *Āṯār*, which provides the cognomens of the kings, and Ibn al-Aṯīr, to whose *Kāmil* al-Maqrīzī recurrently comes back without acknowledgement. It is hard to see why Ibn al-Nadīm and Ibn al-Aṯīr should go unacknowledged. Al-Bīrūnī only provides cognomens for kings, each excerpt being very brief, which may explain why he is never mentioned by name. Al-Iṣfahānī's *Kitāb al-Aġānī* may also have provided some of the verse quotations, but neither the author nor the title is ever cited.[7]

Book titles are rarely given. Even though al-Ṭabarī is mentioned eight times, his book has not been mentioned by title either in this volume or its first part.[8] The other two main sources are mentioned by the title, but each only once. Miskawayh's *Taǧārib* is mentioned in §119, and Ḥamzah's *Kitāb Aḫbār al-Furs* in §4. Orosius' Arabic translation, *Taʾrīḫ al-Rūm*, is only mentioned in §92. The book is of marginal importance in this part, whereas in the first part of al-Maqrīzī, *Ḫabar/Persia*, it was one of the main sources, there mostly quoted as *Kitāb Hurūšiyūš*.[9] The fourth title quoted as an immediate source, is al-Hamdānī's *Iklīl* (§21). In addition, al-Maqrīzī uses extensively two purportedly Middle Persian books in their Arabic translation through Miskawayh's *Taǧārib*. In §§23, 142, and 191, he mentions *ʿAhd Ardašīr*, but in a form that is not exactly or necessarily the title of the book, and in §161, he mentions *Sīrat Anūširwān wa-siyāsatuhu*. Other book titles are not mentioned in this part.

When quoting contradictory opinions, al-Maqrīzī indicates his sources more often. Thus, while he is usually very vague as to whether he is copying al-Ṭabarī, Miskawayh, or Ḥamzah, in §§119–120, he explicitly mentions Miskawayh and Ḥamzah, obviously because the two disagree as to the fate of Bahrām Gūr's

6 Ibn al-Nadīm's *Fihrist* is a somewhat surprising source, but al-Maqrīzī is known to have used it also for some of his other works, see Bauden (2014): 177.

7 For al-Maqrīzī's extensive use of the *Aġānī* in another section, see Webb (2019): 127. Even there, the author is only mentioned twice (§§2.2.1 and 2.2.4) and the title once (§2.2.4).

8 Hämeen-Anttila (2018a).

9 Al-Maqrīzī seems to write the name of Orosius always without vowels. Penelas (2021): 14 draws attention to the vocalisation Harūšiyūš in the unique manuscript of the text, which is also the one al-Maqrīzī was using, so al-Maqrīzī would probably have read it with an A in the first syllable.

body. Likewise, he mentions all three in § 102, which gives two opposite opinions concerning Bahrām b. Sābūr, al-Ṭabarī and Miskawayh heaping laud on him, Ḥamzah heavily criticising him. Something similar happens in § 104 (continued in § 105), where again al-Ṭabarī and Miskawayh are explicitly mentioned in a passage which describes Yazdağird the Sinner in very negative terms. Mentioning both authors seems to act as a kind of certificate for information that is very harsh on the king.

Miskawayh's (d. 421/1030) *Taǧārib al-umam*,[10] is al-Maqrīzī's main source for this part, providing him with more material than all his other sources together. Towards the end of the first part of the Persian section,[11] al-Maqrīzī had already started using this book more extensively, whereas earlier it had only been of marginal importance to him.[12] In the present section, Miskawayh seems to be throughout the main source, when he has sufficient material. For some reason, Miskawayh is extremely succinct in some parts of Sasanian history. Thus, he more or less ignores the events of Ardašīr b. Bābak's reign, deciding instead to include the complete text of his *Testament*.[13] This is why al-Maqrīzī uses Miskawayh only in §§ 11 and 23–54 (the *Testament*), but otherwise records Ardašīr's history on the basis of other sources. Similar gaps in the use of Miskawayh, which can be explained by the lack or paucity of material in the *Taǧārib*, occur in §§ 55–82, 97–103, and 229–241. The end of this section, §§ 296–300, also discusses topics not covered by Miskawayh. In §§ 269–282, al-Maqrīzī abbreviates Miskawayh radically, whereas elsewhere his abbreviations tend to be limited.

Within the material taken from Miskawayh, three larger excerpts are worth special attention. Miskawayh has inserted two complete texts into his *Taǧārib*. *ʿAhd Ardašīr* [The Testament of Ardašīr] (§§ 23–54) purports to be the Arabic translation of the political testament of the first Sasanian ruler, Ardašīr b. Bābak (r. 224–240), a claim that is not supported by modern scholars. There is, however, some uncertainty as to the text's real provenance. It is rather generally considered to be an Arabic translation of a late Sasanian Middle Persian text.[14]

10 Both the editions that I have had at my disposal, by Emāmī and Ḥasan, are unsatisfactory. Throughout, I have given references to Ḥasan's edition and Caetani's facsimile edition of the manuscript al-Maqrīzī was himself using.

11 Hämeen-Anttila (2018a).

12 Cf. Hämeen-Anttila (2018a): 10.

13 Miskawayh, *Taǧārib*, 1:97–107.

14 Grignaschi (1966): 3, Macuch (2009): 181. Note, however, that the translation strategy of the time differs from modern ideals of translation, and very often we should speak of paraphrases rather than translations, see Hämeen-Anttila (2018b): 51–58. Grignaschi (1966):

However, the matter has never been properly studied, and it is also possible that *ʿAhd Ardašīr* is an Arabic composition based on scattered Middle Persian materials, as well as the author's general knowledge of the Sasanian political system, at least on an idealistic level—we should not hasten to assume that the Sasanian Empire was governed as the author of the *Testament* thought it should have been governed. What is certain is that the text does not derive from the third century AD.

Al-Maqrīzī includes in his work the whole *ʿAhd*, as transmitted by Miskawayh. In the holograph, the section which contains this text (§§23–54) is remarkably clear, having no marginal additions or corrections, which is a clear sign that al-Maqrīzī copied the text using a single source, Miskawayh's *Taǧārib*. It is also noteworthy that he does not add any notes of his own or derived from other works, as if he felt that the *ʿAhd* was a more prestigious work, less open to modifications than the text of historians.

The second text included *in toto* is *Sīrat Anūširwān wa-siyāsatuhu* [The Life of Anūširwān and his ways of governing] (§§161–183), also copied from Miskawayh. It claims to be an autobiographical manual of governing and a retrospective analysis of his own reign by the great sixth-century Sasanian king, Kisrá Anūširwān (r. 531–578), the Just King. It would seem rather obvious that in its present form, the work is not a direct translation from Middle Persian, but an Arabic composition, again potentially based on several Middle Persian sources rather than one text. As an appendix to this, al-Maqrīzī, still following Miskawayh, gives (§§184–190) a speech by Anūširwān to his people. Both texts are again remarkably clean.

Other passages from Miskawayh may undergo severe abbreviation and extensive rephrasing with no obvious reason, even though on occasion they may also be quoted almost verbatim. Rephrasing takes place especially towards the end of this section, §§269–282. Partly, this is due to the content of these paragraphs. The earlier text of Miskawayh relates Sasanian history, but when he comes to the Arab conquest, his focus switches to the conquering Arabs. Al-Maqrīzī is not always able to keep the focus on the Persians, either, but he does make an effort to avoid the end of the Sasanians merely becoming part of the history of the conquests.

What is interesting is that we know the very manuscript of Miskawayh that al-Maqrīzī used, MS Ayasofya 3116, as there is a reading note by him on the

46–90, has edited the text from MS Köprülü 1608, fols. 146–166, Miskawayh, *Taǧārib*, and quotations in other sources. There is also an edition by Iḥsān ʿAbbās, *ʿAhd Ardašīr* (Beirut, 1387/1967).

title page of the first volume,[15] and al-Maqrīzī always follows its text. This has, moreover, been edited in facsimile by Leone Caetani.[16] Thus, we can compare al-Maqrīzī's exact source text to his holograph, which allows us to gain information concerning his working methods, with no fear that changes between Miskawayh's and al-Maqrīzī's texts would be due to copyists.[17]

Al-Ṭabarī's (d. 310/923) *Taʾrīḫ* is the second most important source for al-Maqrīzī in this part of his *Ḫabar*. As al-Ṭabarī is also Miskawayh's main source for the Persian kings, the source analysis has to be based on a detailed study of the three texts. In general, al-Maqrīzī only uses al-Ṭabarī as his main source when Miskawayh does not offer sufficient material.

While Miskawayh and al-Ṭabarī are by far al-Maqrīzī's most important sources, Ḥamzah al-Iṣfahānī's (d. 350/961 or 360/971) *Taʾrīḫ* is also used almost throughout the text, with some exceptions, such as the *ʿAhd* and the *Siyāsah*, where al-Maqrīzī only copies from Miskawayh. Ḥamzah's role, though, is mostly auxiliary: he provides additional information to paragraphs that are based on either of the two main sources or even other, less often used sources, but it rarely is, as in § 98, the basis of the paragraph. The two elements of Ḥamzah's work that al-Maqrīzī has systematically used are chronology—which is Ḥamzah's main interest—and the physical descriptions of the Sasanian kings and queens, which Ḥamzah himself got from the Arabic translation of a Middle Persian book only known by its Arabic title *Kitāb al-Ṣuwar* [Book of Pictures].[18] These are given almost systematically, although in a few cases al-Maqrīzī has either forgotten to quote them or decided against doing so. Occasionally, al-Maqrīzī is satisfied with giving only some of the variants for the lengths of a king's rule found in Ḥamzah's work.[19] Other elements have been taken from Ḥamzah only sparingly, most probably because Miskawayh's text usually already covers much of the material Ḥamzah would be able to provide and does so much more extensively.

---

15 See Bauden (forthcoming).

16 Leone Caetani (ed.), *The Tajârib al-Umam or History of Ibn Miskawayh*, I (Leiden–London, 1909).

17 For this reason, I have given throughout references both to one of the printed editions of Miskawayh's *Taǧārib* (ed. Ḥasan) and to Caetani's facsimile edition of MS Ayasofya 3116. When necessary, I have also given reference to the other edition of the same text by Emāmī.

18 See Hämeen-Anttila (2018b): 36–38.

19 Ḥamzah has three lists of the lengths of individual rules in *Taʾrīḫ* 14–15, 19–20, 24–25 = trans. 33–34, 37–39, 43–44. The middlemost list is often ignored by al-Maqrīzī, perhaps because it was already considered erroneous by Ḥamzah himself (*Taʾrīḫ* 21 = trans. 40), but occasionally he ignores one of the other lists, too.

These are the only three works that are quoted throughout this part of the *Ḫabar*. After them, Ibn al-Aṯīr's (d. 630/1160) *Kāmil* is the next in importance, but, rather surprisingly, it is not mentioned by name or title at all in the section concerned with Persia.[20] Al-Maqrīzī may even have started this part of his work relying more heavily on Ibn al-Aṯīr. In § 10, he has first written *wa-kāna ǧadduhu Sāsān šuǧāʿan muġran bi-l-ṣayd*, which is what Ibn al-Aṯīr, *Kāmil*, 1:380, has. Only after this had been written, al-Maqrīzī added in the upper margin *šadīd al-baṭš* (…) *fa-hazamahum*, indicating that these words should be added between *šuǧāʿan* and *muġran*. This addition derives from al-Ṭabarī, *Taʾrīḫ*, which also provides a note on Bābak's hair, also written in the margin, strongly implying that here, which is the first occasion for al-Ṭabarī to appear as source in this part, al-Maqrīzī started by copying Ibn al-Aṯīr and only after having done so took recourse to al-Ṭabarī.

As Ibn al-Aṯīr largely copies al-Ṭabarī and al-Maqrīzī abbreviates and modifies the text he copies, it is often difficult to say with certainty which of the two is al-Maqrīzī's immediate source. It seems, though, that al-Maqrīzī used *Kāmil*, 1:380–384 extensively for §§ 10–20. From § 17 onward, al-Ṭabarī takes precedence over Ibn al-Aṯīr, who only provides some additions to the story as related by Miskawayh and al-Ṭabarī. After § 20, we lose Ibn al-Aṯīr from sight for a longer time, partly due to extensive use of Miskawayh and Ḥamzah. Even when al-Maqrīzī later returns to using al-Ṭabarī, he may not have used Ibn al-Aṯīr until §§ 117–121. From there until § 237, Ibn al-Aṯīr is again used every now and then until he disappears after § 237.

Orosius' book, probably translated into Arabic in the tenth century and mostly quoted as *Kitāb Hurūšiyūš* in the first part of *Ḫabar/Persia*,[21] has almost disappeared from this part of the *Ḫabar*, for the obvious reason that it provides little information on the Sasanians. The only Orosius quotation comes in § 92. Ibn al-Nadīm's (d. 385/995 or 388/998) *Fihrist* is the main source for Mani in §§ 72–77, even though neither the author nor the title is explicitly given.

Al-Hamdānī's (d. 334/945) *Iklīl* provides some information for §§ 21–22. Most of the volumes of this book have disappeared, and it would seem that the information al-Maqrīzī quotes comes from one of the lost volumes or an intermediate source. Abū Nuʿaym's (d. 430/1038) *Dalāʾil* seems to provide information for §§ 235–237, 239–240, although al-Maqrīzī does not quote him sufficiently exactly to exclude the possibility of an intermediate source. In addition to these, there are some sources that have been culled for some specific details,

20 For *Ḫabar/Persia* I, where it may have been used, though probably in only one paragraph (§ 200), see Hämeen-Anttila (2018a): 11.

21 Hämeen-Anttila (2018a): 11–16.

including works by al-Āmidī (d. 371/981) (§ 60), al-Marzubānī (d. 384/994) (§ 60), Ibn Hišām (d. 218/834)/Ibn Isḥāq (d. 150/767) (§§ 62, 63, 64), and al-Suhaylī (d. 581/1185) (§§ 60, 62–64).

While Miskawayh is, overall, al-Maqrīzī's main source for this part, al-Maqrīzī also uses al-Ṭabarī rather extensively. Mostly, this happens when Miskawayh has gaps in his history of the Sasanians, the most conspicuous being in Miskawayh, *Taǧārib*, 1:108–109, where six reigns are covered in a mere eight lines of text in the edition of Ḥasan. Usually, al-Maqrīzī first copies Miskawayh, after which he may add material from al-Ṭabarī, creating an interesting situation where Miskawayh has first abbreviated the text he took from al-Ṭabarī[22] and then al-Maqrīzī brings some of the omitted material back into the text. In § 104, this has resulted in a duplication that clearly shows the process. Al-Ṭabarī has *wa-l-dahāʾ wa-l-mukābadah wa-l-muḫātalah*, which Miskawayh rephrases as *fī l-dahāʾ wa-l-ḫatl*. Al-Maqrīzī misreads the latter as *ḥiyal* and then adds from al-Ṭabarī *makāʾid* (for *mukābadah*) and *muḫātalah*, resulting in *fī l-dahāʾ wa-l-ḥiyal wa-l-makāʾid wa-l-muḫātalah*. Often, though, al-Maqrīzī does not seem to have taken anything from al-Ṭabarī, even when there would have been relevant material that he could have added to his own work.

It is not possible to prove that al-Maqrīzī stopped using al-Ṭabarī as a secondary source for some sections of his work, but this seems a reasonable assumption, because there are long stretches of text where no unequivocal signs of al-Ṭabarī's influence can be detected and the whole text may be derived from Miskawayh and other sources. From § 113 on, the texts of Miskawayh and al-Maqrīzī are largely identical (allowing for occasional additions from especially Ḥamzah). The dependence of al-Maqrīzī on Miskawayh, rather than al-Ṭabarī, is shown by abbreviations and reformulations of al-Ṭabarī's text that are identical in Miskawayh and al-Maqrīzī. Thus, e.g., in § 114, both have the same abbreviations and reformulations of al-Ṭabarī's text. While al-Ṭabarī, e.g., begins the text by *wa-waǧǧaha Bahrām qāʾidan min quwwādihi*, both Miskawayh and al-Maqrīzī read *ṯumma baʿaṯa qāʾidan* (Miskawayh adds *lahu*). The change is slight, but such cases are abundant and their cumulative evidence, together with the identical abbreviations and occasional identical additions (like in § 114 the final comment on the letter's eloquence and fame, missing from al-Ṭabarī), leave no doubt that al-Ṭabarī was not used as the primary source by al-Maqrīzī, and it is dubious whether he systematically used al-Ṭabarī at all after § 113. As Miskawayh himself is very dependent on al-Ṭabarī, there remains, however, an element of uncertainty as to whether al-Maqrīzī has in

22 For Miskawayh's sources, see Arkoun (1970): 120–127.

these sections, after having copied Miskawayh's text, had a look at al-Ṭabarī, but without finding there anything of interest that he would have liked to add to his text. It is probable that he has often not even looked at al-Ṭabarī, as al-Maqrīzī is a very economical writer: if there are no unequivocal signs of al-Ṭabarī's influence in a number of consecutive paragraphs, then, most probably, al-Maqrīzī has stopped checking al-Ṭabarī for these sections.[23]

Though not quoting him systematically, al-Maqrīzī does make occasional use of al-Ṭabarī even after § 113. Thus, e.g., in § 211 there is a clear addition from al-Ṭabarī, *Taʾrīḫ*, 1:1002–1003.[24] That the passage in § 211 is added in the margin shows that even here al-Maqrīzī started by copying Miskawayh as such and only when revising the text had a look at al-Ṭabarī.

Until § 113, al-Maqrīzī may even have preferred al-Ṭabarī when he and Miskawayh both have text that al-Maqrīzī could have used, which probably means that he has first gone al-Ṭabarī through. As al-Ṭabarī and Miskawayh are sometimes almost identical, it needs careful comparison to decide, which text al-Maqrīzī is actually quoting. Thus, e.g., § 66 is almost identical with Miskawayh, *Taǧārib*, 1:108, but the latter lacks the first verse quotation, which unequivocally shows that here, at least, al-Maqrīzī quotes al-Ṭabarī.

In § 83, there are several details that show that, for the first time after the text of *ʿAhd Ardašīr* (§ § 23–54), al-Maqrīzī is back using Miskawayh as his main source. The following passage gives an unequivocal example of how al-Maqrīzī follows Miskawayh, not al-Ṭabarī. Both Miskawayh and al-Maqrīzī read *anna malik al-Furs ṣabiyy yudabbar wa-lā yudrá mā yakūnu minhu*, while al-Ṭabarī reads *anna ahlahā yatalawwamūn ṣabiyyan fī l-mahd lā yadrūna mā huwa kāʾin min amrihi*. The reason for the change to al-Ṭabarī as the main source after the *ʿAhd* is simply that Miskawayh is very concise when writing about the reigns between Ardašīr and Sābūr of Shoulders, compressing everything in less than two pages (*Taǧārib*, 1:107–109).

The order in which al-Maqrīzī has used his sources, or his own notes culled from these sources, can sometimes be conclusively shown. Thus, e.g., in § 222 the comment on the 3,000 free women and the definition of the purpose of the 12,000 servant girls have been written in the margins, and they are missing from Miskawayh. This shows that al-Maqrīzī has first copied the text of Miskawayh

23 However, as al-Ṭabarī is al-Maqrīzī's ultimate source even in these sections, and Bosworth's translation (Bosworth 1999) a valuable tool for understanding the text, I have given references to al-Ṭabarī even in cases where he may not have been directly quoted. These have been marked by "cf."

24 From "led by three of his generals and cavalrymen" until "They all marched." For more examples, see the footnotes to the translation.

and then compared it to Ḥamzah, making the necessary additions in the margins. Al-Ṭabarī contains more or less the same information as Ḥamzah, but the differences in wording show that Ḥamzah has here been al-Maqrīzī's second source.

The paragraph shows that here al-Maqrīzī first copied Miskawayh and then turned to Ḥamzah. After that he may or may not have checked al-Ṭabarī, but this has left no traces in the paragraph. Had al-Maqrīzī checked al-Ṭabarī before Ḥamzah, he would have found the same information already there and would probably have copied it using the wordings of al-Ṭabarī.

Note that Ḥamzah's "regular" material—dates, description of the king/queen—is never added into the margin, as al-Maqrīzī inserts this material regularly and knows that he will take it from Ḥamzah, whereas the marginal additions are usually a kind of afterthought, adding material that al-Maqrīzī did not expect to find, at least not in as great a quantity as he did, thus running out of space. The case of § 222 is different, as it relates to material, copying Miskawayh, he was not expecting to include from Ḥamzah.

Al-Maqrīzī's working methods sometimes shine through in the marginal additions. Thus, we can see how he first copied text from his main source and then added explanations, either his own or ones culled from other sources. The following cases are explanatory additions taken from other sources and added to the text taken from Miskawayh: the words "had recovered from his illness" (§ 245); the synchronisation with the *hiǧrah* (§ 261); the sentence "It is he from whom the Muslims later conquered the country" (§ 212); synchronisation of two events (§ 217); the sentence bridging the transition "The messenger of Abarwīz" (§ 219); the final sentences, from "Then he wrote" onward adding a further detail to the story and a reference to the Qur'ān (§ 221).

In other cases, the marginal additions provide words or sentences erroneously dropped by al-Maqrīzī when first copying the text, as in § 274 (from "from Ḥulwān towards al-Ǧabal with 1,000 mules" until the end of the paragraph).

Sometimes (e.g., fols. 175[b] and 178[b]) al-Maqrīzī left blanks at places where he expected to add more, but never found suitable material or had time to do so. Fols. 176[a]–178[a] contain the life of Hurmuz, which is marked off by such blank spaces before and after it. This also leaves open the possibility that he might have replaced an earlier version by these pages, which might also be implied by the slightly more finalised state of the article on Hurmuz, containing very few corrections and additions in the margins, as if the life was already a more developed draft.

In a number of cases, al-Maqrīzī left blank spaces at the end of major reigns. After he had already begun the next reign, he then came back to fill the blank with text taken from secondary sources, sometimes the text overflowing the space reserved for it so that it has had to be squeezed into the margins or, in the worst cases, written on a separate slip of paper.[25]

Fol. 186[a–b] offers a clear case of this. Al-Maqrīzī started the verso of fol. 186 with a new article, on Šīrūyah, § 241, when he had still some blank space left on the recto, fol. 186[a], having come to the end of § 238 or, possibly, § 239. Even though he had already started writing on fol. 186[b], he clearly intended to add material before it. When he added § 240 and ran out of space, he attached a separate slip of paper and wrote just under two lines on it, upside down. Usually, such attached slips of paper contain a larger amount of material, sometimes written on both sides of the slip.[26] Usually al-Maqrīzī makes such additions in the margin, and one might have expected the addition to have been made in the left margin. There would have been plenty of space in the margin for the two lines he added on the attached note, which shows that he was planning to write more on Kisrá Abarwīz and Šīrīn, but never came to do so. § 240 also ends abruptly in an incomplete sentence (*wa-kāna min ḫabarihi maʿahā*), which would either need a story to be told or at least *mā kāna* to be added, but al-Maqrīzī never closed the text by adding the easy ending of *mā kāna*, leaving it instead open, obviously hoping to find more about Šīrīn before closing the passage.

Likewise, we can see how the article on Kisrá Anūširwān on fol. 164[b] had been started before the article on Qubāḏ on fol. 164[a] was closed. Al-Maqrīzī made two additions to the text in §§ 140–141. The shorter addition, § 141a, has been squeezed into the margin, but the longer note on § 140 (§ 140a) needed more space, so al-Maqrīzī decided in favour of an attached slip of paper.

It seems that sometimes passages in the same section may have been written at widely different times. Until § 107 and again in §§ 132–133,[27] al-Maqrīzī consistently writes the personal name as Sābūr, the only exceptions being § 83, where he first uses Sābūr but then gives the Persian form of the name as Šābūr, and in a poem in § 65.[28] However, in § 107 he uses throughout Šābūr. This article begins a new page, fol. 156[a], and the preceding text (§§ 105–106) has been writ-

25 Leaving blank lines or even pages is also otherwise attested as al-Maqrīzī's working method. For a case of three blank folios in the *Ittiʿāẓ*, see Bauden (2014): 180.

26 There are four such slips in this part: between fols. 155–156 (both sides written full, contains part of § 104, §§ 105–106, and part of § 107); between fols. 163–164 (one side written full, contains § 140a); between fols. 185–186 (two lines only, contains part of § 240); and between fols. 193–194 (one side written full, contains a marginal addition to § 275).

27 After that, the name is only found in §§ 142 and 257, in both as Sābūr.

28 The form Šāhbūr is found twice in § 62, in a comment on a verse by al-Aʿšá. Šābūr is also found twice in § 67 in geographical names, given as their Persian form.

ten on a separate slip of paper attached to the manuscript. The use of the slip shows that al-Maqrīzī ran out of space on fol. 155^b, further showing that fol. 156^a had been written before fol. 155^b was completed. As al-Maqrīzī's source does not change—both § 107 and its surroundings come from al-Ṭabarī—it seems highly probable that § 107 on fol. 156^a was written considerably earlier than the preceding parts and §§ 132–133 and that for some reason al-Maqrīzī had meanwhile changed his way of writing the name. Had the writing of this section, and probably the whole of the *Ḫabar*, been a linear process, it would be inexplicable why he suddenly changed the orthography of the name in one paragraph.

A certain openness of the work to continuous reworking is also implied in the title of the last *faṣl* on the Persians in § 296, which seems to promise a substantial exposé of Zoroastrianism, but most of the space is taken by a single topic, the fire ordeal (§§ 298–299). As the next section, on Israelites, only commences on the recto of fol. 201,[29] al-Maqrīzī would have been at liberty to add as many pages as he wanted, but he never had time to return to this. The manuscript remained open ended at the time of al-Maqrīzī's death.

3 Quoting

There are some governing principles in the way al-Maqrīzī quotes his sources in this section.[30] He attempts to keep focused on Persian history, even when his main sources, Miskawayh and al-Ṭabarī, wander off to other topics. This is especially clear towards the end of this section, where the mainstream historians, based on al-Ṭabarī, switch the focus from the Persians to the conquering Arabs. Al-Maqrīzī does give ample space to some episodes of the conquest, but compared with Miskawayh he manages to remain better focused, not to speak of al-Ṭabarī, who loses his interest in Persian history when he comes to the conquest. In his case, this is natural, though: al-Ṭabarī was writing an annalistic history[31] of the whole world, and as he had much more material on the conquests than on the Persians, it is but natural that the latter fall out of focus.

The Battle of al-Qādisiyyah (§§ 263–267) is a good example of this, taking about 80, 11, and 2 pages, respectively, in al-Ṭabarī, Miskawayh, and al-Maqrīzī.

29 See the table in Bauden (forthcoming).

30 Cf. also Hämeen-Anttila (2018a): 16–26. Note that al-Maqrīzī's way of quoting changes between the various sections, and his strategy in the section on Greeks etc. (cf. Penelas 2021: 10–24) is again different from that in the present section.

31 From the *hiǧrah* onward—earlier sections do not follow this annalistic model, as there is no clear chronology on which to build it.

E.g., the material in § 266 takes nine lines, whereas its source, Miskawayh, uses three full pages, and al-Ṭabarī needs ten pages to cover the same events. For a reader completely unfamiliar with the story, al-Maqrīzī's text may become difficult to follow due to its conciseness. A similar phenomenon may be seen in the discussion of the Ḥīran Laḫmids, who are extensively discussed by al-Ṭabarī, while Miskawayh abbreviates the discussion, and al-Maqrīzī goes even further to keep the focus on the Persians.

Another principle relates to details within the quoted text. Very often al-Maqrīzī drops names, both personal and geographical, which are of no interest to the mainstream of his narrative (e.g., § 12). This is probably partly a practical solution. Where al-Maqrīzī does give foreign names that are not commonly known, he often misreads them. In the first section of Persian history this was even more prominent, al-Maqrīzī both avoiding and misreading, e.g., Greek names.

Arabic historians, in general, are remarkably uninterested in their accuracy, or the lack of it, in copying earlier sources. While al-Maqrīzī often rephrases a passage for no obvious reason (abbreviation, clarification, some hidden agenda), at other times he faithfully transmits passages that would actually benefit from rephrasing. In § 285, the king of China asks the messenger of Yazdağird about the Arabs. Amidst an otherwise perfect sequence of questions and answers, there suddenly comes one exceptional passage (Then the king asked: "Tell me about how they dress themselves." I told him. "And their mounts?") where the second question comes without any introductory formula, such as *qāla: wa-aḫbirnī*. This is already how the text is found in al-Ṭabarī, Miskawayh and al-Maqrīzī faithfully transmitting something that would seem an accidental omission in al-Ṭabarī. Based on this example, the text of al-Ṭabarī might seem sacrosanct, being transmitted for half a millennium with studious consideration of the minutest detail. In most cases, however, his text is freely rephrased without the slightest qualms.

A further characteristic of al-Maqrīzī is that he prefers third-person narration to Miskawayh's ample use of dialogue. Dialogues are by no means lacking in al-Maqrīzī's text, but one rarely finds him changing a third-person narrative into a dialogue, but the reverse happens rather often.

4 Mistakes

It is not uncommon to find mistakes in a text one is reading. The usual suspect is the copyist, who has misunderstood the meaning of the author. In al-Maqrīzī's case, though, we can see exactly how the author himself wrote, thanks to the holograph. Moreover, we have at our disposal the very manuscript of Miskawayh's *Taǧārib* (ed. Caetani) that al-Maqrīzī used. Thus, we have both the manuscript used by al-Maqrīzī and the manuscript he produced on its basis, which enables us to see clearly and exactly how he understood or misunderstood his sources.

In the following, I will take up some examples of different types of al-Maqrīzī's mistakes. Occasionally, these are mere typos, mistakes that have no other reason than carelessness. In § 196, al-Maqrīzī reads *fa-waǧǧaha ilayhi raǧulan min ahl al-raʾy* "he sent against him a discerning man," whereas al-Ṭabarī and Miskawayh (ed. Caetani) read al-Rayy ("a man from Rayy"). Al-Maqrīzī was quite familiar with the city of al-Rayy, which he, e.g., mentions several times in the first part of this section, so that the mistake is due to careless reading or copying.[32] However, al-Maqrīzī's reader may not have been able to notice this, as the sentence makes sense and only a comparison with the source text or parallel tradition shows it to be a mistake.

Al-Maqrīzī freely changes the syntax of the sentences in his sources. In § 199, he seems to have started simplifying Miskawayh's sentence, but then he suddenly comes back to the original wording, without noticing that the parts of the sentence do not match each other. Miskawayh had written (ed. Caetani, p. 222):

بلغه قَتْل آذينجشنس الموجّه لمحاربة بهرام شوبين وانقضاض الجمع الذي …

The syntax is admittedly somewhat complicated, which is probably the reason why al-Maqrīzī started rephrasing the sentence, without realising that he should have rephrased the end of the sentence, too, starting with *inqiḍāḍ*, which he read *infiḍāḍ*:

بلغه أن آذينجسنس الموجّه لمحاربة بهرام شوبين قُتِلَ وانفضاض الجمع الذي …

Another case of a correction left half way can be found in § 193. Miskawayh (ed. Caetani) reads *bi-ḏālika l-dābbah allaḏī*. Al-Maqrīzī changes the demonstrative pronoun from *bi-ḏālika* to *bi-tilka*, but overlooks the masculine relative pronoun and reads *bi-tilka l-dābbah* (fem.) *allaḏī* (masc.).

Sometimes the mistakes cause major changes in the text. In § 213, the text has started changing when Miskawayh rephrased al-Ṭabarī and either he or the copyist of ed. Caetani made a fatal mistake in vocalisation, which al-Maqrīzī

32 See Hämeen-Anttila (2018a), Index.

clearly tried to correct, but ended up in changing the story. Al-Ṭabarī wrote (*Taʾrīḫ*, 1:1003–1004):

وكان شاهين (...) بباب كسرى (...) لموجدة كانت من كسرى عليه وعزله إياه عن ذلك الثغر.

Miskawayh rephrases this, presumably to make the somewhat cumbersome phrase more fluent, but, probably out of mere carelessness, Miskawayh or the copyist of ed. Caetani adds inappropriate vocalisation to *istadʿá*:

وقد كان صاحب ذلك الثغر من قبل كسرى قد استَدعى لموجدة كانت من كسرى عليه.

Without the vowel, this would merely rephrase al-Ṭabarī. Reading *ustudʿiya*, the text would say "he had been summoned (away)," but the vowel sign forces us to read an incomplete sentence: "he had summoned" (whom?). This is where al-Maqrīzī has tried to make sense by adding Heraclius as the object of *istadʿá*:

وقد كان صاحب ذلك الثغر من قبل أبرويز قد استدعى هرقل لموجدة كانت من هرمز.

Thus, instead of the governor having been summoned away, thus enabling Heraclius to move freely into the Persian territory, he is made to invite Heraclius to invade the country. This also shows that at least here al-Maqrīzī did not check al-Ṭabarī or, if he did so, did not stop to read him carefully enough to realise Miskawayh's mistake.

Rephrasing the sentence occasionally reveals gaps in al-Maqrīzī's grammatical perceptivity. In § 277, Miskawayh, his source, writes *wa-*LQBH *Miqlāṣ*. Al-Maqrīzī has understood this as *laqqabahu* "he gave him the cognomen" and rephrased it as *wa-sammāhu*, while it should be read *wa-laqabuhu* "and his cognomen was," which is a common expression in al-Ṭabarī (from where Miskawayh takes the sentence) and Miskawayh. This is also supported by grammar: if we were to read *laqqabahu*, Miqlāṣ should be in the accusative.

Sometimes al-Maqrīzī copies the erroneous form from his source. Thus, al-Ṭabarī, *Taʾrīḫ*, 1:1063, has a grammatically correct sentence:

إن رجلا من أهل إصطخر يقال له فسفروخ بن ماخرشيذان وأخوين له امتعضوا (...)

In Miskawayh (ed. Caetani), p. 268, this has become:

ثم امتعض رجل يقال له بسفروخ وأخوين له (…)

The syntax is less heavy than al-Ṭabarī's, but the rephrasing has gone only half way through (the obliquus *aḫawayn* should have been changed into the nominative *aḫawān* when *inna* was replaced by *ṯumma*). Al-Maqrīzī, § 245, keeps Miskawayh's formulation, without noticing the incongruous grammar.

This example both shows how historians were not always sensitive to rather basic grammatical rules and also how they can simultaneously copy accurately (and mechanically) parts of a text other parts of which they are freely rephrasing without any motif or hidden agenda. There is no great difference between quoting and paraphrasing in most genres of Classical Arabic prose.

Throughout the work, various misunderstandings confirm that al-Maqrīzī did not understand Persian. In § 254, he gives the etymology of Baġdād from an unidentified source, but he misunderstands the first part, which he takes to be *bāġ* "garden, park" and uses his standard etymology for this word, already used in §§ 140a and 224, instead of *baġ*, which must have been in the source he was using, as the later reference to idols shows. In § 224, one finds another example of al-Maqrīzī's lack of Persian, as he divides the Persian origin of the exclamation "Qubāḏ is the King of Kings" onto two lines as *Qubāḏ šāh* / *NŠʾH*.

Poetry is a field where al-Maqrīzī is not at his strongest. Bauden (2014) gives no evidence of al-Maqrīzī's literary education: he was learned in *ḥadīth* and history, but not in *adab*. This is reflected in the low number of verses he quotes throughout the *Ḫabar*. In this part, he only quotes 8 poems, totalling 21 verses on its 125 pages, and even though Persian history is not the densest part of world history as it comes to verses, there are a number of occasions where he could easily have inserted verses: gnomic verses can be fitted anywhere and the Arab connections would have given ample opportunities to quote a large number of verses, especially when it comes to the Laḫmids—in which connection al-Maqrīzī does quote a few verses—and the conquest, where he quotes none.

When he does quote verses, al-Maqrīzī often gets it wrong. The most striking case in this volume comes in § 65, where he continues misvocalising the name al-ʿAbīd as al-ʿUbayd, as he has been doing through the volume (e.g., § 60), but this time the word comes at the end of a line in a poem rhyming in *-īdī* and thus breaks the rhyme.

5 Description of the Manuscripts[33]

This edition is based on the holograph MS Fatih 4340, fols. 137ᵃ–200ᵃ. The whole manuscript consists of 265 leaves, with 25 lines of text on most pages. Most pages contain marginal additions in the hand of al-Maqrīzī.

The text has been compared with MS TKSM A. 2926/5 (MS T), where the part edited here takes fols. 70ᵃ–124ᵇ, with 27 lines per page. The variants and readings of this manuscript have been indicated only when they help us to read the holograph. The whole manuscript comprises 183 leaves plus three unnumbered leaves of Oriental paper (180 × 263 mm.). The manuscript belongs to a set of six volumes (MSS TKSM A. 2926/1–6), and it is copied from the holograph, the marginal corrections of which have been inserted into the text.

The text is further found in the following manuscripts that have not been used for the edition:

Algiers, Bibliothèque nationale MS 1059a;[34]
Cairo, Dār al-Kutub, MS 5251 *Taʾrīḫ*;[35]
MS Aya Sofya 3365, pp. 351–438.[36]

6 The Copying of Manuscript A-2926/5 (MS T)

MS T was copied from the holograph by ʿUmar b. ʿAbd Allāh al-Manẓarāwī in 1489, half a century after the author's death.[37] As a rule, al-Maqrīzī's marginal corrections, marginal commentaries, and the material written on separate slips of paper have been conscientiously copied into MS T.

The copyist of MS T has in general done a very good job: there are few mistakes, passages have not fallen out during the process, and usually, though not

33 The manuscript descriptions rely in large part on Bauden (forthcoming). This section is mainly reproduced from Hämeen-Anttila (2018a): 26–27.

34 Not seen, cf. Bauden (forthcoming) and Fagnan (1893): 439, no. 1589. The Persian section covers fols. 48ᵇ–145ᵃ.

35 Not seen, cf. Bauden (forthcoming) and *Fihris al-kutub*, 8:126. This is a modern copy made in 1353–1354/1934–1935 in seven volumes from the holograph and the photographs of the Istanbul manuscript available in Cairo.

36 Not seen, cf. Bauden (forthcoming). Copied from the holograph, containing on its 542 pages volumes 4 and 5 of the holograph. The manuscript has two separate parts (pp. 1–245; 246–542) by two different hands, bound in Mamlūk leather binding. The part concerned here has 31 lines of writing per page.

37 See Penelas (2021): 27.

always, the copyist is able to read al-Maqrīzī's handwriting even when the latter is not at its clearest. Although the copyist's mistakes are relatively few, there are a handful of them. In § 98, al-Maqrīzī clearly writes the toponym al-Ḥadīṯah, but the copyist gets it as al-Ḥudaybiyah, probably a much more familiar place-name for him, even though far away from the scene of § 98. Another example comes in § 274 with another toponym, Ǧālūlā, which, this time, is not very clear in the holograph. The copyist started writing XLWʾ (where X is an undotted letter, either Ǧ, Ḥ, or Ḫ), and in a misguided effort to correct al-Maqrīzī's text, added the letter N above the *alif* to make it Ḥulwān, mentioned later on in the same paragraph.

Occasionally, the copyist has been successful in correcting the original. In § 11, he corrects al-Maqrīzī's *iṭāʿah* (a mere carelessness on the side of al-Maqrīzī) to *aṭāʿahu* by dropping the dots on the *tāʾ marbūṭah*. In § 82, he noted that a word is missing and left for it a blank space that was never filled in, and in § 153 he corrected al-Maqrīzī's slip of pen (*malikah* for *mallakahu*), again by dropping the dots of the *tāʾ marbūṭah*.[38]

One of the few cases, where we can see the copyist skipping a passage and then having to add it to the margin comes in § 232, where the sentence beginning with "he gave orders to the *marzubāns*" has been dropped from the text of MS T and then added in the margin.

The marginal corrections by al-Maqrīzī in the holograph are carefully copied into MS T and added in their correct place in the main text. There are, though, a few cases, where the copyist has dropped material added by al-Maqrīzī in the margins of the holograph. A good example comes in §§ 140a and 141a. § 140a has been written on a separate slip of paper, as al-Maqrīzī ran out of space when adding material to the text. The copyist of MS T has copied this at the end of § 140, just before the final words of the paragraph (*wa-hiya sittat ṭasāsīǧ*).

However, the copyist has not included § 141a, a marginal note that refers to § 141. Contrary to his habits, al-Maqrīzī has not indicated the place for this note and the copyist may have been uncertain as to where he should put this addition and opted the easy way out by omitting it altogether.

In § 62, al-Maqrīzī has made three marginal correction or additions. While the copyist of MS T takes two of these into account, the third, which is the most crucial as it corrects the beginning of the first line, has not been copied by him. In § 207, a marginal addition has been copied into MS T, except for the last words, beginning with *fa-farra* "and he [Abarwīz] was able to escape."

38 For cases where the attempted correction has not been completely successful or where the copyist seems to have noticed a problem even though he has not known how to correct it, see §§ 10, 80, and 137.

Sometimes the copyist may have left a marginal note away for other reasons. In § 262, the formula *raḍiya llāh ʿanhu* has been added in the margin but is missing from MS T. Al-Maqrīzī has indicated the place where it should go in the text as being after *ilayhi* in *kataba ilayhi* ("he, i.e., al-Muṯanná, wrote to him, i.e., ʿUmar"). However, both al-Ṭabarī and Miskawayh show that it is ʿUmar who is writing the letter, not al-Muṯanná, and this can also be deduced from the context. This may explain why it has not been copied into MS T: rather than inserting it where it is wrongly indicated to belong, but also unwilling to contradict al-Maqrīzī's indication, the copyist may simply have left it away.

The same unwillingness to contradict al-Maqrīzī may be seen in § 158. The holograph reads *al-muqābilah*, but the correction to *al-muqātilah*, also supported by Miskawayh[39] and al-Ṭabarī, is obvious. The copyist of MS T seems to have noticed this, too, as he has left the dot of B away, even though not going as far as to emend the word to *al-muqātilah*. Otherwise, he usually follows the use of diacritics in the original.

The copyist of MS T does not always appear to his profit, though. In § 211, there is a list of three generals. The second of them is introduced by the word *al-ṯānī*, but the word *al-ṯānī* is not very clear in the holograph, and the copyist of MS T has been unable to read it, leaving a framed blank space in his manuscript. The word would have been simple enough to guess, coming in a list of three generals, the first, the [unclear], and the third. It is also far from illegible in the original, even though it could have been clearer. Here, the copyist does not seem to have been very committed to his work.

7 Sasanian Kings and Queens according to al-Maqrīzī

As in Arabic and Persian historiography in general, al-Maqrīzī offers slightly varying lists of Sasanian kings and queens. In § 3, copied from Ḥamzah, he mentions that these were either 24 or 28 in number, repeating the latter number in § 294. Neither, in fact, matches the actual number of kings and queens he mentions, even if we discount the two queens. The tumultuous end of the dynasty introduces many short-lived, and often unwilling, aspirants to the crown, but al-Maqrīzī does not indicate which, if any, of these he does not consider legitimate kings. More probably, he just uses Ḥamzah's numbers without checking them, as he also does in the case of Ḥamzah's miscalculations in §§ 3–5.

39 In ed. Caetani, the dots of T have been written unusually far above the letter, which explains al-Maqrīzī's mistake.

The following gives an overview of the Sasanians according to al-Maqrīzī, the kings and queens numbered from 1 to 35 and marked by boldface, although towards the end of the dynasty, there are many variant versions as to who ruled, in which order, and who were considered kings, who usurpers. The list gives al-Maqrīzī's understanding of the dynasty. The Middle Persian forms of the names and the duration of their reign are mostly taken from Schindel (2013): 815–816.[40]

Bahman §§ 1–2
Sāsān the Elder §§ 1–2
Bābak b. Sāsān the Younger, whose lineage takes him through three ancestors to Sāsān the Elder § 9
1. **Ardašīr b. Bābak** §§ 9–54 (Ardašīr 224–240)
2. **Sābūr b. Ardašīr** §§ 55–67 (Šābuhr 240–272)
3. **Hurmuz b. Sābūr** §§ 68–70 (Ohrmazd 272–273)
4. **Bahrām b. Hurmuz** §§ 71–78 (Warahrān 273–276)
5. **Bahrām b. Bahrām** §§ 78–79 (Warahrān 276–293)
6. **Bahrām b. Bahrām b. Bahrām** § 80 (Warahrān 293)
7. **Narsī b. Bahrām** (no. 5) § 81 (Narseh 293–302/303)
8. **Hurmuz b. Narsī** § 82 (Ohrmazd 302/303–309/310)
9. **Sābūr b. Hurmuz** §§ 83–99 (Šābuhr 309/310–379)
10. **Ardašīr b. Hurmuz** § 100 (Ardašīr 379–383)
11. **Sābūr b. Sābūr** § 101 (Šābuhr 383–388)
12. **Bahrām b. Sābūr** (no. 9) § 102 (Warahrān 388–399)
13. **Yazdağird b. Sābūr** (no. 9) § 103 (Yazdgerd 399–420)
14. **Yazdağird b. Bahrām** §§ 104–106
Kisrá, descendant of Ardašīr (no. 1) §§ 108–111
15. **Bahrām Ǧūr b. Yazdağird** (no. 14) §§ 107–120 (Warahrān 420–438)
16. **Yazdağird b. Bahrām Ǧūr** § 121 (Yazdgerd 438–457)
17. **Hurmuz b. Yazdağird** § 121 (Ohrmazd 457–459, pretender)
18. **Fīrūz b. Yazdağird** §§ 122–129 (Pērōz 457–484)
19. **Balāš b. Fīrūz** § 130 (Walāḫš 484–488)
20. **Qubāḏ b. Fīrūz** §§ 131–141 (Kawād 488–496, 499–531)
Ǧāmāsf b. Fīrūz §§ 135–136 (Ǧāmāsp 496–499)
21. **Kisrá b. Qubāḏ** §§ 142–191 (Ḫosrow 531–578)
22. **Hurmuz b. Kisrá** §§ 192–199 (Ohrmazd 578–590)

40 Cf. also Beeston (1999): xxv–xxvi.

Bahrām Ǧūbīn b. Bahrām-Ǧusnas §§ 207–209 (Warahrān 590–591)

23. **Kisrá b. Hurmuz** §§ 199–240 (Ḫosrow 590, 591–628)
24. **Šīrūyah Qubāḏ b. Kisrá** §§ 241–243 (Kawād 628)
25. **Ardašīr b. Šīrūyah** § 244 (Ardašīr 628–630)
26. **Šahrbarāz Farruḫān Ḫurrahān** §§ 245–247
27. **Būrān bt. Kisrá** §§ 249, 255 (Bōrānduḫt 630–631)
28. **Kisrá b. Qubāḏ** §§ 245, 257 (Ḫosrow around 630)
29. **Fīrūz b. Bahrām Ǧušnas-Banda**, paternal cousin of Kisrá Abarwīz § 257
30. **Āzarmīduḫt bt. Kisrá** §§ 257–259 (Ādarmīgduḫt around 630)
31. **Ḫurdāḏ-Ḫusraw** § 259
32. **Kisrá b. Mihr-Ǧušnas** § 260
33. **Farruḫzāḏ-Ḫusraw b. Kisrá** §§ 259–260
34. **Fīrūz** § 260
35. **Yazdaǧird b. Šahriyār b. Kisrá** (no. 23) §§ 261–294 (Yazdgerd 632–651)

8 Translation and Transliteration of Names

As in the first volume on Persia, my aim has not been to translate the text as it is in al-Ṭabarī, Miskawayh, Ḥamzah, or al-Maqrīzī's other sources, but as it is in al-Maqrīzī. Hence, my translation occasionally differs from Bosworth's, Grignaschi's, and Hoyland's, not necessarily because I would believe them to have mistranslated something but because the meaning of the text has changed when it has been copied and rephrased by al-Maqrīzī. I have tried to translate the text as intended to be understood by al-Maqrīzī and corrected it only when I believe that the change or the mistake has been unintentional. I have followed this policy even when it leads to obscure sentences, which I have then clarified in the footnotes.

Very often, the Sasanian kings speak about themselves in the first-person plural. Where this refers to the king only, I have used the singular in the translation, but where it refers to all the Sasanian kings, or all Iranians, I have retained the plural. In many cases, the reference is not unambiguous, though.

The transliteration of names presents some problems. Following the model I used in the first part of the section on Persian kings,[41] I am more conservative in the edition than in the translation. In the Arabic text, I keep al-Maqrīzī's form, even when it is clearly wrong, if he himself is consistent. Thus, e.g., the name of Barāz (§§ 286–292) appears 17 times in the text, always clearly and unmis-

41 Hämeen-Anttila (2018a): 28–29.

takeably written TR'R (Tarār?). This has been kept in the edition, but to ease comparison with other sources of Sasanian history, in the translation I have used the correct form Barāz, with a note on this at the first occurrence.

In cases where al-Maqrīzī vacillates between several forms, I have chosen the most standard one for use throughout the translation. When a name is written sometimes with and sometimes without diacritics, I have interpreted this to mean that the form with diacritics is what al-Maqrīzī always had in mind, and have added the diacritics to the edition and transliterated accordingly. In some cases, the lack of diacritics is consistent and the form attested several times, like that of Sanǧān written twice ṢNḤ'N (§§ 287, 289) and four times SNḤ'N (§ 292) but never with Ǧ. In these cases, I have retained al-Maqrīzī's form in the edition, taking this as how he would have understood the form, but again using the standard form in the translation.

Plates

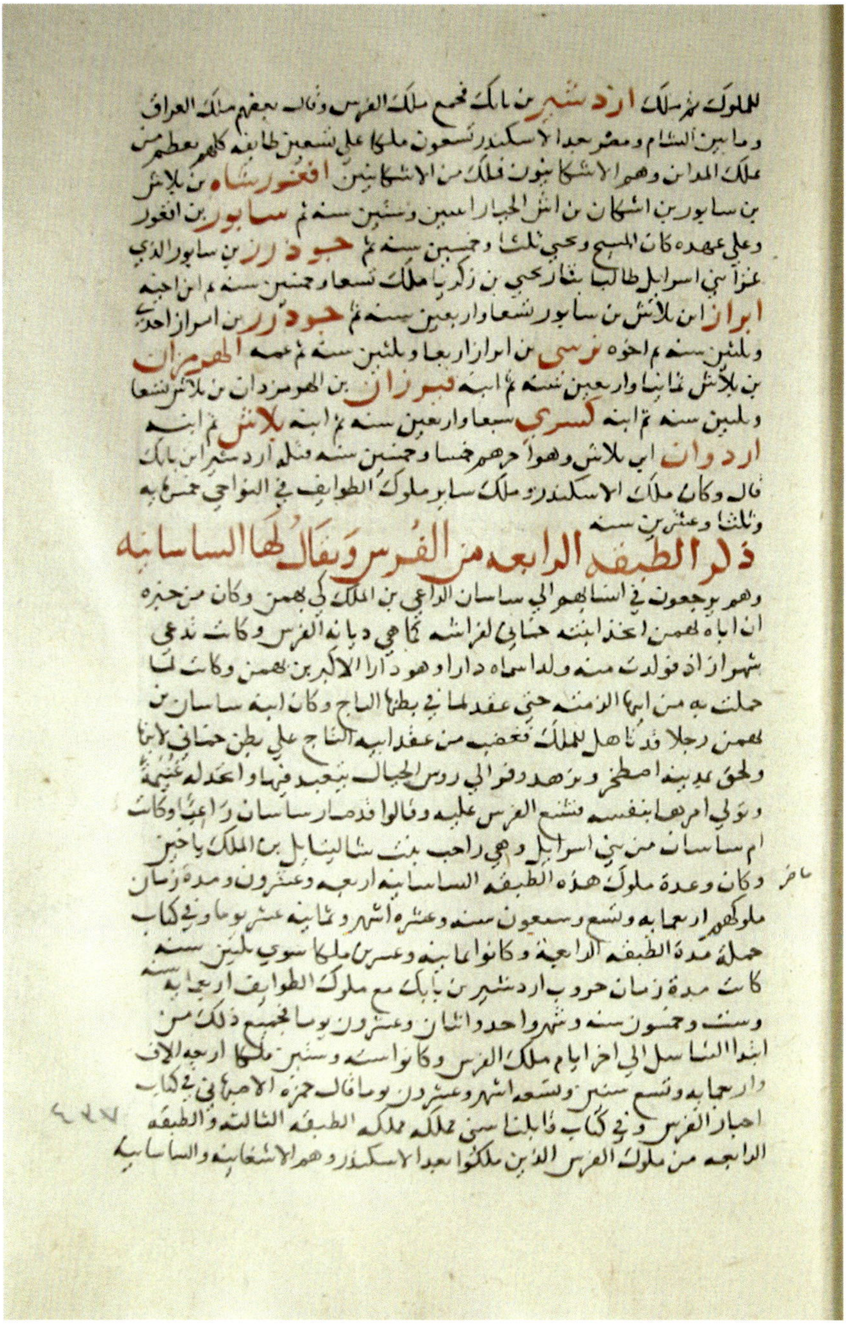

للملوك ثم ملك اردشير بن بابك فجمع ملك الفرس وقال بعضهم ملك العراق
وما بين الشام ومصر بعد الاسكندر تسعون ملكا على تسعين طايفة كلهم يعظم من
ملك المداين وهم الاشكانيون فملك من الاشكانيين افقورشاه بن بلاش
بن سابور بن اشكان بن اش الجبار ستين وستين سنة ثم سابور بن افقور
وعلى عهده كان المسيح ويحيى ثلثا وخمسين سنة ثم جودرز بن سابور الذي
غزا بني اسرايل طالبا بثار يحيى بن زكريا ملك تسعا وخمسين سنة ثم ابن اخيه
ابزان بن بلاش بن سابور تسعا واربعين سنة ثم جودرز بن ابزان احدى
وثلثين سنة ثم اخوه نرسي بن ابزان اربعا وثلثين سنة ثم عمه الهرمزان
بن بلاش ثمانيا واربعين سنة ثم ابنه فيروزان بن الهرمزان بن بلاش تسعا
وثلثين سنة ثم ابنه كسرى سبعا واربعين سنة ثم ابنه بلاش ثم ابنه
اردوان ابن بلاش وهو آخرهم خمسا وخمسين سنة فقتله اردشير بن بابك
قال وكان ملك الاسكندر وملك ساير ملوك الطوايف في النواحي خمسمائة
وثلثا وعشرين سنة

ذكر الطبقة الرابعة من الفرس ويقال لها الساسانية

وهم يرجعون في انسابهم الى ساسان الراعي بن الملك بن بهمن وكان من خبره
ان اباه بهمن اتخذ ابنته خماني لفراشه كما هي ديانة الفرس وكانت تدعى
شهرازاد فولدت منه ولدا سماه دارا وهو دارا الاكبر بن بهمن وكانت لما
حملت به من ابيها الزمته حتى عقد لما في بطنها التاج وكان ابنه ساسان بن
بهمن رجلا قد تاهل للملك فغضب من عقد ابيه التاج على بطن خماني لابنا
ولحق بمدينة اصطخر وتزهد وفر الى روس الجبال يتعبد فيها واتخذ له غنيمة
وتولى امرها بنفسه فتشنع الفرس عليه وقالوا قد صار ساسان راعيا وكانت
ام ساسان من بني اسرايل وهي راحب بنت شالتيال بن الملك باخبر
وكان وعدة ملوك هذه الطبقة الساسانية اربعة وعشرون ومدة زمان
ملوكهم اربعمائة وتسع وسبعون سنة وعشرة اشهر وثمانية عشر يوما وفي كتاب
جملة مدة الطبقة الرابعة وكانوا ثمانية وعشرين ملكا سوى ثلثين سنة
كانت مدة زمان حروب اردشير بن بابك مع ملوك الطوايف اربعمائة سنة
وست وخمسون سنة وشهر واحد واثنان وعشرون يوما فجميع ذلك من
ابتدا الساسانية الى اخر ايام ملك الفرس وكانوا ستة وستين ملكا اربعة الاف
واربعمائة وتسع سنين وتسعة اشهر وعشرون يوما قال حمزة الاصبهاني في كتاب
اخبار الفرس وفي كتاب قابلنا سنى مملكة ملكه الطبقة الثالثة والطبقة ٤٣٧
الرابعة من ملوك الفرس الذين ملكوا بعد الاسكندر وهم الاشغانية والساسانية

PLATE 1 Istanbul/ Süleymaniye Kütüphanesi, MS Ayasofya 3365, p. 437

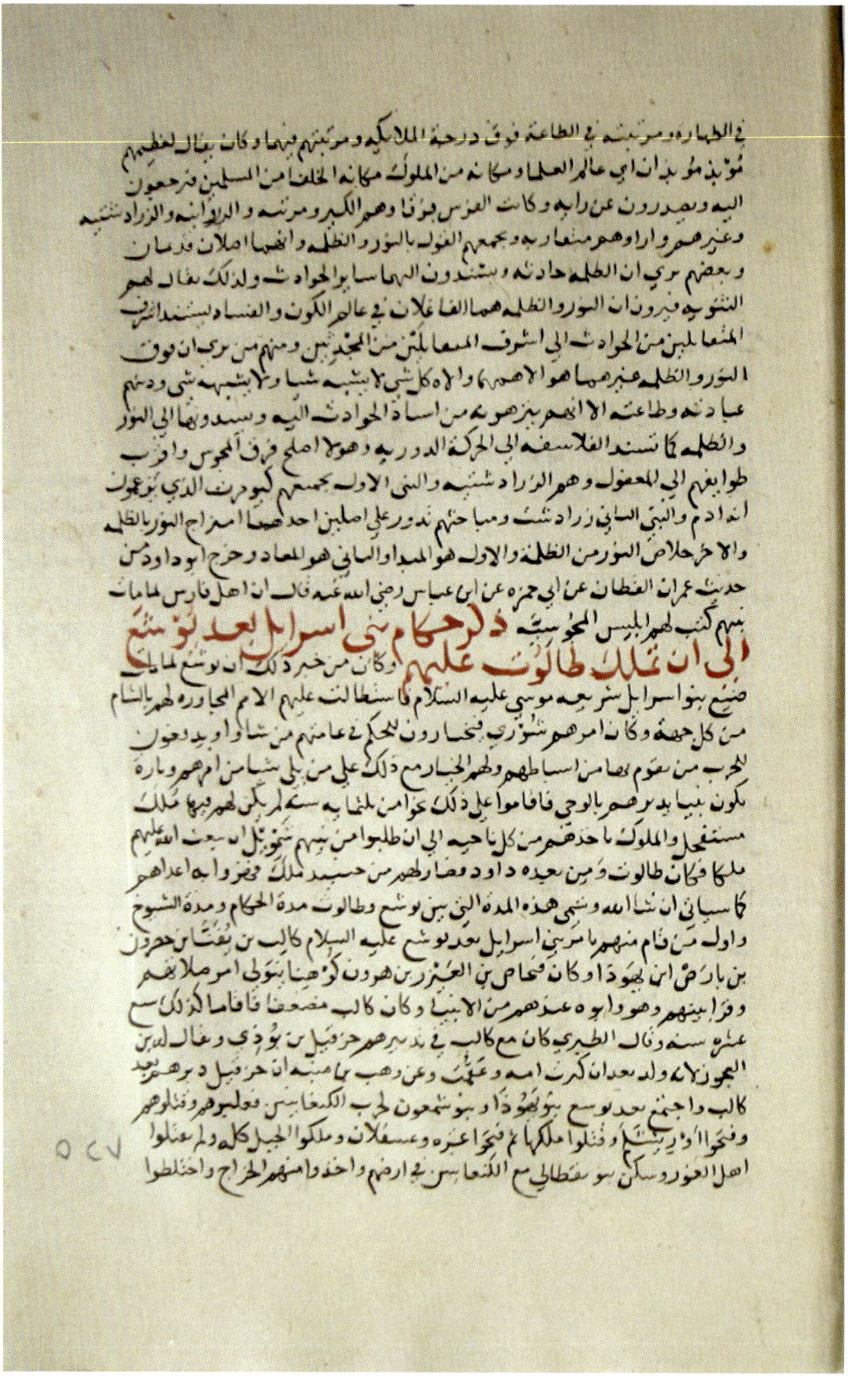

في الطهارة ومرتبته في الطاعة فوق درجة الملائكة ومرتبتهم فيهما وكان يقال لعظيمهم
موبذ موبذان أي عالم العلماء ومكانه من الملوك مكانة الخلفاء من المسلمين فيرجعون
إليه ويصدرون عن رأيه وكانت الفرس ثنوية وهم الكيومرثية والزروانية والزرادشتية
وغيرهم وآراؤهم متقاربة وجميعهم القول بالنور والظلمة وأنهما أصلان قديمان
وبعضهم يرى أن الظلمة حادثة ويسندون إليهما سائر الحوادث ولذلك يقال لهم
الثنوية فيرون أن النور والظلمة هما الفاعلان في عالم الكون والفساد ويسندون أشرف
المتقابلين من الحوادث إلى أشرف المتقابلين من المجذبين ومنهم من يرى أن فوق
النور والظلمة غيرهما هو الإله وأن الإله كل شيء لا يشبه شيئا ولا يشبهه شيء ودينهم
عبادته وطاعته إلا أنهم ينزهونه من إسناد الحوادث إليه ويسندونها إلى النور
والظلمة كما تسند الفلاسفة إلى الحركة الدورية وهؤلاء أصلح فرق المجوس وأقرب
طوائفهم إلى المعقول وهم الزرادشتية والنبي الأول جميعهم كيومرث الذي يزعمون
أنه آدم والنبي الثاني زرادشت ومباحثهم تدور على أصلين أحدهما امتزاج النور بالظلمة
والآخر خلاص النور من الظلمة والأول هو المبدأ والثاني هو المعاد وخرج أبو داود من
حديث عمران القطان عن أبي جمرة عن ابن عباس رضي الله عنه قال إن أهل فارس لما مات
نبيهم كتب لهم إبليس المجوسية

ذكر حكام بني إسرائيل بعد يوشع
إلى أن تملك طالوت عليهم

وكان من خبر ذلك أن يوشع لما مات
ضيع بنو إسرائيل شريعة موسى عليه السلام فاستطالت عليهم الأمم المجاورة لهم بالشام
من كل جهة وكان أمرهم شورى يتخايرون للحكم في عامتهم من شاءوا ويدعون
للحرب من يقوم بها من أسباطهم ولهم الخيار مع ذلك على من يلي شيئا من أمرهم وتارة
يكون نبيا يدبرهم بالوحي فأقاموا على ذلك نحوا من ثلثماية سنة لم يكن لهم فيها ملك
مستقل والملوك تأخذهم من كل ناحية إلى أن طلبوا من نبيهم شمويل أن يبعث الله عليهم
ملكا فكان طالوت ومن بعده داود فصار لهم من حينئذ ملك فقهروا به أعداءهم
كما سيأتي إن شاء الله وتسمى هذه المدة التي بين يوشع وطالوت مدة الحكام ومدة الشيوخ
وأول من قام منهم بأمر بني إسرائيل بعد يوشع عليه السلام كالب بن يوفنا بن حصرون
بن بارص ابن يهوذا وكان فنحاص بن العيزر بن هرون كوهنا يتولى أمر صلاتهم
وقرابينهم وهو وأبوه عندهم من الأنبياء وكان كالب مضعفا فأقام كذلك سبع
عشرة سنة وقال الطبري كان مع كالب في تدبيرهم حزقيل بن بوذي ويقال له ابن
العجوز لأنه ولد بعدما كبرت أمه وعقمت وعن وهب بن منبه أن حزقيل دبرهم بعد
كالب واجتمع بعد يوشع بنو يهوذا وبنو شمعون لحرب الكنعانيين فغلبوهم وقتلوهم
وفتحوا أذربيسق وقتلوا ملكها ثم فتحوا غزة وعسقلان وملكوا الجبل كله ولم يقتلوا ٥٢٧
أهل الغور وسكن بنو نفطالي مع الكنعانيين في أرضهم وأخذوا منهم الخراج واختلطوا

PLATE 2 Istanbul/ Süleymaniye Kütüphanesi, MS Ayasofya 3365, p. 527

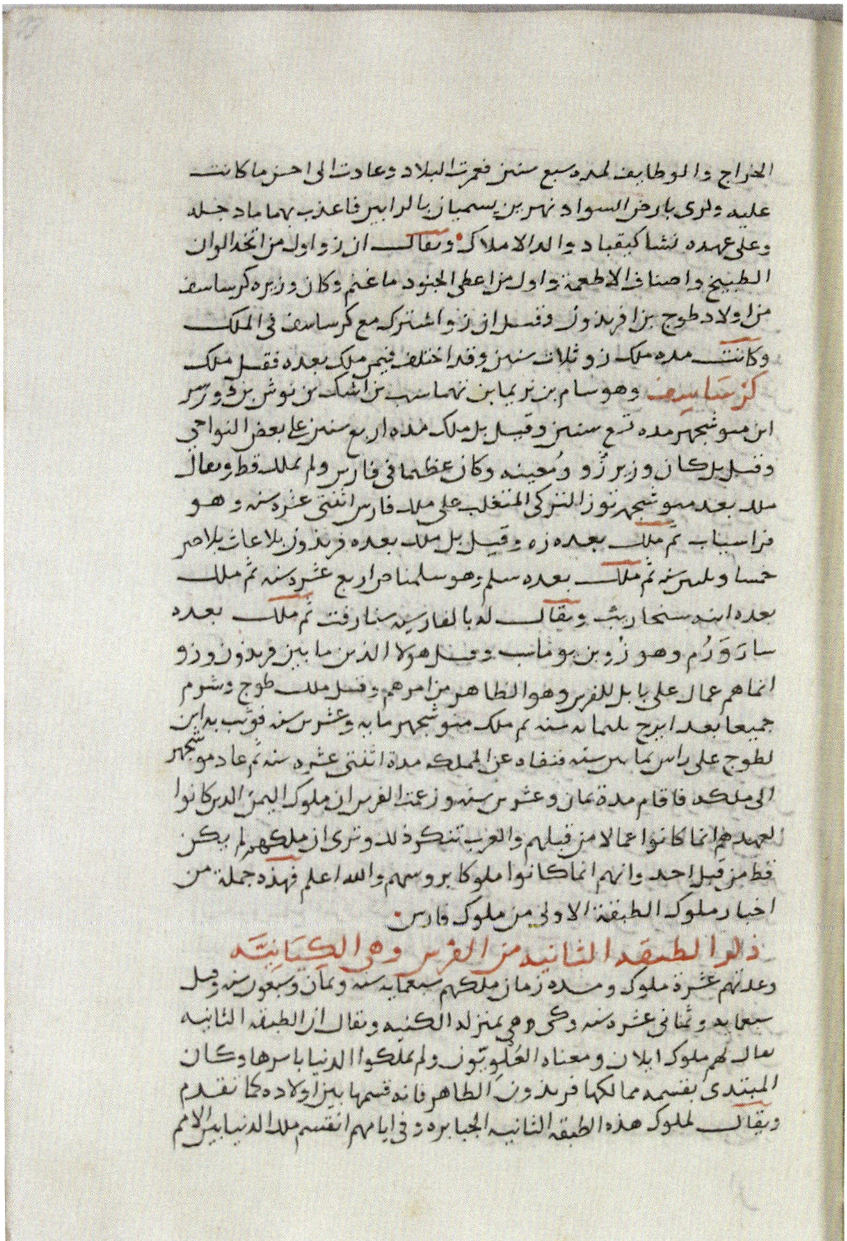
الخراج والوظايف لمدة سبع سنين فعمرت البلاد وعادت الى احسن ما كانت
عليه ويروى بارض السواد نهرين يسميان بالزابين فاعذب بهما ماء دجلة
وعلى عهده نشا كيقباد في الدالاملاك ويقال ان زو اول من اتخذ الوان
الطبيخ واصناف الاطعمة واول من اعطى الجنود ما غنم وكان وزيره كرساسف
من اولاد طوج بن افريدون وقيل ان زو اشترك مع كرساسف في الملك
وكانت مدة ملك زو ثلاث سنين وقد اختلف فيمن ملك بعده فقيل ملك
كرشاسف وهو سام بن نريمان بن طهماسب بن اشك بن نوش بن دورسر
ابن منوشجهر مدة تسع سنين وقيل بل ملك مدة اربع سنين على بعض النواحي
وقيل بل كان وزير زو ومعينه وكان عظيما في فارس ولم يملك قط ويقال
ملك بعد منوشجهر نوذر التركي المتغلب على ملك فارس اثنتي عشرة سنة وهو
فراسياب ثم ملك بعده زو وقيل بل ملك بعده فريدون [illegible]
خمسا وثلثين سنة ثم ملك بعده سلم وهو سلمان اربع عشرة سنة ثم ملك
بعده ابنه سنجاريث ويقال له بالفارسية سنارفت ثم ملك بعده
سادرم وهو زو بن بوماسب وقيل هولا الذين ما بين فريدون وزو
انما هم عمال على بابل للفرس وهو الظاهر من امرهم وقيل ملك طوج وسلم
جميعا بعد ايرج ثلثمائة سنة ثم ملك منوشجهر مائة وعشرين سنة فوثب ابن
لطوج على راس ثمانين سنة فنفاه عن المملكة مدة اثنتي عشرة سنة ثم عاد منوشجهر
الى ملكه فاقام مدة ثمان وعشرين سنة وزعمت الفرس ان ملوك اليمن الذين كانوا
لعهدهم انما كانوا عمالا من قبلهم والعرب تنكر ذلك وترى ان ملكهم لم يكن
قط من قبل احد وانهم انما كانوا ملوكا برؤوسهم والله اعلم فهذه جملة من
اخبار ملوك الطبقة الاولى من ملوك فارس
ذكر الطبقة الثانية من الفرس وهي الكيانية
وعدتهم عشرة ملوك ومدة زمان ملكهم سبعمائة سنة وثمان وسبعون سنة وقيل
سبعمائة وثماني عشرة سنة وكي هي بمنزلة الكنية ويقال ان الطبقة الثانية
يقال لهم ملوك ايلان ومعناه العلويون ولم يملكوا الدنيا باسرها وكان
المبتدي بقسمة ممالكها فريدون الطاهر فانه قسمها بين اولاده كما تقدم
ويقال لملوك هذه الطبقة الثانية الجبابرة وفي ايامهم انقسم ملك الدنيا بين الامم

PLATE 3 Istanbul/ Topkapı Sarayı Müzesi Kütüphanesi, MS A 2926/5, fol. 70a

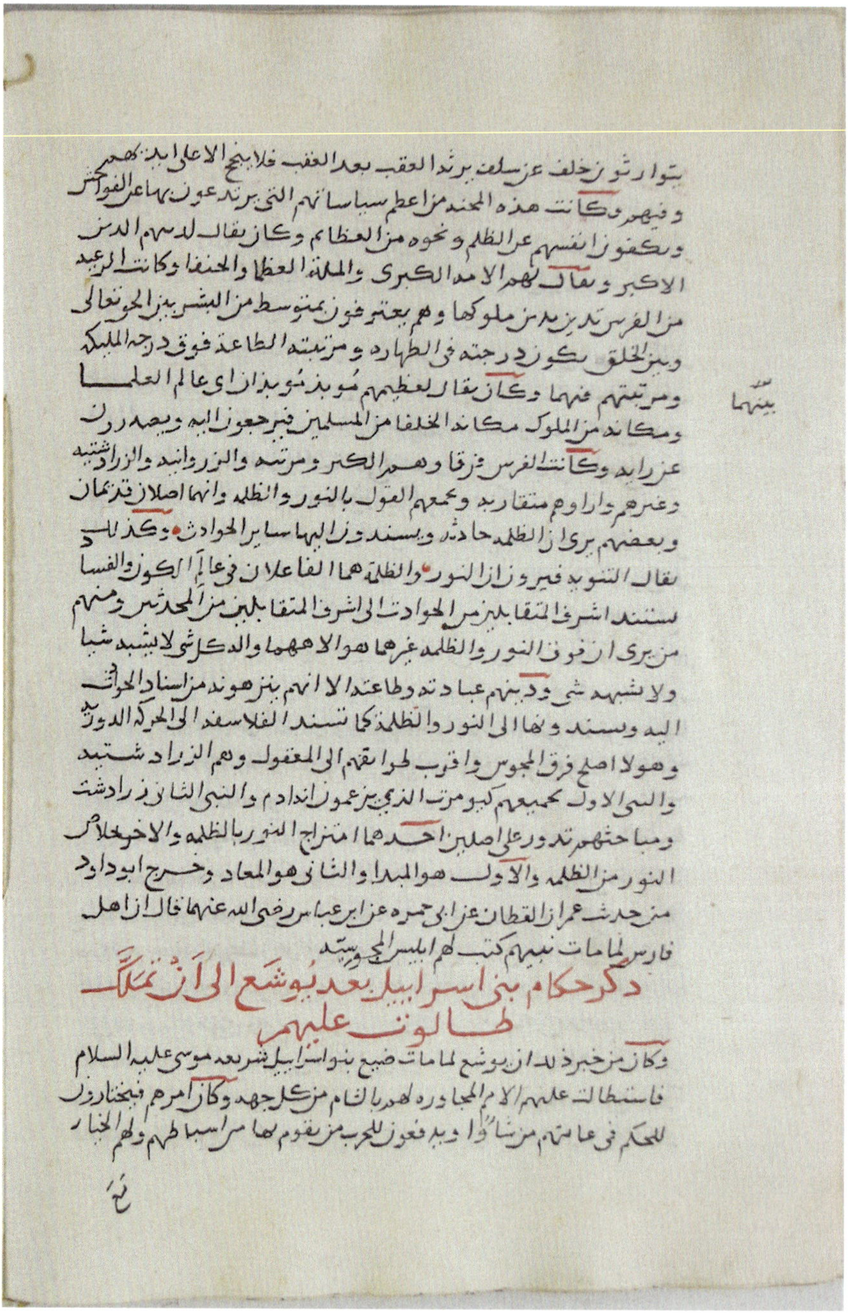

يتوارثون خلف عن سلف يرثونه العقب بعد العقب فلا يبيح الاعلى ابدا لهم
وفيهم وكانت هذه المحنة من اعظم سياساتهم التي يردعون بها عن الفواحش
ويكفون انفسهم عن الظلم ونحوه من العظائم وكان يقال لرئيسهم الديني
الاكبر ويقال لهم الامة الكبرى والملة العظمى والحنفا وكانت الرعية
من الفرس تدين بدين ملوكها وهم يعتقدون بمتوسط من البشر بين الحق تعالى
وبين الخلق تكون درجته في الطهارة ومرتبته الطاعة فوق درجة الملايكة
ومرتبتهم فيهما وكان يقال لعظيمهم موبذ موبذان اي عالم العلما بينهما
ومكانه من الملوك مكانة الخلفا من المسلمين فيرجعون اليه ويصدرون
عن رايه وكانت الفرس فرقا وهم الكثر ومرتبة والزروانية والزرادشتية
وغيرهم واراوهم متقاربة ويجمعهم القول بالنور والظلمة وانهما اصلان قديمان
وبعضهم يرى ان الظلمة حادثة ويسندون اليها ساير الحوادث وكذلك
يقال الثنوية فيرون ان النور والظلمة هما الفاعلان في عالم الكون والفساد
يسندون الاشيا المتقابلين من الحوادث الى الشيين المتقابلين من المحدثين ومنهم
من يرى ان فوق النور والظلمة غيرهما هو الاههما والذي كل شي لا يشبهه شيا
ولا يشبهه شي وذلك بينهم عبادته وطاعته الا انهم ينزهونه من اسناد الحوادث
اليه ويسندونها الى النور والظلمة كما تسند الفلاسفة الى الحركة الدورية
وهولا اصلح فرق المجوس واقرب لحوا نقيهم الى المعقول وهم الزرادشتية
والنبي الاول بجميعهم كيومرث الذي يزعمون انه ادم والنبي الثاني زرادشت
ومباحثهم تدور على اصلين احدهما امتزاج النور بالظلمة والاخر خلاص
النور من الظلمة والاول هو المبدا والثاني هو المعاد وخرج ابو داود
من حديث عمران القطان عن ابي حمزة عن ابن عباس رضي الله عنهما قال ان اهل
فارس لما مات نبيهم كتب لهم ابليس المجوسية

ذكر حكام بني اسرايل بعد يوشع الى ان تملك طالوت عليهم

وكان من خبر ذلك ان يوشع لما مات ضيع بنو اسرايل شرعه موسى عليه السلام
فاستطالت عليهم الامم المجاورة لهم بالشام من كل جهة وكان امرهم فيختارون
للحكم في عامتهم من شاوا ويدفعون للحرب من يقوم بها من اسباطهم ولهم اخبار

PLATE 4 Istanbul/ Topkapı Sarayı Müzesi Kütüphanesi, MS A 2926/5, fol. 124b

PLATE 5 Algiers/ Bibliothèque nationale, MS 1589, fol. 92b

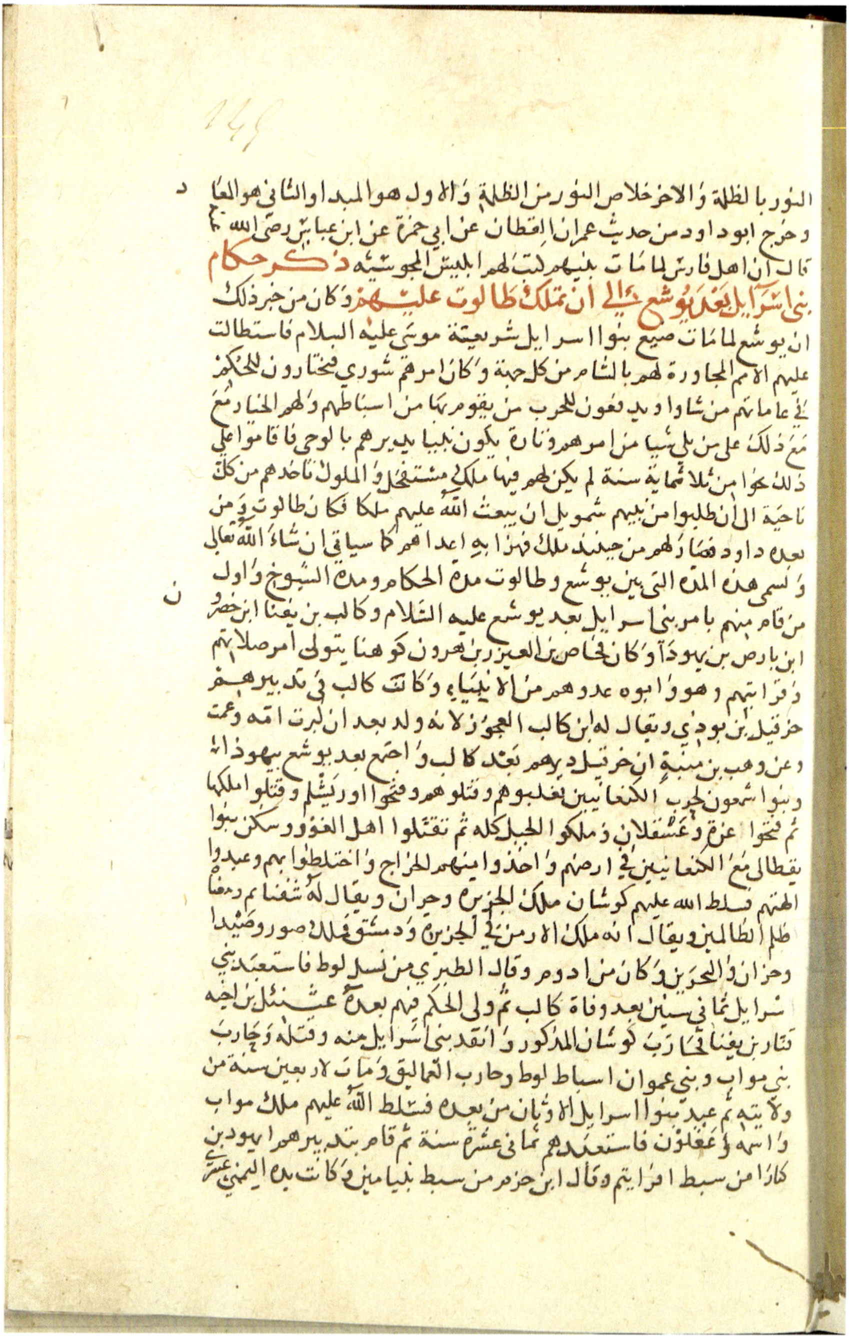

النور بالظلمة والآخر خلاص النور من الظلمة والاول هو المبدا والثاني هو المعاد
وخرج ابو داود من حديث عمران القطان عن ابي حمزة عن ابن عباس رضي الله عنهما
قال ان اهل فارس لما مات نبيهم كتب لهم ابليس المجوسية ذكر حكام
بني اسرايل بعد يوشع الى ان تملك طالوت عليهم وكان من خبر ذلك
ان يوشع لما مات ضيع بنوا اسرايل شريعة موسى عليه السلام فاستطالت
عليهم الامم المجاورة لهم بالشام من كل جهة وكان امرهم شورى يختارون للحكم
في عامتهم من شاووا ويدعون للحرب من يقوم بها من اسباطهم ولهم الخيار مع
مع ذلك على من يلي شيا من امورهم وتارة يكون نبيا يدبرهم بالوحي فاقاموا على
ذلك نحوا من ثلاثماية سنة لم يكن لهم فيها ملك مستقل والملوك تاخذهم من كل
ناحية الى ان طلبوا من نبيهم شمويل ان يبعث الله عليهم ملكا فكان طالوت ومن
بعده داود فصار لهم من حينيذ ملك فهزا به اعداهم كما سياتي ان شاء الله تعالى
وتسمى هذه المدة التي بين يوشع وطالوت مدة الحكام ومدة الشيوخ واول
من قام منهم بامر بني اسرايل بعد يوشع عليه السلام وكالب بن يوفنا ابن حصرون
ابن بارص بن يهوذا وكان فنحاص بن العيزر بن هرون كوهنا يتولى امر صلاتهم
وقرابينهم وهو وابوه عدودهم من الانبياء وكانت كالب في تدبيرهم
حزقيل بن بوذي ويقال له ابن العجوز لانه ولد بعد ان كبرت امه وعمت
وعن وهب بن منبه ان حزقيل دبرهم بعد كالب والاصح بعد يوشع يهوذا
وبنوا شمعون لحرب الكنعانيين فغلبوهم وقتلوهم وفتحوا اورشلم وقتلوا ملكها
ثم فتحوا غزة وعسقلان وملكوا الجبل كله ثم تقاتلوا اهل الغور وسكن بنوا
نفتالي مع الكنعانيين في ارضهم واخذوا منهم الخراج واختلطوا بهم وعبدوا
الهتهم فسلط الله عليهم كوشان ملك الجزيرة وحران ويقال له شفنا ثم رعفا
ظلم الظالمين ويقال انه ملك الارمن في الجزيرة ودمشق وملك صور وصيدا
وحران والبحرين وكان من ادوم وقال الطبري من نسل لوط فاستعبد بني
اسرايل ثماني سنين بعد وفاة كالب ثم ولي الحكم فيهم بعده عثنيل بن اخيه
قناز بن يوفنا فحارب كوشان المذكور وانقذ بني اسرايل منه وقتله وحارب
بني مواب وبني عمون اسباط لوط وحارب العماليق ومات لاربعين سنة من
ولايته ثم عبد بنوا اسرايل الاوثان من بعده فسلط الله عليهم ملك مواب
واسمه عغلون فاستعبدهم ثماني عشرة سنة ثم قام بتدبيرهم ابيود بن
كارا من سبط افرايم وقال ابن حزم من سبط بنيامين وكانت يده اليمنى عسرى

PLATE 6 Algiers/ Bibliothèque nationale, MS 1589, fol. 145a

Abbreviations and Symbols

⟨…⟩	Interpolation (Arabic text)
{…}	Correction
[…]	Word(s) to be overlooked (Arabic text) ; interpolation (translation)
(…)	Blank in the MS
		Used in the Arabic text to indicate the passage to the next folio (number indicated in the left margin)
الأصل	Istanbul, Süleymaniye Kütüphanesi, MS Fatih 4340

 | DOI:10.1163/9789004528765_004

Text and Translation

of al-Maqrīzī's

al-Ḫabar ʿan al-bašar

كتاب الخبر عن البشر

The History of Mankind
Volume V, Section 4:
Persia and Its Kings, Part II

∵

137a

ذكر الطبقة الرابعة من الفرس ويقال لها الساسانية

§1[١] وهم يرجعون في أنسابهم إلى ساسان الراعي بن الملك كي بهمن. وكان من خبره أن أباه بهمن اتخذ ابنته خماني لفراشه كما هي ديانة الفرس وكانت تدعى شهرازاذ. فولدت منه ولدا سماه دارا وهو دارا الأكبر بن بهمن وكانت لما حملت به من أبيها ألزمته حتى عقد لما في بطنها التاج.

§2[٢] وكان ابنه ساسان بن بهمن رجلا قد تأهل للملك فغضب من عقد أبيه التاج على بطن خماني لا بنها ولحق بمدينة إصطخر وتزهد وفر إلى {رؤوس} الجبال يتعبد فيها واتخذ له غُنَيمةً وتولى أمرها بنفسه. فشنع الفرس عليه وقالوا: "قد صار ساسان رَاعِيًا." وكانت أم ساسان من بني إسرائيل وهي راحب بنت شالتيايل بن الملك ياخين وكان (...).

§3[٣] وعدة ملوك هذه الطبقة الساسانية أربعة وعشرون ومدة زمان ملوكهم أربع مائة وتسع وسبعون سنة وعشرة أشهر وثمانية عشر يوما. وفي كتاب: جملة مدة الطبقة الرابعة وكانوا ثمانية وعشرين ملكا سوى ثلاثين سنة كانت مدة زمان حروب أردشير بن بابك مع ملوك الطوائف أربع مائة سنة وست وخمسون سنة وشهر واحد واثنان وعشرون يوما. فجميع ذلك من ابتداء التناسل إلى آخر أيام ملك الفرس وكانوا ستة وستين ملكا أربعة آلاف وأربع مائة وتسع سنين وتسعة أشهر وعشرون يوما.

---

٦ رؤوس: "روس" في الأصل. ٨ راحب: وضع المقريزي رمز "ح" تحت الكلمة إشارة إلى تلفظها بالحاء. || وكان: كشط المقريزي سطرا ونصف سطر ولم يكتب نصا آخر.

---

١ راجع خبر المقريزي (الفرس) ١: ١٩٦–١٩٧.

٢ من تجارب الأمم لمسكويه ١: ٨١.

٣ من تأريخ سني الملوك لحمزة ص ١٤، ٢٥.

 | DOI:10.1163/9789004528765_005

The Fourth Class of Persian (Kings), the Sasanians

§ 1[1] The Sasanians derive their origin from Sāsān the Shepherd, son of King Kay Bahman. Bahman took his daughter Ḫumānī as spouse, as is the religious custom of the Persians.[2] She was called Šihrāzād. She bore her father a son, whom he named Dārā. He was Dārā the Elder b. Bahman. When she was pregnant to her father, she made him crown the child in her womb (as heir-apparent).

§ 2[3] Bahman's son Sāsān b. Bahman was already grown-up and suitable for kingship. When his father crowned Ḫumānī's son in her womb, Sāsān was furious and left for the city of Iṣṭaḫr. He became an ascetic and fled to mountain tops, where he served God and took a little flock of sheep, which he himself herded. The Persians disliked what he did and said: "Sāsān has become a shepherd!" Sāsān's mother was an Israelite, Rāḥab bt. Šālatyāyal, son of King Yāḫīn,[4] and (…) was (…).[5]

§ 3[6] The kings of this Sasanian class[7] were 24 and the sum total of their reigns was 479 years, 10 months, and 18 days. According to one book, the entire period of the fourth class, which consisted of 28 kings, excluding the 30 years Ardašīr b. Bābak fought against the Petty Kings, was 456 years, 1 month, and 22 days. In all, counting from the origin of the humankind until the end of the days of the Persian kings, who were 66 in number, one gets 4,409 years, 9 months, and 20 days.

---

1 Cf. al-Maqrīzī, *Ḫabar/Persia*, 1:196–197 (§ 152).

2 For the *khwēdōdah*, see "Marriage ii. Next of kin marriage in Zoroastrianism," in *EIr*.

3 Miskawayh, *Taǧārib al-umam*, 1:81 = C61; cf. al-Maqrīzī, *Ḫabar/Persia*, 1:188–189, 196–197 (§§ 145, 152).

4 I.e., Shealtiel, son of Jehoiachin, King of Judah (*1 Chronicles* 3:17–18), 6th century BC, also listed as an ancestor of Joseph in *Matthew* 1:12. Cf. also al-Bīrūnī, *al-Āṯār al-bāqiyah*, 28 (as the father of Zarbābīl, the brother of Rāḥab), al-Ṭabarī, *Taʾrīḫ*, 1:689 = trans., 4:83–84, al-Dīnawarī, *Aḫbār* 29, and al-Masʿūdī, *Murūǧ* § 585.

5 Almost two lines have been erased in the holograph, with minimal remnants of writing still visible. MS T has left a short blank space of about 1 1/3 lines. According to al-Ṭabarī, *Taʾrīḫ*, 1:814 = trans., 5:4, Sāsān's mother was Rāmbihišt and derived from a royal line. Cf. § 10.

6 Ḥamzah, *Taʾrīḫ* 14, 25 = trans. 33, 44. Ḥamzah, *Taʾrīḫ* 14, actually counts 429 years, 3 months, and 18 days. Hoyland (2018): 33, note 50, points out that the reigns add up to 449 years, 10 months, and 16 days.

7 For a list of Sasanian kings according to al-Maqrīzī, see above, p. 19–20.

[1]4 § قال حمزة الإصبهاني ⟨في⟩ **كتاب أخبار الفرس**: وفي كتاب: قابلنا سني مملكة مملكة الطبقة الثالثة والطبقة الرابعة من ملوك الفرس الذين ملكوا بعد الإسكندر وهم الأشغانية والساسانية بتاريخ الإسكندر الذي هو مضبوط فطلبنا ما بين ابتداء سني الإسكندر إلى ابتداء سني الهجرة لنجعله أصلا فوجدنا بين سني الإسكندر وبين سني الهجرة وذلك من نصف نهار يوم الاثنين أول يوم من تشرين الأول إلى نصف نهار يوم الخميس أول يوم من المحرم ثلاثمائة ألف | وأربعين ألفا 137b وتسع مائة يوم ويوما واحدا. فتكون هذه الأيام سنين قمرية تسع مائة وإحدى وستين سنة ومائةً وأربعة وخمسين يوما. ويكون سنين شمسية على أن السنة ثلاثمائة وخمسة وستين يوما وربع يوم تسع مائة واثنتين وثلاثين سنة ومائتين وتسعةً وثمانين يوما تبلغ هذه الأيام تسعة أشهر وتسعة عشر يوما.

[2]5 § فزدنا عليها لما بين ابتداء الهجرة إلى انقضاء دولة الفرس بهلك ملكهم يزدجرد أربعين سنة فبلغت مدة ذلك تسع مائة واثنتين وسبعين سنة ومائتين وتسعة وثمانين يوما. حططنا ⟨عن ذلك

٥ الخميس : كتب المقريزي "كذا" فوق الكلمة. ‖ أول يوم : الزيادة بخط المقريزي تحت السطر.
١٠–1.38 عن ... لحصل : الزيادة من تأريخ حمزة.

١ من تأريخ سني الملوك لحمزة ص ١٦–١٧.
٢ من تأريخ سني الملوك لحمزة ص ١٧.

§ 4[8] Ḥamzah al-Iṣfahānī[9] says in *Kitāb Aḫbār al-Furs* [Book of the history of the Persians]:[10] In a book (it is said):[11] We have compared the years of each reign, one by one, of the third and fourth classes of Persian kings, who ruled after Alexander, that is to say, the Ašġānians and the Sasanians, according to the era of Alexander which is determined (in astrological tables).[12] We have studied the period between the beginning of the years of Alexander and those of the *hiǧrah* to take that as our starting point and we have noticed that between the years of Alexander and those of the *hiǧrah*, i.e., from noon, on Monday, the first of Tišrīn I, to noon, on Thursday, the first[13] of Muḥarram, there were 340,901 days. In lunar years, this makes 961 years and 154 days. In solar[14] years, with 365 and 1/4 days to a year, this makes 932 years and 289 days.[15] These 289 days make 9 months and 19 days.

§ 5[16] When we add to this the time from the beginning of the *hiǧrah* to the end of the Persians' kingship when their king Yazdağird died, 40 years,[17] the whole period will be 972 years and 289 days. When we deduct (from that the

8 Ḥamzah, *Taʾrīḫ* 16–17 = trans. 35–36.

9 Ḥamzah al-Iṣfahānī (d. 350/961 or 360/971), historian and philologist, see Mittwoch (1909): 113.

10 In the first part of this section, al-Maqrīzī refers to Ḥamzah's book as *Kitāb Tawārīḫ al-bašar man baqiya minhum wa-man ġabar* [Book of the chronologies of mankind, of those who still remain and those who have passed away] (al-Maqrīzī, *Ḫabar/Persia*, 1:50–51, § 10). Nowadays, the book usually goes by the title *Taʾrīḫ sinī l-mulūk*. For the various titles, see Mittwoch (1909): 129.

11 As he often does, al-Maqrīzī has dropped the title of the book, *Ḫudāynāmah* (cf. Ḥamzah, *Taʾrīḫ* 16), i.e., the translation of the Middle Persian *Ḫwadāynāmag*, for which see Hämeen-Anttila (2018b).

12 Al-Maqrīzī drops the continuation of the sentence that we find in Ḥamzah's *Taʾrīḫ*: "in the calculations of astronomers in their *zīǧs*."

13 The word "first" is missing from the printed edition of Ḥamzah's work, also from ed. Gottwaldt, 17. Al-Maqrīzī has added the words *awwal yawm* in the margin, which shows that the manuscript he used also lacked these words which he then most probably added on his own, without textual evidence.

14 Ḥamzah reads "Chaldaean years."

15 In fact, the number of these days makes about 933 and 1/3 years. The mathematical operations in this and the next paragraph go wrong in Ḥamzah's work, and al-Maqrīzī copies the erroneous results as such, without checking them.

16 Ḥamzah, *Taʾrīḫ* 17 = trans. 36.

17 Hoyland (2018): 36, note 70, points out that Yazdağird died in the year 31, not 40, of *hiǧrah*.

لمدة ملك الأشغانيين مائتين وستا وستين سنة لحصل> لمدة ملك الساسانية من مبدإ ملك أردشير ابن بابك إلى وقت {هلك} يزدجرد سبع مائة وستا وثمانين سنة ومائتين وتسعةً وثمانين يوما.

§6[1] فلما صح لنا من ملك بني ساسان الجملة عدلنا منها إلى التفصيل فاعتبرنا عدد ملوكهم ثم أسماءهم ثم مدة سني كل ملك منهم فأصبنا ثلاثة أسماء لم يذكرها الناقلون وإنما أُتوا في ذلك من أجل تشابه ألفاظ الأسماء نحو يزدجرد ويزدجرد وبهرام وبهرام وبهرام وذلك أن يزدجرد الأثيم والد بهرام جُوْر هو يزدجرد بن يزدجرد الأثيم وهو صاحب شَرْوِيْن الدَسْتَبي لا الأثيم وكان ذا سياسة مرضية وأمانة ورحمة وعطف بخلاف ابنه.

§7 وينشد: [السريع]

يا أيها السائل عن ديننا   نحن على ملة شروين

وكان له مذهب في اللواط وشرب الخمر وينشد: [السريع]

نشربها صرفا بلا مُزْنَةٍ   وندخل القثاء في التين

٢ هلك: "ملك" في الأصل والصواب من تأريخ حمزة.

١ من تأريخ سني الملوك لحمزة ص ١٧.

period of the reign of the Ašġānians, 266 years, we)[18] get 786 years and 289 days for the length of the kingship of the Sasanians from the beginning of the rule of Ardašīr b. Bābak until the death[19] of Yazdağird.

§ 6[20] Now that we have established the total number of the regnal years of the Sasanians, we will move on to a detailed discussion of the number of their kings, their names, and the length of each king's reign. We have also noticed three names that are not mentioned by transmitters (of history). They have erred here because the names resemble each other, like in the case of the two Yazdağirds and the three Bahrāms. Yazdağird the Sinner, father of Bahrām Gūr, was Yazdağird the Sinner b. Yazdağird. The latter Yazdağird was the king of Šarwīn al-Dastabī,[21] not Yazdağird the Sinner. Contrary to his son, he governed well and was trustworthy, compassionate, and gentle.

§ 7 A poet has said:[22] [*al-sarīʿ*]

Oh you, who ask about our religion:
we follow the way (*millah*) of Šarwīn.

Šarwīn followed the way of homosexuality and wine drinking. The poet said (in the same poem): [*al-sarīʿ*]

We drink it unmixed, without water,
and we drive a cucumber into a fig![23]

18 Addition from Ḥamzah.
19 Read *hulk*, following Ḥamzah.
20 Ḥamzah, *Taʾrīḫ* 17 = trans. 36.
21 Ḥamzah relates that Yazdağird sent Šarwīn Barniyān, the chief of the district of Dastabá, to Byzantium as viceregent during the minority of the Byzantine heir-apparent. Cf. also § 103. For the name, see Justi (1895): 290, who suggests reading Narīmān for Barniyān (Yarīnān). Šarwīn and his servant Ḫwarrīn (or Ḫurrīn) seem to have been well-known until at least the tenth century, with a story circulating about them, cf. Abū Nuwās, *Dīwān* 5:144, with Ḥamzah's commentary in 5:146. *Muğmal al-tawārīḫ* 74 (ed. Bahār, p. 95) and al-Dīnawarī, *Aḫbār* 71, give a short description of the story. For a detailed analysis of the story and its development, see Hämeen-Anttila (2022a).
22 The verses resemble some verses by Abū Nuwās, *Dīwān*, 5:57, 293.
23 I.e., practice anal intercourse.

§ 8[١] وقد أسقط الناقلون أيضا من اسمين متفقي اللفظ اسما واحدا وهو بهرام بن بهرام بن بهرام. وأسقطوا أيضا بهرام آخر وهو بهرام بن يزدجرد بن بهرام جور والد فيروز. قال: وأنا أسوق تاريخ سني ملوك بني ساسان على النسق ليظهر منه عُوَارَ ما في النسخ.

§ 9[٢] أزدشير بن بابك. قال غير حمزة: وتسميه اليهود اخشوبروش. وقيل إنه ابن بابك شاه بن ساسان الأصغر بن بابك بن ساسان بن بهافريذ بن مهرمش بن ساسان الأكبر بن بهمن ولقب بالجامع لجمعه ملك الفُرْس ولقب أيضا بابكان.

§ 10[٣] وولد بقرية من رستاق إصطخر يقال لها طبروده. | وكان جده ساسان شجاعا شديد البطش 138a
فحارب وحده ثمانين رجلا ذوي بأس ونجدة فهزمهم مغرى بالصيد وتزوج امرأة من نسل ملوك فارس. فولدت له بابك وله شعر أطول من شبر وصار قيما على بيت نار بإصطخر فلما كبر بابك

---

٥ الأصغر: الزيادة بخط المقريزي في الهامش الأيسر من الأسفل إلى الأعلى + صح، ويشير إليها رمز ⌐ بعد "ساسان". ٧–٨ شديد ... فهزمهم: الزيادة بخط المقريزي في الهامش الأعلى والكلمات الثلاثة الأولى من الأسفل إلى الأعلى والبقية من الأعلى إلى الأسفل. ٩ فولدت ... شبر: الزيادة بخط المقريزي في الهامش الأيسر والكلمات الثلاث الأخيرة منكسة.

---

٤ أزدشير: أضاف المقريزي الحاشية التالية في الهامش الأيمن منكسة: "حـ الراء المهملة فيه أكثر".

---

١ من تأريخ سني الملوك لحمزة ص ١٧–١٨.

٢ من آثار البيروني ص ١٣٦.

٣ من تأريخ الطبري ١: ٨١٤–٨١٥.

§ 8[24] Transmitters have also dropped one of two homophonous names, namely (in the case of) Bahrām b. Bahrām b. Bahrām. They have also dropped another Bahrām, namely Bahrām b. Yazdağird b. Bahrām Gūr, the father of Fīrūz. He (Ḥamzah) said: I will also mention the chronology of the years of the Sasanian kings, in the order (of their reigns), to show the faults there are in the various manuscripts (*nusaḫ*).

§ 9[25] Ardašīr b. Bābak.[26] Someone other than Ḥamzah has said: The Jews call him Aḫšawīrūš.[27] It is said that Ardašīr was the son of Bābakšāh b. Sāsān the Younger b. Bābak b. Sāsān b. Bihāfarīd b. Mihrmaš b. Sāsān the Elder b. Bahman. His cognomen was the Unifier (*al-Ǧāmiʿ*) because he unified the kingship of the Persians. He also had the cognomen Bābakān.[28]

§ 10[29] Ardašīr was born in a village called Ṭīrūdih in the countryside around Iṣṭaḫr.[30] His grandfather Sāsān was brave and fierce. Once he fought single-handedly against eighty strong and brave men and put them all to flight. He also loved hunting. He married a woman belonging to the royal line of the kings of Fārs,[31] who bore him Bābak. Bābak's hair was longer than a span (when he was born). He became the guardian of a fire temple in Iṣṭaḫr.[32]

---

7 Ardašīr : The (letter) R is more common without a dot (marginal gloss in al-Maqrīzī's hand).

---

24 Ḥamzah, *Taʾrīḫ* 17–18 = trans. 37.

25 Al-Bīrūnī, *al-Āṯār al-bāqiyah* 136 (genealogy); cf. al-Ṭabarī, *Taʾrīḫ*, 1:813 = trans., 5:2–3; al-Ṭabarī, *Taʾrīḫ*, 1:688 = trans., 4:82; al-Masʿūdī, *Murūǧ* § 576.

26 Al-Maqrīzī often writes Azdašīr, which is also elsewhere a common, although mistaken, variant of the name.

27 For Ahasverus, see, e.g., al-Bīrūnī, Index; Ibn al-ʿIbrī, *Muḫtaṣar* 52. The Biblical Ahasverus refers to the Achaemenid Artaxerxes I, not the first Sasanian king.

28 Bābakān reflects Middle Persian Bābagān, which is a patronym. All cognomens seem to have been taken from al-Bīrūnī, *al-Āṯār al-bāqiyah* 136–139. Cf. also Justi (1895): 419.

29 Al-Ṭabarī, *Taʾrīḫ*, 1:814–815 = trans., 5:3–6; cf. Ibn al-Aṯīr, *Kāmil*, 1:380–381.

30 Al-Maqrīzī here simplifies al-Ṭabarī. For al-Maqrīzī, Ardašīr was born in the *rustāq* of Iṣṭaḫr, while his source, al-Ṭabarī, says that he was born in the *rustāq* of Ḫīr in the district of Iṣṭaḫr. The reading of the village's name is conjectural. The holograph and MS T read Ṭabrūdih (uncertain vocalisation).

31 Al-Maqrīzī's source, al-Ṭabarī, speaks only of *a* royal family in Fārs, and gives as her name Rāmbihišt.

32 Here, al-Maqrīzī abbreviates his source, which speaks of Sāsān as being (*kāna*, not *ṣāra*) the guardian of the fire temple.

قام بأمره بعد أبيه وولد له ابنه أردشير. فلما بلغ من العمر سبع سنين قدمه أبوه إلى ملك إصطخر فنشأ عنده وحسن قيامه بما وسد إليه.

§ 11[1] وحدثه المنجمون بأنه يملك. ورأى في منامه ذلك فقويت نفسه. وكان حازما أريبا كثير الاستشارة طويل الفكر معتمدا في تدبيره على رجل فاضل من الفرس يعرف بتنسَر كان هربذا فلم يزل يدبر أمره ويجتمع معه على سياسة الملك إلى أن {أطاعه} من جاوره من ملوك الطوائف وعرفوا فضله ودخلوا تحت رايته. فحارب من امتنع منهم عليه وكانت له مكايد وحروب.

§ 12[2] وذكر الطبري عن أهل الكتاب أنه وثب على مضي خمس مائة وثلاث وعشرين سنة مضت من ملك الإسكندر بابل. وفي قول المجوس مائتان وست وستون سنة. وكان أول ما فعل أنه سار

---

١ سبع: أضاف المقريزي كلمة "اربع" في الهامش الأيمن من الأعلى إلى الأسفل وزاد فوقها "ح" (ل "نسخة أخرى") ويشير إليها رمز "٢" بعد كلمة "بما" في آخر الجملة. ٥ أطاعه: في الأصل "اطاعة". ٧–٨ وذكر... سنة: الزيادة بخط المقريزي في الهامش الأيسر ويشير إليها رمز ⌐ بعد "حروب".

---

١ من تأريخ الطبري ١: ٨١٥ وتجارب الأمم لمسكويه ١: ٩٧.

٢ من تأريخ الطبري ١: ٨١٣، ٨١٥–٨١٦.

When he grew up, Bābak inherited his father's position, and a son, Ardašīr, was born to him. When the latter was seven years old, his father sent him to the king of Iṣṭaḫr, with whom he grew up and managed well what was assigned to him.[33]

§ 11[34] Astrologers told Ardašīr that he would become king. He also saw this in a dream, which strengthened his spirit. He was resolute and resourceful, and he often consulted others and pondered matters profoundly. In governing, he relied on an excellent Persian man called Tansar, who was a *hērbad*.[35] Tansar managed his affairs and helped him to govern the kingdom until the neighbouring Petty Kings obeyed Ardašīr,[36] recognised his excellence, and came under his banner. He fought against those who refused to do so. He had many stratagems and battles.

§ 12[37] Al-Ṭabarī[38] has transmitted from the People of the Book that Ardašīr revolted when 523 years had passed since Alexander had taken Babel. According to the Magians, this took place 266 years after that.[39] First he

33 The end may be corrupt. Al-Ṭabarī says that after the death of his foster father Tīrī (whose existence al-Maqrīzī edits away), Ardašīr took over his office and managed it well (*ḥasuna qiyāmuhu bihi*). Al-Maqrīzī has first written *ḥasuna qiyāmuhu bi-mā wussida ilayhi*, but then added in the margin one line *above* this ʾRxʿ (x= B, T, Ṯ, N, Y, without diacritics), which looks as if it was a variant *arbaʿ* "four" for the word "seven" on that line, but the little sign that indicates where the addition should go has been put between *bi-mā* and *wussida ilayhi*. The variant "four" is not found in the other sources. The copyist of MS T has copied this as *arbaʿ* in the margin, not the text itself, clearly equally uncertain as to how to read the lines. Both al-Ṭabarī and Ibn al-Aṯīr lack the end of the sentence.

34 Al-Ṭabarī, *Taʾrīḫ*, 1:815 = trans., 5:7; Miskawayh, *Taǧārib al-umam*, 1:97 = C98; cf. Ibn al-Aṯīr, *Kāmil*, 1:381.

35 For *hērbad* (a category of Zoroastrian priests), see "*hērbed*," in *EIr*. Tansar is best known for his famous letter, commonly called *Tansarnāmah*, purportedly written by him on behalf of Ardašīr defending the latter's policy. It is said to have been translated into Arabic by Ibn al-Muqaffaʿ (d. ca. 139/756), whose translation has later been lost, but the text is preserved in Persian translation in Ibn Isfandiyār, *Tārīḫ* 12–41. See Mīnuwī (1311 AHŠ) and Boyce (1968). It has some similarities with *ʿAhd Ardašīr*, reproduced by al-Maqrīzī below, §§ 23–54.

36 The holograph has *iṭāʿat*, with a clear *tāʾ marbūṭah* and against Miskawayh's (ed. Caetani) clearly vocalised *aṭāʿahu*, but MS T has corrected this.

37 Al-Ṭabarī, *Taʾrīḫ*, 1:813, 815–816 = trans., 5:2, 7–8; cf. Ibn al-Aṯīr, *Kāmil*, 1:380, 381.

38 Abū Ǧaʿfar Muḥammad b. Ǧarīr al-Ṭabarī (d. 310/923), historian and Qurʾān commentator, see Rosenthal (1989), Gilliot (1989), Bosworth (2000), Daniel (2013), and *GAS*, 1:323–328.

39 The first sentences have been added in the margin, and they break the sequence in quoting from al-Ṭabarī, having clearly been added during revision as an afterthought.

من درابجرد إلى موضع سمي جوبابان فقتل ملكها ومضى إلى موضع آخر فقتل ملكه ثم إلى موضع ثالث فقتل ملكه وأقام في كل موضع منها قوما من قبله. وكتب إلى أبيه بابك يأمره أن يثب بملك إصطخر. فثار عليه وقتله وأخذ تاجه.

§13[1] فقام من بعده ابنه وجمع لحرب أردشير بن بابك. فغلبه أردشير وتتوج وجلس على السرير وابتدأ أمره بجد وقوة وجعل له وزيرا ورتب موبذ موبذان وقتل عدة من إخوته وجماعة من أصحابه توهم منهم الفتك به وأوقع بأهل درابجرد وقتل جماعة منهم لعصيانهم عليه. ومضى إلى كرمان وقاتل ملكها قتالا شديدا حتى غلبه عليها وأقام فيها ولدا له. وسار إلى سواحل بحر فارس وملكها وقتل ملكها واستخرج أموالا عظيمة في مطامير كان قد كنزها. وكاتب بقية الملوك يدعوهم إلى طاعته فلم يجيبوه فسار إليهم وقتلهم.

---

٨ في ... كنزها: الزيادة بخط المقريزي في الهامش الأيمن من الأعلى إلى الأسفل، ويشير إليها رمز ⌝ بعد "عظيمة".

---

١ من تأريخ الطبري ١: ٨١٦–٨١٧.

marched from Dārābǧird[40] to a place called Ǧūbānān and killed its king. Then he marched to another place and killed its king, and then to a third place and killed its king. In each place, he settled some people (to govern) on his behalf. Then he wrote to his father Bābak, giving him an order to attack the king of Iṣṭaḫr. Bābak revolted, killed the king, and took his crown.

§13[41] After him, his son rose and gathered an army to fight Ardašīr b. Bābak, but Ardašīr vanquished him, crowned himself, and ascended the throne.[42] His reign began with luck and strength. He appointed a Vizier for himself and organised (people) according to ranks (and appointed)[43] a *mōbad mōbadān*. He killed several of his brothers and companions, who he feared might kill him. Then he fell upon the people of Dārābǧird and killed many of them because they had disobeyed him. From there, he went to Kirmān and fought fiercely against its king until he vanquished him, conquered the town, and appointed there a son of his. Then he went to the shores of the Persian Sea, conquered the area, and killed its king. He extracted great wealth from subterranean storerooms, where it had been buried. To the rest of the kings he sent letters, calling them to obeisance. They did not comply, so he marched against them and killed them.

40 This changes the meaning of al-Ṭabarī, who says that he marched to a place called Ǧūbānān in Dārābǧird (*sāra ilá mawḍiʿ min Dārābǧird yuqālu lahu Ǧūbānān*). Both manuscripts have Darābǧird, but the correct form Dārābǧird appears later in the text.

41 Al-Ṭabarī, *Taʾrīḫ*, 1:816–817 = trans., 5:9–10; Ibn al-Aṯīr, *Kāmil*, 1:381–382.

42 Al-Maqrīzī abbreviates this and makes the text rather misleading for the reader. His text implies that the son of Iṣṭaḫr's deposed king is the one to rise, but what al-Ṭabarī says is that Bābak wrote to Ardawān, asking him permission to crown his son, Sābūr b. Bābak, as the king of Iṣṭaḫr. The permission was not given, and when Bābak died, Sābūr succeeded him and prepared for battle against Ardašīr. Moreover, Ardašīr does not vanquish his brother, but a building conveniently collapses on the latter. This last piece, though, is missing from al-Ṭabarī and has been added by the editors from MS Sprenger, so al-Maqrīzī most probably did not find it in the manuscript of al-Ṭabarī's *Taʾrīḫ* used by him.

43 Al-Maqrīzī seems here to follow Ibn al-Aṯīr, who abbreviates the text beyond recognition. The bracketed words are based on al-Ṭabarī, who also provides the names of the Vizier and the *mōbadān mōbad*. For the *mōbadān mōbad* (usually so also in al-Maqrīzī's text) or high priest, see Christensen (1936): 258–261.

§14[1] وبينا هو كذلك إذ ورد عليه كتاب أردوان فيه: "إنك عدوت طورك واجتلبت حتفك." وأنكر عليه لبسه التاج ومحاربة أهل البلاد وأنه قد بعث إلى ملك الأهواز أن يحمله إليه في وثاق. فكتب إليه: "إن الله تعالى قد حباني بالتاج وملكني البلاد التي افتتحتها وأعانني على من قتلت من الجبابرة والملوك وأنا أرجو أن يمكنني الله منك حتى أبعث برأسك إلى بيت النار الذي أسسته." ثم سار نحو إصطخر وخلف وزيره بأردشيرخره فلم يلبث إلا قليلا حتى أتاه كتاب وزيره بقدوم ملك الأهواز وعوده منكوبا.

§15[2] ثم إن أردشير مضى إلى إصبهان وملكها وقتل | ملكها وعاد إلى فارس وسار يريد ملك 138b
الأهواز. فملك في مسيره عدة مدائن وقتل جماعة من الملوك وغنم غنائم كثيرة وحارب أردوان وملك الأرمانيين فكان يحارب هذا يوما وهذا يوما. فإذا كان يوم ملك الأرمانيين لم يقم له أردشير وإذا كان يوم أردوان لم يقم لأردشير. فصالح عند ذلك أردشير ملك الأرمانيين على أن يكف عنه. وأقبل وقد تفرغ لأردوان على محاربته فلم يلبث أن قتله واستولى على ما كان له فدخل ملك الأرمانيين في طاعته فمن حينئذ دعي أزدشير بشاهنشاه.

§16[3] ثم مضى حتى فتح همذان والجبل وآذربيجان وأرمينية والموصل وملك سواد العراق وعاد إلى إصطخر. ثم سار منها فملك سجستان وجرجان ونيسابور ومرو وبلخ وخوارزم وقتل جماعة وبعث

٣ حباني: وضع المقريزي رمز "ح" تحت الحرف الأول إشارة إلى تلفظه بالحاء. ٣-٤ التي ... والملوك: الزيادة بخط المقريزي في الهامش الأيسر من الأسفل إلى الأعلى والكلمتان الأخيرتان منكستان ويشير إليها رمز ˥ بعد "البلاد". ٤ أرجو: "أرجوا" في الأصل. ١٤–1.48 وقتل ... أناهيذ: الزيادة بخط المقريزي في الهامش الأيسر من الأسفل إلى الأعلى، ويشير إليها رمز ˥ بعد "وخوارزم".

١ من تأريخ الطبري ١: ٨١٧–٨١٨.

٢ من تأريخ الطبري ١: ٨١٨، ٨٢١، ٨١٩.

٣ من تأريخ الطبري ١: ٨١٩–٨٢٠.

§ 14[44] While Ardašīr was doing this, there came to him a letter from Ardawān,[45] saying: "You have trespassed your boundaries and brought upon yourself your own death." He disapproved of him wearing a crown and fighting against other people in the region. He also said that he had sent a word to the king of al-Ahwāz to bring Ardašīr to him in chains. Ardašīr replied "God, He is Exalted, has given me the crown and made me king over the countries I have conquered. He has helped me against those tyrants and kings that I have killed and I hope He will deliver you into my hands, so that I can send your head to the fire temple I have established." Then Ardašīr marched against Iṣṭaḫr, leaving his Vizier in Ardašīr-ḫurrah. Soon, he received a letter from his Vizier, saying that the king of al-Ahwāz had come but had retreated beaten.

§ 15[46] Ardašīr marched against Isfahan and its king, whom he killed before returning to Fārs. Then he marched against the king of al-Ahwāz, conquering on the way several cities, killing a number of kings, and gaining much booty. He fought both against Ardawān and the king of the Aramaeans,[47] fighting against the one and the other on alternate days. When it was the day of the king of the Aramaeans, Ardašīr could not withstand him, but when it was the day of Ardawān, Ardawān could not withstand Ardašīr. So Ardašīr made peace with the king of the Aramaeans, so that the latter left him in peace. After that, he was free to face Ardawān in battle and was soon able to kill him and seize what he had ruled. Then the king of the Aramaeans submitted himself to him. It was then that Ardašīr proclaimed himself the King of Kings (*Šāhanšāh*).

§ 16[48] Ardašīr went on to conquer Hamaḏan, al-Ǧabal, Azerbaijan, Armenia, and Mosul. He also subjected the Sawād of Iraq before returning to Iṣṭaḫr. From there he went to subject Siğistan, Ǧurğan, Nišapur,[49] Marw, Balḫ, and Ḫwarizm. He killed many people, sent their heads to the fire temple of

44 Al-Ṭabarī, *Ta'rīḫ*, 1:817–818 = trans., 5:11–12.

45 The last Ašġānian king, whom al-Maqrīzī mentions in the first part of this section (*Ḫabar/Persia*, 1:342–355, §§ 257–269), but only giving the length of his reign in the various king lists, with no additional information.

46 Al-Ṭabarī, *Ta'rīḫ*, 1:818, 821, 819 = trans., 5:12, 19–20, 14.

47 For Aramaeans (*Armānī*), see al-Masʿūdī, *Tanbīh* 78–79.

48 A-Ṭabarī, *Ta'rīḫ*, 1:819–820 = trans., 5:14–16.

49 Al-Ṭabarī has Abaršahr, but al-Maqrīzī replaces this by the province's capital.

{رؤوسهم} إلى بيت نار أناهيذ وعاد إلى فارس فأتته رسل الملوك بالطاعة له. ثم سار حتى ملك البحرين وعاد فنزل المدائن وتوج ابنه سابور بتاجه.

§17[1] ولم يزل محمود السيرة مظفرا في حروبه منصورا على من يناويه لا ترد له راية ولا يهزم له جيش. وبنى المدائن وكور الكور ورتب المراتب وعمر البلاد وهو الذي جمع كلمة فارس على واحد بعدما كانوا طوائف لا يدين منهم ملك لآخر. ولما استبد أردشير بالأمر وملك العراق كره كثير من تنوخ المقام في ملكه فخرج من كان منهم من قضاعة إلى الشام وهم الذين قدموا مع مالك وعمرو ابني فهم وأذعنت له أهل الحيرة بالطاعة.

§18[2] وذكر حمزة أن أردشير لما ظهر تغلب أول شيء على مدينة إصطخر وتقوى بأهلها فتغلب بهم على من في كُور فارس من ملوك الطوائف. فلما استولى عليها عقد التاج على رأسه ثم نظر في أمور الناس فرأى عدد من حوله من الملوك كثيرا وحوزةَ كل ملك منهم قليلة الخطر ضيقة الرقعة ومؤناتهم على رعيتهم عظيمة. فأنكر الخلاف العارض في ممالكهم مع اتفاقهم في أصل دينهم وعلم أنه لم تجمعهم على الدين إلا ألفة سبقت لهم. فاستخبر من بحضرته من العلماء عن ذلك فعرفوه أن أوائل ملوكهم ما زال أمرهم منتظما لا يتجاوز المُلْك واحدا يجتمع الرعية على طاعته إلى أن ملك دارا بن دارا وكان ⟨من⟩ قتله وتملك الإسكندر ما كان. فعلم أزدشير أنه لا يوصل إلى بث العدل حتى يملكهم واحد.

١ رؤوسهم: "روسهم" في الأصل. ٦-٧ وهم ... فهم: الزيادة بخط المقريزي في الهامش الأيسر من الأسفل إلى الأعلى + صح، ويشير إليها رمز ٦ بعد "الشام". ١٠ وحوزةَ: وضع المقريزي رمز "ح" تحت الحرف الأول إشارة إلى تلفظه بالحاء. ١٤ من: الزيادة يقتضيها السياق.

١ من تأريخ الطبري ١: ٨٢٠-٨٢١.

٢ من تأريخ سني الملوك لحمزة ص ٣٦-٣٧.

Anāhīd,[50] and then returned to Fārs. Messengers from other kings came to him to announce their submission. Finally, Ardašīr marched to conquer Bahrain. When he returned from there, he settled in al-Madāʾin and crowned his son Sābūr (as heir-apparent) with his own crown.

§ 17[51] Ardašīr was praiseworthy in his conduct and victorious in his wars against his enemies. His flags were not forced back nor were his armies put to flight. He built cities, formed administrative districts, established a system of ranks, and made the country flourish. He unified the Persians after they had been divided into petty groups and no king had been subservient to another. When Ardašīr overcame the others and got Iraq under his dominion, many people from among the tribe of Tanūḫ disliked staying under his rule. Those from among them who belonged to Quḍāʿah emigrated to Syria: these were the ones who had come (to Iraq) with Mālik and ʿAmr, the sons of Fahm.[52] The people of al-Ḥīrah submitted to Ardašīr.

§ 18[53] Ḥamzah has said that when he rose, Ardašīr first conquered the city of Iṣṭaḫr and became stronger by its population. With their help, he vanquished the Petty Kings in the districts of Fārs. When he had secured them, he crowned himself. Then he looked into the affairs of people and noticed that around him, there were many kings and each ruled an insignificant and narrow area, yet the burden on their subjects was heavy. He did not like the discord in their kingdoms, as the basis of their religion was one. He understood that only a prior union could have united them in religion. He asked the learned men in his entourage about this, and they informed him that the affairs of their first kings had been well organised and that kingship had not belonged (at a time) to more than one king, whom all obeyed, until Dārā b. Dārā's rule. Then he was killed and Alexander became king and so forth. Ardašīr understood that he could not spread justice until one king ruled them all.

50 For the Zoroastrian goddess Anāhīd, see "Anāhīd," in *EIr* and Saadi-nejad (2021).

51 Al-Ṭabarī, *Taʾrīḫ*, 1:820–821 = trans., 5:17–20.

52 See Bosworth (1999): 20, note 74.

53 Ḥamzah, *Taʾrīḫ* 36–37 = trans. 59, 60.

§19[1] فانتصب لإرسال الكتب إلى من قرب منه من ملوك الطوائف. وما | زال يدبر الأمور 139a حتى قتل تسْعِينَ ملكا من ملوك الطوائف بمملكة إيران شهر في مدة ثلاثين سنة وأقام ملكا بعدها أربع عشرة سنة وعشرة أشهر. وقيل: وستة أشهر. وفي نسخة: تسع عشرة سنة وعشرة أشهر. وبنى عدة مدن منها أردشير خَرِه وهي مدينة فيروزاباد من أرض فارس وكانت تسمى كُوَر. وكُور وَكار اسمان للوَهْدة والحفْرة لا للقبر واللحد فإن الفرس لا تعرف القبور. إنما كانت تغيب الموتى في النواويس. والذي سماها فيروزاباد الأمير عضد الدولة.

§20[2] وبنى أزدشير أيضا مدينة بُه أزدشير وهما مدينتان {إحداهما} بالعراق وهي إحدى مدن المدائن السبع. قيل لها لما عربت: بِهْرَسير. والأخرى بكرمان يقال لها: بردشير. وبنى أيضا بهمن أردشير وهي على دجلة بأرض ميسان تعرف ببهمن شير وبفرات ميسان. وبنى مدينة أشتاذ أرْدشير وتعرف بكرخ ميسان. وبنى رام هرمز إحدى مدن خوزستان وبنى جُستان وعربت فقيل: سوق الأهواز. وبنى أيضا عدة مدن منها مدينة {بنى} سورها على جثث أهلها لأنهم فارقوا

٥ والحفْرة: وضع المقريزي رمز "ح" تحت الحرف الأول إشارة إلى تلفظه بالحاء. ‖ واللحد: وضع المقريزي رمز "ح" تحت الحرف الرابع إشارة إلى تلفظه بالحاء. ٧ إحداهما: "إحدهما" في الأصل. ١٠ أرْدشير: الزيادة بخط المقريزي في الهامش الأيسر. ١١ بنى: "بنا" في الأصل. ‖ سورها: وضع المقريزي رمز "س" تحت الحرف الأول إشارة إلى تلفظه بالسين.

١ من تأريخ سني الملوك لحمزة ص ٣٧، ٢٤، ١٤، ١٩.

٢ من تأريخ سني الملوك لحمزة ص ٣٧–٣٨ ومن الكامل لابن الأثير ١: ٣٨٤.

§ 19[54] Ardašīr set about sending letters to neighbouring Petty Kings. He continued organising his affairs until he had killed 90 of the Petty Kings in the kingdom of Īrānšahr[55] during 30 years. After that he ruled for a further 14 years and 10 months. It is also said: 6 months, and, in one manuscript, 19 years and 10 months. He built several cities, including Ardašīr-ḫurrah, which is now the city of Fīrūzābād in Fārs. It used to be called *kūr*.[56] *Kūr* and *kār* are two nouns that denote a pit or a hole, not a tomb or a grave, as the Persians did not use tombs, but instead buried their dead in sarcophagi. The city was renamed Fīrūzābād by Emir ʿAḍud al-Dawlah.[57]

§ 20[58] Ardašīr also built the city of Bih-Ardašīr, which name actually refers to two cities, one of them in Iraq. This is one of the seven cities of al-Madāʾin. When the name was Arabised, it became Bihrasīr.[59] The other is in Kerman and is (now) called Bardašīr. He also built Bahman-Ardašīr, which is on the Tigris in Maysān and is (now) known as Bahmanšīr or Furāt-Maysān. He built Aštād-Ardašīr,[60] which is (now) known as Karḫ-Maysān. He built Rām-Hurmuz, one of the cities of Ḫuzistan,[61] and Ğustān,[62] which has been rendered into Arabic as Sūq al-Ahwāz. He also built a number of (other) cities, including one whose walls he built on its inhabitants' corpses, because

54 Ḥamzah, *Taʾrīḫ* 37, 24, 14, 19 = trans. 60, 43, 33, 37; Ibn al-Aṯīr, *Kāmil*, 1:384.

55 The Iranian heartland, see "Ērān, Ērānšahr," in *EIr*.

56 Persian *gōr* "grave."

57 The text of Ḥamzah reads ʿAlī b. Būyah, i.e., ʿImād al-Dawlah. ʿAḍud al-Dawlah's name was Abū ʿAlī al-Ḥasan b. Būyah (cf., e.g., Ibn Ḫallikān, *Wafayāt*, 4:50). He died in 372/983, see *EI*[3], s.v. Al-Maqrīzī has taken the name from Ibn al-Aṯīr, *Kāmil*, 1:384.

58 Ḥamzah, *Taʾrīḫ* 37–38 = trans. 60–62; Ibn al-Aṯīr, *Kāmil*, 1:384.

59 Here unequivocally punctuated and vocalised so. Later, al-Maqrīzī consistently writes NHRŠYR (Nahrašīr), which he may have read as Nahr Šīr. This reading comes from Miskawayh (ed. Caetani), which several times misspells the name (e.g., C382).

60 Ḥamzah reads Ašaʾ-Ardašīr (so also in the edition of Gottwaldt, 46—Hoyland 2018: 60 and note 182 on p. 61, has misread this as Anšaʾa-Ardašīr, taking the first word to be Arabic "he founded"). Al-Maqrīzī's form may derive from al-Ṭabarī, *Taʾrīḫ*, 1:820 = trans., 5:16, where the city is mentioned as Astābād-Ardašīr. The form of Ḥamzah is obviously corrupt, but it is possible that al-Maqrīzī had a better manuscript than that on which the modern editions are based. Cf. also Christensen (1936): 91.

61 Both manuscripts read rather consistently Ḫūristān. Following Ibn al-Aṯīr, al-Maqrīzī is here somewhat confused. Ḥamzah first mentions Rām-Ardašīr, the location of which he says he does not know. Then he mentions Rām-Hurmuz-Ardašīr in Ḫuzistan, which he says is usually shortened to Rām-Hurmuz, but he does not say that it was built by Ardašīr. I take it to be a bracketed explanation, a *caveat* for not confusing the unknown Rām-Ardašīr, established by Ardašīr, with the well-known Rām-Hurmuz. Ḥamzah continues with the double city of Hurmuz-Ardašīr, known as Hūğistān Wāğār.

62 Read as in Ḥamzah [Hū]ğistān (Wāğār) "the market of Ḫuzistan."

طاعته وعصوه فجعل ساقا من السور لَبِنًا وساقا جثث القتلى. وقسم مياهَ وادي إصبهان ومياهَ وادي خوزستان. وكان شعاره مُدَنَّر وسراويله أسمانجون وتاجه أخضر في ذهب وبيده رمح قائم.

§ 21 وحكى الهمداني أبو محمد الحسن بن أحمد بن يعقوب في **كتاب الإكليل** أن الأردوانيين نبط الشام والأرمانيين نبط السواد. قال: ولما انقطع ملوك اليونانيين وباخَتْ نائرة حمير حدث أردوان وكان رجلا عاقلا ذا حُنْكة ودَهَاء ونجدة وحلم وحسن تدبير ورَوِيَّة فجمع الجموع وهيأ العُدة. فلما تتامت إليه جموع الفرس واستبد أمره أقبل في جموعه حتى نزل دار مملكة الفرس بالمدائن. فلما نزل أردوان المدائن أحسن السيرة واستعمل على كل كورة رجلا من أشراف الفرس ولم يعرض لأطراف العرب ولم يتناول شيئا من بلادهم وحاسن أهل الحيرة وهم من أعقاب الجند الذين خلفهم تبع هناك وكانوا أهل ثروة ونجدة وبأس.

§ 22 وكان | أردوان مع مداراته لهم خائفا منهم هائبا لهم متقيا لشرهم ونجع فيهم إحسانه 139b
ومداراته فكف بعضهم عن بعض. وكان يخدم أردوان غلام من أبناء أشراف فارس يقال له أزدشير بن بابك حتى إذا كان ليلة من الليالي. وكان أردوان رجلا عالما بصيرا بالنجوم فأبصر نجم

they had disobeyed and defied him. He made one layer[63] of the wall with bricks and another with the bodies of the dead. He distributed the waters of the valleys of Isfahan and Ḫuzistan. His vest was golden, his trousers sky-blue, and his crown green on gold. He was standing and held a spear in his hand.[64]

§ 21 Abū Muḥammad al-Ḥasan b. Aḥmad b. Yaʿqūb al-Hamdānī[65] has narrated in his *Kitāb al-Iklīl* [Book of the Crown] that the Ardawānians are the Nabateans of Syria, whereas the Aramaeans are the Nabateans of the Sawād.[66] He said: When the Greek kings' line ended and the flame of Ḥimyar faded, Ardawān appeared. He was an intelligent man, experienced and shrewd, courageous and discerning, good in governing and reflecting. He gathered troops and made preparations. When all Persians had come to him and he was sole in power, he came with his troops and settled down in the capital of the Persians, al-Madāʾin. After Ardawān had settled in al-Madāʾin he governed well and appointed a Persian nobleman to every administrative district. He did not turn to the region of the Arabs and did not take any of their lands. He treated well the Ḥīrans, who were descendants of the army the Tubbaʿ had left there.[67] They were rich, courageous, and strong.

§ 22[68] Despite treating the Persians gently Ardawān was afraid of them, concerned, and on his guard against their evil. Yet his kindness and gentleness towards them was successful, and he prevented them from fighting with each other. A son of a Persian nobleman, called Ardašīr b. Bābak, served

63 In the holograph, the first word is written with F, the second clearly with Q (*sāqan*) and in MS T both are written with Q.

64 In Ḥamzah, this description is said to come from *Kitāb al-Ṣuwar* [Book of pictures], where the picture of every Sasanian king was drawn, see Hämeen-Anttila (2018b): 36–38. Al-Maqrīzī remains somewhat enigmatic, not explaining what these depictions are.

65 This probably comes from the lost historical volumes IV–VI of al-Hamdānī's *Iklīl*. Al-Ḥasan b. Aḥmad al-Hamdānī (d. 334/945), South Arabian historian. See *GAL S*, 1:409.

66 The use of the term *nabaṭ/anbāṭ* in Classical Arabic is vague. Mostly, it is used to refer to the rural, non-Arabic, mainly Aramaic-speaking population of Iraq and Syria, cf., e.g., Hämeen-Anttila (2006): 36–41.

67 For the term Tubbaʿ, see "Tubbaʿ," in *EI*², 10:575–576. See also al-Maqrīzī, *Ḫabar/Persia*, I § 42.

68 From al-Hamdānī's *Iklīl*. This paragraph resumes the contents of the Middle Persian *Kārnāmag ī Ardašīr*, for which see Grenet (2003), but in a form that differs from the standard version.

ملك قد طلع يريد رأي دولة لمن يسلبه ملكه. ففزع أردوان لذلك وقال لشدة ما دخله وهو يحدث نفسه ولا يرى أن أحدا يسمعه: "أي عبد من عبيدي قام الساعة فركب دابة من دوابي بسرجي ولجامي وخرج يطلب الملك فإنه يظفر به ويسلبني ملكي وملك أصحابي." وإن جارية لأردوان سمعت منه ذلك الحديث وهو يحدث به نفسه ولا يحسب أن أحدا يسمعه. وكانت مصادقة أزدشير فانطلقت من فورها فأخبرته بالذي سمعت من أردوان. فقام من ساعته فركب الدابة التي كان يركبها أردوان بسرجها ولجامها وسار حتى لحق بإصطخر. فأقام بها يدعو إلى نفسه فاجتمع إليه أربعون رجلا من أشراف أبناء فارس فوثبوا على صاحب إصطخر فقتلوه. وذكر الهمداني خبر أزدشير كله.

§23[1] وقال ابن مسكويه: فمن أحسن ما حفظ له عهده إلى الملوك بعده وهذه نسخته: باسم ولي الرحمة. من ملك الملوك أردشير بن بابك إلى من يخلفه بعقبه من ملوك فارس السلام والعافية. أما بعد فإن صنيع الملوك على غير صنيع الرعية فالملك يَطْبَعُه العز والأمن والسرور والقدرة على طباع الأَنَفَةِ والجُرأة والعبث والبَطَر. ثم كلما ازداد في العمر نَفَسًا وفي الملك سلامة زاده في هذه الطبائع الأربعة حتى تُسْلمه إلى سُكْر السلطان الذي هو أشد من سكر الشراب فينسى النكبات والعثرات والغِيَر والدوائر وفحش تسلط الأيام ولُؤْم غلَبَة الدهر فيُرسل يدَه ولسانَه بالفعل والقول. وقد قال

٩ نسخته : بعد هذه الكلمة بياض في الأصل.

١ من تجارب الأمم لمسكويه ١: ٩٧–٩٨.

Ardawān. One night, Ardawān, who was a learned man and able to read the stars, saw that the star of kingship rose, meaning that kingship was for grabs. Ardawān was startled and in the surge of emotion said to himself, believing that no one overheard him: "If any servant of mine rises now and rides one of my horses, on my saddle and using my bridles, and revolts in search of kingship, he will be successful and will grab kingship from me and rule my companions." One of Ardawān's servant girls heard what he was saying to himself, believing that no one was overhearing. She was Ardašīr's friend and went immediately to tell him what she had heard Ardawān say. Ardašīr left at once and rode the horse Ardawān used to ride, using his saddle and his bridles, and went to Iṣṭaḫr. He stayed there calling people to join him. Forty Persian noblemen joined him, attacked the governor of Iṣṭaḫr, and killed him. Al-Hamdānī then narrated the whole story of Ardašīr.

§ 23[69] Ibn Miskawayh[70] has said: One of the most beautiful things preserved from Ardašīr is his testament to the kings who came after him. This is its text: In the name of the Master of Mercy. From the King of Kings Ardašīr b. Bābak to those kings of Persia who will succeed him. Peace and wellbeing (be upon you). Now, a king's actions[71] are not like his subjects' actions. Majesty, security, joy, and power make a king disposed for disdain, insolence, mockery, and arrogance. The longer he lives and the more secure he feels in his kingship, the more these four characteristics grow until they lead him to inebriety of power, which is stronger than inebriety of wine, and he forgets misfortunes, stumbling blocks, vicissitudes of time, calamities, the misery of the power of the days, and the baseness of Time's tyranny, letting loose his hand with actions and his tongue with words. The early (kings) among us have said:

69 Miskawayh, *Taǧārib al-umam*, 1:97–98 = C99. *ʿAhd Ardašīr*, which takes §§ 23–54 in al-Maqrīzī, exists in a separate manuscript (MS Köprülü) edited in Grignaschi (1966): 46–90. Grignaschi's text is mostly superior to that of Miskawayh, who has often misread and/or misunderstood the text. Al-Maqrīzī copies Miskawayh, adding a further layer of misreadings, making it sometimes difficult to gauge how a reader not able to compare the different versions would have understood the text. While al-Maqrīzī is usually rather free with Miskawayh's text, abbreviating and modifying it, in the case of the *Testament* he closely follows his source and adds nothing from other sources.

70 Miskawayh (d. 421/1030), historian. See "Miskawayh," in *EI*², 7:143–144. In modern studies, the name is usually in this form, but al-Maqrīzī and many other Classical authors use the form Ibn Miskawayh.

71 Miskawayh and Grignaschi (1966): 46, read *ṣiyaġ* "character," but both manuscripts have *ṣanīʿ*.

الأولون منا: "عند حسن الظن بالأيام تحدث الغِيَر." وقد كان من الملوك من يُذكِره عِزه الذلَ وأمنه الخوفَ وسروره الكآبَةَ وبطره بالسُوْقَة ولا حزم إلا في جميعها.

§ 24[١] اعلموا أن الذي أنتم لاقون بعدي هو الذي لقيني من الأمور | وهي بعدي واردة عليكم. 140a فيأتيكم السرور والأذى في الملك من حيث أتياني. وإن منكم من سيركب الملك صعبا فيُمْنَى من شِماسِه وجِماحِه وخَبْطه واعتراضه بمثل الذي مُنِيْتُه. ومنكم من سيرث الملك عن الكُفاة المُذَللين له مركبَه وسيجري على لسانه ويُلقَى في قلبه أن قد فُرِغ له وكُفي واكتفى وفَرغَ للسعي في العبَث والملاهي وأن من قبله من الملوك إلى التوطيد له أَجْرَوا وفي التمكين له سَعَوا وأن قد خُص بما حُرِموا وأعطي ما مُنِعوا. فيكثر أن يقول مُسِرا ومُعلِنا: "خصوا بالعمل وخُصِصْتُ بالدِعة وقدموا قبلي إلى الغَرَر وخُلِّفت في الثِقة."

§ 25[٢] وهذا الباب من الأبواب التي تكسِر سُكُورَ الفساد ويُهاج بها قربات البلاء ويغني البصيرَ اللطيفَ ما ينتهك من الأمور في ذلك. فإنا قد رأينا الملكَ الرشيدَ السعيدَ المنصورَ المكْفِيّ المظفرَ الحازم في الفُرصَة البَصيرَ بالعورة اللطيفَ المبسوطَ له في العلم والعمر يجتهد فلا يَعْدو صلاحَ ملكه حياتَه إلا أن يتشبه به مُتَشبه. ورأينا الملكَ القصيرَ عمره القريبة مدته إذا كان سعيه بإرسال اللسان

---

٢ حزم: وضع المقريزي رمز "ح" تحت الحرف الأول إشارة إلى تلفظه بالحاء. ٨ بالدِعة: كذا في الأصل بدال مكسورة. ١٠ قربات: وضع المقريزي رمز "ك" (لـ "كذا") فوق الكلمة إشارة إلى شكه في صحة قراءتها. ١٢ يَعْدو: "يَعْدوا" في الأصل.

---

١ من تجارب الأمم لمسكويه ١: ٩٨.

٢ من تجارب الأمم لمسكويه ١: ٩٨.

"Misfortunes fall upon you when you believe good of the days." There were kings whose grandeur reminded them of lowliness, whose feeling of security reminded them of fear, whose joy reminded them of sorrow, and whose pride reminded them of ordinary people. There is no resolution if one does not have all these features.

§ 24[72] Know that after me you will encounter the same things that I have encountered and they will fall upon you after me. Joy and trouble of kingship will come to you just as they came to me. Some of you will find kingship hard to handle and will have to face its restiveness and recalcitrance, its stamping and resistance just as I did. Others will inherit it from competent predecessors, who have subjected it. Such a king will say aloud and think in his heart that all has been done for him and taken care of. He will be content and occupy himself with play and amusement, thinking that the earlier kings worked to consolidate his power and strived for his benefit and that he has been given what his predecessors were deprived of and that he has received what they lacked. He repeats both openly and in secret that his predecessors were given toil but he was given ease: "They went before me through perils, and I inherited peace."

§ 25[73] This is one of the ways that break[74] the inebriety of corruption, and through it the proximities[75] of affliction are awakened. The affairs that have been profaned in that will be enough for an acute observer.[76] We have seen how a rightly-guided, fortunate, and victorious king, protected and triumphant, resolute when opportunity strikes, perspicacious of weaknesses, subtle and endowed with much knowledge and long life, strives yet his kingship does not thrive after the end of his life, if (his successor) does not follow his way. We have also seen how a short-lived king, who does not rule long, freely lets his tongue speak and his hand act without premeditation and

72 Miskawayh, *Taǧārib al-umam*, 1:98 = C99–100.

73 Miskawayh, *Taǧārib al-umam*, 1:98 = C100–101.

74 Miskawayh and both manuscripts read *taksiru*, but Grignaschi (1966): 47, *yukthiru* "increase" is obviously better.

75 Miskawayh and both manuscripts read *qurubāt*, but Grignaschi (1966): 47, who reads *qarāʾin* "effects" is obviously better.

76 Grignaschi (1966): 47, reads *wa-yuʿmī l-baṣīra ʿan al-laṭīf mā yanhatiku min al-umūr fī ḏālika*. Miskawayh's and al-Maqrīzī's sentence hardly makes real sense. Grignaschi's texts would translate as "and (even) an intelligent person is made blind of the (at first) minor profanation of affairs."

بما قال واليد بما عملت بغير تدبير يُدْرِك أفسدَ جميعَ ما قُدِّم له من الصلاح قبلَه ويُخلِّف المملكة خرابا على من بَعدَه.

§ 26[1] وقد علمتُ أنكم سَتُبلون مع الملك بالأزواج والأولاد والقُرَباء والوزراء والأخْدان والأنصار والأصحاب والأعوان والمتنصحين والمتقربين والمضحكين المُزَينين. كل هؤلاء إلا قليلا أنْ يأخذ لنفسه أَحَبُ إليه من أن يُعطي منها. وإنما عمله لِسُوْقِ يومه وحياةِ غَدِه فنصيحة الملوك فضْل نصيحته لنفسه وغاية الصلاح عنده صلاحُ نفسه وغاية الفساد عنده فسادها. يجعل نفسَه هي العامّة والعامّة هي الخاصة فإن خُص بنعمة دون الناس فهي عنده نعمة عامة وإذا عَم الناسَ بالنصر على العدو والعدل في البَيْضَة والأمْن على الحُرَم والحِفظ للأطراف والرأفة من المَلِك | 140b والاستقامة مِن المُلْك ولم يُخْصَصْ من ذلك بما يرضيه سمى تلك النعمةَ نعمةً خاصةً. ثم أكثر شَكِيَّةَ الدهر ومَذَمةِ الأمور. يقيم للسلطان سُوقَ المودة ما أقام له سُوقَ الأرباح. ولا يعلم ذلك الوزيرُ والقرينُ أن في التماس الربح على السلطان فسادَ جميع الأمور. وقد قال الأولون منا: "رشاد الوالي خير للرعية من خِصْب الزمان."

§ 27[2] واعلموا أن المُلْك والدِيْنَ أخوان لا قِوامَ لأحدهما إلا بصاحبه لأن الدينَ أُسُ المُلْك وعماده وصار المُلْك بعدُ حارسَ الدين. فلا بد للمُلك من أُسّه ولا بد للدين من حارسه. فإن ما لا حارس له ضائع وإن ما لا أُسَّ له مهدوم. وإن رأسَ ما أخاف عليكم مُبادَرةُ السَفِلَةِ إياكم إلى دراسة الدين ⟨وتلاوته والتفقه فيه فتحملكم الثقة بقوة السلطان⟩ على التهاون بهم. فتحدث في الدين رياسات مُسْتَسِرات فيمن قد وَتَرتم وجفَوتم وحَرَمتم وأخفتم وصغرتم من سَفِلَة الناس والرعيةِ وحَشْوِ العامة

٥ لنفسه: في الأصل "لنفسَه". ١٠ ومَذَمةِ: كذا في الأصل لـ "مَذَمةَ". ١٦ وتلاوته ... السلطان: الزيادة من تجارب الأمم لمسكويه.

١ من تجارب الأمم لمسكويه ١: ٩٨-٩٩.

٢ من تجارب الأمم لمسكويه ١: ٩٩.

corrupts everything good that he received from those before him and how he leaves the kingdom in ruins to those after him.

§ 26[77] I know that you and the kingdom will be put to test through spouses, children, relatives, Viziers, friends,[78] aids, companions, helpers, advisers, favourites, buffoons, and barbers. All these, except for a few, take rather than give and they work for their day's benefit and their future's provision: the advice they give to kings is merely the left-overs of the advice they give to themselves. For them, the furthest limit of welfare is their faring well and the furthest limit of deprivation is their being deprived. They consider themselves general and the general they consider specific. If they receive something others do not, in their opinion that is the common good. When all people enjoy victory over enemies and justice in general, safety of inviolability, protection of frontiers, clemency of the king, and order in the kingdom, but they do not get a large enough share of this, they call it a restricted benefit. Then they will keep complaining about the times and blame the affairs. They barter their love of the ruler for profit. Such Viziers or companions do not understand that in trying to profit from the ruler lies the corruption of all affairs. Our forefathers have said: "A just governor is better for the subjects than fertile times."

§ 27[79] Know that kingship and religion are brothers and each only survives through the other. Religion is the foundation of kingship and its support, and kingship becomes the guardian of religion. Kingship needs its foundation and religion its guardian. What has no guardian will disappear and what has no foundation will collapse. What I most fear for you is that lowly people will be more eager than you to study religion, (interpreting it and becoming learned in it while you trust in the might of kingship, which will lead you)[80] to think lightly of them, so that within religion there arise hidden leaders among those lowly people, subjects, and general riffraff whom

77 Miskawayh, *Taǧārib al-umam*, 1:98–99 = C101–102.

78 Miskawayh and Grignaschi (1966): 48, read *quranāʾ* "companions."

79 Miskawayh, *Taǧārib al-umam*, 1:99 = C102–103. The idea of kingship and religion as twins is one of the most widely spread Middle Persian sayings, see Shaked (1984): 31–40. In al-Masʿūdī, *Murūǧ* § 586, this is attributed to Ardašīr's *Waṣiyyat Ardašīr li-bnihi Sābūr*, which is probably a variant title for the *ʿAhd*.

80 The text in brackets, already missing from Miskawayh (ed. Caetani) has been added from Miskawayh (ed. Ḥasan). Al-Maqrīzī would probably have understood the mutilated sentence as "more eager than you to study religion despite others despising him."

ولم يجتمع رئيس في الدين مُسِرٌّ ورئيس في المُلك معلن في مملكة واحدة قط إلا انتزع الرئيسُ في الدين ما في يد الرئيس في المُلك لأن الدينَ أُسٌّ والمُلك عماد وصاحب الأس أولى بجَمْع البنيان من صاحب العماد.

§ 28[1] وقد مضى قبلنا ملوك كان الملِك منهم يتعهد الجُملةَ بالتفسير والجماعاتِ بالتفصيل والفراغَ بالأَشْغال كتعهده جسدَه بقص فضول الشعَرِ والظُفُرِ وغَسْلِ الدَرَن والغَمَرِ ومداواة ما ظهر من الأدواء وما بطَنَ. وقد كان من أولٰئك الملوك مَن صحة مُلكه أَحبُ إليه من صحة جسده وكان بما يُخلِفه من الذِكْرِ المحمود أفرحَ وأَبْهَجَ منه بما يسمعه بأذنه في حياته فتتابعت تلك الأملاك بذلك كأنهم ملِك واحد وكَأَن أرواحَهم روح واحدة يمكن أولهم لآخرهم ويُصَدق آخرُهم أولَهم بجميع أنباء أسلافهم ومَوارِيثِ آرائهم وصِياغات عقولهم عند الباقي منهم بعدهم فكأنهم جلوس معه يُحدثونه ويشاورونه حتى كان على رأس دارا بن دارا ما كان وغلَبة الإسكندر على ما غلب من ملكنا. فكان إفسادُه أمرَنا وتفريقُه جماعتَنا وتخريبه عمران مملكتنا أبلغَ له فيما أراد من سفك دمائنا. فلما أذن الله في جمع مملكتنا | ودَولةِ أحسابنا كان من ابتعاثه إيانا ما كان. وبالاعتبار تَتَّقَى 141a
الغِيَر ومَن يَخْلُفنا أوجَدُ للاعتبار منا لما استدبروا من أعاجيب ما أَتى علينا.

§ 29[2] اعلموا أن سلطانكم إنما هو على أجساد الرعية وأنه لا سلطان للملوك على القلوب. واعلموا أنكم إن غلبتم الناس على ذات أيديهم فلن تغلبوهم على عقولهم. واعلموا أن العاقل سَالّ عليكم لسانَه

---

١ من تجارب الأمم لمسكويه ١: ٩٩.

٢ من تجارب الأمم لمسكويه ١: ٩٩–١٠٠.

you have wronged, been harsh to, deprived, frightened, and belittled. When there is a secret leader in religion and a public leader in kingship in one kingdom, the leader in religion will always snatch what there is in the hand of the leader in kingship because religion is the foundation and kingship only its support. The one who is the foundation is better entitled to the whole building than the one who is the support.

§ 28[81] Before me, there have been kings who attended to the whole by scrutiny,[82] to groups by dividing them, and to (excessive) leisure by activity, just as they attended to their own body by cutting excessive hair, clipping nails, washing dirt and foul smell off their body, and treating both visible and internal diseases with medicine. The health of their kingdom was dearer to some of those kings than their own bodily health. They were happier and more delighted by the praised memory they left behind than (the flattery) they heard by their own ears during their lifetime. Those kings followed each other in this as if they were one king and their souls were one soul. The predecessor made (kingship) possible for his successor, and the latter followed the ways of his ancestors and the heritage of their opinions and the compositions of their reason, preserved among those of them who remained behind. It was as if the ancestors were still with them, speaking to them and advising them. (This went on) until the misfortune of Dārā b. Dārā and the conquest of our kingdom by Alexander. He destroyed our affairs, disunited our community, and ruined our flourishing kingdom. This was his ultimate aim, rather than merely spilling our blood. When God again allowed the unification of our kingdom and the return of our nobility to power, He sent me. By learning a lesson, misfortunes may be avoided. Those who will come after me may learn even more than I did when they consider all the wonders that befell me.

§ 29[83] Know that you can only rule over the bodies of your subjects. Kings cannot rule over their hearts. Know also that even though you may take control of what there is in the hands of people, you cannot take control of their reason. Know that an intelligent man (left without)[84] uses his tongue against

81 Miskawayh, *Taǧārib al-umam*, 1:99 = C103–104.

82 I follow MS Köprülü's reading *bi-l-taftīš*, see Grignaschi (1966): 49, note 19.

83 Miskawayh, *Taǧārib al-umam*, 1:99–100 = C104–105.

84 Miskawayh (ed. Caetani), followed by al-Maqrīzī, lacks the word *al-maḥrūm* (cf. Grignaschi 1966: 50), without which the sentence does not really make sense.

وهو أقطع سيفيه وإن أشد ما يضربكم به من لسانه ما صَرَّفَ الحِيْلَةَ فيه إلى الدِين فكأن بالدِين يحتج وللدين فيما يظهر يغضب فيكون للدين بكاؤه وإليه دعاؤه وهو أوجَد للتابعين والمصَدقين وَالمناصحينَ والمؤازرينَ منكم لأن بغْضةَ الناس هي موكلة بالملوك ومحبتهم ورحمتهم موكلة بالضعفاء المغلوبين. وقد كان من قبلنا من الملوك يحتالون لعقول من يحذرون بتخريبها. فإن العاقل لا تنفعه نحيزته إذا صُيِّر عقلُه خرابا. وكانوا يحتالون للطاعنين بالدين على الملوك فيسمونهم المبتدعين فيكون الدين هو الذي يقتلهم ويُريح الملوك منهم. ولا ينبغي للملك أن يعترف للعُباد والنُساك أن يكونوا أولى بالدين ولا أَحْدَبَ عليه ولا أغضب له منه ولا ينبغي للملك أن يدَع النُساكَ بغير الأمر والنهي لهم في نسكهم فإن خروجَ النساك وغير النساك من الأمر والنهي عيب على الملوك وعيب على المملكة وثلمة يتسنمها الناس بيِّنَة الضرر للملك ولمن بعده.

§30[1] واعلموا أن مَصيْر الوالي إلى غير أخْدَانه وتقريبه غير وزرائه فتح لأبواب المحجوب عنه علمُها. وقد قيل: "إذا استوحش الوالي ممن لم يُوطن نفسَه عليه أطبقت عليه ظُلَم الجهالة." وقيل: "أخوف ما تكون العامة آمن ما تكون الوزراء." اعلموا أن دولتكم تؤتى من مكانين أحدهما غلَبة بعض الأمم المخالفة لكم والآخر فساد أدبكم. ولن يزال حريمكم من الأمم محروسا ودينكم من غلبة الأديان محفوظا ما عُظِمَت فيكم الولاةُ. ولَيس تعظيمُهم بترك كلامهم ولا إجْلالُهم بالتنحي عنهم ولا المحبةُ لهم بالمحبة لكل ما يحبون ولكن تعظيمهم تعظيم أديانهم وعقولهم وإجلالُهم إجلال منزلتهم من الله ومحبتُهم محبة إصابتهم وحكاية الصَواب عنهم.

٤ يحتالون: وضع المقريزي رمز "ح" تحت الحرف الثاني إشارة إلى تلفظه بالحاء. ٥ نحيزته: وضع المقريزي رمز "ح" تحت الحرف الثاني إشارة إلى تلفظه بالحاء. ٧ أحْدَبَ: وضع المقريزي رمز "ح" تحت الحرف الثاني إشارة إلى تلفظه بالحاء.

١ من تجارب الأمم لمسكويه ١: ١٠٠.

you, and his tongue is sharper than his sword. The worst he hits you with his tongue is when he uses religion for his schemes. He seems to be arguing by religion and is ostensibly enraged on its behalf. He weeps for religion and calls to it and he will find more followers and approvers, advisers and helpers than you because people hate kings and love and pity those who are weak and vanquished. Some kings before my time outwitted those they feared by corrupting their reason. Natural disposition does not benefit an intelligent man when his reason is corrupt. The former kings used to plot against those who used religion to calumniate kings. This they did by calling them heretics. Thus, it would be because of religion that they were killed and kings could get rid of them. A king should not acknowledge pious people and ascetics to be more entitled to religion than he, more caring for it, or more vigilant on its behalf. A king should not let ascetics be above commands and prohibitions just because they are ascetics. If ascetics and others stop obeying commands and prohibitions, it is a shame on kings and their kingdom and a fault that people will notice, clearly detrimental to the king and his successors.

§ 30[85] Know that when a ruler approaches others than only his intimate companions and brings closer to himself others than only his Viziers, he opens the door to what had remained unknown to him until then. It is said that when a ruler avoids people other than those to whom he is accustomed, then the darkness of ignorance will cover him. It is also said that the more people are afraid (of the king), the more Viziers feel safe. Know that your rule is threatened by two things. The one is that an enemy country vanquishes you and the other is that your manners become corrupt.[86] You will remain safe from foreign peoples and your religion preserved from being vanquished by other religions, as long as rulers will be respected among you. Respecting them does not mean not speaking to (advise) them and honouring them does not mean retreating (in awe) from them and loving them does not mean loving everything they love. Respecting them means respecting their religion and their reason, honouring them means honouring their place vis-à-vis God, and loving them means loving it when they hit the mark and telling others what they have done right.

---

85 Miskawayh, *Taǧārib al-umam*, 1:100 = C105–106.

86 The text reads *adabikum*, which is also how Miskawayh reads, but the continuation makes it clear that *dīnikum* "your religion," Grignaschi (1966): 51, is the better variant.

§ 31[١] واعلموا أنه لا سبيل إلى أن يُعظم الوالي | إلا بالإصابة في السياسة. ورأسُ إصابة السياسة 141b
أن يفتح الوالي لمن قبَله من الرعية بابين أحدُهما باب رقةٍ ورحمةٍ ويُسْرٍ وتَهَلُّل وانبساط وانشراح. والآخر بابُ غِلظَةٍ ووحْشةٍ وتعَنُت وتشدد وإمساك ومباعدة وإقصاء ومخالفة ومنع وقطوب وانقباض ومَحَقَرة إلى أن يبلغ القتلَ.

§ 32[٢] واعلموا أني لم أسم هذا البابَ بابَ رِفق وباب عُنفٍ ولكني سميتها جميعا بابَي رفق لأن فتح باب المكروه مع باب الشرور هو أوشك لغلقه حتى لا يُبتلى به أحد وفي الرعية من الأهواء الغالبة للرأي والفجور المستثقل للدين والسَفِلة الحَنِقةِ على الوجُوه بالنَفاسَة والحسَد ما لا بد معه أن يُقرن بباب الرأفة باب الغِلْظة وبباب الاستبقاء باب القتل. وقد يفسِد الوالي بعضَ الرعية من حرصه على صلاحها ويَغلُظ عليها من رقته لها ويَقتل فيها من حرصه على حياتها.

§ 33[٣] واعلموا أن قتالكم الأعداء من الأمم قبل قتالِكم الأدبَ من أنفُس رعيتكم ليس بحفظ ولكنه إضَاعَة. وكيف يُجاهَد العدو بقلوب مختلفة وأيد مُتَعادِيَة وقد علمتم أن الذي بُني عليه الناسُ وجُبلت عليه الطباع حُب الحياة وبُغْض الموت. فلا دفع ولا مَنْع ولا صبر ولا محاماة مع هذا إلا

٤ ومَحَقَرة: وضع المقريزي رمز "ح" تحت الحرف الثاني إشارة إلى تلفظه بالحاء.

١ من تجارب الأمم لمسكويه ١: ١٠٠.

٢ من تجارب الأمم لمسكويه ١: ١٠٠.

٣ من تجارب الأمم لمسكويه ١: ١٠٠-١٠١.

§ 31[87] Know that there is no way for a ruler to be respected, except by correct governing, and the main thing in correct governing is that the ruler opens two gates for the people he governs. One is the gate of graciousness, mercy, and ease,[88] of delight, happiness, and relaxation. The other is the gate of harshness, coldness,[89] harassment, sternness, withdrawal, distancing, removal, opposition, deprival, scowling, disheartening, and scorn, even killing.

§ 32[90] Know that I do not call these gates[91] the gate of graciousness and the gate of harshness, but I call both of them the gates of graciousness, because the opening of the gate of discomfort together with the gate of joy[92] is more prone to closing it, so that no one would be afflicted by it. Among people, there are desires that overcome discernment, immorality burdensome to religion, and lowly people furiously grudging and envious of important people. Thus, the gate of harshness has to be attached to the gate of graciousness and the gate of killing to the gate of letting live. A ruler may destroy some of his subjects while being eager for the wellbeing of the majority, he may be harsh towards some because of his mildness towards others, and he may kill some of them for his eagerness of others remaining alive.

§ 33[93] Know that fighting enemy peoples before fighting the (bad) habits in your subjects' souls is not protection but waste. How could the enemy be fought with hearts at variance with each other and hands inimical towards each other? You know that people have been built and their characters moulded on the love of life and the hatred of death.[94] Withal, there is no way to repel and to bar, to be patient and to defend except in one of two ways. Either

87 Miskawayh, *Taǧārib al-umam*, 1:100 = C106–107.

88 Miskawayh reads *bišr* "joy."

89 Miskawayh reads *ḫašyah* "fear."

90 Miskawayh, *Taǧārib al-umam*, 1:100 = C107.

91 In singular in the text, but the sense necessitates reading *bi-hāḏayni l-bābayn*, as in Miskawayh and Grignaschi (1966): 52.

92 I follow Grignaschi's (1966): 52, emendation *šurūr* "evils" > *surūr* "joy."

93 Miskawayh, *Taǧārib al-umam*, 1:100–101 = C107–108.

94 Grignaschi (1966): 53, adds a sentence which makes the following more understandable: "War distances life and brings death closer." This has been added to Miskawayh (ed. Ḥasan) but is missing from C.

بأحد وجهين. إما نية والنيَّة ما لن يقدر عليه الوالي عند الناس بعد النية التي تكون في أول الدولة وإما بحُسْن الأدب وإصابة السياسة.

§ 34[1] واعلموا أن بَدءَ ذهاب الدول من قِبل إهمال الرعية بغير أشغال معروفة ولا أعمال معلومة. فإذا فشا الفراغ تولد منه النَظَر في الأمور والفِكر في الأصول. فإذا نظروا في ذلك نظروا فيه بطبائع مختلفة فتختلف بهم المذاهب ويتولد من اختلاف مذاهبهم تعاديهم وتضاغنهم وتطاعنهم وهم في ذلك مجتمعون في اختلافهم على بُغض الملوك لأن كل صنف منهم إنما يجري إلى فجيعة الملك بملكه ولكنهم لا يجدون سُلما إلى ذلك أوثقَ من الدين ولا أكثر اتّباعا ولا أعَزّ امتناعا ولا أشد على الناس صَبْرا. ثم يتولد من تعاديهم أن الملِكَ لا يستطيع جَمعهم على هَوًى واحد. فإذا انفرد بَبَعْضِهم فهو عدو | بقيتهم. ثم يتولد من عداوتهم كثرتهم فإن من شأن العامة الاجتماع على استثقال الولاة 142a والنفاسة عليهم لأن في الرعية المحروم والمضروب والمُقَام عليه وفيه وفي حَميمه الحُدود والداخِل عليه بعز الملك الذل في نفسه وخاصته. فكل هؤلاء يجري إلى متابعة أعداء الملك. ثم يتولد من كثرتهم أن يجْبُن الملك عن الإقدام عليهم. فإن إقدام الملك على جميع الرعية تغْرِير بملكه ونفسه ويتولد من جُبن الولاة عن تأديب العامة تضييع الثغور التي فيها الأمم من ذوي الدِيْن وذوي البأس لأن الملِك إن سد الثغور بخاصته المناصحين له وخلَت به العامة الحاسدة المُعادِية لم يَعُد بذلك تدريبهم في الحرب وتقويتهم في السلاح وتعليمهم المكيدة مع البغضة فهم عند ذلك أقوى عدو وأحضره وأخلقه بالظَفر. ولا بد من استطراد هذا كله إذا ضُيّع أوله.

٢ وإما: كتب المقريزي في الهامش الأيسر أمام هذه الكلمة رمز "ك" (لـ "كذا") إشارة إلى شكه. ١٤ يَعُد: كتب المقريزي فوق هذه الكلمة رمز "ك" (لـ "كذا") إشارة إلى شكه في صحة قراءتها.

١ من تجارب الأمم لمسكويه ١: ١٠١.

through setting a goal, but a ruler[95] will not be able to do so among the population after the goal that was set at the beginning of the rule, or through good habits and correct governing.

§ 34[96] Know that the beginning of the fall of dynasties comes from letting people (occupy themselves) with other than their usual occupations and ordinary duties. When leisure spreads (among people),[97] it creates speculation concerning affairs and consideration of their foundations. When they start speculating, they will do so with different mentalities, which will lead to differences of opinion. The differences of opinion will cause enmity, rancour, and backbiting between them. Despite their differences they agree on hating their king because each group aims to cause a misfortune to the king in his kingship. The most certain way to achieve this is through religion, which brings them more followers than any other way, which is the most difficult to prevent, and which makes people more patient. From their mutual enmity the king will not be able to unify them behind one aim. If he joins some of them, the others will become his enemies. Their enmity then makes them numerous. Ordinary people tend to unite in the dislike and envy of rulers, as among people some will have been deprived of something, beaten, punished, he himself or his family, or humbled by the royal might, he himself or his closest. All these are ready to follow the enemies of the king. Because of their number, the king is afraid of facing them, because if the king faces all his subjects he exposes both his person and his kingship to danger. When the ruler is afraid of correcting his people, he will lose his frontier zones where he has religious and strong people. If he mans these with people loyal to him, he will be left with the envious and inimical people, who cannot be trained for war, strengthened with weapons, or taught stratagems because of their hatred (of the king). Thus, they are the strongest enemy, the closest, and the most prone to win. There is no doubt all this will follow, once the beginning has been lost.

---

95 Miskawayh (ed. Caetani) is somewhat unclear but seems to read *al-mawālī* "subjects," for *al-wālī*.

96 Miskawayh, *Taǧārib al-umam*, 1:101 = C108–110.

97 Addition from Miskawayh (ed. Ḥasan), but missing from C.

§ 35[١] فمن أَلْفَى منكم الرعيةَ بعدي وهي على حال أقسامها الأربعة التي هي أصحابُ الدِين والحَرب والتدبير والخِدمة من ذلك الأساورة صنف والعُبادُ والنساكُ وسَدَنة النيران صنف والكُتّاب والمنجمون والأطِباء صنف والزُراع والمُهّان والتجار صنف فلا يكونن بإصلاح عبيده أشد اهتماما منه بإحياء تلك الحال وتفتيش ما يَحدُث فيها من الدخلات ولا يكونن لانتقاله عن الملك بأجزع منه من انتقال صنف من هذه الأصناف إلى غير مرتبته لأن تنقل الناس عن مراتبهم سريع في نقل الملِك عن ملكه إما إلى خلع وإما إلى قتل فلا يكونن من شيء من الأشياء أوحش بتّةً من رأس صار ذنبا أو ذنبٍ صار رأسا أو يَد مشغولة أحدثت فراغا أو كريمٍ ضَريرٍ أو لئيم مَرِحٍ. فإنه يتولد من تنقل الناس عن حالاتهم أن يلتمس كل امرئ منهم أشياء فوق مرتبته. فإذا انتقل أوشك أن يَرى أشياء أرفع مما انتقل إليه فيغبط ويُنافس. وقد علمتم أن من الرعية أقواما هم أقرب الناس من الملوك حالا وفي تنقل الناس عن حالاتهم مَطمَعةٌ للذين يلون الملوك في الملك ومَطمَعة للذين دُون الذين يلون الملوك في تلك الحال وهذا لقاح بوار المُلْك.

§ 36[٢] ومَن الفَى منكم الرعية وقد | أضيع أول أمرها فألقاها في اختلاف من الدِيْن واختلاف من المراتب وضياع من العامة وكانت به على المكاثرة قوة فليكاثر بقوته ضَعفَهم وليبادر بالأخذ بأكظامهم قبل أن يُبادروا بالأخذ بكظمه ولا يقولن: "أخاف العَسفَ." فإنما يخاف العسفَ من يخاف جريرةَ العسف على نفسه. فأما إذا كان العسفُ لبعض الرعية صلاحا لبقيتها وراحة له ولمن 142b

١٣ وضياع: كتب المقريزي حرف العين فوق السطر.

١ من تجارب الأمم لمسكويه ١: ١٠١-١٠٢.

٢ من تجارب الأمم لمسكويه ١: ١٠٢.

§ 35[98] Some of you will perhaps find after me people divided into four classes, namely men of religion, war, administration, and service. From these, one group consists of cavalrymen, one of religious people, ascetics, and keepers of fires, one of scribes, astrologers, and doctors, and one of farmers, artisans, and merchants.[99] If he finds people divided into these four classes, the king should by no means be more concerned with his own bodily wellbeing[100] than with preserving this situation and scrutinising what changes take place. He should fear less being removed from his kingship than the transition of one of these groups to a rank not its own. If people start moving from their ranks, the king will soon be moved from his kingship, either by being deposed or killed. Let the king not be worried about anything as much as he is worried about a head becoming a tail or a tail becoming a head, or of a hand occupied in work becoming unoccupied, or of a nobleman in need, or of an ignoble one exuberant. When people start moving from their positions, everyone will desire what is above his rank. Hardly has he moved upward, when he already sees a rank even higher than the one he moved into, and he will envy that and aspire to it. You know that some people are next to the king in position. When people move from position to position, those closest to the king covet kingship and those below them covet their position. This is the seed that leads to the destruction of kingship.

§ 36[101] Some of you will find the first step of deterioration in people's affairs having already been taken. He will find[102] people differing in matters of religion and rank and the general public having been lost, but he will still have power to resist them. Let him use his power against their weakness and let him quickly act against them before they act against him. Let him by no means say: "I fear being harsh." Let him fear being harsh who fears that the guilt of his harshness falls upon him. However, when harshness towards some is for the benefit of others and for the peace of the king himself and the

98 Miskawayh, *Taǧārib al-umam*, 1:101–102 = C110–111.

99 Grignaschi (1966): 87, n. 36, considers this a later gloss. This division of people into different classes, or estates, is found in a number of sources, such as the *Tansarnāmah* 12–13 (= Ibn Isfandiyār, *Tārīḫ* 19–20), translated in Boyce (1968): 37–38.

100 Al-Maqrīzī's reading does not make real sense, and the translation is based on reading *bi-iṣlāḥ ǧasadihi* as in Miskawayh (also quite clearly so in C110) and Grignaschi (1966): 55.

101 Miskawayh, *Taǧārib al-umam*, 1:102 = C111–112.

102 Reading *alfāhā* with Grignaschi (1966): 55. Miskawayh (ed. Caetani) could equally well be read *alqāhā*.

بقي معه من الرعية من النغَلِ والدَغَلِ والفساد فلا يكونن إلى شيء بأسرع منه إلى ذلك فإنه ليْسَ نَفسَه ولا أهلَ موافقته يَعْسِفُ ولكنما يعسف عدوَه. ومن ألفى منكم الرعيةَ في حال فسا⟨د⟩ها ولم ير بنَفسِه عليها قوة في صلاحها فلا يكونن لقميصٍ قَمِلٍ بأسرع خَلْعًا منه لما لَبِس من ذلك الملك وليأته البوار إذا أتاه وهو غير مذكور بشُؤمٍ ولا مُنوَّهٍ به في دنياه ولا مهتوك به سِترَ ما في يديه.

§ 37[١] واعلموا أن فيكم من يستريح إلى اللهو والدَعَةِ ثم يديم من ذلك ما يورثه خُلقا وعادة فيكون ذلك لقاح جِد لا لَهْوَ فيه وتعب لا خَفْضَ فيه مع الهُجْنة في الرأي والفضيحة في الذِكر. وقد قال الأولون منا: "لَهْوُ رَعية الصِدْق بتفريط الملوك ولهو ملوك الصدق بالتودد إلى الرعية." واعلموا أن من شاء منكم ألا يَسَيْر بسيرة إلا قُرِظَتْ له فعَل ومن شاء منكم بعَث العيونَ على نفسه فأذكاها فلم يكن الناس بعَيْب نفوسهم بأعلم منه بعيبه.

§ 38[٢] ثم إنه ليس منكم ملك إلا كثير الذكر لمن يلي الأمرَ بعدَه. ومن فساد الرعية نشرُ أمور ولاة العهود فإن في ذلك من الفساد أن أوله دخول عداوة مُمضَّة بين الملك وولي عهده وليس يتعادَى متعاديان بأشد من أن يسعى كل واحد منهما في قطع سُؤْلِ صاحبه. وهكذا الملك وولي عهده لا يَسُر الأرْفعَ إلا وَضْعُ سُؤْلِه في فَنَائه ولا يَسُر هذا الأوْضَعَ أن يُعطَى الآخر سُؤْلَه في البقاء ومتى يكن فرَحُ أحدهما في الراحة من صاحبه يدخل كُلَ واحد منهما وحشةٌ من صاحبه في طعامه

١ من تجارب الأمم لمسكويه ١: ١٠٢.

٢ من تجارب الأمم لمسكويه ١: ١٠٢.

rest of the people, who remain with him, free from resentment, corruption, and decay, then he should quickly turn to it, as he is not harsh towards himself or his followers, but only towards his enemies. If one of you finds people in a state of corruption and does not consider himself powerful enough to correct them, let him resign kingship quicker than he would put away a lice-infested shirt. Let it then perish without him being considered ill-omened nor spoken of throughout the world nor having his honour blemished.

§ 37[103] Know that some of you will enjoy play and comfort. Enjoying this for a longer while, it will become his nature and his habit, and this will be the seed of trouble, not joy, and of toil without rest, causing shortcomings of reason and shame for reputation. Our predecessors have said that the joy of sincere subjects is to praise[104] their kings and the entertainment of sincere kings is to love their subjects. Know that those of you who want to lead a life only to be lauded may do so. Those of you who want, may commission some to keep an eye on him, so that he can correct himself, so that people would not know their faults better than he his.

§ 38[105] Each king among you will invest considerable thought to who is going to inherit his kingship. Making public the affair of heir-apparent corrupts people. The first corruption is that there will be bitter enmity between the king and his heir-apparent. The worst two enemies do to each other is that they seek to frustrate each other's wishes. So it is with the king and the heir-apparent. The higher of them will not be pleased to see the lower have his wish[106] fulfilled and see him pass away, and the lower will not be pleased to see the higher have his wish fulfilled and remain alive. As both would be gladdened to get rid of the other, so both are suspicious of the other

103 Miskawayh, *Taǧārib al-umam*, 1:102 = C112.

104 Both manuscripts have clearly *tafrīṭ*, but I translate from Miskawayh, who reads *taqrīẓ*. Cf. also Grignaschi (1966): 56.

105 Miskawayh, *Taǧārib al-umam*, 1:102 = C112–113. For choosing the heir-apparent, cf. *Tansarnāmah* 26–41 (= Ibn Isfandiyār, *Tārīḫ* 28–36) and Boyce (1968): 51–63. The passage in the *Tansarnāmah* has been lengthened by adding two enframed stories. The theme of selecting the heir-apparent was current at the time of Khusraw Anūširwān (cf., e.g., Procopius, *Hist.* I.xxi.17–22), to whose time the *Testament* is often considered to date.

106 Al-Maqrīzī's text is corrupt, reading *lā yasurru l-afraʿa illā waḍʿu suʾlihi*, which does not make much sense, and the translation is based on Miskawayh, who has *lā yasurru l-arfaʿa an yuʿṭā l-awḍaʿu suʾlahu*.

وشرابه ومتى تداينا بالتُهَمَة يتخِذ كل واحد منهما وغرًا على إحْياء صاحبه. ثم تنساق الأمور إلى هلاك أحدهما لما لا بد منه من الفناء فتفضي | الأمور إلى الآخَر وهو حنق على جيل من الناس 143a يرى أنه موتور إن لم يحرمهم ويضعهم وتنزل بهم التي كانوا يريدون إنزالها به لو ولوا. فإذا وضع بعضَ الرعية وأسخط بعضا على هذه الجهة تولد من ذلك ضَغَن وسَخَط من الرعية. ثم ترامى ذلك إلى بعض ما أحذر عليكم بعدي.

§ 39[١] ولكن ليتخير الوالي منكم لله ثم للرعية ثم لنفسه وليا للعهد من بعده ثم يكتب اسمه في أربع صحائف فيختمها بخاتمه فيضعها عند أربعة نفر من خيار أهل مملكته ثم لا يكون منه في سر ولا علن أمر يستدل به على ولي العهد لا في إدْناء وتقريب يعرف به ولا في إقصاء وتَنكُبٍ يُستراب له وليتّق ذلك في اللحظة والكلمة. فإذا هلك جُمعت تلك الكتب التي عند الرهط الأربعة إلى النسخة التي عند الملك فَفُضِضْنَ جميعا ثم نُوِّه بالذي وُضع اسمه في جميعهن فيلقى المُلْكَ إذا لقيه بحداثة عهده بحال السُوْقَة فيلبَس ذلك الملك إذا لبِسَه ببَصَرِ السُوقة وسمعها ورأيها. فإن في سُكر السلطان الذي سيناله ما يكتفي به له من سُكْر ولاية العهد مع سُكْر المُلْك فيصم ويَعْمى قبل لقاء المُلْك كصَمم

١ إحْياء : الزيادة بخط المقريزي في الهامش الأيسر. ١٠ بحداثة : وضع المقريزي رمز "ح" تحت الحرف الثاني إشارة إلى تلفظه بالحاء.

١ من تجارب الأمم لمسكويه ١: ١٠٢-١٠٣.

when eating or drinking. When they are suspicious of each other they take for themselves (friends, confidants, and family, and they both feel)[107] hatred against the friends[108] of the other. This will undoubtedly lead to the death of one of them, and the affairs will come into the hands of the other, who will be enraged at some people, thinking that he has to take his revenge by depriving them and lowering them and letting them taste what they would have wanted him to taste had they won. When he thus lowers some people and angers others, this will create more rancour and anger from people and lead to what I warn you, who come after me, from.

§ 39[109] But let the ruler among you select an heir-apparent to succeed him thinking first of God, then of people, and only then of himself. He should write the heir-apparent's name on four sheets and seal them with his seal. These sheets he should give to four of his kingdom's best men. He should show neither in privacy nor in public any signs from which it could be deduced who the heir-apparent is. The heir-apparent should not be revealed by proximity and closeness nor by distancing and avoiding (the other potential candidates), which would cause suspicions. The king should avoid this in his looks and words. When the king dies, the documents, which these four people have, should be compared with the copy the king had. The seals should simultaneously be broken and the name that is found in all the documents should be read aloud and the heir-apparent proclaimed king. Then the heir-apparent becomes king having only just before been a commoner, and he will have been able to see, hear, and think in the way of people. He will, in any case, be inebriated by kingship, which is quite enough without the inebriation of having been heir-apparent before becoming king. If not, he will have been deaf and blind like a king even before his kingship. Becoming king, this would add deafness and blindness to what he already had

---

107 Addition from Miskawayh (ed. Ḥasan). Al-Maqrīzī's reading derives from Miskawayh (ed. Caetani).

108 Part of the sentence is missing here. Miskawayh (ed. Caetani) reads *yattaḫiḏu kullu wāḥid minhumā waġaran ʿalā iḥyāʾ/aḥibbāʾi* (written without diacritics in C) *ṣāḥibihi*. Al-Maqrīzī reads this word as *iḥyāʾ*, which would give something like "each of them feels hatred against letting the other live." *Iḥyāʾ* is written in the margin, which implies that al-Maqrīzī did go through this passage but failed to notice that Miskawayh (ed. Caetani) was already corrupt. The translation is based on an emended reading *yattaḫiḏu kullu wāḥid minhumā aḥibbāʾa wa-aḫdānan wa-ahlan. ṯumma yadḫulu kulla wāḥid minhumā waġar ʿalā aḥibbāʾi ṣāḥibihi*. (cf. Miskawayh, ed. Ḥasan).

109 Miskawayh, *Taǧārib al-umam*, 1:102–103 = C113–115.

الملوك وعماهم ثم يلقى الملك فيزيده صَمما وعَمى معما يلقي من ولاية العهد من بطرِ السلطان وحِيْلَة العُتَاة وبغي الكذابين وتمقه النمامين وتحميل الوشاة بينه وبين من فوقه.

§ 40[١] ثم اعلموا أنه ليس للملك أن يكذب لأنه لا يقدر أحد على استكراهه. وليس له أن يغضب لأن الغضبَ والعداوة لَقاح الشر والندامة وليس له أن يلعب ولا يعبث لأن العبث واللعب من عمل الفُرّاغ وليس له أن يفرغ لأن الفراغ من أمر السوقة وليس له أن يحسُد إلا ملوك الأمم على حسن التدبير وليس له أن يخاف لأن الخوف من المعور وليس له أن يتسلط إذ هو مُعور. واعلموا أن زين الملوك في استقامة الحال أن لا تختلف منه ساعات العمل والمباشرة وساعات الفراغ والدَعَة وساعات الركوب والنزهة فإن اختلافها منه خِفة وليس للملك أن يخِف.

§ 41[٢] اعلموا أنكم لن تقدروا على ختم أفواه الناس من الطعن والإزراء عليكم ولا قدرة بكم على أن تجعلوا القبيح حسنا. واعلموا أن لباس الملك ومطعمه مقارب للباس السوقة ومطعمهم وبالحَرى | 143b أن يكون فرحهما بما نالا من ذلك واحدا. وليس فضل الملك على السوقة إلا بقدرته على اقتناء المحامد واستفادة المكارم فإن الملك إذا شاء أحسن وليس السوقة كذلك واعلموا أنه يحق على الملك منكم أن يكون ألطف ما يكون نظرا أعظم ما يكون خَطَرا وألا يُذهِبَ حُسنَ أثره في الرعية خَوفُه لها. وألا يستغني بتدبير اليوم عن تدبير غد وأن يكون حذره للملاقين أشد من حذره للمباعدين وأن يتقي بطانة السوء أشد من اتقائه عامة السُوء. ولا يطمعن ملك في إصلاح العامة إذا لم يبدأ بتقويم الخاصة.

٦ المعور: كتب المقريزي فوق هذه الكلمة رمز "ك" (لـ "كذا") إشارة إلى صحة قراءتها. ‖ مُعور: كتب المقريزي فوق هذه الكلمة رمز "ك" (لـ "كذا") إشارة إلى صحة قراءتها. ١٠ وبالحَرى: وضع المقريزي رمز "ح" تحت الحرف الرابع إشارة إلى تلفظه بالحاء.

١ من تجارب الأمم لمسكويه ١: ١٠٣.

٢ من تجارب الأمم لمسكويه ١: ١٠٣.

as heir-apparent: arrogance of power, scheming of the impudent, injustice of liars, embellishment of calumniators, and the imposition of slanderers between himself and those above him.

§ 40[110] Know that the king should never lie, because he cannot be compelled (to do so). He should not be angry, because anger and enmity create evil and remorse. He should not joke and play, because joking and playing are the work of people at leisure, and he should never be at leisure, because leisure belongs to common people. He should only envy kings of other nations for their good governing. He should not be afraid, because being afraid means being exposed to fear and being exposed to fear one cannot rule. Know that the ornament of kings in keeping everything in good order is that his hours of work and toil, leisure and calm, and riding and pleasure should not vary. Their variance is lightmindedness, and a king should not be lightminded.

§ 41[111] Know that you will not be able to seal people's mouths from calumniating and derogating you. You cannot make beautiful what is ugly. Know that a king's clothes and his meals resemble those of commoners, and it is appropriate that the pleasure which the king and commoners get from this should be the same. The king has no other excellence over commoners except his ability to acquire glorious deeds and noble characteristics. If the king so wishes, he is able to do good, but this is not the case with commoners. Know that it is the obligation of the king from among you that he should be as discerning in his considerations as possible and as impressive in his importance as possible, and his fear of people should not carry away the effects of his good deeds among population. He should not be content with the measures he takes for today without planning those of tomorrow. He should beware more of those he meets than those who are far away. He should beware of bad confidants more than of other bad things. A king should not dream of putting people in order as long as he does not begin with correcting his own entourage.

110 Miskawayh, *Taǧārib al-umam*, 1:103 = C115.

111 Miskawayh, *Taǧārib al-umam*, 1:103 = C115–116.

§ 42[1] واعلموا أن لكل ملك بطانة وأن لكل رجُل من بطانته بطانة ثم لكل امرئ من بطانة البطانة بطانة حتى يجتمع في ذلك أهل المملكة. فإذا أقام الملك بطانته على حال الصواب أقام كل امرئ منهم بطانته على مثل ذلك حتى يجتمع على الصلاح عامة الرعية. اعلموا أن الملك منكم قد تهون عليه العيوب لأنه لا يَستَقبِل بها وإن عملها حتى يرى أن الناس يتكاتمونها بينهم كمكاتمتهم إياه تلك العيوب. وهذا من الأبواب الداعية إلى طاعةِ الهوى وطاعةُ الهوى داعية إلى غلبته فإذا غلب الهوى اشتد علاجه من السوقة المغلوب فضلا عن الملك الغالب. اتقوا بابا واحدا طال ما أمنته فضرني وحَذِرته فنفعني. احذروا إفشاء السر عند الصغار من أهليكم وخدمكم فإنه لا يصغر أحد منهم على حمل ذلك السر كاملا لا يقول منه شيئا حتى يضعَه حيث تكرهون إما سقطا وإما غِشا والسَقَط أكثر ذلك. اجعلوا حديثكم لأهل المراتب وحِباءكم لأهل الجهاد وبِشْرَكم لأهل الدين وسركم عند من يلزمه خير ذلك وشره وزَينه وشينه.

§ 43[2] اعلموا أن صحة الظنون مفاتيح اليقين وإنكم ستستيقنون بعض رعيتكم بخير وشر وستظنون ببعضهم خيرا أو شرا. فمن استيقنتم منه بالخير والشر فليستيقن منكم بهما ومن ظننتموهما به فليظنهما بكم في أمره. فعند ذلك يبدو من المحسن إحسانه فيخالف الظن فيغتبط ومن المسيء إساءته فيصدق الظن به فيندم. واعلموا أن للشيطان في ساعات من الدهر طمعا في السلطان عليكم منها ساعة | الغضب والحرص والزهو فلا تكونوا له في شيء من ساعات الدهر أشدَّ قتالا منكم عندهن 144a
حتى يتقشعن. وكان يقال: "اتق مقارنة الحريص الغادر فإنه إن رآك في القُرْب رأى منك أخبث حالاتك وإن رآك في الفضول لم يدعك وفضولك." أسْعِدوا الرأي على الهوى فإن ذلك تمليك

١٣ يبدو: "يبدوا" في الأصل.

١ من تجارب الأمم لمسكويه ١: ١٠٣–١٠٤.

٢ من تجارب الأمم لمسكويه ١: ١٠٤.

§ 42[112] Know that all kings have their confidants, each of these has his confidants, and each of these has again his confidants until the whole population of the kingdom is involved. If the king keeps his confidants in order, each of these keeps his similarly in order until the whole population is in order. Know that to some kings among you, his own faults may appear insignificant as he does not have to face them, even though he may have some, as he thinks that people will cover them up among themselves just as they cover them up from him. This is a gate leading to obeying one's desires, and obeying one's desires leads to their getting the better of you. When desire wins, it is hard to cure ordinary, dominated people, not to speak of the dominating king. Beware of a gate which, as long as I trust it, harms me, and as long as I beware of it, benefits me. Beware of spreading your secrets to lowly ones in your household and among your servants, because none of them is so insignificant that he could not keep that whole secret without revealing any of it until he reveals it to whom you would not have liked it to be revealed, either by carelessness or by disloyalty, mostly by carelessness. Confide your words to people of rank, give your gifts to people of fighting, your friendly smile to people of religion, and your secrets to those upon whom they are incumbent, both good and bad secrets, adornments and blemishes.

§ 43[113] Know that correct suppositions are the key to certainty. You will know with certainty that some of your subjects will have good and bad in them, while others you suppose to have the one or the other. Let those in whom you know with certainty good and bad be certain that they may receive both from you. Let those whom you suppose to have them both suppose them both from you in their affairs, too. This will bring visible the goodness of the good, (even when) contradicting your supposition, and they will have reason to rejoice. The badness of the bad will also become visible and prove your supposition right in their case, and they will have reason to regret. Know that there are moments when Satan desires to take possession of you. These include moments of anger, greed, and pride. Never fight more firmly against him than in these moments until they pass away. It used to be said: "Beware of associating with greedy and deceitful people. If they see you from close range, they will only see your worst moments and if they see you doing something in excess, they will not let you and your excesses in peace." Help

112 Miskawayh, *Taǧārib al-umam*, 1:103–104.

113 Miskawayh, *Taǧārib al-umam*, 1:104 = C118–119.

للرأي. واعلموا أن من شَأن الرأي الاستخذاء للهوى إذا جرى الهوى على عادته. وقد عرفنا رجالا كان الرجل منهم يؤنِس من قوة طباعه ونَبالة رأيه ما تُريه نفسُه أنه على إزاحة الهوى عنه وإن جرى على عادته ومُعاودته الرأي وإن طال به عهده قادر لثقة يجدها بقوة الرأي. فإذا تمكن الهوى منه فسخ عزمَ رأيه حتى تسميه كثير من الناس ناقصا في العقل. فأما البُصَراء فيستبينون من عقله عند غلبة الهوى عليه ما يُستبان من الأرض الطيبة الموات.

§ 44[1] واعلموا أن في الرعية صنفا من الناس هم بإساءة الوالي أفرحُ منهم بإحسانه. وإن كان الوالي لم يتَرْهم وكان الزمان لم ينكَبهم وذلك لاستِطْراف حادثات الأخبار فإن استِطراف الأخبار معروف من أخلاق حَشْوِ الناس. ثم لا طُرفةَ عندهم فيما ⟨اشتهر⟩ فجمعوا في ذلك سرور كل عدو لهم ولعامتهم معما وتروا به لنفسهم وولاتهم فلا دَواء لأولٰئك إلا بالأشغال. وفي الرعية صنف وتَروا الناسَ كلهم وهم الذين قووا على جفوة الولاة. ومن قوي على جفوتهم فهو غير سَادٍّ ثغرا ولا مناصح إماما. ومن غَش الإمامَ فقد غش العامة وإن ظن أنه للعامة مناصح. وكان يقال: "لم ينصح عملا من غش عامله."

§ 45[2] وفي الرعية صنف تركوا إتيان الملوك من قبَل أبوابهم وأتوهم من قبل وزرائهم فليعلم الملك منكم أن من أتاه من قِبل بابه فقد آثره بنصيحته إن كانت عنده ومن أتاه من قبل وزرائه فهو مُؤْثِر للوزير على الملك في جميع ما يقول ويفعل. وفي الرعية صنف دعوا إلى أنفسهم الجاه بالآباء

٨ اشتهر: الزيادة من تجارب مسكويه.

١ من تجارب الأمم لمسكويه ١: ١٠٤–١٠٥.

٢ من تجارب الأمم لمسكويه ١: ١٠٥.

reason against desire,[114] that will keep reason in power. Know that reason tends to submit to desire when desire is let to run its course. We have known men who trusted the strength of their nature and the nobility of their reason because their soul showed them that they would be able to abolish desire from them, even after it had been left to run its course, and to make their reason return (to power), even after a long while, because they trusted in the power of their reason. But when desire had a grip on them it dissolved the determination of their reason, so that finally many people considered them deficient in reason. As for discerning people, when desire is about to take over, they inspect their reason (to separate good from bad), just as a fruitful land is inspected (and separated) from a barren one.

§ 44[115] Know that among people there are some who take more delight in the bad deeds of a ruler than in his good deeds, even if the ruler has not wronged them and they have not been afflicted by the time. This is because they find pleasure in misfortunes, which is a well-known characteristic of the riffraff. In their opinion, there is no pleasure, except in what (becomes commonly known).[116] Thus, they combine the joy of all their (the kings') enemies and the people's enemies with the wrong they do to themselves and to their rulers. These people cannot be cured except by keeping them occupied in toil. Then there are among people others who wrong all the people. They are those who encourage (kings) to be harsh to them (their subjects). Who encourages (kings) to be harsh does not protect frontiers or give sincere advice to the Imam.[117] Who deceives the Imam, has deceived all people, even though he might think that he is sincere to people. It used to be said: "He who deceives the governor is not sincere to the district."

§ 45[118] Among people there are some who do not come to the king directly but through his Viziers. Let all kings among you know that when someone comes directly to you, he prefers being sincere to you if he has advice to give, but if he comes to you through your Viziers, he prefers the Vizier over the king in all that he says or does. Then there are those who claim high rank

114 This is also the reading of Miskawayh. MS Köprülü (Grignaschi 1966: 61) has a better reading *istaʿīnū bi-l-raʾy* "seek help from reason against desire."

115 Miskawayh, *Taǧārib al-umam*, 1:104–105 = C119–120.

116 Miskawayh reads *lā ṭurfata ʿindahum fīmā štahar* and Grignaschi (1966): 61, *lā ṭurfata ʿindahum illā fīmā štahar*. In translation, I follow Grignaschi's text and take this to mean that the riffraff enjoys spreading gossips about the ruler's bad deeds.

117 This is a rare case of Islamic terminology finding its way into the *ʿAhd*.

118 Miskawayh, *Taǧārib al-umam*, 1:105 = C120.

ووجدوا ذلك عند المغفلين نافقا وربما قرب الملك الرجلَ من أولٰئك لغير نبل في رأي ولا إجزاء في العمل ولكن الآباء أغروه به.

§ 46[1] وفي الرعية صنف أظهروا التواضع واستَشعَروا الكِبرَ فالرجل منهم يعظ الملوك زاريا عليهم بالموعظة يجد ذلك أسهل طريقي طعنه عليهم ويسمى هوا | ذلك وكثير ممن معه تَحرّيا للدين. فإن أراد 144b الملك هوانَهم لم يعرف لهم ذنبا يهانون عليه وإن أراد إكرامهم فهي منزلة حَبَوا بها أنفسهم على رَغم الملوك. وإن أراد إسكاتهم كان السماع في ذلك أنه استثقل ما عندهم من حفظ الدين وإن أمروا بالكلام قالوا "إنما يُفسِد ولا يُصلح." فأولٰئك أعداء الدول وآفات الملوك فالرأي للملوك تقريبهم من الدنيا فإنهم إليها أجروا وفيها عملوا ولها سعوا وإياها أرادوا. فإذا تلوثوا فيها بدت فضائحهم وإلا فإن فيما يحدثون ما يجعل للملوك سُلّما إلى سفك دمائهم. وكان بعض الملوك يقول: "القتل أقل للقتل." وفي الرعية صنف أتوا الملوك من قبل النصائح لهم والتمسوا صلاح منازلهم بإفساد منازل الناس فأولٰئك أعداء الناس وأعداء الملوك ومن عادى الملوك وجميع الناس الرعية فقد عادى نفسَه.

§ 47[2] واعلموا أن الدهرَ حاملكم على طبقات منهن حال السخاء حتى تدنوا من السرَف ومنهن حال التقتير حتى تقرب من البخل ومنهن حال الأناة حتى تصير إلى البلادة ومنهن حال المناهزة

---

١ من تجارب الأمم لمسكويه ١: ١٠٥.

٢ من تجارب الأمم لمسكويه ١: ١٠٥.

through ancestors.[119] They find this useful among inattentive people. A king may draw close one of these not because of any nobility of opinion or sufficient deeds, but because the (mention of) ancestors makes him want (to have) him (in his entourage).[120]

§ 46[121] Then there are those among people who simulate humility, while they feel superiority. Some of these preach to kings, scolding them in their sermons, finding this the easiest of the two ways[122] to calumniate them. They, and many others, call this "striving for religion." If the king wants to bring them down, he cannot find any fault with them for which to do so. If he honours them, then it will be they who have given this to themselves despite the king's will (and they will not be grateful). If he wants to silence them, he will be said to have done so because he found it difficult that they defended the religion. If he allows them to speak, they will say: "He corrupts and does no good." They are enemies of empires and misfortunes of kings. For the king, the right thing to do is to bring them closer to world(ly goods), because that is what they want, strive, and work for. That is what they really want. When they are tarnished by it, their shamefulness will become evident. If not, then there will be something in their deeds that gives the king an excuse to shed their blood. Some king has said: "Killing (one person) diminishes killing." Then there are some among people who come to the king ostensibly to give him advice while they, in fact, are after their own benefit to ruin others. These are enemies of people and the king. Who is inimical to the king and all people[123] is also his own enemy.

119 Miskawayh (ed. Caetani) reads *bi-l-ābāʾ* (the first vowel explicitly, but erroneously written as long A: to make sense, one should read *bi-l-ibāʾ*) *wa-l-radd lahu* "through forefathers and declining." Cf. MS Köprülü (Grignaschi 1966: 62), which reads *bi-l-taʾabbī wa-l-radd lahu*. Al-Maqrīzī understood this as translated above, as is shown by the end of the paragraph (*aġrawhu*, pl., refers back to al-ʾBʾ, which has to be read *al-ābāʾ*, not *al-ibāʾ*, which would call for a singular). A few orthographic changes have changed the passage from describing a person who endeavours to reach a high position by ostensibly simulating reluctance to accept it into one who uses his ancestors to claim high rank.

120 Al-Maqrīzī has changed Miskawayh's (ed. Caetani) *wa-lākinna l-ābāʾ* (explicitly with an initial long A) *wa-l-radd aġrayāhu bihi* into *wa-lākinna l-ābāʾ aġrawhu bihi*, thus trying to make sense of Miskawayh (ed. Caetani) by dropping *wa-l-radd*, which has become incongruous after the change from *al-ibāʾ* to *al-ābāʾ*.

121 Miskawayh, *Taǧārib al-umam*, 1:105 = C120–121.

122 Both al-Maqrīzī and Miskawayh refer to "two ways" without explanations, whereas MS Köprülü (Grignaschi 1966: 62) simply speaks of "an easy way."

123 Both manuscripts read here *al-nās al-raʿiyyah*, while Miskawayh and Grignaschi (1966): 63, have *al-raʿiyyah*. Al-Maqrīzī probably first wrote *al-nās* and then copied the word *al-raʿiyyah* from Miskawayh. The expression *al-nās wa-l-raʿiyyah* is used in § 27.

حتى تدنو من الخفة ومنهن حال الطلاقة في اللسان حتى تدنو من الهذَر ومنهن حال الأخذ بحكم الصمت حتى تدنو من العي. فالملك منكم جدير أن يبلغ من كل طبقة في محاسنها حَدّها فإذا وقف على الحدود التي ما وراءها سَرَف ألجم نفسَه عما وراءها.

§48[1] واعلموا أن الملك منكم ستعرض له شهوات في غير ساعاتها والملك إذا قدَّر ساعة العمل وساعة الفراغ وساعة المطعم وساعة المشرب وساعةَ الفضيلَة وساعة اللهو كان جديرا ألا يُعرَف منه الاستِقْدام بالأمور ولا الاستئخار عن ساعاتها فإن اختلاف ذلك يورث مضرتين إحداهما السُخْف وهي أشد الأمرين والأخرى نقص الجَسَد بنقص أقواته وحركاته.

§49[2] واعلموا أن من ملوككم من سيقول: "لي الفضل على من كان قبلي من آبائي وعمومتي ومن وَرِثت عنه هذا الأمرَ" لبعض الإحسان يكون منه. فإذا قال ذلك سُوْعِدَ عليه بالمتابعة له فليعلم ذلك الملك والمتابعون إنما وضعوا أيديَهُم وألسنَتَهم في قَصْب آبائه من الملوك وهم لا يشعرون. ولَبالحرى أن يشعر بعض المتابعين له فيُغَمِضُ على ما يَحزُنه من ذلك.

§50[3] واعلموا أن ابن | الملك وأخاه وعَمه وابن عمه كلهم يقول: "كِدْت أكون ملكا وبالحَرَى ألا 145a
أموت حتى أكون ملكا." فإذا قال ذلك قال ما لا يسر الملكَ فإن كتمه فالداء في كل مكتوم وإن أظهره كلِم في قلب الملك كَلْما يكون لقاحا للتباين والتعادي. وستجد القائل ذلك من التابعين والمحتملين والمُتَمنِينَ ما تمنى لنفسه ما يريده إلى ما اشتاق إليه شوقا. فإذا تمكن في صدره الأمل

---

١ تدنو[١] : في الأصل "تدنوا". ‖ تدنو[٢] : في الأصل "تدنوا". ٢ تدنو : في الأصل "تدنوا". ١١ ولَبالحرى : وضع المقريزي رمز "ح" تحت الحرف السادس إشارة إلى تلفظه بالحاء. ‖ يَحزُنه : وضع المقريزي رمز "ح" تحت الحرف الثاني إشارة إلى تلفظه بالحاء. ١٢ وبالحَرَى : وضع المقريزي رمز "ح" تحت الحرف الخامس إشارة إلى تلفظه بالحاء. ١٥ والمحتملين : وضع المقريزي رمز "ح" تحت الحرف الخامس إشارة إلى تلفظه بالحاء.

---

١ من تجارب الأمم لمسكويه ١: ١٠٥–١٠٦.

٢ من تجارب الأمم لمسكويه ١: ١٠٦.

٣ من تجارب الأمم لمسكويه ١: ١٠٦.

§ 47[124] Know that time will bring you to various situations. One is the state of generosity verging on extravagance. Another is economising verging on stinginess. Another is deliberation verging on stupidity. Another is seizing the opportunity[125] verging on fickleness. Another is a freely flowing tongue verging on blabbering. Another is keeping to the rule of silence verging on inability to speak. A king among you should reach out in each situation for its maximal merits, and when he comes to the limit beyond which there is only extravagance, he should bridle himself from going any further.

§ 48[126] Know that kings from among you will be subject to desires in inappropriate moments. When a king sets his times for work and leisure, eating and drinking, usefulness and entertainment, he should not be known to advance or postpone matters from their set times. Doing so causes two kinds of harm. The worse of the two is (reputation for) fickleness, and the other is the bodily harm caused by lack of nutrition and exercise.

§ 49[127] Know that some among your kings will say: "I am better than my fathers and uncles and others before me, from whom I inherited this!" (He will say so) because of some good deed he has done. When he says so, he will be supported by his followers. Let that king and his followers know that they have set their hand and their tongue to slaughter[128] his royal fathers unknowingly. Most probably some of the followers notice this, but they close their eyes to what saddens them.

§ 50[129] Know that the king's sons, brothers, paternal uncles, and paternal cousins will all say: "I almost became king. It becomes me to become king before I die." Saying this openly will not delight the king, and if the aspirant hides it, it is a hidden disease. If he reveals it, he will wound the heart of the king in a way that will lead to alienation and enmity. The one who says so will find[130] some who will follow him, some who will tolerate this, and some who will hope for themselves what he hopes for himself, and this will add to

124 Miskawayh, *Taǧārib al-umam*, 1:105 = C121–122.
125 Miskawayh makes this explicit by reading (*al-munāhazah*) *li-l-furṣah*.
126 Miskawayh, *Taǧārib al-umam*, 1:105–106 = C122–123.
127 Miskawayh, *Taǧārib al-umam*, 1:106 = C123.
128 Grignaschi (1966): 64, reads *qaḍb*.
129 Miskawayh, *Taǧārib al-umam*, 1:106 = C123–124.
130 Reading *sa-yaǧidu l-qāʾilu*, as in Grignaschi (1966): 64, against both manuscripts and Miskawayh (ed. Caetani), which explicitly reads *sa-taǧidu l-qāʾila*.

لم يرج النَيل له إلا في اضطراب الحبْل وزعزعة تدخل على الملِك وأهل المملكة. فإذا تمنى ذلك فقد جعل الفسادَ سُلما إلى الصلاح ولم يكن الفسادُ سُلما إلى صلاح قط. وقد رسمت لكم في ذلك مثالا لا مَخرجَ لكم منه إلا به. اجعلوا أولاد الملك من بنات عمومتهم ثم لا يصلح من أولاد بنات الأعمام إلا كامل غير سخيف العقل ولا عازب الرأي ولا ناقص الجوارح ولا معيوب عليه في دين فإنكم إذا فعلتم ذلك قل طلاب المُلْك وإذا قل طلابه استراح كل امرئ على جديلته وعرف حاله وغض بصره ورضي بمعيشته واستطاب زمانه.

§ 51[1] واعلموا أنه سيقول قائل من عُرْض رعيتكم أو من ذوي قرابتكم: "ما لأحد علي فضل ولو كان لي ملك!" فإذا قال ذلك فإنه قد تمنى الملك وهو لا يشعر ويوشك أن يتمناه بعد ذلك وهو يشعر فلا يرى ذلك من رأيه خَطَلا ولا من فعله زللا. وإنما يستخرج ذلك فراغُ القلب واللسانِ مما يكلّف أهل الدين والكتّاب والحُساب أو فراغ اليد مما يكلّف الأساورة أو فراغ البدن مما يكلّف التجار والمِهَنَة والخدَم. واعلموا أن الملكَ ورعيتَه جميعا يحق عليهم ألا يكون للفراغ عندهم موضع فإن التضْييعَ في فراغ الملك وفسادَ المملكة في فراغ الرعية.

§ 52[2] واعلموا أنا على فضل قوتنا وإجابة الأمور إيانا وحِدَّة دولتنا وشدة بأس أنصارنا وحُسْن نية وزرائنا لم نستطع إحْكامَ تفتيش الناس حتى بلغنا من الرعية مكروهها ومن أنفسنا مجهودَها. واعلموا أنه لا بد من سَخَط سيحدث منكم على بعض أعوانكم المعروفين بالنصيحة لكم ولا بد من رضًى سيحدث لكم من بعض أعدائكم المعروفين بالغش لكم فلا تحدِثوا عند ما يكون من ذلك انقباضا عن المعروف بالنصيحة ولا استرسالا إلى | المعروف بالغش. 145b

---

١ الحبْل: وضع المقريزي رمز "ح" تحت الحرف الثالث إشارة إلى تلفظه بالحاء.

---

١ من تجارب الأمم لمسكويه ١: ١٠٦.

٢ من تجارب الأمم لمسكويه ١: ١٠٦–١٠٧.

his yearning.[131] When this wish takes a firm grip of his heart, he only wishes to reach this through disturbances and troubles that fall on the king and the inhabitants of the kingdom. Wishing this he has set corruption as a way to wellbeing. Corruption, however, is never a way to wellbeing! I have already given you an example of that from which you cannot get rid of except by following it (my example). Let the sons of the king be from the daughters of his paternal uncles. From the sons of the daughters of paternal uncles only a perfect one will do, one not simple-minded nor halfwit, perfect of limbs, unblemished in religion. When you do so, those who seek kingship will be few, and when they are few, all will be in peace according to their nature and know their place, lower their eyes (from higher positions) and be satisfied with their own life and enjoy their time.

§ 51[132] Know that some among your subjects or relatives will say: "No one is better than I! Oh, if only I were king!" When he says so, he unconsciously wishes to become king and is on the brink of consciously wishing it. He cannot see that this is a fallacy and mistaken action. He is led to this by not occupying his heart and his tongue with what people of religion, scribal office, and accounting do, or occupying his hand with what horsemen do, or occupying his body with what merchants, artisans, and servants do. Know that neither king nor his subjects should have too much leisure. Waste lies in the leisure of a king and corruption of a kingdom lies in the leisure of a people.

§ 52[133] Know that despite my great power and my control of affairs, the vehemence of my rule, the strength of my helpers, and the good intentions of my Viziers, I have not been able to examine people('s affairs)[134] without forcing on people what they dislike and on myself toil and trouble. Know that you will certainly be annoyed by some of your helpers, who are known for their advice to you, and that you will be satisfied with some of your enemies, who are known to deceive you. Do not, on such occasions, refrain from kindness towards the one known for his advice or friendliness towards the one known for deceit.

131 Miskawayh (ed. Caetani) reads explicitly *yurīduhu*, followed by al-Maqrīzī. Grignaschi (1966): 64, reads *yazīduhu*, which is the better variant.

132 Miskawayh, *Taǧārib al-umam*, 1:106 = C124, 126. Note that pages 125 and 126 have changed places in Caetani's facsimile edition of Miskawayh.

133 Miskawayh, *Taǧārib al-umam*, 1:106–107 = C126, 125.

134 MS Köprülü (Grignaschi 1966: 65) reads *ḥaml al-nās ʿalá ḏālika* "we have not been able to bring people to that," i.e., that they would not have too much leisure, as in § 51.

§ 53[1] قد خلّفت لكم رأيي إذ لم أستطيع تخليفَ بدني وقد حَبوتكم بما حَبَوت به نفسي وقضيتُ حقكم فيما آسيتكم به من رأيي فاقضوا حَقّي بالتشفيع لي في صلاح أنفسكم والتمسك بعهدي إليكم فإني قد عهدت إليكم عهدي وفيه صلاح جميع ملوككم وعامتكم وخاصتكم ولن تضيعوا ما احتفظتم بما رسمت لكم ما لم تصنعوا غيره فإذا تمسكتم به كان علامة في بقائكم ما بقي الدهر.

§ 54[2] ولو لا اليقين بالبوار النازل على رأس الألف من السنين لظننت أني قد خلّفت فيكم ما إن تمسكتم به كان علامة في بقائكم ما بقي الدهر. ولكن القضاء إذا جاءت أيامه أطعتم أهواءكم واستثقلتم ولاتكم وأمنتم وتنقلتم عن مراتبكم وعصيتم خياركم وكان أصغر ما {تخطئون} فيه سُلما إلى أكبر منه حتى تفتقوا ما رتقنا وتضيعوا ما حفظنا. والحق علينا وعليكم ألا تكونوا للبوار أغراضا وفي الشؤم أعلاما فإن الدهْر إذا أتى بالذي تنتظرون اكتفى بوَحْدَته. ونحن ندعو الله لكم بنماء المنزلة وبقاء الدولة دعوةً لا يُفنيها فناء قائلها حتى المنقلَب ونسأل الله الذي عجل بنا وخلّفكم أن يرعاكم رعاية يرعى بها ما تحت أيديكم ويكرمكم كرامةً يُهين بها من ناوأكم ونستودعكم الله وديعةً يكفيكم بها الدهرَ الذي يُسْلمكم إلى زيَاله وغِيَره وعداوته والسلام على أهل الموافقة ممن يأتي عليه العهدُ من الأمم الكائنة بعدي. (...)

§ 55[3] سابور الجنود بن أزدشير بن بابك كان يلقب نَبَرْدَه. فلما أكثر من الغزو قيل له سابور الجنود قام بملك فارس بعد أبيه أردشير وله قصص وأنباء. منها أن أردشير بن بابك لما أفضى إليه الملك أسرف في قتل الأشكانية من ملوك الطوائف حتى أفناهم بسبب أن ساسان الأكبر بن بهمن

١ أستطيع: كذا في الأصل لـ"أستطع". ‖ حَبَوت: وضع المقريزي رمز "ح" تحت الحرف الأول إشارة إلى تلفظه بالحاء. ٧ تخطئون: "تخطُون" في الأصل. ٩ ندعو: "ندعوا" في الأصل. ١٣ بعدي: بعد هذه الكلمة بياض سطر في الأصل.

١ من تجارب الأمم لمسكويه ١: ١٠٧.

٢ من تجارب الأمم لمسكويه ١: ١٠٧.

٣ من تأريخ الطبري ١: ٨٢٢–٨٢٤.

§ 53[135] Now, I have left you my wisdom as I could not leave you my body. I have given you the same gift that I gave to myself. I have fulfilled my duty toward you by sharing my understanding with you. Fulfil your duty toward me by using my intercession for your wellbeing and following my testament to you. I have now given you my testament, in which you will find the wellbeing of all your kings, commoners, and people of rank. You will not lose what you guard by what I have described to you as long as you do not do otherwise. If you keep to it, it will be a sign for you as long as time itself remains.

§ 54[136] Were it not for the certainty of the destruction that will come at the end of the millennium, I would think that if you just kept to what I have left to you it will be a sign of your existence as long as time itself remains. But when the destined days are completed you will obey your desires and find your rulers burdensome, believing that you will be safe. You shall be moving from one rank to another and disobeying the best among you. Your small mistakes will lead you to bigger ones until you tear to parts what I have mended and you will lose what I have guarded. Yet it is your duty and mine that you should not set yourselves as targets for destruction and become sign posts of calamities. When Time brings you what you have been waiting for, it will be enough on its own (to destroy you). I pray to God that He raise your position and keep your empire, a prayer which will not vanish when the one who expressed it has vanished but will remain until the return of times. I ask God, who takes me soon away and leaves you behind, to guard you in a way that will keep safe what you have and to keep you honoured while humiliating your enemies. I leave you to God for Him to keep safe from the Time that delivers you to its end, its vagaries, and its enmity. Peace be upon those who agree with this testament among peoples that will come after me.

§ 55[137] Sābūr of the Armies b. Bābak. His cognomen was Nabardah.[138] He was called Sābūr of the Armies because he made so many campaigns. He became the king of Fārs after his father Ardašīr. There are many stories and reports about him. For example, when he became king, Ardašīr b. Bābak massacred Aškānians from among the Petty Kings until he (nearly) extinguished them. This he did because Sāsān the Elder b. Bahman had sworn an

135 Miskawayh, *Taǧārib al-umam*, 1:107 = C125.
136 Miskawayh, *Taǧārib al-umam*, 1:107 = C125, 127.
137 Al-Ṭabarī, *Taʾrīḫ*, 1:822–824 = trans., 5:23–25.
138 Al-Bīrūnī, *al-Āṯār al-bāqiyah* 136, reads Tīrdah (for Tīrdād).

كان آلى أَلِيَّةً أنه إن ملك يوما من الدهر لم يبق من نسل أشك بن ⟨خره⟩ أحدا. وأوجب ذلك على عقبه وأوصاهم أن لا يبقوا منهم أحدا إن هم ملك منهم أحد. فكان أول من ملك من نسل ساسان أردشير فقتلهم جميعا رجالهم ونساءهم بحيث لم يبق منهم أحدا غير جارية وجدها في دار المملكة فأعجبه حسنها. | وكانت ابنة الملك المقتول فأخفت نسبها وذكرت أنها كانت خادما لبعض 146a نساء الملك وأنها بكْر فاتخذها لنفسه فعلقت منه. فلما أمنته أخبرته أنها من نسل أشك. فنفر منها ودعا شيخا مسنا من ثقات أصحابه وأخبره خبرها وأمره بقتلها. فمضى بها ليقتلها فأخبرته أنها حبلى فأودعها سربا في الارض وقطع مذاكيره وجعلها في حُق وختم عليه وعاد إلى أردشير فأخبره أنه أودع المرأة الأرض ودفع إليه الحق وسأله أن يختم عليه بخاتمه ويودعه بعض خزائنه ففعل.

§56[1] وأقامت الجارية عند الشيخ حتى وضعت غلاما فسماه شاه بور بعد أن عرف طالعه وأنه يدل على أنه سيملك. وغبر أردشير دهرا لا يولد له حتى دخل ذلك الشيخ الأمين الذي عنده الصبي فوجده محزونا فقال: "ما يحزنك أيها الملك؟" فقال: "كيف لا أحزن وقد ضربت بسيفي ما بين المشرق والمغرب حتى ظفرت بحاجتي وصفا لي ملك آبائي. ثم أهلك ولا يعقبني فيه عقب ولا يكون لي فيه بقية." فقال له الشيخ: "سرك الله أيها الملك وعمرك! لك عندي ولد طيب نفيس فادع بالحُقّ الذي استودعتك وختمته بخاتمك أريك برهان ذلك." فدعا أزدشير بالحُق ثم فض ختمه فوجد فيه مذاكير الشيخ وكتابا فيه: "إني لما اختبرت خبر حَمل فلانة التي علقت من ملك الملوك

١ أشك : كتب المقريزي فوق الكلمة رمز "ك" (ل " كذا") إشارة إلى شكه في صحة قراءتها. ‖ خره : بياض في الأصل والزيادة من تأريخ الطبري. ٦ ثقات : الزيادة بخط المقريزي في الهامش الأيمن من الأعلى إلى الأسفل + صح، ويشير إليها رمز ⌝ بعد "من". ١٥ خبر : الزيادة بخط المقريزي في الهامش الأيمن من الأعلى إلى الأسفل + صح، ويشير إليها رمز ⌝ بعد "اختبرت".

١ من تأريخ الطبري ١: ٨٢٤–٨٢٥.

oath that if he were one day to become king, he would leave none alive from the offspring of Ašk b. [Ḫurrah].[139] This he also made incumbent on his descendants ordering them to leave none alive if one of them became king. The first among the offspring of Sāsān to become king was Ardašīr, and he killed them all, men as well as women, so that he left none alive except for a girl he found in the royal palace. Her beauty pleased him. She was the daughter of the king that had been killed, but she hid her lineage and claimed to be a servant of one of the king's women and a virgin. Ardašīr took her for himself, and she became pregnant of him. When she thought she was safe, she told him that she was of the family of Ašk, but Ardašīr shunned her and summoned an old man, a trusted companion of his, told him about her, and ordered him to kill her. The old man went to kill her, but she said she was pregnant. He put her in an underground cellar, cut off his own genitals, and put them into a box, which he sealed. Then he returned to Ardašīr and told him that earth now covered the woman. He also gave Ardašīr the box and asked him to seal it with his own seal and keep it safe in his treasuries, which the king did.

§ 56[140] The girl stayed with the old man until she gave birth to a son, whom he named Šāhbūr after he had studied his ascendant, which indicated that he would become king.[141] A long time passed, and no other child was born to Ardašīr. One day the loyal old man, in whose care the child was, came to the king, found him sad, and asked: "O King, what makes you sad?" The king answered: "How could I not be sad? I have fought with my sword in the East and the West until I have accomplished what I wanted and the kingdom of my ancestors has become securely mine. Yet I will die with no offspring of mine to succeed me and nothing will remain of me here." The old man said: "May God gladden you, o King, and make you prosper! You do have an excellent and precious son in my care. Call for the box which I entrusted to you and which you sealed with your own seal, and I will prove it to you." Ardašīr did so, broke the seal, and found in the box the genitals of the old man, together with a letter, which said: "I came to know that the girl was pregnant by the King of Kings Ardašīr. He had given me orders to kill her,

---

139 The space for the name of Ašk's father has been left blank in both manuscripts and is here added from al-Ṭabarī.

140 Al-Ṭabarī, *Taʾrīḫ*, 1:824–825 = trans., 5:25–26.

141 The name Šāhpūr means "king's son."

أردشير حين أمر بقتلها لم استحل إتلاف زرع الملك الطيب فأودعتها بطن الأرض كما أمر ملكنا وتبرَّأت إليه من نفسي لئلا يجد عاتب إلى دمي سبيلا.“

§ 57[1] فأمر أزدشير أن يجعل الغلام مع مائة غلام وقيل: مع ألف غلام من أترابه وأشباهه في الهيئة والقامة. ثم يدخل بهم عليه جميعا حتى لا يُفَرِق بينهم زِيّ. ففعل الشيخ ذلك فعند ما نظر إليهم أردشير قبلت نفسُه ابنَه من بينهم فأمر أن يُعطَوا صوالجة ويخرجوا تجاه الإيوان فلعبوا جميعا بالكرة وهو في الإيوان على سريره فدخلت الكرةُ الإيوانَ فلم يجسر أحد من الغلمان إليه وأقدم سابور من بينهم فدخل الإيوان. فاستدل أردشير بدخوله عليه وإقدامه وجرأته مع ما كان من قبول نفسه له حين رآه ورقته له دون أصحابه أنه ابنه. فقال له: ”ما اسمك؟“ فقال: ”شاه بور.“ فعند ذلك شهر أمره | وعقد له التاج من بعده. 146b

§ 58[2] فبلا منه أهل فارس في حياة أبيه عقلا وفضلا وعلما وشدة بطش وبلاغة منطق ورأفة بالرعية. فلما مات أردشير وعقد التاج على رأسه اجتمع إليه العظماء فدعوا له بطول البقاء وأطنبوا في ذكر والده وبثوا فضائله. قال لهم إنهم لم يكونوا يستدعون إحسانه بشيء يعدل عنده ذكرهم أباه بخير ووعدهم الخير. ثم أمر بما في الخزائن من الأموال فوسع بها على الناس من الجنود والوجوه وأهل الحاجة وكتب إلى عماله بالكُوَر والنواحي ففعلوا مثل ذلك في الأموال التي كانت بها. فعم إحسانه البعيد والقريب والخاص والعام والشريف والوضيع. ثم تخير العُمال واستقصى النظر في أمورهم وأمور الرعية فبان لكل أحد فضله وحسن سيرته.

---

٧ بينهم: وضع المقريزي رمز ”٢“ فوق هذه الكلمة ولكن لا توجد حاشية في الهامش.

---

١ من تأريخ الطبري ١: ٨٢٥.

٢ من تأريخ الطبري ١: ٨٢٥–٨٢٦.

but I did not consider it lawful to waste the good seed of the King. I endowed her to the belly of the earth, just as the King had given me orders to and then cleared myself of any suspicion, so that no one could find fault with me."[142]

§ 57[143] Ardašīr gave orders for the boy to be put amongst a hundred other boys—or a thousand other boys—of the same age and similar to him in form and stature. Then they were all to be brought to him, so that their clothing would not distinguish them. The old man did this. When Ardašīr looked at the boys, his soul accepted his own son from among them. He ordered them to be given polo mallets and be sent to play in front of the *īwān*. They all played ball while Ardašīr sat on his throne in the *īwān*. The ball rolled into the *īwān*, and none of the boys ventured to follow it. Only Sābūr was bold enough to enter. Ardašīr gathered from this and his courage and fearlessness that he was his son, as well as from his own natural affection and tenderness toward him rather than toward any of the other boys when he saw him. Ardašīr asked him: "What is your name?" He replied: "Šāhbūr." Then Ardašīr made the matter public and crowned him (as heir-apparent to rule) after him.

§ 58[144] Already at the time of his father, the people of Fārs noticed that Sābūr had reason, excellence, knowledge, strength, eloquence, and kindliness towards people. When Ardašīr died, and Sābūr was crowned, the noblemen came together and prayed for a long life for him. They spoke long about his father and his excellence. Sābūr said to them that they could not have appealed to his benevolence by anything better than by speaking well of his father. He promised them all good. Then he gave orders to give generously of the wealth in the treasury to the army, nobility, and those in need. He also wrote to his governors in different provinces and districts, and they did the same with the wealth they had. Thus, Sābūr's benevolence reached near and far, to the elect and the commoners, to the noble and the lowly. Then he elected his governors and investigated their affairs and the affairs of people. Everyone could see his excellence and his good way of life.

142 In reformulating the text, al-Maqrīzī has changed the focus of the last sentence. In al-Ṭabarī's version, it is the girl who is protected from gossip, not the old man.

143 Al-Ṭabarī, *Taʾrīḫ*, 1:825 = trans., 5:26–27.

144 Al-Ṭabarī, *Taʾrīḫ*, 1:825–826 = trans., 5:27–28.

§ 59[١] فانتشر ذكره في الآفاق حتى فاق جميع الملوك وسار إلى مدينة نصيبين لإحدى عشرة مضت من ملكه وبها جنود الروم. فحاصرهم مدة ثم رحل عنها لحادث أتاه خبره بخراسان حتى أحكم أمره ثم عاد إلى نصيبين فنزل عليها. فاتفق أن سور المدينة تصدع وانفرجت منه فرجة فدخل منها وقتل المقاتلة وسبى وأخذ الأموال وكانت عظيمة. ثم سار إلى الشام وبلاد الروم فافتتح مدنا كثيرة وأخذ ملك الروم من أنطاكية بعدما حاصرها مدة حتى ملكها وساقه فيمن ساق من الأسرى حتى أسكنهم جندي سابور وجعل ملك أنطاكية يبني شادروان تستر بنفسه على أن يجعل عرضه ألف ذراع. فبناه الرومي بقوم أشخصهم له من الروم فلما تم بناؤه جذع أنفه وأطلقه وقيل: قتله.

§ 60[٢] وكان بجبال تكريت بين الموصل والفرات مدينة يقال لها الحَضْر. والحَضْر حصن عظيم كالمدينة على شاطئ الفرات وهو الذي ذكره عدي بن زيد العِبادي في قوله من قصيدة: [الخفيف]

وأخو الحَضْرِ إذ بناه وإذ دجـ ـلةُ تُجبَى إليه والخابورُ
شَادَه مَرْمرًا وجَلّله كِلْـ ـسًا فلِلطَيْر في ذُراه وُكُورُ

٥ الروم من : الزيادة بخط المقريزي في الهامش الأيسر من الأسفل إلى الأعلى + صح، ويشير إليها رمز ⌐ بعد "ملك". ٨ الحَضْر : وضع المقريزي رمز "ح" تحت الحرف الثالث إشارة إلى تلفظه بالحاء. ‖ والحَضْر: وضع المقريزي رمز "ح" تحت الحرف الرابع إشارة إلى تلفظه بالحاء.

١ من تأريخ الطبري ١: ٨٢٦–٨٢٧.

٢ من تأريخ الطبري ١: ٨٢٧، ٨٣٠.

§ 59[145] Sābūr's fame spread in all directions until he had surpassed all other kings. In the twelfth year of his reign he went to Nisibis, where the Byzantine army was stationed. For a long time, he laid siege on the city, but then he had to leave because he heard that something had happened in Ḫurasan. He took care of the matters (there) and returned to Nisibis and encamped outside of the city. One of the city walls happened to crack so that there appeared a gap in it. Sābūr entered from there and fought against the enemy army, taking prisoners and winning enormous booty. Then he marched to Syria and the Byzantine territory and conquered many cities, managing to capture the Byzantine king in Antioch after he had laid siege on that city for a long time. When he had conquered the city, he took the Byzantine king and the other prisoners and settled them in Gundīsābūr. He forced the king of Antioch[146] himself build the dam of Tustar. Its width was to be 1,000 cubits. The Byzantine built it with the help of people he brought from Byzantium. When the dam had been built, Sābūr cut his nose and released him. Others say that he killed him.

§ 60[147] In the mountains of Tikrit, between Mosul[148] and the Euphrates, there is a city called Hatra. It is a huge fortress, like a city, on the bank of the Euphrates. It is mentioned by ʿAdī b. Zayd al-ʿIbādī in his *qaṣīdah*:[149] [*al-ḫafīf*]

(Where is now) the ruler of Hatra, to whom
the taxes of the Tigris and Ḫabur were brought?
He raised it from marble and coated with
lime, yet birds (now) nest on its top.

145 Al-Ṭabarī, *Taʾrīḫ*, 1:826–827 = trans., 5:28–31. Al-Maqrīzī, *Ḫabar/Greeks* § 141 dates this to the time of Ardašīr.

146 A few lines earlier al-Maqrīzī had first written *wa-aḫaḏa malik Anṭākiyā*, but then added in the margin *al-Rūm min*, to be inserted between *malik* and *Anṭākiyā* ("the king of Antioch" > "the king [of the Byzantines from] Antioch"). Here, he has forgotten to make a similar correction and speaks of the king of Antioch, instead of the Byzantines. Al-Ṭabarī uses the personal name of Valerian (Riyānūs), and the confusion has arisen when al-Maqrīzī rephrased the passage, omitting, as usual, the personal name, which was of no interest to him.

147 Al-Ṭabarī, *Taʾrīḫ*, 1:827, 830 = trans., 5:31–33.

148 Al-Ṭabarī reads the Tigris.

149 For ʿAdī (seventh century), see GAS, 2:178–179. This *qaṣīdah* is perhaps the most famous example of the motif *Ubi sunt* in Classical Arabic poetry, see, e.g., Kilpatrick (2003): 206, 255.

لم يهبْه رَيْبُ المنونِ فبادَ الـ   ملْكُ عنه فبابُه مَهْجُورُ

وذكره أبو دُؤَاد الإيادي واسمه عند المرزباني حارثة بن عمران بن الحجاج وعند | الآمدي حوثرة 147a
ابن الحجاج وعند السهيلي حنظلة بن شرقي وذلك في قوله من أبيات. وقيل: بل هي لخلف الأحمر
ويقال لحماد الراوية: [الخفيف]

٥ وأرى الموتَ قد تدلَّى من الحَضْـ   ـرِ على رَبّ أهلِه السَّاطِرُونْ
    صرعتْه الأيامُ من بعدِ مُلْكٍ   ونعيمٍ وجَوْهَرٍ مَكْنُونْ

والساطرون بالسريانية هو الملك واسمه الضَّيْزَنُ بن مُعاوية بن العُبَيْد بن الأجرام بن عمرو بن النخع بن
سَليح بن حُلْوان بن الحاف بن قضاعة. قال ابن الكلبي: هو قضاعي من العرب الذين تَنَخُوا بالسَّوَاد
فسُمُّوا تَنُوخ أي أقاموا بها وهم قبائل شتى. وأم الضَّيْزَنْ جَيْهَلَة وبها كان يُعرف وهي أيضا قضاعية
١٠ من بني تزيد بالتاء المثناة من تحت.

٣-٤ وقيل ... الراوية : الزيادة بخط المقريزي في آخر السطر في الهامش الأيسر من الأسفل إلى الأعلى.
٥ الحَضْر : وضع المقريزي رمز "ح" تحت الحرف الثالث إشارة إلى تلفظه بالحاء.   ٨ الحاف : وضع
المقريزي رمز "ح" تحت الحرف الثالث إشارة إلى تلفظه بالحاء.

The uncertainties of fate did not stand in his awe:
his kingship ended, and his gate is (now) deserted.[150]

Abū Du'ād al-Iyādī, whose name al-Marzubānī gives as Ḥāriṯah b. ʿImrān b. al-Ḥağğāğ and al-Āmidī as Ḥawṯarah b. al-Ḥağğāğ and al-Suhaylī as Ḥanẓalah b. Šarqī, mentions (the king) in the following verses, which are also attributed to Ḫalaf al-Aḥmar or Ḥammād al-Rāwiyah:[151] [*al-ḫafīf*]

I see how death has come down from Hatra
on the lord of his people, al-Sāṭirūn.
Days have brought him down after kingship
and happiness and treasured jewel.[152]

Al-Sāṭirūn is Syriac and means "the king."[153] His name was al-Ḍayzan b. Muʿāwiyah b. al-ʿAbīd[154] b. al-Ağrām b. ʿAmr b. al-Naḫaʿ b. Salīḥ b. Ḥulwān [b. ʿImrān][155] b. al-Ḥāfi b. Quḍāʿah. Ibn al-Kalbī has said that he was a Quḍāʿite from among the Arabs who settled (*tanaḫū*)[156] in the Sawād and were therefore called Tanūḫ. They consist of various tribes. The mother of al-Ḍayzan was Ğayhalah, and he was known by her name (i.e., as Ibn Ğayhalah). She was a Quḍāʿite, too, from the tribe of Tazīd.[157]

150 The poem is in the metre *ḫafīf*.

151 The last sentence concerning the attribution to Ḫalaf and Ḥammād is written in the margin, and even the last letters of the sentence referring to al-Āmidī have been squeezed together, which implies that the sentence was added to the text when the verse had already been written. For Abū Du'ād (mid-sixth century), see *GAS*, 2:167–169. For the learned scholars al-Marzubānī (d. 384/994), see *EI*², s.v., 6:634–635; Abū l-Qāsim al-Āmidī (d. 371/981), see *EI*³, s.v.; al-Suhaylī (d. 581/1185), see *EI*², s.v., 12:756, and *Rawḍ*, 1:326. For the philologists Ḫalaf al-Aḥmar (d. ca. 180/796), see *GAS*, 2:460–461; and Ḥammād al-Rāwiyah (d. ca. 155–158/771–774), see *GAS*, 1:366–368.

152 The poem is in the metre *ḫafīf*.

153 For al-Sāṭirūn, see Justi (1895): 282–283 (Sanatrūk). Cf. al-Suhaylī, *Rawḍ*, 1:323–324.

154 Al-Maqrīzī consistently vocalises al-ʿUbayd, even in a verse where it goes against the rhyme (§ 64).

155 Addition from al-Ṭabarī.

156 Al-Maqrīzī adds an explanation to this rare verb, for which see Ibn Manẓūr, *Lisān al-ʿarab*, 2: 56b: *ay aqāmū bihā*.

157 Al-Maqrīzī adds vocalisation note: "With a T, with two dots below," which is a mistake for "with two dots above."

§61[1] وقال أبو جعفر الطبري إن الضيزن جرمقاني وكان من ملوك الطوائف يقدمهم إذا اجتمعوا لحرب عدو من غيرهم. وملك أرض الجزيرة وكان معه من بني عُبيد بن الأجرام وقبائل قضاعة ما لا يحصَى وبلغ ملكه الشام وتطرف بعضَ السواد في غيبة سابور بخراسان. وفي ذلك يقول عمرو ابن ألَة بن جدي بن الرُها بن غَنْم بن حُلْوان بن عمران بن الحاف بن قضاعة: [السريع]

لقيناهم بجمع من عِلَافٍ وبالخيل الصَلَادِمَةِ الذُكورِ
فلاقَتْ فارسٌ منا نكالا وقتّلنا هَرابِذَ شَهْرَزُورِ
دلفنا للأعاجم من بَعيْدٍ بجمع مِلْجَزِيرَةَ كالسَّعِيرْ

وقوله: "مِلْجَزيرة" يريد: "من الجزيرة." فلما أخبر سابور مما كان من الضيزن شخص إليه حتى أناخ على الحَضْر وقد تحصن به. فزعم ابن الكلبي أن سابور أقام عليه أربع سنين لا يقدر على هدمه ولا الوصول إلى الضيزن.

§62 وذكر ابن هشام عن ابن إسحٰق أن الذي غزا ساطِرون ملك الحَضْر سابور ذو الأكتاف لحصره سنتين. قال السهيلي: وذكر الأعشى في شعره حولين لا يقدر على فتح الحصن. قلت: يشير إلى قول الأعشى أبي بصير ميمون بن قيس بن جندل بن شراحيل بن عوف بن سعد بن ضُبَيَعَة

٣-٤ وفي ... بن١ : كشط المقريزي عبارة أخرى قبل أن يصححها كما هي الآن. ٤ بن جدي : الزيادة بخط المقريزي في الهامش الأيمن من الأعلى إلى الأسفل + صح، ويشير إليها رمز ⌐ بعد "ألَة". || الحاف : وضع المقريزي رمز "ح" تحت الحرف الثالث إشارة إلى تلفظه بالحاء. ٩ الحَضْر : وضع المقريزي رمز "ح" تحت الحرف الثالث إشارة إلى تلفظه بالحاء. ١١ عن ... إسحٰق : الزيادة بخط المقريزي في آخر السطر في الهامش الأيسر.

١ من تأريخ الطبري ١: ٨٢٧-٨٢٨.

§ 61[158] Abū Ǧaʿfar al-Ṭabarī has said: al-Ḍayzan was *ǧurmuqānī*[159] and one of the Petty Kings. He led them when they joined forces to fight against an outer enemy. He ruled the Ǧazīrah and was supported by innumerable people from Banū ʿAbīd b. al-Aǧrām and the tribes of Quḍāʿah. His rule reached as far as Syria. When Sābūr was absent in Ḫurasan, he made an excursion into parts of the Sawād, and it is about this that ʿAmr b. Alah b. Ǧudayy b. al-Dahāʾ[160] b. Ġanm b. Ḥulwān b. ʿImrān b. al-Ḥāfi b. Quḍāʿah says:[161] [*al-sarīʿ*]

We encountered them with a host of (Banū) ʿIlāf
  and strong-hoofed stallions.
The Persians received from us an exemplary punishment,
  and we massacred the *hērbads* of Šahrazūr.
Slowly we advanced from afar against the Persians
  with a host from the Ǧazīrah (*mil-Ǧazīrah*) like a blazing fire.[162]

By *mil-Ǧazīrah* he means *min al-Ǧazīrah* "from the Ǧazīrah." When he heard what al-Ḍayzan had done, Sābūr marched against him until he encamped in front of Hatra, where al-Ḍayzan had withdrawn. Ibn al-Kalbī[163] claims that Sābūr stayed there for four years without being able to destroy it and get at al-Ḍayzan.

§ 62[164] Ibn Hišām has transmitted from Ibn Isḥāq that it was Sābūr of Shoulders (Ḏū l-Aktāf) who attacked Sāṭirūn, King of Hatra, and laid siege on him for two years. Al-Suhaylī has said that al-Aʿšā mentions in his poem two years during which he could not conquer the fortress. I say that he refers to the words in a *qaṣīdah* by al-Aʿšā Abū Baṣīr Maymūn b. Qays b. Ǧandal b. Šarāḥīl

158 Al-Ṭabarī, *Taʾrīḫ*, 1:827–828 = trans., 5:32–33.

159 I.e., from Bā-Ǧarmā. The term is also used for one group of Nabateans, see Hämeen-Anttila (2006): 40, deriving their origin from the ancient Assyrians.

160 Vocalisation from al-Ṭabarī.

161 For ʿAmr b. Alah, see Nöldeke (1879): 38 and al-Iṣfahānī, *Aġānī*, 2:37.

162 Al-Maqrīzī seems to have taken the reading from al-Iṣfahānī, *Aġānī* 2:37, though there the name of the city is given as Nahr Šīr. Al-Ṭabarī reads *ka-l-ǧazīrati fī l-saʿīrī* "like an island amidst a blazing fire." The poem is in the metre *wāfir*.

163 Hišām b. Muḥammad al-Kalbī (d. ca. 206/821), early historian and an important source for al-Ṭabarī, see *GAS*, 1:269–271.

164 Al-Suhaylī, *Rawḍ*, 1:326; al-Ṭabarī, *Taʾrīḫ*, 1:828–829 = trans., 5:34. ʿAbd al-Malik b. Hišām (d. 218/834), Egyptian historian and genealogist. See *GAS*, 1:297–298. Muḥammad b. Isḥāq (d. 150/767), historian, author of the first biography of the Prophet Muḥammad. See *GAS*, 1:288–290.

ابن قَيْس بن ثعلبة وهو الحِصْن بن عُكَابة بن صَعْب بن علي بن بكر بن وائل الملقب الصَناجة من قصيدة: [المتقارب]

ألم تر للحَضْر إذ أهله   بنعمى وهل خالد من نَعِمْ
أقام به شاهبور الجنو   د حَولين يَضرب فيه القُدُم
فهل زادَه رَبُه قوةً   ومثل مُجاوِره لم يَقِمْ
وكان دعا قومَه دَعوةً   هلموا إلى أمركم قد صَرِم
فموتوا كراما بأسيافكم   أرى الموتَ يجشمه من جَشَم

§63[1] قال السهيلي: غير أن ابن إسحٰق قال: كان المستبيح للحَضْر سابور ذو الأكتاف | وجعله غيره 147b سابور بن أردشير بن بابك وهو أول من جمع ملك فارس وأذل ملوك الطوائف حتى دان الكل له والضيزن كان من ملوك الطوائف. فيبعد أن تكون هذه القصة لسابور ذي الأكتاف وهو سابور ابن هرمز لأنه كان بعد سابور الأكبر بدهر طويل وبينهما ملوك وهم هرمز بن سابور وبهرام بن هرمز وبهرام بن بهرام وبهرام الثالث ونرسي بن بهرام وبعده كان ابنه سابور ذو الأكتاف. وقول الأعشى: "شاهبور الجنود" بخفض الدال يدل على أنه ليس بشاهبور ذي الأكتاف. ثم إن النَضِيرَةَ

١–٢ من قصيدة: الزيادة بخط المقريزي في الهامش الأيمن من الأعلى إلى الأسفل + صح. ٣ ألم ... للحَضْر: زاد المقريزي في الهامش الأيمن من الأسفل إلى الأعلى: "ألم تري الحضْرَ" وهو الصواب. وكتب فوق كلمة "تري" رمز "ح" (لـ "نسخة أخرى"). ٥–٧ فهل ... جَشَم: كتب المقريزي الأبيات الثلاثة الأخيرة في الهامش الأيسر. والبيت الأول من الأسفل إلى الأعلى والبيتين الثاني والثالث من الأعلى إلى الأسفل.

٤ القُدُم: أضاف المقريزي الحاشية التالية في الهامش الأيسر: "جمع قدوم."

١ من تأريخ الطبري ١: ٨٢٩.

b. ʿAwf b. Saʿd b. Ḍubayʿah b. Qays b. Ṯaʿlabah, who was called al-Ḥiṣn, b. ʿUkābah b. Ṣaʿb b. ʿAlī b. Bakr b. Wāʾil, whose cognomen was al-Ṣannāǧah:[165] [*al-mutaqārib*]

Have you not seen Hatra when its people
  were in bliss? Yet can one eternally enjoy?[166]
Šāhbūr of the Armies stayed there
  for two years striking with his axes (*al-qudum*).
Did his Lord give him more strength?
  Pivots like his do not stand still.[167]
He called his people:
  "Come, your affairs have already been set!
Die a noble death with a sword in hand!
  I see men ready to undergo death!"[168]

§ 63[169] Al-Suhaylī has said: Except that Ibn Isḥāq has said:[170] The one who looted Hatra was Sābūr of Shoulders, while others say it was Sābūr b. Ardašīr b. Bābak. He was the first to join together all the kingship of Fārs and to humble the Petty Kings, so that they all became subservient to him. Al-Ḍayzan was one of the Petty Kings, so that it is improbable that this story relates to Sābūr of Shoulders, who was Sābūr b. Hurmuz, because he came a long time after Sābūr the Elder and there were several kings between them, namely Hurmuz b. Sābūr, Bahrām b. Hurmuz, Bahrām b. Bahrām, the third Bahrām, and Narsī b. Bahrām, and it was only after the last that there came his son Sābūr of Shoulders. Al-Aʿšā's Šāhbūr of the Armies, the last word in the genitive, indicates that it was not Šāhbūr of Shoulders. Then al-Naḍīrah

---

7 *al-qudum* : The plural of *qudūm* (axe) (marginal gloss in al-Maqrīzī's hand).

---

165 For al-Aʿšā (d. 5/625 or later), see *GAS*, 2:130–131. For the poem, see al-Aʿšā, *Dīwān* 28–34, poem 4, here vv. 60–62, 64–65.

166 While MS T takes into account two of al-Maqrīzī's marginal comments, the third, which corrects the beginning of the first line to *a-lam taray-i l-Ḥaḍra*, is dropped by the copyist. Note that al-Ṭabarī also has the inferior variant *a-lam tara li-l-Ḥaḍri*.

167 The second hemistich, which refers to the turning of fates, is translated on the basis of al-Ṭabarī, who reads *wa-miṯlu maḥāwirihī lam yaqum*. The verse refers to the besieged king, not Sābūr.

168 The poem is in the metre *mutaqārib*.

169 Al-Suhaylī, *Rawḍ*, 1:328; al-Ṭabarī, *Taʾrīḫ*, 1:829 = trans., 5:34–35 (latter half).

170 *Anna* may be a mistake, and one should probably read: Someone other than Ibn Isḥāq (*ġayr Ibn Isḥāq*).

بنت الضيزن عركت أي حاضت فأخرجت إلى ربَض المدينة وكانت من أجمل نساء زمانها. وكانت سُنّتهم في الجارية إذا حاضت أخرجوها إلى الربَض. وكان سابور من أجمل رجال زمانه. فرأى كل واحد منهما صاحبه وعلى سابور تاج من ذهب مكلل بالزبرجد والياقوت وقد لبس ثياب ديباج فعشقته وعشقها. فأرسلت إليه: "ما تجعل لي إن دللتك على ما تهدم به سور هذه المدينة وتقتل أبي؟" فقال: "حكمك وأرفعك على نسائي وأخصك بنفسي دونهن."

§ 64[1] فاختلف في السبب الذي دلته عليه. فقال ابن إسحٰق: فلما أمسى ساطرون شرب حتى سَكِر فأخذت مفاتيح باب الحَضْر من تحت رأسه فبعثت بها مع مولى لها. ففتح الباب فدخل سابور فقتل سَاطِرُون واستباح الحضر وخربه وسار بها معه فتزوجها. وقال المسعودي: دلته على مَنْهَر واسع كان يدخل منه الماء إلى الحَضْر فقطع لهم الماء أو دخلوا منه.

§ 65[2] وقال الطبري: قالت: "عليك بحمامة ورقاء مطوقة فأخضب رجليها بحيض جارية بكرٍ زرقاء. ثم أرسلها فإنها تقع على حائط المدينة فتقع المدينة." وكان ذلك طلسم المدينة لا يهدمها غيره. ووعدته النضيرة أنها تسقي الحرس الخمر: "فإذا صرعوا فاقتلهم وادخل المدينة." ففعل سابور ذلك فسقطت الأسوار ودخلها عنوة وقتل الضيزن فأبيدت قضاعة الذين كانوا مع الضيزن حتى لم يبق منهم باق وأصيبت قبائل بني حلوان فانقرضوا وقال عمرو بن آلةَ—وفى نسخة أَلَاهٍ—يذكر من هلك في تلك الوقعة وكان مع الضيزن: [الوافر]

---

٢ حاضت : وضع المقريزي رمز "ح" تحت الحرف الأول إشارة إلى تلفظه بالحاء. ٣-٤ وعلى ... ديباج: الزيادة بخط المقريزي في الهامش الأيسر من الأسفل إلى الأعلى، ويشير إليها رمز ˥ بعد "صاحبه". ٧ الحَضْر : وضع المقريزي رمز "ح" تحت الحرف الثالث إشارة إلى تلفظه بالحاء. ١١ ووعدته : كشط المقريزي عبارة أخرى (خمس كلمات تقريبا) قبل أن يكتب هذه الكلمة وأطال الخط بين العين والدال لملء البياض. ١٥ وكان ... الضيزن : الزيادة بخط المقريزي في آخر السطر في الهامش الأيسر من الأسفل إلى الأعلى + صح.

---

١ من مروج الذهب للمسعودي رقم ١٤٠٩.

٢ من تأريخ الطبري ١: ٨٢٩.

bt. al-Ḍayzan came into her periods, i.e., menstruated,[171] and she was sent to the outskirts of the city. She was one of the most beautiful women of her time. It was their habit that when a girl came into her periods, they sent her to the outskirts of the city. Sābūr was one of the most beautiful men of his time. They happened to see each other. Sābūr had a golden crown set with emeralds and rubies and he wore silken clothes.[172] She fell in love with him, and he with her. She sent him a message: "What shall you give me if I show you how to destroy the walls of the city and kill my father?" He replied: "Whatever you want. And I will raise you above my other wives and I will select you specifically for myself instead of the others."

§ 64[173] There is some disagreement concerning the means by which al-Naḍīrah guided Sābūr against her father. Ibn Isḥāq has said that one evening Sāṭirūn drank wine until he was drunk. Al-Naḍīrah took the keys of the gate of Hatra from under his pillow and sent a slave of hers to take them to Sābūr, who opened the gate and entered the city, killing Sāṭirūn and pillaging Hatra, reducing it to ruins. Then he took her with him and married her. Al-Masʿūdī[174] has said that she guided him to a wide channel through which water flowed to Hatra. Sābūr cut off their water[175] or entered the city through the channel.

§ 65[176] Al-Ṭabarī has said that al-Naḍīrah said to Sābūr: "Take a silver-coloured collared pigeon and smear[177] its feet with menstrual blood of a young blue-eyed virgin. Let it then loose. It will sit on the city wall, and the city will fall." That was the talisman of the city and the only way to destroy it. Al-Naḍīrah promised him that she would give the guards wine: "When they are dead drunk, kill them and enter the city." Sābūr did so, the walls collapsed, and he took the city by force and killed al-Ḍayzan. Thus were exterminated the Quḍāʿah who were with al-Ḍayzan, so that none of them was left alive. Also the tribes of Banū Ḥulwān were afflicted, and they became extinct. ʿAmr b. Alah—or in another manuscript Alāh—who was with al-Ḍayzan, said about those who died in this battle: [*al-wāfir*]

171 The explanation is al-Maqrīzī's.
172 The description of Sābūr is not from al-Ṭabarī.
173 Al-Suhaylī, *Rawḍ*, 1:327, which is also the source for the quotation from al-Masʿūdī, *Murūǧ* § 1409.
174 Abū l-Ḥasan ʿAlī al-Masʿūdī (d. 345/956), historian, see Khalidi (1975) and Shboul (1979).
175 This version is found in, e.g., al-Maqdisī, *Badʾ*, 3:157.
176 Al-Ṭabarī, *Taʾrīḫ*, 1:829 = trans., 5:35–36.
177 Al-Ṭabarī speaks about writing (something).

148a
ألم يُخْبِرك والأنباء تَنْمي   بما لاقت سَراةُ بَني العُبَيد |
ومَصْرعُ ضَيزنٍ وبَني أبيه   وأَحلاسِ الكتائب مِن تَزيد
أتاهم بالفيول مُخَلَّلاتٍ وبالأ   بطال شابورُ الجُنودِ
فهدَّم مِن أَواسي الحَضْر صخرًا   كأنّ ثِفاله زُبَر الحديد

§66[١] وأخرب سابور المدينة وحَرق خزائن الضيزن بعدما أخذ جميع ما فيها واحتمل النضيرة فأعرس بها بعين التمر. فذكر أنها لم تزل ليلتها تضوّر من خشونة فرشها وكانت الفرش من حرير حشوه القز وقيل: كان حشوه زَغَب الطير. فالتمس ما كان يؤذيها فإذا ورقة آس ملتزقة بعَكْنَة من عكَنها قد أثرت فيها ويقال: كان يُنظر إلى مخها في ساقها من لين بشرتها فقال لها سابور: "ويحك بأي شيء كان يغذوك أبوك؟" قالت: "بالزبد والمخ وشُهْد الأبكار من النحل وصفو الخمر." قال: "وأبيك لأنا أقرب عهدا بك وأوتر لك من أبيك الذي غذاك بما تذكرين!" ثم أركب رجلا فرسا جموحا وربط غدائرها بذنبه ثم استركضها فقطعتها قطعا فذلك قول الشاعر: [الخفيف]

أقفرَ الحَضْر من نضِيْرةَ فالمِـ   ـرْباع منها فجانب الثرثارِ

٢ وأَحلاسِ: وضع المقريزي رمز "ح" تحت الحرف الثالث إشارة إلى تلفظه بالحاء. ٣ مُخَلَّلاتٍ: كتب المقريزي فوق الكلمة "صح". ٥ وحَرق ... فيها: الزيادة بخط المقريزي في الهامش الأيمن من الأعلى إلى الأسفل، ويشير إليها رمز ⌐ بعد "المدينة". ٩ النحل: وضع المقريزي رمز "ح" تحت الحرف الرابع إشارة إلى تلفظه بالحاء.

١ يُخْبِرك: أضاف المقريزي الحاشية التالية في الهامش الأيمن: "يُحزِنك" ووضع رمز "ح" تحت الحرف الثاني إشارة إلى تلفظه بالحاء وو رمز "خ" (لـ "نسخة أخرى") فوق الكلمة.

١ من تأريخ الطبري ١: ٨٢٩–٨٣٠.

With reports coming in, does it not make you sad,[178]
what the leading men of Banū ʿAbīd have undergone,[179]
as well as the fall of al-Ḍayzan and the sons of his father
and his companions of Tazīd, who rode with his troops:
Sābūr of the Armies marched against them with
elephants draped (in armour)[180] and heroes,
destroying Hatra's column of stone,
whose foundation stones were like pieces of iron.[181]

§ 66[182] Sābūr destroyed the city and burned al-Ḍayzan's treasuries after having taken everything out of them. He carried away al-Naḍīrah, marrying her at ʿAyn al-Tamr. It is said that she writhed with pain the whole night because her bed was too rough, even though it was of silk stuffed with raw silk or, it is also said, with fluff. Sābūr examined what was paining her and found that a myrtle leaf had stuck at the folds of her belly and left a mark there. It is said that the marrow of her leg could be seen, so soft (and transparent) was her skin. Sābūr said to her: "Woe to you, what did your father give you to eat?" She replied: "Cream, marrow, honey from virgin bees, and clear wine." He said: "By your father, I have known you less time than your father and am still dearer[183] to you than your father, who used to feed you with what you said!" Then he made a man ride an unbroken horse, to whose tail he tied her hair.[184] Then he spurred it on, and it tore her to parts. The poet refers to this in his verse: [*al-ḫafīf*]

Hatra is now desolate without Naḍīrah,
as are al-Mirbāʿ and the banks of al-Ṯarṯār.[185]

178 Al-Maqrīzī has first written *a-lam yuḫbirka* "has it not told you" and then corrected himself in a marginal note.

179 Al-Maqrīzī reads al-ʿUbayd, again vocalising this wrong, even against the rhyme.

180 Reading with al-Ṭabarī *muǧallalāt*, as against al-Maqrīzī's *muḫallalāt*, even though al-Maqrīzī explicitly marks this as the correct reading by adding a minuscule *ṣaḥḥa* over the line.

181 The metre of the poem is *wāfir*.

182 Al-Ṭabarī, *Taʾrīḫ*, 1:829–830 = trans., 5:36–37; cf. Miskawayh, *Taǧārib al-umam*, 1:108 = C129–130.

183 I prefer al-Ṭabarī's reading *awṯar* to al-Maqrīzī's *awtar*, even though the former is grammatically irregular (for *āṯar*).

184 E.g., al-Masʿūdī, *Murūǧ* § 1410, speaks more logically of *two* horses that tore her apart.

185 The poem is in the metre *ḫafīf*.

وقد أكثر الشعراء من ذكر الضيزن هذا في أشعارهم وإياه عنا عدي بن زيد العبادي من قصيدة: [الخفيف]

وأخو الحَضر إذ بناه وإذ دجلة تُجبَى إليه والخابور

§67[1] وذكر حمزة أن سابور الجنود ملك بعد أزدشير بن بابك اثنتين وثلاثين سنة وأربعة أشهر. وفي نسخة: ثلاثين سنة وخمسة عشر يوما. وفي أخرى: ثلاثين سنة وشهرا إلا يومين. وفي أيامه ظهر ماني الزنديق وادعى النبوة فتبعه خلق كثير عرفوا بالمانوية. وسابور هو الذي بنى شادروان تستر أحد عجائب الدنيا وأنشأ مُدنا منها ني شابور من مدن فارس وعربت فقيل: سابور. وكانت مدينة من إنشاء طهمورث خربها الإسكندر ونسي اسمها. ومنها فيروز شابور وتسمى بالعربية الأنبار من مدن العراق. ومنها آنْديُو سابور من مدن خوزستان وعربت فقيل: جندي سابور واشتقت بالفارسية من الخير فمعنى آنديو اسم أنطاكية وبه اسم للخير فيكون المعنى: خير من أنطاكية. وبناها على صورة رقعة الشطرنج يخرق في وسطها ثمانية طرق في ثمانية طرق. وكانوا يبنون | المدْن على تصوير أشياء 148b
وكانت مدينة السُوْس على صورة باز ومدينة تستر على صورة فَرَس. وكان شعار سابور أسمانجون وسراويله وشي أحمر وتاجه أحمر في خضرة وهو قائم بيده رمح وهو أول من ملك الحيرة. (...)

٦ وادعى ... بالمانوية: الزيادة بخط المقريزي في الهامش الأيمن من الأعلى إلى الأسفل، ويشير إليها رمز ⌜ بعد "الزنديق". ٧ سابور: وضع المقريزي ثلاث نقط تحت السين إشارة إلى تلفظه بالسين. ١٣ الحيرة: بعد هذه الكلمة بياض بقدر أربع كلمات في الأصل.

١ من تأريخ سني الملوك لحمزة ص ١٩، ٢٤، ١٤، ٣٨-٣٩.

Many poets have mentioned this al-Ḍayzan in their poems. In his *qaṣīdah*, ʿAdī b. Zayd al-ʿIbādī refers to him: [*al-ḫafīf*]

(Where is now) the ruler of Hatra, to whom
the taxes of the Tigris and Ḫabur were brought?[186]

§ 67[187] Ḥamzah has mentioned that Sābūr of the Armies ruled after Ardašīr b. Bābak for 32 years and 4 months or, according to another manuscript, 30 years and 15 days, and according to yet another 30 years and a month less two days. It was at his time that there appeared the heretic Mani, who claimed prophethood. Many people followed him, and they are known as the Manichaeans.[188] Sābūr is the one who built the dam of Tustar, which is one of the wonders of the world. He built several cities, including Nī-Šābūr in Fārs,[189] which in Arabic is called Sābūr. It is a city established by Ṭahmūraṯ and destroyed by Alexander, so that even its (original) name has been forgotten. He also built Fīrūz-Šābūr, which in Arabic is called al-Anbār, of the cities of Iraq, and (Bih-az)-Andīw-Sābūr of the cities of Ḫuzistan.[190] In Arabic, it is called Ǧundī-Sābūr. In Persian, it is derived from "good." The meaning of Andīw is the name of Antioch, and *bih* is a noun meaning "good," so the meaning (of the whole name) is "Better than Antioch."[191] He built it in the form of a chessboard, pierced by eight roads by eight. They used to build cities in the form of various things. The city of al-Sūs was built in the form of a hawk and the city of Tustar in the form of a horse. The vest of Sābūr was sky-blue, his trousers were red embroidery, and his crown was red on green. He was standing with a spear in his hand. He was the first to rule al-Ḥīrah. (…)

186 The poem is in the metre *ḫafīf*.

187 Ḥamzah, *Taʾrīḫ* 19, 24, 14, 38–39 = trans. 37, 43, 33, 62–63.

188 For Mani and the Manichaeans in Islamic sources, see Reeves (2011).

189 Al-Maqrīzī, who clearly reads Nī-Šābūr, confuses here between Nišapur and Bī-Šābūr, which are both mentioned by Ḥamzah. Al-Maqrīzī takes the name of the more famous city and combines it with the description of the less famous one. Throughout the text, al-Maqrīzī is eclectic with the names of the established or conquered cities, mentioning some, but leaving others unnamed, with no obvious logic.

190 *Bih-az* has been added from Ḥamzah.

191 In al-Maqrīzī, this remains a bit enigmatic, but Ḥamzah is much clearer. Al-Maqrīzī, who drops *Bih-az-*, seems to be copying something he does not himself fully understand.

§68[1] هرمز البَطَلُ الجَرِيءُ بن سابور الجنود بن أزدشير بن بابك. عهد إليه أبوه عندما حضره الموت وكان يشبه في عظم خَلْقه وبطشه وجُرْأته بأردشير جده إلا أنه غير لا حق به في رأيه وتدبيره وله أخبار عظيمة. وكانت أمه من بنات مهرك الملك الذي قتله أردشير بن بابك وتتبع نسله فقتلهم لأن المنجمين أخبروه أنه يكون من نسله من يملك. فهربت أم هرمز إلى البادية وكانت ذات عقل وجمال وكمال. فوقعت عند بعض الرعاة حتى خرج سابور يوما متصيدا فأمعن في طلب الصيد واشتد به العطش فرأى أخبية فقصدها وقد غاب الرعاء عنها. فطلب الماء فناولته امرأة ماء فرأى جمالا فائقا وقواما حسنا وبينا هو يتأملها إذ حضر الرِعاء فسألهم عنها {فادعى} بعضهم أنها ابنته. فسأله أن يزوجه بها فأجابه إلى ذلك. فصار بها إلى منزله وأمر بها فأصلح شأنها وخلا بها فامتنعت عليه مرارا حتى عجب من قوتها. فلما طال عليه أمرها وفحصه عنها أخبرته أنها إنما هي ابنة مهرك وأنها إنما فعلت ما فعلت خوفا عليه من أبيه أردشير. فعاهدها على ستر أمرها عن أبيه ووطأها فولدت له هرمز في سِتْر وخفية حتى أتت له سنون. فاتفق أن أردشير ركب يوما وعاد فدخل على ابنه سابور منزله على حين غفلة. فرأى هرمز وقد ترعرع وبيده صولجان يلعب به وهو يصيح في أثر الكُرَة. فأنكره وأخذ يتأمله فرأى المشابه فيه. وكانت صفات آل أزدشير لا تخفى بعلامات فيهم من حسن الوجوه وعبالة الخلق. فاستدناه وسأل سابور عنه فخر له ساجدا واعترف بالخطأ وحدثه

---

٢ وبطشه : الزيادة بخط المقريزي في آخر السطر في الهامش الأيسر من الأسفل إلى الأعلى. ٣ مهرك : وضع المقريزي رمز "ك" (لـ "كذا") فوق هذه الكلمة إشارة إلى شكه في صحة قراءتها. ٧ فادعى : "فادعا" في الأصل. ١٠ أبيه : الزيادة بخط المقريزي في الهامش الأيسر من الأسفل إلى الأعلى، ويشير إليها رمز ⌐ بعد "من".

---

١ من تأريخ الطبري ١: ٨٣١–٨٣٣.

§ 68[192] Hurmuz the Courageous Hero[193] b. Sābūr of the Armies b. Ardašīr b. Bābak. When his father was dying, he appointed Hurmuz as his successor. In the size of his body, his strength, and his courage, Hurmuz resembled his grandfather Ardašīr, but he lacked the latter's reason and ability to govern. There are wonderful stories about him. His mother was a daughter of the king Mihrak, whom Ardašīr b. Bābak had killed, pursuing his offspring and killing them, too, because astrologers had told him that a descendant of Mihrak would one day rule as king. The mother of Hurmuz had escaped to the desert. She was intelligent, beautiful, and in every way perfect. She lived with some shepherds. One day Sābūr went hunting, eagerly riding after the game, until he was very thirsty. He saw some tents and headed towards them. The shepherds were away, and when he asked for water, it was given to him by a woman whom he saw to be extremely beautiful and to have a nice stature. While he was looking at her, the shepherds returned. He asked them about her, and one of them claimed that she was his daughter. Sābūr asked for her hand in marriage, and the shepherd agreed to this. Sābūr took her home, giving orders to prepare her properly. When he was alone with her, she refused his advances several times, so that he was astonished by her strength. When this continued long enough, he asked her about this (behaviour), and she told him that she was the daughter of Mihrak and had done what she had done out of fear of Sābūr's father Ardašīr. Sābūr promised to keep her secret from his father. Then he had intercourse with her, and she bore him Hurmuz in secrecy. One day, when the boy was a few years old, Ardašīr rode off, but then returned and went unnoticed to the house of his son Sābūr.[194] He saw Hurmuz, who had grown to be a flourishing lad. In his hand, he held a polo mallet, with which he was playing, running after the ball and shouting. Ardašīr had not seen him earlier and started looking at him and saw a (family) resemblance in him. The features[195] of Ardašīr's family could not be hidden because they had certain characteristics in them, such as a beautiful face and stout form. Ardašīr told the boy to come closer and asked Sābūr about him. Sābūr fell on his knees and confessed his guilt, telling

192 Al-Ṭabarī, *Taʾrīḫ*, 1:831–833 = trans., 5:40–42.

193 Cf. al-Bīrūnī, *al-Āṯār al-bāqiyah* 136.

194 Al-Maqrīzī condenses the narrative here and makes it rather hard to follow. Al-Ṭabarī, *Taʾrīḫ* 1:832, explains that Ardašīr had something to tell to Sābūr.

195 Al-Ṭabarī speaks specifically of the *kayiyyah*, i.e., the royalty.

بما كان منه. فسر أردشير وقال: "الآن تحققت ما ذكره المنجمون من تملك ولد مهرك وأن الذي يملك منهم إنما هو هرمز إذ كانت أمه من نسل مهرك والآن قد زال ما كان في نفسي من ذلك."

§69[1] فلما قام سابور بعد موت | أبيه أردشير ولى ابنه هرمز خراسان وبعثه إليها. فاستقبل عمله 149a بقوة وقمع من كان يليه من ملوك الأمم وزاد في التجبر فوشي به إلى سابور أنه يريد الأمر لنفسه وأنه إن دعاه للحضور لم يحضر. فبلغ ذلك هرمز فخلا بنفسه وقطع يده وحسمها وألقى عليها ما يحفظها وأدرجها في ثوب نفيس وبعث بها في سفط إلى سابور وكتب إليه يعلمه بما نقل الأعادي عنه وأنه فعل بيده ما فعل ليزيل عنه التهمة. وذلك أنه كان من رسم الفرس ألا يملكوا ذا عاهة. فلما وصل ذلك إلى سابور تقطع أسفًا وحَسْرةً وكتب إلى هرمز بما أصابه من الغم واعتذر إليه وأعلمه أنه لو قطع بدنه عضوا عضوا لم يقدم عليه أحدا.

§70[2] فلما مات سابور وعقد التاج على رأس هرمز دعا له العظماء فأحسن جوابهم ووعدهم {بالخير}. وكانوا يعرفون منه صدق الحديث فأحسن السيرة فيهم وعدل في رعيته وسلك سبيل آبائه وكوّر كُوْرة رام هرمز. وكان شعاره أحمر موشّى وسراويله أخضر وتاجه أيضا أخضر في ذهب وبيده اليمنى رمح وفي يسراه ترس. وكانت مدة ملكه سنة وعشرة أشهر وفي نسخة سنتين.

١١ بالخير: في الأصل "بالخبر" وهو خطأ ظاهر.

١ من تأريخ الطبري ١: ٨٣٣.

٢ من تأريخ الطبري ١: ٨٣٣ ومن تأريخ سني الملوك لحمزة ص ٣٩، ١٤، ٢٤.

how this had happened. Ardašīr, however, was delighted and said: "Now I am convinced of[196] the saying of the astrologers about a descendant of Mihrak coming to rule as king. The one to rule will be Hurmuz, as his mother is from the offspring of Mihrak. Now, I am freed of what has been burdening my mind."

§ 69[197] When he became king after the death of his father Ardašīr, Sābūr appointed his son Hurmuz over Ḫurasan and sent him there. Hurmuz started his governorship energetically[198] and suppressed the neighbouring kings of other peoples and acted increasingly forcefully. He was slandered to Sābūr, and it was claimed that he wanted the kingship for himself and that if he were to be called to the court he would not obey. Hurmuz heard about this, withdrew to his rooms, and cut off his hand. He put preservatives on the severed hand, wrapped it in an expensive cloth, and sent it in a basket to Sābūr with a note, in which he explained what his enemies had said about him and that he had cut his hand, so that no suspicions would remain about him. The habit of the Persians was that they did not appoint king anyone with a physical defect. When the basket and the note came to Sābūr, he was pulled down by grief and sorrow and replied to Hurmuz, telling him about his sadness and apologising to him. He also let him know that he would not prefer anyone else above him even if he were to cut off his whole body, limb by limb.

§ 70[199] When Sābūr died and Hurmuz was crowned, the noblemen prayed for him and he replied in a beautiful way, promising good to them. They knew that he was truthful, and he behaved well towards them and was just to people, following the way of his fathers. He established the district of Rām-Hurmuz. His vest was red and embroidered and his trousers green and his crown green on gold. In his right hand, he had a spear and in his left a shield. The length of his reign was 1 year and 10 months or, according to another manuscript, 2 years.

---

196 Al-Ṭabarī reads *taḥaqqaqa* "it has become true."

197 Al-Ṭabarī, *Taʾrīḫ*, 1:833 = trans., 5:42–43.

198 Al-Maqrīzī misreads al-Ṭabarī's *fa-staqalla bi-l-ʿamal* "[he] adopted an independent policy" (trans. Bosworth) as *fa-staqbala* and then slightly modifies the passage by adding *bi-quwwah* to make better sense of it.

199 Al-Ṭabarī, *Taʾrīḫ*, 1:833 = trans., 5:43; Ḥamzah, *Taʾrīḫ* 39, 14, 24 = trans. 63, 33, 43. Ḥamzah, *Taʾrīḫ* 14 = trans. 33, gives another variant, 1 year and 12 days.

§71[1] بهرام بن هرمز البطل بن سابور الجنود بن أردشير بن بابك وكان يلقب يردخار. قام بملك فارس بعد موت أبيه هرمز البطل فظهر عن حلم وتُؤَدَة. فاستبشر الناس بولايته فأحسن السيرة واتبع في سياسة الناس آثار آبائه وقتل ماني الزنديق وداعيتهم بعدما هرب سنين.

§72[2] وكان من خبر ماني بن فُتّق بن تيتك من الحسركانية وأمه ميس ويقال: أوتاخيم ويقال: مار مريم من الأشغانية. كان أسقفا وكان أَحْنف الرجل اليمنى وأصل أبيه من هَمَذان ونزل المدائن في بيت الأصنام فكان يحضرها كما يحضر الناس. فهتف به ذات يوم هاتف: "يا فُتّق لا تأكل لحما ولا تشرب خمرا ولا تنكح بَشَرا." وكرر ذلك عليه دفعات في ثلاثة أيام. فسار حتى نزل بقوم في نواحي دستميسان يُعرفون بالمغتسلة وهم من فِرَقِ الصابئة يغسلون جميع ما يأكلونه ولهم أقاويل شنيعة. وهم ممن يقول بالأصلين كما يقول المانوية ويعظمون النجوم. فأقام فيهم وتبع | مذهبهم وكانت 149b امرأته حاملا بماني. فلما ولدته ببابل سنة أربع من ملك أردوان الأخير كانت ترى له المنامات الحسنة وكانت ترى كأنه أخذ منها وصعد به إلى السماء ثم يُرد. فربي ماني مع أبيه فتق على ملته وصار يتكلم في صغره بالحكمة.

---

٤ خبر: الزيادة بخط المقريزي في آخر السطر في الهامش الأيسر. ‖ الحسركانية: كتب المقريزي تحت السين ثلاث نقط يعني أنها مهملة. ٥ أَحْنف: وضع المقريزي رمز "ح" تحت الحرف الثاني إشارة إلى تلفظه بالحاء. ١٠ ببابل ... الأخير: الزيادة بخط المقريزي فوق السطر في الهامش الأعلى من الأسفل إلى الأعلى.

---

١ من تأريخ سني الملوك لحمزة ص ٤٠ وراجع تأريخ الطبري ١: ٨٣٤.

٢ من فهرست ابن النديم ص ٣٩١-٣٩٢.

§ 71[200] Bahrām b. Hurmuz the Hero b. Sābūr of the Armies b. Ardašīr b. Bābak. His cognomen was Yardḫār.[201] He became King of Fārs after the death of his father Hurmuz the Hero. He was mild and forbearing, and people rejoiced in his reign. He ruled well and followed the ways of his fathers in governing. He killed Mani the Heretic, the Propagandist after he had been on the run for many years.

§ 72[202] Mani b. Qunnaq b. Tītak[203] was from al-Ḫusrakāniyyah.[204] His mother was Mays or, according to others, Ūtāḫīm, and it is also said that (she was) Mār Maryam from among the Ašġānians. He was a bishop and had a deformed right foot. His father originated from Hamadan and settled in al-Madā'in in the temple of idols.[205] Mani's father used to be in the presence of those idols, as people used to do, when one day he heard a voice saying: "O Qunnaq, eat no meat, drink no wine, and marry no human being." This happened several times during three days. He left and settled in the region of Dastmaysān among some people, who were known as *al-Muġtasilah*, being one group of the Sabians,[206] who wash everything they eat. They have disgusting doctrines and they are among those who believe in two principles, just like the Manichaeans, and they worship heavenly bodies. Qunnaq stayed with them, following their doctrine. His wife was pregnant with Mani. When she gave birth to him in Babel in the fourth year of the reign of Ardawān the Last, she had several favourable dreams about him. She saw him taken from her and raised to heaven, before being returned to her. Mani grew up with his father Qunnaq in his religion and in his childhood he started speaking wisely.

---

200 This paragraph resembles al-Ṭabarī, *Ta'rīḫ*, 1:834 = trans., 5:45. The last sentence comes from Ḥamzah, *Ta'rīḫ* 40 = trans. 64.

201 Cf. al-Bīrūnī, *al-Āṯār al-bāqiyah* 136 (Bardǧār).

202 Ibn al-Nadīm, *Fihrist* 391–392; cf. Reeves (2011): 36–37. In §§ 72–77, al-Maqrīzī deviates from his source more than usually, which implies that he either has used an additional source or received the information from some intermediate source, which had done so.

203 Both names would appear to be corruptions of Fattiq < Pattīg. Ibn al-Nadīm reads Fattaq ibn Bābak (read Bātak).

204 Al-Maqrīzī's sentence is an anacoluthon. Ibn al-Nadīm reads al-Ḥaskāniyyah.

205 Ibn al-Nadīm only says that he settled in al-Madā'in, where there is a temple of idols.

206 For Ṣābians, see "*ṣābi'a*," in *EI*², 8:675–678. *Al-Muġtasilah* have sometimes been identified with the Mandaeans.

§73[1] فلما بلغ تمام اثنتي عشرة سنة زعم أنه أتاه الوحي من ملك جِنان النور وهو الله تعالى. وكان الملك الذي أتاه بالوحي يسمى التَوْم بالنبطية ومعناه القَرِين بالعربية. فقال له التوْم فيما جاءه به من الوحي: "اعتزل هذه الملة فلست من أهلها وعليك بالبَراهِمَة وترك الشهوات ولم يأن لك أن تظهر لحداثة سِنك." وكان مجيء الوحي إليه لسنتين خلتا من ملك أردشير بن بابك. فلما تم له أربع وعشرون سنة {أتاه} التَوْم فقال: "قَدْ حَان لك أن تخرج فتنادي بأمرك." فخرج في اليوم الذي ملك فيه سابور بن أزدشير بن بابك وهو يوم الأحد أول نيسان والشمس في برج الحمل. وخرج معه رجلان قد تبعاه على دينه وهما شمعون ودكوا وخرج معه أبوه فُتَّق.

§74[2] وكان قد ظهر قبله بنحو مائة سنة مرقيون. ثم ظهر ابن ديصان بعد مرقيون بنحو ثلاثين سنة وقيل له ابن ديصان لأنه ولد على نهر يقال له ديصان. وادعى ماني أنه البارقليط الذي بشر به المسيح عيسى بن مريم عليه السلام. واستخرج ملته من المجوسية والنصرانية وجال في البلاد أربعين سنة يدعو الناس. فكان ممن دعاه فاستجاب لدعائه فيروز أخو سابور بن أزدشير بن بابك فأوصله إلى أخيه سابور الجنود. فلما دخل عليه كبر في عينه وبالغ في تعظيمه بعدما كان قد عزم على قتله فعندما وقعت عينه عليه داخلته له هيبة وسُر به. فسأله سابور عن مذهبه فشرحه له وقام وقد

---

٢ بالنبطية: الزيادة بخط المقريزي في الهامش الأيسر من الأسفل إلى الأعلى، ويشير إليها رمز ⌐ بعد "التَوْم". ٤ وكان ... بابك: الزيادة بخط المقريزي في الهامش الأيمن منكسة، ويشير إليها رمز ⌐ بعد "سِنك". ٥ أتاه: في الأصل "انام" وهو خطأ ظاهر. ‖ حَان: وضع المقريزي رمز "ح" تحت الحرف الأول إشارة إلى تلفظه بالحاء. ١١ يدعو: "يدعوا" في الأصل. ١٣ فشرحه ... وقد: الزيادة بخط المقريزي في الهامش الأيسر من الأسفل إلى الأعلى + صح، ويشير إليها رمز ⌐ بعد "مذهبه".

---

١ من فهرست ابن النديم ص ٣٩٢.

٢ من فهرست ابن النديم ص ٣٩٢.

§ 73[207] When he was twelve years of age, Mani claimed to have received revelation from the King of the Gardens of Light, who is God, He is Exalted. The angel that brought him the revelation was called al-Tawm in Nabatean, which in Arabic means companion.[208] In the revelation he brought him, al-Tawm said: "Leave this religion, you do not belong to it, and join the Barāhimah[209] and forsake your desires. It is not yet time for you to appear due to your young age." The revelation came to him when two years had passed from the reign of Ardašīr b. Bābak.[210] When he was 24 years of age, al-Tawm came to him and said: "Now it is time for you to come out and propagate your cause." He came out on the very day when Sābūr b. Ardašīr b. Bābak became king, which was Sunday, the first of Nisan, the Sun being in the sign of Aries. Together with him there came out two other men, his followers in his religion, Simon and Dakwā.[211] His father Qunnaq followed him, too.

§ 74[212] About a hundred years before Mani, there had appeared Marcion. Then some thirty years after Marcion, there appeared Bardaisan.[213] He is called Bardaisan (Ibn Dayṣān) because he was born by the river called Dayṣān. Mani claimed being the Paraclete, about whom the Messiah, Jesus, son of Mary, peace be upon him, had given good tidings. Mani derived his religion from Magianism and Christianity and travelled around for forty years summoning people. Among those whom he summoned and who answered his call was Fīrūz, brother of Sābūr b. Ardašīr b. Bābak, who introduced him to his brother, Sābūr of the Armies. When Mani entered, he looked magnificent in Sābūr's eyes, and Sābūr treated him with excessive honour, even though he had earlier decided to have him killed. But now that he saw him, he was filled with awe and delighted by him. Sābūr asked him about his religion, and Mani explained it to him. Then Mani left, after

207 Ibn al-Nadīm, *Fihrist* 392; cf. Reeves (2011): 37–38.

208 "Nabatean" refers to the local languages of Iraq and Syria, primarily various forms of Aramaic. *Tawm* comes from Syriac *tūmā* "twin" (Arabic *taw'am*). The Manichaean *tawm* is actually more than a mere companion, being rather the inseparable equivalent of a human being in the spiritual world. *Qarīn* has similar connotations, meaning also "companion-spirit."

209 For the *barāhimah* (Brahmins), see *EI*[3], s.v. Al-Maqrīzī has, however, misread his source, Ibn al-Nadīm, who reads *al-nazāhah* "being unblemished."

210 This sentence does not come from Ibn al-Nadīm, and it has been added to the margin.

211 See Reeves (2011): 26, note 34. Ibn al-Nadīm reads Zakwā.

212 Ibn al-Nadīm, *Fihrist*, 392; cf. Reeves (2011): 38–39.

213 For Marcion (d. 160), see BeDuhn (2015). For Bardaisan (d. 222), see "Bardesanes," in *EIr*.

وعده أن يعود إليه بعدما سأله أن يعز أصحابه في جميع مملكته وأن يسيروا حيث شاؤوا فأجابه سابور إلى ذلك.

§75[1] وكان ماني قد دعا أهل الهند والصين وخراسان فاستجاب له خلق كثير. وخلف على كل ناحية رجلا من ثقات أصحابه يقوم بأمر شريعته. وكان من شريعته أن مبدأ العالَم من أصلين هما النور والظُلمة فالنور هو الله تعالى والظُلمة هي الشيطان. وله في صفة الإلاه تعالى وفي كيفية {بدء} التناسل ووجود المخلوقات وكيف تسلك طريقته كلام طويل. وفرض على قومه سبع | 150a صلوات في كل يوم وليلة وأوجب عليهم أن يستقبلوا في صلاتهم الشمس بعد مسحهم الأعضاء بالماء وحرم عليهم عبادة الأصنام [و]وتحريم أكل اللحوم بأسرها وتحريم شرب الخمر والإعراض عن الكذب وتحريمه وتحريم الزنا والقتل والسرقة والسحر وأوجب تعظيم يوم الأحد على العامة وتعظيم يوم الاثنين على الخاصة. وله زيادة على مائة كتاب وهو ينتقص جميع الانبياء عليهم السلام في كتبه ويزري عليهم ويرميهم بالكذب وأن الشياطين استحوذت عليهم وتكلمت على ألسنتهم ويسمي الأنبياء شياطين.

§76[2] فلما كانت أيام بهرام بن هرمز جمع له العلماء فناظروه لأنه قدم عليه ودعاه إلى دينه فأجابه. وطلب منه أن يجمع له أصحابه المانوية ليعرفهم فجمعهم له. وعندما ناظره علماء المجوس من فارس حجوه وألزموه الحجة على {رؤوس} الملإ. فأمر به بهرام فقتل وسلخ جلده وحشي تبنا وعلق على باب مدينة جندي سابور. وتتبعت المانوية فقتلوا حيث وجدوا وفر طائفة منهم إلى بلاد الترك. وكان قتله بعد مضي شهر من سنة أربع وستين وخمسمائة من سني الإسكندر بن فلبش المجدوني. وتزعم

٦ بدء: في الأصل "بدو". ٨ ووتحريم: الزيادة بخط المقريزي في الهامش الأيمن من الأعلى إلى الأسفل، ويشير إليها رمز ⌐ بعد "الاصنام و". وكتب حرف الواو مرة في المتن ومرة أخرى في الهامش. ١٠-١٢ وله ... شياطين: الزيادة بخط المقريزي في آخر السطر في الهامش الأيسر، معظمها منكسة وآخرها في الهامش الفوقي من الأعلى إلى الأسفل. ١٥ رؤوس: "روس" في الأصل. ١٦ وفر ... الترك: الزيادة بخط المقريزي في الهامش الأيمن من الأعلى إلى الأسفل، ويشير إليها رمز ⌐ بعد "وجدوا".

١ من فهرست ابن النديم ص ٣٩٢-٣٩٣، ٣٩٦-٣٩٧، ٣٩٨.

٢ من تأريخ سني الملوك لحمزة ص ٤٠ ومن فهرست ابن النديم ص ٣٩٧، ٣٩٨، ٤٠٠-٤٠١.

having promised Sābūr to return and asked him to honour his companions throughout the whole kingdom and to allow them to go wherever they wanted to. Sābūr promised this.

§ 75[214] Mani had summoned people in India, China, and Ḫurasan, and many had answered his call. In every region, he left behind a trusted companion of his to take care of his religion. According to his religion, the origin of the world derives from two Principles, Light and Darkness. Light is God, He is Exalted, and Darkness is Satan. Mani has long expositions describing God, He is Exalted, and the nature of the origin of procreation, and the existence of all created beings, and how his way is to be followed. He ordered his people to pray seven times a day and to face the Sun while praying and after having washed their limbs with water. He forbade them to worship idols,[215] eat any kind of meat, or drink wine. He ordered them to turn away from lying and forbade lying, adultery, killing, stealing, and magic. He ordered ordinary people to hallow Sunday and the elect to hallow Monday. He wrote more than a hundred books. In his books, he found fault with every prophet, peace be upon them, and belittled them, accusing them of lying. He also said that satans had taken possession of them and spoken in their voices, and he called prophets satans.

§ 76[216] At the time of Bahrām b. Hurmuz, Bahrām gathered learned men to dispute with Mani, who had come to him and summoned him to his religion. Bahrām answered the call and asked him to gather his Manichaean followers, so that he would recognise them. Mani did so. When they disputed with Mani, the learned Magians of Fārs defeated him with their arguments and forced him to accept them in the presence of the heads of the assembly. Bahrām ordered Mani to be killed, and he was skinned and the skin filled with straw and hung at the gate of the city of Gundīsābūr. Manichaeans were tracked down and killed wherever they were found. Some escaped to the land of the Turks. Mani was killed one month into the year 564 according to the years of Alexander, son of Philip, the Macedonian. The Manichae-

214 Ibn al-Nadīm, *Fihrist* 392–393, 396–397, 398; cf. Reeves (2011): 39.

215 The syntax is here somewhat ungrammatical.

216 Ḥamzah, *Taʾrīḫ* 40 = trans. 64; Ibn al-Nadīm, *Fihrist* 397, 398, 400–401; cf. Reeves (2011): 227–228.

المانوية أنه قيل: ماني ارتفع إلى جنان النور نخلفه من بعده سيس الإمام وتوارثت خلافته من بعد سيس جماعة وكانت إمامتهم لا تتم إلا ببابل ولا يجوز أن يكون الإمام بغيرها. فلما كانت الملة الإسلامية وتمزق ملك فارس قدمت المانوية من بلاد الترك إلى العراق وكثروا في أيام خالد بن عبد الله القسري أيام ملك بني أمية فإن خالدا كان يعني بهم. فلم يزالوا إلى أيام المأمون والمعتصم وأخرجوا من العراق غير مرة آخرها في أيام المقتدر فلحقوا بخراسان واستتر من نفي منهم.

§77[1] واجتمع من المانوية بسمرقند نحو الخمس مائة فأراد صاحب خراسان قتلهم فبعث ملك الصين فيهم ويهدد أنه إن قتل منهم أحد قتل من في مملكة الصين من المسلمين فكف عنهم. وآخر ما عرف من المانوية ببغداد في أيام معز الدولة ابن بويه نحو {ثلاثمائة} نفس. ثم تفانوا حتى لم يبق منهم قبل الأربعمائة من سني الهجرة إلا خمسة نفر. ولا أعلم اليوم أحد ينتحل مذهبهم ولله الحمد. وكان شعار بهرام أحمر وسراويله حمراء وتاجه على لون السماء وعليه شُرَفَتا ذهب وفي يده اليمنى رمح وفي اليسرى سيف وهو معتمد عليه.

٨ ثلاثمائة: "ثلاثة" في الأصل وهو خطأ ظاهر كما تشير كلمة "نفس" والتصحيح من فهرست ابن النديم، ص ٤٠١. ٩ أحد: كذا في الأصل لـ "أحدا".

١ من فهرست ابن النديم ص ٤٠١ ومن تأريخ سني الملوك لحمزة ص ٤٠.

ans claim that it is said[217] that Mani rose to the Gardens of Light and was succeeded by Sīs, the Imam.[218] After Sīs, Mani's Caliphate was inherited (in succession) by a number of people. The appointment as Imam had to take place in Babel, and it was not allowed for the Imam to live elsewhere. With the coming of the religion of Islam and the collapse of the kingdom of Fārs, Manichaeans returned from the land of the Turks to Iraq and became numerous under the governorship of Ḫālid b. ʿAbd Allāh al-Qasrī during the reign of Umayyad kings.[219] Ḫālid was concerned with them, and they remained there until the reigns of al-Maʾmūn and al-Muʿtaṣim. They were evicted from Iraq several times, the last of them during the reign of al-Muqtadir,[220] and they went to Ḫurāsān and those who were expelled hid themselves.

§ 77[221] Around 500 Manichaeans gathered in Samarqand. The governor of Ḫurāsān wanted to kill them, but the king of China sent him a message, threatening to kill all Muslims in the Chinese Empire if he were to kill even a single one of them, so he refrained from doing so. The last Manichaeans in Baġdād were about 300 persons[222] during the reign of Muʿizz al-Dawlah b. Būyah.[223] Then they disappeared so that before the year 400 of the *hiǧrah* [1010 AD] only five persons remained. Today, I know no one who would embrace their religion, glory be to God![224] Bahrām's vest was red, his trousers red, and his crown was sky-blue with two golden merlons. In his right hand, he had a spear, and in the left, a sword on which he was leaning.

---

217 The syntax is somewhat confused, and MS T reads *qatl*. The source, Ibn al-Nadīm, *Fihrist* 397, reads: *qāla l-Mānawiyyah: lammā rtafaʿa Mānī ilá Ǧinān al-nūr aqāma qabla irtifāʿihi Sīs al-imām baʿdahu*. In the holograph, the middlemost letter of Sīs is not provided with diacritics.

218 For Sīs, i.e., Sisinnios, see Reeves (2011): 257, note 219.

219 For the Umayyad governor Ḫālid al-Qasrī (d. 126/743), see "Khālid al-Ḳasrī," in *EI*^{2}, 4:925–927.

220 Al-Maʾmūn (r. 198–218/813–833); al-Muʿtaṣim (r. 218–227/833–842); al-Muqtadir (r. 295–320/908–932).

221 Ibn al-Nadīm, *Fihrist* 401; cf. Reeves (2011): 228–229; Ḥamzah, *Taʾrīḫ* 40 = trans. 64 (end).

222 Following Ibn al-Nadīm. Both manuscripts read "about three persons," but the singular *nafs* shows that the word *miʾa* has accidentally been dropped.

223 For Muʿizz al-Dawlah (r. in Iraq 334–356/945–967), see "Muʿizz al-Dawla," *EI*^{2}, 7:484–485.

224 This is al-Maqrīzī's own addition.

§78[1] وملك بعده ابنه بهرام الثاني فكان ملكه تسع سنين. وفي نسخة: ثلاث [ثلاث] سنين وثلاثة أشهر وثلاثة أيام. وكان عامل سابور بن أزدشير بن بابك | وابنه هرمز ثم بهرام بن هرمز بعد مهلك 150b عمرو بن عدي بن نصر بن ربيعة على ربيعة ومُضَر وسائر بادية العراق والجزيرة والحجاز امرؤ القيس {البدء} بن عمرو بن عدي. وهو أول من تنصر من ملوك آل نصر بن ربيعة وعمال الفرس وعاش في قول هشام بن محمد الكلبي مملكا في عمله مائة وأربع عشرة سنة منها في زمن سابور بن أزدشير ثلاثا وعشرين سنة وشهر وفي زمان هرمز ⟨بن⟩ سابور بن أردشير سنة وعشرة أيام وفي زمن بهرام ابن هرمز بن سابور ثلاث سنين وثلاثة أشهر وثلاثة أيام وفي زمان بهرام بن بهرام بن هرمز ثماني عشرة سنة. (...)

§79[2] بهرام شاه يذه بن بهرام بن هرمز بن ⟨سابور بن⟩ أزدشير بن بابك. ولي بعد أبيه بهرام بن هرمز. فلما عقد التاج على رأسه دعا العظماء له بمثل ما كانوا يدعون لآبائه فرد عليهم ردا حسنا وأحسن فيهم السيرة وكان ذا علم بالأمور وقال: "إن ساعدنا الدهر نقبل ذلك بالشكر وإن يكن غير ذلك نرضى بالقسم." فأقام ملكا ثلاثا وعشرين سنة وقيل: سَبْع عشرة سنة. وقيل: ثماني عشرة سنة. وكان شعاره أحمر مُوشى وسراويله خضراء وتاجه على لون السماء بين مشرفتي ذهب وهلال ذهب يقعد على سريره وفي يمناه قوس مُوتَّرة وفي يسراه ثلاث نشابات.

١ ثلاث : كرر المقريزي هذه الكلمة لأنها في آخر السطر، ثم في أول السطر التالي. ٤ البدء : "البدو" في الأصل. ٥ مملكا : الزيادة بخط المقريزي في الهامش الأيسر من الأسفل إلى الأعلى + صح، ويشير إليها رمز ⌐ بعد "الكلبي". ٦ هرمز : الزيادة بخط المقريزي في الهامش الأيسر من الأعلى إلى الأسفل + صح، ويشير إليها رمز ⌐ بعد "زمان". || بن : ساقط في الأصل والزيادة يقتضيها السياق. ٨ سنة : بعد هذه الكلمة بياض بقدر كلمة في الأصل. ٩ سابور بن : ساقط في الأصل والزيادة من تأريخ الطبري وتأريخ سني الملوك لحمزة.

١ من تأريخ الطبري ١: ٨٣٤–٨٣٥ و من تأريخ سني الملوك لحمزة ص ١٤، ١٩، ٢٤.

٢ من تأريخ الطبري ١: ٨٣٤–٨٣٥ ومن تأريخ سني الملوك لحمزة ص ٤٠، ١٤، ١٩، ٢٤–٢٥.

§ 78[225] After Bahrām, there reigned his son, the second Bahrām. His (the first Bahrām's) reign lasted for 9 years or, according to another manuscript, 3 years, 3 months, and 3 days.[226] After the death of ʿAmr b. ʿAdī b. Naṣr b. Rabīʿah, the governor for Sābūr b. Ardašīr b. Bābak and his son Hurmuz and then Bahrām b. Hurmuz over Rabīʿah and Muḍar and the rest of the (tribes of the) desert of Iraq, the Ǧazīrah, and Ḥiǧāz was Imruʾ al-Qays al-Badʾ b. ʿAmr b. ʿAdī, who was the first among the kings of the family of Naṣr b. Rabīʿah and the governors of the Persians to convert to Christianity. According to Hišām b. Muḥammad al-Kalbī he lived, holding this position, for 114 years, 23 years and a month of this during the reign of Sābūr b. Ardašīr, a year and 10 days during the reign of Hurmuz b. Sābūr b. Ardašīr, and 3 years, 3 months, and 3 days during the reign of Bahrām b. Hurmuz b. Sābūr and 18 years during the reign of Bahrām b. Bahrām b. Hurmuz. (…)

§ 79[227] Bahrām Šāh-Yadah[228] b. Bahrām b. Hurmuz b. (Sābūr b.) Ardašīr b. Bābak ruled after his father Bahrām b. Hurmuz. When he was crowned, the noblemen prayed for him like they had prayed for his fathers, and he answered them beautifully. He conducted himself well with them, and he was knowledgeable in his affairs. He said: "If fate helps us, we will accept it thankfully, but if it is otherwise, we will resign to what we are given." He reigned for 23 years or, according to others, 17 years or 18 years.[229] His vest was red and embroidered, his trousers green, and his crown was sky-blue between two golden merlons and a golden crescent. He was sitting on his throne, with a drawn bow in his right hand and three arrows in the left.

225 Al-Ṭabarī, *Taʾrīḫ*, 1:834–835 = trans., 5:43–45; Ḥamzah, *Taʾrīḫ* 14, 19, 24 = trans. 33, 37, 43.

226 The mention of 9 years is slightly inaccurate, whether it is to be understood as 9 years vs. 3 years, 3 months, and 3 days or as 9 years, 3 months, and 3 days vs. 3 years, 3 months, and 3 days. Ḥamzah gives three different lengths for his reign: 3 years, 3 months, and 3 days; 9 years and 3 months; or 3 years and 3 months.

227 Al-Ṭabarī, *Taʾrīḫ*, 1:834–835 = trans., 5:464; Ḥamzah, *Taʾrīḫ* 40, 14, 19, 24–25 = trans. 64, 33, 37, 43.

228 Cf. al-Bīrūnī, *al-Āṯār al-bāqiyah* p, 137 (Sāhandah, for Šāh-Yadah).

229 Ḥamzah only gives 23 or 17 years. 18 years may have been generated by taking the 18 years mentioned in the previous paragraph as the total number of Bahrām's regnal years.

§ 80[1] وملك بعده ابنه بهرام ويقال له بهرامان شكان شاه بن بهرام شاه يده بن بهرام بن هرمز ابن سابور بن أردشير بن بابك. وإنما قيل له: شكان شاه لأن الفرس كان ملكهم إذا جعل ابنه أو أخاه ولي عهده لقبه بشاهِيّة بلَدٍ فيدعى بذلك اللقب طول حياة أبيه أو أخيه. فإذا انتقل الملك إليه سمي شاهنشاه وعلى هذا جرى أمر بهرام الملقب كرمان شاه وكان أنوشروان يلقب في حياة أبيه قباذ تفَذْشَخار كرشاه وهو التملك على طبرستان لأن تَفْر اسم الجبَل وفَذْشخار اسم السهل والسفح وكر اسم التِلال والهِضاب وشكان اسم لسجستان. ولما عقد التاج على رأسه واجتمع العظماء دعوا له بالبركة في الولاية وطول ⟨العمر و⟩رد عليهم أحسن الرد. وكان قبل أن يفضي الملك إليه مملكا على سجستان فكان شعاره على | لون السماء موشى وسراويله حمراء {ويقعد} على السرير معتمدا بيده 151a على سيفه وتاجه أخضر بين شُرُفَتَي ذهب.

§ 81[2] وملك بعده أخوه نرسي ولقبه نخجيركان بن بهرام بن بهرام شاه بن بهرام بن هرمز بن سابور ابن أردشير بن بابك. فلما عقد التاج على رأسه وحضر الأشراف وعدهم خيرا وأمرهم بمعاونته على أمره ثم سار فيهم أعدل سيرة. وقال يوم ملك: "إنا لن نضَيع شكر الله على ما أنعم به علينا."

٧ العمر و: الزيادة من تأريخ الطبري. ٨ ويقعد: "ويقعده" في الأصل.

١ من تأريخ سني الملوك لحمزة ص ٤٠ و من تأريخ الطبري ١: ٨٣٥.

٢ من تأريخ الطبري ١: ٨٣٤ و من تأريخ سني الملوك لحمزة ص ٤١.

§ 80[230] After Bahrām Šāh-Yadah, there reigned his son Bahrām, who was called Bahrāmān Šakānšāh[231] b. Bahrām Šāh-Yadah b. Bahrām b. Hurmuz b. Sābūr b. Ardašīr b. Bābak. He was called Šakānšāh because when the king of Persia nominated his son or his brother as heir-apparent, he gave him the title of the king of a particular place. As long as his father or brother lived, he was addressed by that title. When he later became king, he was called the King of Kings (*šāhanšāh*). This is how it was that Bahrām bore the title of Kirmānšāh, and during the life of his father Qubād, Anūširwān was called Tafadšaḫār[232] Karšāh, which refers to the rule over Ṭabaristān because *tafar* means "mountain" and *faḏšaḫār* mean "plain; rocky surface" and *kar* means "hills; mountains."[233] *Šakān* is the name of Siǧistān. When he was crowned, the noblemen assembled and prayed for him blessing in rule and long (life).[234] He replied to them beautifully. Before becoming king, he had ruled Siǧistān. His vest was sky-blue and embroidered and his trousers red. He sat on a throne leaning with his hand on his sword. His crown was green between two golden merlons.

§ 81[235] After Bahrām, there reigned his brother Narsī, whose cognomen was Naḫǧīrakān,[236] b. Bahrāmšāh b. Bahrām b. Bahrām b. Hurmuz b. Sābūr b. Ardašīr b. Bābak. When he was crowned, he promised in the presence of the nobility all good and gave them orders to help him in his affairs. Then he acted most justly towards them. The day he became king, he said: "We will not neglect to be thankful to God for what He has mercifully given us."

230 Ḥamzah, *Taʾrīḫ* 40 = trans. 64–65; al-Ṭabarī, *Taʾrīḫ*, 1:835 = trans., 5:47.

231 Al-Ṭabarī has erroneously *šāhanšāh*. For the cognomen Šakānšān (better: Sakānšāh), see al-Bīrūnī, *al-Āṯār al-bāqiyah* 137.

232 Hoyland (2018): 65, reads Yaqarsaǧān. Both al-Maqrīzī and Hoyland have misunderstood the syntax in Ḥamzah's sentence and taken the preposition *bi-* as part of the word (read as Ta- or Ya-). One should read *kāna* (…) *yulaqqab* (…) *bi-Fadišḫārkaršāh*. The first part of the word reflects Middle Persian *Padašḫwārgar*, see, e.g., Christensen (1936): 348. Ḥamzah's erroneous etymological notes, both here and in Abū Nuwās, *Dīwān*, 2:106, show that already he was confused and probably misunderstood his source. This is further proof that Ḥamzah could not read Middle Persian, cf. Hämeen-Anttila (2018b): 118.

233 From Middle Persian *gar*, see MacKenzie (1971), s.v.; Zakeri (2008): 32; and Daryaee (2009): 84, and notes 55–56. The other etymologies are incorrect.

234 Addition from al-Ṭabarī. MS T has tried to correct this by adding the determinate article to *radd* (*al-radd*).

235 Al-Ṭabarī, *Taʾrīḫ*, 1:835 = trans., 5:48, and Ḥamzah, *Taʾrīḫ* 41 = trans. 65.

236 Cf. al-Bīrūnī, *al-Āṯār al-bāqiyah* 137.

فأقام تسع سنين وكان شعاره وشي أحمر وسراويله موشاة على لون السماء وهو معتمد على سيفه بيديه جميعا وتاجه أخضر.

§ 82[١] فملك بعده ابنه هرمز الملقب كونده بن نرسي بن بهرام بن بهرام شاه بن بهرام بن هرمز بن سابور الجنود بن أزدشير بن بابك. وكان فظا فوجل الناس منه وخشوا غلظته وشدته. فلما جلس على السر⟨ير⟩ أعلمهم أنه علم تخوفهم من شدته وقال لهم: "إني قد بدلت ما كان في خلقي من الفظاظة والغلظة بالرقة والرأفة." فوفى بما قال ورفق بالرعية وسار فيهم أعدل سيرة. وحرص على العمارة وانتعاش الضعفاء وأقام ثلاث عشرة سنة وقيل: سَبْع سنين وقيل: سَبْع سنين وخمسة أشهر وقيل: ست سنين وخمسة ⟨أشهر⟩. وأنشأ بلد خوزستان في كورة رامهرمز وكان شعاره وَشي أحمر وسراويله موشاة بلون السماء ويقوم معتمدا على سيفه وتاجه أخضر. ومات عن غير ولد فشق على الناس خروج الملك عن ذريته وفحصوا عن نسائه فوجدوا بامرأة منهن حمل. فعقدوا التاج على بطنها. وقيل إنه أوصى بالملك لذلك الحمل في بطن أمه.

§ 83[٢] فولدت تلك المرأة سابور وهو ذو الأكتاف بن هرمز بن نرسي بن [ابن] بهرام بن بهرام بن هرمز بن سابور الجنود بن أزدشير بن بابك. وكان يلقب شابور هُويه سُنَبا ومعنى هويه: الكَتِف ومعنى سُنَبا: نقّاب. فقالت العَرب: ذو الأكتاف. وذلك أنه غزا العرب وكان ينّقب أكتافهم فيجمع

---

٥ السرير: كذا في الأصل. لم يكتب المقريزي نهاية الكلمة. ١٠ حمل: كذا في الأصل لـ"حملا". ١٢ ابن: كشط المقريزي كلمة أخرى وكرر كلمة "ابن". ١٣ هرمز بن: الزيادة بخط المقريزي في الهامش الأيمن من الأعلى إلى الأسفل + صح، ويشير إليها رمز ⌐ بعد "بهرام بن".

---

١ من تأريخ الطبري ١: ٨٣٥-٨٣٦ و من تأريخ سني الملوك لحمزة ص ٤١، ١٤، ١٩، ٢٤.

٢ من تأريخ سني الملوك لحمزة ص ٤١ ومن تجارب الأمم لمسكويه ١: ١٠٩.

He ruled for 9 years. His vest was red and embroidered, his trousers were embroidered in sky-blue, and he leaned with both his hands on a sword and his crown was red.

§ 82[237] After Narsī, there reigned his son Hurmuz, called Kawandah,[238] b. Narsī b. Bahrāmšāh b. Bahrām b. Bahrām b. Hurmuz b. Sābūr of the Armies b. Ardašīr b. Bābak. He was coarse and people were afraid of him, fearing his roughness and violence. When he ascended the throne, he told them that he knew them to be afraid of his strength and said: "I have changed my coarseness and roughness to mildness and clemency." He kept his word and was merciful to people, behaving most justly towards them. He was keen to keep the land cultivated and to help the weak. He ruled for 13 years or, according to others, for 7 years or 7 years and 5 months or 6 years and 5 (months).[239] He built the town of Ḫūzistān in the district of Rām-Hurmuz.[240] His vest was red embroidery and his trousers were embroidered in sky-blue. He stood, leaning on his sword, and his crown was green. He died childless. It was hard for people to see kingship leave his offspring, so they inspected his womenfolk and found one woman pregnant. They put the crown on her belly or, according to others, he had bequeathed kingship to the child in his mother's womb.

§ 83[241] That woman gave birth to Sābūr, who is Sābūr of Shoulders (Ḏū l-Aktāf) b. Hurmuz b. Narsī b. Bahrām b. Hurmuz b. Sābūr of the Armies b. Ardašīr b. Bābak. He was called Šābūr Hūyah-sunbā. The meaning of *hūyah* is "shoulder" and of *sunbā* "piercer."[242] The Arabs called him Ḏū l-Aktāf, because he campaigned against the Arabs and used to pierce their shoulders,

237 Al-Ṭabarī, *Taʾrīḫ* 1:835–836 = trans. 5:49–50; Ḥamzah, *Taʾrīḫ* 41, 14, 19, 24 = trans. 65, 33, 37, 43.

238 Cf. al-Bīrūnī, *al-Āṯār al-bāqiyah* 137 (Kūhbad).

239 The word "month" is added from al-Ṭabarī. The copyist of MS T has noticed that something is missing and left a blank space.

240 While abbreviating it, al-Maqrīzī has confused the passage from Ḥamzah, who says that Hurmuz built in Ḫūzistān, in the district of Rām-Hurmuz, a *rustāq* called Wahišt-Hurmuz.

241 Ḥamzah, *Taʾrīḫ* 41 = trans. 65–66; Miskawayh, *Taǧārib al-umam*, 1:109 = C132; and cf. al-Ṭabarī, *Taʾrīḫ*, 1:836–837 = trans., 5:50–52.

242 Cf. al-Bīrūnī, *al-Āṯār al-bāqiyah* 137. For this epithet, correctly Hūbah-sunbā(n), see Hämeen-Anttila (2018b): 113, note 179.

بين كتفي الرجلين منهم بحلقة ويخلي عنهما. ولسابور هذا | قصص وأنباء وكان من أمره أنه لما 151b ولد استبْشر الناس بولادته وبثوا خبره في الآفاق وكتبوا الكتب بوصية أبيه هرمز له بالملك من بعده ووجهوا البُرد بها إلى الأطراف وتقلد الوزراء والكتّاب والعمال الأعمال التي كانوا يعملونها في أيام أبيه. فشاع الخبر وفشا في أطراف المملكة أن ملك الفرس صبي يُدبّر ولا يُدْرَى ما يكون منه. فطمع فيهم وفي مملكتهم الروم والترك والعرب وكانت بلاد العرب أقرب بلاد أعدائهم إليهم وكانوا من أحوج الأمم إلى تناول شيء من المعاش لسوء حالهم وشظف عيشهم. فسار جمع عظيم منهم في البحر من ناحية بلاد عبد القيس والبحرين وكاظمة حتى أناخوا براشهر وسواحل أردشير خره وأسياف فارس وغلبوا أهلها على مواشيهم وحُرُوثهم ومعايشهم وأكثروا الفساد في تلك البلاد ومكثوا بذلك حينا لا يغزوهم أحد من الفرس لقلة الهيبة وانتشار الأمر وكثرة المدَبّرين ولأن الملك طفل حتى ترعرع سابور.

§ 84[1] وكان أول ما عرف من حُسن تدبيره أنه استيقظ ليلة من الليالي وهو في قصر المملكة بمدينة {طيسبون} من المدائن الغربية فسمع في السحر ضوضاء الناس. فسأل عن ذلك فقيل له: "هذه ضجة الناس عند ازدحامهم على الجسر بدجلة في وقت إقبالهم عليه وإدبارهم منه." فأمر باتخاذ جسر آخر حتى يكون معبرا للمقبلين والآخر معبرا للمدبرين فلا يزدحم الناس في المرور عليهما. فعقد الجسر الذي أمر به قبل غروب الشمس من يومه بحذاء الجسر القديم. فاستراح الناس بعد ذلك من المخاطرة بأنفسهم في الجواز على الجسر واستبشر العظماء بما ظهر من فطنته على صغر سنه.

---

١ بحلقة: وضع المقريزي رمز "ح" تحت الحرف الثاني إشارة إلى تلفظه بالحاء. ٥ بلاد: الزيادة بخط المقريزي في الهامش الأيسر من الأسفل إلى الأعلى + صح، ويشير إليها رمز ⌐ بعد "وكانت". ١٢ طيسبون: "بطيسبون" في الأصل. ‖ من ... الغربية: الزيادة بخط المقريزي في الهامش الأيسر من الأسفل إلى الأعلى + صح، ويشير إليها رمز ⌐ بعد "طيسبون". ‖ السحر: وضع المقريزي رمز "ح" تحت الحرف الرابع إشارة إلى تلفظه بالحاء. ١٥ بحذاء: وضع المقريزي رمز "ح" تحت الحرف الثاني إشارة إلى تلفظه بالحاء.

---

١ من تأريخ الطبري ١: ٨٣٧–٨٣٨.

joining together by shoulders two men with a ring and then leaving[243] them so. There are many stories and reports about this Sābūr. When he was born, people rejoiced in his birth and spread the news to all directions, writing letters about how his father Hurmuz had bequeathed the kingship to him. They sent the letters through mail to all directions. Viziers, scribes, and governors were confirmed in the positions they had had during the reign of his father. The news spread and diffused to all corners of the kingdom that the king of Persia was a mere child, who was himself governed, and no one knew what would become of him. The Byzantines, Turks, and Arabs coveted the kingdom of the Persians. The country of the Arabs was the closest of their enemy countries. They were also the people most in need of laying their hands on some means of livelihood because of their poor condition and the hardships of their way of life. A large number of them came over the sea from the direction of the country of ʿAbd al-Qays and Bahrain and Kāẓimah and settled in Rāšahr and the coast of Ardašīr-ḫurrah and the shores of Fārs. They took from the inhabitants their cattle, fields, and livelihoods and caused much havoc in those areas. They stayed there for some time without any of the Persians attacking them, because they had little fear of the Persians, whose command was divided, who had many governors, and whose king was a child. So it was until Sābūr grew up.

§ 84[244] Sābūr's administrative ability was first noticed when he woke up one night in his royal palace in the city of Ṭaysabūn,[245] which is one of the Western al-Madāʾin. In the morning, he heard the clamour of people and asked what it was. He was told that that was the noise of people jostling each other on the bridge over the Tigris, when some were coming and others going. He gave orders to build another bridge, so that there would be separate bridges for those coming and those going and people would not need to jostle each other in trying to pass. Before evening that very day the second bridge had been built opposite the old bridge and people were no more risking their lives in crossing the river. The noblemen rejoiced in the sagacity this showed despite Sābūr's young age.

243 Ḥamzah says that he took them prisoners in this condition, which makes better sense.

244 Al-Ṭabarī, *Taʾrīḫ*, 1:837–838 = trans., 5:52–53.

245 Al-Maqrīzī has first written *bi-Ṭaysabūn*, as in al-Ṭabarī, but then added before it *bi-madīnat*, so literally the translation should read "in one of the cities of Ṭaysabūn."

§85[1] وكانت النجابة تتبين فيه كل يوم أضعاف ما تتبين في غيره وجعل الوزراء يعرضون عليه أمر الدولة شيئا بعد شيء. فكان مما عرضوا عليه أمر الجنود التي في الثغور وإن أكثرهم قد أَخَلّ وعظموا عليه الأمر بعد الأمر. فقال لهم: "لا يكبرن عليكم هذا فإن الحيلة فيه يسيرة." وأمر بالكتاب إلى أولٰئك الجنود جميعا بأنه "انتهى إلى طول مكثكم في النواحي التي أنتم فيها وعُظْم غنائكم عن إخوانكم وأوليائكم. فمن أحب منكم الانصراف إلى | أهله فلينصرف مأذونا له في ذلك. ومن أحب 152a أن يستكمل الفضل بالصبر في موضعه عرف له ذلك." وتقدم إلى من اختار الانصراف في لزوم أهله وبلاده إلى وقت الحاجة إليه. فلما سمع الوزراء ذلك من قوله ورأيه استحسنوه وقالوا: "لو كان هذا قد أطال تجربة الأمور وسياسة الجنود ما زاد رأيه على ما سمعنا منه."

§86[2] ثم تتابعت آراؤه في تقويم أصحابه وقمع أعدائه حتى تمت له ست عشرة سنة وأطاق حملَ السلاح وركوب الخيل واشتد عظمه جمع إليه رؤساء أصحابه وأجناده. ثم قام فيهم خطيبا فذكر الله تعالى وذكر ما أنعم به عليه وعليهم بآبائه وما أقاموا من أَرَبهم ونفَوا من أعدائهم وما اختل من أمورهم في الأيام التي مضت من أيام صباه وأعلمهم أنه يستأنف العمل في الذب عن البيضة وأنه عزم على الشخوص إلى بعض الأعداء لمحاربته في ألف رجل من المقاتلة. فنهضوا بأجمعهم داعين شاكرين وسألوه أن يقر بموضعه ويوجه القواد والجنود ليكفوه ما قَدّر من الشخوص فيه. فأبى أن يجيبهم إلى المقام. فسألوه الازدياد على العِدة التي ذكرها فأبى.

---

١ من تجارب الأمم لمسكويه ١: ١٠٩.

٢ من تجارب الأمم لمسكويه ١: ١٠٩–١١٠.

§ 85[246] Every day Sābūr showed double the eminence others showed, and little by little Viziers started introducing him to the matters of the Empire. Among other things, they told him about the troops that were in frontier garrisons and most of whom had deserted. They presented the matters, one after the other,[247] to him as huge problems, but he replied: "Do not let yourselves be distressed by this because it is easy to solve." He ordered letters to be written to all those troops as follows: "I have heard about your long stay in the region where you are and how greatly you have been missing your brethren and friends. Whoever wants to return to his family may do so with permission. For those who want to fulfil their service by patiently staying where they are this shall be recognised." Further, he allowed those who decided to return to stay with their family in their own country until they would again be needed. When the Viziers heard such words from him and saw his reason, they applauded and said: "Had he long experience in leading troops he could not have done better than what we just heard!"

§ 86[248] Sābūr expressed his opinions, one after the other, to put his companions right and to subdue his enemies. When he was sixteen years of age and able to carry arms and ride horses and his strength had grown, he called together all the chiefs of his companions and of armies and stepped forth to deliver a speech. He mentioned God, He is Exalted, and how He had been gracious to him and to them through his fathers and how these had fulfilled their wishes[249] and what enemies they had expelled, but how the situation had deteriorated during the days that had passed of his youth. He then told them that he would start anew the work by driving (enemies) away from the treasured heartland (of Iran). He had decided to march against some of the enemies in person to fight them with a group of a thousand warriors. They all rose up, blessing and thanking him, but asking him to stay where he was and to send generals and armies to appear in person in his stead. Sābūr refused to listen to them and to stay. Then they asked him at least to raise the number he had mentioned, but he refused to do so, too.

246 Miskawayh, *Taǧārib al-umam* 1:109 = C132–133; cf. al-Ṭabarī, *Taʾrīḫ*, 1:837 = trans., 5:53.

247 Al-Maqrīzī follows Miskawayh's text and reads *al-amr baʿd al-amr*, but this may merely echo the expression *šayʾan baʿd šayʾ* in the previous sentence. Dropping *baʿd al-amr* makes the sentence more logical: "they presented the matters to him as a huge problem."

248 Miskawayh, *Taǧārib al-umam*, 1:109–110 = C133; cf. al-Ṭabarī, *Taʾrīḫ*, 1:838 = trans., 5:54.

249 Al-Ṭabarī reads *adabihim*, but Miskawayh and both manuscripts have *arabihim* (*irabihim*).

§ 87[1] ثم انتخب ألف فارس من صناديد جنده وأبطالهم وأغنيائهم وتقدم اليهم في المضي لأمره ونهاهم عن الإبقاء على العرب وعلى من لقوا منهم ووصاهم ألا يعرجوا على مال ولا غنيمة ولا يلتفتوا إليه. ثم سار بهم حتى أوقع بمن انتجع بلاد فارس من العرب وهم غَارُّوْنَ فقتل منهم أَبْرَحَ القتل وأسر أعنف الأسْر وهرب بقيتهم. ثم قطع البحر في أصحابه فورَد الخَطّ واسْتَبْرى بلاد البحرين يقتل أهلها ولا يقبل فداء ولا يعرج على غنيمة. ثم مضى على وجهه فورد هجر وبها ناس من تميم وبكر بن وائل وعبد القيس فسفك فيهم من الدماء سَفْكًا سالت كسيل المطر حتى كان الهارب منهم يرى أن لن ينجيه غار ولا جبل ولا بحر ولا جزيرة.[2]

§ 88 ثم عطف إلى بلاد عبد القيس فأباد أهلها إلا من هرب منهم فلحق بالرمال. ثم أتى اليمامة فقتل بها مثل تلك المقتلة ولم يمر بماء من مياه العرب إلا غوّره ولا جُبّ من جبابهم إلا طمّه. ثم أتى قرب المدينة فقتل من وجد | [من وجد] هنالك من العرب وأسر. ثم عطف نحو بلاد بكر 152b وتَغْلِب وفيما بين مملكة فارس ومناظر الروم بأرض الشام فقتل من وجد بها من العرب وسَبَى وطَمَّ مياههم. ثم أسكن قوما من بني تغلب ومن سكن منهم البحرين دَارِيْن والخَطّ ومن كان من عبد القيس وطوائف تميم هجر ومن كان من بكر بن وائل بكرمان وهم الذين يُدْعَون بَكْر إيادٍ ومن كان منهم من بني حنظلة بالرُمَيلَة من بلاد الأهواز. وبَنَى بالسواد مدينة بُزُرْج سابور وهي عُكْبرا وبنى الأنبار وبنَى السُوْس والكرخَ.

١٣ تميم : صحح المقريزي الكلمة بعد أن كشط كلمة أخرى.

١ من تجارب الأمم لمسكويه ١: ١١٠.

٢ من تجارب الأمم لمسكويه ١: ١١٠.

§ 87[250] Sābūr selected a thousand cavalrymen of the most seasoned in his army and their heroes and the richest[251] ones. He gave them orders to accomplish what he wanted and forbade them to let alive any of the Arabs they would meet. He also told them not to turn to looting the property, but to ignore it. He marched with them until they suddenly attacked those of the Arabs who had resorted to the regions of Fārs. He massacred them and took prisoners most brutally, while the rest escaped. Then he crossed the sea with his companions, coming to al-Ḫaṭṭ. He marched through the country of Bahrain, killing its inhabitants and not accepting ransom or turning to loot. Then he continued, coming to Hağar, where there were people from Tamīm, Bakr b. Wā'il, and ʿAbd al-Qays. He shed their blood, so that it flowed like a torrent of rain and those who tried to escape thought that neither caves nor mountains, neither seas nor islands could save them.

§ 88[252] Then Sābūr turned to the country of ʿAbd al-Qays, killing all except those who managed to flee and reach the desert. He continued to al-Yamāmah and massacred people there in the same way. When he passed by any springs of the Arabs, he destroyed them, or any of their wells, he filled them in. Then he came close to Medina and killed the Arabs he found there and took prisoners. Then he turned towards the countries of Bakr and Taġlib and the area between the kingdom of Fārs and the watch towers of the Byzantines in the country of Syria. He killed the Arabs he found there and took prisoners, filling in their springs. Then he settled in Dārīn and al-Ḫaṭṭ some of Banū Taġlib and those of them who were settled in Bahrain and he settled in Hağar those who were from ʿAbd al-Qays and the groups of Tamīm, and he settled in Kirmān those who were from Bakr b. Wā'il—they are those who are called Bakr Iyād—and he settled in al-Rumaylah in al-Ahwāz those of them who were from Banū Ḥanẓalah. In the Sawād, he built the city of Buzurğ-Sābūr, which is (now called) ʿUkbarā, and he built al-Anbār, al-Sūs, and al-Karḫ.

250 Miskawayh, *Tağārib al-umam*, 1:110 = C133–134, cf. al-Ṭabarī, *Ta'rīḫ*, 1:838–839 = trans., 5:54–55.

251 The word *aġniyā'* is an addition to the text of al-Ṭabarī by Miskawayh. It probably relates to Sābūr's interdiction against looting, the richest cavalrymen being less prone to start looting against the king's command.

252 Miskawayh, *Tağārib al-umam*, 1:110 = C134–135; cf. al-Ṭabarī, *Ta'rīḫ*, 1:839–840 = trans., 5:55–57.

§ 89[1] ثم غزا بعد ذلك أرض الروم فسَبَى منها سَبْيا كثيرا وبنى بخراسان نيسابور. ثم هادن قسطنطين ملك الروم الذي بنى قسطنطينية وهو أول من تَنصَّر من ملوك الروم. فلما هلك تفرق ملكه حتى قام لليانوس بملك الروم وكان لا يدين بدين النصرانية فهدم الكنائس وقتل الأساقفة وجمع جموعا من الروم والخزر ومن كان في مملكته من العرب ليقاتل سابور. فانتهزت العرب الفرصة في الانتقام من سابور بما كان من قتله العرب واجتمعوا إلى ليانوس وهم مائة وسبعون ألف مقاتل من العرب فبعث بهم مع بطريق له في مقدمته فساروا إلى فارس حنقين موتورين حتى طرقوا بلاد فارس. وذلك أن سابور لم يقتصر في إسرافه في قتل العرب على الانتقام ممن أذنب وتجاوز حده بل قتل البريء وسفك من الدماء ما لا يحصى كثرة.

§ 90 وسبب ذلك أن الفرس لم تزل تحدث أن الملك ينتقل عنهم إلى قبيل من نسل اهل كوثا وهي المدينة التي ولد بها إبرٰهيم الخليل عليه السلام ولذلك أسقطوا كثيرا من أهل السواد من دواوينهم في أزمنة طويلة. فلما كانت غلبة العرب على أطراف فارس أوقع بهم سابور يريد استئصالهم خوفا من انتقال الملك إليهم لأنهم من ولد إبرٰهيم عليه السلام ولم يعلم البائس أن الله تعالى جعل زوال ملك فارس على أيدي أصحاب محمد رسول الله صلى الله عليه وسلم الذين هم قريش أولاد إسمٰعيل بن إبرٰهيم عليهما السلام ليقضي الله أمرا كان مفعولا. وإذا أراد الله بقوم سوءا فلا مرد له.

§ 91[2] فلما انتهى إلى سابور | كثرة من مع لليانوس من الجنود وشدة بصائرهم وحَنَقِ العرب وعدد 153a
الروم والخَزَر هاله ذلك ووجه عيونا تأتيه بأخبارهم ومبلغ عددهم وشجاعتهم وعُدتهم. فاختلفت

---

٧ حتى ... فارس: الزيادة بخط المقريزي في آخر السطر في الهامش الأيسر من الأسفل إلى الأعلى + صح.

---

١ من تجارب الأمم لمسكويه ١: ١١٠، ١١١ ومن تأريخ الطبري ١: ٨٤٠–٨٤١.

٢ من تجارب الأمم لمسكويه ١: ١١١.

§ 89[253] Then Sābūr attacked the country of the Byzantines and took many captives. In Ḫurāsān, he built Nīsābūr. Then he made a truce with Constantine,[254] the king of Byzantium, who is the one who built Constantinople. He was the first Byzantine king to convert to Christianity. When he died, his kingship was divided until Julian[255] became the king of Byzantium. He did not follow Christianity, but destroyed churches and killed bishops. He collected great numbers of Byzantines, Ḫazars, and those Arabs who lived in his kingdom to fight against Sābūr. The Arabs used the opportunity to take revenge on Sābūr for having killed Arabs. They flocked around Julian.[256] They were 170,000 Arab warriors. Julian sent them under the command of one of his Patricians in the vanguard. They marched to Fārs, enraged and ready to take revenge. This was because when Sābūr had killed an excessive number of Arabs as a revenge he did not restrict himself and kill only those who had done wrong and committed crimes, but he killed the innocent, too, shedding immeasurable quantities of blood.

§ 90 The reason for this was that there circulated among the Persians a story that kingship would leave them and go to a tribe from the offspring of the Kūṯaeans. Kūṯā is the city in which Abraham the Friend, peace be upon him, was born. This is why they had been striking from their registers many people of the Sawād during long times. When the Arabs conquered outlying parts of Fārs, Sābūr attacked them, wishing to uproot them in fear of the kingship moving to them, as they were children of Abraham, peace be upon him. The wretch did not know that God, He is Exalted, had set the end of the kingdom of Fārs at the hands of the companions of Muḥammad, God's Messenger, may God honour him and grant him peace, who were the Qurayš, sons of Ishmael, son of Abraham, peace be upon them, so that God would fulfil what was to happen. When God wishes evil to a people, there is no turning it aside.

§ 91[257] When Sābūr heard how large an army Julian had with him, how sharp their insight was, the rage of the Arabs, and the number of the Byzantines and Ḫazars, he was frightened and sent spies to bring him reports about them, their number, their courage, and their equipment, but when

253 Miskawayh, *Taǧārib al-umam*, 1:110, 111 = C135; al-Ṭabarī, *Taʾrīḫ*, 1:840–841 = trans., 5:57, 58–59.

254 Constantine I (r. 324–337).

255 R. 361–363.

256 Here written Liyānūs.

257 Miskawayh, *Taǧārib al-umam*, 1:111 = C137; cf. al-Ṭabarī, *Taʾrīḫ*, 1:841 = trans., 5:60.

عليه أقاويل أولٰئك العيون فيما أتوه به من الأخبار عن لليانوس وجنده فتنكر سابور وسار في ثقاته ليعاين عسكرهم. قلت: هكذا ذكر الطبري وابن مسكويه أن اسم ملك الروم الذي قصد محاربة سابور لليانوس.

§92[1] وذكر هروشيوش في تاريخ الروم وهو أقعد بأخبارهم من العراقيين أن قسطنطين باني قسطنطينية وأول من تنصر من ملوك الروم لما مات استخلف على الملك ابنه قسطنطين فأقام أربعا وعشرين سنة ومات. فولي الأمر بعده يِليان قيصر بن مَخْشَنْطِيُش وكان يعبد الأوثان فعبأ لمحاربة الفرس فسار وقتل في {مسيره} وكانت ولايته سنة واحدة. وولي بعده يليان بن قسطنطين قيصر سنة واحدة وغزا أرض الفرس فأحيط بعسكره فاضطر إلى مصالحة سابور ملك الفرس وانصرف فمات. وولي بعدَه بَلَنْسِيَان بن [ابن] قسطنطين قيصر. فظهر أن صاحب حرب سابور إنما هو يليان بن قسطنطين وهو الثالث من ملوك الروم بعد قسطنطين المؤمن باني قسطنطينية.

---

٧ مسيره: "مسيرة" في الأصل.

---

١ من كتاب هروشيوش ص ٣٧٢-٣٧٤.

they returned to him, the spies brought conflicting reports about Julian and his army. Sābūr donned a disguise and went with some of his confidants to inspect the enemy camp. I say:[258] This is what al-Ṭabarī and Ibn Miskawayh say, that the name of the Byzantine King, who fought Sābūr, was Julian (Lulyānūs).

§ 92[259] Orosius, however, mentions in *Taʾrīḫ al-Rūm* [History of the Romans]—and he has more profound knowledge about their stories than Iraqi historians[260]—that when Constantine, the builder of Constantinople and the first of the Byzantine kings to convert to Christianity, died, he left his son Constantine to reign.[261] He reigned for 24 years. When he died, he was succeeded by Julian (Yuliyān) the Caesar, son of Maxentius.[262] He worshipped idols and prepared to fight the Persians. He went there but was killed on the way.[263] He reigned for only one year. After him, there ruled Julian (Yuliyān), son of Constantine the Caesar, for one year. He attacked the country of Fārs, but, together with his army, was surrounded and had to sue Sābūr, the king of Persia, for peace. Afterwards, he returned and died. After him, there reigned Valentinian (Balansiyān),[264] son of Constantine the Caesar's son. It would appear that the one who fought against Sābūr was Julian (Yuliyān), son of Constantine, the third of the Byzantine kings after Constantine the Believer, founder of Constantinople.

---

258 Addition by al-Maqrīzī.

259 *Kitāb Hurūšiyūš* 372–374. In the first part of this section, Orosius' book is quoted as *Kitāb Hurūšiyūš*, *Taʾrīḫ Rūmah*, or *Taʾrīḫ madīnat Rūmah* (Hämeen-Anttila 2018a: 26). Note that the title *Taʾrīḫ al-Rūm* could also be translated as *History of the Byzantines*.

260 This relates to al-Maqrīzī's opinion that historians of a nation should be given precedence in writing the history of their nation. For this reason, he explicitly prefers Persian national history, the early parts of which are legendary, to Orosius, when writing about the Persians (Hämeen-Anttila 2018a: 6). Now, following the same principle, he prefers Orosius on matters Byzantine.

261 Constantine II (r. 337–361).

262 Julian (r. 361–363). For Maxentius (r. 306–312), see al-Maqrīzī, *Ḫabar/Greeks* §§ 169, 181, and Penelas' notes (2021: 163, note 476; 171, note 505). Cf. also al-Maqrīzī, *Ḫabar/Greeks* § 196.

263 Al-Maqrīzī reads *fī Masīrah* (with *tāʾ marbūṭah*) and probably took this as a place name ("he died in Masīrah").

264 Valentian I (r. 364–375).

§93[١] وكان مما جنى سابور على نفسه وتخلص منه بحسن الاتفاق أنه لما قرب من عسكر البطريق الذي كان على المقدمة وكان اسمه يوسانوس ومعه العرب والخزَر وجه قوما ليتجسسوا الأخبار ويأتوه بحقائقها. فنذرت بهم الروم فأخذوهم ودفعوهم إلى يوسانوس فأقر من جملتهم رجل واحد وأخبر بالقصة على وجهها وبمكان سابور وسأله أن يدفع معه جندا فيدفع إليهم سابور. فأرسل يوسانوس رجلا من بطانته إلى سابور يعلمه ما ألقى إليه من أمره وينذره. فارتحل سابور من الموضع الذي كان فيه وصار إلى عسكره. ثم زحف لليانوس بمسألة العرب له فقاتل سابور وفض جموعه وقتل منهم مقتلة عظيمة وهرب سابور فيمن بقي معه واحتوى لليانوس على | مدينة طيسبون محلة 153b
سابور وظفر ببيوت أمواله وخزائنه التي فيها.

§94[٢] واجتمع إلى سابور من آفاق بلاده جنوده وحارب لليانوس واسترد منه مدينة طيسبون واختلفت الرسل بينه وبين لليانوس. فاتفق في أثناء ذلك أن لليانوس بينا هو جالس في فسطاطه والرسل تختلف بينهما إذ جاءه سهم غرب في فؤاده ⟨و⟩سقط ومات. فهال جنده ما أصابه واجتمعوا إلى القائد يوسانوس وملكوه عليهم فأظهر دين النصرانية فأجابه جنده على التدين بها. وبلغ سابور الخبر كله فبعث إلى قواد الروم يقول: "إن الله تعالى قد أمكننا منكم وأدالنا عليكم بظلمكم إيانا وتخطيكم إلى بلادنا. وإنا نرجو أن تهلكوا ببلادنا جوعا من غير أن نهز لقتالكم سيفا أو نشرع له رمحا فسرحوا إلينا رئيسا إن كنتم رأستموه عليكم." فعزم يوسانوس على إتيان سابور بنفسه لما

١٤ نرجو: "نرجوا" في الأصل.

١ من تجارب الأمم لمسكويه ١: ١١١–١١٢.

٢ من تجارب الأمم لمسكويه ١: ١١٢.

§ 93[265] One of the cases where Sābūr brought harm on himself but, by lucky coincidence, got away with it, was when he came close to the camp of the Patrician, who was in charge of the vanguard. His name was Jovian (Yūsānūs),[266] and he had Arabs and Ḫazars with him. Sābūr sent some people to reconnoitre the situation and bring him exact information. The Byzantines, however, were on their guard and caught them, taking them to Jovian. Among them, one single man confessed and told him the matter as it was, including where Sābūr was. This man asked to be given some troops so that he could turn Sābūr over to them. Jovian, however, sent a man from among his confidants to Sābūr and told him what had been suggested to him and warned him. Sābūr moved from the place he had been in and returned to his army. Julian advanced at the request of the Arabs and fought Sābūr, dispersing his troops and massacring many of them. Sābūr fled with the remaining men, and Julian took possession of the city of Ṭaysabūn, the capital of Sābūr, getting hold of the treasuries and wealth that were there.

§ 94[267] The armies of Sābūr came to him from all parts of his kingdom, and he returned to fight Julian, regaining the city of Ṭaysabūn. Messengers went to and fro between him and Julian. During this time, it happened that while Julian was in his pavilion and messengers were coming and going between them, an arrow shot from afar pierced his heart, and he fell down dead. His armies were frightened by what had happened and went to the general Jovian and proclaimed him king over them. He disclosed to them that he was Christian, and the troops accepted his religion.[268] Sābūr heard about all this and sent a message to the generals of the Byzantines, saying: "God, He is Exalted, has given you to my power and has given us the upper hand because of the wrong you have committed against us, forcing your way into our country. We hope that you will perish of hunger in our country without us having to draw our swords or raise our spears against you in battle. If you have elected a leader, send him to us." Jovian decided to go himself to Sābūr because

265 Miskawayh, *Taǧārib al-umam*, 1:111–112 = C137–138; cf. al-Ṭabarī, *Taʾrīḫ*, 1:841–842 = trans., 5:59–60. In *Ḫabar/Greeks* § 198, al-Maqrīzī relates these events differently.

266 Jovian (r. 363–364).

267 Miskawayh, *Taǧārib al-umam*, 1:112 = C138–140; cf. al-Ṭabarī, *Taʾrīḫ*, 1:842–843 = trans., 5:61–62.

268 Miskawayh, following al-Ṭabarī, writes more extensively on Jovian's Christianity both in this and the preceding paragraph. Al-Maqrīzī, who otherwise copies these paragraphs almost as they are, has heavily edited away the Christian aspects, perhaps because they take the focus away from the Sasanians.

كان بينه وبينه من إنذاره والمن عليه فلم يوافقه أحد من قواده على ذلك فاستبد برأيه. وجاء إلى سابور في ثمانين رجلا من أشراف من في عسكره وعليه تاجه. فتلقاه سابور بنفسه وسجد كل منهما لصاحبه وتعانقا ثم أكلا ونعما وانصرفا. فكتب سابور إلى قواد جند الروم ورؤسائهم يعلمهم أنهم لو ملكوا غير يوسانوس لجرى هلاكهم في بلاد فارس ولكن تمليكهم إياه ينجيهم من سطوته. ثم قوى يوسانوس بكل جهده.

§ 95[1] وقال له عند منصرفه: "إن الروم قد شنوا الغارة على بلادنا وقتلوا بشرا كثيرا وقطعوا بأرض السواد من الشجر والنخل ما كان بها وخربوا عمرانها. فإما أن تدفعوا إلينا قيمة ما أفسدوا وخربوا وإما أن تعوضونا من ذلك نصيبين وحيزها." فأجاب يوسانوس وأشراف جنده إلى ذلك ودفعوا إلى سابور مدينة نصيبين. فلما بلغ ذلك أهلها جلوا عنها إلى مدن الروم خوفا على أنفسهم من سابور لمخالفته ملتهم. فنقل سابور اثني عشر ألف أهل بيت من أهل إصطخر وإصبهان وكور أخر من بلاده إلى نصيبين فأسكنهم إياها. وانصرف يوسانوس إلى الروم وملكها قليلا | ومات. 154a

§ 96[2] وضري سابور على العرب فقتلهم ونزع أكتاف رؤسائهم زمانا طويلا فسمته العرب ذا الأكتاف. ثم إنه استصلح العرب وأسكن بعض تغلب وعبد القيس وبكر بكرمان وتوّج والأهواز. وذكِر أن سابور بعد أن أثخن في العرب وأجلاهم عن النواحي التي كانوا صاروا إليها مما خرب من نواحي فارس والبحرين واليمامة ثم هبط إلى الشام وصار إلى حَد الروم أعلم أصحابه أنه عزم على دخول بلاد الروم حتى يبحث عن أسرارهم ويعرف أخبار ملكهم وعدد جنودهم. فدخل إلى الروم فجال فيها حينا وبلغه أن قيصر أولم وليمة وأمر بجمع الناس ليحضروا طعامه. فانطلق سابور

---

٨ وحيزها: وضع المقريزي رمز "ح" تحت الحرف الثاني إشارة إلى تلفظه بالحاء. ١٥ حَد: وضع المقريزي رمز "ح" تحت الحرف الأول إشارة إلى تلفظه بالحاء.

---

١ من تجارب الأمم لمسكويه ١: ١١٢-١١٣.

٢ من تجارب الأمم لمسكويه ١: ١١٣ ومن تأريخ الطبري ١: ٨٤٣-٨٤٤.

of what was between them, he having warned Sābūr and Sābūr being thus indebted to him. None of his generals agreed with him on this, but he was adamant and, wearing the crown, he went to Sābūr with eighty nobles from his camp. Sābūr came personally to meet him. They bowed to each other and embraced each other. Then they ate together in comfort before returning to their camps. Then Sābūr wrote to the generals and leaders of the Byzantine army, telling them that had they elected anyone else than Jovian as their king, they would all have perished in the country of Fārs. However, their having elected him saved them from his power. He made his utmost to strengthen Jovian.

§ 95[269] When Jovian was returning to Byzantium, Sābūr said to him: "The Byzantines have raided our country, killed many people, and cut down trees and palms in the Sawād, ruining cultivated areas. Either you have to pay us the price of what you have destroyed and ruined or you must give us Nisibis and its surroundings as replacement." Jovian and the nobles of his army accepted this and gave Sābūr the city of Nisibis. When its inhabitants heard of this, they emigrated to Byzantine cities, fearing Sābūr for their lives, as Sābūr opposed their religion. Sābūr moved 12,000 noblemen from Iṣṭaḫr, Isfahan, and other provinces of his country to Nisibis and settled them there. Jovian returned to Byzantium, where he ruled for a short while before he died.

§ 96[270] For a long time Sābūr fought against the Arabs, killing them and dislocating the shoulders of their leaders, which is why the Arabs called him Ḏū l-Aktāf. Finally, he made peace with them and settled some of Taġlib, ʿAbd al-Qays, and Bakr in Kirmān, Tawwaǧ, and al-Ahwaz. It is said that Sābūr massacred Arabs and drove them away from the areas into which they had forced their way, laying waste parts of Fārs, Bahrain, and al-Yamāmah. Then he turned to Syria and proceeded until the Byzantine border. He let his companions know that he had decided to go to the Byzantine dominion to study their secrets and reconnoitre their kingdom and the number of their armies. He went to Byzantium, wandering there for a while. Then he heard that the Caesar was going to give a banquet and had invited everybody

269 Miskawayh, *Taǧārib al-umam*, 1:112–113 = C140–141; cf. al-Ṭabarī, *Taʾrīḫ*, 1:843 = trans., 5:62–63.

270 Miskawayh, *Taǧārib al-umam*, 1:113 = C141 (beginning); al-Ṭabarī, *Taʾrīḫ*, 1:843–844 = trans., 5:63–64.

بِهَيْئة السُؤّال حتى شهد ذلك الجمع لينظر إلى قيصر ويعرف هيأته وحاله في طعامه. ففُطِن له فأُخِذ وأمر به قيصر فأدرج في جلد ثور. ثم سار بجنوده إلى أرض فارس ومعه سابور على ذلك من حاله فأكثر من القتل وخراب المدائن والقرى وقطْع النخل والأشجار حتى انتهى إلى مدينة جندي سابور وقد تحصن أهلها فنصب عليها المجانيق وهدم بعضها.

§97[١] فبينا هم كذلك ذات ليلة إذ غفل الروم الموكلون بحراسة سابور. وكان يقربه قوم من سبي الأهواز فأمرهم أن يلقوا على القد الذي كان عليه زيتا من زقاق كانت بقربهم ففعلوا ذلك فلان الجلد فانسل منه. ولم يزل يدب حتى دنا من باب المدينة وأخبر حراسها باسمه فأدخلوه المدينة. فاجتمع إليه أهلها وسروا به سرورا كثيرا وارتفعت أصواتهم بالحمد والتسبيح فانتبه أصحاب قيصر بأصواتهم. وجمع سابور من كان في المدينة وخرج سحرا من ليلته فقتل الروم وأخذ قيصر أسيرا وغنم أمواله ونساءه. ثم أثقله بالحديد وأمره بعمارة ما أخرب وألزمه بنقل التراب من أرض الروم إلى المدائن وجندي سابور حتى يرم به ما هدم منها وألزمه أن تغرس الزيتون مكان النخل والشجر الذي عقره. ثم قطع عقبه وبعث به إلى بلاد الروم على حمار وقال: "هذا جزاؤك ببغيك علينا."

154b §98[٢] ثم أقام سابور حينا وغزا الروم فقتل من أهلها وسبى سبيا كثيرا وأسكنهم مدينة بناها | بناحية السوس سماها إيران شهر وأنزل بالحديثة قوما منهم. وكان كلما ظفر بملك ألزمه أن يعيد

---

٩ سحرا: وضع المقريزي رمز "ح" تحت الحرف الثاني إشارة إلى تلفظه بالحاء. ١٥ وأنزل ... منهم: الزيادة بخط المقريزي فوق السطر في الهامش الأعلى منكسة. ‖ بالحديثة: وضع المقريزي رمز "ح" تحت الحرف الرابع إشارة إلى تلفظه بالحاء.

---

١ من تأريخ الطبري ١: ٨٤٤–٨٤٥.

٢ من تأريخ الطبري ١: ٨٤٥ و من تأريخ سني الملوك لحمزة ص ٤١–٤٢.

to join it. Disguised as a beggar Sābūr went there to witness the occasion and to take a look at the Caesar and see his form and manner while eating. He was, however, recognised and captured. The Emperor ordered him to be imprisoned in a bull's hide. Then the Caesar marched with his armies to Fārs, carrying Sābūr along in this state. The Caesar killed numerous people and destroyed cities and villages, cutting down date palms and trees until he came to the city of Gundīsābūr, whose inhabitants had fled to the fortress. The Caesar set mangonels against it and destroyed part of the city.

§ 97[271] One night, the Byzantines set to guard him were inattentive to Sābūr. Close by, there were some prisoners from al-Ahwāz, and Sābūr ordered them to pour on his leather straps olive oil from skins that were nearby. The hide softened, and Sābūr was able to slip free. Then he crept close to the gate of the city and informed the guards who he was. They let him into the city where people surrounded him and greatly rejoiced in seeing him. They raised their voice to thank God and praise Him. The Caesar's troops woke to their voices. Sābūr rounded up everybody in the city and the next morning he attacked, killing the Byzantines and taking the Caesar prisoner. He also looted their property and made prisoners of their women. He put the Caesar in heavy irons and ordered him to rebuild what he had ruined. He forced him to bring soil from Byzantium to al-Madā'in and Gundīsābūr so that he could repair what he had destroyed. He also forced him to plant olive trees in place of the palm trees and others that had been rooted. Then he cut his hamstrings and sent him back to Byzantium riding a donkey, saying: "This is your reward for having wronged us."

§ 98[272] For some time Sābūr raided Byzantium, killing people and taking numerous prisoners, which he settled in a city he built close to al-Sūs and called Īrānšahr.[273] Some of their people he settled in al-Ḥadīṯah.[274] Always[275] when he vanquished a king, he ordered him to rebuild everything

---

271 Al-Ṭabarī, *Ta'rīḫ*, 1:844–845 = trans., 5:64–65.

272 Al-Ṭabarī, *Ta'rīḫ*, 1:845 = trans., 5:65–66 (beginning and the note on medicine); Ḥamzah, *Ta'rīḫ* 41–42 = trans. 66–67.

273 The full name of the city, according to al-Ṭabarī, was Īrānšahr-Sābūr.

274 The copyist of MS T reads this as al-Ḥudaybiyah, even though the dots of Ṯ are very clear in the holograph.

275 Al-Maqrīzī has read Ḥamzah carelessly, as the latter only speaks of the Byzantine king. That the mistake is in reading, rather than writing, is shown by al-Maqrīzī also changing Ḥamzah's *wa-lammā* into *kullamā*, thus ruling out the possibility that al-Maqrīzī has just forgotten to add *al-Rūm* after *malik*.

كلما خربه وأن يكون إعادته لما كان باللَبِن والطين بالآجُرّ والجص. فسوَّر مدينة جندي سابور نصفه باللبن ونصفه بالآجُر {وبنى} عدة مدن بسجستان والسند ونصب بقرية جرواآن نارا سماها نَار شروس آذران ووقف عليها قرية. ونقل طبيبا من الهند وأسكنه الكرخ من السُوْس. فلما مات ورث طبه أهل السوس فصاروا أعلم العجم بالطب. وأقام سابور منذ ولد إلى تمام ثلاثين سنة بجندي سابور ثم تحول إلى المدائن الشرقية {وبنى} بها الإيوان فصارت المدائن الشرقية دار الملك بعدما كانت طيسبون دار الملك وبقي الإيوان بعده. فأقام بها باقي عمره حتى مات عن اثنتين وسبعين سنة كان ملكا في جميعها.

§99[١] وكان شعاره مُورد مُوَشى وسراويله حمراء موشاة وتاجه على لون السماء حواليه ملون بالذهب بين شرفتي ذهب وهلال ذهب في وسطه وكان يقعد على السرير وبيده طبرزين. وفي زمانه كان آذُرباد الذي أذيب الصُفْر على صدره. وهلك في عهده عامله على ضاحية مضر وربيعة امرؤ القيس البَدْءِ بن عمرو بن عدي بن ربيعة بن مضر فاستعمل على عمله ابنَه عمرو بن امرئ القيس فبقي في عمله بقية ملك سابور وجميع أيام أخيه أردشير بن هرمز بن نرسي وبعض أيام سابور بن سابور ذي الأكتاف.

---

٢ وبنى: "وبنا" في الأصل. ٥ وبنى: "وبنا" في الأصل. ٥-٦ الشرقية ... بعده: الزيادة بخط المقريزي في الهامش الأيسر من الأسفل إلى الأعلى، ويشير إليها رمز ⌐ بعد "المدائن". ١٠ ضاحية: وضع المقريزي رمز "ح" تحت الحرف الثالث إشارة إلى تلفظه بالحاء.

---

١ من تأريخ سني الملوك لحمزة ص ٤٢ ومن تأريخ الطبري ١: ٨٤٥-٨٤٦.

he had destroyed, insisting that he should rebuild in baked bricks and lime everything that had been built in mud bricks and clay. In Gundīsābūr, he rebuilt half of the walls in mud bricks, half in baked bricks. He built several cities in Siǧistān and al-Sind. In the village of Ǧarwāʾān[276] he established a fire, which he named the Fire of Surūš-Ādurān.[277] He endowed it a village. Then he brought a physician from India and settled him in al-Karḫ of al-Sūs. When the physician died, the people of al-Sūs inherited his practice and became the most knowledgeable of the Persians in medicine. From the time he was born until he was thirty,[278] Sābūr stayed in Gundīsābūr before moving to the Eastern al-Madāʾin, where he built an *īwān* and the Eastern al-Madāʾin became the royal capital after that had been Ṭaysabūn. The *īwān* remained after him, and he stayed there for the rest of his life until he died in the age of 72, having reigned as king during all those years.

§ 99[279] Sābūr's vest was rose-coloured and embroidered and his trousers red and embroidered. His crown was sky-blue, the edges coloured in gold, between two golden merlons with a golden crescent in between. He sat on his throne with an axe in his hand. During his time, there lived Ādurbād,[280] on whose breast molten brass was poured. It was also in his time that his governor of the region of Muḍar and Rabīʿah died, Imruʾ al-Qays al-Badʾ b. ʿAmr b. ʿAdī b. Rabīʿah b. Muḍar, and Sābūr appointed in his stead his son, ʿAmr b. Imriʾ al-Qays, who remained in office for the rest of Sābūr's life and all the days of his brother Ardašīr b. Hurmuz b. Narsī and some of the days of Sābūr b. Sābūr of Shoulders.

---

276 Ḥamzah reads Ḥarwān.

277 Text: Šurūs.

278 Al-Maqrīzī has read Ḥamzah's *ṯamān(in) wa-ṯalāṯīn* "thirty-eight" as *tamām ṯalāṯīn*.

279 Ḥamzah, *Taʾrīḫ* 42 = trans. 66 (and cf. Ḥamzah, *Taʾrīḫ* 78); al-Ṭabarī, *Taʾrīḫ*, 1:845–846 = trans., 5:67.

280 Ḥamzah reads erroneously Izdiyād (so also in the edition of Gottwaldt, p. 53, but the mistake was already corrected to Azerbad in Gottwaldt's translation, p. 39). For the *mōbadān mōbad* Ādurbād ī Mahrspandān and his ordeal, see *EIr*, s.v.

§100[1] ولما احتضر سابور ذي الأكتاف عهد بالملك لأخيه أردشير الجَميل بن هرمز بن نرسي بن بهرام بن بهرام بن هرمز بن سابور الجنود بن أزدشير بن بابك لصغر سن ابنه. فلما عقد التاج على رأسه دخل عليه العظماء ودعوا له بالنصر وشكروا أخاه سابور ذي الأكتاف فأحسن جوابهم وأعلمهم موقع ما كان من شكرهم لأخيه. فلما استقر به الملك قراره عطف على العظماء وذوي الرئاسة فقتل منهم خلقا كثيرا. فخلعه الناس بعد أربع سنين من ملكه وكان شعاره وشي مُدنر على لون السماء وسراويله موشاة بحمرة وبيمناه رمح ويسراه معتمد بها على سيفه وتاجه أخضر.

§101[2] وملك بعده ابن أخيه سابور بن سابور ذي الأكتاف وقد أدرك وخرج عن الطفولية فاستبشرت الرعية برجوع الملك إليه وتلقاهم هو أجمل | اللقاء. وكتب إلى عماله يأمرهم بحسن 155a السيرة والرفق بالرعية وأمر وزراءه وكتابه بذلك وخطبهم خطبة بليغة. ولم يزل عادلا في رعيته متحننا عليهم لما تبين له من مودتهم ومحبتهم وطاعتهم وخضع له عمه أردشير المخلوع ومنحه الطاعة. ولم يزل على ذلك إلى أن قطع العظماء وأهل البيوتات أطناب فسطاط كان قد ضرب عليه في حجرة من حجره فسقط عليه فقتله. وكانت مدة ملكه خمس سنين. وذكر حمزة أنه ملك اثنتين وثمانين سنة. وقيل: خمسين سنة وأربعة أشهر. قال: وفي نسخة أنه ملك خمس سنين. وفي أخرى أنه هو الذي

١ بالملك لأخيه: كتب المقريزي كلمة "بالملك" فوق السطر وكلمة "لأخيه" في الهامش الأيسر. ٢ لصغر... ابنه: الزيادة بخط المقريزي في الهامش الأيسر من الأعلى إلى الأسفل + صح، ويشير إليها رمز ⌐ بعد "بابك". ٧ ابن أخيه: كتب المقريزي كلمة "ابن" فوق السطر وكلمة "أخيه" في الهامش الأيسر. ١٠ متحننا: وضع المقريزي رمز "ح" تحت الحرف الثالث إشارة إلى تلفظه بالحاء.

١ من تأريخ الطبري ١: ٨٤٦ ومن تأريخ سني الملوك لحمزة ص ٤٢.

٢ من تأريخ الطبري ١: ٨٤٦ ومن تأريخ سني الملوك لحمزة ص ٤٢، ١٤، ١٩، ٢٥.

§ 100[281] When he was about to die, Sābūr of Shoulders[282] bequeathed the kingship to his brother Ardašīr the Beautiful[283] b. Hurmuz b. Narsī b. Bahrām b. Bahrām b. Hurmuz b. Sābūr of the Armies b. Ardašīr b. Bābak, because his own son was still young. When Ardašīr was crowned, the noblemen came to him and prayed for his victory and praised his brother Sābūr of Shoulders. Ardašīr answered them beautifully and told them how deeply moved he was for them praising his brother. When he was firmly in power, he turned against the noblemen and leaders and killed many of them. People deposed him after four years of his reign. His vest was speckled in sky-blue and embroidered and his trousers were embroidered in red. In his right hand, he held a spear, and he leaned with his left on his sword. His crown was green.

§ 101[284] After Ardašīr the Beautiful, there reigned his nephew Sābūr b. Sābūr of Shoulders, who meanwhile had grown up and reached adulthood. People rejoiced in seeing kingship return to him, and he received people in a most beautiful manner. He wrote to his governors, ordering them to behave well and kindly towards people. He also ordered his Viziers and scribes to do the same and gave them an eloquent speech. He remained just and compassionate towards his subjects, as he saw their love, affection, and obedience to him. His deposed uncle Ardašīr also submitted to him and was obedient. In the end, the noblemen and members of the great families cut the ropes of the pavilion which had been erected for him in one of his rooms, and it collapsed on him and killed him. The length of his reign was five years. Ḥamzah has mentioned that he reigned for 82 years or, according to others, 50 years and 4 months.[285] He said that in one manuscript it was said that he ruled

281 Al-Ṭabarī, *Taʾrīḫ*, 1:846 = trans., 5:67–68; Ḥamzah, *Taʾrīḫ* 42 = trans. 67.

282 The wrong grammatical form, the genitive Ḏī l-Aktāf for Ḏū l-Aktāf, results from al-Maqrīzī rephrasing al-Ṭabarī. The latter has correctly *ṯumma qāma bi-l-mulk baʿda Sābūr Ḏī l-Aktāf*. When rephrasing this al-Maqrīzī has made Sābūr the subject of the sentence, but kept the genitive Ḏī l-Aktāf. A few lines later, he also uses the genitive instead of the expected accusative Ḏā l-Aktāf in a case where al-Ṭabarī only reads Sābūr.

283 Cf. al-Bīrūnī, *al-Āṯār al-bāqiyah* 137.

284 Al-Ṭabarī, *Taʾrīḫ*, 1:846 = trans., 5:68; Ḥamzah, *Taʾrīḫ* 42, 14, 19, 25 = trans. 67, 33, 37, 43.

285 50 years and 4 months is probably a misreading of Ḥamzah, *Taʾrīḫ* 14, which speaks of 5 years and 4 months.

عقد على بطن أمه التاج وفيه نظر. قال: وكان شعاره أحمر موشى وسراويله لون السماء وتحت شعاره شعار أصفر وتاجه أخضر في حمرة بين شرفتين من ذهب وهلال من ذهب بيده قضيب حديد على طرفه رأس طائر معتمد بيسراه على مقبض سيفه.

§102[1] وملك بعده أخوه بهرام بن سابور ذي الأكتاف وكان يلقب بكرمان شاه لأن سابور ولاه كرمان. فكتب إلى قواده كتابا يحثهم فيه على الطاعة ويأمرهم بتقوى الله تعالى والنصيحة للملك وبنى بكرمان مدينة. قال الطبري: وكان حسن السياسة لرعيته محمودا في أموره. وقال ابن مسكويه: فمضت محمودة وكان جميل السياسة محببا. وقال حمزة: وكان فظا ذاهبا بنفسه لم يقرأ طول أيامه قصة ولا نظر في مظلمة. فلما مات وجدوا الكتب الواردة عليه من الكوَر مختومة ما فكها بعد. وملك اثنتي عشرة سنة وقيل: إحدى عشرة سنة. وأمر أن يكتب على ناووسه: "قد علمنا أن هذا الجسد سيودع هذه البنية فلا ينفعه رأي شفيق كما لا يضره نُبو عدو." وكان شعاره لون السماء موشى وسراويله حمراء موشاة وتاجه أخضر بين ثلاث شرفات ذهب وبيده اليمنى رمح وهو باليسرى معتمد على سيفه. قال الطبري: وكان ملكه إحدى عشرة سنة وإن ناسا من الفتاك ثاروا إليه فقتله رجل منهم برمية رماها إياه بنشاب.

٧ محببا: وضع المقريزي رمز "ح" تحت الحرف الثاني إشارة إلى تلفظه بالحاء.

١ من تأريخ الطبري ١: ٨٤٧ ومن تجارب الأمم لمسكويه ١: ١١٣.

for 5 years and in another that he was the one on whose mother's belly the crown was set, but this is debatable. His vest was red and embroidered and his trousers sky-blue. Under his vest he had a yellow shirt, and his crown was green on red between two golden merlons and a golden crescent. In his (right) hand, he had an iron staff that had on its top a bird's head, and with his left hand he leaned on the hilt of his sword.

§ 102[286] After Sābūr, there reigned his brother Bahrām b. Sābūr of Shoulders, who was called Kirmānšāh[287] because Sābūr had given him Kirmān to rule. He wrote to his generals urging them to obedience and ordering them to fear God, He is Exalted, and to be sincere to the king. He built the city of Kirmān. Al-Ṭabarī has said that he governed his people well and his deeds were laudable. Ibn Miskawayh has said that (his days)[288] went in a laudable way and he was lovable and governed beautifully. Ḥamzah has said that he was coarse and conceited[289] and during all his days he did not read any reports nor did he look at any complaints. When he died, letters that had arrived to him from the districts were found with their seals still unbroken. He ruled for 12 years or, according to others, 11 years. He gave orders that it should be written on his mausoleum: "I knew that this body would be placed in this building and the opinion of the compassionate would no more benefit it nor could the rise of an enemy harm it." His vest was sky-blue and embroidered and his trousers red and embroidered. His crown was green between three golden merlons. In his right hand, he had a spear and he was leaning with the left on his sword. Al-Ṭabarī has said that his reign lasted for 11 years and that some murderers attacked him. He was killed by one of them, who shot him with an arrow.

286 Al-Ṭabarī, *Ta'rīḫ*, 1:847 = trans., 5:69; Miskawayh, *Taǧārib al-umam*, 1:113 = C142; Ḥamzah, *Ta'rīḫ* 42, 14, 19, 25 = trans. 67, 33, 38, 43.

287 Cf. al-Bīrūnī, *al-Āṯār al-bāqiyah* 137.

288 Added from Miskawayh.

289 Translating from Ḥamzah *zāhiyan*.

§ 103[١] وملك بعده ابنه يزدجرد الخَشِن ويقال: المُجْرِم والأثيم | والفَظّ. ويقال له بالفارسية: دِفْر وبَدَه كُرْبن بهرام كرمان شاه بن سابور ذي الأكتاف. وقال هشام بن الكلبي: إن يزدجرد الأثيم هو أخو بهرام كرمان شاه وليس بابنه وإنه يزدجرد بن سابور ذي الأكتاف. وقال حمزة: وفي نسخة أن يزدجرد الأثيم والد بهرام جور هو يزدجرد بن يزدجرد الأثيم وهو صاحب شَرْوين الدَسْتَبِي لا الأثيم. وكان ذا سياسة مرضية وأمانة ورحمة وعطف بخلاف ابنه وبلغ من وفائه أن ملكا من ملوك الروم كان في زمانه حضرته الوفاة وله ابن صغير فأوصى إلى يزدجرد هذا أن ينفذ من رجال مملكته خليفة له إلى بلاد الروم يضبط على ابنه عمله إلى أن يبلغ مبلغ الرجال. فأنفذ إليها شَرْوين بن بَزْنيَان رئيس كُورَة دَسْتَبي وملكه على بلاد الروم فضبطها له عشرين سنة. ثم أدى الأمانة في رده مملكة الروم على ابنه واسترداده شروين منها بعد أن اختط مدينة بها وسماها بَاإِشَرْوَان ثم عُربت فقيل: بَاجَرْوان. 155b

§ 104[٢] وقال الطبري وابن مسكويه يزيد أحدهما على الآخر إن يزدجرد الأثيم كان فظا غليظا ذا عيوب كثيرة. وكان من أشد عيوبه وضعه ذكاء ذهن وحسنَ أدب كانا فيه وصنوف من العلم قد مهرها وعلمها غير موضعها. وكثرت رؤيته في الضار من الأمور واستعماله كل ما عنده من ذلك في

---

١ بعده ابنه : كتب المقريزي الكلمتين فوق السطر في الهامش الأيسر. ٢ هشام ... الكلبي : الزيادة بخط المقريزي في الهامش الأيسر من الأسفل إلى الأعلى + صح، ويشير إليها رمز ⌐ بعد "وقال". ٥ ابنه : كتب المقريزي فوق الكلمة "صح". ١١ يزيد ... الآخر : الزيادة بخط المقريزي في الهامش الأيسر من الأسفل إلى الأعلى + صح، ويشير إليها رمز ⌐ بعد "مسكويه".

---

١ من تأريخ الطبري ١: ٨٤٧ ومن تأريخ سني الملوك لحمزة ص ٤٣، ١٩.

٢ من تأريخ الطبري ١: ٨٤٧–٨٤٨ ومن تجارب الأمم لمسكويه ١: ١١٣.

§ 103[290] After Bahrām, there reigned his son Yazdağird the Rough or, according to others, the Criminal or the Sinner or the Coarse.[291] In Persian, he is called Difr and Badahkur,[292] b. Bahrām Kirmānšāh b. Sābūr of Shoulders. Hišām b. al-Kalbī has said that Yazdağird the Sinner was Bahrām Kirmānšāh's brother, not his son, and that he was Yazdağird b. Sābūr of Shoulders. Ḥamzah has said that in one manuscript it is said that Yazdağird the Sinner, the father of Bahrām Gūr, was Yazdağird the Sinner b. Yazdağird and that it was the older Yazdağird who was king at the time of Šarwīn al-Dastabī,[293] not the Sinner. People were pleased with his governing, and he was trusted, merciful, and kind, contrary to his son. His faithfulness was such that when a contemporary Byzantine king was dying and leaving behind a small son, the king expressed his will that this Yazdağird would send someone from his kingdom to Byzantium to act as his viceregent and control the affairs for his son until the latter grew up. Yazdağird sent Šarwīn b. Barniyān, the head of the district of Dastabá and gave him the kingship of Byzantium, which he kept for him for twenty years. Then Yazdağird returned the trust by giving the kingdom of Byzantium back to the deceased king's son and calling Šarwīn back after he had designed a city there, calling it Bāʾišrawān, which was then Arabised as Bāğarwān.

§ 104[294] Al-Ṭabarī and Ibn Miskawayh have said, the one adding to what the other wrote, that Yazdağird the Sinner was coarse and rough, full of faults. One of the worst was that he put in wrong use the keenness of his mind and the excellent learning he had, as well as the various[295] sciences that he had mastered. He also studied many harmful things and used all

290 Al-Ṭabarī, *Taʾrīḫ*, 1:847 = trans., 5:70; Ḥamzah, *Taʾrīḫ* 43, 19, 17 = trans. 68, 36–37.

291 For "the Sinner," cf. al-Bīrūnī, *al-Āṯār al-bāqiyah* 137. For the Coarse, *al-Ḫashin*, cf. Ḥamzah, *Taʾrīḫ* 19.

292 The latter cognomen is clearly *bazahgar* "sinful," but the former is unclear. Nöldeke (1879): 72–73, note 4, followed by Hoyland (2018): 68, note 219, suggests *dabz* "thick; coarse." Discussing the word *difahrī* (probably "outcast") in Abū Nuwās' famous *fārisiyyah*, *Dīwān*, 5:143–146 (no. 148, verse 21), Mīnuwī (1332 AHŠ): 16, referring to an oral communication by Bailey and later followed by Harb (2019): 11, suggests a derivation from Middle Persian *dēpahr* (Nyberg 1974, s.v.; in modern transliteration *dēbahr*, see MacKenzie, s.v., and Durkin-Meisterernst 2004: 148–149), which might also be considered for Difr. Cf also Christensen (1936): 264.

293 Cf. § 6.

294 Al-Ṭabarī, *Taʾrīḫ*, 1:847–848 = trans., 5:70–71; Miskawayh, *Tağārib al-umam*, 1:113 = C142–143.

295 This should be in accusative, *ṣunūfan*, as in al-Ṭabarī.

الدَهاء والحِيَل والمكائد والمخاتلة مع فِطنة كانت له بجهات الشر وشدة عجبه بما عنده من ذلك. واستخف بكل علم وأدب واحتقر ذلك واستطال على الناس بما عنده وكان مع ذلك غَلِقًا سَيِّئ الخلق رديء الطِعْمة حتى بلغ من شدة غلقه وحِدّته أن كان يستعظم صغير الزلات ويسير السقطات ولا يرضى في عقوبتها إلا بما لا يُسْتَطاع أن يَبلغ مِثلَها. ثم لم يقدر أحد من بطانته وإن كان لطيف المنزلة منه أن يشفع لمن ابتلي به وإن كان ذنب المبتلَى به يسيرا. ولم يكن يأتمن أحدا على شيء من الأشياء ولم يكن يكافئ على حسن البلاء وكان يعتد بالحسيس من العُرْف إذا ولاه ويستجزل ذلك فإن جسر على | كلامه أحد في أمر قال له: "ما قَدْر جَعالتك في هذا الأمر الذي 155a
كلمتنا فيه وما الذي بُذل لك؟" وما أشبه ذلك.

§105[1] وكان إذا بلغه عن أحد من بطانته أنه صافى رجلا من أهل صناعته أو طبقته نحاه عن خدمته. وكان قد استوزر عند ولايته نرسي حكيم دهره وكان كاملا في أدبه فاضلا في جميع مذاهبه فأملت الرعية بما كان عليه نرسي من الفضائل أن ينزع يزدجرد عن رديء أخلاقه فكان ما أملوه بعيدا. فلما اشتدت إهانته للأشراف والعظماء ولقيت الرعية منه عنتا وحمل على الضعفاء وأكثر من سفك الدماء وتسلط على الناس تسلطا لم يبتلوا بمثله اجتمعوا وشكوا إلى ربهم ما نزل بهم من ظلمه وتضرعوا وابتهلوا إليه في تعجيل إنقاذهم منه. فزعموا أنه كان بجرجان فرأى ذات يوم وقد تطلع من قصره فرسا عائرا لم يُرَ مثله قط في الخيل حسن صورة وتمام خلق حتى وقف على بابه. فتعجب الناس منه لأنه كان متجاوز الأمر. فأمر يزدجرد أن يسرَج ويلجم ويدخل عليه فحاول ساسته وأصحاب مراكبه إلجامه وإسراجه فلم يمكن أحدا منهم من نفسه. فخرج | يزدجرد 155b
بنفسه فألجمه بيده وأسرجه ولببه فلم يتحرك. فلما استدار به ورفع ذنبه ليثفره رمحه الفرس على فؤاده

٩ نحاه: وضع المقريزي رمز "ح" تحت الحرف الثاني إشارة إلى تلفظه بالحاء.

١ من تأريخ الطبري ١: ٨٤٨–٨٥٠ ومن تجارب الأمم لمسكويه ١: ١١٤ ومن تأريخ سني الملوك لحمزة ص ١٤، ٢٥.

abilities he had in slyness and plotting, ruses and deception with his cleverness in various evil things and his self-admiration in all this. He disdained all fields of knowledge and education and despised them. With all this, he became overbearing to people. In addition, he was sullen, bad-natured, and ill-mannered, so that his sullenness and vehemence reached such limits that he considered small slips and minor mistakes enormous and was not satisfied unless they were punished unbearably severely. None of his confidants, even if he were in a close position, could intercede on behalf of those who suffered from him, even though the sufferer's fault had been minor. He did not trust anybody with anything, nor did he recompense those who had bravely undergone difficulties. Even a paltry kindness from himself he considered enormous. If anyone dared to speak to him in any matter, he asked him: "How much did they give you as bribes to speak to me about this matter? How much did you get?" etc.

§105[296] If he heard that one of his confidants was friendly with someone in the same profession or the same class, Yazdağird sent him away from his service. At the beginning of his reign, he had appointed as Vizier the Sage of his Age, Narsī, who had a perfect education and was excellent in every way. People hoped that Narsī's virtues would turn Yazdağird away from his vices, but they hoped in vain. Yazdağird's scorn for noblemen and nobility grew hard to bear, and people were afflicted by him. The weak were oppressed, and much blood was shed by him. He governed people so ruthlessly that they had never before suffered so much, and the noblemen and nobility came together and complained to their Lord Yazdağird's tyranny that had overcome them. They prayed humbly and supplicated Him to hasten to release them from him. It is claimed that Yazdağird was in Ğurğān. One day, looking out of the palace window he saw a stray horse, the like of which had never been seen; beautifully formed and of a perfect build. It stopped at the palace gate. People admired the exceptional horse. Yazdağird gave orders to put a saddle and bridles on it and to bring it to him. The grooms and masters[297] of the stables attempted to do so, but the horse did not let them approach. Yazdağird himself came and with his own hand put a saddle and bridles on it and harnessed it, while it did not move. Then Yazdağird went around it and raised its tail to put on the crupper, and the horse kicked him so hard in the

296 Al-Ṭabarī, *Taʾrīḫ*, 1:848–850 = trans., 5:71–74; Miskawayh, *Tağārib al-umam*, 1:114 = C143–144 (contributing little, if anything); Ḥamzah, *Taʾrīḫ* 14, 25 = trans. 33, 43. Ḥamzah, *Taʾrīḫ* 19 = trans. 37, also gives 82 years.

297 In singular, master, in al-Ṭabarī.

رمحة هلك منها مكانه. ثم لم يعاين ذلك الفرس فأكثرت الفُرْس في حديثه وظنت الظنون وكان أحسنهم مذهبا من قال: "إن الله تعالى استجاب دعاءنا." وكان ملكه إحدى وعشرين سنة وخمسة أشهر وثمانية عشر يوما وقيل: اثنتين وعشرين سنة وخمسة أشهر وستة عشر يوما.

§106[١] ولما هلك عمرو بن امرئ القيس البدءِ بن عمرو بن عدي بن نصر في عهد سابور بن سابور ذي الأكتاف استخلف سابور على عمله أوس بن قَلام بن بُطَيْنا بن جُمَيْهِر بن لحيان العمليقي. فثأر به بعد خمس سنين جحجبا بن عتيك من بني فاران بن عمرو بن عمليق فقتله وهلك في عهد بهرام بن سابور ذي الأكتاف. فاستخلف بعده في عمله امرأ القيس البَدءِ بن عمرو بن عدي خمسا وعشرين سنة وهلك في عهد يزدجرد الأثيم. فاستخلف يزدجرد مكانه ابنَه النعمٰن بن امرئ القيس البدءِ. وكان شعار يزدجرد أحمر وسراويله على لون السماء وتاجه كذلك وبيده رمح.

§107[٢] ولما مات ملك بعده ابنه | بِهْرام جُور ويقال: كُور بن يزدجرد الخَشِن ويقال له: المُجْرِم 156a
والأثيم والفَظّ بن بهرام كرمان شاه بن شابور بن شابور ذي الأَكْتَاف بن هرمز بن نَرْسي بن بهرام ابن بهرام شاه بن هرمز بن شابور بن شابور الجنود بن أزدَشير بن بابك. أسلمه أبوه يزدجرد الأثيم أول ما ولد إلى المنذر بن النعمٰن وكَفَّلَه إياه رغبة في أن تحضنه العرب وتتولى تربيته. فسار به

٦ جحجبا : وضع المقريزي رمز "ح" تحت الحرف الثاني إشارة إلى تلفظه بالحاء. ١١ شابور١ : كتب المقريزي فوق هذه الكلمة "صح". || شابور٢ : كتب المقريزي فوق هذه الكلمة "صح". ١٢ بهرام : كتب المقريزي فوق هذه الكلمة "صح". || شابور١ : كتب المقريزي فوق هذه الكلمة "صح". || شابور٢ : كتب المقريزي فوق هذه الكلمة "صح". ١٣ أول ... ولد : الزيادة بخط المقريزي في الهامش الأيمن من الأعلى إلى الأسفل + صح، ويشير إليها رمز ˥ بعد "الأثيم".

١ من تأريخ الطبري ١: ٨٥٠ ومن تأريخ سني الملوك لحمزة ص ٤٣.

٢ من تأريخ الطبري ١: ٨٥٤–٨٥٧.

heart that he died on the spot. The horse was never seen thereafter. Persians spoke much about this and had various opinions, but the best opinion was expressed by those who said: "God, He is Exalted, answered our prayers." He reigned for 21 years, 5 months, and 18 days or, according to others, 22 years, 5 months, and 16 days.[298]

§ 106[299] ʿAmr b. Imriʾ al-Qays al-Badʾ b. ʿAmr b. ʿAdī b. Naṣr died during the reign of Sābūr b. Sābūr of Shoulders, and Sābūr appointed to his position Aws b. Qalām b. Buṭaynā b. Ǧumayhir b. Liḥyān al-ʿImlīqī, but after five years Ǧaḥǧabā b. ʿAtīk of Banū Fārān b. ʿAmr b. ʿImlīq rouse against him and killed him. He died during the reign of Bahrām b. Sābūr of Shoulders, who appointed to his position after him Imruʾ al-Qays al-Badʾ b. ʿAmr b. ʿAdī[300] for 25 years. He died during the reign of Yazdaǧird the Sinner, and Yazdaǧird appointed to his position his son al-Nuʿmān b. Imriʾ al-Qays al-Badʾ. Yazdaǧird's vest was red and his trousers sky-blue, as was his crown, too, and he had a spear in his hand.

§ 107[301] When Yazdaǧird died, there reigned after him his son Bahrām Gūr or, according to others, Kūr[302] b. Yazdaǧird the Rough or, according to others, the Criminal or the Sinner or the Coarse b. Bahrām Kirmānšāh b. Šābūr b. Šābūr of Shoulders b. Hurmuz b. Narsī b. Bahrām b. Bahrāmšāh b. Hurmuz b. Šābūr b. Šābūr of the Armies b. Ardašīr b. Bābak. As soon as he was born, his father, Yazdaǧird the Sinner, entrusted him to al-Mundir b. al-Nuʿmān, because he wanted the Arabs to raise him and be responsible for his edu-

298 The various suggested lengths of Yazdaǧird's reign are primarily taken from Ḥamzah, although al-Ṭabarī contains much the same information. Al-Maqrīzī's 22 years, 5 months, and 18 days does not come as such from either source, but it is most probably a mix between al-Ṭabarī's 22 years, 5 months, and 16 days, and Ḥamzah's 21 years, 5 months, and 18 days (p. 25—on p. 14, Ḥamzah gives 21 years, 5 months, and 16 days).

299 Al-Ṭabarī, *Taʾrīḫ*, 1:850 = trans., 5:74–75; Ḥamzah, *Taʾrīḫ* 43 = trans. 68. The genealogies have been supplemented from another source and partly contradict al-Ṭabarī. Ḥamzah, *Taʾrīḫ* 78, is a possible source.

300 This is al-Maqrīzī's mistake. The genealogy of the Ḥīran Laḫmids is already confused in al-Ṭabarī, who gives the cognomen al-Badʾ to both Imruʾul-Qayses, as already pointed out by Bosworth (1999):74, note 198. Cf. Toral-Niehoff (2014): 223–224. Here we have the second Imruʾ al-Qays al-Badʾ (II) b. ʿAmr b. Imriʾ al-Qays al-Badʾ (I) b. ʿAmr b. ʿAdī.

301 Al-Ṭabarī, *Taʾrīḫ*, 1:854–857 = trans., 5:81–85.

302 Persian *gūr* "wild ass." For the cognomen, cf. al-Bīrūnī, *al-Āṯār al-bāqiyah* 137.

المنذر إلى أحْيائه واختار لرضاعه ثلاث نسوة ذوات أجسام صحيحة وأذهان ذكية وآداب حسنة من بنات الأشراف منهن عربيتان وعجمية فأرضعنه ثلاث سنين. فلما بلغ خمس سنين أحضر له مؤدبِيْن فعلموه الكتابة والفقه والرمي بطلبٍ من بهرام لذلك. وأحضر له حكيما من حكماء الفرس فتعلم ووعى كلما عُلمه بأدنى تعليم. فلما بلغ اثنتي عشرة سنة تعلم كلما أفيد وفاق معلميه. فأمرهم المنذر بالانصراف وأحضر معلمي الفروسية فأخذ بهرام عنهم كلما ينبغي له. ثم صرفهم المنذر وأحضر خيل العرب للسباق فسبقها فرس أشقر للمنذر فقربه لبهرام يده فقبله.

§108[١] ثم ركبه يوما للصيد فرأى عانة حمر وحش فرمى عليها وقصدها. فإذا هو بأسد قد أخذ عَيْرا منها تناول ظهره بفمه فرماه بهرام بسهم فنفذ فيه وفي العَيْر ووصل إلى الأرض فساخ السهم إلى ثلثه فتعجب من كان معه من ذلك. وأقبل على الصيد واللهو حتى مات أبوه يزدجرد. فاتفق عظماء الدولة على أن لا يملكوا أحدا من ذرية يزدجرد لسوء سيرته فيهم وعلى أن لا يملكوا بهرام {لنَشئه} في العرب وتخلقه بأخلاقهم. وملكوا رجلا من عقب أردشير بن بابك يقال له: كسرى. فجمع بهرام المنذر وابنه النعمٰن بن المنذر وأشراف العرب وذَكَّرَهُم إحسان أبيه إليهم وشدته على الفرس فوعدوه من أنفسهم النصر والمعونة. وتكفل له المنذر بالأمر وجهز ابنه النعمٰن على عشرة آلاف

---

٣ له : الزيادة بخط المقريزي في الهامش الأيمن من الأعلى إلى الأسفل + صح، ويشير إليها رمز ⌝ بعد "وأحضر". ١٠ لنَشئه : "لنَشْوه" في الأصل.

---

١ من تأريخ الطبري ١: ٨٥٧–٨٥٩ ومن تجارب الأمم لمسكويه ١: ١١٥–١١٦.

cation. Al-Munḏir brought the child to the tribes and selected three noble women to give suck to him, all of healthy body, sharp mind, good education, and noble descent. Two of them were Arabs and the third Persian. They gave him suck for three years. When Bahrām was five years old, al-Munḏir brought him teachers, who, on the request of Bahrām himself, taught him writing, law,[303] and archery. Al-Munḏir also brought him a Persian sage,[304] and the child learned quickly and retained in memory everything that he was taught. When he was twelve years of age, he had learned everything that had been taught to him and had become better than his teachers, whom al-Munḏir ordered to leave. Instead, he brought teachers of horsemanship. Bahrām learned from them all that he needed, and al-Munḏir sent them away. Then al-Munḏir brought Arab horses to race, and a reddish horse of his won the race. He led this horse to Bahrām with his own hand, and Bahrām accepted it.

§ 108[305] One day Bahrām rode off to hunt and saw a herd of wild asses. He shot arrows at them and started pursuing them, but suddenly there was a lion, which attacked one of the asses, sinking its teeth into its back. Bahrām shot an arrow at it, and it pierced the lion and the ass and hit the ground sinking into it for a third of its length. Those who were present were astonished by this. Bahrām concentrated on hunting and pleasures until his father Yazdağird died. The noblemen of the Empire decided that they would not choose the king from among the descendants of Yazdağird because of the latter's evil ways with them and that they would not (specifically) choose Bahrām because he had grown up among the Arabs, adopting their customs. Instead, they elected a man from among the offspring of Ardašīr b. Bābak, called Kisrá. Bahrām met al-Munḏir and his son al-Nuʿmān b. al-Munḏir and the nobles of the Arabs, reminded them of the good deeds his father had done them and his father's harshness towards the Persians. The Arabs promised to assist and help him. Al-Munḏir took this on himself and furnished his son al-Nuʿmān with 10,000 horsemen to march to Nahrašīr and

303 The term *fiqh* is difficult to translate here. I prefer the slightly anachronistic "law" (*fiqh* usually referring to Islamic law) to "knowledge (in general); understanding," as the former was a more common meaning in al-Maqrīzī's time, whether or not it was already so in al-Ṭabarī's time. Cf. also Bosworth (1999): 83.

304 Al-Ṭabarī speaks of a number of sages from Persia and Byzantium, as well as Arab storytellers.

305 Al-Ṭabarī, *Taʾrīḫ*, 1:857–859 = trans., 5:85–89; Miskawayh, *Taǧārib al-umam*, 1:115–116 = C146.

فارس إلى نَهْرشِيْر {وطيسبون} مدينتي الملك. وأمره | أن يعَسْكر قريبا منهما ويبعث طلائعه إليهما 156b وأن يقاتل من قاتله ويُغِير على البلاد. ففعل ذلك فبعث عظماء فارس إلى المنذر بحواني صاحب رسائل يزدجرد ليعلم خبره فأدخله على بهرام فلم يسجد له. فكلمه بهرام ووعده أحسن وعد ورده إلى المنذر وأمره أن يُجيبه فقال: "إن الملك بهرام أرسل النعمٰن إلى ناحيتكم. وقد ملكه الله بعد أبيه." فاشار بأن يسير المنذر ببهرام إلى مدينة الملك ليجتمع إليه الأشراف والعظماء ويشاوروا في ذلك فقبل رأيه وأعاده.

§109[1] ثم سار بعد عوده بيومين في ثلاثين ألفا مِن فرسان العرب ومعه بهرام حتى وافى المدينة. فصعد بهرام منبرا من ذهب مكلل بالجواهر وحضر عظماء الفرس. فذكروا فظاظة يزدجرد والد بهرام وسوء سيرته وكثرة قتله وإخراب البلاد وأنهم من أجل هذا صرفوا الملك عن ولده. فقال بهرام: "لست أكذبكم وما زلت زاريا عليه ولم أزل أسأل الله تعالى أن يملكني لأصلح ما أفسد وأسُد الثغور وأنفي أهل الفساد فإن أتت لملكي سنة ولم أف لكم بهذه الأمور تبرأت من الملك طائعا. وأشهد الله تعالى وملائكته ومُوْبذان مُوبذ بذلك." فرضي أكثر الناس إلا طائفة كان رأيها مع كسرى فإنها تكلمت. فقال بهرام: "فإني مع ما ضمنته لكم واستحقاقي للملك وإنه حق لي قد رضيت أن يوضع التاج والزينة بين أسدَين ضاريين. فمن تناوله فهو الملك." فأظهروا الرضا وقالوا:

---

١ وطيسبون: في الأصل "وطسون" وأضاف المقريزي فوق الكلمة، وهي غير معجمة، رمز "ك" (لـ "كذا") إشارة إلى شكه في صحة قراءتها. ٢ بحواني: في الأصل الكلمة غير معجمة وأضاف المقريزي فوقها رمز "ك" (لـ "كذا") إشارة إلى شكه في صحة قراءتها.

---

١ من تأريخ الطبري ١: ٨٥٩–٨٦١ ومن تجارب الأمم لمسكويه ١: ١١٦–١١٧.

Ṭaysabūn, the royal cities, and told him to encamp close by the cities and to send his vanguards to them and to fight those who attacked them and to raid the country. Bahrām did so, and the noblemen of Fārs sent to al-Munḏir Ḥawānī,[306] Yazdaǧird's head of chancery, to get to know what al-Munḏir was up to. Al-Munḏir, however, brought him to Bahrām. Ḥawānī did not bow in front of him,[307] but Bahrām spoke to him and gave him good promises, sending him back to al-Munḏir and ordering the latter to reply to him. Al-Munḏir said: "King Bahrām sent al-Nuʿmān to your region. God has appointed him king after his father." Ḥawānī suggested that al-Munḏir should come with Bahrām to the royal city to meet the noblemen and the nobility and to negotiate with them. Al-Munḏir accepted his advice and sent him back.[308]

§109[309] Two days after Ḥawānī's return, al-Munḏir, together with Bahrām, marched out with 30,000 Arab cavalrymen. When they came to the city, Bahrām ascended the golden *minbar* encrusted with jewels. The Persian noblemen were present and spoke about the coarseness of Yazdaǧird, the father of Bahrām, and about his bad ways and how he had killed numerous people and laid waste many regions. They said that because of this they had turned the kingship away from his offspring. Bahrām replied: "I do not say that you are lying. I found fault with him myself, too, and kept asking God, He is Exalted, that He make me king so that I could put in order what he had corrupted, repair what he had broken, and drive away corrupt people. If I rule a year without fulfilling my promise to you, I will voluntarily resign from kingship. I call God, He is Exalted, His angels, and the *mōbadān mōbad* to be my witnesses in this." Most people were satisfied with this, but some remained on the side of Kisrá and expressed their opinion. Bahrām replied to them: "I have already given you a guarantee and it is my right to become king and I deserve kingship, yet I consent to the crown and the regalia being put between two ferocious lions, and let the one who takes them be king." They accepted this and said: "If we persist in denying Bahrām the kingship,

---

306 The first letter explicitly marked as Ḥ.
307 Al-Ṭabarī explains this by his confusion in front of Bahrām's majestic appearance, but al-Maqrīzī's readers will more probably have understood this as lack of respect.
308 The paragraph has been heavily abbreviated from al-Ṭabarī's text and is somewhat hard to follow on its own, especially as the original Arabic text uses few personal names.
309 Al-Ṭabarī, *Taʾrīḫ*, 1:859–861 = trans., 5:89–90; Miskawayh, *Taǧārib al-umam*, 1:116–117 = C148–150.

"إن تمادينا على صرف الملك عن بهرام لم نأمن هلاك الفرس على يده بمن يرى رأيه ولكثرة من استجاش من العرب. وقد عرض علينا ما لم يَدْعُه إليه أحد ولو لا ثقته ببطشه وجرأته ما وعد من نفسه بذلك. فإن فعل ما وصف فما الرأي إلا تسليم الملك إليه والسمع والطاعة له. وإن يهلك عجزا وضعفا فنحن {بُرآء} منه آمنون لشره وغائلته وافترقوا على ذلك."

§110[1] وجلس بهرام من الغد وحضر من كان ينازعه فقال: "إما أن تجيبوني عما تكلمت به أمسِ وإما أن تسكتوا باخعين لي بالطاعة." فقال القوم: "قد | رضينا بحكمك وأن يوضع التاج والزينة بين 157a
الأسدين كما ذكرت بحيث رسمت وتنازعاهما أنت وكسرى." فأتي بالتاج والزينة وتولى حمل ذلك مُوبذان موبذ الذي كان يعقد التاج على رأس كل ملك تملك فوضعهما ناحية. وجاء أصبهبذ مع ثقات القوم بأسَدَين ضاريين مجوعَين مُشْبِلَين فوقف أحدهما عن جانب الموضع الذي وضع فيه التاج والزينة والآخر بحذائه وأرخى وثاقهما. ثم قال بهرام لكسرى: "دونك التاج والزينة." فقال كسرى: "أنت أولى مني لأنك تطلب الملك بوراثة وأنا فيه دخيل." فلم يكره بهرام قوله لثقته بنفسه وحمل جرزا وتوجه نحو التاج والزينة فقال له موبذان موبذ: "استماتتك في هذا الأمر الذي تقدم عليه هو تطوع منك لا عن رَأيِيْ ولا عن رأي أحد من الفرس ونحن {بُرآء} إلى الله من إتلاف نفسك." فقال بهرام: "نعم أنتم {بُرآء} ولا وِزْرَ عليكم."

§111[2] ثم أسرع نحو الأسدين. فلما رأى موبذان موبذ جِده هتف به وقال: "بُح بذنوبك وتب منها ثم أقْدِم إن كنت لا محالة مُقْدِما." فباح بهرام بما سلف من ذنوبه ثم مشى نحو الأسدَيْن فبدرَه أحدُهما. فلما دنا من بهرام وثب وثبة فإذا هو على ظهر الأسد وعَصَر جنبي الأسد بفخذيه حتى أثْخَنَه وجعل

---

٤ بُرآء: "بُراآ" في الأصل. ٧ حمل ذلك: الزيادة بخط المقريزي في آخر السطر في الهامش الأيسر. ١٢ جرزا: كتب المقريزي فوق الكلمة رمز "ك" (لـ "كذا") إشارة إلى شكه في صحة قراءتها. ١٣ بُرآء: "بُراآ" في الأصل. ١٤ بُرآء: "بُراآ" في الأصل. ١٦ محالة: وضع المقريزي رمز "ح" تحت الحرف الثاني إشارة إلى تلفظه بالحاء.

---

١ من تأريخ الطبري ١: ٨٦١–٨٦٢ ومن تجارب الأمم لمسكويه ١: ١١٧.
٢ من تأريخ الطبري ١: ٨٦٢ ومن تجارب الأمم لمسكويه ١: ١١٧–١١٨.

we cannot be sure that he and those with him would not cause the destruction of the Persians, as he has raised numerous Arabs. Now he has suggested something that no one asked from him. If he were not so certain about his strength and courage, he would not have promised this. If he does what he says, then we have to let him become king and we must hear and obey him. If, however, he perishes because of weakness and incapability, we are innocent and safe from his evil and ruin." Having agreed on this they left.

§ 110[310] The next day Bahrām sat on the throne. Those who disputed with him were also there, and Bahrām said: "Either give me an answer to what I suggested yesterday or remain quiet and obey me." They answered: "We accept your suggestion that the crown and the regalia are to be put between two lions, like you said and where you suggested, and then you and Kisrá will face them." The crown and the regalia were brought to them. The *mōbadān mōbad*, who used to crown every king, carried them and put them on one side. Then the *iṣbahbad*[311] and some trusted men brought two ferocious lions, which were hungry and had cubs. One stopped close to where the crown and the regalia were and the other was opposite it. Then the *iṣbahbad* loosened their chains, and Bahrām said to Kisrá: "There's the crown and the regalia for you!" Kisrá replied: "You are better entitled to begin, as you claim kingship by inheritance, whilst I am a newcomer." Bahrām did not dislike what he said, as he was confident in himself. He took a mace and headed for the crown and the regalia. The *mōbadān mōbad* said: "It is on your own accord that you risk your life in this matter you are going to engage in, not because of my opinion or any other Persian's. We are innocent in front of God, if you now waste your own life," Bahrām replied: "Yes, you are innocent and you will not be held responsible."

§ 111[312] Then Bahrām hurried towards the lions. When the *mōbadān mōbad* saw that he was in earnest, he cried to him: "Confess your sins and repent of them! Then proceed if indeed you have to proceed." Bahrām confessed all the sins he had committed and then continued towards the lions. One of them hastened against him. When it drew closer Bahrām jumped on its back and pressed the lion's flanks with his thighs, exhausting it. He also started to

310 Al-Ṭabarī, *Taʾrīḫ* 1:861–862 = trans. 5:90–92; Miskawayh, *Taǧārib al-umam*, 1:117 = C150–152.

311 For the military leader *iṣbahbad*, see "*spāhbed*," in *EIr*.

312 Al-Ṭabarī, *Taʾrīḫ*, 1:862 = trans., 5:92–93; Miskawayh, *Taǧārib al-umam*, 1:117–118 = C152–153.

يضرب رأسه بالجُرز. ثم قرب من الأسد الآخر فلما تمكن منه قبض على أذنيه وعرَكهما بكلتا يديه ولم يزل يضرب رأسه برأس الأسد الذي ركب ظهره حتى دمغهما ثم قتلهما ضربا على رأسيهما بالجرز. وذلك كله بمشهد من جميع من حضر ذلك المحفل وبمرأى من كسرى. فتناول بهرام التاج والزينة. فكان كسرى أول من هتف به وقال: "عمر الله بهرام الذي يسمع له من حوله ويطيع ورزقه الله ملك أقاليم الأرض السبعة." ثم هتف جميع من حضر ذلك المجلس وقالوا: "أذْعَنَّا للملك بهرام ورضينا به ملكا." وكثر الدعاء والضجيج.

§ 112[1] ولقي الرؤساء المنذر بعد ذلك وسألوه أن يكلم بهرام في التعمد لإساءتهم والصفح عنهم. فسأله فأسعفه الملك بطلبته. ثم | جلس بهرام وهو ابن عشرين سنة سبعة أيام متوالية للجند والرعية 157b يعدهم الخير من نفسه ويحضهم على تقوى الله تعالى وطاعته. وغبر زمانا يحسن السيرة وينعم النظر ويعمر البلاد ويدر الأرزاق. ثم آثَر اللهو على ذلك وكثرت خلواته بأصحاب الملاهي والجواري وأخذ الناس بأن يعملوا من كل يوم نصفه ثم يستريحوا ويتوفروا على الأكل والشرب واللهو وأن يشربوا بالجواشنة والأكاليل. فعز المغنون في أيامه حتى بلغ رسم كل دَسْت من الجواسنة مائة درهم. ومر يوما بقوم يشربون على غير ملهين فقال: "أليس قد نهيتكم عن الإغفال عن الملاهي؟" فقاموا إليه وسجدوا قائلين: "طلبناه بزيادة على مائة درهم فلم نقدر عليه." فدعا بالدواة والمهراق

---

٩ تعالى : كتب المقريزي الكلمة فوق السطر. ١٢ الجواسنة : كتب المقريزي فوق الكلمة رمز "ك" (لـ "كذا") إشارة إلى شكه في صحة قراءتها.

---

١ من تأريخ الطبري ١: ٨٦٢-٨٦٣ ومن تجارب الأمم لمسكويه ١: ١١٨ ومن تأريخ سني الملوك لحمزة ص ٤٣.

hit its head with his mace. Then he approached the other lion. When he was close by, he took a grip of its ears and pulled them with both his hands. He banged the heads of the two lions together until he had smashed their skulls and then killed them off with his mace. All this was done in full view of everybody present on the occasion and with Kisrá seeing everything. Bahrām took the crown and the regalia. Kisrá was the first to address him, saying: "May God give long life to Bahrām, whom those around him hear and obey, and may God give him the kingship of the seven climes of earth." All who were present addressed him and said: "We submit ourselves to King Bahrām and accept him as king." There were many blessings and much noise.

§ 112[313] After that, the leaders met al-Mundir and pleaded with him, asking him to speak to Bahrām so that he would forgive them and ignore their bad deeds. Al-Mundir did so, and the king granted him his wish. Then Bahrām, who was twenty years of age, gave audiences to the army and people for seven consecutive days, promising them good things and urging them to fear God, He is Exalted. For some time he behaved well, took pains to look into matters, made the country flourish, and bestowed lavish provisions. But then he started preferring pleasure to that and often withdrew with musicians and slave girls. People started working only half of the day, resting the other half, eating and drinking well and enjoying themselves. They drank (while being entertained) by musicians (*ǧawāšinah*)[314] and wore diadems, singers (*muġannūn*) becoming so expensive during his days that the rate for one group (*dast*) of musicians was a hundred dirhams. One day Bahrām went by some people who were drinking without entertainers (*mulhīn*), and said to them: "Have I not forbidden you (to feast) without music!" They rose up, bowed to him, and replied: "We have tried to find a musician, offering more than a hundred dirhams, but we could not find anyone." Bahrām ordered ink

313 Al-Ṭabarī, *Taʾrīḫ*, 1:862–863 = trans., 5:93; Miskawayh, *Taǧārib al-umam*, 1:118 = C153; Ḥamzah, *Taʾrīḫ* 43 = trans. 68.

314 The two attestations of *ǧawāšinah*/*ǧawāsinah* in this paragraph and their source, Ḥamzah, are possibly the only attestations of the plural of *ǧūsān* (*gōsān*) in Arabic. The word is once written with Š by al-Maqrīzī, once with an undotted S. The printed edition of Ḥamzah reads *al-ḥawāšiyah*. In Islamic sources, *gōsān* seems to refer to musicians/singers in general, rather than singers of tales (*pace* Boyce 1957). In any case, it will have been a rare word already at the time of Ḥamzah, and would not have been readily understood by al-Maqrīzī and his audience.

وكتب إلى ملك الهند يستدعي مُلْهِين فأنفذ إليه اثني عشر ألف رجل منهم ففرقهم على بلدان مملكته فتناسلوا بها وسمي نسلهم الزُط.

§113[1] فلما أمعن في اللهو كثرت ملامة رعيته إياه على ذلك وطمع من حوله من الملوك في استباحة بلاده والغلبة على ملكه. وكان أول من سبق إلى مغالبته خاقان ملك الترك فإنه غزاه في مائتين وخمسين ألفا من الأتراك. فبلغ الفرس إقبال خاقان في هذا الجمع فهالهم ذلك. ودخل إليه من عظمائهم قوم من أهل الرأي فقالوا: "أيها الملك قد أزِفَك من بائقة هذا العدو ما يشغلك عما أنت فيه من اللهو والتلذذ فتأهب له كيما يلحقك منه أمر يلزمك فيه مَسَبة وعار." وكان بهرام لثقته بنفسه ورأيه يجيب القوم بأن الله ربنا قوي ونحن أولياؤه. ثم يقبل على المثابرة واللزوم لما هو فيه من اللهو والصيد إلى أن أظهر ذات يوم التجهز إلى آذربيجان لينسك في بيت نارها ويتوجه منها إلى أرمينية ويطلب الصيد في آجامها ويلهو في مسيره في سبعة رهط من العظماء وأهل البيوتات وثلاث مائة رجل من رابطته ذوي بأس ونجدة. واستخلف أخاه نرسي على ما كان يدبر من ملكه. فلم يشك الناس | حين بلغهم مسير بهرام فيمن سار بهم واستخلافه أخاه في أن ذلك هرب 158a ⟨من⟩ عدوه وإسلام لملكه وتوامروا في إنفاذ وفد إلى خاقان والإقرار له بالخراج مخافة منه أن يستبيح بلادهم ويصطلم مقاتلتهم ووجوههم إن هم لم يفعلوا ذلك ويبادروا إليه.

§114[2] فبلغ خاقان الذي أجمع عليه الفرس من الانقياد والخضوع له فأمنهم وترك كثيرا من الجند والاستعداد. وأتى بهرامَ عينٌ له من جهة خاقان فأخبره بحاله وحال جنده وفتورهم عن

١٣ من: الزيادة يقتضيها السياق.

١ من تأريخ الطبري ١: ٨٦٣-٨٦٤ ومن تجارب الأمم لمسكويه ١: ١١٨.

٢ من تجارب الأمم لمسكويه ١: ١١٩.

and parchment (*muhrāq*) to be brought and wrote to the king of India asking for entertainers (*mulhīn*). The king of India sent him 12,000 of them, and Bahrām divided them between the various parts of his kingdom, where they begat offspring, who are nowadays called gypsies (al-Zuṭṭ).

§113[315] When Bahrām devoted himself to pleasures, people started blaming him for that. Kings around him grew desirous of seizing his country and vanquishing his kingdom. The first who challenged him was the Ḫāqān, the king of the Turks, who marched against him with 250,000 Turks. The Persians heard of the Ḫāqān approaching with such numbers and were scared. Some of the discerning noblemen entered on Bahrām and said: "O King, a misfortune caused by the enemy is approaching and you have to give attention to it, rather than to the entertainments and pleasures you are involved in. Prepare for it, so that you will not gain permanent blame and shame." Bahrām, who was confident of himself and his understanding, kept answering them: "God, our Lord, is strong and will protect us." He persevered in pleasures and hunting, until one day he let all see that he prepared to go to Azerbaijan in order to perform the rites of its fire temple. From there, he would go with a group of seven noblemen and members of noble families and three hundred strong and courageous men from his guard to Armenia to hunt in its forests and to enjoy himself on the way. He left his brother Narsī to govern the kingdom. When they heard that Bahrām had gone with his retinue and left his brother Narsī to govern, people were certain that he was fleeing from the enemy and surrendering his kingship. They negotiated with each other and decided immediately to send an embassy to the Ḫāqān, promising to pay him tribute, fearing that otherwise he would loot their country and kill their warriors and prominent men.

§114[316] The Ḫāqān heard that the Persians had humbly decided to submit to him and felt safe with them.[317] Thus, he left much of his army and equipment behind. Having spied on the Ḫāqān, a spy came to Bahrām and informed him about the Ḫāqān and his army and how they neglected the serious-

---

315 Al-Ṭabarī, *Taʾrīḫ*, 1:863–864 = trans., 5:94–95; Miskawayh, *Taǧārib al-umam*, 1:118 = C153–154.

316 Miskawayh, *Taǧārib al-umam*, 1:119 = C155; cf. al-Ṭabarī, *Taʾrīḫ*, 1:864 = trans., 5:95–96.

317 Al-Ṭabarī's formulates this differently (*fa-ammana* [read so for the edition's *āmana*] *nāḥiyatahu wa-amara ǧundahu bi-l-tawarruʿ*) and clearly refers to giving a guarantee, as also Bosworth (1999): 95, understands it. Even though a similar reading is possible here, I think the context would better support reading *aminahum* and translating as above.

الجد الذي كانوا عليه. فسار في العدة الذين كانوا معه فبيت خاقان وقتله بيده وانهزم من سلم من القتل منهم وخلفوا عسكرهم وأثقالهم. فأمعن بهرام في طلبهم بقتلهم ويحوي الغنائم ويسبي الذراري وانصرف هو وجنده سالمين وظفر بتاج خاقان وإكليله وغلب على بلاد الترك وبخع له أهل البلاد المتاخمة لما غلب عليه بالطاعة وسألوه أن يَحُد لهم حدا بينه وبينهم فلا يتعدوه.

§ 115[1] ثم بعث قائدا إلى ما وراء النهر فأثخنهم وأقروا بالعبودية وأداء الجزية. وانصرف بهرام بالغنائم العظيمة والتاج والإكليل وما فيهما من الياقوت الأحمر وسائر الجواهر فنحلها بيت النار بآذربيجان. ورفع الخراج عن الناس ثلاث سنين وقسم في الفقراء مالا عظيما وفي البيوتات وأهل الأحساب عشرين ألف ألف درهم وكتب كتبا إلى الآفاق يذكر فيها أن الخبر كان ورد عليه بورود خاقان بلاده وأنه مجد الله تعالى وتوكل عليه وسار في سبعة رهط من أهل البيوتات وثلاثمائة فارس من نخبة رابطته على طريق آذربيجان وجبل القبق حتى نفذ إلى براري خوارزم ومفاوزها فأبلاه الله أحسن بلاء وذكر في الكتاب ما وضعه عن الناس من الخراج وهذا الكتاب كان بليغا والفرس يحفظونه.

§ 116[2] ويقال إن بهرام ترك من حق بيت المال من الخراج سبعين ألف ألف درهم بقسط تلك السنة وكان هذا مقدار ما بقي منه ثم أمر بترك الخراج كله ثلاث سنين أخر. ثم لما انصرف بهرام من غزوة خاقان | مظفرا قصد الهند فتحكى له حكايات عظيمة وأمور كبار تولاها وغلب 158b

---

٦ فنحلها: وضع المقريزي رمز "ح" تحت الحرف الثالث إشارة إلى تلفظه بالحاء. ٨ ألف¹: كتب المقريزي فوق هذه الكلمة "صح". ١٠ القبق: كتب المقريزي رمز "ك" (لـ "كذا") إشارة إلى شكه في صحة قراءتها. ١٣ ألف¹: كتب المقريزي فوق هذه الكلمة "صح".

---

١ من تجارب الأمم لمسكويه ١: ١١٩.

٢ من تجارب الأمم لمسكويه ١: ١١٩.

ness of their situation. Bahrām marched with the men he had and attacked the Ḫāqān by night, killing him with his own hand. Those of the Turks who survived the massacre fled, leaving their camp and their baggage, Bahrām pursued them assiduously, killing, looting, and taking their family members prisoners. Finally, he and his army returned safe. Bahrām got possession of the Ḫāqān's crown and his diadem and vanquished the country of the Turks. When he vanquished the Ḫāqān, people of the neighbouring region submitted themselves to him and asked him to draw a border between them and him, promising not to cross it.

§ 115[318] Then Bahrām sent a general to Transoxania. He vanquished people there, and they admitted being his slaves and promised to pay him the head tax. Bahrām returned with much booty, the crown, and the diadem, and all the red rubies and other jewels that had been encrusted in them. These he donated to the fire temple in Azerbaijan. He freed people from taxes for three years and distributed much property to the poor and gave 20,000,000 dirhams to great families and noblemen. Then he wrote letters to all directions informing people that this had happened because the Ḫāqān had invaded his country and that he had glorified God, He is Exalted, and trusted in Him, marching with seven members of noble families and 300 cavalrymen selected from his guard through Azerbaijan and Ǧabal al-Qabaq until he passed the deserts and plains of Ḫwārizm. God had supported him. He mentioned in the letter how he had freed people from taxes. This letter is very eloquent, and the Persians preserve it.[319]

§ 116[320] It is said that Bahrām forgave tax arrears to the treasury for 70,000,000 dirhams for that year. This much had remained unpaid. Then he gave orders to free people from all taxes for three more years. After he returned from his victorious campaign against the Ḫāqān Bahrām went to India. Wonderful stories about great feats, which he took on himself to perform and in which he was victorious, are told about him. The king of India

318 Miskawayh, *Taǧārib al-umam*, 1:119 = C155; cf. al-Ṭabarī, *Taʾrīḫ*, 1:864–865 = trans., 5:96–97.

319 This letter is given in, e.g., *Nihāyat al-arab* 264–266.

320 Miskawayh, *Taǧārib al-umam*, 1:119 = C155–156; cf. al-Ṭabarī, *Taʾrīḫ*, 1:866–868 = trans., 5:99–103.

عليها وزوجه ملك الهند ابنته ونحله الدبيل ومكران وما يليها فضمها بهرام إلى أرض فارس وحُمل خراجها إليه. ثم أغْزَى بهْرامُ مهرنرسي وهو من ولد بهمن بن إسفنديار بن يستاسف إلى بلاد الروم في أربعين ألف مقاتل وأمره أن يقصد عظيمها ويناظره في أمر الإتاوة وغيرها. فتوجه مهرنرسي في تلك العدة ودخل إلى قسطنطينية فهادنه ملك الروم وانصرف بجميع ما أراد بهرام وبلغ مبلغا عظيما بهيبة بهرام وبما تمكن له في قلوب الملوك وأهل الأطراف والجند من جودة الرأي وحسن التدبير والشجاعة ونفاذ العزيمة وقلة الأتكال على غيره.

§117[1] وذكر أن بهرام بعد فراغه من أمر خاقان وأمر ملك الروم والسند مضى إلى بلاد السودان من ناحية اليمن فأوقع بهم وقتل منهم مقتلة عظيمة وسبى منهم خلقا وانصرف إلى مملكته وولى نرسى خراسان وأمره أن ينزل مدينة بلخ. فبلغه أن بعض رؤساء الديلم جمع جمعا كبيرا وأغار على الري وأعمالها فغنم {وسبى} وخرب البلاد وقرر على أهل البلاد إتاوة تحمل إليه. فبعث مرزبانا على عسكر كثيف إلى الري وأمره أن يضع على الديلمي من يطمعه في البلاد ويغريه بقصدها. ففعل ذلك وجمع الديلمي جموعه وقصد الري. فلما بلغ بهرام ذلك كتب إلى نرسي يأمره بالمسير إلى الديلمي وعين له موضعا يقيم به. ثم سار جريدة في نفر من خواصه إلى عسكره المقيم بالموضع

---

١ ونحله : وضع المقريزي رمز "ح" تحت الحرف الثالث إشارة إلى تلفظه بالحاء. ٢ وهو ... يستاسف : الزيادة بخط المقريزي في آخر السطر في الهامش الأيسر من الأسفل إلى الأعلى. || يستاسف : وضع المقريزي ثلاث نقط تحت الكلمة إشارة إلى تلفظها بالسين. ١٠ وسبى : "وسبا" في الأصل.

---

١ من تجارب الأمم لمسكويه ١: ١٢٠ ومن تأريخ الطبري ١: ٨٦٥ ومن الكامل لابن الأثير ١: ٤٠٤-٤٠٥.

gave his daughter in marriage to him and donated him al-Daybul[321] and Makrān and the adjacent areas. Bahrām attached these to the country of Fārs, and their taxes were carried to him. Then he sent Mihr-Narsī, a descendant of Bahman b. Isfandiyād b. Yustāsf,[322] on a campaign to Byzantium with 40,000 warriors and ordered him to find their ruler and demand from him the taxes and other things. Mihr-Narsī marched with these men to Constantinople, and the king of Byzantium sued for truce. Mihr-Narsī returned with everything fulfilled that Bahrām had wanted and reached great things because people were afraid of Bahrām and because of what all kings, people of various regions, and the army felt in their heart concerning his good reason, excellent governing, courage, determination, and his independence from relying on others.

§ 117[323] It is said that after he was finished with the Ḫāqān and the kings of Byzantium and al-Sind, Bahrām went to the land of the Blacks through Yemen. He attacked them and massacred them in great numbers and took many captives, after which he returned to his kingdom and appointed Narsī[324] over Ḫurāsān and gave him orders to settle in the city of Balḫ. Then he heard that one of the leaders of the Daylamites had collected a great army and raided Rayy and its district, looting, taking prisoners, destroying the country, and setting on the inhabitants a tax to be carried to him. Bahrām sent a *marzubān* with a large army to Rayy, giving him orders to have someone make the Daylamite covetous of the region and entice him to attack it (again). The *marzubān* did so and the Daylamite again collected his troops and headed for Rayy. When he heard of this, Bahrām wrote to Narsī giving him orders to march against the Daylamite, specifying the place where he should stay. Then Bahrām himself rode with a detachment of his companions and joined the army that was staying in the place he had

321 Written in both manuscripts al-DBYL. Miskawayh (ed. Caetani) is not quite clear but seems correctly to read al-Daybul.

322 Later sources, e.g., Firdawsī, read Isfandiyār, but the form with a final -D (or -Ḏ) represents an older form. Yustāsf is a rather common misreading for Bištāsb/Guštāsb.

323 Miskawayh, *Taǧārib al-umam*, 1:120 = C157; al-Ṭabarī, *Taʾrīḫ*, 1:865 = trans., 5:97 (a few sentences from the beginning); Ibn al-Aṯīr, *Kāmil*, 1:404–405.

324 The name Mihr-Narsī is often abbreviated to Narsī, as already mentioned by al-Ṭabarī, *Taʾrīḫ*, 1:868 = trans., 5:103 (cf. Miskawayh, *Taǧārib al-umam*, 1:119), although al-Maqrīzī does not copy this into § 116. According to al-Ṭabarī, though, this Narsī is Bahrām's brother, not the Mihr-Narsī mentioned above.

الذي عينه. والديلمي لا يعلم بوصوله وقد قوي طمعه في البلاد فعبى بهرام أصحابه وسار نحو الديلمي حتى لقيه وباشر القتال بنفسه فأخذ الديلمي أسيرا وانهزم الديلم. فأمر فنودي فيهم بالأمان فعادوا بأجمعهم فأمنهم ولم يقتل منهم أحدا وأحسن إليهم وأفرج عن الديلمي رئيسهم وجعله من خواصه. وقد قيل إن هذه الحادثة كانت قبل محاربة خاقان ملك الترك.

§118[1] ولما ظفر بهرام بالديلم أمر ببناء مدينة سماها فيروز بهرام. وقيل | إنه استوزر نَرْسي وأعلمه 159a
أنه ماض إلى الهند في خفية. وسار من غير أن يعرفه أحد حتى دخل بلاد الهند غير أن الهند يرون شجاعته وقتله السباع فيعجبون له إلى أن ظهر فيل قطع السبيل وقتل خلقا كثيرا فخرج إليه بهرام ومعه من جهة الملك من يدله عليه حتى وقف على الأجمة التي فيها الفيل فصعد قاصد الملك شجرة. وعبر بهرام بمفرده إلى الأجمَة إلى أن قرب منه فرماه بسهم وقع بين عينيه وتابع الرمي بالنشاب حتى أثخنه وللفيل صياح عظيم. ثم حمل على الفيل وأخذ مشفره ولم يزل يطعنه حتى صرعه واحتز رأسه وخرج به وعاد. فأكرمه عند ذلك ملك الهند وأحسن إليه وسأله عن حاله فذكر أن ملك فارس سخط عليه ففر منه.

§119[2] وكان لملك الهند عدو فقصده فأذعن ذلك العدو وسأل الملك في العفو عنه فنهاه بهرام عن ذلك وأشار بمحاربته. فلما {التقى} الجمعان قال بهرام لأساورة الهند: "احفظوا لي ظهري." ثم حمل

٣ رئيسهم: الزيادة بخط المقريزي في الهامش الأيسر من الأسفل إلى الأعلى + صح، ويشير إليها رمز ⌐ بعد "الديلمي". ٧ أن: الزيادة بخط المقريزي في الهامش الأيمن من الأعلى إلى الأسفل + صح، ويشير إليها رمز ⌐ بعد "إلى". ٩ أن: الزيادة بخط المقريزي في الهامش الأيمن من الأعلى إلى الأسفل + صح، ويشير إليها رمز ⌐ بعد "إلى". ١٤ التقى: "التقا" في الأصل.

١ من تأريخ الطبري ١: ٨٦٦–٨٦٧.

٢ من تأريخ الطبري ١: ٨٦٧–٨٦٨ ومن تجارب الأمم لمسكويه ١: ١٢٠.

specified without the Daylamite being aware of his arrival. The Daylamite had become very covetous of the country. Bahrām prepared his troops and marched towards the Daylamites until they met, and Bahrām took personally part in the battle. He took the Daylamite as prisoner, and the Daylamite troops fled. Bahrām gave orders that a herald should proclaim that they were given indemnity. All the Daylamites returned, and he gave them a guarantee of safety and did not kill any of them but was kind to them. He also let free the leader of the Daylamites and took him among his own companions. It is also said that this happened before he fought the Ḫāqān, the king of the Turks.

§ 118[325] When Bahrām had vanquished the Daylamites, he ordered a city to be built, which he called Fīrūz-Bahrām. It is said that he appointed Narsī[326] as his Vizier and told him that he would secretly go to India. He left without anybody knowing and came to India. The Indians saw his courage and how he killed beasts and admired him. When an elephant appeared, attacking passers-by and killing many, Bahrām set out for it with a man whom the king had given him to show the way. He came to the thicket in which the elephant lived. The king's guide climbed up a tree while Bahrām continued alone to the thicket until he was close to the elephant. He shot an arrow and hit it between the eyes and then let other arrows follow until he had exhausted the elephant, which trumpeted furiously. Then he attacked it and grasped its trunk and kept hitting it until he brought it down and cut off its head, which he took with him when returning. The king of India showed him great honour and did well to him and asked about his story. Bahrām told him that the king of Fārs had been angered at him and that he was fleeing from him.

§ 119[327] The king of India had an enemy, against whom he marched. That enemy was ready to submit and asked the king for pardon, but Bahrām advised against this and suggested meeting him in battle.[328] When the two armies met, Bahrām said to the Indian cavalrymen: "Cover me!" Then

---

325 Al-Ṭabarī, *Ta'rīḫ*, 1:866–867 = trans., 5:99–101; cf. Ibn al-Aṯīr, Kāmi, l 1:405.

326 According to al-Ṭabarī, this was Mihr-Narsī, cf. § 117, note 324. Ibn al-Aṯīr reads Narsī.

327 Al-Ṭabarī, *Ta'rīḫ*, 1:867–868 = trans., 5:101–103; Miskawayh, *Taǧārib al-umam*, 1:120; cf. al-Ṭabarī, *Ta'rīḫ*, 1:865 = trans., 5:97; Ibn al-Aṯīr, *Kāmil*, 1:405–406.

328 Al-Maqrīzī has rephrased al-Ṭabarī and inverted the roles of the king and his enemy. In al-Ṭabarī's version, it is the enemy who marches against the king, and the king considers surrendering. Ibn al-Aṯīr, *Kāmil*, 1:405, reads *wa-kāna li-hāḏā l-malik ʿadūw fa-qaṣadahu fa-staslama l-malik wa-arāda an yuṭīʿa wa-yabḏula l-ḫarāǧ fa-nahāhu Bahrām.*

بنفسه حملة منكرة وجعل يضربهم ويرميهم بالنشاب حتى هزمهم. فغنم ملك الهند ما كان معهم وحينئذ أعطى بهرام الديبل ومكران وأنكحه ابنته فعاد بهرام إلى مملكته وضم ذلك إلى أرض فارس. ثم خرج في آخر ملكه إلى ماه يريد الصيد فشد على عَيْر وأمعن في طلبه فارتطم في ماء في سَبخة وغرق هناك. فسارت والدته إلى ذلك الموضع بأموال عظيمة وأقامت قريبا منه وأمرت بإنفاق تلك الأموال على من يخرجه. فنقلوا طينا كثيرا وحَمْأة كثيرة وجمعوا منه إِكَامًا عظيما فلم يقدروا على جثة بهرام. هكذا ذكر أبو علي ابن مِسْكَويه في **تجارب الأمم**.

§ 120[1] وذكر حمزة الإصفهاني أن بهرام كتب على ناووسه أنه: "بعد أن مُكِن لنا في الأرض فبَقَّيْنا بها آثارا محمودة اقتُصِرَ بنا على هذا المحل وقد كنا من سكوننا إياه على يقين." وكان شِعاره على لون السماء وسراويله أخضر {مُوَشّى}. قال ابن مسكويه: وكان ملكه ثلاثا وعشرين سنة. وقال حمزة: ملك ثلاثا وعشرين سنة. | وقيل: تسع عشرة سنة. وذكر أبو جعفر محمد بن جرير الطبري أنه ملك 159b ثماني عشرة سنة وعشرة أشهر وعشرين يوما. وقيل: كان ملكه ثلاثا وعشرين سنة وعشرة أشهر وعشرين يوما.

§ 121[2] ثم ملك بعده ابنه يزدجرد بن بهرام جور ويقال له: يزدجرد شاه دوست أَيْ اللَّيِّن. ولما لبس التاج جلس للناس ووعدهم وذكر أباه ومناقبه وأعلمهم أنه إن كانوا فقدوا منه طول {جلوسه} لهم فإن خلوته إنما كانت في مصالحهم وكيد أعدائهم وأنه قد استوزر نرسي صاحب أبيه. وعدل في

---

٩ مُوَشّى: "مُوَشا" في الأصل. ١٤ جلوسه: "جلوسهم" في الأصل. ١٥ وعدل: وضع المقريزي رمز ⌐ بين الواو و"عدل" إشارة إلى زيادة في الهامش الأيسر ولكن لا توجد أي زيادة على الصفحة.

---

١ من تأريخ سني الملوك لحمزة ص ٤٣، ١٤، ١٩، ٢٥ ومن تجارب الأمم لمسكويه ١: ١٢٠ ومن تأريخ الطبري ١: ٨٧١.

٢ من تأريخ الطبري ١: ٨٧١–٨٧٢ ومن تجارب الأمم لمسكويه ١: ١٢٠ ومن تأريخ سني الملوك لحمزة ص ٤٣، ١٤، ٢٥.

he attacked by himself with formidable force, hitting the enemy (with his sword) and shooting arrows at them until he had driven them away. The king of India got everything they had as booty. It was then that he gave al-Daybul[329] and Makrān to Bahrām as well as his daughter in marriage. Bahrām returned to his kingdom and appended these provinces to the country of Fārs. At the end of his reign, Bahrām went to Māh to hunt there. He rode hard after a wild ass and followed it, but fell into a bog eye and drowned there. His mother came to that place with loads of money and settled close to it giving orders to use the money to get the body up. People dug out a lot of clay and mud, heaping it up in great mounds but could not find Bahrām's body. This was related by Abū ʿAlī b. Miskawayh in *Taǧārib al-umam* [Trials of the Nations].

§ 120[330] Ḥamzah al-Iṣfahānī has mentioned that Bahrām had it written on his sarcophagus: "Once I had been given power on earth and I left there my praised traces. Now I have been confined to this place, but I was always aware that I would find my place here." His vest was sky-blue and his trousers green and embroidered. Ibn Miskawayh has said that his reign was 23 years. Ḥamzah has said that his reign was 23 years or, according to others, 19 years.[331] Abū Ǧaʿfar Muḥammad b. Ǧarīr al-Ṭabarī mentions that he reigned for 18 years, 10 months, and 20 days. It is also said that his reign was 23 years, 10 months and 20 days.

§ 121[332] After Bahrām, there reigned his son Yazdağird b. Bahrām Gūr, who is called Yazdağird Šāhdūst,[333] or the Gentle. After he had been crowned, he received people, made promises to them, and mentioned his father's virtues, telling them that even though they might have missed long receptions from him, his withdrawal had been for their own benefit and a ruse against their enemies. He also told them that he had appointed as Vizier Narsī, his father's companion.[334] He was just to his subjects, subdued his enemies, did

329 Written al-DxYL (x = undotted letter B, T, Ṯ, N, or Y).

330 Ḥamzah, *Taʾrīḫ* 43, 14, 19, 25 = trans. 5:68–69, 33, 38, 44; Miskawayh, *Taǧārib al-umam*, 1:120 = C158; al-Ṭabarī, *Taʾrīḫ*, 1:871 = trans., 5:106.

331 Ḥamzah, *Taʾrīḫ* 25 = trans. 44, mentions 19 years and 11 months.

332 Al-Ṭabarī, *Taʾrīḫ*, 1:871–872 = trans., 5:106–109; Miskawayh, *Taǧārib al-umam*, 1:120 = C158–159; Ḥamzah, *Taʾrīḫ* 43, 14, 25 = trans. 69, 33, 44; Ibn al-Aṯīr, *Kāmil*, 1:407. Ḥamzah, *Taʾrīḫ* 19, and Hoyland (2018): 38, also give 18 years and 5 months.

333 Cf. al-Bīrūnī, *al-Āṯār al-bāqiyah* 137 (Sipāhdūst).

334 Al-Ṭabarī reads Mihr-Narsī. Ibn al-Aṯīr reads Narsī.

رعيته وقمع أعداءه وأحسن إلى جنده ورأف برعيته. وكان له ابنان أحدهما يسمى هرمز والآخر فيروز. وكان لهرمز سجستان فغلب على الملك بعد هلاك أبيه يزدجرد ففر منه أخوه فيروز ولحق ببلاد الهياطلة وأخبر ملكها بقصته مع أخيه هرمز وأنه أولى بالملك منه وسأله أن يمده بجيش يقاتل به أخاه فأبى عليه ملك الهياطلة وقال: "سأعلم علمه ثم أمدك إن كنت صادقا." فلما عرف ملك الهياطلة أن هرمز ملك ظلوم غشوم قال: "إن الجور لا يرضاه الله ولا يصلح عليه الملك ولا تقوم عليه سياسة ولا يحترف الناس فى ملك الملك الجائر إلا بالجور وفي هذا هلاك الناس وخراب الأرض." فأمد فيروز ودفع إليه الطالقان فأقبل فيروز من عنده بجيش طخارستان وطوائف خراسان وسار إلى أخيه هرمز وهو بالري. وكانت أمهما واحدة وكانت بالمدائن تدبر ما يليها من الملك. فظفر فيروز بأخيه فحبسه وقيل: قتله. وكان ملك الروم قد منع حمل الخراج إلى يزدجرد فوجه إليه نرسي في العدة التي أنفذه أبوه بهرام فيها فبلغ إرادته. وكان ملك يزدجرد ثماني عشرة سنة وأربعة أشهر وثمانية عشر يوما وقيل: أربع عشرة سنة وأربعة أشهر وثمانية عشر يوما. وكان شعاره أخضر وسراويله موشاة سوداء وشيها ذهب وتاجه بلون السماء وإذا قعد على سريره اعتمد على سيفه.

§122[1] وملك | فيروز بن يزدجرد بن بهرام جور بعد أن قتل أخاه هرمز وثلاثة نفر من أهل 160a بيته. ويقال لفيروز هذا فيروز مردانه. فأظهر العدل وحسن السيرة وكان يتدين إلا أنه كان محدودا {مشؤُومًا} على رعيته. لحط الناس في زمانه سبع سنين متوالية فغارت فيها جميع الأنهار والقني والعيون وقل ماء دجلة وقحلت الأشجار والغياض وتماوتت الوحوش والطيور وجاعت

٦ يحترف: وضع المقريزي رمز "ح" تحت الحرف الثاني إشارة إلى تلفظه بالحاء. ١٣ سيفه: كتب المقريزي هذه الكلمة فوق السطر. ١٤ وملك: الزيادة بخط المقريزي في آخر السطر في الهامش الأيسر من الأسفل إلى الأعلى + صح. ١٦ محدودا: وضع المقريزي رمز "ح" تحت الحرف الثاني إشارة إلى تلفظه بالحاء. ‖ مشؤُومًا: "مَشؤُمًا" في الأصل. ١٧ وقل ... دجلة: الزيادة بخط المقريزي في الهامش الأيسر من الأسفل إلى الأعلى + صح، ويشير إليها رمز ˥ بعد "العيون".

١ من تأريخ الطبري ١: ٨٧٢–٨٧٤ ومن تجارب الأمم لمسكويه ١: ١٢٠–١٢١.

good to his army, and was kind to people. He had two sons, Hurmuz and Fīrūz. Hurmuz had Siğistān, and after their father Yazdağird's death he took the kingship. His brother Fīrūz fled from him and went to the land of the Hephthalites and told their king his story with his brother Hurmuz and said that he was better entitled to be king than his brother, asking the king to help him with an army with which he could fight against his brother. The king of the Hephthalites refused, but said: "Once I know more about this, I will help you if you have spoken the truth." When the king of the Hephthalites knew that Hurmuz was a tyrannical and unjust king, he said: "God is not pleased with tyranny, and a kingdom based on tyranny does not thrive. Good governance cannot be based on it, and people will not succeed under a tyrannical king except through injustice. Therein lies the destruction of people and the ruination of a country." The king then helped Fīrūz, and Fīrūz gave him al-Ṭālaqān. Fīrūz went from there with the army of Tuḫāristān and groups from Ḫurāsān and marched against his brother Hurmuz, who was in Rayy. They had the same mother, who was in al-Madāʾin governing that part of the kingdom. Fīrūz defeated and imprisoned, or according to others killed, his brother. The king of Byzantium had refused to bring tribute to Yazdağird, and Fīrūz sent against him Narsī with an army as large as that which Yazdağird's father Bahrām had sent with him, and achieved what he wanted. The reign of Yazdağird was 18 years, 4 months, and 18 days or, according to others, 14 years, 4 months, and 18 days. His vest was green, his trousers black and embroidered with gold, and his crown sky-blue. Sitting on his throne he leaned on his sword.

§ 122[335] After he had killed his brother Hurmuz and three members of his family, Fīrūz b. Yazdağird b. Bahrām Gūr became king. This Fīrūz is called Fīrūz the Manly (Mardānah).[336] He was just, behaved well, and was religious except that he was unlucky and ill-omened for his people. In his time, there was dearth of rain for seven consecutive years. All rivers, *qanāts*,[337] and springs dried up, the water level of the Tigris was low, trees and thickets withered, wild animals and birds died, and cattle and horses (*dawābb*)

335 Al-Ṭabarī, *Taʾrīḫ*, 1:872–874 = trans., 5:109–112; Miskawayh, *Tağārib al-umam*, 1:120–121 = C159–160.

336 Cf. al-Bīrūnī, *al-Āṯār al-bāqiyah* 137.

337 Underground irrigation canal, see "*kāriz*," in *EIr*.

الأنعام والدواب حتى كانت لا تطيق أن تحمل حمولة وعم أهل البلاد الجهد والمجاعة. فأحسن فيروز إلى الناس وقسم ما في بيوت الأموال وكف عن الجباية وساسهم أحسن سياسة وكتب إلى جميع أعماله أنه لا خراج عليكم ولا جزية ولا سخرة وأنه قد ملككم أنفسكم. وأمرهم بالسعي فيما يقوتهم ويصلحهم. ثم كتب إليهم في إخراج الهُري والطعام من المطامير لكل من كان يملك شيئا من ذلك مما يَقوت الناس والتآسي فيه وترك الاستئثار به وأن يكون حال أهل الفقر {والغنى} وأهل الشرف والضِعَة في التآسي واحدة وأنه إن بلغه أن إنسانا مات جوعا عاقب أهل تلك المدينة أو القرية أو الموضع الذي مات فيه ونكل بهم أشد النكال. فلم يعرف أنه هلك في تلك المجاعة أحد من رعيته جوعا إلا رجل واحد من رستاق كورة أردشير خره. فلما حييت بلاده وأغاثه الله وعادت المياه وصلحت الأشجار واستوسق الملك أثخن في الأعداء وقهرهم.

§123[1] {وبنى} مدنا {إحداها} بالري وأخرى بين جرجان وصول وأخرى بناحية آذربيجان وسماها بأسماء مشتقة من اسمه. {وابتنى} حائطا وراء النهر بين ملك فارس وأرض الترك وهو حائط ممتد من الجبل طول أربعة فراسخ يدخل مع بحر الخزر ليحول بين ناحية صول التركي وبينه. فجاء طوله أربعة وعشرين {فرسخا} وتممه أنوشروان بعد ذلك. واستتم بناء سور مدينة جي وأمر بقتل نصف يهود إصبهان وإسلام صبيانهم في بيت نار سروشاذُران ليكونوا عبيدا. وسبب ذلك أنهم | شَرحوا 160b جلد ظهري رجلين من الهرابذة ثم ألصقوا أحد الجلدين بالآخر ودبغوهما.

٥ والغنى: "والغنا" في الأصل. ٦ بلغه: كشط المقريزي بعض الكلمات كانت قبل هذه الكلمة ثم أطال الباء لملء البياض. ١٠ وبنى: "وبنا" في الأصل. || إحداها: "احدها" في الأصل. ١١ وابتنى: "وابتنا" في الأصل. ١٣ فرسخا: "فرسا" في الأصل. ١٤ شَرحوا: وضع المقريزي رمز "ح" تحت الحرف الثالث إشارة إلى تلفظه بالحاء.

١ من تجارب الأمم لمسكويه ١: ١٢١ ومن تأريخ سني الملوك لحمزة ص ٤٤.

hungered, so that they did not have the strength to carry burdens. All the people of the country suffered and were left hungry. Fīrūz did good to people and distributed what there was in the treasuries and refrained from collecting taxes and governed them well. He wrote to all districts that they were exempt from land tax and head tax, as well as corvée, and that he had given them power over themselves. He gave them orders to be diligent in doing what would give them food and make their situation better. Then he wrote to them ordering anyone who had something with which people could nourish themselves to open their granaries and bring out food from storehouses and share it, giving up their privileged position, so that poor and rich, noble and lowly would all be equal in sharing. He added that if it became known to him that a single person had died of hunger, he would punish the whole population of that city or village or place where he had died and make them a severe warning example. It is not known that any of his subjects would have died in this famine except one man from the rural district of Ardašīr-ḫurrah. When his country again flourished and God helped him and waters returned and trees flourished again and ruling became possible, he smashed his enemies and overpowered them.

§ 123[338] Fīrūz built several cities, one of them in Rayy, another between Ǧurǧān and (Bāb) Ṣūl,[339] and a third in the direction of Azerbaijan, and he named these by names derived from his own. He also built a wall in Transoxania between the kingdom of Fārs and the country of the Turks. It is a long wall extending from al-Ǧabal for four *farsaḫs* and ending in the sea of the Ḫazars to separate the region of the Turkish Ṣūl from his.[340] Its length was 24 *farsaḫs*, and later Anūširwān completed it. Fīrūz also finished building the walls of the city of Ǧay and ordered half of the Jews of Isfahan to be killed and their small children to be given as slaves to the fire temple of Surūšādurān. The reason for this was that they had flayed the skin from the backs of two *hērbads*, attached the skins together, and tanned them.

338 Miskawayh, *Taǧārib al-umam*, 1:121 = C160; Ḥamzah, *Taʾrīḫ* 44 = trans. 69; cf. al-Ṭabarī, *Taʾrīḫ*, 1:874 = trans. 5:112–113.

339 The addition of Bāb is based on al-Ṭabarī. While Ḥamzah and Miskawayh leave these cities unnamed, al-Ṭabarī, *Taʾrīḫ*, 1:874 = trans., 5:112–113, mentions their names.

340 For the royal title of Ṣūl, cf. al-Bīrūnī, *al-Āṯār al-bāqiyah* 116.

§124[1] وسار بجنوده نحو خراسان يريد حرب أخشنواز ملك الهياطلة لأشياء كانت في نفسه ولأن الهياطلة كانوا يأتون الذكران ويرتكبون الفواحش. فخافه أخشنواز لعلمه أنه لا طاقة له به فتحيل عليه حتى قهره وقتله وعامة من كان معه. وذلك أن رجلا من أصحاب أخشنواز تنصح إليه وقال: "إني رجل كبير السن قريب الأجل وقد فديت الملك وأهل مملكته بنفسي. فاقطع يدي ورجْليّ وأظهر في جسمي وجَنْبَيّ آثار السياط من العقوبات وألقني في طريق فيروز وأحسن إلى ولدي وعيالي بعدي فإني أكفيك أمر فيروز." ففعل ذلك أخشنواز بذلك الرجل وألقاه على طريق فيروز.

§125[2] فلما مر به أنكر حاله ورأى شيئا فظيعا فسأله عن أمره. فأخبره أن أخشنواز فعل به ذلك لأنه قال له: "لا قوام لك بالملك فيروز وجنوده." وأشار عليه بالانقياد له والعبودية. فرق له فيروز ورحمه وأمر بحمله معه فأعلمه على وجه النصح له فيما زعم أنه يدله على طريق قريب مختصر لم يدخل أحد منه قط إلى أخشنواز على طريق المفازة وسأله أن يشتفي له منه. فاغتر فيروز بذلك منه وأخذ الأقطع بالقوم في الطريق الذي ذكره له. ولم يزل يقطع بهم مفازة بعد مفازة وكلما شكوا عطشا أعلمهم أنهم قد قربوا من الماء ومن قطع المفازة حتى إذا بلغ بهم موضعا أعلمهم أنهم لا يقدرون فيه على تقدم ولا تأخر وبين لهم أمره. فقال أصحاب فيروز لفيروز: "قد كنا حذرناك هذا أيها الملك فلم تحذر. فأما الآن فلا بد من المضي فإنه لا سبيل إلى الرجوع. فلعلك توافي القوم على الحالات كلها."

١ بجنوده: وضع المقريزي رمز "٢" فوق الكلمة وكرر هذا الرمز في الهامش الأيمن ولاكن لا توجد أي زيادة فيه.

١ من تجارب الأمم لمسكويه ١: ١٢١.

٢ من تجارب الأمم لمسكويه ١: ١٢١–١٢٢.

§124[341] Then Fīrūz marched with his armies towards Ḫurāsān to fight Aḫšunwār, the king of the Hephthalites,[342] because of some things he had in his mind and also because the Hephthalites used to have sex with males and committed other atrocities. Aḫšunwār was afraid of him. He knew he did not have the strength to resist him, so he used a ruse to overpower and kill Fīrūz and most of the men with him. This went as follows: One of Aḫšunwār's companions advised him, saying: "I am an old man, soon to die. I can redeem the king and the people of the kingdom by my own life. Cut my hands and feet and leave marks of whipping on my body and my flanks. Then throw me on the road Fīrūz takes, but take good care of my children and family after me. I will take care of Fīrūz for you." Aḫšunwār did so and threw the man on the road Fīrūz was taking.

§125[343] When he went by, Fīrūz found the old man's situation disturbing and disliked what he saw and asked what had happened to him. The man said that Aḫšunwār had done this to him because he had said: "You will not be able to resist king Fīrūz and his armies." He had suggested to the king that he should submit himself and become Fīrūz's slave. Fīrūz was moved by this and felt sorry for the man and ordered him to be carried with them. The man told him, claiming this to be sincere advice, that he could lead them a shorter and nearer way through the desert, which had never been used by anybody except by Aḫšunwār himself. He also asked him to take revenge on Aḫšunwār for him. Fīrūz was deceived by this and selected for his men the shorter way that the man had suggested to him. They marched through desert after desert. When they complained of thirst the man told them that they were already close to water and about to get across the desert. Finally, they reached a certain place where he told them[344] that they would not be able either to proceed or go back and explained to them how the matters were. The companions of Fīrūz said to Fīrūz: "O King, we warned you about this, but you did not listen to us. Now, we can only go on, as there is no turning back anymore. Perhaps you can provide for the people under any circumstances."

341 Miskawayh, *Taǧārib al-umam*, 1:121 = C160–161; cf. al-Ṭabarī, *Taʾrīḫ*, 1:874–875 = trans., 5:112–114.

342 Al-Maqrīzī consistently writes the name of Aḫšunwār with a final Z as do many others, Firdawsī included. Miskawayh (ed. Caetani) also mostly writes the name with Z.

343 Miskawayh, *Taǧārib al-umam*, 1:121–122 = C161–162; cf. al-Ṭabarī, *Taʾrīḫ*, 1:874–875 = trans., 5:113–114.

344 Miskawayh and al-Ṭabarī have more naturally *ʿalima* "he knew," for al-Maqrīzī's *aʿlamahum*. Miskawayh (ed. Caetani) vocalises this as *ʿalima*. Ibn al-Aṯīr, *Kāmil*, 1:408, has both: *ḥattá idhā ʿalima annahum lā yaqdirūn ʿalá l-ḫalāṣ aʿlamahum ḥālahu.*

§126[1] فمضوا لوجوههم وقتل العطش أكثرهم وصار فيروز بمن معه إلى عدوهم. فلما أشرفوا عليهم وهم بأسوأ حال من الضر والضعف دعوا أخشنواز إلى الصلح على أن يخلي سبيلهم حتى ينصرفوا إلى بلادهم على أن يجعل | له فيروز عهد الله وميثاقه ألا يغزوهم ولا يروم أرضهم ولا 161a يبعث إليهم جندا يقاتلهم ويجعل بين المملكتين حدا لا يجوزه. فرضي أخشنواز بذلك وكتب له به كتابا مختوما وأشهد له على نفسه شهوده. ثم {خلى} سبيله فانصرف. فلما صار إلى مملكته حمله الأَنَفُ على معاودة أخشنواز. فكان عاقبة غدره أن هلك هو وجنوده وذلك أنه غزاه بعد أن نهاه وزراؤه وخاصته عن ذلك لما فيه من نقض العهد فلم يقبل منهم وأبى إلا ركوب رأيه. وكان فيمن نهاه عن ذلك رجل كان يَخُصُّه ويقتدي برأيه يقال له مَرْبوذ. فلما رأى لجاجته كتب ما دار بينهما في صحيفة وسأله أن يختم عليها. ومضى فيروز لوجهه نحو بلاد أخشنواز. فلما بلغ منارة كان بناها بهرام جور فيما بين تخوم بلاد خراسان وبلاد الترك لئلا يجوزها الترك إلى خراسان لميثاق كان بين التُرْك والفرس على تَرْك الفريقين التَّعَدِّي لها. وكان فيروز عاهد أخشنواز أن لا يجاوزها إلى بلاد الهياطلة.

§127[2] أمر فيروز فصمد فيها خمسون فيلا وثلاث مائة رجل فجُرت أمامه جَرا وأتبعها وزعم أنه يريد بذلك الوفاء وترك مجاوزة ما عاهد عليه. فلما بلغ أخشنواز ذلك من فعل فيروز بعث إليه يقول: "إن الله عز وجل لا يُماكِر ولا يخادع. فانته عما انتهى عنه أسلافك ولا تقدم على ما لم يقدموا عليه." فلم يحفل فيروز بقوله ولم يكترث لرسالته وجعل يحب محاربة

٥ خلى: "خلا" في الأصل. ٩ نحو: وضع المقريزي رمز "ح" تحت الحرف الثاني إشارة إلى تلفظه بالحاء.
١٦ يحب: وضع المقريزي رمز "ح" تحت الحرف الثاني إشارة إلى تلفظه بالحاء.

١ من تجارب الأمم لمسكويه ١: ١٢٢.
٢ من تجارب الأمم لمسكويه ١: ١٢٢.

§126[345] So they went on. Thirst killed most of them. Fīrūz and those still remaining with him finally came to their enemy. When they came there, totally worn out by afflictions and weakness, they sued Aḫšunwār for peace. If he let them return to their country, Fīrūz promised to swear by God that he would no more raid them nor desire their land or send armies to fight them and he would set a boundary between the two kingdoms, which he would not cross. Aḫšunwār was satisfied with this. Fīrūz wrote him a sealed letter and provided witnesses against himself, after which Aḫšunwār let him go, and Fīrūz returned. But when he was back in his kingdom, his pride urged him to return to Aḫšunwār, and the result of this betrayal was death for him and his armies. This happened as follows: Even though his Viziers and confidants forbade him because he would be breaking his oath, he marched against Aḫšunwār, without listening to the advisers and following only his own opinion. One of those who forbade him was a man whom Fīrūz had selected for himself and whose advice he usually followed, called Marbūd.[346] When Marbūd saw how obstinate the king was, he wrote on a sheet what happened between them and asked the king to seal the document. Then Fīrūz went his way to the country of Aḫšunwār. He came to the border post which Bahrām Gūr had erected as a boundary between the land of Ḫurāsān and the land of the Turks, so that the Turks would not cross over to Ḫurāsān, following a pact that was between the Turks and the Persians to give up animosities between each other. Fīrūz had sworn to Aḫšunwār that he would not pass by the post to the land of the Hephthalites.

§127[347] Now Fīrūz gave orders for fifty elephants and three hundred men to drag the post before him. He followed it and said that he wanted thus to keep true to his pact, not passing by what he had promised not to pass by. When he heard what Fīrūz was doing Aḫšunwār sent him a word: "God, He is Mighty and Majestic, neither deceives nor plots. Stop doing what your ancestors did not do and do not venture what they never ventured!" Fīrūz ignored his words and did not heed his message. He urged Aḫšunwār to join

345 Miskawayh, *Taǧārib al-umam*, 1:122 = C162–163; cf. al-Ṭabarī, *Taʾrīḫ*, 1:275–276 = trans., 5:114–115.

346 So also in Miskawayh while al-Ṭabarī has MZDBWḎ, which Bosworth (1999): 115, hesitantly reads Muzdbuwaḏ, obviously on the basis of Justi (1895): 218. Another possibility would be to read this as Mardbūd, cf. Justi (1895): 196.

347 Miskawayh, *Taǧārib al-umam*, 1:122 = C163–165; cf. al-Ṭabarī, *Taʾrīḫ*, 1:876–877, 878–879 = trans., 5:115–116, 118–119.

أخشنواز ويدعوه إليها وجعل أخشنواز يمتنع من محاربته ويتكرهها لأن جل محاربة الترك إنما هو بالخداع والمكر والمكائد. ثم إن أخشنواز أمر بحفر خلف عسكره خندق عرضه عشرة أذرع وعمقه عشرون ذراعا وعُمِّي بخشب ضعاف وألقي عليه تراب. ثم ارتحل في جنده ومضى غير بعيد. فبلغ فيروز رِحْلَة أخشنواز بجنده من معسكره فلم يشك أن ذلك هزيمة منهم وأنه قد انكشف وهرب. فأمر بضرب الطبول وركب بجنده في | طَلَب أُخشنواز وأصحابه وأغذوا السير وكان مسلكهم على 161b ذلك الخندق. فلما بلغوه اقتحموه على عماية فتردى فيه فيروز وعامة جنده فهلكوا من آخرهم.

§128[1] وعطف أخشنواز على عسكر فيروز واحتوى على كل شيء فيه وأسر موبذان موبذ وأسر قباذ بن فيروز. وصارت فيروز دخت بنت فيروز فيمن صار في يده من نساء فيروز. ثم استخرج جثة فيروز ومن سقط معه فجعلها في النواويس. وقيل: إن فيروز لما انتهى إلى الخندق الذي حفره أخشنواز ولم يكن {مُغَطى} عقد عليه قناطر وجعل عليها أعلاما له ولأصحابه يقصدونها في عودهم وجاز إلى القوم. فلما التقى العسكران احتج عليه أخشنواز بالعهود التي بينهما وحذره عاقبة الأمر فلم يرجع فنهاه أصحابه فلم يرجع وضعفت نياتهم في القتال. فلما {أبى} إلا القتال رفع أخشنواز نسخة العهد على رمح وقال: "اللهم خذ بما في هذا الكتاب وقلده بغيه." ثم قاتله فانهزم فيروز وعسكره وضلوا عن مواضع القناطر فسقطوا في الخندق فهلك فيروز وأصحابه وغنم أخشنواز أموالهم ودوابهم وجميع ما معهم وغلب على عامة خراسان.

٧–٨ وأسر ... فيروز١: الزيادة بخط المقريزي في الهامش الأيسر من الأسفل إلى الأعلى + صح، ويشير إليها رمز ⌐ بعد "موبذ". ١٠ مُغَطى: "مُغَطا" في الأصل. ١٢ أبى: في الأصل "أبا".

---

١ من تجارب الأمم لمسكويه ١: ١٢٢ ومن تأريخ الطبري ١: ٨٢٦.

battle[348] and called him to fight, but Aḫšunwār kept refusing. He disliked battles because the Turks mainly fight by deceiving, plotting, and stratagems. Aḫšunwār gave orders to dig a trench behind his camp, ten cubits wide and twenty deep, and this was covered by small sticks and some soil thrown over them. Then he set to move with his army and went a short way. Fīrūz heard that Aḫšunwār was on the move from his camp with his troops and was certain that they were fleeing and Aḫšunwār was running away. He gave orders for the drums to be sounded and rode with his army after Aḫšunwār and his companions. They moved quickly forward and their route took them over that trench. When they came there, they plunged blindly into it. Fīrūz and his whole army perished to the last man.

§128[349] Aḫšunwār turned to the camp of Fīrūz and looted it. He took as prisoners the *mōbadān mōbad* and Qubād b. Fīrūz. Among the womenfolk of Fīrūz, Fīrūzduḫt bt. Fīrūz fell into his hands. Then he lifted up the bodies of Fīrūz and those who had fallen with him and put them in coffins. It is also said that when Fīrūz came to the trench which Aḫšunwār had dug, it was not covered, and he had bridges built and marked for himself and his companions to use when they returned. Then they crossed over to the enemy. When the two armies met, Aḫšunwār reminded him of the treaties they had and warned him about the outcome of the affairs, but Fīrūz did not listen to them. His own companions forbade him, too, but he did not care. Their motivation to fight was weak, and when Fīrūz stubbornly insisted on fighting, Aḫšunwār raised a copy of the treaty on a spear head and said: "O God, act upon what is written in this document and collar him with his injustice!"[350] Then he attacked, and Fīrūz and his army fled. They missed the places where the bridges were and fell into the trench. Fīrūz and his companions perished, and Aḫšunwār looted their property and their horses and everything they had with them. He also conquered most of Ḫurasan.

348 Miskawayh reads *yastaṭʿim* while al-Maqrīzī seems to read *yuḥibbu*, although the dot under B is not quite clear and the word could also be *yaḥuṯṯu*.

349 Miskawayh, *Taǧārib al-umam*, 1:122 = C165 (only the beginning); al-Ṭabarī, *Taʾrīḫ*, 1:826 = trans., 5:115–116.

350 This is obviously reminiscent of the similar scene in the battle of Ṣiffīn, where copies of the Qurʾān were raised on spear heads.

§129[1] فسار إليه رجل من عظماء أهل فارس يقال له سوخَرّا في زي محتسب. وقيل: بل كان فيروز استخلفه على ملكه لما سار. وكان له سجستان فلقي أخشنواز ملك الهياطلة وأخرجه من خراسان واستعاد منه كلما وجده مما كان في عسكر فيروز من سبي وغيره. وافتك من الأسار قباذ ابن فيروز وعاد. فعظمته الفرس حتى لم يكن أحد فوقه إلا الملك فقط. وكانت مملكة الهياطلة طخارستان. وكان فيروز قد أعطى لملكهم لما ساعده على حرب أخيه الطالقان وكان ملك فيروز مردانه بن يزدجرد سبعا وعشرين سنة. وقيل: سبع عشرة سنة. وفي نسخة: ستا وعشرين سنة. وقيل: إحدى وعشرين سنة. وكان شعاره أحمر وسراويله على لون السماء موشاة بالذهب وتاجه على لون السماء وبيده رمح وهو على سريره.

§130[2] ثم ملك بعد فيروز ابنه | بلاش كرمان مايه بن فيروز مردانه بن يزدجرد شاه دوست بن 162a
بهرام جور أربع سنين. وكان حسن السيرة حريصا على العمارة. وبلغ من حسن نظره أنه كان لا يبلغه أن بيتا خرب وجلا أهله عنه إلا عاقب صاحب القرية التى فيها ذلك البيت على تركه إنعاشهم وسد فاقتهم حتى لا يضطروا إلى الجلاء عن أوطانهم. وكانت ثيابه خضرا وسراويله حمراء موشحة بسواد وبياض وتاجه على لون السماء وبيده الرمح. {وبنى} مدينتين {إحداهما} بساباط المدائن والأخرى بجانب حلوان.

---

١ عظماء: الزيادة بخط المقريزي في الهامش الأيسر من الأسفل إلى الأعلى + صح، ويشير إليها رمز ˥ بعد "من". ٣-٤ وافتك ... فيروز: الزيادة بخط المقريزي في الهامش الأيسر من الأعلى إلى الأسفل + صح، ويشير إليها رمز ˥ بعد "وغيره". ١٣ وبنى: "وبنا" في الأصل. || إحداهما: "احدىهما" في الأصل.

---

١ من تأريخ الطبري ١: ٨٧٧، ٨٧٩-٨٨٠ ومن تأريخ سني الملوك لحمزة ص ٤٤، ١٤، ٢٥.

٢ من تجارب الأمم لمسكويه ١: ١٢٣ ومن تأريخ الطبري ١: ٨٨٢-٨٨٣ ومن تأريخ سني الملوك لحمزة ص ٤٤.

§ 129[351] Then a Persian nobleman called Sūḫrā[352] marched against Aḫšunwār, wearing the garment of an officer (*muḥtasib*),[353] but it is also said that Fīrūz had left him in charge of the kingdom when he had marched against Aḫšunwār. Sūḫrā ruled Siǧistān and set himself out against Aḫšunwār, the king of the Hephthalites, drove him out of Ḫurāsān, and took back all prisoners and everything else that Aḫšunwār had taken from the camp of Fīrūz. He freed Qubād b. Fīrūz and other prisoners. When he returned, the Persians praised him highly, so that above him there was only the king. The kingdom of the Hephthalites was Tuḫāristān. Fīrūz had given al-Ṭālaqān to their king when the king had helped him to fight his brother.[354] The reign of Fīrūz the Manly b. Yazdağird was 27 years[355] or, according to others, 17 years, or, in one manuscript, 26 years[356] or, according to others 21 years. His vest was red, his trousers sky-blue and embroidered with gold, and his crown was sky-blue and in his hand he held a spear and he was on his throne.

§ 130[357] After Fīrūz, there reigned his son Balāš Kirmānmāyah[358] b. Fīrūz the Manly b. Yazdağird Šāhdūst b. Bahrām Gūr for four years. He ruled well and was eager to make the country flourish. A good example of his acumen is that when he heard that a house had become ruined and its inhabitants had had to leave their home, he would punish the owner of the village in which this happened because he had neglected keeping them in good shape and helping them out of their poverty, so that they would not have needed to leave their native village. His clothes were green, his trousers red with black and white stripes, and his crown was sky-blue. In his hand, he held a spear. He built two cities, one in Sābāṭ al-Madā'in and the other close to Ḥulwān.

---

351 Al-Ṭabarī, *Ta'rīḫ*, 1:877, 879–880 = trans., 5:116–117, 120–121; Ḥamzah, *Ta'rīḫ* 44, 14, 25 = trans. 69, 33, 44.

352 Al-Maqrīzī explicitly writes Sūḫarrā.

353 Ibn al-Aṯīr, *Kāmil*, 1:409, reads *ka-l-muḥtasib*, but has a manuscript variant *ka-l-muḫtabir*.

354 Cf. § 121.

355 This seems to come from Ḥamzah, *Ta'rīḫ* 14, where the length of the reign is given as 27 years and one day.

356 This may be a mistake derived from Ḥamzah, *Ta'rīḫ* 19 = trans. 38, where Fīrūz's predecessor Bahrām b. Yazdağird, who is not mentioned on the other two lists of Ḥamzah, is said to have ruled for 26 years and one month. There, Fīrūz is said to have ruled for 29 years and one day, a variant not given by al-Maqrīzī.

357 Miskawayh, *Taǧārib al-umam*, 1:123 = C165; al-Ṭabarī, *Ta'rīḫ*, 1:882–883 = trans., 5:126–127; Ḥamzah, *Ta'rīḫ* 44 = trans. 70.

358 Cf. al-Bīrūnī, *al-Āṯār al-bāqiyah* 137 (Garānmāyah).

§131[١] ثم ملك بعده أخوه قباذ تنك رأي بن فيروز. وكان قد صار إلى خاقان يستنصره على أخيه بلاش ويذكر أنه أحق بالملك منه. فبقي هناك أربع سنين ثم جهزه خاقان. فلما عاد وبلغ نيسابور بلغه موت أخيه بلاش. وكان في وقت اجتيازه تزوج بها ابنة رجل من الأساورة متنكرا وواقعها فحملت بأنوشروان. فلما عاد في هذا الوقت الذي ذكرناه سأل عن الجارية فأتي بها وبابنه أنوشروان فتبرك به وبها. ولما بلغ حدود فارس والأهواز {بنى} مدينة أَرَّجَان {وبنى} حلوان {وبنى} عدة مدن. وكان من آرائه الجيدة وعزائمه النافذة قبضه على خاله سُوخَرًّا.

§132[٢] وكان سبب ذلك أن فيروز لما جرى عليه ما جرى من الهياطلة كان سوخرا يخلفه على مدينة الملك بالمدائن. فجمع جموعا كثيرة من الفرس وقصد أخشنواز ملك الهياطلة وحاربه وانتقم منه وتحكم عليه. وكان وقع في يده دفاتر الديوان الذي صحب فيروز فتقاضى جميع ما كان في خزائنه وخزائن قواده وأهله وطلب الوجوه من الأساورة الذين بقوا في يد أخشنواز. ولم يزل يحارب أخشنواز ويكيده ويبلغ منه ما يتحكم به عليه حتى استنقذ جميع من في يده من الفرس وأكثر ما احتوى عليه من خزائن فيروز. فكان له أثر حسن عند الفرس وعند ابني فيروز | أعني بلاش وقباذ 162b فعظموه ورفعوا منزلته إلى حيث ليس بينه وبين الملك إلا مرتبة واحدة. فتولى سياسة الأمن بحُنكة وتجربة واستولى على الأمر ومال إليه الناس واستخفوا بقباذ وتهاونوا به. فلم يحتمل قباذ

١ أخوه: بعد هذه الكلمة بياض بقدر نصف سطر في الأصل. ٥ بنى١: "بنا" في الأصل. ‖ وبنى٢: "وبنا" في الأصل. ‖ حلوان: وضع المقريزي رمز "ح" تحت الحرف الأول إشارة إلى تلفظه بالحاء. ‖ وبنى٣: "وبنا" في الأصل.

١ من تجارب الأمم لمسكويه ١: ١٢٣.
٢ من تجارب الأمم لمسكويه ١: ١٢٣.

§ 131[359] After Balāš, there reigned his brother Qubād Tankra'y[360] b. Fīrūz. He had gone to the Ḫāqān to ask help against his brother Balāš, saying that he was better entitled to kingship than his brother. He stayed there for four years, after which the Ḫāqān prepared (an army) for him. When he was returning and had reached Nīsābūr, he heard that his brother Balāš had died. Earlier, when he had passed through, he had married there in disguise the daughter of a cavalryman and slept with her. She had become pregnant with Anūširwān. Now that Qubād returned during the time we are speaking about, he asked about the girl, and she and his son Anūširwān were brought to him. Qubād rejoiced in both of them. When he reached the boundaries of Fārs and al-Ahwāz, he built the cities of Arrağān, Ḥulwān, and a number of others. One of his good ideas and penetrating determinations was to arrest his maternal uncle Sūḫrā.

§ 132[361] The reason for this was that when these things happened between Fīrūz and the Hephthalites, Sūḫrā had been left behind to govern the royal capital in al-Madā'in. Sūḫrā collected a large army of Persians and marched after Aḫšunwār, the king of the Hephthalites, and fought against him taking on him his revenge and getting him in his power. Sūḫrā had recovered the account books of the *dīwān*, which had travelled with Fīrūz, and demanded back all that had been in Fīrūz's treasury and the treasuries of his generals and his family. He also demanded back the leading cavalrymen, who were still in the hands of Aḫšunwār. He continued making war on Aḫšunwār and tricking him and getting back what he had appropriated until he had rescued every Persian that had been in his hands and most of what he had got from Fīrūz's treasuries. He had a good reputation among Persians and the two sons of Fīrūz, I mean Balāš and Qubād. They exalted him and raised his position so high that there was only one degree between him and the king. He took care of the administration of peace with dexterity and experience and took possession of affairs, and people inclined towards him, thinking little of Qubād and disdaining him. Qubād could not bear this and wrote to

359 Miskawayh, *Tağārib al-umam*, 1:123 = C165–166; cf. al-Ṭabarī, *Ta'rīḫ*, 1:883–885 = trans., 5:128–131.

360 Cf. al-Bīrūnī, *al-Āṯār al-bāqiyah* 137 (Nīkrāy).

361 Miskawayh, *Tağārib al-umam*, 1:123 = C166–167; cf. al-Ṭabarī, *Ta'rīḫ*, 1:885 = trans., 5:131–132.

ذلك وكتب إلى سابور الرازي الذي يقال للبيت الذي هو منه مهران وكان إصبهبذ البلاد في القدوم عليه فيمن قبله من الجند. فقدم بهم سابور فواضعه قباذ قِتالَ خاله سُوخرًا وأمره فيه بأمره على لطف وكتمان شديد خفي. فغدا سابور على قباذ فوجد عنده سوخرا جالسا فمشى نحو قباذ مجاوزا له وتغفل سوخرا فلم يأبه سوخرا لأرب سابور حتى ألقى في عنقه وهقا كان معه. ثم اجتذبه فأخرجه فأوثقه واستودعه السجن.

§ 133[١] فحينئذ ضربت الفرس المثل بأن قالوا: "نقَصَت ريح سُوخرا وهبت ريح مهران." ثم قتل قباذ سوخرا وكان هذا رأيا تم على سكون ولم يضطرب فيه أمر وقدم سابور عوضا عن سوخرا وكان مما أساء فيه التدبير والرأي حتى اجتمعت كلمة موبذان موبذ وجماعة الفرس على حبسه وإزالة ملكه عنه أنه اتبع رجلا يقال له مزدك بن بامداذاي موبذ موبذان مع أصحاب له يقال لهم: العَدْلية.

§ 134[٢] قالوا: "إن الله تعالى إنما جعل الأرزاق في الأرض مبسوطة ليقسمها عباده بينهم بالتآسي ولكن الناس تظالموا." وزعموا أنهم آخِذون للفقراء من الأغنياء ويَرُدون من المكْثِرين على المقلين

---

٢ قباذ : الزيادة بخط المقريزي في الهامش الأيمن + صح، ويشير إليها رمز ⌐ بعد "فواضعه". ٧ وقدم ... سوخرا : الزيادة بخط المقريزي في آخر السطر في الهامش الأيسر من الأسفل إلى الأعلى + صح. ٩ بن ... موبذان : الزيادة بخط المقريزي في الهامش الأيمن ويشير إليها رمز ⌐ بعد "مزدك". || بامداذاي : وضع المقريزي رمز "ك" (لـ "كذا") فوق الكلمة إشارة إلى شكه في صحة قراءتها.

---

١ من تجارب الأمم لمسكويه ١: ١٢٣–١٢٤.

٢ من تجارب الأمم لمسكويه ١: ١٢٤.

Sābūr al-Rāzī, whose family was called Mihrān. Sābūr was the *iṣbahbad* of the Land,[362] and Qubād gave him orders to come to him with the soldiers he had. Sābūr came with them, and Qubād made a deal with him that he would fight against his maternal uncle Sūḫrā. He gave him orders concerning this in a most delicate manner and under the strictest secrecy. Next morning Sābūr came to Qubād and found Sūḫrā sitting with him. He went towards Qubād, passing by Sūḫrā, without taking any notice of him, and Sūḫrā paid no attention to what Sābūr was up to until Sābūr threw a rope he had with him around his neck and drew him out, chaining him and putting him into prison.

§ 133[363] It was then that the Persians coined the saying: "Sūḫrā's wind blew out, and Mihrān's wind rose."[364] Later, Qubād killed Sūḫrā. This was a decision executed in silence, and there was no confusion because of it. Qubād also raised Sābūr replacing Sūḫrā with him. Then there was an example of bad reasoning and policy, which lead the *mōbadān mōbad* and many Persians to agree on imprisoning Qubād and deposing him. This was his following a man called Mazdak[365] b. Bāmdādān, the *mōbad mōbadān*,[366] and his followers, who were called egalitarians (*al-ʿadliyyah*).

§ 134[367] The Mazdakites said that God, He is Exalted, has spread provisions on earth for His servants to divide equally between themselves, but people wrong each other. They claimed that they took from the rich and gave to the poor and to those who had little. They also said that if someone had more

---

362 For the supreme commander *Ērān iṣbahbad*, or the *iṣbahbad* of the Land, see "*ispahbadh*," in *EI*², 4:207–208.

363 Miskawayh, *Taǧārib al-umam*, 1:123–124 = C167–168; cf. al-Ṭabarī, *Taʾrīḫ*, 1:885 = trans., 5:132.

364 *Nihāyat al-arab* 295, offers what seems to be a better variant of the saying: *ḫamadat nār Sūḫrā wa-habbat rīḥ Sābūr* "Sūḫrā's fire went out, and Sābūr's wind started blowing."

365 For Mazdak, see Christensen (1936): 330–357, and Crone (1991).

366 Mazdak's father's name and the claim that Mazdak was the *mōbadān mōbad*, are not found in Miskawayh or al-Ṭabarī. Several Arabic sources, including Ḥamzah, *Taʾrīḫ* 82, claim that Mazdak was a *mōbad*, but al-Bīrūnī, *al-Āṯār al-bāqiyah* 254, is one of the few to make him a *mōbadān mōbad*. MS T reads the father's name as Madādāy. In the holograph, the last letter looks more like Y than N. In § 142, al-Maqrīzī clearly reads Bāmārd.

367 Miskawayh, *Taǧārib al-umam*, 1:124 = C168; cf. al-Ṭabarī, *Taʾrīḫ*, 1:885–886 = trans., 5:132–133.

وأنه من كان عنده فضل في المال والقوت أو النساء والأمتعة فليس هو أولى به من غيره. فاغتنم السفلة ذلك وكاتفوا مزدك وأصحابه حتى قوي أمره. فكانوا يدخلون على الرجل في داره فيغلبونه على ماله ونسائه فلا يستطيعون الامتناع منهم. وقواهم قبول الملك رأيهم ودخوله معهم. فلم يلبثوا إلا قليلا حتى صار الرجل لا يعرف أباه ولا الأب ولده ولا يملك أحد شيئا مما يتسع به. وصيروا قُباذ في مكان لا يصل إليه غيرهم فيه.

§135[1] وكان مزدك يزعم أنه يدعو إلى شريعة إبرٰهيم[⌐] عليه السلام حسب ما دعا إليه زرادشت. ووافق | زرادشت في بعض ما جاء به وزاد ونقص واستحل المحارم والمنكرات وسَوى بين الناس 163a في الأموال والأملاك والنساء والعبيد والإماء حتى لا يكون لأحد على أحد فضل في شيء البتة. فكثر أتباعه من السفلة والأغتام حتى صاروا عشرات ألوف. فكان مزدك يأخذ امرأة هذا فيسلمها لهذا وكذا في الأموال والإماء والعقار والضياع. فاستولى على الأمر وعظم شأنه حتى قال يوما للملك قباذ: "اليوم نوبتي من امرأتك أم أنوشروان." فأجابه إلى ذلك. فقام أنوشروان إليه ونزع خفيه بيديه وقبل رجليه وشفع إليه حتى لا يتعرض لأمه وله حكمه في سائر ملكه فتركها. وحرم مزدك ذبح الحيوان وقال: "يكفي في طعام الإنسان ما تنبته الأرض وما يتولد من الحيوان كالبيض واللبن والجبن والسمن." فلما عظمت البلية به على الناس اجتمعت الفرس حين رأوا فساد الملك قباذ على تمليك أخيه جاماسف الملقب مكاريق بن فيروز.

---

٦ حسب ... زرادشت: الزيادة بخط المقريزي في الهامش الأيسر من الأسفل إلى الأعلى + صح، ويشير إليها رمز ⌐ بعد "السلام". ١٣ مزدك: الزيادة بخط المقريزي في آخر السطر في الهامش الأيسر. ١٥ الملقب مكاريق: الزيادة بخط المقريزي في آخر السطر في الهامش الأيسر.

---

١ من الكامل لابن الأثير ١: ٤١٣ ومن تجارب الأمم لمسكويه ١: ١٢٤.

property and provisions, women and goods than he needed, he had no more right to that (surplus) than anybody else. Lowly people used the opportunity and supported Mazdak and his followers, so that he grew strong. They would force their way into a man's house and take his property and women, and he could not defend himself against them. They were strengthened by the king accepting their doctrines and entering their group. Soon a man did no more know who his father was nor the father who his son was and no one owned anything that would have made his life comfortable. They moved Qubād into a place where no one except they had an access.

§135[368] Mazdak claimed that he called people to the religion of Abraham, peace be upon him, like Zarathustra had done.[369] He agreed with Zarathustra in some of his teachings, but added things and took others away, made permissible what had been forbidden or censured, and made people equal in money, property, women, slaves, and slave girls, so that no one would have more of anything than anyone else. He got many followers from among the lower classes and riffraff until they numbered in tens of thousands. Mazdak took the wife of one man and gave her to another and the same with money, slave girls, immovables, and villages. He started running the affairs and his importance grew until one day he said to king Qubād: "Today is my turn with your wife, the mother of Anūširwān." Qubād accepted this, but Anūširwān rose, took the slippers off Mazdak's feet with his own hands, kissed his feet, and pleaded that he would not interfere with his mother; otherwise, he could have his say in all the rest of the kingdom. Mazdak did leave her in peace. Mazdak forbade the slaughter of animals and said: "It is enough for a human being to eat of what the earth grows and what is produced by animals, such as eggs, milk, cheese, and butter." When people suffered more and more because of him and saw the corruption of King Qubād, the Persians decided to transfer kingship to his brother Ǧāmāsf, whose cognomen was Makārīq,[370] b. Fīrūz.

368 Ibn al-Aṯīr, *Kāmil*, 1:413; Miskawayh, *Taǧārib al-umam*, 1:124 = C 168 (last sentence); cf. Ibn al-Aṯīr, *Kāmil*, 1:434.

369 This is probably a confusion between Zarathustra, the founder of Zoroastrianism, and the second Zarathustra, for whom, see Crone (1991): 7–18, and cf. §142. The first Zarathustra is occasionally linked to Abraham and sometimes even equated with him, see, e.g., Asadī Ṭūsī, *Garšāspnāmah*, p. 385 (v. 50).

370 Cf. al-Bīrūnī, *al-Āṯār al-bāqiyah* 137 (Nigārīn).

§136[1] وقد حكي أيضا أن المزدكية هم الذين أجلسوا جاماسف ليكون الملك من قبلهم لا منة لغيرهم عليه إلا أن الحكاية الأولى أشبه بالحق. ولم يَعُدوا جاماسف ملكا لأنه أقيم في أيام فتنة مزدك. وذلك أنه لما مضى عشر سنين من ملك قباذ اجتمع موبذان موبذ والعظماء وخلعوه وقالوا له: "إنك قد أثمت باتباعك مزدك وما عمله أصحابه بالناس وليس ينجيك إلا إباحة نفسك وأزواجك." وأرادوه على أن يُسَلم نفسه اليهم ليذبحوه ويقربوه للنار. فامتنع من ذلك فحبسوه وتركوه لا يصل إليه أحد. وخرج زرمهر بن سوخرا فقتل من المزدكية خلقا وأعاد قباذ إلى ملكه وأزال أخاه جاماسف.

§137[2] وقيل: بل تحيلت أخت قباذ فتمت لها الحيلة حتى أخرجت قباذ من الحبس. وذلك أنها أتت الحبس الذي فيه قباذ وحاولت الدخول إليه فمنعها الموكل به وطمع أن يفضحها بذلك السبب وأعلمها بذلك وراودها عن نفسها. فأطمعته بأنها غير مخالفة له في شيء مما يهواه منها. فأذن لها حتى دخلت وأقامت عند قباذ يوما. ثم أمرت فلف قباذ في بساط وحمل على عاتق غلام قوي ضابط كان معه في | الحبس. فلما مر الغلام بوالي الحبس سأله عما يحمله فاضطرب. فلحقته أخت قباذ 163b
وأخبرته أنه فراش حيضتها وأنها إنما خرجت لتتطهر وتنصرف فصدقها ولم يمس البساط ولم يدن منه استقذارا له على مذهبهم. وخلى عن الغلام الحامل لقباذ فمضى به وخرجت في أثره وهرب قباذ فلحق بأرض الهياطلة ليستمد ملكها فيحارب من خالفه. فيقال إنه في مسيره هذا نزل بإيرشهر

٢-٣ ولم ... مزدك: الزيادة بخط المقريزي في الهامش الأيمن من الأعلى إلى الأسفل + صح، ويشير إليها رمز ⌐ بعد "بالحق". ٢ في أيام: كشط المقريزي عبارة أخرى قبل أن يصححها كما هي الآن.

١ من تجارب الأمم لمسكويه ١: ١٢٤ ومن تأريخ الطبري ١: ٨٨٥-٨٨٦.

٢ من تجارب الأمم لمسكويه ١: ١٢٤-١٢٥ ومن تأريخ سني الملوك لحمزة ص ١٤، ٢٥.

§ 136[371] It is also related that the Mazdakites were the ones who set Ǧāmāsf on the throne, so that he would owe his kingship to them and no one else. The first version, however, is more probably true. They (Persian historians) do not count Ǧāmāsf as king because he was proclaimed king during the rebellion of Mazdak. When ten years had passed of the reign of Qubād, the *mōbadān mōbad* and the noblemen decided to depose Qubād, saying to him: "You have sinned by following Mazdak and what his companions have done to people. Nothing will now save you except that you give yourself and your women up." They wanted him to give himself up so that they could slaughter him and offer him to fire. Qubād refused to do so, so they imprisoned him and left him so that no one had access to him. Zarmihr b. Sūḫrā rebelled and killed many of the Mazdakites before returning Qubād on the throne and deposing his brother Ǧāmāsf.

§ 137[372] It is also said that Qubād's sister came up with a ruse, with which she managed to get Qubād out of prison. She came to the prison Qubād was in and tried to gain access to him. The warden prevented her and wanted to violate her. He told her as much and tried to seduce her. She fed his desire, implying that she would surrender herself willingly to everything he wanted from her. So he let her enter the prison, and she stayed the day with Qubād. Then she gave an order (to Qubād's servant) to wrap Qubād in a rug. This was carried on his shoulder by a strong and powerful servant, who was with him in the prison. When the servant walked past the prison warden, the warden asked what he was carrying. The servant got confused, but Qubād's sister hastened to tell him that it was her menstrual bed and that she was just going away to cleanse herself and she would be back. The warden believed her and did not touch the rug or come close to it because in their religion menstruation is considered impure. So he let the servant go, and the latter carried Qubād away, and she followed him. Qubād escaped to the land of the Hephthalites, seeking help from their king and fighting against those who opposed him. It is said that during this journey Qubād alighted in Abaršahr[373] and

371 Miskawayh, *Taǧārib al-umam*, 1:124 = C168–169 (beginning); al-Ṭabarī, *Taʾrīḫ*, 1:885–886 = trans., 5:132–134.

372 Miskawayh, *Taǧārib al-umam*, 1:124–125 = C169–170; Ḥamzah, *Taʾrīḫ* 14, 25 = trans. 34, 44; cf. al-Ṭabarī, *Taʾrīḫ*, 1:886–888 = trans., 5:135–139. Ḥamzah, *Taʾrīḫ* 20 = trans. 38, also mentions 68 or 43 years.

373 In the holograph, this looks more like Īršahr, which is also how Ḥamzah reads it, but cf. al-Ṭabarī. MS T leaves the letter B/Y undotted.

على رجل من عظمائها فتزوج بابنة له مُعْصِر وإنها أم كسرى أنوشروان وإن نكاحه لأم أنوشروان في سفره هذا كان. ثم إن قباذ رجع من سفره هذا بابنه أنوشروان وغلب على أخيه جاماسف بعد أن ملك أخوه ست سنين. ثم غزا الروم وافتتح آمد {وبنى} مدنا وملك ابنه كسرى أنوشروان وأعطاه خاتمه ثم هلك. فكان ملكه بسني ملك أخيه جاماسف ثلاثا وأربعين سنة وقيل: إحدى واربعين سنة.

§138[1] ويقال إن الخزر خرجت في أيامه وأغارت على بلاده فبلغت الدينور. فوجه قائدا من عظماء قواده في اثني عشر ألفا فوطئ بلاد أران وفتح ما بين النهر المعروف بأرش إلى شروان. ثم إن قباذ لحق به وبنى مدينة البيلقان ومدينة بردعة ونفا الخزر. ثم {بنى} سُدا فيما بين أرض شروان وباب ⟨اللان⟩ {وبنى} على السد مدنا كثيرة خربت بعد بناء باب الأبواب.

§139[2] وكان سبب هلاكه سوء رأيه وفساد عقيدته وضعف ملكه. وذلك أنه لما {التقى} الحٰرث ابن عمرو بن حُجْر الكندي والنعمٰن بن المنذر بن امرئ القيس قتله وأفلت المنذر بن النعمٰن الأكبر. وملك الحٰرث بن عمرو ما ⟨كان⟩ يملك النعمٰن. فبعث قباذ بن فيروز إلى الحٰرث بن عمرو الكندي أنه: "قد كان بيننا وبين الملك الذي كان قبلك عهد. وإني أحب لقاءك." وكان قباذ زنديقا يظهر الخير ويكره سفك الدماء ويداري أعداءه فيما يكره. وكثرت الأهواء في زمانه واستضعفه الناس حتى وهى ملكه ومرج أهل فارس بانتشار الزندقة فيهم. فخرج إليه الحٰرث بن عمرو في عدد وعدة

٣ وبنى: "وبنا" في الأصل. ٤–٦ إحدى ... ويقال: الزيادة بخط المقريزي في آخر السطر في الهامش الأيسر من الأسفل إلى الأعلى + صح. ٨ بنى[٢]: "بنا" في الأصل. ٩ اللان: بياض في الأصل بقدر كلمة والزيادة من الكامل لابن الأثير. ‖ وبنى: "وبنا" في الأصل. ١٠ التقى: "التقا" في الأصل. ١٢ كان: ساقط في الأصل والزيادة يقتضيها السياق. ١٥ حتى ... فيهم: الزيادة بخط المقريزي في الهامش الأيسر من الأسفل إلى الأعلى + صح، ويشير إليها رمز ⌐ بعد "الناس".

١ من الكامل لابن الأثير ١: ٤١٤.

٢ من تجارب الأمم لمسكويه ١: ١٢٥.

was hosted by one of its noblemen. Qubād married a pubescent daughter of his, and she became the mother of Kisrá Anūširwān and it was on this journey that Qubād married her. Then Qubād returned from this journey with his son Anūširwān and vanquished his brother Ǧāmāsf after the latter had ruled for six years. Then Qubād raided the Byzantines, conquered Āmid, and built several cities. He appointed his son Kisrá Anūširwān as king, gave him his signet ring, and died. Including the years of his brother Ǧāmāsf's reign, his reign lasted for 43 years or, according to others, 41 years.

§138[374] It is said that the Ḫazars rebelled during Qubād's reign and raided his country up to al-Dīnawar. Qubād sent one of his great generals with 12,000 men, and the general subjected the country of Arrān and conquered the area from the river known as Ariš[375] until Širwān. Then Qubād joined him and built the city of al-Baylaqān and the city of Barda'ah. He drove (*nafā*)[376] the Ḫazars away and built a wall between the land of Širwān and Bāb (Allān).[377] Opposite the wall, he built several cities, which later fell in ruin after Bāb al-Abwāb had been built.

§139[378] The reason why Qubād perished was his bad reasoning, corrupt doctrines, and weakness of rule. This was as follows: When al-Ḥāriṯ b. 'Amr b. Ḥuǧr al-Kindī and al-Nu'mān b. al-Munḏir b. Imri' al-Qays met, al-Ḥāriṯ killed al-Nu'mān, but al-Munḏir b. al-Nu'mān al-Akbar escaped. Al-Ḥāriṯ b. 'Amr now ruled what al-Nu'mān had ruled. Qubād b. Fīrūz sent to al-Ḥāriṯ b. 'Amr al-Kindī a message, saying: "I had an agreement with the king before you. Now, I would like to meet you." Qubād was Manichaean (*zindīq*)[379] and showed goodness and disliked shedding blood. He treated enemies gently when these did something he disliked. There were, at his time, numerous heresies, and people considered him weak so that his kingdom was weakened, and the people of Fārs grew restless with Manichaeism spreading among them. Al-Ḥāriṯ b. 'Amr came with a number of men in arms to meet

374 Ibn al-Aṯīr, *Kāmil*, 1:414.
375 Ibn al-Aṯīr reads al-Rass.
376 Ibn al-Aṯīr reads *wa-baqiya*, which is probably wrong.
377 Left blank in both manuscripts. The addition is from Ibn al-Aṯīr.
378 Miskawayh, *Taǧārib al-umam*, 1:125 = C170–171; cf. al-Ṭabarī, *Ta'rīḫ*, 1:888–889 = trans., 5:139–140.
379 As the previous paragraphs have shown, Qubād followed Mazdak rather than Mani, but the term *zindīq* is vague, covering Manichaeans, Mazdakites, and other heresies. In translation, I follow the most common meaning of the word.

حتى التقيا. فأمر قباذ بطبق من تمر فنزع نواه وأمر بطبق آخر فجعل فيه | تمر بنواه. ثم وضعا بين 164a أيديهما وجعل الذي فيه النوا بين يدي الحٰرث بن عمرو والذي لا نوى فيه بين يدي الملك قباذ. وكان الحٰرث يأكل التمر ويلقي {النوى} والملك يأكل التمر ولا يحتاج إلى إلقاء النوى فقال للحٰرث: "ما لك لا تأكل كما آكل؟" فقال الحٰرث: "إنما يأكل {النوى} إبلنا وغنمنا." وعلم أن قباذ يهزأ به. ثم افترقا على الصلح وعلى أن لا يتجاوز الحٰرث وأصحابه الفرات.

§140[1] إلا أن الحٰرث استضعفه وطمع فيه فأمر أصحابه أن يَعْبُروا الفرات ويغيروا في السواد. فأتى الصريخ قباذ وهو بالمدائن فأرسل إلى الحٰرث بن عمرو أن لصوصا من العرب قد أغاروا على السواد وأنه يحب لقاءه. فلقيه فقال قباذ كالعاتب: "لقد صنعت صنعا ما صنعه أحد قبلك." فطمع الحٰرث في لين كلامه فقال: "ما علمت ولا شعرت ولا أستطيع ضبط لصوص العرب وما كُل العرب تحت طاعتي وما أتمكن منهم إلا بالمال والجنود." فقال له قباذ: "فما الذي تريد؟" قال: "أريد أن تطعمني من السواد ما أتخذ به سلاحا." فأمر له بما يلي جانب العرب من أسفل الفرات وهي ستة طسَاسِيج.

§140a | وكانت أرض فارس في قديم الأيام مقاسمات. فلما كانت أيام قباذ أبي كسرى 163b أنوشروان نزل من تعب ناله في بستان منفردا بنفسه. فإذا بامرأة وبين يديها صغيرة. فأضافته المرأة وصارت الصغيرة تمد يدها إلى شجرة رمان والعجوز تمنعها. فغلبت على أمر العجوز وقطعت رمانة فضربتها العجوز ضربا مبرحا. فقال قباذ: "لم ضربت هذه الصغيرة على هذا القدر الطفيف الخسيس

٣ النوى١ : "النوا" في الأصل. ٤ النوى : "النوا" في الأصل. ١٣–7.194 وكانت ... البيادر : كتب المقريزي هذا الفصل على ورقة صغيرة.

١ من تجارب الأمم لمسكويه ١: ١٢٥.

him. When they met, Qubād gave orders for a plate of dates to be brought with their pits removed. Then he gave orders for another plate to be brought, containing dates with their pits. These plates were then set before them, the one of dates with pits in front of al-Ḥāriṯ b. ʿAmr and the one without in front of the king. Al-Ḥāriṯ ate dates and threw their pits away, while the king ate but had no pits to throw away. Then he said to al-Ḥāriṯ: "What's the matter with you? Why don't you eat like me?" Al-Ḥāriṯ replied: "Camels and sheep eat the pits where we come from." He understood that Qubād was jesting with him. Then they separated in peace on the condition that al-Ḥāriṯ and his companions would not cross the Euphrates.

§ 140[380] Al-Ḥāriṯ, however, thought Qubād weak and became covetous of him. He ordered his companions to cross the Euphrates and raid the Sawād. Qubād heard the cries of people when he was in al-Madāʾin and sent a word to al-Ḥāriṯ b. ʿAmr saying that Arab robbers had raided the Sawād and that he wanted to meet him. When they met, Qubād rebuked him: "You have done a deed no one has done before." Al-Ḥāriṯ grew covetous because of Qubād's soft words and replied: "I did not know nor did I realise this. I cannot hold in order all Arab robbers because not all Arabs obey me and I cannot cope with them except by money and arms." Qubād asked what he wanted, and he said: "I want you to provide for me from the wealth of the Sawād, so that I can buy weapons." Qubād gave him the area at the lower Euphrates closest to the Arabs, which formed six administrative districts (*ṭassūǧ*).

§ 140a[381] In ancient times, the lands of Fārs were (considered as) partnerships (between the king and the landowner). During the time of Qubad, father of Kisrá Anūširwān, the king once alighted in a garden to rest, being all alone. There he saw a woman with a little girl. The woman offered him hospitality, and the little one kept stretching her hand towards a pomegranate tree and the old woman was telling her off. Despite this, the little one was able to pick a pomegranate, and the old woman started beating her severely. Qubād asked her: "Why do you beat the girl for this insignificant and little

380 Miskawayh, *Taǧārib al-umam*, 1:125 = C171–172; cf. al-Ṭabarī, *Taʾrīḫ*, 1:889 = trans., 5:140–141.

381 On a separate slip of paper. MS T includes the text of § 140a, inserted there at the end of § 140, before the final words of that paragraph (*wa-hiya sittat ṭasāsīǧ*).

من رمانة؟" فقالت: "يا سيدي لنا فيها شريك وفي جميع الباغ شريك غائب ويقبح بالشريك الحاضر خيانة الشريك الغائب سيما إذا كان عدلا أمينا." فقال قباذ: "ومن شريكك؟" قالت: "الملك قباذ. له فيها بحق القسمة نصيب ويقبح بالفقير ذي المروءة خيانة الغني ذي العدالة والأمانة." فبكى قباذ وقال: "صدقت. وأقبح منه أن يكون الملك الغني العدل الأمين الذي هو أعدل وقد سلطه الله وملكه ومكنه وأقدره في عباده وبلاده أن لا يساعدك على أمانتك." ثم لحق بعسكره وجمع جيشه إلى مجلسه وأخبرهم خبر العجوز ولم يرم حتى جعل أرض فارس مقاطعات بخراج يؤخذ من الناس إذا حازوا ما في البيادر.

164a §141[1] | فأرسل الحٰرث بن عمرو الكندي إلى تبع وهو باليمن: "إني قد طمعت في ملك الأعاجم وقد أخذت منه ستة طسَاسيج. فاجمع الجنود وأقبل فإنه ليس دون مُلكهم شيء لأن الملك عليهم لا يأكل اللحم ولا يستحل هراقة الدماء. وله دين يمنعه من ضبط الملك فبادر بعدتك وجندك." فجمع تبع الجنود وسار حتى نزل الحيرة وقرب من الفرات فآذاه البق. فأمر الحٰرث بن عمرو أن يشق له نهرا إلى النجف ففعل وهو نهر الحِيْرة. فنزل عليه ووجه ابن أخيه شمرا ذا الجناح إلى قباذ فقاتله. فهزمه شمر حتى لحق بالري. ثم أدركه بها فقتله. وكان شعار قباذ على لون السماء موشحا بالبياض والسواد وسراويله حمراء وتاجه أخضر يعتمد على سيفه وهو على السرير. وملك بعده ابنه كسرى أنوشروان. ويقال إنه كان يجبى لقباذ السواد دون سائر أعماله وما كان تحت يده وسلطانه مائة ألف ألف وخمسين ألف ألف مثقال.

---

١ شريك: الزيادة بخط المقريزي في الهامش الأيمن من الأسفل إلى الأعلى + صح، ويشير إليها رمز ⌐ بعد "فيها". ٧ حازوا: وضع المقريزي رمز "ح" تحت الحرف الأول إشارة إلى تلفظه بالحاء. ١٥-١٦ دون ... مثقال: الزيادة بخط المقريزي في آخر السطر في الهامش الأيسر، آخرها من الأعلى إلى الأسفل.

---

١ الباغ: أضاف المقريزي الحاشية التالية في الهامش الأيسر من الأسفل إلى الأعلى "الباغ البستان بالفارسية".

---

١ من تجارب الأمم لمسكويه ١: ١٢٦ ومن تأريخ سني الملوك لحمزة ص ٤٤.

matter of one pomegranate?" She replied: "Dear Sir, we have a partner in this pomegranate and the whole *bāġ*, an absent partner. It is wrong for the present partner to deceive the absent partner, especially if he is just and reliable." Qubād asked: "And who is your partner?" She replied: "King Qubād. He has the right to a share because of partnership. It would be ugly for a virtuous poor to deceive a rich man, who is just and reliable." Qubād burst in tears and said: "You have said the truth, and even uglier it would be if the rich, just, and reliable king, who is more just (than you) and whom God has made king and given power to, and whose position He has strengthened, putting him in charge of His servants and His country, that this king would not help you in keeping your tryst." Then he returned to his camp and collected his army into his audience hall and told them the story of the old woman. He did not leave his place before he had divided the country of Fārs in shares with the tax collected from people when they had received theirs from the threshing floor.

§ 141[382] Al-Ḥāriṯ b. ʿAmr al-Kindī sent a word to the Tubbaʿ, who was in Yemen: "I have become covetous of the kingdom of the Persians (*al-Aʿāǧim*). I have already taken six *ṭassūǧs* from them. Collect your army and come, as there is nothing to protect their kingdom because their king does not eat meat and does not allow shedding blood. He professes a religion which makes it impossible for him to retain his kingdom. Make haste with your army!" The Tubbaʿ collected his armies and marched to al-Ḥīrah close to the Euphrates. There he was pestered by midges. He ordered al-Ḥāriṯ b. ʿAmr to dig a canal for him until al-Naǧaf. This was done, and this is the canal of al-Ḥīrah. The Tubbaʿ encamped there and sent his nephew Šamir Ḏū l-Ǧanāḥ against Qubād, and they fought with each other. Šamir put Qubād to flight, and he fled to Rayy, where Šamir caught and killed him. Qubād's vest was sky-blue with black and white stripes, his trousers red, and his crown green. Enthroned, he leaned on his sword. After him, there reigned his son Kisrá Anūširwān. It is said that of all the dominions under his rule the Sawād alone brought him 150,000 *miṯqāls* in taxes.

---

2 *bāġ* : *al-Bāġ* means "garden" in Persian (marginal gloss in al-Maqrīzī's hand).

---

382 Miskawayh, *Taǧārib al-umam*, 1:126 = C172–173; Ḥamzah, *Taʾrīḫ* 44 = trans. 70; cf. al-Ṭabarī, *Taʾrīḫ*, 1:889–890 = trans., 5:141–142.

§141a[١] هذا وهم لأن قباذ هذا هو والد كسرى أنوشروان الذي ولد رسول الله في أيامه والتبابعة انقطع ملكهم قبل تمزق أهل اليمن من مأرب بدهر وتمزق أهل اليمن كان قبل الإسلام {بثماني} مائة سنة أو أكثر. وكذلك الحٰرث بن عمرو إنما ملك بعد المنذر والمنذر من بني نصر وبنو نصر إنما خرجوا من اليمن في وقت التمزق. ولعل قباذ صاحب تبع إنما هو قباذ أحد ملوك الطوائف أو هو كيقباذ أول الملوك الكيانية.

164b §142[٢] | كسرى أنوشروان بن قباذ بن فيروز بن يزدجرد بن بهرام جور بن يزدجرد الأثيم بن بهرام ابن سابور بن سابور ذي الأكتاف بن هرمز بن نرسي بن بهرام بن بهرام شاه بن هرمز بن سابور بن سابور الجنود بن أردشير بن بابك. ويلقب بالعادل. ولما لبس التاج خطب الناس فحمد الله وأثنى عليه وذكر ما ابتلي به الناس من فساد أمورهم ودينهم وأولادهم ووعدهم أنه يصلح ذلك. فاستقبل الأمر بجد وسياسة وحزم وكان جيد الرأي كثير النظر صائب التدبير طويل الفكر ويستشير مع ذلك. فجدد سيرة أردشير بن بابك ونظر في عهده وأخذ نفسه به وأدب رعيته وبطانته وبحث عن سياسات الأمم واستصلح لنفسه منها ما رضيه. ونظر في تدبير أسلافه المستحسنة فاقتدى بها. فكان أول ما بدأ به أن أبطل ملة زرادشت الثاني الذي كان من أهل فسا وكان ممن دعا الناس إليها مزدك بن بامارد. وكان مما أمر به الناس وزينه لهم وحثهم عليه التأسي في أموالهم وأهاليهم.

١–٥ هذا ... الكيانية : أول الفصل في الهامش الأيمن من الأسفل إلى الأعلى وآخره في الهامش الأعلى من الأسفل إلى الأعلى. ١ كسرى : وضع المقريزي ثلاث نقط تحت الحرف الثاني إشارة إلى تلفظه بالسين. ٢ بثماني : "بثمان" في الأصل. ٨–٩ ولما ... ذلك : الزيادة بخط المقريزي، أولها في الهامش الأيسر من الأسفل إلى الأعلى وآخرها في الهامش الأعلى من الأعلى إلى الأسفل. ١٤ بامارد : وضع المقريزي رمز "ك" (لـ "كذا") فوق الكلمة إشارة إلى شكه في صحة قراءتها.

---

١ راجع الكامل لابن الأثير ١: ٤٢٢.

٢ من تجارب الأمم لمسكويه ١: ١٢٧–١٢٨.

§ 141a[383] This is a mistake. This Qubād is the father of Kisrá Anūširwān, during whose reign the Messenger of God was born, whereas the rule of the Tubbaʿs ended a long time before the dispersal of the people of Yemen from Maʾrib. The dispersal of the people of Yemen was 800 or more years before Islam. Moreover, al-Ḥāriṯ b. ʿAmr ruled after al-Munḏir, who belonged to Banū Naṣr, and Banū Naṣr left Yemen at the time of the dispersal. Perhaps the Qubād, contemporary of the Tubbaʿ, was Qubād, one of the Petty Kings, or Kay Qubād, the first of the Kayanian kings.

§ 142[384] Kisrá Anūširwān b. Qubād b. Fīrūz b. Yazdağird b. Bahrām Gūr b. Yazdağird the Sinner b. Bahrām b. Sābūr b. Sābūr of Shoulders b. Hurmuz b. Narsī b. Bahrām b. Bahrāmšāh b. Hurmuz b. Sābūr b. Sābūr of the Armies b. Ardašīr b. Bābak. He was called the Righteous.[385] When he was crowned, he spoke to people. First, he praised and glorified God and mentioned how people had suffered from the corruption of their affairs, religion, and children and promised that he would put things right again. He started ruling with diligence,[386] good governance, and determination. He was discerning and considered matters carefully, he governed well, pondered long on matters, and, despite this, also asked advice from others. He revived the ways of Ardašīr b. Bābak and perused his *Testament*, following it and educating his subjects and his confidants. He studied the ways of governing among other nations and adopted for himself what he deemed good. He looked at how those of his ancestors had ruled whom he thought good and followed their example. He started by suppressing the religion of the second Zarathustra, who was from Fasā.[387] One of those who called people to this religion was Mazdak b. Bāmārd.[388] He, for example, ordered people to share both wealth and women,[389] made them think this was good, and urged them to do so.

---

383 Ibn al-Aṯīr, *Kāmil*, 1:422. Given as a marginal note on fol. 164ᵃ and referring to the mention of the Tubbaʿ in § 141.

384 Miskawayh, *Taǧārib al-umam*, 1:127–128 = C176–177; cf. al-Ṭabarī, *Taʾrīḫ*, 1:893 = trans., 5:148.

385 Cf. al-Bīrūnī, *al-Āṯār al-bāqiyah* 138.

386 Miskawayh (ed. Caetani) explicitly vocalises *bi-ǧidd*.

387 See § 135, note 369.

388 Al-Ṭabarī reads Bāmdād, Miskawayh (ed. Caetani) Qāmārd. Cf. § 133.

389 Literally, "family," but here this seems to refer to womenfolk, even though Mazdak was rumoured to have abolished paternity, too.

§143[1] وذكر أن ذلك من البر الذي يرضاه الله تعالى ويثيب عليه أحسن الثواب وأنه لو لم يكن من الدين لكان مكرمة في الفعال ورضًا في التفاوُض. فحض السفلة بذلك على الأشراف واختلط أجناس اللُؤَماء بعناصر الكرماء وسهل سبيل الظلمة إلى الظلم والعُهّار إلى قضاء نهمتهم وإلى الوصول إلى الكرائم فشمل الناس بلاء عظيم. فلما أبطل الملك أنوشروان ملة هذين قتل عليه بشرا كثيرا وسفك من الدماء ما لا يحصى كثرة ممن كان لا ينتهي حتى قيل إنه قتل منهم في ضحوة نهار مائة ألف إنسان. وقتل قوما من المانَوِيَّة وثبَّت ملة المجوسية القديمة. وكتب في ذلك كتبا بليغة إلى أصحاب الولايات والإصْبَهْبَذين.

§144[2] وقوى الملك بعد ضعفه بإدامة النظر وهَجْر الملاذ وترك اللهو إلا في أوقات يسيرة حتى نظم أموره. وقوى جنوده بالأسلحة والكراع وعمر البلاد وحفظ الأموال وفرق منها ما لا يسع حِفْظه من الأَرْزَاق والصِلَات الموضوعة مواضعها وسد الثغور ورد كثيرا من | الأطراف التي غلب عليها 165a الأمم بعلل وأسباب شتى منها السِنْد والرخج وزابلستان وطخارستان ودورستان وغيرها. وقتل أمةً يقال لها: البافرز. واستبقى منهم من فرقهم واستعبدهم واستعان بهم في حروبه. وأُسِرَتْ له أمة أخرى يقال لهم: صُوْل. وقُدِم بهم عليه فقتلهم واستبقى ثمانين رجلا من كُمَاتهم. وعمل أعمالا عظيمة منها بنيانه الحصون والآطام والمعاقل لأهل بلاده لتكون حرزا لهم يلجؤون إليها من عدو إن دهمهم.

٤ أنوشروان: زاد المقريزي الحروف الثلاثة الأولى في الهامش الأيسر من الأسفل إلى الأعلى + صح، ويشير إليها رمز ⌐ بعد "الملك".

١ من تجارب الأمم لمسكويه ١: ١٢٨.

٢ من تجارب الأمم لمسكويه ١: ١٢٨.

§ 143[390] Mazdak said that all this was part of the piety which God, He is Exalted, liked and for which He would give a most beautiful reward and that even if this were not a religious obligation it would still be a noble thing to do and something that could be negotiated to everybody's satisfaction. With this, he urged lowly people against nobles. Various reprehensible people got thus mixed up with the noblest. He made it easy for wrong-doers to do wrong and for adulterers to satisfy their cravings and get at noble ladies. People suffered greatly from this. King Anūširwān suppressed the religion of these two and killed numerous people because of this and shed immeasurable quantities of blood of those who refused to give their religion up. It is said that in a single morning he killed 100,000 people. He also killed some Manichaeans and made the religion of ancient Magianism firmly established. He wrote eloquent letters about this to governors and *iṣbahbads*.[391]

§ 144[392] By constant consideration and avoidance of pleasures and entertainment, except at given times, Anūširwān strengthened kingship after it had been weak. He put his affairs in order and strengthened his armies with weapons and mounts. He made the country flourish and took good care of (state) property. What could not be kept in store he distributed as salaries and gifts in a proper way. He put the frontiers in order and in various ways won back many regions that other peoples had conquered, such as al-Sind, al-Ruḫḫaǧ, Zābulistān, Ṭuḫāristān, Dardistān,[393] and others. He killed a people called al-Bāfirz,[394] leaving alive only those he resettled (in various parts of the kingdom),[395] enslaving them and using them as auxiliaries in his wars. Another nation was made his prisoners, called Ṣūl. They were brought to him and he killed them all, leaving alive only 80 of their most valiant warriors. He completed mighty feats, including the building of fortresses, fortifications, and strongholds for his people to protect them, so that they could seek refuge in them if the enemy were suddenly to attack.

390 Miskawayh, *Taǧārib al-umam*, 1:128 = C177; cf. al-Ṭabarī, *Taʾrīḫ*, 1:893 = trans., 5:148.

391 Cf. the *Tansarnāmah*, for which, see above, note 35. Often this work is seen as deriving from Kisrá Anūširwān's time.

392 Miskawayh, *Taǧārib al-umam*, 1:128 = C177–178; cf. al-Ṭabarī, *Taʾrīḫ*, 1:894 = trans., 5:150–151.

393 In both manuscripts Dūristān, while Miskawayh reads Darwistān. Note that MS T has been misbound. Its fol. 93[b] ends in § 139 and the text continues on fol. 95[a–b], before coming back to fol. 94[a–b].

394 Al-Ṭabarī reads al-Bāriz.

395 The bracketed words come from al-Ṭabarī.

§ 145[1] فكان من ثمرة هذه الأعمال أن خاقان واسمه سنحبوا كان في ذلك الوقت أمنع التُرْك وأشجعهم وهو الذي قاتل وَرْز ملك الهياطلة غير هائب كثرة الهياطلة ومَنَعَتهم وبأسَهُم. فقتل وَرْزَ وعامةَ جنده وغنم أموالهم واحتوى على بلادهم إلا ما كان كسرى غلب منها. وأقبل في جموعه مع أمم استمالهم وهم أبْجَر وبنجر وبلنجر وبلغت عدة الجميع مائة ألف وعشرة آلاف مقاتل أنجاد. فأرسل إلى كسرى يتوعده ويطلب منه أموالا وأنه إن لم يُعَجِل بالبعثة إليه بما سأله وَطئ بلاده وناجزه. فلم يحفل كسرى به ولم يجبه إلى ما سأل لتحصينه نواحيه لا سيما ناحية صُوْل التى أقبل منها خاقان ولِمَنَاعَة السُبُل والفجاج ولمعرفته بمقدرته على ضبط ثغر أرمينية. فأقدم خاقان على ناحية صول من نواحي جرجان فرأى من الحصون والرجال الذين أعدهم كسرى ما لا حيلة له فيه فانصرف خائبا.

§ 146[2] وأما تدبيره للمزدكية فإنه ضرب أعناق رؤسائهم وقسم أموالهم في أهل الحاجة وقتل جماعة كثيرة ممن دخل على الناس في أموالهم وأهاليهم ممن عُرف ورد الأموال إلى أربابها. وأمر بكل مولود اختلف فيه أن يلحق بمن هو في سِيْما ذلك منهم إذا لم يعرف أبوه وأن يُعطَى نصيبا من مال الرجل الذي يُسنَد إليه إن قبِله الرجل وبكل امرأة غُلِبَت على نفسها أن يؤخذ الغالب لها حتى يغرم لها مهرها ويُرضي | أهلها. ثم تُخير المرأة بين الإقامة عنده وبين تزويج غيره إلا أن 165b
يكون لها زوج أول فترد إليه. وأمر بكل من كان أضَرّ برجل في ماله أو ركب أحدا بمظلمة أن

١ سنحبوا: النون غير معجمة ووضع المقريزي فوق الكلمة رمز "ك" (لـ"كذا") إشارة إلى شكه في صحة قراءتها.
٥ إن: الزيادة بخط المقريزي في الهامش الأيمن من الأعلى إلى الأسفل + صح، ويشير إليها رمز ⌜ بعد "وأنه".
٦ يحفل: وضع المقريزي رمز "ح" تحت الحرف الثاني إشارة إلى تلفظه بالحاء.

١ من تجارب الأمم لمسكويه ١: ١٢٨.
٢ من تجارب الأمم لمسكويه ١: ١٢٩.

§ 145[396] One of the fruits of these labours was the following: The Ḫāqān, whose name was Sinḥibū,[397] was at that time the strongest and the most courageous of the Turks—he was the one who had fought Warz, the king of the Hephthalites, without being afraid of the number of the Hephthalites and their strength and power. Sinḥibū killed Warz and most of his army and looted their properties and took over their country, except for what Kisrá had conquered. Then Sinḥibū advanced with his armies and the peoples he had won over to his side—the Abǧar, Banǧar, and Balanǧar—so that the number of all his troops went up to 110,000 brave soldiers. He sent a word to Kisrá, threatening him and demanding money, and said that if Kisrá would not speedily send him what he demanded he would invade his country and fight him. Kisrá was not frightened by this and did not do what he demanded, because he had fortified his borders, especially the border of Ṣūl, from which direction the Ḫāqān was approaching. He also trusted in the inaccessibility of the roads and mountain paths and knew that he would be able to keep the frontier of Armenia. The Ḫāqān approached from the direction of Ṣūl in Ǧurǧān and saw the fortresses and the men Kisrá had equipped. Seeing that he could do nothing there he turned away disappointed.

§ 146[398] This is how Anūširwān dealt with the Mazdakites: He executed their leaders and gave their property to those in need. He killed great numbers of those who had taken other people's property or their women, of those who were known, and returned the properties to their rightful owners. He gave orders that every child, about whose (father) there was no clarity, was to be attached to him in whose family he was,[399] and the child should be given a share in the property of the man in whose care he was, if that man accepted him. In the case of every woman who had been forcibly taken, his taker was to pay her bridal money to her and satisfy her family, after which the woman was given the choice of staying with him or marrying another, except when she had an earlier husband, in which case she was returned to him. Kisrá gave orders that everyone who had harmed someone by taking

396 Miskawayh, *Taǧārib al-umam*, 1:128 = C178–179; cf. al-Ṭabarī, *Taʾrīḫ*, 1:895–896 = trans., 5:152–153.

397 Al-Ṭabarī reads Sinǧibū, but the holograph has explicitly Ḥ, like Miskawayh, who reads Sinḥiwā.

398 Miskawayh, *Taǧārib al-umam*, 1:129 = C179–181; cf. al-Ṭabarī, *Taʾrīḫ*, 1:897–898 = trans., 5:155–157.

399 The text of Miskawayh, followed by al-Maqrīzī, is corrupt and the ultimate source, al-Ṭabarī, is already problematic, but this seems to be the general sense.

يؤخذ منه الحق ثم يعاقب الظالم بعد ذلك بقدر جُرْمه. وأمر بعيال ذوي الأحساب الذين مات قيمهم فكتبوا له فأنكح بناتهم الأكفاء وجعل جهازهم من بيت المال وأنكح بنيهم من سويات الأشراف وأغناهم وأمرهم بملازمة بابه ليُستعان بهم في أعماله. وخيّر نساء والده أن يقمن مع نسائه فيؤاسَيْنَ ويُصَيّرن في الإجْرَاء أمثالهن أو يبتغي لهن أكفاءهن من البُعُولة. وأمر بكَرْي الأنهار وحفر القُنِيّ وإسلاف العُمَّار وتقويتهم وأمر بإعادة كل جسر قُطع وكل قنطرة كسِرَت وكل قرية خرِبت وأن ترد إلى أحسن ما كانت عليه. وأمر بتسهيل سُبُل الناس {وبنى} في الطرق القصور والحصون. وتخيَّر الحكام والعمال وتقدم إلى من ولى منهم أبلغ التقدم وتقدم بكتب سِيَر أردشير ووصاياه فاقتدى بها وحمل الناس عليها.

§ 147[1] فلما انتظمت له هذه الأمور واستوسق ملكه ووثق بجنده وقوته سار نحو أنطاكية فافتتحها. وأمر أن تُصَور له المدينة على ذرعها وطرقها وعدة منازلها وأن {يبْنى} على صورتها له مدينة إلى جانب المدائن. فبنيت المدينة المعروفة بالرومية. ثم حمل أهل أنطاكية حتى أسكنهم إياها. فلما دخلوا باب المدينة مضى أهل كل بيت منهم إلى ما يشبه منازلهم التي كانوا فيها بأنطاكية. ثم قصد لمدينة هرقل فافتتحها ثم الإسكندَرية وأذعن له قيصر وحمل إليه الفدية.

---

٦ وبنى : "وبنا" في الأصل. ١٠ يبْنى : "يبنا" في الأصل.

---

١ من تجارب الأمم لمسكويه ١: ١٢٩.

some of his property or doing some other wrong to him should recompense it and then be punished according to his crime. He gave orders that he should be informed concerning the children of persons of nobility whose guardian had died. He gave their daughters in marriage to their equals and provided their dowry from the treasury and their sons he married to their equals in nobility, giving them riches and ordering them to attach themselves to his court so that he could use them when needed. For the wives of his father he gave the choice of staying with his wives, where they would be treated as equals and would receive the same stipend, or that he would find them husbands, who were their equals. Then he ordered canals and *qanāts* to be dug and money to be lent to cultivators so that they would be strengthened. He further ordered every bridge that had been destroyed and every stone bridge that had been broken and every village that had been reduced to ruins to be rebuilt even better than they had used to be. He gave orders to level the roads used by people and to build castles and fortresses alongside roads. He chose administrators and governors. To those of them whom he appointed he gave precise orders, and he himself perused books about the ways and admonitions of Ardašīr (*bi-kutub siyar Ardašīr wa-waṣāyāhu*) and followed their advice and brought people to (act according to) them.

§ 147[400] When these affairs were in order, and he was able to rule and to trust his army and his strength, Kisrá marched towards Antioch and conquered it. He gave orders that a plan of the city was to be drawn for him to scale with roads and the right number of houses, and another city to be built according to this plan at the side of al-Madāʾin, to be known as al-Rūmiyyah. Then he settled the people of Antioch there. When the Antiochians entered the gates of the new city, the inhabitants of each house went to the replica of the house they used to have in Antioch. Then Kisrá marched to the city of Heraclea and conquered it, then further to Alexandria. The Caesar submitted himself to him and paid him ransom money.

400 Miskawayh, *Taǧārib al-umam*, 1:129 = C181; cf. al-Ṭabarī, *Taʾrīḫ*, 1:898 = trans., 5:157–159.

§148[1] وسبب ذلك أن كسرى أنوشِروان كان بينه وبين قيصر ملك الروم هدنة فوقع بين الحٰرث ابن أبي شَمِر ملك عرب الشام من قبل قيصر وبين المنذر بن النعمٰن ملك العرب بالعراق من قبل كسرى فأغار على المنذر بن النعمٰن وقتل من أصحابه مقتلة عظيمة وغنم أمواله. فكتب كسرى إلى قيصر يذكر ما بينهما من العهد والصلح ويعلمه ما لقي المنذر من الحٰرث ويسأله أن يأمر برد ما أخذ للمنذر وأن يدفع إليه ديات من قتل من أصحابه وينصف المنذر منه. وإن لم | يفعل انتقض الصلح. 166a
ووالى الكتب. فلما لم يفعل سار كسرى في بضعة وتسعين ألفا ومر على الجزيرة فأخذ مدينة دارا والرها وعبر إلى الشام فأخذ مدينة منبج وحلب وأنطاكية وكانت أفضل مدائن الشام ومدينة أفامية ومدينة حمص ومدنا كثيرة متاخمة لهذه البلاد عنوة. واحتوى على ما فيها من الأموال وغيرها وسبى أهل أنطاكية ونقلهم إلى أرض السواد وأنزلهم المدينة التى بناها كما تقدم ذكره. وكَوَّر لهذه المدينة خمسة طساسيج وأجرى على من أنزلهم بها الأرزاق وأقام عليهم رجلا من نصارى الأهواز ليأنسوا به فإنهم كانوا نصارى. فابتاع منه قيصر مدن الشام ومصر بأموال عظيمة

---

٢ شَمِر: كشط المقريزي ما يلي الشين ثم صحح الكلمة كما هي الآن. ٣ المنذر بن: الزيادة بخط المقريزي في الهامش الأيسر من الأسفل إلى الأعلى + صح، ويشير إليها رمز ⌐ بعد "على". ‖ النعمٰن وقتل: كشط المقريزي عبارة أخرى قبل أن يصححها كما هي الآن.

---

١ من تأريخ الطبري ١: ٩٥٨–٩٦٠ ومن تجارب الأمم لمسكويه ١: ١٢٩.

§148[401] The reason for this was that there had been a truce between Kisrá Anūširwān and the Caesar, the king of Byzantium, but then there occurred (a conflict)[402] between al-Ḥāriṯ b. Abī Šamir,[403] the king of the Arabs of Syria on behalf of the Caesar, and al-Munḏir b. al-Nuʿmān, the king of the Arabs of Iraq on behalf of Kisrá. Al-Ḥāriṯ attacked al-Munḏir b. al-Nuʿmān and killed several of his companions, looting his property. Kisrá wrote to the Caesar, reminding him of their treaty and peace agreement and telling him what al-Ḥāriṯ had done to al-Munḏir, asking him to give orders to return to al-Munḏir what had been taken from him and to pay him the blood money for his companions who had been killed, so that al-Munḏir would get justice from him. If the Caesar would not do this, the treaty would have been broken. Kisrá sent several letters, but the Caesar did nothing. Finally, Kisrá marched with an army of more than 90,000 men through the Ǧazīrah, capturing by force the cities of Dārā and al-Ruhā, crossing over to Syria and taking the cities of Manbiǧ, Aleppo, and Antioch, which was the best city in Syria, as well as the cities of Apamea and Ḥimṣ and many others, adjacent to these, taking all the money and property that was in them. He took the inhabitants of Antioch as prisoners and moved them to the Sawād, settling them in the city he had built, as we have already mentioned,[404] and creating five *ṭassūǧs* for this city. To those who settled there he gave their livelihood and placed a Christian from al-Ahwāz to govern them, so that they would feel familiar with him, because they themselves were Christians. The Caesar bought back from him the cities of Syria and Egypt with a huge sum of money, which he sent to

401 Al-Ṭabarī, *Taʾrīḫ*, 1:958–960 = trans., 5:252–255; Miskawayh, *Taǧārib al-umam*, 1:129 = C181 (the last sentence).

402 In a long and meandering sentence, al-Ṭabarī does, finally, come to the subject of *waqaʿa, nāʾirah*, but al-Maqrīzī has lost track of the syntax in reproducing the passage and omits it.

403 Al-Ṭabarī reads Ḫālid b. Ǧabalah, which Bosworth (1999): 252, note 611, corrects to al-Ḥāriṯ b. Ǧabalah. It is not clear what al-Maqrīzī's source for the correction is. Nöldeke (1879): 238, notes 2 and 3, followed by Bosworth, explains al-Ṭabarī's forms Yaḫṭiyānūs (dropped by al-Maqrīzī) and al-Ḥāriṯ, for Justinian and Ḫālid, with reference to Pahlavi orthography and postulates an ultimately Pahlavi source for this version, but this is purely speculative and not based on any existing Pahlavi source or even attested Pahlavi forms of these names. As can be seen from the case of the hypothetical Pahlavi *Alexander Romance* (see Hämeen-Anttila 2018b: 45–51), this is a hazardous project, which may result in the creation of "ghost works" that never really existed.

404 See §147.

حملها إليه وضمن له مالا يحمله كل سنة على أن لا يغزو بلاده وصار يحملها كل عام. فسار كسرى أنوشروان من الروم وأخذ نحو الخزَر فقتل منهم وغنم وأخذ منهم بثأر رعيته.

§149[1] ثم مضى يريد اليمن حتى بلغها فسكر نحو عدن ناحية من البحر بين جبلين بالصخور وعمد الحديد بعد ما قتل وغنم وعاد إلى المدائن وقد اتسع ملكه. فملك النعمٰن بن المنذر على الحيرة وسار إلى الهياطلة مطالبا لهم بدم فيروز جده. وذلك بعد أن صاهر خاقان واستعان به فأتاهم فقتل ملكهم واستأصل أهل بيته وتجاوز بلخ وما وراءها وأنزل جنوده فرغانة. ثم انصرف إلى المدائن وغزا البرجان. ثم رجع وبعث قوما إلى اليمن لقتل الحبشة الذين بها في جند من الديلم. فقتلوا مسروقا الحبشي باليمن. وفتح كور اليمن. واتفق لكسرى في ذلك شيء عجيب فإنه أنفذ ستمائة رجل إلى ثلاثين ألفا فقتلوهم كلهم حتى لم ينج منهم إلا من {ألقى} بنفسه في البحر فغرق فيه.

§150[2] فلما دانت له بلاد اليمن وجه منها إلى سرنديب من بلاد الهند قائدا من قواده في جند كثيف. فقاتل ملكها وقتله واستولى عليها وحمل إلى كسرى منها أموالا عظيمة وجواهر كثيرة. فأقام كسرى أنوشروان مظفرا منصورا تهابه جميع الأمم ويحضر بابه وفود الترك والصين والخزَر ونظرائهم. وكان مكرما للعلماء. وكان لما غزا برجان ثم رجع {بنى} الباب والأبواب وذلك أن أرمينية وآذربيجان كان بعضها للروم وبعضها للخزر {فبنى} قباذ بن فيروز سورا مما يلي بعض الناحية. فلما ملك كسرى أنوشروان وقوي أمره وغزا فرغانة وبرجان | كتب إلى ملك الترك يسأله الموادعة 166b

٤ وعاد ... الحيرة: الزيادة بخط المقريزي في الهامش الأيمن من الأعلى إلى الأسفل + صح، ويشير إليها رمز ⌝ بعد "وغنم". ٨–٩ وفتح ... فيه: الزيادة بخط المقريزي في الهامش الأيسر، ويشير إليها رمز ⌜ بعد "باليمن". ٨ لكسرى: وضع المقريزي ثلاث نقط تحت الحرف الثالث إشارة إلى تلفظه بالسين. ٩ ألقى: "القا" في الأصل. ١٣ بنى: "بنا" في الأصل. ١٤ فبنى: "فبنا" في الأصل.

١ من تجارب الأمم لمسكويه ١: ١٢٩ ومن تأريخ الطبري ١: ٨٩٩ ومن تأريخ سني الملوك لحمزة ص ٤٦.

٢ من تأريخ الطبري ١: ٩٦٥، ٨٩٩ ومن تجارب الأمم لمسكويه ١: ١٢٩–١٣٠.

him, also promising money to be brought to him every year, in recompense for him not attacking his country. This used then to be brought to Kisrá every year. Kisrá Anūširwān then left Byzantium and went to the Ḫazars, killing many of them, looting, and taking his revenge on them on behalf of his subjects.

§149[405] Then Kisrá marched to Yemen. Close to Aden, he blocked part of the sea between two mountains with boulders and iron columns after having killed and looted. After expanding his kingdom, he returned to al-Madāʾin. He appointed al-Nuʿmān b. al-Mundir as the king of al-Ḥīrah and marched against the Hephthalites to revenge the blood of his grandfather Fīrūz. This happened after he had married the Ḫāqān's daughter and could use his help. He attacked them and killed their king and rooted his family. Then he went beyond Balḫ and settled his armies in Farġānah. Then he returned to al-Madāʾin, raided al-Burǧān, and returned. He sent some people in an army of Daylamites to Yemen to kill the Ethiopians who were there. They killed Masrūq the Ethiopian in Yemen and conquered the districts of Yemen. This was a real miracle! Kisrá sent 600 men against 30,000, and the 600 killed all the 30,000, so that none of them escaped the slaughter except for those who threw themselves into the sea and drowned there.

§150[406] When Yemen was subjected to him, Kisrá sent one of his generals from there to Serendip of India with a large army. The general fought against its king, killed him, and conquered the country, bringing back to Kisrá huge amounts of money and numerous jewels. Kisrá Anūširwān remained victorious and triumphant. All peoples stood in his awe, and embassies from the Turks, Chinese, Ḫazars, and others came to his court. He was generous to learned men. Having campaigned in Burǧān[407] and then returned home, he built al-Bāb wa-l-Abwāb. This was because parts of Armenia and Azerbaijan belonged to the Byzantines and parts to the Ḫazars. Qubād b. Fīrūz had built a wall on the side of a certain area. When Kisrá Anūširwān became king and his position was strengthened and he had raided Farġānah and Burǧān, he wrote to the king of the Turks asking him to a friendly meeting and propos-

405 Miskawayh, *Taǧārib al-umam*, 1:129 = C181; al-Ṭabarī, *Taʾrīḫ*, 1:899 = trans., 5:160; Ḥamzah, *Taʾrīḫ* 46 = trans. 72.

406 Al-Ṭabarī, *Taʾrīḫ*, 1:965 = trans., 5:264 and 1:899 = trans., 5:160; Miskawayh, *Taǧārib al-umam*, 1:129–130 = C182.

407 In this paragraph without the definitive article *al-*, cf. §149.

والاتفاق ويخطب إليه ابنته ورغب في صهره. فتزوج كل منهما ابنة الآخر فأما كسرى فإنه أرسل إلى خاقان بنتا كانت قد تبنتها بعض نسائه وذكر أنها ابنته وأرسل خاقان ابنته.

§ 151[١] ثم اجتمعا فأمر أنوشروان جماعة من ثقاته أن يكبسوا طرفا من عسكر الترك ويحرقوا فيه ففعلوا. فلما أصبحوا شكا خاقان ذلك فأنكر أنوشروان أن يكون علم به. ثم أمر بمثل ذلك بعد ليال. فلما أصبح الترك شكوا ذلك فرفق بهم أنوشروان واعتذر إلى خاقان. ثم أمر أن {يلقى} في ناحية من عسكره النار. وكان في تلك الناحية أكواخ من حشيش. فلما أصبح شكا إلى خاقان وقال: "كافيتني بالتهمة." فحلف خاقان أنه لم يعلم بشيء من ذلك فقال أنوشروان: "إن جندنا قد كرهوا صلحنا لانقطاع الغزو والغارات. ولا آمن أن يحدثوا حدثا يفسد ما بيننا فتعود العداوة. والرأي أن تأذن لي في بناء سور يكون بيني وبينك أجعل عليه أبوابا فلا يدخل عليك إلا من تريد ولا يدخل إلينا إلا من نريد." فأجابه إلى ذلك {فبنى} أنوشروان حينئذ السور من البحر وألحقه. { برؤوس} الجبال وعمل عليه أبواب الحديد ووكل به من يحرسه.

§ 152[٢] فقيل لخاقان: "إنه قد خدعك وزوجك غير ابنته وتحصن منك حتى لم تقدر أن تصل إليه." وهذا السور هو سُد دَرْبَند وهي الباب والأبواب. {وبنى} عنده مدينة وأسكنها قوما. {وبنى} هناك

---

٥ شكوا ذلك : الزيادة بخط المقريزي في آخر السطر في الهامش الأيسر من الأسفل إلى الأعلى. ‖ يلقى : "يلقا" في الأصل. ١٠ فبنى : "فبنا" في الأصل. ‖ برؤوس : "بروس" في الأصل. ١٣ سُد ... والأبواب : الزيادة بخط المقريزي في الهامش الأيسر من الأسفل إلى الأعلى + صح، ويشير إليها رمز ⌐ بعد "هو". ‖ وبنى[١]: "وبنا" في الأصل. ‖ وبنى[٢] : "وبنا" في الأصل.

---

١ من الكامل لابن الأثير ١: ٤٤١.

٢ من الكامل لابن الأثير ١: ٤٤١ ومن تأريخ سني الملوك لحمزة ص ٤٥، ٤٧.

ing to his daughter and urging him[408] to marry his daughter respectively. The kings married each other's daughter, but Kisrá only sent the Ḫāqān a girl one of his wives had adopted, claiming her to be his daughter, while the Ḫāqān sent him his own daughter.[409]

§ 151[410] When they met, Anūširwān gave some of his confidants an order to attack one part of the Turks' camp and set it on fire. They did this, and next morning the Ḫāqān complained about it. Anūširwān denied knowing anything about this. Some days later he again commanded his men to do so, and the next morning the Turks were again complaining about this. Anūširwān was kind to them and apologised to the Ḫāqān. Later, he ordered one part of his own camp to be set on fire, where there were some reed huts. The next morning, he complained to the Ḫāqān and said: "You have paid me back in kind, based on suspicion only!" The Ḫāqān swore that he knew nothing of all this, and Anūširwān said: "Our armies[411] hate the peace we have made, because they will miss campaigns and raids. I fear that they may do something to spoil our relations and return the enmities as they were. The thing to do now is that you allow me to build a wall between us. I'll put some gates there, so that only those you want may enter your country, and only those we want may enter our country." The Ḫāqān accepted this, and Anūširwān built a wall from the sea unto the mountain tops. He made iron gates for it and appointed men to guard them.

§ 152[412] Someone said to the Ḫāqān: "He deceived you. First he gave someone other than his daughter to you in marriage. Then he made a fortress for himself, so that you cannot get at him." This wall is the wall of Darband, also known as al-Bāb wa-l-Abwāb. Anūširwān built there a city and settled

---

408 The holograph seems to read RĠB (*raġiba*), which is also how the copyist of MS T has read it, but it might be possible read this as *raġġabahu*, which would fit the context better. The translation is based on that reading.

409 For the assumed unwillingness of Sasanian kings to give their daughters to foreign kings in marriage, see Christensen (1936): 313, based on Ibn al-Balḫī, *Fārsnāmah* 97–98. See also Vacca (2017): 98–99.

410 Ibn al-Aṯīr, *Kāmil*, 1:441.

411 In singular in the text, as also in Ibn al-Aṯīr, and grammatically this could only refer to Anūširwān's army, but it seems more natural to assume that it refers to both armies.

412 Ibn al-Aṯīr, *Kāmil*, 1:441; Ḥamzah, *Ta'rīḫ* 45, 47 = trans. 71–72; cf. Miskawayh, *Taǧārib al-umam*, 1:129–130 = C182, and al-Ṭabarī, *Ta'rīḫ*, 1:899 = trans., 5:161. This paragraph is one of the few where al-Maqrīzī abbreviates Ḥamzah's text.

عدة مدن وجعل على كل باب قصرا من حجارة وأسكن في كل طرف قائدا بقطعة من الجيش. وأطعمهم ما يلي ذلك الصُقع من الضياع وجعلها بعدهم وقفا على أولادهم. وخلع على كل قائد يوم أنفذه إلى حفظ الثغر الموسوم به قباء ديباج مصورا بنوع من التصوير وسمى ذلك القائد باسم تلك الصورة نحو بغَّران شاه شروان شاه فيلان شاه ألان شاه. واختص منهم بسرير من فضة قائدا فسمى سرير شاه وقيل له بالعربية: ملك السرير. والسرير غير عربي بل له اسم فارسي واقع على التخت الصغير. فجاء طول هذا السد من البحر إلى الجبل نحوا من عشرين فرسخا. وأخذ جميع ما كان بأيدي الروم من أرمينية فلم تزل أرمينية بأيدي الفرس حتى جاء الله بالإسلام فخلت تلك الحصون حتى خربت فاستولى عليها الخزر والروم. وفي أيام أنوشروان ولد عبد الله بن عبد المطلب لأربع وعشرين سنة من ملكه. ثم ولد رسول الله صلى الله عليه وسلم في الثانية والأربعين وقيل: لإحدى وأربعين من ملكه.

§ 153[1] وبعث أنوشروان إلى المنذر بن النعمٰن الأكبر وأمه ماء السماء امرأة من اليمن فملكه الحيرة وما كان يليه آل الحٰرث بن عمرو فرد الأمر إلى نصابه. وذلك أن المنذر أقبل إلى أنوشروان وقد علم خلافه على أبيه في مذهبه | في اتباعه مزدك. فجلس أنوشروان وأذن للناس إذنا عاما فدخل 167a

---

١–٦ وأسكن ... فرسخا: الزيادة بخط المقريزي في الهامش الأيمن منكسة وآخرها في الهامش الأعلى من الأسفل إلى الأعلى + صح، ويشير إليها رمز ⌝ بعد "حجارة". ٩–١٠ وقيل ... وأربعين: الزيادة بخط المقريزي في الهامش الأيمن + صح، ويشير إليها رمز ⌝ بعد "والأربعين". ١٢ إلى[٢]: كشط المقريزي ما يلي الألف (يبدو أنه كتب أولا "اليه")، ثم صحح الكلمة كما هي الآن. ‖ أنوشروان: الزيادة بخط المقريزي في الهامش الأيمن من الأسفل إلى الأعلى + صح، ويشير إليها رمز ⌝ بعد "إلى".

---

١ من تجارب الأمم لمسكويه ١: ١٣٠.

people in it. He also built several other cities there. At every gate, he built a stone castle and in each he settled a general with some men and provisioned them from the villages nearby. He also set it as an endowment for their children after them. When he sent a general to keep guard in the fortress to which he was appointed, he bestowed upon him a robe of silk brocade, decorated with something, and the general was given a title in accordance with that decoration, like Buġrānšāh, Širwānšāh, Fīlānšāh, and Alānšāh. For one of them, he specifically gave a silver throne, and that general was known as Sarīršāh or, in Arabic, the King of the Throne. The word *sarīr* is not originally Arabic.[413] Nay, it is a Persian word referring to a small couch. The length of this wall from the sea to the mountain was about twenty *farsaḫs*. Then he conquered everything the Byzantines had had of Armenia, which remained in the hands of the Persians until God brought Islam forth and these fortresses were deserted so that they became ruined and the Ḫazars and Byzantines took them over. During the time of Anūširwān, ʿAbd Allāh b. ʿAbd al-Muṭṭalib[414] was born in the 24th year of his reign. The Messenger of God, may God honour him and grant him peace, was born on the 42nd or, according to others, 41st year of his reign.[415]

§ 153[416] Anūširwān sent a word to al-Mundir b. al-Nuʿmān the Elder—his mother was Māʾ al-Samāʾ, a woman from Yemen—and made him the king[417] of al-Ḥīrah and of what the family of al-Ḥāriṯ b. ʿAmr had governed, thus putting the matters back to what they had been. This was as follows: Al-Mundir came to Anūširwān, knowing that Anūširwān had opposed his father concerning his religious ideas in following Mazdak. Anūširwān sat down and

413 The titles refer to ethnic groups, rather than animals as suggested by Hoyland (2018): 71, note 238. It is not clear why al-Maqrīzī's source, Ḥamzah, says that *sarīr* would be a loanword from Persian. For the kingdom of the Christian Avars, called the kingdom of the *sarīr*, see Vacca (2017): 8, with further references.

414 The Prophet Muḥammad's father.

415 Bosworth (1999): 161, following Nöldeke (1879): 168, notices a gap in the text of al-Ṭabarī, and emends it slightly differently: ʿAbd Allāh "was born during his reign [in the twenty-fourth year of this, and that he died] in the forty-second year of his dominion." As the Prophet is said to have been orphaned before his birth, both emendations are equally possible. I have not been able to ascertain where al-Maqrīzī gets his emendation from.

416 Miskawayh, *Taǧārib al-umam*, 1:130 = C182 (beginning only); cf. al-Ṭabarī, *Taʾrīḫ*, 1:899–900 = trans., 5:161; Ibn al-Aṯīr, *Kāmil*, 1:434–435.

417 The holograph reads erroneously *malikat* (MLKT-, with *tāʾ marbūṭah*) *al-Ḥīrah*, al-Maqrīzī being misled by the mention of Māʾ al-Samāʾ. The copyist of MS T has corrected the obvious slip of pen and reads *mallakahu*.

عليه مزدك ثم دخل عليه المنذر. فقال أنوشروان: "إني كنت تمنيت أمنيتين أرجو أن يكون الله عز وجل جمعهما لي." فقال {مزدك}: "ما هما أيها الملك؟" قال: "تمنيت أن أملك فاستعمل هذا الرجل الشريف" يعني المنذر "وأن أقتل هذه الزنادقة." فقال له مزدك: "أوتستطيع أن تقتل الناس كلهم؟" فقال: "وإنك هاهنا يابن الزانية؟ والله ما ذهب نتن ريح جوربيك من أنفي منذ قبلت رجليك إلى يومي هذا." وأمر به فقتل وصلب.

§154[١] وولى المنذر وطلب الحٰرث بن عمرو بن حجر وكان بالأنبار. فخرج هاربا في صحابته وماله وولده فتبعه المنذر بالخيل من تغلب وبهرا وإياد. وحفر أنوشروان خندقا من هيت حتى أتى كاظمة مما يلي البصرة وينفذ إلى البحر وجعل عليه المناظر ليرد العَرب عن الغَيْث في أطراف السواد وما يليه. فخربت عانات وهيت بذلك السبب. وكان من أحسن ما دبره أنوشروان في استغزار الأموال وتثميرها أنه بعد فراغه من الثغور وملوك الأطراف وتوظيفه الوظائف على أقاصي الملوك من الترك والخزر والهند وغيرهم وبيعه مدن الشام ومصر والروم على ملك الروم بأموال عظيمة وإلزامه جزية يحملها في كل سنة على أن لا يغزو بلاده نظر في الخراج وأبواب الأموال التي كان يستأديها الملوك قبله من بلاده. فإذا رسوم الناس كانت جارية على الثلث من الارتفاع خراجا ومن بعض الكُوَر الربع ومن بعضها الخمس ومن بعضها السدس على حسب شربها وعمارتها ومن جزية الجماجم شيئا معلوما.

---

٢ مزدك: "موبذان" في الأصل والصواب من الكامل لابن الأثير. ٧–٩ وحفر ... السبب: الزيادة بخط المقريزي في الهامش الأيمن من الأعلى إلى الأسفل وآخرها في الهامش الأسفل من الأسفل إلى الأعلى، ويشير إليها رمز ⌐ بعد "وإياد".

---

١ من تجارب الأمم لمسكويه ١: ١٣٠ ومن الكامل لابن الأثير ١: ٤٣٥.

allowed everyone to come forward. First Mazdak came to him and then al-Munḏir. Anūširwān said: "I have two wishes, both of which I hope God, He is Mighty and Majestic, will grant me." Mazdak[418] asked: "What are they, O King?" He replied: "I wished that I would become king so that I could appoint this noble man"—referring to al-Munḏir—"and that I could kill these heretics." Mazdak asked him: "Can you then kill all the people?" Anūširwān said: "What! Are you still here, you son-of-a-bitch? By God, until this very day the stench of your socks still lingers in my nostrils from the time I had to kiss your feet."[419] He gave an order, and Mazdak was killed and crucified.

§ 154[420] Anūširwān appointed al-Munḏir, who went after al-Ḥāriṯ b. ʿAmr b. Ḥuǧr, who was in al-Anbār, but he fled from there with his companions, property, and children. Al-Munḏir followed him with some cavalrymen from Taġlib, Bahrā, and Iyād. Anūširwān had a trench dug from Hīt to Kāẓimah, near Basra, and until the sea. He built watch towers over it to keep the Arabs from the rain(-time pastures) at the outskirts of the Sawād and its vicinity. This was the reason ʿĀnāt and Hīt became ruins. An example of how well Anūširwān arranged financial matters to make property abundant and flourishing is that when he was done arranging the affairs of the frontiers and the kings of the surrounding countries and imposing duties on the more distant kings of the Turks, Ḫazars, Indians, and others and had sold the cities of Syria, Egypt, and Byzantium back to the king of the Byzantines for an enormous sum of money and forced him to send him ǧizyah every year, so that he would not attack his country, he considered taxation and the various sorts of income that kings before him had demanded from the country. He found out that the rates (of taxation) varied from a third of the product to a fourth, fifth, or sixth in some districts, according to water supply and cultivation, in addition to a certain sum of poll tax.

---

418 The text reads *fa-qāla mūbaḏān*, which is a mistake. Ibn al-Aṯīr has correctly *fa-qāla Mazdak*.
419 See § 135.
420 Miskawayh, *Taǧārib al-umam*, 1:130 = C183 (latter half); Ibn al-Aṯīr, *Kāmil*, 1:435; cf. al-Ṭabarī, *Taʾrīḫ*, 1:960 = trans., 5:255.

§ 155[1] وكان الملك قباذ بن فيروز تقدم في آخر ملكه بمسح الأرض سهلها وجبلها ليصح الخراج عليها. فمسحت غير أن قباذ هلك قبل أن يستحكم له أمر تلك المساحة. فلما ملك أنوشروان أمر باستتمامها وإحصاء النخل والزيتون والجماجم. ثم أمر الكتّاب فأخرجوا جُمل ذلك غير مفصلة وأذن للناس إذنا عاما وأمر كاتب خراجه أن يقرأ عليهم الجُمل المستخرجة من أصناف الغلات وعدد النخل والزيتون والجماجم. فقرأ ذلك عليهم ثم قال لهم كسرى: "إنا قد رأينا أن نضع على ما أُحْصي من جُربان هذه المساحة ومن النخل والزيتون والجماجم وضائع | ونأمر بأنجامها في السنة 167b في ثلاثة أنجم. ونجمع في بيوت أموالنا من الأموال ما لو أتانا عن ثغر من ثغورنا أو طرف من أطرافنا فتق أو شيء نكرهه واحتجنا إلى تداركه أو حَسْمه ببذلنا فيه مالا كانت الأموال عندنا مُعَدّةً موجودة ولم نرد استئناف اجتبائها على تلك الحال. فما ترون فيما رأينا وأجمعنا عليه؟"

§ 156[2] فلم يشر عليه أحد منهم بمشورة ولم ينبس بكلمة. فكرر كسرى هذا القول عليهم ثلاث مرات. فقام رجل من عُرضهم وقال لكسرى: "أتَضَع أيها الملك عمرك الله خالدا من هذا الخراج على الفاني من كَرْم يموت وزرع يهيج ونهر يغيض وعين أو قناة ينقطع ماؤها؟" فقال له كسرى: "يا ذا الكلفة {المشؤوم} من أي طبقات الناس أنت؟" قال: "أنا رجل من الكتّاب." فقال كسرى: "اضربوه بالدوي حتى يموت." فضربوه بها الكتّاب خاصة تبريا منهم إلى كسرى من رأيه وما جاء منه حتى قتلوه وقال الناس: "نحن راضون أيها الملك بما أنت ملزمنا من خراج."

§ 157[3] فاختار كسرى رجالا من أهل الرأي والنصيحة فأمرهم بالنظر في أصناف ما ارتفع إليه من المساحة وعَددِ النخلِ والزيتونِ {ورؤُوسِ} الجزية ووَضْعِ الوضائع على ذلك بقدر ما يرون أن

١٠ كسرى : كشط المقريزي كلمة أخرى قبل أن يصححها كما هي الآن. ١٣ المشؤوم : "المشوم" في الأصل. ١٧ ورؤُوسِ : "وروسِ" في الأصل.

١ من تجارب الأمم لمسكويه ١: ١٣٠.

٢ من تجارب الأمم لمسكويه ١: ١٣٠–١٣١.

٣ من تجارب الأمم لمسكويه ١: ١٣١.

§155[421] Towards the end of his reign, King Qubād b. Fīrūz had commissioned a cadastral survey of land, plains as well as mountains, so that the taxation should be correct. This had been started but Qubād had died before the survey had been completed. When he began his reign, Anūširwān gave orders to complete the survey and to count the date palms, olive trees, and heads. Then he gave orders to his scribes to calculate the sum totals of these without specification. Then he issued a general summons to people and ordered his scribe of taxation to read out to them the calculated sum totals of various crops, and the number of date palms, olive trees, and heads. After this had been done, Kisrá said to them: "We have decided to set rates on arable land (*ǧurbān*), as revealed in this survey, on date palms, olive trees, and heads. We will order taxes to be collected in three instalments during the year. We will collect money into our treasury so that if something were to arise or occur to our dislike in one of our frontier fortresses or borderlands and we needed to set it right or to settle it by spending some money, we would have money at hand and would not need to start collecting taxes on that occasion. What do you think of this that we have thought and decided?"

§156[422] No one suggested anything nor even said a word. Kisrá repeated the question three times. Finally, a man rose from their midst and said: "O King, may God let you live long, are you setting an eternal basis for this tax on perishable vines, which may die, crops, which may wither, rivers, which may dwindle, and springs and *qanāts*, which may dry up?" Kisrá replied to him: "You ill-omened nuisance! From which class of people are you?" When the man told him that he was a scribe, Kisrá said: "Beat him dead with inkstands!" Other scribes, specifically, beat him to dissociate themselves from his opinion and his comments in the eyes of Kisrá, until they killed him. Then people said: "O King, we are satisfied with the tax you are setting on us!"

§157[423] Kisrá selected some intelligent and sincere men and gave them orders to inspect the various classes (of crops) that the measuring had revealed and the number of date palms, olive trees, and heads for poll tax and to establish rates for them according to what they thought would be

421 Miskawayh, *Taǧārib al-umam*, 1:130 = C183–184; cf. al-Ṭabarī, *Taʾrīḫ*, 1:960–961 = trans., 5:255–257.

422 Miskawayh, *Taǧārib al-umam*, 1:130–131 = C184–185; cf. al-Ṭabarī, *Taʾrīḫ*, 1:961 = trans., 5:257.

423 Miskawayh, *Taǧārib al-umam*, 1:131 = C185–186; cf. al-Ṭabarī, *Taʾrīḫ*, 1:961–962 = trans., 5:257–258.

فيه صلاح رعيته ورفاهة عيشهم ورفْع ذلك إليه. فتكلم كل امرئ منهم بمبلغ رأيه في ذلك وفي قدر الوضائع وأداروا الأمر بينهم. فاجتمعت كلمتهم على وضع الخراج على ما يعْصم الناس والبهائم وهو الحنطة والشعير والأرز والكرم والرطاب والنخل والزيتون. وكان الذي وضعوا على كل جَرِيْبِ أرضٍ من مزارع الحنطة والشعير درهمًا وعلى كل جريب كَرْم ثمانية دراهم وعلى كل جريب أرض رطاب سبعة دراهم وعلى كل أربع نخلات فارسية درهما وعلى كل ست نخلات دقل مثل ذلك وعلى كل ستة أصول زيتون مثل ذلك. ولم يضعوا إلا على كل نخل في حديقة أو مجتمع غير شاذ وتركوا ما سوى ذلك من الغلات السَبْع.

168a §158[١] فقَوِي الناس في معايشهم وألزَموا الناس الجزية ما خلا أهل البيوتات | والعظماء والمقابلة والهرابذة والكتّاب ومن كان في خدمة الملك. وصيروها على طبقات إثنا عشر درهما وثمانية وستة وأربعة على قدر إكثار الرجل وإقلاله. ولم يلزموا الجزية من كان {أتى} له من السنين دون العشرين أو فوق الخمسين ورفعوا هذه الوضائع إلى كسرى. فرضيها وأمر بإمضائها والاجتباء عليها في ثلاثة أنجم كل سنة وسماها أبراسيار وتأويله الأمر المتراضى به. وهي الوضائع التي {اقتدى} بها أمير المؤمنين عمر بن الخطاب رضي الله عنه حين افتتح بلاد الفرس وأمر باجتباء الناس من أهل الذمة عليها إلا أنه وضع على كل جريب عامر على قدر احتماله مثل الذي وضع على الأرض المزروعة وزاد على كل جريب أرض مزارع حنطة أو شعير قفيزًا من حنطة إلى القفيزين ورزق منه الجند. ولم يخالف بالعراق خاصة وضايع كسرى على جُرْبان الأرض وعلى النخل والزيتون والجماجم وألغَى ما كان كسرى ألغاه في معايش الناس. ولم يزل السواد في ملك النبط والفرس

٣ كل: الزيادة بخط المقريزي في الهامش الأيسر من الأسفل إلى الأعلى + صح، ويشير إليها رمز ⌐ بعد "على". ١٠ أتى: "أتا" في الأصل. ١٢ اقتدى: "اقتدا" في الأصل. ١٥ كل: الزيادة بخط المقريزي في الهامش الأيسر من الأعلى إلى الأسفل + صح، ويشير إليها رمز ⌐ بعد "على".

١ من تجارب الأمم لمسكويه ١: ١٣١.

for the common good and the ease of his subjects' life and to report back to him. Each man spoke according to his understanding about this and the rates, and they consulted each other until they were unanimous in setting the tax on what preserved men and animals, namely, wheat, barley, rice, grapes, clover, date palms, and olive trees. For every *ǧarīb* of cultivated land, they set one dirham for wheat and barley, eight dirhams for grapes, seven dirhams for clover, and for four Persian date palms one dirham, for six *daqal* date palms the same, for six olive tree stacks the same. They only set the tax on date palms in gardens or growing together, not on those growing in isolation. Crops other than these seven they left untaxed.

§ 158[424] People's living conditions ameliorated. They also set poll tax on everyone, except for those belonging to noble houses, noblemen, soldiers,[425] *hērbads*, scribes, and all those who were in the king's service. They set poll tax in classes of twelve, eight, six, and four dirhams, according to the person's wealth. They exempted from poll tax those under twenty years of age or above fifty. They presented these rates to Kisrá, who approved of them and gave orders to implement them and collect the taxes based on them in three instalments every year. Those he called *abrāsiyār*, which means "the matter mutually agreed upon."[426] These were the rates that the Commander of the Believers ʿUmar b. al-Ḫaṭṭāb, may God be pleased with him, used as a model when he conquered the land of the Persians. ʿUmar gave orders to collect taxes from protected peoples according to these rates. He, however, set on every *ǧarīb* lying fallow the same tax according to its potential as was on cultivated land. On every cultivated *ǧarīb* of wheat or barley he also added from one to two *qafīz* of wheat,[427] which he used to provide for the army. In the specific case of Iraq, he did not contradict the rates of Kisrá as per *ǧarīb* of land, date palms, olive trees, and heads. He also excluded from tax the same means of sustenance that Kisrá had exempted. The cultivation of the Sawād had continued on the basis of share cropping during the rule

424 Miskawayh, *Taǧārib al-umam*, 1:131 = C186–187; cf. al-Ṭabarī, *Taʾrīḫ*, 1:962–963 = trans., 5:259–261.

425 The holograph reads *al-muqābilah*, but the correction, also supported by Miskawayh and al-Ṭabarī, is obvious. In Miskawayh (ed. Caetani), the dots of T are written unusually much above the letter, which may explain al-Maqrīzī's mistake.

426 It is not clear what Middle Persian word lies behind this. *Abar rasīdan* "to come to" might come into question.

427 One would expect "or barley," but both al-Maqrīzī and his immediate source, Miskawayh, as well as his ultimate source, al-Ṭabarī, only mention wheat here.

مقاسمة إلى أيام قباذ بن فيروز فإنه فرض على كل جريب درهمين وألزم الناس المساحة وأطلقوا في أملاكهم وكانوا ممنوعين منها إلى وقت القسمة. فهلك قباذ قبل إتمام ذلك. فلما ملك أنوشروان تممه وأخذ الناس به على ما تقدم ذكره. فارتفع أول سنة بمائة ألف ألف وخمسين ألف ألف درهم من الدراهم التي وزن الدرهم منها مثقال.

§159[1] ومن عجيب صنع الله تعالى لكسرى أن الحبشة لما أخذت اليمن وأخرجت رجالها واستفرشت النساء حتى قدم سيف بن ذي يزن إلى كسرى. فأقام ببابه سبع سنين حتى وصل إليه ورفع إليه خبر الحبشة وما حل منهم بالحُرَم. وكان كسرى غيورا فرحمه وقال: "سأنظر في أمرك فأفكر." ثم قال: "لا يجوز لي في ديني أن أغرر بجيشي فأحملهم في البحر إلى مغوثة من ليس على ديني ولكن في سجوني من قد استحق القتلَ. والصوابُ أن أرمي بهم في نحر هذا العدو. فإن ظفروا جعلت لهم البلاد طعمة وإن هلكوا لم آثم فيهم." فأمر بجمع | المحبسين فبلغ عددهم ثماني 168b مائة وتسعةَ رجال أكثرهم من ولد ساسان وولد بهمن بن إسفندياذ. وولى عليهم وَهْرَز وهو من ولد وَهْرَز بن فريد بن ساسان بن بهمن بن إسفندياذ. فقال له سيف بن ذي يزن: "يا ملك الملوك أين يقع هؤلاء ممن خلفت ورائي؟" فقال كسرى: "أخبرك أن كثير الحطب يكفيه قليل النار."

---

٦ واستفرشت: كتب المقريزي الحرفين الأخيرين في الهامش الأيسر.

١ من تأريخ سني الملوك لحمزة ص ٤٦.

of the Nabateans and the Persians until the time of Qubād b. Fīrūz, who set two dirhams on every *ǧarīb* and made people take a cadastral survey. The peasants were freed (to act as they liked) with their property. They had been forbidden (to use the crop) before the time of the division.[428] Qubād, however, died before accomplishing this. When Anūširwān came to rule he saw this to completion and made people act upon it as has been mentioned. The first year he received as taxes 150,000,000 dirhams, with one dirham weighing one *miṯqāl*.

§159[429] One of the wondrous things God, He is Exalted, did for Kisrá was the following: When the Ethiopians conquered Yemen expelling their men and using their women, Sayf b. Ḏī Yazan came to Kisrá and stayed at his gate for seven years until he gained access to him and raised with him the issue of the Ethiopians, telling him what atrocities they had done to women. Kisrá was concerned with women's honour, felt pity for him, and said that he would look into this. He gave it some thought and then said: "According to my religion, it is not appropriate for me to put my army in danger by taking it overseas to aid people who do not follow my religion. In my prisons I have, however, men who deserve death. I think that it is well to send them to fight this enemy. If they win, I shall make over to them that country as a means of subsistence, but if they die, I shall have done no wrong to them." He gave orders to gather these prisoners, whose number rose to 809 men, most of them descendants of Sāsān and of Bahman b. Isfandiyād. He appointed over them Wahriz,[430] who descended from Farīd[431] b. Sāsān b. Bahman b. Isfandiyād. Sayf b. Ḏī Yazan said to him: "O King of Kings, what use are these against those I have left behind!" Kisrá replied: "I tell you that a little fire is enough to consume much firewood."

428 For a story related to this, see §140a.

429 Ḥamzah, *Taʾrīḫ* 46 = trans. 72–73; cf. al-Ṭabarī, *Taʾrīḫ*, 1:947–948 = trans., 5:239.

430 Al-Maqrīzī systematically vocalises Wahraz.

431 Ḥamzah reads Bih-Āfarīdūn, which may be a mixture between Bihāfarīd and Ferīdūn. Al-Maqrīzī repeats the name of Wahriz here and calls Wahriz a descendant of *Wahriz b.* Farīd, which seems to be a simple mistake.

§160[1] فساروا في ثماني سُفن غرق منها اثنتان ونجت ست. فخرجوا من السفن فأمر وَهْرَز أصحابه أن يأكلوا فأكلوا. ثم عمد إلى باقي المطعوم فغرقه في البحر. فقال أصحابه: "عمدت إلى زادنا فأطعمته السمك." فقال: "إن عشتم أكلتم السمك وإن لم تعيشوا فلا تأسفوا على عدم الطعام مع تلف الأرواح." ثم عمد إلى سُفُنِه فأحرقها ثم قال لأصحابه: "يجب أن تختاروا لأنفسكم الفوز بمجاهدة هؤلاء فإن الهلاك في استعمال التقصير." ثم حمل في الستمائة الذين بقوا معه من الفرس على الحبشة. وجعل شعاره اسم الله ثم اسم الملك فهزموهم بإذن الله. وأتى القتل عليهم في خمس ساعات من نهار ذلك اليوم. فاشتهر هذا الظفر عند ملوك الأمم.

§161[2] قال ابن مسكويه: **ذكر قطعة من سيرة أنوشروان وسياساته** كتبتها على ما حكاه أنوشروان نفسه في كتاب عمله في سيرته وما ساس به مملكته. قال ابن مسكويه: وقرأت فيما كتبه أنوشروان من سيرة نفسه قال: كنت يوما جالسا بالدَسْكَرَة وأنا سائر إلى هَمَذَان لنُصَيِّف هناك وقد أُعِدَّ طعام الرسل الذين بالباب من قبل خاقان والهياطلة والصين وقيصر وبعبور إذ دخل رجل من الأساورة مخترطا سيفه حتى وصل إلى الستر وقطع الستر في ثلاثة أماكن وأراد الدخول حيث نحن والوثوب علينا. فأشار علي بعض خدمي أن أخرج إليه بسيفي فعلمت أنه إن كان إنما هو رجل واحد فسوف يحال بيننا وبينه وإن كانوا جماعة فإن سيفي لا يغني شيئا. فلم أَخِفَّ ولم أتحرك عن مكاني فأخذه بعض الحرس فإذا رجل رازي من حشمنا وخاصتنا. فلم يشكوا أن من هو على رأيه

١٣ إن: الزيادة بخط المقريزي في الهامش الأيسر من الأسفل إلى الأعلى + صح، ويشير إليها رمز ⌐ بعد "أنه".

١ من تأريخ سني الملوك لحمزة ص ٤٦–٤٧.

٢ من تجارب الأمم لمسكويه ١: ١٣٢.

§160[432] These men set off on eight ships, of which two sank and six came safely over. When they had disembarked, Wahriz gave orders for his men to eat. When they had eaten, he took the remaining provisions and threw them into the sea, whilst his companions protested: "You took our supplies and fed them to the fish!" He replied: "If you remain alive, you can eat the fish, and if not, you will not grieve for the lack of food after having lost your lives." Then he went to the ships, burned them, and said to his companions: "Now you have to choose for yourselves victory by fighting against those people the best you can. Falling short means to die." He attacked the Ethiopians with the remaining 600 Persians and made his battle-cry the name of God and then the name of the king. With God's permission, they put the enemy to flight, and for five hours of that day the enemy were being killed. This victory became famous among kings of various nations.

§161[433] Ibn Miskawayh has said: Mention of a part of *Sīrat Anūširwān wa-siyāsatuhu* [The life of Anūširwān and his way of governing], which I copied according to what Anūširwān himself said in a book he wrote about his life and about how he governed his kingdom. Ibn Miskawayh said: I read from what Anūširwān has written about his own life, saying: One day, I was sitting in al-Daskarah, being on my way to Hamaḏan to spend the summer there. Supper had been prepared for the messengers, who were in the court, sent by the Ḫāqān and the Hephthalites, the Chinese, the Caesar, and the Baʿbūr,[434] when suddenly a cavalryman entered with a sword in hand. He came to the curtain, which he pierced in three places, attempting to get at me.[435] One of the servants suggested that I should take my sword and stand against him, but I knew that if he was alone, he would be stopped before he could reach me, and if they were many, my sword would not help me. Hence, I did not

432 Ḥamzah, *Taʾrīḫ* 46–47 = trans. 73.

433 Miskawayh, *Taǧārib al-umam*, 1:132 = C187–188. *The Life of Anūširwān* (§§161–183 in al-Maqrīzī) has been translated from Miskawayh with extensive notes by Grignaschi (1966): 16–45.

434 Thus in both manuscripts. Miskawayh reads Baġbūr. Baġbūr, or Faġfūr, refers to the king of China.

435 The text has first-person plural forms, which I take to refer to the king, using *pluralis maiestatis*, rather than to the king and his guests.

كثير فسألوني أن لا أجلس ولا أحضر الشُرْبَ في جماعة حتى | يستبين الأمر. فلم أجبهم إلى ذلك 169a
لِئَلَّا ترى الرسل مني جبنا نخرجت لشربي.

§ 162[1] فلما فرغنا هَدَّدْت الرازي بقطع اليمين والعقوبات وسألته أن يصدقني عن الذي حمله على ذلك وأنه إن صدقني لم تنله عقوبة بعد ذلك. فذكر أن قوما وضعوا من قبل أنفسهم كتبا وكلاما وذكروا أنه من عند الله تعالى أشاروا عليه بذلك وأخبروه أن قتله إن قتلني يدخله الجنة. فلما فحصت عن ذلك وجدته حقا فأمرت بتخلية الرازي وبرد ما أخذ منه من المال وتقدمت بضرب أولٰئك الذين انتحلوا الدِينَ وأشاروا به عليه حتى لم أدع منهم أحدا.

§ 163[2] وقال أنوشروان: إني لما أحضرت القوم الذين اختلفوا في الدين وجمعتهم للنظر فيما يقولونه بلغ من جرأتهم وخبثهم وقوة شياطينهم أن لم يبالوا بالقتل والموت في إظهار دينهم الخبيث حتى أني سألت أفضلهم رجلا على {رؤوس} الناس عن استحلاله قتلي فقال: "نعم استحل قتلك وقتل من لم يطاوعنا على ديننا." فلم آمر بقتله حتى إذا حضر وقت الغداء أمرت أن يُحْتبس للغداء وأرسلت إليه بطُرَف من الطعام وأمرت الرسول أن يبلغه عني أن بقائي أنفع له مما ذكر. فأجاب رسولي أن: "ذلك حق ولكن سألني الملك أن أصْدُقه ذات نفسي ولا أكتمه شيئا مما أدين به وإنما أدين بما أخذته من مُؤَدِبي."

١٠ رؤوس: "روس" في الأصل.

١ من تجارب الأمم لمسكويه ١: ١٣٢.

٢ من تجارب الأمم لمسكويه ١: ١٣٢.

stir or move from my place. One of the guards stopped him. The attacker was a man from Rayy, one of my special entourage. People were certain that there would also be others with the same intention and asked me not to sit there nor to take part in drinking in company until the matter had been investigated. I ignored them so that the messengers would not see an act of cowardice from me, and I went to take part in the drinking.

§ 162[436] Once I was free, I threatened the man from Rayy with cutting his right hand and other punishments. I ordered him to tell me the truth about his attack and said that if he told me the truth, he would not be punished. He told me that some people had written some books and words they claimed to have received from God, He is Exalted, and suggested this attack to him, telling him that if he killed me and was himself killed in doing so, this would bring him to the Paradise. I examined this, found it to be true, and gave orders to let the man from Rayy free and to return to him his wealth that had been confiscated. Then I gave orders to execute those who had invented that religion and suggested the attack to the man, and I left none of them alive.

§ 163[437] Anūširwān said: I had the people who disagreed about religion brought to my presence to inspect what they were saying. Their insolence and wickedness and the strength of their demons was such that they did not care about being killed and put to death for exhibiting their wicked religion. I even asked the best of them, who was above the chiefs of the people, whether it would be licit to kill me, and he answered: "Yes, I consider it licit to kill you and anybody who does not obey us in our religion." Yet I did not give orders to kill him, but when the time to eat came I gave orders to detain him and sent him choice dishes to eat.[438] I told the messenger to give him my greetings that it was more profitable for him that I stayed alive than what he had suggested. He answered to my messenger: "This is quite true, but the king asked me to tell in truth what I had in my mind without concealing anything of my religion, and I do follow what I have received from my teacher."

436 Miskawayh, *Taǧārib al-umam*, 1:132 = C188.

437 Miskawayh, *Taǧārib al-umam*, 1:132 = C188–189.

438 Miskawayh (ed. Caetani) reads *ṭaraf*, and Grignaschi (1966): 17, translates "une portion," clearly reading it so, too. Al-Maqrīzī unequivocally vocalises *ṭuraf*.

§164[1] وقال أنوشروان: لما غدر بي قيصر وغزوته فذل وطلب الصلح وأنفذ إلي بمال وافر عن الخراج والفدية تصدقت على مساكين الروم وضعفاء مزارعيها مما بعث إلي قيصر بعشرة آلاف دينار. وذلك فيما وطئته من أرض الروم دون غيرها.

§165[2] قال: ولما هممت بتصفح أمر الرعية بنفسي ورفع البلاء والظلم عنهم وما ينوبهم من ثقل الخراج فإن فيه مع الأجر تزيين المملكة وغِناهم وقدرة الوالي على ما يجب أن يستخرج منهم إن هو احتاج إلى ذلك. وقد كان في آبائنا من يرى أن وضع الخراج عنهم السنة والسنتين والتخفيف أحيانا مما يقويهم على عمارة أرضيهم. فجمعت العمال ومن يؤُدي الخراج فرأيت من تخليطهم ما لم أر له حيلة إلا التعديل والمقاطعة على بلدة بلدة | وكُورة كُوْرَةٍ ورُسْتاق رستاق وقرية قرية ورجل 169b رجل. واستعملت عليهم أهل الثقة والأمانة في نفسي وجعلت في كل بلد مع كل عامل أمناء يحفظون عليه. ووليت قاضي كل كورة النظر في أهل كورته وأمرت أهل الخراج أن يرفعوا ما يحتاجون إلى رفعه إلينا إلى القاضي الذي وليته أمر كورتهم حتى لا يقدر العامل أن يزيد شيئا وأن يؤَدوا الخراج بمشهد من القاضي وأن يُعطَى به البراءة وأن يرفع خراج من هلك منهم ولا يُرَادُ الخراج ممن لم يدرك من الأحداث وأن يرفع القاضي وكاتب الكُوْرة وأمين أهل البلد والعامل محاسبتهم إلى ديواننا وفرقت الكتب بذلك.

§166[3] وقال: رفع إلينا مُوبذان مُوبذ أَن قوما سماهم من ذوي الشرف بعضهم بالباب كان شاهدا وبعضهم ببلاد أخر دينهم مخالف لما ورثنا عن نبينا وعلمائنا وإنهم يتكلمون بينهم سرا ويدعون إليه الناس وأن ذلك مفسدة للمْلك حيث لا تقوم الرعية على هوى واحد فيُحَرمون جميعهم ما يُحَرِم الملك ويستحلون ما يستحل الملك في دينه. فإن ذلك إذا اجتمع للملك قوِيَ جُنده لأجل الموافقة

---

١ من تجارب الأمم لمسكويه ١: ١٣٣.

٢ من تجارب الأمم لمسكويه ١: ١٣٣.

٣ من تجارب الأمم لمسكويه ١: ١٣٣.

§ 164[439] Anūširwān said: When the Caesar deceived me, I attacked him. He was humbled and sued for peace, sending me a great sum of money as tribute and ransom. From the ten thousand *dīnārs* that the Caesar sent me, I gave alms to the poor in Byzantium and their poor cultivators. This was in the part of what I had conquered from Byzantium only.

§ 165[440] Anūširwān said: I wanted personally to examine the affairs of people to free them of suffering and iniquity and the heaviness of recurring taxation. Besides the (divine) recompense, such deeds embellish the kingdom, bring prosperity to the subjects, and make it possible for the ruler to levy taxes, when he needs to. Among my ancestors, there had been some who thought that freeing people of taxes for a year or two and making taxation lighter for them at times enables them to cultivate their land better. I gathered my governors and tax collectors and saw such a confusion that I did not know any remedy other than straightening things up and assessing the share of each country, each district, each *rustāq*, each village, and each man, one by one. To this task I appointed people whom I considered trusted and reliable. I appointed my trusted men to every place, to be with every governor and to keep an eye on them. I made it the task of every judge in his district to inspect its inhabitants. Then I told the tax collectors that whatever they were going to send me they should first take it to the judge I had appointed to take care of the affairs of the district, so that the governor could not add anything and that they should submit the taxes in the presence of the judge and receive a receipt. I also told them that the tax of those who had died should be exempted and no tax should be collected from youths who had not come of age. The judge, the scribe of the district, the trusted man of the local people, and the governor should submit their accounts to my registers. I sent letters around concerning this.

§ 166[441] Anūširwān said: The *mōbadān mōbad* made me aware that the religion of some nobles, whom he named, some present in the court, others away in other places, differed from what we had inherited from our prophet and our men of religion and that they were secretly speaking with each other and calling others to their religion. The *mōbadān mōbad* also expressed that this was destructive to the kingdom as people would not be unanimous in

439 Miskawayh, *Tağārib al-umam*, 1:133 = C189.
440 Miskawayh, *Tağārib al-umam*, 1:133 = C189–190.
441 Miskawayh, *Tağārib al-umam*, 1:133 = C190–181.

بينهم وبين الملك فاستظهر على قتال الأعداء. فأمرت بإحضار أولٰئك المختلفين في الأهواء وأن يناظروا حتى يقفوا على الحق ويقرروا به وأمرت أن يُقْصَوا من مدينتي وعن بلادي ومملكتي ويتتبع كل من هو على هواهم فيفعل به ذلك.

§167[1] وقال: إن الترك الذين في ناحية الشمال كتبوا إلينا بما قد أصابهم من الحاجة وأنهم لا يجدون بدا إن لم نعطهم شيئا من أن يغزونا وسألونا خصالا أحدها أن نتخذهم جُندًا ونُجْري عليهم ما يعيشون به وأن نعطيهم من أرض الكنج وبلنجر وتلك الناحية ما يتعيشون منه. فرأيت أن أسير في ذلك الطريق إلى باب صُول وأحببت أن تعرف الملوك الذين من قبلنا هناك نشاطنا للأسفار وقوتنا عليها متى هممنا وأن يروا ما رأوا من هيبة الملوك وكثرة الجنود وتمام العُدة وكمال السلاح وما يقوون به على أعدائهم ويعرفون به قوة من خلفهم إن | هم احتاجوا إليه. وأحببنا بمسيرنا أن يَجْري 170a
لهم على أيدينا الجوائز والحملان والقُرْب من المجلس واللطف في الكلام ولنزيدهم بذلك مودة لنا ورغبة فينا وحرصا على قتال أعدائنا. وأحببت أيضا التعهد لحصونهم وأن أسأل أهل الخراج عن أمرهم في مسيرنا.

§168[2] فسرت في طريق هَمَذان وآذربيجان. فلما بلغت باب الصُوْل ومدينة فيروز خسره رممت تلك المدائن العتيقة والحدود وأمرت ببناء حصون أخر. فلما بلغ خاقان الخزر نزولنا هناك تخوف

٧ الذين: الزيادة بخط المقريزي في آخر السطر في الهامش الأيسر من الأسفل إلى الأعلى.

١ من تجارب الأمم لمسكويه ١: ١٣٤.

٢ من تجارب الأمم لمسكويه ١: ١٣٤.

forbidding what the king forbids and allowing what the king allows in his religion. When people do unanimously back their king, his army will be strong because they and the king are in accord with each other and, hence, they will be able to overcome the enemy in battle. I gave orders for these dissenters to be brought into my presence and that they should be debated until they acknowledged the truth and accepted it. Then I ordered them to be expelled far away from my city, my country, and my kingdom. Everybody who followed their ideas should be traced and treated like this.

§ 167[442] Anūširwān said: The Turks who live in the North wrote to us about the poverty that had stricken them, so that if we were not to give them something, they would have to raid us. They made us some requests, one of which was that we enlist them in the army and pay them salaries with which they could live and that we give them something in the lands of al-Kanǧ,[443] Balanǧar, and that region that would support them. I thought it best to march to that direction until Bāb Ṣūl. I wanted the kings set by us there to know our zeal for campaigns and our strength to do so whenever we wanted and again to feel the same awe for the king and the numerous armies, well-equipped and fully-armed, which would make them strong against their enemies, and to know the strength of those behind them if they were to need them. During the campaign, I wanted to give them their stipends and (flocks of) sheep with my own hands, as well as to allow them the proximity of audience and gentle words. By this I wanted to increase their love for me and their hopes in me and their eagerness to fight my enemies. I also wanted to use the campaign to get to know their fortresses and to ask the tax collectors about their affairs.

§ 168[444] I took the way of Hamaḏān and Azerbaijan and when I came to Bāb al-Ṣūl[445] and the city of Fīrūz-Ḫusrah I had those ancient cities and borders repaired and gave orders to build further fortresses. When the Ḫāqān of the Ḫazars heard that we had encamped there, he was afraid that I was planning

---

442 Miskawayh, *Taǧārib al-umam*, 1:134 = C191–192.

443 The holograph has one dot below the line (al-Kabḥ or al-KaXǧ, with X for an undotted letter). MS T has interpreted this as al-Kabḥ. Miskawayh (ed. Caetani) reads al-Kanḥ. Grignaschi (1966): 34–35, note 29, has not been able to identify the place, but on p. 35, note 31, he refers to a Syriac source, which mentions the tribe of Kangarāyē, which might support reading al-Kanǧ.

444 Miskawayh, *Taǧārib al-umam*, 1:134 = C192–193.

445 Here written with the determinate article.

أن نغزوه فكتب أنه لم يزل منذ ملكت تحت موادعتي وأنه يرى الدخول في طاعتي سعادة. ورأى بعض قواده لما شاهد حاله تركه فأتانا في ألفين من أصحابه فقبلناه وأنزلناه مع أساورتنا في تلك الناحية وأجرينا عليه وعلى أصحابه الرزق. وأمرت لهم بحصن كان هناك وأمرت بمصلّى لأهل ديننا وجعلت فيه موبذا وقوما نساكا وأمرتهم أن يعلّموا من دخل في طاعتنا من الترك ما في طاعة الولاة من المنفعة العاجلة في الدنيا والثواب الآجل في الأخرى وأن يحثوهم على المودة والعدل والنصيحة ومجاهدة العدو وأن يعلّموا أحداثهم رأينا ومذهبنا. وأقمت لهم في تلك التخوم الأسواق وأصلحت طرقهم وقومت السكك. ونظرنا فيما اجتمع لنا هناك من الخيل والرجال فإذا هو بحيث لو كان في وسط فارس لكان منزلنا بها فاضلا.

§169[١] قال: ولما {أتى} للملكا ثمان وعشرين سنة جددت النظر في أمر المملكة والعدل على الرعية والنظر في أمرهم وإحصاء مظالمهم وإنصافهم. وأمرت موبذ كل بلد ومدينة وثغر وجند بإنهاء ذلك إلي وأمرت بعرض الجند من كان منهم بالباب بمشهد مني ومن غاب في الثغور والأطراف بمشهد القائد وباذوسبان والقاضي وأمين من قبلنا. وأمرت بجمع أهل كور الخراج في كل ناحية من مملكتي إلى مصرها مع القائد وقاضي البلد والكاتب والأمين. وسرحت من قبلي من عرفت نصيحته وأمانته ونسكه وعلمه ومن جربت ذلك منه | إلى كل مصر ومدينة حيث أولئك العمال 170b
وأهل الأرض ليجمعوا بينهم وبين أرضيهم وبين وضيعهم وشريفهم وأن يرفع الأمر كله على حقه وصدقه فيما نفذ فيه لهم أمرا وصح فيه القضاء ورضي به أهله فرغوا منه هنالك وما أشكل عليهم رفعوه إلي.

---

٩ أتى: في الأصل "اتا".

---

١ من تجارب الأمم لمسكويه ١: ١٣٤–١٣٥.

an attack on him and wrote to me that since the beginning of my reign he had been on good terms with me and considered it a blessing to enter my service. Seeing his state, one of his generals thought it wise to leave him and came to me with 2,000 men. I accepted him and settled him among my cavalrymen in that area, giving him and his men provisions. I ordered them to settle in a fortress that was there. I also gave a praying place to the people of my religion and settled there a *mōbad* and some pious people and gave them orders to teach those Turks who entered my service what immediate benefits there were in this world for obeying rulers and what ultimate reward there would be in the world to come. They were to encourage them to love, justice, sincerity, and waging war against the enemies. They were also to teach their young our ways and doctrines. I erected for them in those regions market places, repaired their roads, and made their lanes straight. Then I inspected the horses and men we had there and found them to be such that even had it been in the middle of Fārs, it would have been a suitable place for us to settle.

§ 169[446] Anūširwān said: When I had reigned for 28 years, I inspected again the affairs of the kingdom to see whether people were treated justly, inspecting their affairs, going through their complaints, and dealing justice to them. I gave orders to the *mōbad* of each place, city, fortress, and army to send me their reports. I also gave orders to review the army, both those men who were in my presence in the palace and those who were away in the fortresses and provinces in the presence of their general, *bādūsbān*,[447] judge, and a trusted man sent by me. I gave orders to gather the whole population of a tax district everywhere in my kingdom to their capital city in the presence of their general, the local judge, the scribe, and the trusted man. Further, I sent to every capital and every city, where those governors and inhabitants were, someone whose sincerity, trustworthiness, piety, and knowledge I knew and had tested, so that they would bring together the people and their lands, the lowly and the noble. If the whole affair, which they were executing, was reported according to truth and veracity, and the judgment was clearly right and people were satisfied with it, they would finish it there, but if something were to be unclear, they would report it back to me.

446 Miskawayh, *Taǧārib al-umam*, 1:134–135 = C193–194.

447 *Pādusbān*, provincial civil governor, cf. Christensen (1936): 134 and Nöldeke (1879): 151–152, note 2.

§170[١] وبلغ من اهتمامي بتفقد ذلك ما لو لا الذي أدارى من الأعداء والثغور لباشرت أمر الخراج والرعية بنفسي قرية قرية حتى أتعهدها وأكلم رجلا رجلا من أهل مملكتي غير أني تخوفت أن يضيع بذلك السبب أمر هو أعظم منه والأمر الذي لا يغني فيه أحد غِنَائي ولا يقدر على إحكامه غيري ولا يكفينيه كاف مع الذي في الشخوص إلى قرية قرية من المؤنة على الرعية من جندنا ومن لا نجد بدا من إشخاصه معنا. وكرهنا أيضا إشخاصهم إلينا مع تخوفنا أن يشغل أهل الخراج عن عمارة أرضيهم أو يكون فيهم من يدخل عليه في ذلك مؤنة في تكلف السيْر إلى بابنا وقد ضيع قُراه أنهاره وما لا يجد بدا من تعهده في السنة كلها في أوقات العمارة. ففعلنا ذلك بهم ووكلنا بهم موبذان موبذ وكتبنا به الكتب وسرحنا من وثقنا به ورجونا أن يجري مجرانا وشخصنا وقلدناه ذلك.

§171[٢] قال: ولما أمن الله تعالى جميع أهل مملكتنا من الأعداء فلم يبق منهم إلا نحو ألفي رجل من الديلم الذين عَسُر افتتاح حِصْنهم لصعوبة الجبال عليها لم نجد شيئا أنفع لمملكتنا من أن نفحص عن الرعية وأولٰئك الأمناء الذين وصيناهم بإنصاف أهل الخراج. وكان بلغنا أن أولٰئك الأمناء لم يبالغوا على قدر رأينا في ذلك. فأمرت بالكتب إلى قاضي كورة كورة وأن يجمع أهل الكورة بغير علم عاملهم وأولي أمرهم فيسألهم عن مظالمهم وما استخرج منهم ويفحص عن ذلك بمجهود رأيه ويبالغ فيه ويكتب حال رجل رجل منهم ويختم عليه بخاتمه وخاتم الرِضَا من أهل تلك الكورة ويبعث به إلي ويُسَرح ممن يجتمع رأي أهل الكورة عليه بالرضا نفرا وإن أحبوا أن يكون فيمن يشخص بعض سَفِلَتِهم أيضا فُعِل ذلك.

١ من[١] : الزيادة بخط المقريزي في الهامش الأيسر من الأسفل إلى الأعلى + صح، ويشير إليها رمز ⌐ بعد "وبلغ". ٦ عليه : الزيادة بخط المقريزي في الهامش الأيسر من الأسفل إلى الأعلى + صح، ويشير إليها رمز ⌐ بعد "يدخل". ٩ أمن : وضع المقريزي فوض الكلمة رمز "٢" وكرر هذا الرمز في الهامش الأيسر ولكن ولا توجد أي حاشية فيه. ١٥ أهل : الزيادة بخط المقريزي في الهامش الأيسر من الأسفل إلى الأعلى + صح، ويشير إليها رمز ⌐ بعد "رأي".

١ من تجارب الأمم لمسكويه ١: ١٣٥.

٢ من تجارب الأمم لمسكويه ١: ١٣٥.

§ 170[448] I was so concerned with investigating this that had it not been for my worries with enemies and frontiers I would have investigated the taxation and people personally, village by village, to become acquainted with them. I would have spoken to each man in my kingdom, but I was afraid lest something even more important would then be lost, something which only I could take care of and which no one else could achieve and which no one could have done in my stead. In addition, it would have burdened people if I had personally gone to each village with my army and all those who should have come with me. Likewise, I disliked the idea of making them come to me, because I was afraid that that would have occupied tax payers from cultivating their land and somebody would have borne the costs caused by the travel to my court. He would have had to neglect his villages and his canals and everything else he should have been doing during the whole year, especially at the time of cultivation. This is why we did what we did with them and put the *mōbadān mōbad* in charge of them and sent letters about this and sent people we trusted, hoping that they would fulfil our role and represent us and we appointed them to do so.

§ 171[449] Anūširwān said: When God, He is Exalted, had made all the inhabitants of my kingdom safe from enemies, there only remained about 2,000 Daylamites, whose fortress was difficult to conquer because of the terrain in the mountains. I could not find anything that would have been more useful for my kingdom than inspecting the situation of people and those trusted men I had appointed to be just to the tax payers, as I had heard that those trusted men did not exert themselves as much as I would have liked them to. I gave orders to send a letter to the judge of each district, telling him to gather the people of the district without the knowledge of the governor and those in charge and to ask them whether they had complaints and how much was taken from them. The judge was to investigate this to the best of his abilities and exert himself. Then he was to write down the report of every single man and to seal it with his own seal and the seal of someone whom the people of the district accepted and to send it to me. He was also to send some men on whom the people of the district would agree and if they wished they could also send someone from among the lower classes as well.

448 Miskawayh, *Taǧārib al-umam*, 1:135 = C194–195.
449 Miskawayh, *Taǧārib al-umam*, 1:135 = C195–196.

§ 172[١] فلما حضروا جلست | للناس وأذنت لهم بمشهد من عظماء أرضنا وملوكهم وقضاتهم 171a وأحرارهم وأشرافهم. ونظرت في تلك الكتب والمظالم {فأية} مظلمة كانت من العمال ومن وكلائنا أو من وكلاء أولادنا ونسائنا وأهل بيتنا حططنا عنهم بغير بينة لعلمنا بضَعْف أهل الخراج عنهم وظلم أهل القوة من السلطان لهم. {وأية} مظلمة كانت لبعضهم من بعض وصحت لنا أمرت بإنصافهم قبل البراح وما أشكل أو وجب الفحص عنه بشهود البلد وقاضيها سَرّحت معه أمناء من الكتّاب وأمينا من فقهاء ديننا وأمينا ممن وثقنا به من خدمنا وحاشيتنا فأحكمت ذلك إحكاما وثيقا.

§ 173[٢] ولم يجعل الله تعالى لذوي قرابتنا وخدمنا وحاشيتنا منزلة عندنا دون الحق والعدل. فإن من شأن قرابة الملك وحاشيته أن يستطيلوا بعزة وقوة. فإذا أهمل السلطان أمرهم هلك من جاوروه إلا أن يكون فيهم متأدب بأدب ملكه محافظ على دينه شفيق على رعيته وأولٰئك قليل فدعانا الذي أطلعنا عليه من ظلم أولٰئك أن لا نطلب البينة عليهم فيما ادعي قبلهم. ولم نُرِدْ ظلم أحد أيضا ممن كان عزيزا بنا منيعا بمكانه ومنزلته عندنا فإن الحق واسع للضعفاء والأقوياء والفقراء والأغنياء ولكنا لما أشكلت الأمور في ذلك علينا كان الحمل على خواصنا وخدمنا أحب إلينا من أن نحمل على ضعفاء الناس ومساكينهم وأهل الفاقة والحاجة منهم.

---

٢ فأية: "فأيت" في الأصل. ٤ وأية: "وأيت" في الأصل.

---

١ من تجارب الأمم لمسكويه ١: ١٣٥–١٣٦.

٢ من تجارب الأمم لمسكويه ١: ١٣٦.

§ 172[450] When they came, I gave them an audience in the presence of our country's noblemen, their kings, their judges, their free men, and their nobility. I looked at these letters and complaints, and whatever complaints there were against the governors and my agents and the agents of my sons and wives and family members, I accepted without proof because I knew how weak tax payers are against them and how unjust people in power can be. Whatever complaints they had against each other, when these seemed clear[451] to me I gave orders to put them right before they left, but if something was complicated or needed more investigation together with local witnesses and the local judge, in these cases I sent with them a trusted man[452] from among the scribes and another one from among the lawyers of our religion and a third from among my trusted servants and entourage, and I made the process robust and reliable.

§ 173[453] God, He is Exalted, has not given my relatives and servants and entourage a position higher in my eyes than truth and justice. It is natural for the relatives and entourage of kings to become arrogant because of their might and power, and if the ruler ignores this, their neighbours[454] will perish, except when there is among them someone who follows the king's exemplary behaviour (*adab*), sustains his religion, and is compassionate toward his subjects, but these are few. What I had seen of the injustice of these made me not to demand proof against them when they were accused. Yet I did not want to do injustice to any of those who were powerful thanks to us and protected by their position. The truth applies for the weak and the powerful, the poor and the rich, but when things were difficult for us (to decide), I preferred putting the burden on my entourage and servants rather than on weak and poor people and those in need and penury.

450 Miskawayh, *Taǧārib al-umam*, 1:135–136 = C196–197.

451 Al-Maqrīzī reads *wa-ṣaḥḥat*, while Miskawayh, whom I follow in translation, has *wa-waḍaḥat*.

452 Al-Maqrīzī reads *umanāʾ*, which I take to be a slip for Miskawayh's *amīn*, and I translate accordingly in singular.

453 Miskawayh, *Taǧārib al-umam*, 1:136 = C197.

454 Both manuscripts seem to read *ǧāwara*, although the dot under Ǧ is not quite clear in either. Miskawayh has *ḥāwarūhu*, which also lies behind Grignaschi's translation (1966: 22, "ceux qui ont le droit de lui adresser la parole"), but al-Maqrīzī's reading seems preferable.

§174[1] وعلمنا أن أولٰئك الضعفاء لا يقدرون على ظلم من حولنا. وعلمنا مع ذلك أن {الذين} أقدمنا عليهم من خاصتنا يرجعون من نعمتنا وكرامتنا إلى ما لا يرجع إليه أولٰئك الضعفاء. ولعمري إن أحب خواصنا إلينا وأبرَّ خدمنا في أنفسنا الذين يحفظون سيرتنا في الرعية ويرحمون أهل الفاقة والمسكنة وينصفونهم فإنه قد ظلَمَنا من ظلَمَهم وجار علينا من جار عليهم وأراد تعطيل ذمتنا التي هي حِرْزهم {وملجأهم}.

§175[2] قال: ثم كتَب إلينا على رأس سبع وثلاثين سنة من ملكنا أربعة | أصناف من الترك من 171b ناحية الخزَر ولكل صنف منهم ملك يذكرون ما دخل عليهم من الحاجة وما لهم من الحظ في عبوديتنا. وسألونا أن نأذن لهم في القدوم بأصحابهم لخدمتنا والعمل بما نأمرهم به وألا نحقد عليهم ما سلف منهم قَبْل مُلكِنا وأن ننزلهم منزلة سائر عبيدنا فإنا سنرى في كل ما نأمرهم به من قتال وغيره كأفضل ما نَرَى من أهل نصيحتنا. فرأيت في قبولي إياهم عدة منافع منها جَلَدهم وبأسُهُم ومنها أني تخوفت أن تحملهم الحاجة على إتيان قيصر أو بعض الملوك فيقووا بهم علينا وقد كان فيما سلف يستأجر قيصر منهم لقتال ملوك ناحيتنا {بأغلى} الأجرة. فكان لهم في ذلك القتال بعض الشوكة بسبب أولٰئك الأتراك لأن الترك ليس عنْدهم لذة الحياة فهو يُجَرِّئهم مع شقاء معيشتهم على الموت.

§176[3] فكتبت إليهم: "إنا نقبل من دخل في طاعتنا ولا نبخل على أحد بما عندنا." وكتبت إلى مرزبان الباب آمُره أن يدخلهم أولا فأولا. فكتب إلي أنه قد أتاه منهم خمسون ألفا بنسائهم وأولادهم وعيالاتهم وأتاه من رؤسائهم ثلاثة آلاف بأهل بيتهم ونسائهم وأولادهم وعيالاتهم. ولما بلغني ذلك أحببت أن أقربهم إلي ليعرفوا إحساني إليهم فيما أكرمهم به وأعطيهم وليطمئنوا

---

١ الذين : "الذي" في الأصل. ٥ وملجأهم : "وملجأوهم" في الأصل وكتب المقريزي الأحرف الثلاثة الأخيرة في الهامش الأيسر. ١٢ بأغلى : "بأغلا" في الأصل.

---

١ من تجارب الأمم لمسكويه ١: ١٣٦.

٢ من تجارب الأمم لمسكويه ١: ١٣٦.

٣ من تجارب الأمم لمسكويه ١: ١٣٦-١٣٧.

§ 174[455] I knew that these weak people could not wrong those around me. I also knew that if I decided something against my companions, they would recuperate thanks to my mercy and generosity, whereas weak people would not be able to do the same. By my life, those of my closest companions that I love most and those of my servants who are the most upright in my eyes are those who follow my way with people and are compassionate and just to needy and poor people. Those who wrong them wrong me and those who oppress them oppress me, wishing to do away with the protection I give them, which is their retreat and sanctuary.

§ 175[456] Anūširwān said: At the beginning of my 37th regnal year four different groups of Turks from the region of the Ḫazars, each having their own king, wrote to me, telling me how they were stricken by poverty and how happy they would be to enter my service. They asked me permission to enter my service with their companions to do whatever I told them to and that I would not bear grudge for what they had done earlier, before my kingship. They asked me to settle them among my other servants, and we would see that they would obey our commands to fight or do something else just as well as my own most sincere people. I saw many benefits in accepting them: they were hardy and strong, and I was afraid least their poverty turn them to the Caesar or some other king, who would then gain strength from them against me. In earlier times, the Caesar had hired some of them with very high pay to fight against some kings close to us, and the Byzantines had had some sting in that battle thanks to those Turks, because the Turks do not know the pleasures of life, which makes them reckless of death, due to their wretched life.

§ 176[457] I wrote back to them, saying that I would receive those who wanted to enter my service and I would not be miserly towards anyone. I also wrote to the *marzubān* of al-Bāb and gave him orders to let them come in the order they came. He wrote back, telling me that 50,000 of them had come, together with their women, children, and dependents. 3,000 of their chiefs had come to him with the members of their noble houses and women and children and dependents. When I heard this, I wanted to bring them closer to me so that they would recognise how well I acted towards them by being generous and giving them (presents). I also wanted them to feel secure with our generals,

455 Miskawayh, *Taǧārib al-umam*, 1:136 = C197–198.
456 Miskawayh, *Taǧārib al-umam*, 1:136 = C198–199.
457 Miskawayh, *Taǧārib al-umam*, 1:136–137 = C199–200.

إلى قوادنا حتى إذا أردنا تسريحهم مع بعض قوادنا كان كل واحد بصاحبه واثقا فشخصت إلى آذربيجان فلما نزلت آذربيجان أذنت لهم في القدوم. وأتاني عند ذلك طرائف من هدايا قيصر وأتاني رسول خاقان الأكبر ورسول خوارزم ورسول ملك الهند والداْور وكابُلْشاه وصاحب سرنديب وصاحب كَلَه وكثير من الرسل وتسعة وعشرون ملكا في يوم واحد.

§177[1] وانتهيت إلى أولٰئك الأتراك الثلاثة والخمسين الألف فأمرت أن يُصَفّفوا هناك وركبت لذلك. فكان يومئذ من أصحابي ومن قدم علي ومَن دخل في طاعتي وعبودتي من لم يسَعْهم مرج كان طوله نحو عشرة فراسخ. فحمدت الله تعالى كثيرا وأمرت أن يصف أولٰئك | الأتراك في أهل 172a بيوتاتهم على سَبْع مراتب ورَأَسْتُ عليهم منهم وأقطعتهم وكسوت أصحابهم وأجريت عليهم الأرزاق وأمرت لهم {بالمياه} والأرضين وأسكنت بعضهم مع قائد لي ببرجان وبعضهم بآذربيجان وقسمتهم في كل ما احتجنا إليه من الثغور وضممتهم إلى المرزبان. فلم أزل أرى من مناصحتهم واجتهادهم فيما توجهوا له ما يسرني في جميع المدائن والثغور وغيرها.

§178[2] قال: وكتب إلي خاقان الأكبر يعتذر إلي من بعض غدراته ويسأل المراجعة والتجاوز وذكر في كتابه ورسالته أن الذي حمله على عداوتي وغزو أرضي من لم ينظر له وناشدني الله أن أتجاوز عنه وتوثق إلي بما أطمئن إليه. وذكر أن قيصر أرسل إليه وزعم أنه يستأذنني في قبول رسله وأنه لا يعمل في قبول رسول أحد إلا بما أمرته لا يجاوز أمري ولا يرغب في الأموال ولا في

٨ منهم: كشط المقريزي كلمة أو كلمتين قبل أن يكتب الكلمة كما هي الآن. ٩ بالمياه: "بالمياة" في الأصل.

١ من تجارب الأمم لمسكويه ١: ١٣٧.

٢ من تجارب الأمم لمسكويه ١: ١٣٧.

so that when I would send them somewhere with one of the generals each would trust the other. So, I went personally to Azerbaijan. When I settled there, I gave them permission to come to me. At the same time, there came to me some rare presents from the Caesar and a messenger from the great Ḫāqān, and another from Ḫwārizm, and a third from the king of India, as well as from al-Dāwar and Kābulšāh and the ruler of Serendip and the ruler of Kalah and many other messengers and 29 kings in a single day.

§ 177[458] So, I came to those 53,000 Turks and ordered them to line up. Then I rode to inspect them. That day there were so many of my companions and those who had now come to me and entered my service and servanthood that there was not enough place for them in a meadow about ten *farsaḫs* long. I gave much praise to God, He is Exalted, and gave orders that those Turks with their noble families were to be arranged[459] in seven ranks. I appointed for them chiefs from among themselves, gave them fiefs, clothed their companions, and gave them rations. I ordered them to be given water sources and land and settled some of them with one of my generals in Burǧān, some in Azerbaijan, and I sent a group of them to every fortress where they were needed. I attached them to the *marzubān*. Later, I was delighted by what I kept seeing of their sincerity and effort in what they did in every city and fortress and elsewhere.

§ 178[460] The Great Ḫāqān wrote to me, apologising for some of his betrayals and asking for a return of confidence and forgiveness. In his letter and message, he mentioned how he had been led to become my enemy and raid my country by someone who had not helped him.[461] He implored me by God to forgive him and was ready to give us guarantees that I could feel assured with. He said that the Caesar had sent him messages and claimed he was asking my permission to receive his messengers and said that he would not receive messengers from anyone without my permission and would not break my orders or request money or friendship from anyone, except when

458 Miskawayh, *Taǧārib al-umam*, 1:137 = C200–201.

459 Al-Maqrīzī reads *yuṣaffu*, which is a mistake for Miskawayh's *yuṣannafu*.

460 Miskawayh, *Taǧārib al-umam*, 1:137 = C201–202.

461 Al-Maqrīzī and Miskawayh read *lam yunẓar lahu*. I follow Grignaschi (1966): 25, who translates "ne lui avait point prêté assistance," clearly based on reading *man lam yanṣur lahu*.

المودات لأحد إلا برضاي. وكان دَسِيْس لي في الترك كاتبني بندم خاقان وندم أصحابه على غدره وعداوته إياي. فأجبته: "إني لعمري ما أبالي أبطبيعة نفسك وغريزتك غدرت بنا أم أطعت غيرك في غدرك بنا. وما ذنبك في طاعة من أطعتَ في ذلك إلا كذنبك فيما فعلتَه برأي نفسك. وإنك قد استحققت أشد العقوبة."

§179[1] وكتبت: "إني لا أظن شيئا مما وجب بيني وبينكم إلا وقد صَنَعْتهُ ولا أظن شيئا من الوثيقة بقي لكم إلا وقد وثقت لنا به قبل اليوم ثم غدرتم. فكيف نطمئن إليك ونثق بقولك ولسنا نأمنك على مثل ما فعلت من الغدر ونقض العهد والكذب في اليمين. وذكرت أن رسل قيصر عندك ووقفنا على استئذانك إيانا فيهم. ولست أنهاك عن مودة أحد." وكرهتُ أن يَرَى أني أتخوف مصادقته وأهاب ذلك منه فأحببت أن أعلمه أني لا أبالي بشيء مما يجري بينهما. ثم سرحت لمرمة المدائن والحصون التي بخراسان وجمع الأطعمة والأعلاف إليها وما يحتاج إليه الجند وأمرتهم أن | [172b] يكونوا على استعداد وحذر ولا يكون من غفلتهم ما كان في المرة الأولى.

§180[2] قال: وكان شكري لله تعالى لما وهبني وأعطاني متصلا بنِعَمه الأوَل التي وهبها لي في أول خلقه إياي. {فإنما} الشكر والنعم عدلان ككفتي الميزان أيهما رجح بصاحبه احتاج الأخف إلى أن يزاد فيه حتى يعادل صاحبه. فإذا كانت النعم كثيرة والشكر قليلا انقطع الحمل وهلك ظهر الحامل. وإذا كان ذلك مستويا استمر الحامل فكثير النعم يحتاج صاحبها إلى كثير الشكر وكثير الشكر يجلب كثير النعم. ولما وجدت الشكر بعضه بالقول وبعضه بالعمل نظرت في أحب الأعمال إليه فوجدته الشيء الذي أقام به السموات والأرض وأقام به الجبال وأجرى به الأنهار وبَرَأَ به

١٣ فإنما: "فايما" في الأصل.

١ من تجارب الأمم لمسكويه ١: ١٣٧–١٣٨.

٢ من تجارب الأمم لمسكويه ١: ١٣٨.

I allowed him to do so. I had a secret agent among the Turks, and he wrote to me about how the Ḫāqān and his companions regretted having betrayed me and become my enemies. I wrote back to the Ḫāqān: "By my life, I do not care whether you betrayed me through your own nature and disposition or because you obeyed someone. Your guilt in obeying someone is quite as much as your guilt in doing what you did on your own. You deserve a heavy punishment."

§ 179[462] I also wrote: "I think that whatever obligations there were between us I have fulfilled and I think that whatever guarantees you have you have already given before this day and then betrayed me. How could I feel assured and trust your word, since we cannot trust you not to betray us in the way you did earlier, breaking our agreement and your own oath? Then you mentioned that the messengers of the Caesar have come to you. We understand that you ask our permission to receive them. I do not forbid you to be friendly with anybody." I disliked the idea that he would think that I was afraid of their friendship and feared it. I wanted him to know that I did not care at all about what was going on between them. Then I sent a word to repair cities and fortresses in Ḫurasan and to collect food and fodder in them and what else the army would need and gave them orders to be prepared and on their guard, so that they would not again be negligent like they had been the first time.

§ 180[463] Anūširwān said: My gratitude towards God, He is Exalted, for what He had given and donated me was linked to His first blessings that He had given me in the first place by creating me. Gratitude and blessing are balanced weights, like those of scales: if one side outweighs the other, the lighter side needs more to be added to in order to retain the balance. When blessings outweigh gratitude, the burden is impossible to carry and the back of the bearer breaks, but when they are balanced, the bearer will be able to go on. Many blessings call for much gratitude, and much gratitude draws on itself more blessings. I noticed that some gratitude may be expressed by words and some by deeds. Then I looked at deeds and found out that the most pleasing of them to Him is something by which the heaven and earth are supported and the mountains kept upright and the rivers running and by which He has

462 Miskawayh, *Taǧārib al-umam*, 1:137–138 = C202.
463 Miskawayh, *Taǧārib al-umam*, 1:138 = C202–203.

البريةَ وذلك الحق والعدل. فلزمته ورأيت ثمرة الحق عمارة البلدان التي بها معاش الناس والدواب والطير وسكان الأرض ولما نظرت في ذلك وجدت المقاتلة أُجَرَاء لأهل العمارة ووجدت أيضا أهل العمارة أُجَرَاء للمقاتلة.

§ 181[1] فأما المقاتلة فإنهم يطلبون أجورهم من أهل الخراج وسكان البلدان لمدافعتهم عنهم ومجاهدتهم من ورائهم. فحق على أهل العمارة أن يوفوهم أجورهم فإن عمارتهم تتم بهم. وإن أبطؤوا عليهم أوهنوهم فقَوِيَ عدوهم. فرأيت من الحق على أهل الخراج ألا يكون لهم من عمارتهم إلا ما أقام معايشهم وعمروا به بلدانهم. ورأيت ألا أجتاحهم وأستفرغ ذات أيديهم للخزائن والمقاتلة فإني إذا فعلت ذلك ظلمت المقاتلة مع ظلم أهل الخراج. وذلك أنه إذا فسد 〈العامر فسد〉 المعمور وذاك أهلُ الأرضِ والأرضُ فاته إذا لم يكن لأهل الخراج ما يُعَيْشُهم ويعمرون به بلادهم هلكت المقاتلة الذين قوتهم بعمارة الأرض وأهل العمارة فلا عمارة للأرض إلا بفضل ما في يد أهل الخراج. فمن الإحسان إلى المقاتلة والإكرام لهم أن أرفق بأهل الخراج وأعمر بلادهم وأدع لهم فضلا في معايشهم فأهل الأرض وذوو الخراج أيدي المقاتلة والجند وقُوتُهم والمقاتلة أيضا أيدي أهل الخراج وقوتهم. | 173a فلقد فكرت وميزت ذلك جهدي وطاقتي فما رأيت أن أفضل هؤلاء على أولٰئك ولا أولٰئك على هؤلاء إذ وجدتهما كاليدين المتعاونين والرجلين المترافدين. ولعمري ما أعفى أهلَ الخراج من الظلم من أضر بالمقاتلة ولا كف الظلم عن المقاتلة من تعدى على أهل الخراج. ولو لا سفهاء الأساورة لأبقوا على الخراج والبلاد إبقاء الرجل على ضَيْعَته التي منها معيشته وحياته وقوته ولو لا جهال أهل الخراج لكفوا عن أنفسهم بعض ما يحتاجون إليه من المعايش إيثارا للمقاتلة على أنفسهم.

٨ العامر فسد : ساقط في الأصل والزيادة من تجارب الأمم لمسكويه ويقتضيها السياق. ١٢ وذوو: في الأصل "وذووا". ١٤ المتعاونين : كذا في الأصل لـ "المتعاونتين". || المترافدين : كذا في الأصل لـ "المترافدتين".

١ من تجارب الأمم لمسكويه ١: ١٣٨-١٣٩.

created the creation, namely truth and justice. So I kept to them and saw that the fruit of truth is the flourishing of the land, which gives provision to people, beasts, birds, and all other inhabitants of the world. Looking further at this I found out that soldiers are salaried servants of cultivators and cultivators salaried servants of soldiers.

§ 181[464] Soldiers earn their wages from tax payers and the inhabitants of the country because they defend them and strain themselves on their behalf. Thus, it is incumbent on cultivators to pay the soldiers' wages in full, as their cultivation is perfected by them. If they delay or lose vigour, their enemies will grow stronger. I also saw it to be right that tax payers should not retain from their cultivation more than what is enough for them to survive and cultivate their land with, but I also saw that I should not destroy them and take all they have for the treasury and soldiers. If I did so, I would wrong both soldiers and tax payers, because when the (cultivator suffers),[465] cultivation, that is peasants and the soil, suffers and if tax payers do not have enough to live on and to cultivate their land with, soldiers will also perish, as their provisions come from cultivation of the land and from cultivators. There will be no cultivation of land except through the surplus in the hands of tax payers. To be able to do good to soldiers and to be generous to them, one has to be kind to tax payers and make their land flourish and leave them some surplus for their living. People in the countryside and tax payers are the hands of soldiers and their strength, while soldiers are the hands of tax payers and their strength. I have thought about this and made my utmost to discern things, and I realised that I should not prefer the ones over the others, since I had found them to be like a pair of hands, each helping the other, or feet, each supporting the other. By my life, one does not protect tax payers from injustice by harming soldiers, nor does one restrain injustice from soldiers by assailing tax payers. Were not some cavalrymen stupid, they would care for taxes and the country as well as a man cares for his village from which he receives his means of living and life and strength, and were not some tax payers ignorant they would refrain from keeping some of what they need and prefer soldiers over themselves.

464 Miskawayh, *Taǧārib al-umam*, 1:138–139 = C203–205.
465 Addition from Miskawayh.

§182[1] قال: ولما فرغنا من إصلاح العامة والخاصة بهذين الركنين من أهل الخراج والمقاتلة وكان ذلك ثمرة العدل الذي به دبر الله العظيم خلائقه وشكرت الله تعالى على نعمته في أداء حقه على مواهبه وأحكمنا أمور المقاتلة وأهل الخراج ببسط العدل أقبلنا بعد ذلك على السِيَر والسُنَن. ثم بدأنا بالأعظم فالأعظم نفعا لنا والأكبر فالأكبر عائدة على جندنا ورعيتنا. ونظرنا في سيَر آبائنا من لدن بستاسف إلى ملك قباذ أقرب آبائنا منا. ثم لم نترك صلاحا في شيء من ذلك إلا أخذنا به ولا فسادا إلا أعرضنا عنه. ولم يدْعُنا إلى قبول ما لا خير فيه من السُنن حب الآباء ولكنا آثرنا حب الله وشكره وطاعته.

§183[2] ولما فرغنا من النظر في سير آبائنا وبدأنا بهم وكانوا أحق بذلك فلم ندع حقا إلا آثرناه. ثم لما وجدنا الحق أقرب القرابة نظرنا في سِيَر أهل الروم والهند فاصطفينا محمودها وجعلنا عيار ذلك عقولنا وميزناه بأحلامنا فأخذنا من جميع ذلك ما زين سلطاننا وجعلناه سُنّة وعادةً ولم تنازعنا أنفسنا إلى ما تميل إليه أهواؤنا. وأعلمناهم ذلك وأخبرناهم به وكتبنا إليهم بما كرهنا لهم من السير ونهيناهم عنه وتقدمنا إليهم فيه غير أنا لم نكره أحدا على غير دينه وملته ولم نلزمهم ما قِبلنا ولا مع ذلك أنفنا من تعلم ما عندهم. فإن الإقرار بمعرفة الحق والعلم والاتباع له من أعظم ما تزينت به الملوك الآنفة من التعلم والحمية من طلب العلم ولا يكون عالما من لم يتعلم. ولما استقصيت ما عند هاتين الأمتين | من حكمة التدبير والسياسة ووصلت بين مكارم أسلافي وما أحدثته برأيي وأخذت 173b
به نفسي وقبلته عن الملوك الذين لم يكونوا منا وثَبَتُّ على الأمر الذي نلت به الظفَر والخير رفضت سائر الأمم لأني لم أجد عندهم رأيا ولا عقولا ولا أحلاما .ووجدتهم أصحاب بغي وحسد وكَلَب

٢ به: الزيادة بخط المقريزي في الهامش الأيسر من الأعلى إلى الأسفل + صح، ويشير إليها رمز ˥ بعد "الذي".
١١ ما: الزيادة بخط المقريزي في الهامش الأيسر من الأعلى إلى الأسفل + صح، ويشير إليها رمز ˥ بعد "إلى".
١٣ أنفنا: كشط المقريزي عبارة أخرى قبل أن يصححها كما هي الآن.

١ من تجارب الأمم لمسكويه ١: ١٣٩.
٢ من تجارب الأمم لمسكويه ١: ١٣٩.

§ 182[466] Anūširwān said: When I had put the affairs of commoners and the elite right through these two pillars, tax payers and soldiers, and this was the fruit of justice by which the Great God governs His creation, I thanked God, He is Exalted, for His favours by rendering Him His right for His gifts. When I had, thus, put the affairs of the soldiers and tax players on a firm basis by spreading justice, I proceeded to norms and laws, beginning with the most important ones as to usefulness to us and the greatest ones for the benefit for my armies and subjects. I looked at the norms of my ancestors from Bistāsf to King Qubād, the closest of my fathers. I followed everything that was useful, but turned away from everything that was harmful. The love of my ancestors did not incite me to accept any laws in which there was no good, as I preferred the love of God, thankfulness to Him, and obedience to Him over it.

§ 183[467] I started by looking at the norms of my ancestors, because they had the right to come first, and I always prefer doing what is right. When I had finished that, I realised that the right thing was to proceed in the order of proximity. I looked at the norms of the Byzantines and the Indians, selecting what was praiseworthy, using my reason as a touching stone for this. I made a selection on the basis of my discernment and took from all what would adorn my rule and I set that as a law and a habit. My soul did not draw me to what my desires would be taking me to. I informed them (my subjects) about this (the new laws and habits) and let them know them and wrote to them, telling them what norms I disliked and forbade them from and I commanded them to follow this. However, I never forced anyone to a religion and religious community not their own nor did I force them to join what I had accepted (as religion). Despite this, I did not disdain from learning from what they (the foreign nations) had, as accepting the truth and knowledge and following it is one of the greatest adornments of earlier kings in learning and zeal of searching for knowledge. He who does not learn is not learned. When I had exhausted what these two nations had of the wisdom of governing and ruling and I had adopted the noble features of my predecessors and what I had by my own reason innovated and accepted from foreign kings and I was on a firm basis in the affair with which I had reached victory and good, I abandoned (the norms of) the remaining nations because I found them lacking in reason, intelligence, and understanding. I found them to be

466 Miskawayh, *Taǧārib al-umam*, 1:139 = C205–206.
467 Miskawayh, *Taǧārib al-umam*, 1:139 = C206–207.

وحرص وشح وسوء تدبير وجهالة ولؤم عهد وقلة مكافأة. وهذه أمور لا تصلح عليها ولاية ولا تتم بها نعمة.

§184[1] ولما فرغ أنوشروان من أمور ممالكه وهذبها جمع إليه الأساورة والقواد والعظماء والمرازبة والنساك والموابذة وأماثل الناس وخطبهم فقال: أيها الناس أحضروني فهمكم وارعوني أسماعكم وناصحوني أنفسكم فإني لم أزل واضعا سيفي على عنقي منذ وليت عليكم غرَضًا للسيوف والأسنة. كل ذلك للمدافعة عنكم والإبقاء عليكم وإصلاح بلادكم مرة بأقصى المشرق وتارة في آخر المغرب وأخرى في ناحية الجنوب ومثلها في جانب الشمال ونقلت الذين اتهمتهم إلى غير بلادهم ووضعت الوضائع في بلدان الترك وأقمت بيوت النيران بقسطنطينية ولم أزل أصعد جبلا شامخا وأنزل عنه وَأَطَأُ حُزُونَه بعد سهوله وأصبر على المخمصة والمخافة وأكابد البرد والحر وأركب هول البحر وخطر المفازة إرادة هذا الأمر الذي قد أتمه الله تعالى لكم من الإثخان في الأعداء والتمكن في البلاد والسَعَة في المعاش ودَرَك العز وبلاغ ما نلتم. فقد أصبحتم بحمد الله ونعمته على الشرف {الأعلى} من النعمة والفضل الأكبر من الكرامة والأمن. قد هزم الله تعالى أعداءكم وقتلهم فهم بين مقتول هالك وحي مطيع لكم سامع.

§185[2] وقد بقي لكم عَدوٌّ عددهم قليل وبأسهم شديد وشوكتهم عظيمة. وهؤلاء الذين بقوا أخوف عندي عليكم وأحْرَى أن يهزموكم ويغلبوكم من الذين غلبتموهم من أعدائكم أصحاب السيوف والرماح والخيول. فإن أنتم أيها الناس غلبتم عدوكم هذا الثاني غَلَبْتُكُم لعدوكم الذين قاتلتم وحاصرتم | 174a فقد تم لكم الظفر والنصر وتمت فيكم القوة وتم بكم العز وتمت عليكم النعمة وتم لكم الفضل وتم لكم الاجتماع والألفة والنصيحة والسلامة. وإن أنتم قصرتم ووهنتم وظفر هذا العدو بكم فإن الظفر الذي كان منكم على عدوكم بالمغرب والمشرق والجنوب والشمال لم يكن ظفرا منكم. فاطلبوا أن

٩ حُزُونَه: وضع المقريزي رمز "ح" تحت الحرف الأول إشارة إلى تلفظه بالحاء. ١١ الأعلى: "الاعلا" في الأصل. ١٥ وأحْرَى: وضع المقريزي رمز "ح" تحت الحرف الثاني إشارة إلى تلفظه بالحاء.

١ من تجارب الأمم لمسكويه ١: ١٤٠.

٢ من تجارب الأمم لمسكويه ١: ١٤١.

companions of injustice, envy, rage, greed, avarice, bad governing, stupidity, treason, and lack of gratitude. These are things upon which good governing cannot be based, and no (divine) favour comes from them.

§ 184[468] When Anūširwān had finished arranging the affairs of his kingdoms, he brought to his presence all the cavalrymen, generals, noblemen, *marzubāns*, pious men, *mōbads*, and exemplary people and said: O people, listen to me with comprehension, allow me your attention, and be sincere to yourselves. I have carried my sword on my back since I started reigning over you and I have been the target of swords and spears, all this to defend and preserve you for the benefit of your country, at times in the far East, at others in the remote West, now in the South, and then again in the North. I have moved those to another country about whom I had suspicions and I have established rates (of taxation) for the countries of the Turks. I have established fire temples in Constantinople. I have ascended high mountains and descended them, I have trampled rough terrains after level ground. I have patiently suffered hunger and fear, enduring cold and heat, facing perils of the sea and dangers of the desert, seeking what God, He is Exalted, has now perfected for you, wearing out your enemies and taking possession of countries and procuring prosperity of life, attaining glory and reaching what you now have. Through God's glory and mercy you have now attained the highest glory of His favour and the excellence of His generosity and safety. God, He is Exalted, has driven away your enemies and killed them, so that now they are either killed and perished or alive and obedient and subservient to you.

§ 185[469] But there still remains an enemy, few in numbers, but great in strength and might. I think that this enemy that still remains is more formidable and more probable to defeat and vanquish you than the ones you have slain, the ones who had swords, spears, and horses. O people, if you slay this second enemy of yours like you did the ones whom you fought and besieged, then victory and triumph will be completely yours! Then your power will have been perfected and your might become complete, and God's favour will have been perfected for you and excellence consummated in you, as will have been your community, your concord, your sincerity, and your safety. But if you fall short and grow feeble, and that enemy vanquishes you, then the victory you had over your enemies in the West and East, South and North was not a real victory. Do your best to fight this remaining enemy as

468 Miskawayh, *Taǧārib al-umam*, 1:140 = C207–208.
469 Miskawayh, *Taǧārib al-umam*, 1:141 = C208–210.

تقتلوا من هذا العدو الباقي مثل الذي قتلتم من ذلك العدو الماضي وليكن جدكم في هذا واجتهادكم واحتشادكم أكبر وأجل وأحزم وأعزم وأصح وأسد. فإن أحق الأعداء بالاستعداد له أعظمهم مكيدة وأشدهم شوكة. وليس الذي كنتم تخافون من عدوكم الذي قاتلتم بقريب من هؤلاء الذين آمركم بقتالهم الآن. فاطلبوه وصلوا ظفرا بظفر ونصرا بنصر وقوة بقوة وتأييدا بتأييد وحزما وعزما بعزم وحزم وجهادا بجهاد. فإن بذلك اجتماع صلاحكم وتمام النعمة عليكم والزيادة في الكرامة من الله تعالى لكم والفوز برضوانه في الآخرة.

§186[1] ثم اعلموا أن عدوكم من الترك والروم والهند وسائر الأمم لم يكونوا ليبلغوا منكم إن ظهروا عليكم وغلبوكم مثل الذي يبلغ هذا العدو منكم إن غلبكم. فإن بأس هذا العدو أشد وكيده أكبر وأمره أخوف من ذلك العدو. وأيها الناس إني قد نصَبْتُ لكم كما رأيتم ولقيت ما قد علمتم بالسيف والرمح والمفاوز والبحار والسهولة والجبال أقارع عدوا عدوا وأكالب جندا جندا وأكابد ملكا ملكا لم أتضرع إليكم هذا التضرع في قتال أولٰئك الجنود والملوك ولم أسألكم هذه المسألة في طلب الجد منكم والاجتهاد والاحتفال والاحتشاد. وإنما فعلت هذا اليوم لعظم خطره وشدة شوكته ومخافة صولته بكم. وإن أنا أيها الناس لم أغلب هذا العدو {وأنفه} عنكم فقد أبقيت فيكم أكبر الأعداء ونفيت عنكم أضعفها فأعينوني على نفي هذا العدو المخوف عليكم القريب الدار منكم. فأنشدكم الله أيها الناس لما أعنتموني عليه حتى أنفيه عنكم وأخرجه من بين أظهركم فيتم بلائي عندكم وبلاء الله تعالى فيكم عندي وتتم النعمة علي وعليكم والكرامة من | الله تعالى لي ولكم ويتم هذا العز والنصر 174b
وهذا الشرف والتمكين وهذه الثروة والمنزلة.

١٣ وأنفه: "وانفيه" في الأصل.

١ من تجارب الأمم لمسكويه ١: ١٤٠–١٤١.

you fought the past enemy. Let your eagerness, exertion, and concentration be even greater and mightier, more determined and more resolute, sounder and more correct, because one should prepare best for the enemy which is the most cunning and the strongest. What you feared from the enemies you fought is not even close to these that I now tell you to fight against. Search for and attach a new victory to your earlier victory, a new triumph to your earlier triumph, strength to strength and divine succour to divine succour, determination and resoluteness to resoluteness and determination, striving to striving. Through this you will reach your perfect wellbeing, your complete favour, and an addition of generosity from God, He is Exalted, towards you and the great triumph through His pleasure in the Hereafter.

§186[470] Know also that your enemies from among the Turks, Byzantines, Indians, and other peoples would not have caused such damage to you, had they won and vanquished you in the way this enemy will do if he were to vanquish you. The strength of this enemy is stronger, his cunning greater, and his force more formidable than those of the earlier enemies. O people, I have exhausted myself on your behalf, as you have seen, and I have suffered, as you know, from swords and spears, deserts and seas, plains and mountains, battling one enemy after the other, fighting one army after the other, standing against one king after the other, without ever imploring you to fight against these armies and kings so much as I now do. I have never before asked you so urgently to be eager, exert yourselves, to be concerned, and to concentrate. Today I do so, because of the greatness of the hazard, the strength of the enemy's power, and the fear of his attack against you. O people, if I do not win this enemy and drive him away, I have left the worst of enemies among you, while driving away weaker ones. Help me drive this enemy away, which one has to fear for you and which lives close by you. I implore you by God, o people! When you have helped me drive him away and oust him from amidst you, my tribulation on your behalf has been fulfilled and God's, He is Exalted, tribulation in you for me has been fulfilled, and His favour to me and to you has been fulfilled and God's, He is Exalted, generosity to me and to you has been fulfilled, and this glory and victory, this eminence and establishment, this wealth and position have been fulfilled.

470 Miskawayh, *Taǧārib al-umam*, 1:140–141 = C210–211.

§187[1] يأيها الناس إني تفكرت بعد فراغي من كتابي هذا وما وصفت من نعم الله تعالى علينا في الأمر الذي لما غلب دَارَا الملوكَ والأمم وقهرها واستولى على بلادها ثم لما لم يُحكِم أمر هذا العدو هلك وهلكت جنوده بعد السلامة والظفر والنصر والغلبة. وذلك أنه لم يرض بالأمر الذي تم له به الملك واشتد به له السلطان وقوي به على الأعداء وتمت عليه به النعمة وفاضت عليه من وجوه الدنيا كلها الكرامة حتى احتيل له بوجوه النميمة البغي. فدعا البغي الحسدَ فتقوى به وتمكن ودعا الحسد {بغض} أهل الفقر لأهل الغنى وأهل الخمول لأهل الشرف. ثم أتاهم الإسكندر على ذلك من تفرق الأهواء واختلاف الأمور وظهور البغضاء وقوة العداوة فيما بينهم والفساد منهم. ثم ارتفع ذلك إلى أن قتله صاحب حرسه وأمينه على دمه للذي شمل قلوب العامة من الشَر والضغينة وثبت فيها من العداوة والفرقة. فكفى الإسكندر مؤونة نفسه وقد اتعظت بذلك اليوم وذكرته.

§188[2] يأيها الناس فلا أسمعن في هذه النعمة تفرقا ولا بغيا ولا حسدا ظاهرا ولا سِعَاية ولا وشايَة فإن الله تعالى قد طهر من ذلك أخلاقنا ومُلْكَنا وأكرم عنه ولايتنا. وما نلت ما نلته بنعمة ربنا وحمده بشيء من هذه الأمور الخبيثة التي نفتها العلماء وعافتها الحكماء ولكني نلت هذه الرتب بالصحة والسلامة والحب للرعية والوفاء والعدل والاستقامة والتؤدة. وإنما تركنا أن نأخذ عن هذه الأمم التي سميناها أعني الترك والبربر والزنج وأهل الجبال وغيرهم مثل ما أخذنا عن الهند والروم لظهور هذه الأخلاق فيهم وغلبتها عليهم. ولم تصلح أمةٌ قط ولا مَلِكُها على ظهور هذه الأخلاق فيها. وإن أول ما أنا ناف وتارك من هذه الأمور هذه الأخلاق التي هي {أعدى} أعدائكم.

٦ بغض: "بعض" في الأصل. ١٧ أعدى: "اعدا" في الأصل.

١ من تجارب الأمم لمسكويه ١: ١٤١.

٢ من تجارب الأمم لمسكويه ١: ١٤١–١٤٢.

§ 187[471] O people, after I had finished this letter of mine with its description of God's, He is Exalted, favours on us, I thought about Darius, who, after having vanquished kings and nations and made them subservient to him, had a firm grip on countries. But as he did not deal firmly with this enemy, he and his armies perished after having been successful and victorious, triumphant and conquering. That was because he was not satisfied with what had made his kingship complete, his rule strong, and him stronger than his enemies and with the divine favour that had been completed for him, with signs of respect flowing to him from all parts of the world. He was tricked to injustice through slander, and injustice called envy, which grew strong and powerful, and envy made the poor hate[472] the rich and the low hate the noble. Then there came Alexander when their desires had become various and their affairs contradictory, hatred had become visible, corruption and mutual enmity had become strong. This escalated until the commander of his guard and the man trusted for his life killed him because of the evil and rancour that filled the hearts of the common people and the enmity and disunion that had become firmly established in their hearts. Alexander did not need to exert himself. I have taken heed of the warning of that day and I remember it.

§ 188[473] O people, may I not hear in this divine favour any disunion, injustice, open envy, slander, or defamation. God, He is Exalted, has purified my character and my kingship from all that and has generously purified our rule from that. None of what I have achieved, have I achieved through these wicked things that learned scholars forbid and wise men dismiss, thanks to the favour of our Lord and His glory. I have reached these ranks through soundness, safety, and love of people, faithfulness, justice, honesty, and deliberateness. I have desisted from taking anything from these nations that I have mentioned—I mean the Turks, Berbers, Zanǧ, peoples of the mountains, and others—contrary to what I have taken from the Indians and the Byzantines, because these features are manifest in them and preponderant on them. No people and no king will flourish if these characteristics appear in them. The first thing I drive away and leave are these characteristics, which are your worst enemies.

471 Miskawayh, *Taǧārib al-umam*, 1:141 = C211–212.

472 Reading *buġḍ*. Both manuscripts, as well as Miskawayh, read *wa-daʿā l-ḥasadu baʿḍa ahl al-faqr*.

473 Miskawayh, *Taǧārib al-umam*, 1:141–142 = C212–213.

§189[١] يأيها الناس إن في ما بسط الله تعالى علينا من السلامة والعافية والاستصلاح غنًى لنا عما نطلب بهذه الأخلاق المردية {المشؤومة}. فاكفوني في ذلك أنفسكم فإن | قهر هذه الأعداء أحب 175a إلي وخير لكم من قهر أعدائكم من الترك والروم. فأما أنا يأيها الناس فقد طبت نفسا بترك هذه الأمور ومحقها وقمعها ونفيها عني لا حاجة لي بما فيها ولا بالذي علي منها. فطيبوا أنفسا بالذي طبت به نفسا منكم. يأيها الناس إني قد أحببت أن أنفي عنكم عدوكم الباطن والظاهر. فأما الظاهر منهما فإنا بحمد الله ونعمته قد نفيناه وأعاننا الله تعالى عليه وخضدنا شوكته وأحسنتم فيه وأجملتم وآسَيْتم واجتهدتم. فافعلوا في هذا العدو كما فعلتم في ذلك العدو واعملوا فيه كالذي عملتم في ذلك واحفظوا علي ما أوصيكم به فإني شفيق عليكم ناصح لكم.

§190[٢] يأيها الناس من أحيا هذه الأمور فينا فقد أفسد بلاءه عندنا بقتاله من كان يقاتلنا من أعدائنا فإن هذه أكثر مضرة وأشد شوكة وأعظم بلية وأضر تبعة. واعلموا أن خيركم من جمع إلى بلائه السالف عندنا المعونة لنا على نفسه في هذا الغابر. واعلموا أن من غلبه هذا غلب عليه ذاك ومن غلب هذا فقد قهر ذاك وذاك أن بالسلامة والمودة والألفة والاجتماع والتناصح منكم يكون العز والقدرة ومع التحاسد والبغي والنميمة والتشتت يكون ذهاب العز وانقطاع القوة وهلاك الدنيا والآخرة. فعليكم بما أمرناكم به واحذروا ما نهيناكم عنه ولا قوة إلا بالله. عليكم بمؤاساة أهل الفاقة وضيافة السابلة وأكرموا جوار من جاوركم وأحسنوا صحبة من دخل من الأمم فيكم فإنهم في ذمتي لا تجبهوهم ولا تظلموهم ولا تسلطوا عليهم ولا تحرجوهم فإن الإحراج يدعو إلى المعصية. ولكن اصبروا لهم على بعض الأذى واحفظوا أمانتكم وعهدكم واحفظوا ما عهدت إليكم من هذه الأخلاق فإنا لم نر سلطانا قط ولا أمة هلكوا إلا بترك هذه الأخلاق ولا صلحوا إلا معها وبالله ثقتنا في الأمور كلها.

٢ المشؤومة: "المشومة" في الأصل.   ١١ الغابر: وضع المقريزي فوق هذه الكلمة رمز "ك" (لـ "كذا") إشارة إلى شكه في صحة قراءتها.   ١٦ تحرجوهم: وضع المقريزي رمز "ح" تحت الحرف الثاني إشارة إلى تلفظه بالحاء. ‖ الإحراج: وضع المقريزي رمز "ح" تحت الحرف الرابع إشارة إلى تلفظه بالحاء. ‖ يدعو: "يدعوا" في الأصل.

١ من تجارب الأمم لمسكويه ١: ١٤٢.

٢ من تجارب الأمم لمسكويه ١: ١٤٢.

§189[474] O people, the safety, health, and wellbeing that God, He is exalted, has spread over us make it unnecessary that I would aspire for more through these ill-omened, destructive characteristics. Beware them, because vanquishing these enemies pleases me more and is better for you than vanquishing your enemies from among the Turks and the Byzantines. O people, I am pleased to have left these things, eradicating, and suppressing them and driving them away from me. I do not need what they have for or against me. Be pleased with what I am pleased with for you. O people, I want to drive away your inner and outer enemies. With God's glory and His favour the outer ones God, He is Exalted, has already helped me to drive away. We have cut the outer enemies' stings, and you have done well in this and properly, sharing the troubles and exerting yourselves. Do with this enemy as you did with that and treat it like you treated that. Keep the advice I give you, because I wish you well and am sincere to you.

§190[475] O people, if one of you revives these things among us, he has forfeited the trouble he has seen by fighting against the enemies that fought against me. These enemies are more harmful and stronger, a greater disaster and of more nefarious results. Know that the best of you is the one who combines with his earlier trouble he has seen for me the help he gives me against his own soul in this matter. Know that who will be vanquished by this, will also be vanquished by those and he who vanquishes this has also vanquished those. By safety, love, friendship, union, and mutual sincerity might and power are born, whereas mutual envy and injustice, slander and disunion, cause the departure of might, the end of power, and perdition in both this world and the Hereafter. Keep well what I tell you to and beware of what I forbid you from. There is no might except God's! Share with the poor and host the traveller. Respect the rights of your neighbours and be good companions to peoples who enter among you, because I protect them. Do not confront them and do not wrong them, do not impose yourselves on them and do not coerce them, because coercion calls to disobedience. Instead, be patient towards them even if they cause some harm, and keep your tryst and your pact. Keep also what I have said to you concerning these characteristics, because I have never seen a ruler or a nation perish except when they have left these characteristics and they have not flourished except with them. In God I trust in all matters.

---

474 Miskawayh, *Taǧārib al-umam*, 1:142 = C213–214.

475 Miskawayh, *Taǧārib al-umam*, 1:142 = C214–215.

§191[1] وكان شعاره أبيض ووشيه ألوان مختلفة وسراويله على لون السماء وكان يعتمد على سيفه. وكانت مدة ملكه إلى أن هلك سبعا وأربعين سنة وسبعة أشهر. وكان عمر بن الخطاب رضي الله عنه يكثر | الخلوة بقوم من الفرس {يقرؤون} عليه سياسات الملوك ولا سيما ملوك العجم الفضلاء وسيما 175b أنوشروان فإنه كان معجبا بها كثير الإقتداء بها. وكان أنوشروان مقتديا بسيرة أردشير آخذًا نفسه بها وبعهده الذي تقدم في خبره مطالبا به غيره. وكان أردشير متبعا لبهمن وكورش مقتديا بهما فهؤلاء جلة ملوك الفرس وفضلاؤهم الذين ينبغي أن يقتدى بأفعالهم ويتعلم سياساتهم ويتشبه بهم. (...)

§192[2] | هرمز الملقب ترك زاذ بن كسرى أنوشروان بن قباذ. أمه ابنة خاقان الأكبر. كان كثير 176a الأدب حسن النية في الإحسان إلى الضعفاء والمساكين إلا أنه كان يحمل على الأشراف فعادوه وأبغضوه. فعلم بذلك منهم وكان في نفسه منهم مثل ما كان في أنفسهم منه. وكان من سيرته المرتضاة أنه تحرى الخير والعدل على الرعية وتشدد على العظماء المستطيلين على الضعفاء. وبلغ من عدله أنه كان يسير إلى الماه ليصيف هناك. فأمر فنودي في مسيره ذلك في مواضع الحرث أن {يتحامى} ولا يسير فيها الراكب لئلا يضروا بأحد. ووكل بعض أساورته بتعهد ما يجري في عسكره ومعاقبة من تعدى أمره وتغريمه عوضا لصاحب الحرث.

§193[3] وكان ابنه كسرى برويز في عسكره فعار مركب من مراكبه فوقع في محرثة من المحارث التي كانت في طريقه فرتع فيها وأفسد منها. فأخذ ذلك المركب ورفع إلى الرجل الذي وكل بمعاقبة

---

٣ يقرؤون: "يقرون" في الأصل. ٦ ملوك: الزيادة بخط المقريزي في الهامش الأيمن من الأسفل إلى الأعلى + صح، ويشير إليها رمز ⌐ بعد "جلة". ٧ بهم: بعد هذه الكلمة بياض بقدر تسعة عشر سطرا في الأصل. ٨ كان: كتب المقريزي أولا "وكان"، ثم كشط الواو. ١٢ يتحامى: في الأصل "يتحاما". ١٣ بعض أساورته: الزيادة بخط المقريزي في الهامش الأيسر من الأعلى إلى الأسفل + صح، ويشير إليها رمز ⌐ بعد "ووكل".

---

١ من تأريخ سني الملوك لحمزة ص ٤٥، ١٤.

٢ من تجارب الأمم لمسكويه ١: ١٤٢–١٤٣.

٣ من تجارب الأمم لمسكويه ١: ١٤٣.

§191[476] Anūširwān's vest was white with embroidery in variegated colours and his trousers sky-blue. He used to lean on his sword. The length of his reign until he died was 47 years and 7 months. ʿUmar b. al-Ḫaṭṭāb, may God be pleased with him, used to withdraw himself with some Persians, who read to him (books of) kings' ways of governing, and especially excellent Persian (*al-ʿAǧam*) kings', and even more especially Anūširwān's,[477] who was much admired and imitated for his governing. Anūširwān modelled himself after Ardašīr, emulating his ways of governing and following his *ʿAhd* [Testament], which has been mentioned above, and demanding others to follow it, too. Ardašīr, for his part, was following Bahman and Cyrus and emulating their example. These are the most exalted Persian kings and the best of them, and it behoves to model oneself on their deeds and to learn their ways of governing and to imitate them.[478]

§192[479] Hurmuz, called Turkzād,[480] b. Kisrá Anūširwān b. Qubād. His mother was the daughter of the Great Ḫāqān. He was very learned and full of good intentions of doing good to the weak and the poor, but he attacked the nobility, and these became inimical to him and hated him. He realised this and felt the same towards them in his heart. Of his good ways is that he pursued what was good and was just to his people and harsh on the noblemen, who were overbearing toward the weak. His justice reached to the following: When he was travelling to al-Māh to spend the summer there, he gave orders to announce that when they were travelling through cultivated areas, riders should take care not to ride through cornfields, in order not to cause damage to anyone. He appointed some cavalrymen to keep an eye on what was going on in the convoy and to punish those who broke his order and to fine them to pay back to the owner of the field.

§193[481] Hurmuz's son Kisrá Abarwīz was in the convoy, and one of his horses wandered off to a cultivated field, which was on their way, and grazed there and spoiled some of it. The horse was captured and taken to the man who

476 Ḥamzah, *Taʾrīḫ* 45, 14 = trans. 71, 34 (beginning). Ḥamzah, *Taʾrīḫ* 20, 25 = trans. 38, 44, give 47 years, 7 months and some days or 48 years.

477 This can also be taken as a reference to *Siyāsat Anūširwān*, which is not explicitly mentioned but can be implied from *siyāsāt al-mulūk … wa-siyyamā Anūširwān*.

478 Nineteen last lines of fol. 175ᵃ have been left blank.

479 Miskawayh, *Taǧārib al-umam*, 1:142–143 = C215–216; cf. al-Ṭabarī, *Taʾrīḫ*, 1:988–989 = trans., 5:295–296.

480 Cf. al-Bīrūnī, *al-Āṯār al-bāqiyah* 138.

481 Miskawayh, *Taǧārib al-umam*, 1:143; cf. al-Ṭabarī, *Taʾrīḫ*, 1:989–990 = trans., 5:296–297.

من أفسد هو أو دابته شيئا من المحارث وتغريمه فلم يقدر الرجل على إنفاذ أمر هرمز في ابنه ولا أحد من حشمه. فرفع ما {رُئي} من إفساد ذلك المركب إلى هرمز فأمره أن يجذع أذنيه ويبْتُر ذنبه ويغرم أبرويز. فخرج الرجل لإنفاذ الأمر فدس له أبرويز رهطا من العظماء ليسألوه التغييب في أمره فلقوه وكلموه في ذلك فلم يجب إليه. فسألوه أن يؤخر ما أمر به هرمز حتى يكلموه فأمر بالكف عنه. فلقي أولٰئك الرهط هرمز وأعلموه أن بتلك الدابة الذي عار زعارة وأنه أخذ للوقت وسألوه أن يأمر بالكف عن جذعه وتبتيره لما فيه من سوء الطيرة. فلم يجبهم وأمر بالمركب فجذع أذناه وبتر ذنبه وغرم أبرويز ما يغرم غيره في هذا الحد فأمضى ما أمر به ثم ارتحل.

§194[1] وركب ذات يوم في أوان إيناع الكرم إلى ساباط المدائن وكان ممره على بساتين وكروم. فاطّلَع بعض أساورته في كَرْم فرأى فيها حِصْرِما فأصاب منه عناقيد ودفعها إلى غلامه وقال: "اذهب بها إلى المنزل واطبخها بلحم واتخذ منها مرقة فإنها نافعة في | هذا الأبان." فأتاه حافظ ذلك 176b الكرم فلزمه وصرخ. فبلغ إشفاق الرجل من عقوبة هرمز على تناوله من ذلك الكرم أن دفع إلى حافظ الكرم منطقة محلاة بذهب كانت عليه عوضا له من الحصرم الذي رزأه من كرمه وافتدى بها نفسه ورأى أن قبض الحافظ إياها منه وتخليته عنه مِنَّةً من بها عليه. فهذه كانت سيرة هرمز في العدل والضبط والهيبة. وكان مظفرا لا يمد يده إلى شيء إلا وأتاه. وكان مع ذلك أديبا دَاهِياً إلا عِرْقًا قد نزَعَه أخواله من التُرْك وكان لذلك مُقْصِياً للأشراف وأهل البيوتات والعلماء. وقيل إنه قتل ثلاثة عشر ألف رجل وستمائة رجل ولم يكن له رأي إلا في تألف السَفِلة واستصلاحهم

٢ ما: الزيادة بخط المقريزي في الهامش الأيسر من الأعلى إلى الأسفل + صح، ويشير إليها رمز ⌐ بعد "فرفع". || رُئي: في الأصل "راي". ١٢ محلاة: وضع المقريزي رمز "ح" تحت الحرف الثاني إشارة إلى تلفظه بالحاء.

١ من تجارب الأمم لمسكويه ١: ١٤٣-١٤٤.

was appointed to punish those who, or whose horses, spoiled any cultivated fields, and to fine them. The man could not execute the order of Hurmuz concerning Hurmuz's son or any of his servants, so he reported to Hurmuz that this horse had been seen doing damage. Hurmuz gave him an order to cut the ears of the horse and crop its tail and fine Abarwīz. The man went to execute the order, but Abarwīz sent some noblemen to ask him to overlook this matter. They tried to convince him but he refused to do so. Then they asked him to postpone executing the order of Hurmuz, so that they could address Hurmuz first. The man gave orders to refrain from it for a while. Those noblemen went to Hurmuz and told him that the horse[482] was malicious and that it had been taken away quickly. They asked him to give an order to refrain from cutting its ears and cropping its tail because of the bad omen that would contain. Hurmuz did not accede and confirmed the order to cut its ears and to crop its tail. Abarwīz was also made to pay the same fine as others for the same offence. The man executed this command and then moved on.

§ 194[483] Once, when grapes were ripening, Hurmuz rode to Sābāṭ al-Madāʾin. His route took him through orchards and vineyards. One of his cavalrymen saw a vineyard with some unripe grapes. He took a few bunches and gave them to his servant, saying: "Take these to the camp, cook them with some meat, and make a broth. It is good for health at this time of the year." The guardian of the vineyard came to him, gripped him, and shouted at him. The cavalryman was so afraid of being punished by Hurmuz for having taken something from the vineyard that he gave the guardian his belt adorned with gold in recompense for the unripe grapes he had taken and so ransomed himself free. He considered it a favour to himself by the guardian that the latter accepted the belt from him and let him go. This was the way of Hurmuz in justice, punctuality, and awe felt for him. He was always successful: whatever he set out to do, he accomplished. He was learned and shrewd, but had inherited one feature from his Turkish maternal relatives. This is why he was harsh to the nobles and members of the great families and learned men. It is said that he had 13,600 men killed. He only liked the company of low

482 Miskawayh (ed. Caetani) reads *bi-ḏālika l-dābbah allaḏī*. Al-Maqrīzī changes the demonstrative from *bi-ḏālika* to *bi-tilka*, but overlooks the masculine relative pronoun and reads *bi-tilka l-dābbah* (fem.) *allaḏī* (masc.).

483 Miskawayh, *Taǧārib al-umam*, 1:143–144 = C217–219; cf. al-Ṭabarī, *Taʾrīḫ*, 1:990 = trans., 5:297–298.

عليه. وحبَسَ خلقا من العظماء وحط مراتب خلق وقصَّر بالأساورة ففسدت عليه نيات جنده من الكبراء واتصل ذلك بما جناه على بهرام شُوبِيْن فكان ذلك سبب هلاكه.

§195[١] وذلك أنه خرج على هرمز خوارج منهم شَابَة ملك التُّرْك الأعظم وصار إلى باذغيْس وذلك بعد إحدى عشرة سنة من ملكه. وخرج عليه ملك الروم في ثمانين ألف مقاتل قاصدا له وخرج عليه ملك الخزَر حتى صار إلى باب الأبواب وخرج عليه من العَرَب خلق نزلوا في شاطئ الفرات وشنوا الغارة على أهل السواد. واجترأ عليه أعداؤه وغزوا بلاده فأما شابة ملك الترك فإنه أرسل إلى هرمز وإلى عظماء الفرس يؤذنهم بإقباله ويقول: "رُمُّوا لي قناطر أنهار وأودية اجتاز عليها إلى بلادكم واعقدوا القناطر على كل نهر لا قنطرة له. وافعلوا ذلك فى الأنهار والأودية التي عليها مسلكي من بلادكم إلى بلاد الروم فإني مُجْمع على المسير إليها من بلادكم."

§196[٢] فاستفظع هرمز ما ورد عليه من ذلك وشاور فيه فأجمع رأيهم على قصد ملك الترك وصرف العناية إليه. فوجه إليه رجلا من أهل الرأي يقال له بهرام بن بهرام جسنس ويعرف بشوبين. فاختار بهرام من الجند اثني عشر ألف رجل من الكهول دون | الشباب وكانت عدة 177a
من يشمل عليه الديوان سبعين ألف مقاتل فمضى بهرام بجد وإغذاذ حتى جاز هراة وباذغيس ولم يشعر شابة ببهرام حتى نزل بالقرب منه مُعَسْكِرًا. فجرت بينهما رسائل وحروب قتل فيها بهرامُ شابَةَ برمية رماه بها بهرام واستباح عسكره وأقام موضعه. فوافاه برموذة بن شابة وكان يُعْدل بأبيه فحاربه فهزمه وحصره ببعض الحصون حتى استسلم له فوجهه أسيرا إلى هرمز وغنم كنوزا عظيمة.

١٥ بها بهرام: الزيادة بخط المقريزي في الهامش الأيسر من الأعلى إلى الأسفل + صح، ويشير إليها رمز ⌐ بعد "رماه".

١ من تجارب الأمم لمسكويه ١: ١٤٤.

٢ من تجارب الأمم لمسكويه ١: ١٤٤.

people and wanted to please them. He imprisoned a number of noblemen and lowered the ranks of many people. He was negligent of cavalrymen, and the opinions of the higher ranks in his army concerning him deteriorated. He also wronged Bahrām Čūbīn, which was the reason of his downfall.

§ 195[484] This went as follows: Some people rebelled against Hurmuz, among them Šābah, the Great King of the Turks, who marched to Bādġīs in the twelfth[485] year of Hurmuz's reign. At the same time, the king of the Byzantines marched against him with 80,000 men and the king of the Ḫazars rebelled against him, marching to Bāb al-Abwāb, and many of the Arabs rebelled and settled on the banks of the Euphrates, raiding the people of the Sawād from there. All his enemies grew bold with him and raided his country. Šābah, the king of the Turks, sent a word to Hurmuz and the Persian noblemen asking permission to march further and saying: "Repair for me the bridges over rivers and valleys, so that I can cross them to your country, and build stone bridges over rivers that do not have a bridge. Do this to rivers and valleys that are on my way from your country to the country of the Byzantines, because I will be marching there through your country."

§ 196[486] Hurmuz found the situation threatening and took counsel with his men. They decided to turn their attention to the king of the Turks and take care of him (first). Hurmuz sent against him a discerning man[487] by the name of Bahrām b. Bahrām-Ǧusnas, known as Čūbīn. Bahrām selected 12,000 seasoned men, no youngsters, from the army. The number of soldiers in the register was 70,000. Bahrām advanced with diligence and speed until he had passed Herat and Bādġīs. Šābah only grew aware of Bahrām, when Bahrām set his camp close to his. There followed an exchange of letters and some battles, in which Bahrām killed Šābah by shooting an arrow. Bahrām let his soldiers raid Šābah's camp. Bahrām stayed where he was, and Barmūdah b. Šābah came to him. Barmūdah was equal to his father. Bahrām fought him, put him to flight, and besieged him in one of the fortresses until he surrendered. Bahrām sent him as a prisoner to Hurmuz and looted great treasures.

484 Miskawayh, *Taǧārib al-umam*, 1:144 = C219–220; cf. al-Ṭabarī, *Taʾrīḫ*, 1:991–992 = trans., 5:298–301.

485 Al-Ṭabarī says that this happened in (*fī*) the eleventh year, but Miskawayh, and following him al-Maqrīzī, say that this took place after (*baʿd*) the eleventh year.

486 Miskawayh, *Taǧārib al-umam*, 1:144 = C220–221; cf. al-Ṭabarī, *Taʾrīḫ*, 1:992 = trans., 5:301–303.

487 Thus in al-Maqrīzī, who reads *al-raʾy* for al-Rayy ("a man from Rayy"), as in al-Ṭabarī and Miskawayh.

§197[١] فيقال إنه حمل إلى هرمز من الأموال والجواهر والآنية والأمتعة مما غنمه وقر مائتي ألف وخمسين ألف بعير في مدة تلك الأيام. فشكره هرمز على ذلك إلا أنه أراد منه أن يتقدم بمن معه إلى بلاد الترك فكاتبه في ذلك فلم ير بهرام ذلك صوابا. ثم خاف بهرام سطوة هرمز وحُكي له أن الملك يستقل ما حمله إليه من الغنائم في جنب ما وصل إليه وأنه يقول في مَجالِسه: "بهرام قد تَرفه واستطاب الدَعَة." وبلغ ذلك الجند نخافوا مثل خوفه.

§198[٢] فيقال إن بهرام جمع وجوه عسكره فأجلسهم على مراتبهم. ثم خرج عليهم في زي النساء وبيده مِغْزل وقطن. ثم جلس في موضعه وحمل لكل واحد من أولٰئك مغزل وقطن فوضع بين أيديهم فامتعضوا من ذلك وأنكروه. فقال بهرام: "إن كتّاب الملك ورد علي بذلك فلا بد من امتثال أمره إن كنتم طائعين." فأظهروا أنفَةً وحَمية وخلعوا هرمز وأظهروا أن ابنه أبرويز أصلح للملك منه. وساعدهم على ذلك خلق ممن كان بحَضْرة هرمز وأنفذ هرمز جيشا كثيفا مع آذيجسنس لمحاربة بهرام.

§199[٣] وأشفق أبرويز من الحديث وخاف سطوة أبيه فهرب إلى آذربيجان. فاجتمع إليه هناك عدة من المرازبة والإصبهبذين فأعطوه بيعتهم. ولم يظهر أبرويز شيئا وأقام بمكانه إلى أن بلغه أن آذيجسنس الموجه لمحاربة بهرام شوبين قُتِل وانفضاض الجمع الذي معه واضطراب أمر | أبيه 177b
هرمز. وكتبت إليه أخت آذيجسنس وكانت تِرْبَه تخبره بضعف أبيه هرمز وأعلمته أن العظماء

١٠ مع : كشط المقريزي عبارة أخرى قبل أن يصححها كما هي الآن. ‖ آذيجسنس : في الأصل "اذىجسس". ١٤ آذيجسنس : في الأصل "ادىحسس".

١ من تجارب الأمم لمسكويه ١: ١٤٤.
٢ من تجارب الأمم لمسكويه ١: ١٤٥.
٣ من تجارب الأمم لمسكويه ١: ١٤٥ ومن تأريخ سني الملوك لحمزة ص ٤٧، ١٤.

§ 197[488] It is said that during those days 250,000 camel loads of booty, money, jewels, vessels, and goods were carried to Hurmuz, who thanked Bahrām for this, but he also wanted Bahrām and his army to push forward into the realm of the Turks, writing to him and telling him to do so. Bahrām, however, did not consider this wise. He was afraid of Hurmuz's anger, though. He was also told that the king belittled the booty that had been carried to him, compared to what had come to him (Bahrām) and kept saying to his companions: "Bahrām has made his life pleasant and now prefers comfort." This reached also the troops, who were as worried about this as he.

§ 198[489] It is said that Bahrām called the leaders of his army together and seated them according to their ranks. Then he came to them in a dress, with a spindle and some cotton in hand. He sat in his place, and a spindle and some cotton was put in front of each of the army leaders, who resented this and disapproved of it. Bahrām said to them: "A letter from the king came to me with such orders, and we must follow his orders, if you want to be obedient to him." The men disdained this and were enraged by it. They renounced Hurmuz, expressing that his son Abarwīz was better suited to being king. Many of those who were in Hurmuz's presence helped them in this. Hurmuz sent a large army led by Ādīn-Ǧusnas[490] to fight Bahrām.

§ 199[491] Abarwīz was concerned with this talk, fearing the wrath of his father, and fled to Azerbaijan, where a great number of *marzubāns* and *iṣbahbads* joined him and gave him their allegiance. Abarwīz, however, did not initiate anything but stayed where he was until he heard that Ādīn-Ǧusnas, who had been sent to fight Bahrām Čūbīn, had been killed[492] and that the troops that were with him had been scattered and the affairs of his father Hurmuz had become confused. The sister of Ādīn-Ǧusnas wrote to him—she was of his age—and told him about the weakness of his father Hurmuz and let him know that the noblemen and the leaders had decided

488 Miskawayh, *Taǧārib al-umam*, 1:144 = C220–221; cf. al-Ṭabarī, *Ta'rīḫ*, 1:993 = trans., 5:303.

489 Miskawayh, *Taǧārib al-umam*, 1:145 = C221.

490 For the name, see Bosworth (1999): 306, note 716, who, following de Blois, suggests reading Ādur-Gushnasp.

491 Miskawayh, *Taǧārib al-umam*, 1:145 = C221–222; Ḥamzah, *Ta'rīḫ* 47, 14 = trans. 74, 34. Ḥamzah, *Ta'rīḫ* 20, 25 = trans. 38, 44, give 23, 13, or 12 years.

492 The syntax in the rest of the sentence has been changed from that of Miskawayh and is incorrect.

والوجوه قد أجمعوا على خلعه وأعلمته أن چوبين إن سبقه إلى المدائن احتوى على الملك. ولم يلبث العظماء بعد ذلك أن وثبت على هرمز وفيهم بيدويه وبسطام خالا أبرويز فخلعوه وسَمَلُوا عينيه وتركوه تحرجا من قتله. فلما بلغ ذلك أبرويز بادر بمن معه وسبق بهرام إلى المدائن وتتوج. فكانت مدة هرمز إحدى عشرة سنة وسبعة أشهر وعشرة أيام. وكان شعاره أحمر مُوَشَّى وسراويله على لون السماء موشى وتاجه أخضر ويعتمد إذا جلس على سريره بيُسْراه على سيفه وبيُمْناه جرز. ولم يُسْمَل من ملوك قبله ولا بعده غيره.

§200[1] ومن محاسن سيره أنه لما فرغ من بناء داره التي بشرق دجلة مقابل المدائن عمل وليمة عظيمة وأحضر الناس من الأطراف فأكلوا. ثم قال: "هل رأيتم في هذه الدار عيبا؟" فكلهم قال: "لا عيب فيها." فقام رجل وقال: "فيها ثلاثة عيوب فاحشة. أحدها أن الناس يجعلون دورهم في الدنيا وأنت جعلت الدنيا في دارك فقد أفرطت في توسيع صحونها وبيوتها فتتمكن الشمس منها في الصيف والسموم فيؤذي ذلك أهلها ويكثر فيها في الشتاء البرد. والثاني أن الملوك ينزلون في البناء على الأنهار لتزول همومهم وأفكارهم بالنظر إلى المياه ويترطب الهواء وتضيء أبصارهم. وأنت تركت دجلة وبنيتها في القفر. والثالث أنك جعلت حُجْرة النساء مما يلي الشمال من مساكن الرجال وهو أدوم هبوبا فلا يزال الهواء يجيء بأصوات النساء وريح طيبهن وهذا مما تمنعه الغيرة والحَمِية."

---

٣ تحرجا: وضع المقريزي رمز "ح" تحت الحرف الثاني إشارة إلى تلفظه بالحاء. ٤ مُوَشَّى: كذا في الأصل.

---

١ من الكامل لابن الأثير ١: ٤٧١.

to depose him and told him that if Čūbīn[493] reached al-Madāʾin before him he would get the kingship. Soon after this, the noblemen attacked Hurmuz. Among them, there were Bindūyah[494] and Bisṭām, the maternal uncles of Abarwīz. They deposed Hurmuz and blinded his eyes, but left him alive, shrinking from regicide. When Abarwīz heard of this, he hurried with his troops to al-Madāʾin, outdoing Bahrām, and crowned himself. Hurmuz reigned for 11 years, 7 months, and 10 days. His vest was red with embroidery, his trousers sky-blue with embroidery, and his crown green. Sitting on his throne, he leaned with his left hand on his sword, holding a mace in his right hand. Neither before nor after him were kings blinded.

§ 200[495] Of his excellent ways was that when Hurmuz had finished building his palace east[496] of the Tigris, opposite al-Madāʾin, he organised a big celebration and invited people from everywhere. The guests ate, and then he asked them: "Do you see any defects in this palace?" All assured that it had no defects, but then someone rose and said: "It has three ugly defects. The first is that people build their houses in the world, but you have put the whole world into your house by exaggerating the size of its courtyards and chambers, so that in summer it is wide open to sun and hot winds, which will harm its inhabitants. In winter, it will be very cold. The second is that kings reside in palaces built[497] on river banks so that looking at the water frees them of worried thoughts, air is pleasantly humid, and water glitters under their eyes. But you have left the Tigris and built your palace in the desert. The third is that you have set women's apartments[498] on the north side of men's apartments, and wind more often blows from the North, so that it will carry women's voices and the scent of their perfume to men. Yet this is something jealousy and passion should prevent."

493 Written here with a Č with three dots.

494 Almost always explicitly written with Y as Bīdūyah. There is only one case, § 204, where this has been correctly written with N.

495 Ibn al-Aṯīr, *Kāmil*, 1:471.

496 The printed edition of Ibn al-Aṯīr reads *allatī tušrifu ʿalá Diğlah* "which overlooked the Tigris," but the holograph has clearly and explicitly *bi-šarq Diğlah*, which is, indeed, a better reading. For a similar story about three defects, cf. the story of al-Manṣūr (r. 136–158/754–775) and the Byzantine ambassador, concerning Baghdad, see al-Ḫaṭīb, *Taʾrīḫ Baġdād*, 1:78, and El Cheikh (2004): 151.

497 Ibn al-Aṯīr reads *yatawaṣṣalūna fī l-bināʾ*.

498 In the singular in the text, but the expected plural is used a few lines later in § 201. In Ibn al-Aṯīr both are in the singular.

§ 201[١] فقال هرمز: "أما سعة الصحون والمجالس فخير المساكن ما سافر فيه البصر وشدة الحر والبرد يُدفَعان بالخيّش والملابس والنيران. وأما مجاورة الماء فكنت عند أبي وهو يشرف على دجلة فغرقت سفينة تحته فاستغاث من فيها إليه وأبي يتأسف عليهم ويصيح بالسفن التي تحت | داره 178a ليلحقوهم. فإلى أن يلحقوهم غرقوا جميعهم. فجعلت على نفسي أني لا أجاور سلطانا هو أقوى مني. وأما عمل حجر النساء في جهة الشمال فإنا قصدنا به أن الشمال أرق هواء وأقل وخامة والنساء يلازمن البيوت فعمل لذلك. وأما الغَيْرة فإن الرجال لا يخلون بالنساء وكل من يدخل هذه الدار إنما هو مملوك وعبد مقيم. وأما أنت فما أخرج هذا منك إلا بغض لي فخبرني سببه."

§ 202[٢] فقال الرجل: "لي قرية ملك كنت أنفق حاصلها على عيالي فغلبني فلان المرزبان وأخذها مني. فقصدت أتظلم منذ سنين فلم أصل إليك. فقصدت وزيرك وتظلمت إليه فلم ينصفني وأنا أؤدي خراج القرية حتى لا يزول اسمي عنها. وهذا غاية الظلم أن يكون غيري يأخذ دخلها وأنا أؤدي خراجها." فسأل هرمز وزيره فصدقه وقال: "خفت أن أعلمك فتؤدب المرزبان." فأمر هرمز أن يؤخذ من المرزبان ضعف ما أخذ وأن يستخدمه صاحب الضيعة في أي شغل شاء سنتين وعزل وزيره وقال في نفسه: "إذا كان الوزير يراعي الظالم فبالحَرَى أن غيره يُراعيه." فأمر باتخاذ صندوق وكان يقفله ويختمه بخاتمه ويتركه على باب داره وفيه خرق {فيلقى} فيه رقاع المظلومين. وكان

---

١٤ فيلقى: "فيلقا" في الأصل. || رقاع: كشط المقريزي كلمة أخرى قبل أن يصححها كما هي الآن.

---

١ من الكامل لابن الأثير ١: ٤٧١–٤٧٢.

٢ من الكامل لابن الأثير ١: ٤٧٢.

§ 201[499] Hurmuz replied: "As to the size of the courtyards and halls, the best place to live is where your eyes may roam. Excessive heat or cold can be prevented by canvases, clothing, and fire. As to being near water, I was once with my father, who was looking at the Tigris. A boat happened to sink under his eyes, and those in it cried to him for help. My father was sorry for them and shouted to men in the boats that were sailing under his palace to go and help them, but before they reached them, they had all drowned. Then I decided that I would never live next to a power greater than mine. As to women's apartments being on the north side, I considered that the air is milder in the north and less polluted and women keep to their houses. This is why it was done so. As to jealousy, men will not be alone with women, and those who enter this house are either *mamlūks* or resident slaves.[500] As to you, you said this only because you hate me. Tell me why!"

§ 202[501] The man replied: "I have a king's village, the produce of which used to provide for my family, but a certain *marzubān* took it from me by force. Since two years[502] I have tried to complain about this, but I have not gained access to you. I went to your Vizier and complained to him, but he did not give me justice. Now I pay the tax for the village in order to keep it under my name. It is injustice in extreme that someone else takes the profit, while I pay the tax." Hurmuz asked his Vizier about this, and the Vizier admitted it, saying: "I was afraid to let you know lest you punish the *marzubān*."[503] Hurmuz gave orders that double the amount of what the *marzubān* had gained was to be taken from him and that the owner of the village could use him for any labour he wanted for two years. Hurmuz also deposed his Vizier, saying to himself: "Viziers keep an eye on wrongdoers, but it is appropriate that someone keeps an eye on them." He gave orders to make a box, which he then locked and sealed with his own seal. The box, which had little holes, was left by the gate of his palace. Those who had been wronged could throw their complaints in it, and Hurmuz opened it every week, finding the

499 Ibn al-Aṯīr, *Kāmil*, 1:471–472.

500 In the Islamic context, *mamlūk* primarily refers to military slaves, see "*mamlūk*," in *EI*², 6:314–321. For *ʿabd muqīm*, Ibn al-Aṯīr has *ʿabd li-qayyim* "slave belonging to a custodian."

501 Ibn al-Aṯīr, *Kāmil*, 1:472.

502 The holograph seems to read *sinīn*, and MS T clearly reads so. However, Ibn al-Aṯīr has *sanatayn*, which also matches with the punishment of the *marzubān*, who has to serve the owner of the village for precisely two years.

503 Ibn al-Athīr reads *fa-yuʾḏiyanī* "lest he (the *marzubān*) punish me."

يفتحه كل أسبوع ويكشف المظالم. ثم أفكر وقال: "أريد أعرف ظلم الرعية ساعة بساعة." فاتخذ سلسلة طرفها في مجلسه في السقف والطرف الآخر خارج الدار في روزنة وفيها جَرَسٌ فكان المتظلم يحرك السلسلة فيتحرك الجرس فيُحضِره ويكشف ظلامته. (...)

§203[١] | كِسْرَى أَبْرَوِيْز الملقب بالملك العزيز بن هرمز بن كسرى أنوشروان. كان قد خرج خوفا 178b من أبيه هرمز إلى آذربيجان واجتمعوا عليه كما تقدم. فلما بلغه خلع أبيه وسمل عينيه بادر إلى المدائن وتتوج وجمع إليه الوجوه والأشراف وجلس لهم على سريره ومناهم ووعدهم وقال: "إن أبانا هرمز كان لكم قاضيا عادلا ومن نيتنا لكم البر والإحسان فعليكم بالسمع والطاعة." فاستبشر به الناس ودعوا له. فلما كان اليوم الثاني أتى أباه فسجد له وقال له: "عمرك الله أيها الملك إنك تعلم أني بريء مما أتاه إليك المنافقون وإنما هربت خوفا منك." فصدقه هرمز وقال له: "يا بني لي إليك حاجتان فاسعفني بهما. {إحداهما} أن تنتقم لي ممن عاون على خلعي والسمل لعيني ولا تأخذك بهم رأفة. والأخرى أن تؤنسني كل يوم بثلاثة نفر لهم أصالة رأي وتأذن لهم في الدخول علي." فتواضع له أبرويز وقال: "عمرك الله أيها الملك إن المارق بهرام قد أظلنا ومعه الشجاعة والنجدة ولسنا نقدر أن نمد يدا إلى من آتى عليك ما آتى فإنهم وجوه أصحابك. ولكن إن أدالني الله تعالى من المنافق فأنا خليفتك وطوع أمرك."

§204[٢] ثم إن أبرويز خرج إلى النهروان لما وردها بهرام شوبين وواقفه وجعل النهر بينه وبينه. ودار بينهما كلام كثير. كل ذلك يدور على استصلاح بهرام فلا يرد عليه بهرام إلا ما يسوءه حتى يئس

---

٣ ظلامته: بعد هذه الكلمة بياض بقدر سبعة أسطر في الأصل. ١٠ إحداهما: "احدهما" في الأصل.

---

١ من تجارب الأمم لمسكويه ١: ١٤٥.

٢ من تجارب الأمم لمسكويه ١: ١٤٦.

complaints therein. Then he thought some more and said: "I want to know the wrong deeds done to people hourly." He installed a chain, one end of which was in the ceiling of his hall and the other in a window outside the palace. There was a little bell, and when the claimant touched the chain, the bell rang, and the king could have him brought in to hear his complaint.[504]

§ 203[505] Kisrá Abarwīz, called the Mighty King,[506] b. Hurmuz b. Kisrá Anūširwān had gone to Azerbaijan, being afraid of his father Hurmuz. As has already been mentioned, people joined him there. When Abarwīz heard that his father had been deposed and his eyes blinded, he hurried to al-Madāʾin, crowned himself, and called the leaders and the noblemen. He sat on the throne, made promises and raised hopes, saying: "My father Hurmuz was a just judge to you, and it is my will to be righteous and do good. It is upon you to hear and obey." People were happy with him and prayed for him. The next day he went to see his father, prostrated himself before him, and said: "May God grant you long life, o King. You know that I am innocent of what the hypocrites did to you. I fled because I was afraid of you." Hurmuz believed him and said: "My son, I have two requests, which I want you to grant me. One is that you take revenge for me on those who helped to depose me and blind my eyes. Feel no compassion for them. The second is that you give me for company every day three men, who have clarity of reason, and let them come to me." Abarwīz agreed to this and said: "May God give you long life, o King! That turncoat Bahrām is already close by. He has courage and bravery, and I cannot, at present, touch those who did what they did to you, because they are the leaders of your companions, but if God, He is Exalted, gives me ascendancy over the hypocrite, I will be your representative and follow your order."

§ 204[507] Abarwīz went to Nahrawān when Bahrām Čūbīn came there. He took position opposite him with the river between them. They had a long discussion, Abarwīz trying all the while to reconcile with Bahrām, who only replied in abusive terms. Finally, Abarwīz lost all hope of reconciliation and

504 Seven last lines of fol. 178ᵃ have been left blank.

505 Miskawayh, *Taǧārib al-umam*, 1:145 = C222–223; cf. al-Ṭabarī, *Taʾrīḫ*, 1:995–996 = trans., 5:306–307.

506 Cf. al-Bīrūnī, *al-Āṯār al-bāqiyah* 138.

507 Miskawayh, *Taǧārib al-umam*, 1:146 = C223–224; cf. al-Ṭabarī, *Taʾrīḫ*, 1:996–998 = trans., 5:307–310.

منه وأجمع على حربه. ولهما أخبار كثيرة وأحاديث طويلة آخرها أن أبرويز ضعف عنه بعد أن قتل بيده ثلاثة نفر من الأتراك كانوا ضمنوا لبهرام قتل أبرويز ووعدهم بمال عظيم. وكان هؤلاء الثلاثة من أشد الأتراك وأعظمهم أجساما وشجاعة. ثم رأى أبرويز من أصحابه فتورا وحرض أصحابه فتبين منهم فشلا فصار إلى أبيه وشاوره فرأى له المصير إلى ملك الروم. فأحرز نساءه وشخص في عدة يسيرة فيهم بندويه وبسطام وكردي أخو بهرام شوبين فإنه كان ماقتا له شديد الطاعة لأبرويز. فلما خرجوا من المدائن خاف القوم من بهرام وأشفقوا أن يرد هرمز إلى الملك ويكاتب ملك الروم عن هرمز في ردهم فيتلفوا فأعلموا ذلك أبرويز واستأذنوه في | إتلاف أبيه فلم يُحِر جوابا. 179a

§ 205[1] فانصرف بيدويه وبسطام وطائفة معهما إلى هرمز حتى أتلفوه خنقا. ثم رجعوا إلى أبرويز وقالوا: "سر على خير طائر." فحثوا دوابهم وصاروا إلى الفرات فقطعوه وأخذوا طريق المفازة بدلالة رجل يقال له خرشينان وصاروا إلى بعض الديارات التي في أطراف العمارة. فلما أوطنوا الراحة لحقتهم خيل بهرام. فلما نذروا بهم أَنبّه بيدويه أبرويز من نومه وقال له: ."احتل لنفسك فإن القوم قد أظلوك." فقال كسرى أبرويز: "ما عندي حيلة." فقال بيدويه: "فإني سأحتال لك بأن أبذل نفسي دونك." قال: "وكيف ذلك؟" قال: "تدفع إلي بزتك وزينتك لأعلو الدير وتنجو أنت ومن معك من وراء الدير. فإن القوم إذا وصلوا إلي ورأوا هَيئَتك علي اشتغلوا عن غيري وطاولْتهم حتى تفوتَهم."

---

٤ فأحرز: وضع المقريزي رمز "ح" تحت الحرف الثالث إشارة إلى تلفظه بالحاء. ١١ احتل: وضع المقريزي رمز "ح" تحت الحرف الثاني إشارة إلى تلفظه بالحاء. ١٣ لأعلو: "لاعلوا" في الأصل. || وتنجو: "وتنجوا" في الأصل.

---

١ من تجارب الأمم لمسكويه ١: ١٤٦.

decided to fight him. There are a lot of stories and long narratives about them. After having killed with his own hand three Turks, who had promised Bahrām to kill him and had been promised great wealth for that, Abarwīz grew weaker than Bahrām. These three Turks were among the strongest of the Turks and the greatest both in size and in courage. After this, Abarwīz saw laxity in his companions. He tried to urge them on but noticed that they had lost their courage. He went to his father and asked his opinion. Hurmuz thought it best for him to go to the king of the Byzantines. Abarwīz sent his womenfolk to a secure place and left in a small company, including Bindūyah, Bisṭām, and Kurdī, the brother of Bahrām Čūbīn, who loathed his brother and was extremely loyal to Abarwīz. When they left al-Madāʾin, people were afraid of Bahrām and were concerned that he would restore Hurmuz on the throne and write to the king of the Byzantines on his behalf to return the fugitives, who would then perish. They told this to Abarwīz and asked permission to murder his father, but he gave them no answer.

§ 205[508] Bindūyah, Bisṭām, and a few others with them turned back and strangled Hurmuz to death. Then they returned to Abarwīz and said: "Travel with the best of omens!" They urged their horses and rode to the Euphrates, crossing it. They took the way through the desert, being guided by a man called Ḫuršīdān.[509] They rode until they came to a monastery, which was close to cultivated area. When they encamped in the inner courtyard, the cavalry of Bahrām was approaching them. When the fugitives saw this, Bindūyah wakened Abarwīz and said: "Save yourself, the pursuers are almost here!" Kisrá Abarwīz said that he had no way to save himself, but Bindūyah replied: "I will save you by sacrificing myself." Kisrá asked how this was to happen, and Bindūyah explained: "Give me your clothes and your ornaments! I will go on the roof of the monastery, while you and the others escape from the rear. When the enemies come here and see your clothes on me, they will not care about the others. I will delay them so that you can escape."

508 Miskawayh, *Taǧārib al-umam*, 1:146 = C224–225; cf. al-Ṭabarī, *Taʾrīḫ*, 1:998–999 = trans., 5:310.

509 The text clearly reads Ḫuršīnān, but I follow Miskawayh and al-Ṭabarī. For the name, see Bosworth (1999): 310, note 726.

§206[1] ففعلوا ذلك وبادروهم حتى تواروا بالجبل. ثم وافاهم خيل بهرام وعليهم قائد يقال له بهرام بن سياوش. فاطلع عليه بِنْدَويه من فوق الدير وعليه بزة أبرويز. فأوهمه أنه هو وسأله أن ينظره إلى غد ليصير في يده سِلْما ويصير إلى بهرام شوبين. فأمسك عنه وحفظ الدير بالحرس ليلته فلما أصبح اطلع عليه في بزته وحليته وقال: "إن علي وعلى أصحابي بقية شغل من استعداد لصلوات وعبادات فأمهلنا." ولم يزل يدافع حتى مضى عامة النهار وأمعن أبرويز وعلم أنه قد فاتهم. ففتح الباب حينئذ وأعلم بهرام بأمره فانصرف به إلى شوبين فحبسه في يد بهرام بن سياوش.

§207[2] وأما بهرام شوبين فإنه دخل المدائن وجلس على سرير الملك وجمع العظماء فخطبهم وذم أبرويز. ودار بينهم كلام فكان كلهم منصرفا عنه إلا أنه تتوج وانقاد له الناس خوفا. ثم إن بهرام ابن سياوش واطأ بيدويه على الفتك بخوبين فظهر شوبين على ذلك فقتله وأفلت بيدويه ولحق بآذربيجان. وسار أبرويز —وقد لقيه حسان بن حنظلة بن أبي رهم بن حسان بن حية بن سعنة بن الحٰرث بن الحويرث بن ربيعة بن مالك بن سَفَر بن هِنْي بن عمرو بن الغوث بن طيء الذي يقال له فارس الضُبَيْب وهي فرسه فحمله على الضبيب ففر فولاه لما ملك سميساط وقاليقلا— حتى أتى أنطاكية وكاتب ملك الروم موريق ويقال: مَوْرِيْجِيُش قيصر منها وراسله بجماعة ممن كان معه

٩ بخوبين: كذا في الأصل، يعني أن الحرف بين الجيم والشين. ١٠–١٢ وقد ... حتى: الزيادة بخط المقريزي في الهامش الأيمن من الأسفل إلى الأعلى، ويشير إليها رمز ⌐ بعد "أبرويز". ١٣ موريق ... قيصر: الزيادة بخط المقريزي تحت السطر في الهامش الأسفل + صح.

١ من تجارب الأمم لمسكويه ١: ١٤٦–١٤٧.

٢ من تجارب الأمم لمسكويه ١: ١٤٧.

§206[510] They did this and hurried away before Bahrām's cavalry arrived and concealed themselves in the mountain. Then the men of Bahrām came to the monastery, led by a general named Bahrām b. Siyāwuš. Bindūyah showed himself from the top of the monastery, clad in the garment of Abarwīz, giving Bahrām b. Siyāwuš the impression that he was Abarwīz. Bindūyah asked respite until the next day, and then he would surrender peacefully and come to Bahrām Čūbīn. Bahrām b. Siyāwuš refrained from forcing his way to him and set guards to keep an eye on the monastery that night. Next morning, Bindūyah again appeared in Abarwīz's clothes and his ornaments, saying: "I and my companions have still some preparations to do for the prayers and worship." Bahrām b. Siyāwuš again gave him some respite, and Bindūyah kept asking him for more time until the whole day had passed. Meanwhile Abarwīz rode post haste. In the end, Bindūyah knew that Abarwīz had escaped from them. Then he finally opened the gate and told Bahrām b. Siyāwuš how things were. The latter took him to Čūbīn, who consigned Bindūyah to Bahrām b. Siyāwuš's custody.

§207[511] Meanwhile, Bahrām Čūbīn had entered al-Madā'in and ascended the royal throne. He called the noblemen together and spoke to them, blaming Abarwīz. There was a long exchange between him and the noblemen, who all turned away from him. He, however, crowned himself, and people followed him for fear. Bahrām b. Siyāwuš agreed with Bindūyah to murder Čūbīn,[512] but the latter got hunch of this and had him killed. Bindūyah was able to slip away and fled to Azerbaijan. Abarwīz went on—he had been met by Ḥassān b. Ḥanẓalah b. Abī Ruhm b. Ḥassān b. Ḥayyah b. Saʿnah b. al-Ḥāriṯ b. al-Ḥuwayriṯ b. Rabīʿah b. Mālik b. Safar b. Hiny b. ʿAmr b. al-Ġawṯ b. Ṭayyi' who was called the Rider of al-Ḍubayb, which was his horse. He let Abarwīz ride al-Ḍubayb, and Abarwīz was able to escape. When he became king, he appointed Ḥassān as the king of Sumaysāṭ and Qālīqalā[513]—until he came to Antioch. From there, he wrote to the king of the Byzantines Mauricius (Mawrīq), also called Mawrīǧiyuš Qayṣar. He sent to him some people he had

510 Miskawayh, *Taǧārib al-umam*, 1:146–147 = C225–226; cf. al-Ṭabarī, *Ta'rīḫ*, 1:999 = trans., 5:310.

511 Miskawayh, *Taǧārib al-umam*, 1:147 = C226–227; cf. al-Ṭabarī, *Ta'rīḫ*, 1:999–1000 = trans., 5:310–313.

512 Here Ǧ/Č written with three dots above the letter.

513 The addition, written in the margin, is not from Miskawayh. Much of the addition has been copied to MS T, but the last words, beginning with "and Abarwīz was able to escape," have been dropped.

179b وسأله نصرته فأجابه | إلى ذلك. وانساقت الأمور بالمقادير إلى أن زوجته قيصر ابنته مريم وحملها إليه وبعث إليه بتياذوس أخيه ومعه ستون ألف مقاتل عليهم رجل يقال له سرجس يتولى تدبير أمرهم ورجل آخر يقال كان يُعدَل بألف رجل معظم في الروم. وسأله ترك الإتاوة التي كان آباؤه {يسألونها} ملوك الروم إذا هو ملك. فاغتبط بهم أبرويز وأراحهم خمسة أيام. ثم عرضهم وعَرَّف عليهم العرفاء في القوم تياذوس وسرجس والكمي الذي وصفناه وسار بهم حتى نزل من آذربيجان في صحراء تدعَى الدِنق.

§ 208[١] فوافاه هناك بيدويه ورجل من إصبهذي الناحية يقال له موسِيْل في أربعين ألف مقاتل وانقض إليه الناس بالخيل من إصبهان وخراسان وفارس. وانتهى إلى شوبين مكانه فشخص نحوه من المدائن. فجرت بينهما حروب شديدة قتل فيها الكمي الرومي بضربة ضربه بها بعض الفرس على رأسه فقَدَّ رأسه ويده. وعار فرسه بنصف بدنه الباقي إلى معركة أبرويز ومُعَسْكَره فاستضحك أبرويز وعظم ذلك على الروم وكثر الكلام فيه وعوتب وقيل: "هذا جزاؤنا منك. يقتل كمينا وواحد عصره في طاعتك وبين يديك فتضحك." فاعتذر بأن قال: "إني والله ما ضحكت لما تكرهون ولقد شق علي أن فقدت مثله أكثر مما شق عليكم ولكني رأيتكم تستصغرون شأن بهرام شوبين وتنكرون هربي منه. فذكرت ذلك من قولكم الآن وعلمت أنكم برؤيتكم هذه الضربة وأثرها على هذا الكمي تعذروني وتعلمون يقينا أن هربي إنما كان من أمثال هؤلاء القوم الذين هذا مبلغ نكايتهم في الأبطال." ويقال إن أبرويز حارب بهرام شوبين منفردا من العسكر بأربعة عشر رجلا منهم كردي أخو بهرام وبيدويه وبسطام حربا شديدة وصل فيها بعضهم إلى بعض.

١ قيصر: الزيادة بخط المقريزي فوق السطر في الهامش من الأسفل إلى الأعلى. ٤ يسألونها: "يسلونها" في الأصل.

١ من تجارب الأمم لمسكويه ١: ١٤٨–١٤٩.

with himself and asked for help. Mauricius answered to him, and things went their way. The Caesar even gave his daughter Maryam to him in marriage and sent her to him. He also sent to him his brother Theodosius with 60,000 soldiers led by a man called Sergius, who was in charge of their affairs, and another man, about whom it was said that he equalled a thousand men and who enjoyed much respect among the Byzantines. Mauricius asked Abarwīz to abandon the tribute his ancestors had demanded from the Byzantine kings as soon as he would become king. Abarwīz was delighted with the men and let them rest for five days. Then he inspected them and appointed officers over them. Theodosius, Sergius, and the warrior we described were among them. Abarwīz marched out with these and camped in Azerbaijan on a plain called al-Danaq.

§ 208[514] Bindūyah and an *iṣbahbad* of that region, called Mušel (Mamikonean), with 40,000 soldiers joined Abarwīz there, and people rushed to him on horseback from Isfahan, Ḫurāsān, and Fārs. Bahrām Čūbīn heard where he was and set out for him from al-Madāʾin. Fierce battles took place between them, and the Byzantine warrior was killed in one of these by one of the Persians with one stroke on his head, which detached his head and one of his hands. His horse wandered back to where the troops and the camp of Abarwīz were, carrying the remaining half of his body. Abarwīz laughed at this, which enraged the Byzantines. There was much talk about this, and he was blamed for it. People said to him: "Is this the reward you give us? Our warrior, unique in his time, is killed in your service and under your very eyes and you just laugh?" Abarwīz apologised and said: "By God, I did not laugh at what you think, and it is heavier for me to lose a man like him than it is for you. But I saw how you belittled the matter of Bahrām Čūbīn and disapproved of my fleeing from him. Now I remembered what you had said and knew that when you saw this stroke and its effect on this warrior you would forgive me and know for sure that my flight was from people who can cause such damage to heroes." It is said that Abarwīz fought Bahrām Čūbīn separately, without the army, with fourteen men, including Kurdī, the brother of Bahrām, Bindūyah, and Bisṭām in a fierce battle in which they met each other.

514 Miskawayh, *Taǧārib al-umam*, 1:148–149 = C227–228; cf. al-Ṭabarī, *Taʾrīḫ*, 1:1000 = trans., 5:313 (only the beginning).

§ 209[1] والمجوس تحكي حكايات عظيمة لا فائدة في حكاياتها. وجملتها أن أبرويز استظهر استظهارا يئس معه بهرام شوبين وعلم أنه لا حيلة له فيه فانحاز عنه نحو خراسان. ثم صار إلى الترك وصار أبرويز إلى | المدائن بعد أن فرق في جنود الروم أموالا عظيمة وصرفهم إلى ملك الروم. وفي نسخة: 180a أنه لما صرف الروم الذين أنجدوه إلى بلادهم جهز معهم هدايا جليلة إلى مَوْريق. ثم بعث بعض أساورته بهدايا وأموال عظيمة ليخطب مريم بنت موريق. فحملها إليه بجهاز عظيم جدا فحظيت عنده. ولبث بهرام شوبين في الترك مكرما عند الملك حتى احتال له أبرويز بتوجيه رجل يقال له هرمز إلى الترك بجوهر نفيس وغيره حتى احتال لخاتون امرأة الملك ولاطفها بذلك الجوهر وغيره من الهدايا حتى دست لبهرام من قتله فاغتم الملك خاقان لموته وأرسل إلى أخته كُرْدِيَّة وامرأته يعلمهما بلوغ الحادث ببهرام منه ويسأل أن يتزوجها. وطلق امرأته خاتون بهذا السبب فأجابته كردية جوابا لينا وضمّتْ من كان مع أخيها شوبين من المقاتلة إليها.

§ 210[2] وخرجت بهم من بلاد الترك إلى حدود مملكة فارس. فأتبعها ملك الترك أخاه بُطرا في اثني عشر ألف فارس فقاتلته كُرديّة وقتلته بيدها ومضت حتى تلقتها خيول الفرس وكتبت إلى أخيها كردي فأخذ لها أمانا من أبرويز. فلما قدمت عليه اغتبط بها وتزوج بها أبرويز. ثم كانت من

٣–٦ وفي ... عنده : الزيادة بخط المقريزي في الهامش الأيمن من الأعلى إلى الأسفل وآخرها في الهامش الأعلى من الأسفل إلى الأعلى، ويشير إليها رمز ⌐ بعد "الروم".

---

١ من تجارب الأمم لمسكويه ١: ١٤٨.

٢ راجع تأريخ الطبري ١: ١٠٠١.

§ 209[515] The Magians tell exaggerated stories about this, not worth repeating. The result was that Abarwīz overcame Bahrām Čūbīn, who became desperate and knew that there was no way to resist Abarwīz, so he withdrew to Ḫurāsān and from there to the Turks. After having distributed great sums of money to the Byzantine army and sent them back to the king of the Byzantines Abarwīz went to al-Madāʾin. According to one manuscript,[516] when he sent the Byzantines, who had helped him, back to their country, he sent with them valuable gifts to Mauricius. Then he sent one of his cavalrymen with gifts and huge sums of money to propose to Maryam, the daughter of Mauricius, who sent her daughter to him with a huge dowry. She found favour with her husband. Bahrām Čūbīn stayed among the Turks, respected by the king until Abarwīz managed to plot against him. He sent a man called Hurmuz to the Turks. He had a precious jewel and other valuables with him and he managed to impress the Ḫātūn, the wife of the king. He obliged her with that jewel and other gifts, and she sent some people to kill Bahrām. The king, the Ḫāqān, grieved for his death and sent a word to Kurdiyyah, Bahrām's sister, and to his wife, telling them[517] what had happened to Bahrām and asking her to marry him. He divorced his former wife, the Ḫātūn, because of this. Kurdiyyah politely refused and took over to herself the soldiers that had been with her brother Čūbīn.

§ 210[518] Kurdiyyah left the country of the Turks with these soldiers, moving towards the kingdom of Fārs. The king of the Turks sent after her his brother Buṭrā[519] with 12,000 horsemen, but Kurdiyyah fought him and killed him with her own hand. She then went forward until she met with the cavalry of the Persians and wrote to her brother Kurdī. Kurdī acquired an indemnity from Abarwīz. When Kurdiyyah came to him, Abarwīz liked her and

515 Miskawayh, *Taǧārib al-umam*, 1:148 = C228–229; cf. al-Ṭabarī, *Taʾrīḫ*, 1:1000–1001 = trans., 5:313–316.

516 The addition, until "she found favour with her husband," is not from Miskawayh. It is not clear, whether "another manuscript" refers to another manuscript of Miskawayh's *Taǧārib al-umam* or, more probably, some other text.

517 Al-Maqrīzī uses here dual (*yuʿlimuhumā*), not realising that Kurdiyyah was Bahrām's sister-consort. Miskawayh has correctly *yuʿlimuhā*. In this light, the passage should be translated "sent a word to Kurdiyyah, Bahrām's sister and wife," but I have preferred the above translation, which, I believe, is how a contemporary reader would have taken it. In the following sentence, al-Maqrīzī is back to using the singular.

518 Miskawayh, *Taǧārib al-umam*, 1:148 = C229–230; cf. al-Ṭabarī, *Taʾrīḫ*, 1:1001 = trans., 5:317.

519 In al-Ṭabarī, *Taʾrīḫ*, 1:1001, it is the Ḫāqān's brother, N.ṭrā, who is supposed to marry Kurdiyyah.

أبرويز سوء سياسة في جنده حتى ظهر الروم عليه. وذلك أنه لم يزل يلاطف ملك الروم الذي كان نصره ويهاديه إلى أن وثب الروم عليه في شيء أنكروه منه فقتلوه في الليل. قتله بعض غلمانه بموافقة فوقا. ويقال: فوقاص أحد بطاركة الروم فاستبد فوقاص وقتل أولاد موريق.

§ 211[١] وقد فر أحدهم إلى أبرويز فامتعض وأخذته الحفيظة فآوى ابن الملك المقتول وقد التجأ إليه وتَوَّجَه ومَلَّكه على الروم ووجه معه جنودا كثيفة. وجعل عليها ثلاثة من قواده وأساورته أحدهم موران على جيش لغزو بلاد الشام فدوخها وأخذ القدس. والثاني شاهين على جيش إلى مصر ففتحها وملك الإسكندرية. والقائد الثالث فرخان ويدعى شهربراز ومعه جيش لغزو قسطنطينية وإليه مرجع القائدين وكان أعظمهم. فساروا جميعا مع شهربراز فدوخ بهم البلاد وملك بيت المقدس وأخذ خشبة الصليب وبعث بها إلى أبرويز في أربع وعشرين سنة من ملكه.

§ 212[٢] ثم احتوى على مصر والإسكندرية وبلاد نوبة وبعث مفاتيح مدينة الإسكندرية إلى أبرويز في سنة ثمان وعشرين من ملكه. وقصد قسطنطينية فأناخ على ضفة الخليج القريب منها وخيم هنالك. فأمره أبرويز نخرب بلاد الروم غضبا بما انتهكوا من ملكهم وانتقاما له. ولم يخضع لابن ملكهم المقتول أحد ولا منحوا الطاعة غير أنهم قتلوا الملك الذي ملكوه بعد أبيه المسمى

٢-٣ في[٢] ... موريق: الزيادة بخط المقريزي في الهامش الأيسر منكسة إلا أولها، ويشير إليها رمز ⌐ بعد "فقتلوه". وكشط المقريزي بعض الكلمات في آخر هذه الزيادة. ٤ وقد ... إلى: كشط المقريزي عبارة أخرى قبل أن يصححها كما هي الآن. ٥-٨ وجعل ... جميعا: الزيادة بخط المقريزي في الهامش الأيسر وآخرها في الهامش الأسفل من الأعلى إلى الأسفل + صح، ويشير إليها رمز ⌐ بعد "كثيفة". ١٣ منحوا: وضع المقريزي رمز "ح" تحت الحرف الثالث إشارة إلى تلفظه بالحاء.

١ من تجارب الأمم لمسكويه ج ١ ص ١٤٨ ومن تأريخ الطبري ١: ١٠٠٢-١٠٠٣.

٢ من تجارب الأمم لمسكويه ١: ١٤٨-١٤٩.

married her. After that Abarwīz mismanaged his army and the Byzantines overwhelmed him.[520] This happened so that he kept being compliant towards the king of the Byzantines, who had helped him, and kept sending him gifts until the Byzantines attacked their king because of something they disapproved of. He was killed at night by one of his slaves in concordance with Phocas (Fūqā), also called Fūqāṣ, one of the patricians of Byzantium.[521] Phocas killed the sons of Mauricius.

§ 211[522] One of Mauricius' sons fled to Abarwīz, who was annoyed and resented the murders. He gave asylum to the son of the murdered king, after he had taken refuge with him. Abarwīz crowned him and proclaimed him the king of the Byzantines. He sent a large army with him, led by three of his generals and cavalrymen, one of them Mūrān,[523] who led an army that attacked Syria, subjugated it, and captured Jerusalem. The second was Šāhīn, who led an army to Egypt, which he conquered, taking Alexandria. The third general was Farruḫān, also called Šahrbarāz.[524] He had with him an army to attack Constantinople, and he had authority over the other two generals, being the greatest of them. They all marched with Šahrbarāz, who with their help subjugated the country and took Jerusalem, taking the wooden cross and sending it to Abarwīz in the 24th year of his reign.

§ 212[525] Then Šahrbarāz captured Egypt, Alexandria, and the country of Nubia and sent the keys of the city of Alexandria to Abarwīz in the year 28 of his reign. Then he went towards Constantinople and encamped on the bank of the strait, close to the city, and put his tents there. Abarwīz ordered him to destroy the Byzantine country as he was angered at how they had abused their king and wanted to take revenge for him. None of the Byzantines followed the son of the king they had killed or obeyed him, but they did kill the king whom they had appointed after his father, called Phocas, when his

520 In Miskawayh, this is the heading of the next paragraph (*Ḏikr sūʾ siyāsah …*).

521 Al-Maqrīzī reads *al-baṭārikah* for what, properly, should be *al-baṭāriqah*, and may well have understood this as "one of the patriarchs."

522 Miskawayh, *Taǧārib al-umam*, 1:148 = C230; al-Ṭabarī, *Taʾrīḫ*, 1:1002–1003 = trans., 5:318–321. For §§ 211–221, see Hämeen-Anttila (2022b).

523 In al-Ṭabarī, the name is given as Rumyūzān, for whom see Bosworth (1999): 318, note 745.

524 In §§ 216–217, Šahrbarāz and Farruḫān are given as brothers.

525 Miskawayh, *Taǧārib al-umam*, 1:148–149 = C230–231; cf. al-Ṭabarī, *Taʾrīḫ*, 1:1002–1003 = trans., 5:319–320.

فوقا لما ظهر من فجوره وسوء تدبيره وملكوا عليهم رجلا يقال له هرقل وهو الذي أخذ المسلمون منه البلاد. فلما رأى هرقل عظيم ما فيه الروم من تخريب جنود | فارس بلادهم وقتلهم مقاتلتهم 180b وسبيهم ذراريهم واستباحتهم أموالهم تضرع إلى الله تعالى وأكثر الدعاء والابتهال.

§ 213[1] فيقال إنه رأى في منامه رجلا ضخما رفيع المجلس عليه. فدخل عليهما داخل فألقى ذلك الرجل عن مجلسه وقال لهرقل: "إني قد سلمته في يدك." فلم يقصص رؤياه تلك في يقظته على أحد حتى توالت عليه أمثاله. فرأى في بعض لياليه كأن رجلا دخل عليهما وبيده سلسلة طويلة فألقاها في عنق صاحبه أعني صاحب المجلس الرفيع عليه. ثم دفعه إليه وقال له: "ها قد دَفَعْتُ إليك كسرى برمته." فلما تتابعت عليه هذه الأحلام قصها على عظماء الروم وذوي العلم منهم فأشاروا عليه أن يغزوه. فاستعد هرقل واستخلف ابنه على مدينة قسطنطينية وأخذ غير الطريق الذي فيه شهرابراز وسار حتى وغل في بلاد أرمينية ونزل نصيبين سَنَةً. وقد كان صاحب ذلك الثغر من قبل أبرويز قد استدعى هرقل لموجدة كانت من هرمز.

١–٢ وهو ... البلاد: الزيادة بخط المقريزي تحت السطر في الهامش الأسفل من الأعلى إلى الأسفل + صح.
٥ على أحد: الزيادة بخط المقريزي في الهامش الأيسر من الأسفل إلى الأعلى + صح، ويشير إليها رمز ⌐ بعد "يقظته".

---

١ من تجارب الأمم لمسكويه ١: ١٤٩.

immorality and bad governing became apparent. Instead, they appointed a man called Heraclius as king over them. It is from him that the Muslims later conquered the country. When Heraclius saw the threatening situation the Byzantines were in, with the armies of Fārs devastating the country, killing their soldiers, taking their families as prisoners, and plundering their property, he humbled himself in front of God, He is Exalted, praying and supplicating fervently.

§ 213[526] It is said that Heraclius saw in a dream a corpulent man in a lofty assembly hall.[527] Someone entered on them, threw that man from the assembly hall, and said to Heraclius: "I have given him into your hands." When he woke up, Heraclius told no one about his dream, until he had had several similar ones. One night he dreamed that a man entered on them with a long chain in his hand, which he threw on the neck of his companion, that is to say the man in the lofty assembly hall.[528] Then he pushed him to Heraclius and said: "Here, I have given Kisrá completely into your hands." When he kept having these dreams, he told the Byzantine noblemen and knowledgeable men about them, and they suggested that he should lead a campaign against Kisrá. Heraclius made preparations and left his son in charge of the city of Constantinople. Then he took a road other than the one leading to where Šahrbarāz[529] was and penetrated the country of Armenia. He stayed a year in Nisibis. The governor of that frontier province, set by Abarwīz, had summoned Heraclius because of something he resented in Hurmuz.[530]

526 Miskawayh, *Taǧārib al-umam*, 1:149 = C231–232; cf. al-Ṭabarī, *Taʾrīḫ*, 1:1003 = trans., 5:320–321.

527 Both Miskawayh and al-Maqrīzī add ʿLYH (*rafīʿ al-maǧlis* ʿLYH). A comparison with al-Ṭabarī shows what the problem is. Al-Ṭabarī has *rafīʿ al-maǧlis* ʿalayhi *bizzah qāʾiman fī nāḥiyah ʿanhu* "in a lofty assembly hall, wearing a (magnificent) garb and standing at one side" (Bosworth 1999: 320, translates somewhat differently). Miskawayh has dropped the end of the expression (this has been added in square brackets to the edition, though), probably understanding ʿLYH as *ʿaliyyuhu*, and al-Maqrīzī follows him.

528 Here, too, Miskawayh and al-Maqrīzī have the additional ʿLYH (cf. the previous note), which Miskawayh has added to the text when rephrasing al-Ṭabarī.

529 The name is written here as ŠHRʾBRʾZ, with an additional *alif*.

530 Miskawayh (ed. Caetani) writes *qad istadʿá li-mawjidah kānat min Kisrá*, explicitly vocalising the verb in the active voice, which hardly makes sense. It has to be read in the passive voice, saying that the governor had been summoned (*ustudʿiya*) away because Kisrá (not Hurmuz) had been angry with him, the point being that the frontier province lacked its commander, which is even more clearly expressed by al-Ṭabarī. Al-Maqrīzī has copied the active form (*istadʿá*) from Miskawayh, but has added Hiraql as its object, the governor being thus made to summon Heraclius there, instead of being himself summoned away. For the correct version, see § 215.

§ 214[1] وأما شهربراز فكانت كتب كسرى أبرويز ترد عليه في الجثوم على الموضع الذي هو به وترك البراح. ثم بلغ أبرويز تساقط هرقل في جنوده إلى نصيبين فوجه لمحاربته رجلا من قواده يقال له زَاهزَاد في اثني عشر ألف رجل من الأنجاد. وأمره أن يقيم بنينوى وهي التي تدعى الآن الموصل على شاطئ دجلة ويمنع الروم أن يجوزوها. وكان أبرويز بلغه خبر هرقل وأنه مُغِذٌ وهو يومئذ مقيم بدسكرة الملك. فنفذ زاهزاذ لأمر أبرويز وعسكر حيث أمره فقطع هرقل دجلة في موضع آخر إلى الناحية التي كان فيها جند فارس فأذكى زاهزاذ العيون عليه. فانصرفوا إليه وأخبروه أنه في سبعين ألف مقاتل. فأيقن زاهزاذ أنه ومن معه من الجند عاجزون عن مناهضته فكتب إلى أبرويز غير مرة أن هرقل دهمه بمن لا طاقة له ولمن معه بهم لكثرتهم وحُسن عدتهم.

§ 215[2] كل ذلك يجيبه أبرويز بأنه إن عجز عن الروم فلن يعجز عن استقبالهم بمن معه وبذل دمائهم في | طاعته. فلما تتابعت على زاهزاذ جوابات أبرويز بذلك عبأ جنده وناهض الروم بهم. 181a فقتلت الروم زاهزاذ وستة آلاف رجل وانهزمت بقيتهم وهربوا على وجوههم. وبلغ أبرويز ذلك فهده مصابهم وانحاز من دسكرة الملك إلى المدائن وتحصن بها لعجزه عن محاربة هرقل. وسار هرقل حتى كان قريبا من المدائن. فلما استعد أبرويز لقتاله انصرف راجعا إلى بلاد الروم. وكتب أبرويز إلى قواد الجند الذين انهزموا أن يدلوه على كل رجل منهم ومن أصحابه ممن فشل في تلك الحروب ولم يرابط مركزه فيها بأن يعاقب فأحوجهم هذا إلى الخلاف عليه وطلب الحيل لنجاتهم منه. وكتب مع ذلك إلى شهربراز يأمره بالقدوم عليه ويستعجله في ذلك ويصف له ما نال هرقل منه ومن بلاده.

---

٤ وكان: كشط المقريزي كلمة أخرى قبل أن يصححها كما هي الآن. ٨ أن ... دهمه: كشط المقريزي عبارة أخرى قبل أن يصححها كما هي الآن. ٩ بمن معه: الزيادة بخط المقريزي تحت السطر في الهامش الأسفل من الأعلى إلى الأسفل. ١٢ وانحاز: وضع المقريزي رمز "ح" تحت الحرف الثالث إشارة إلى تلفظه بالحاء. ١٥ فأحوجهم: وضع المقريزي رمز "ح" تحت الحرف الثالث إشارة إلى تلفظه بالحاء. || الحيل: وضع المقريزي رمز "ح" تحت الحرف الثالث إشارة إلى تلفظه بالحاء.

---

١ من تجارب الأمم لمسكويه ١: ١٤٩.

٢ من تجارب الأمم لمسكويه ١: ١٤٩–١٥٠.

§ 214[531] Šahrbarāz had received letters from Kisrá Abarwīz ordering him to stay where he was and not to move from there. Then Abarwīz heard that Heraclius had come down on Nisibis with his armies and sent one of his generals, called Rāhzād,[532] with 12,000 men to fight him, giving him orders to stay in Nineveh, which is nowadays called Mosul, on the bank of the Tigris, and to prevent the Byzantines from crossing over. Abarwīz had heard about Heraclius marching post haste. Abarwīz himself was at that time staying in the King's Daskarah.[533] Rāhzād obeyed Abarwīz's command and encamped where he had been ordered to encamp, but Heraclius crossed the Tigris at another place to that side of the river where the Persian army was. Rāhzād sent spies to spy on him. They came back and told him that Heraclius had 70,000 men. Rāhzād became convinced that he and his army would not be able to offer resistance to him, so he wrote several times to Abarwīz, telling him that Heraclius had taken him unawares with an army so numerous and so well equipped that he and his men would not be able to offer resistance.

§ 215[534] To all this Abarwīz merely replied that if unable to resist the Byzantines, Rāhzād would at least be able to march against them with his men to shed their blood in his obeisance. When Rāhzād kept receiving such answers from Abarwīz, he arranged his troops and set himself against the Byzantines, who killed him and 6,000 of his men, while the rest fled wherever they could. Abarwīz heard about this, and the disaster crushed him. He withdrew from the King's Daskarah to al-Madā'in and fortified himself there because he was unable to fight Heraclius. Heraclius marched until he was close to al-Madā'in. When Abarwīz was preparing for battle, Heraclius turned away and returned to Byzantium. Abarwīz wrote to the generals of the armies that had fled and gave them orders to show him every single man in their troops who had acted cowardly in those wars and had not kept his position, so that they could be punished. This was what made them oppose him and try to find a way to save themselves from him. Despite this, Abarwīz wrote to Šahrbarāz, giving him an order to come to him in all haste and telling him what Heraclius had done to him and his country.

531 Miskawayh, *Taǧārib al-umam*, 1:149; cf. al-Ṭabarī, *Taʾrīḫ*, 1:1004 = trans., 5:322–323.

532 Consistently written Zāhzād in al-Maqrīzī.

533 For *Daskarat al-malik*, see Christensen (1936): 449–450.

534 Miskawayh, *Taǧārib al-umam*, 1:149–150 = C232–233; cf. al-Ṭabarī, *Taʾrīḫ*, 1:1004–1005 = trans., 5:323.

§216[١] ويحكى أن أبرويز عرف امرأة من فارس لا تلد إلا الملوك الأبطال. فدعاها وقال: "إني أريد أن أبعث إلى الروم جيشا واستعمل عليهم رجلا من بنيك. فأشيري علي أيُهم أستعمل." فوصفت أولادها فقالت: "هذا فرخان أنفذ من سنان. وهذا شهربراز أحكم من كذا. وهذا فلان أروغ من كذا. فاستعمل أيهم شئت." فاستعمل شهربراز فسار إلى الروم فظهر عليهم وهزمهم وخرب مدائنهم. فلما ظهرت فارس على الروم جلس فرخان يشرب فقال لأصحابه: "لقد رأيت كأني جالس على سرير كسرى." فبلغت أبرويز فكتب إلى شهربراز: "إذا أتاك كتابي هذا فابعث إلي برأس فرخان." فكتب إليه: "أيها الملك إنك لن تجد مثل فرخان. فإن له نكاية في العدو وصوتا فلا تفعل." فكتب إليه: "إن في رجال فارس خلفا منه فعجل علي برأسه." فراجعه فغضب أبرويز ولم يجبه وبعث بريدا إلى أهل فارس: "أني قد نزعت عنكم شهربراز واستعملت فرخان." ثم دفع إلى البريد صحيفة صغيرة وقال: "إذا ولي الفرخان الملك وانقاد له أخوه فأعطه الصحيفة."

§217[٢] فلما قرأ شهربراز الكتاب قال: "سمعا وطاعة." ونزل عن سريره وجلس فرخان ودفع الصحيفة إليه فقال: | "ائتوني بشهربراز." فقدمه ليضرب عنقه فقال: "لا تعجل حتى أكتب وصيتي." قال: "افعل." فدعا بسفط وأعطاه ثلاث صحائف وقال: "كل هذا راجعت فيك كسرى وأنت أردت أن تقتلني بكتاب واحد." فرد فرخان الملك على أخيه شهربراز فكتب شهربراز إلى هرقل قيصر ملك الروم: "إن لي إليك حاجة لا تحملها البُرْد ولا تبلغها الصحف. فالقني ولا تلقني إلا في خمسين روميا فإني أيضا ألقاك في خمسين فارسيا." فأقبل هرقل في خمس مائة رومي وجعل يضع 181b

٢ أيُهم: كذا في الأصل. ١٠ الصحيفة: الزيادة بخط المقريزي في الهامش الأيمن من الأعلى إلى الأسفل + صح، ويشير إليها رمز ⌐ بعد "فأعطه". ١٦ خمسين: وضع المقريزي تحت الحرف الثالث ثلاث نقط إشارة إلى تلفظه بالسين.

١ من تجارب الأمم لمسكويه ١: ١٥٠.

٢ من تجارب الأمم لمسكويه ١: ١٥٠–١٥١.

§ 216[535] It is narrated that Abarwīz knew a woman from Fārs who only gave birth to heroic kings. He called her and said: "I want to send an army against the Byzantines and appoint one of your sons over it. Advise me on which of them I should appoint." She described her sons, saying: "Now, Farruẖān is more penetrating than a spear, Šahrbarāz is firmer than such-and-such, and the third is more cunning than so-and-so. Appoint whomever you want to." Abarwīz appointed Šahrbarāz, who marched to Byzantium, attacking the Byzantines, forcing them to flee, and destroying their cities. When the Persians had won the Byzantines, Farruẖān sat down to drink and said to his companions: "I have seen myself in a dream sitting on Kisrá's throne." Abarwīz heard about this and wrote to Šahrbarāz: "When my letter arrives to you, send me the head of Farruẖān." Šahrbarāz replied to him: "O King, you will not find another one like Farruẖān. He causes damage to the enemies and has a reputation among them. Don't do this." Abarwīz wrote back: "There are among the men of Fārs others to replace him, so send me his head at once!" Šahrbarāz argued against this, and it angered Abarwīz, who did not reply, but instead sent a messenger to the people of Fārs saying that he had deposed Šahrbarāz and appointed instead Farruẖān. He also gave a small note to the messenger and said: "When Farruẖān has taken over the kingship and his brother obeys him, give him this note."

§ 217[536] When he read the letter, Šahrbarāz said: "I hear and I obey." He descended from the throne, and Farruẖān ascended it. The note was given to him, and he said: "Bring me Šahrbarāz." When Farruẖān prepared to cut his head, Šahrbarāz said: "Don't make so much haste! Let me first write my will." Farruẖān consented to this. Šahrbarāz called for the basket (in which he kept his papers), gave three sheets (from there) to Farruẖān, and said: "All of these I wrote back to Kisrá about you, but you would execute me after a single letter!" Farruẖān returned the kingship to his brother Šahrbarāz, who wrote to Heraclius the Caesar, the king of the Byzantines: "I have something to ask you that I cannot say in a letter and that no note can convey. Meet me with only fifty Byzantines and I will also meet you with only fifty Persians." Heraclius approached with 500[537] Byzantines, sending spies before him along

535 Miskawayh, *Taǧārib al-umam*, 1:150 = C233–234; cf. al-Ṭabarī, *Taʾrīẖ*, 1:1006–1008 = trans., 5:326–328.
536 Miskawayh, *Taǧārib al-umam*, 1:150–151 = C235–236; cf. al-Ṭabarī, *Taʾrīẖ*, 1:1008–1009 = trans., 5:328–330.
537 Al-Ṭabarī has the exaggerated number of 500,000.

العيون بين يديه في الطريق وخاف أن يكون قد مكر به حتى أتاه عيونه أنه ليس معه إلا خمسون رجلا. ثم بسط لهما والتقيا في قبة ديباج ضربت لهما واجتمعا ومع كل واحد منهما سكين. ودَعَوا ترجمانا بينهما فقال شهربراز: "إن الذين خربوا مدينتك وبلغوا منك ومن جندك ما بلغوا أنا وأخي بشجاعتنا وكيدنا وإن كسرى أبرويز حسدنا فأراد أن أقتل أخي فأبيت. ثم أمر أخي أن يقتلني فقد خلعناه جميعا فنحن نقاتله معك." قال: "قد أصبتما ووفقتما." ثم أشار أحدهما إلى صاحبه أن السر إنما يكون بين اثنين فإذا جاوز اثنين فشا. قال صاحبه: "أجل." فقاما جميعا إلى الترجمان بسكينيهما فقتلاه واتفقا على قتال أبرويز. وفي أيام أبرويز كانت وقعة ذي قار فانتصرت العرب فيها على فارس. ومنها ذلت الفارس ورق أمرها وذلك بعد قتله النعمٰنَ بن المنذر وقد رماه تحت أرجل الفيلة واستباحة أمواله وأهله وولده وبيعهم بأوكس الأثمان.

§218[١] ثم كانت لأبرويز حيلة على ملك الروم. وذلك أنه كان قد وجه رجلا من جلة أصحابه في جيش جرار إلى بلاد الروم كما تقدم ذكره {فأنكى} فيهم وبلغ منهم وفتح الشامات وبلغ الدرب فى آثارهم فعظم أمره. وخافه أبرويز وكاتبه بكتابين يأمره في أحدهما أن يستخلف على جيشه من يثق به ويقبل إليه. ويأمره في الآخر أن يقيم بموضعه فإنه لما تدبر أمره وأجال الرأي لم يجد من يسد مسده

٨–٩ وذلك ... الأثمان: الزيادة بخط المقريزي في آخر السطر في الهامش الأيسر من الأسفل إلى الأعلى + صح. ١١ كما ... ذكره: الزيادة بخط المقريزي في الهامش الأيسر من الأعلى إلى الأسفل + صح، ويشير إليها رمز ⌐ بعد "الروم". ‖ فأنكى: "فانكا" في الأصل.

---

١ من تجارب الأمم لمسكويه ١: ١٦٢.

the road, as he was afraid that Šahrbarāz might be trying to deceive him. But his spies came back, telling him that Šahrbarāz had only fifty men with him. (A carpet) was spread for them, and they met in a silk tent that was raised for them. They met there, both having a dagger with him. They called for an interpreter, and Šahrbarāz said: "It was I and my brother who with our courage and cunning destroyed your city and caused such damage to you and your army. Now Kisrá Abarwīz has become envious of us. He wanted me to kill my brother. I refused, and then he ordered my brother to kill me. We have, both of us, given him up and will fight with you against him." Heraclius replied: "You have found what you were looking for." Then one of them signalled to the other that a secret remains a secret only between two people and when it goes beyond that, it will spread. The other agreed, and they rose together with their daggers, killed the interpreter, and agreed to fight against Abarwīz. The battle of Ḏū Qār took place during the reign of Abarwīz. It was won by the Arabs, and from then on, the Persians became humbled and their affairs precarious. This happened after Abarwīz had killed al-Nuʿmān b. al-Munḏir, whom he threw under the feet of elephants, and let his property, family, and children be plundered and sold for the lowest of prices.

§ 218[538] Abarwīz, however, resorted to a trick against the king of the Byzantines. He had sent one of his chief companions[539] with a huge army to the Byzantine territory, as we have related,[540] and he caused great damage among them. He also conquered Syria and reached al-Darb, pursuing the Byzantines. He grew powerful, and Abarwīz became fearful of him. He sent him two letters, in one of which he ordered him to leave someone whom he trusted to take over the command of the army and to come to him. In the other, he ordered him to stay where he was, because when he, Abarwīz, had further considered the matter and thought about it, he had realised that no one could take his place and if he were to leave his place (as the commander

538 Miskawayh, *Taǧārib al-umam*, 1:162 = C257–258.

539 Interestingly, this person is only identified in the next paragraph as Šahrbarāz. The whole episode, §§ 218–221, comes through Miskawayh, *Taǧārib al-umam*, 1:162–164 = C257–261, from a source other than al-Ṭabarī, and it is conspicuous that the only name mentioned by Miskawayh is that of Kisrá Abarwīz. The Persian general, the Byzantine king, the messenger, and the monk, all remain anonymous. As the whole text otherwise comes, almost letter by letter, from Miskawayh, it is obvious that the name of Šahrbarāz has been deduced by al-Maqrīzī on the basis of § 212.

540 § 212. The cross reference is by al-Maqrīzī, and it is not found in Miskawayh.

ولم يأمن الخلل إن غاب عن موضعه. وأرسل بالكتابين رسولا من ثقاته وقال له: "أوصل الكتاب الأول بالأمر بالقدوم فإن خَفّ لذلك فهو ما أردتُ. وإن كره وتثاقل عن الطاعة | فاسكت عليه 182a أياما ثم أعلمه أن الكتاب الثاني ورد عليك وأوصله إليه ليقيم بموضعه."

§ 219[١] فخرج رسول أبرويز حتى ورد على شهربراز صاحب الجيش ببلاد الشام فأوصل الكتاب إليه. فلما قرأه قال: "إما أن يكون كسرى قد تغير لي وكره موضعي أو يكون قد اختلط عقله بصرف مثلي وأنا في نحر العدو." فدعا أصحابه وقرأ عليهم الكتاب فأنكروه. فلما كان بعد ثلاثة أيام أوصل قاصد أبرويز الكتاب الثاني بالمقام وأوهمه أن رسولا ورد به. فلما قرأه قال: "هذا تخليط." ولم يقع منه موقعا. ودس إلى ملك الروم من ناظره في إيقاع صلح بينهما على أن يخلي الطريق لملك الروم حتى يدخل بلاد العراق على غرة من أبرويز وعلى أن لملك الروم ما يغلب عليه من دون العراق وللفارسي ما وراء ذلك إلى بلاد فارس. فأجابه ملك الروم إلى ذلك وتنحى الفارسي عنه في ناحية من الجزيرة وأخذ أفواه الطرق. فلم يعلم أبرويز حتى ورد خبر ملك الروم عليه من ناحية قرقيسا وهو غير مستعد وجنده متفرقون في أعماله.

§ 220[٢] فوثب من سريره مع قِرَاءة الخبر وقال: "هذا وقت حِيْلة لا وقت شِدّة." وجعل ينكتُ في الأرض مليا. ثم دعا برق وكتب فيه كتابا صغيرا بخط دقيق إلى صاحبه بالجزيرة يقول فيه: "قد

---

٧ قاصد أبرويز: الزيادة بخط المقريزي في الهامش الأيمن من الأعلى إلى الأسفل + صح، ويشير إليها رمز ⌜ بعد "أوصل".

---

١ من تجارب الأمم لمسكويه ١: ١٦٢-١٦٣.

٢ من تجارب الأمم لمسكويه ١: ١٦٣-١٦٤.

of the army), he, Abarwīz, was afraid that some damage might ensue.[541] He sent the two letters with a trusted messenger, advising him: "Give him the first letter, which orders him to come here. If he is fine with that, I have got what I wanted, but if he dislikes it and is reluctant to obey, let him be for a couple of days. Tell him then that another letter has arrived and give it to him, so that he will stay where he is."

§ 219[542] The messenger of Abarwīz left and came to Šahrbarāz, the leader of the army in Syria, and gave him the (first) letter. When Šahrbarāz read it, he thought: "Either Kisrá has changed his attitude towards me and dislikes what I have achieved or his reason has left him, as he calls me back while I am busy fighting the enemy." He called his companions and read the letter to them, and all disapproved of it. After three days, the messenger of Abarwīz gave him the second letter, which contained the order to remain where he was, and implied that a messenger had just brought it. Šahrbarāz read it and thought: "This is all confused!" He did not care to obey it, but sent a messenger to the king of the Byzantines to negotiate a peace between them on the condition that he leave the way free for the king of the Byzantines to enter Iraq without Abarwīz noticing and that the king of the Byzantines would get what he conquered except for Iraq itself, and the Persian[543] would get everything else, until the country of Fārs. The Byzantine king accepted this, and the Persian withdrew to one part of the Ǧazīrah and guarded the mouths of the roads. Abarwīz noticed nothing until he received word of the Byzantine king approaching from the direction of Qirqīsiyā. Abarwīz was unprepared and his army was dispersed in various provinces.

§ 220[544] When he read the report Abarwīz jumped from his throne and said: "Now is the time for cunning, not strength." He tapped the soil[545] for a while and then asked for some parchment to be brought and wrote a small-size letter with thin script to his general in the Ǧazīrah saying: "You will remem-

541 Compared with §§ 216–217, it is clear that both stories have the common core of Abarwīz sending two letters to Šahrbarāz, but otherwise the stories have little in common. A third version, based on Ibn al-ʿAmīd, *al-Maǧmūʿ al-mubārak*, is told in al-Maqrīzī, *Ḫabar/Greeks* § 262. Cf. also al-Masʿūdī, *Murūǧ* § 647 and ps.-al-Ǧāḥiẓ, *Tāǧ*, 180.

542 Miskawayh, *Taǧārib al-umam*, 1:162–163 = C258–259.

543 This expression comes from Miskawayh, who does not identify the general. Al-Maqrīzī has kept Miskawayh's vague formulation, even though he has already given the name of the Persian general.

544 Miskawayh, *Taǧārib al-umam*, 1:163–164 = C259–260. Cf. al-Masʿūdī, *Murūǧ* § 647.

545 This is a sign of being deep in thought, cf. Hämeen-Anttila (2020): 89 and note 128.

علمت ما كنت أمرتك به من مواصلة صاحب الروم وإطماعه في نفسك وتخلية الطريق له حتى إذا تورط في بلادنا أخذتُه من أمامه وأخذتَه أنت ومن ندبنا لذلك من خلفه فيكون ذلك بواره. وقد تم في هذا الوقت ما دبرناه وميعادك في الإيقاع به يوم كذا.» ثم دعا راهبا كان في دير بجانب مدينته وقال: «أي جارٍ كنتُ لك؟» قال: «أفضل جار.» قال: «فقد بدت لنا إليك حاجة.» قال الراهب: «الملك أجل من أن يكون له حاجة إلى مثلي ولكني أبذل نفسي في الذي يأمر الملك به.» قال أبرويز: «تحمل لي كتابا إلى فلان صاحبي.» قال: «نعم.» قال أبرويز: «فإنك تجتاز بأصحابك النصارى فأخفه.» قال: «نعم.» فلما ولى عنه الراهب قال له أبرويز: «أعلمت ما في الكتاب؟ قال: «لا.» قال: «فلا تحمله حتى | تعلم ما فيه.» 182b

§ 221[1] فلما قرأه أدخله في جيبه ثم مضى فلما صار في عسكر الروم نظر إلى الصلبان والقسيسين وضجيجهم بالتقديس والصلوات احترق قلبه لهم وأشفق مما خاف أن يقع بهم. وقال في نفسه: «أنا شر الناس إن حملت بيدي حتف النصرانية وهلاك هؤلاء الخلق.» فصاح: «أنا قد حملني كسرى رسالة ومعي كتاب منه.» فأخذوه فوجدوا الكتاب معه وقد كان أبرويز وجه رسولا قبل ذلك اختصر الطريق حتى مر بعسكر الروم كأنه رسول إلى أبرويز من صاحبه الذي طابق ملك الروم ومعه كتاب فيه: «أن الملك قد كان أمرني بمقاربة ملك الروم وأن أخدعه وأخلي له الطريق فيأخذه

---

١ القرآن، سورة الروم، الآيات ٣-١.

ber that I ordered you to make contact with the Byzantine to make him desirous of you changing sides and I ordered you to leave the roads open for him, so that he becomes entangled in our country. Then I will attack him from front and you and those who we have commissioned to do so from behind. That will be his end! What we have planned is now going to happen. You are to attack him on the day so-and-so." Then he called a monk from a monastery close to his city and said: "What kind of a neighbour have I been to you?" The monk replied that he had been a very good neighbour, and Abarwīz went on: "Now I have something to ask from you." The monk replied: "The king is all too great to have to ask something from a nobody like myself, but I am ready to sacrifice myself to accomplish what he commands." Abarwīz said: "Would you carry a letter of mine to my commander so-and-so?" The monk promised to do this, and Abarwīz continued: "You will have to cross the area of your coreligionists, Christians, but hide the letter from them." The monk promised to do so. When he was ready to go, Abarwīz asked: "Do you know what there is in the letter?" The monk said he did not, and Abarwīz said: "Don't carry it without first reading it."[546]

§ 221[547] When the monk had read the letter, he put it in his pocket and left. When he was in the Byzantine camp and saw the crosses and the priests and heard their voices chanting glorifications and prayers, his heart burned for them and he was concerned about what would fall on them. He thought: "I will be the worst of all people if I carry by my own hand the destruction of Christianity and the death of all these people." Then he shouted: "Kisrá has given me a letter to carry! I have it on me!" They took him and found the letter. Before this Abarwīz had sent another messenger, who took shortcuts and went by the camp of the Byzantines as if he were a messenger going to Abarwīz from the general who had come into an understanding with the Byzantine king. He carried a letter, which said: "The king gave me orders to make friends with the Byzantine king in order to deceive him. He also ordered me to let him pass freely so that the king may attack him from the

546 For reading a letter before carrying it, cf. Kay Kāʾūs, *Qābūsnāmah* 97. For the story of the letter, see also Christensen (1936): 447–448; al-Masʿūdī, *Murūǧ* § 647; and ps.-al-Ǧāḥiẓ, *Tāǧ* 180–187.

547 Miskawayh, *Taǧārib al-umam*, 1:164 = C260–261. The reference to the Qurʾān is well known. It could derive from al-Ṭabarī, *Taʾrīḫ*, 1:1005 = trans., 5:324, or Ibn al-Aṯīr, *Kāmil*, 1:479.

الملك من أمامه وآخذه أنا من خلفه. وقد فعلت ذلك. فرأى الملك في إعلامي وقت خروجه إليه.“ فأخذ ملك الروم الرسول وقرأ الكتاب وقال: ”عجبت أن يكون هذا الفارسي دَاهَن على كسرى.“ وبينا هو في ذلك إذ وافاه أبرويز فيمن أمكنه من جنده فوجد ملك الروم قد {ولى} هاربا. فاتبعه يقتل ويأسر من أدرك. وبلغ شهرباز صاحب الجيش ببلاد الشام هزيمة الروم فأحب أن يجلي نفسه ويستر ذنبه لما فاته ما دبر. فخرج خلف الروم الهاربين فلم يسلم منهم إلا القليل وكتب إلى أبرويز: ”إنني قد عملت الحيلة على الروم حتى صاروا في العراق.“ فأرسل من {رؤوسهم} شيئا كثيرا. وفي هذه الحادثة أنزل الله تعالى: ﴿الم غُلِبَتِ ٱلرُّومُ فِي أَدْنَى ٱلْأَرْضِ﴾[١] الآية.

§ 222[٢] ثم كان أبرويز سبب هلاك نفسه. وذلك أنه تجبر واحتقر العظماء وعتا واستخف بما لا يستخف به الملك الحازم. وكان من أشد ملوك فارس بطشا وأنفذهم رأيا وبلغ من البأس والنجدة ومن مساعدة الأقدار وجمع الأموال ما لم يجمعه أحد من الملوك قبله وبلغت خيله قسطنطينية وإفريقية. وكان له في داره ثلاث آلاف حرة واثنتا عشرة ألف جارية للغناء ولصنوف الخدمة وألف فيل إلا فيلا واحدا وخمسون ألف دابة. ورتب في حَرَسه ستة آلاف رجل وكان في إصطبله

---

٢ ملك الروم: الزيادة بخط المقريزي في آخر السطر في الهامش الأيسر من الأسفل إلى الأعلى. ٣ ولى: ”ولا“ في الأصل. ٤ شهرباز: الزيادة بخط المقريزي في الهامش الأيسر من الأسفل إلى الأعلى + صح، ويشير إليها رمز ⌐ بعد ”وبلغ“. ٥–٧ وكتب ... الآية: الزيادة بخط المقريزي في الهامش الأيمن من الأعلى إلى الأسفل إلا آخرها + صح، ويشير إليها رمز ⌐ بعد ”القليل“. ٦ رؤوسهم: ”روسهم“ في الأصل. ٩–١٠ من[١] ... الأقدار: الزيادة بخط المقريزي في الهامش الأيمن منكسة + صح، ويشير إليها رمز ⌐ بعد ”وكان“. ١٠ الأموال: كشط المقريزي كل ما قبل اللام النهاية ثم صحح الكلمة كما هي الآن. ‖ قبله: كتب المقريزي هذه الكلمة فوق السطر. ١١ وكان له: كشط المقريزي ما يلي الألف ثم صحح العبارة كما هي الآن. ‖ في ... حرة: الزيادة بخط المقريزي في الهامش الأيمن + صح، ويشير إليها رمز ⌐ بعد ”له“. ‖ ألف: كشط المقريزي ما يلي الألف، ثم صحح الكلمة كما هي الآن وأطال الفاء لملء البياض. ‖ للغناء ... الخدمة: الزيادة بخط المقريزي في الهامش الأيسر من الأسفل إلى الأعلى + صح، ويشير إليها رمز ⌐ بعد ”جارية“.

---

١ من تجارب الأمم لمسكويه ١: ١٦٤.

٢ من تجارب الأمم لمسكويه ١: ١٦٤ ومن تأريخ سني الملوك لحمزة ص ٤٧.

front and I from behind. I have done this. The king may now decide whether to inform me when he will set out for him." The king of the Byzantines caught the messenger, read the letter, and thought: "I did wonder why that Persian was deceiving Kisrá!" While he was thinking about this, Abarwīz attacked him with what he had been able to assemble of his army and found that the king of the Byzantines had turned away, fleeing. Abarwīz followed him, killing and taking prisoner whomever he could catch. Šahrbarāz, the leader of the army in Syria heard about the defeat of the Byzantines and wanted to clear himself of suspicions and hide his guilt, as he had already lost what he had planned. He followed the fleeing Byzantines and left only few of them alive. Then he wrote to Abarwīz: "I deceived the Byzantines and lured them into Iraq." He sent (to Abarwīz) a large number of their leaders. About this occurrence God, He is Exalted, says: "*Alif, lām, mīm.* The Byzantines have been vanquished in a country close by" etc.[548]

§ 222[549] Abarwīz caused his own downfall, because he was tyrannical and despised the noblemen, was insolent, and belittled what a judicious king would not belittle. However, he was one of the strongest kings of Fārs, with a piercing reason. He had such strength and courage, such assistance from destiny, and such sums of money that no king had gathered before him. His cavalry reached Constantinople and Ifrīqiyah, and in his palace he had 3,000 free women and 12,000 servant girls for singing and for various kinds of services, one thousand elephants less one, and 50,000 horses. He had 6,000 men in his guard and 8,500 horses in his stable for him to ride, 12,000 pack

548 Qur'ān (*al-Rūm*), 30:1–3.

549 Miskawayh, *Taǧārib al-umam*, 1:164 = C261–262; Ḥamzah, *Ta'rīḫ* 47 = trans. 74; cf. al-Ṭabarī, *Ta'rīḫ*, 1:1041 = trans., 5:376–377.

ثمانية آلاف وخمس مائة دابة لركابه خاصة واثنا عشر ألف بغل لأثقاله وعشرون ألف بختي ومن الجواهر والأواني والآلات ما يليق بذلك. وأمر أن يُحْصَى ما اجتبي من خراج بلاده وسائر أبواب المال سنة ثماني عشرة من ملكه فرفع إليه أن الذي اجتبي في تلك السنة من الخراج وسائر الأبواب ستمائة ألف ألف درهم.

§ 223[١] وفي نسخة: أنه | كان في يده السواد وأرض العجم دون أعمال العَرَب وأن حد مملكته إلى هِيْت. وكان ما وراء ذلك من الموصل والجزيرة والشام بيد الروم. فكانت جباية مملكته فى سنة ثماني عشرة من ملكه أربعمائة ألف ألف وعشرين ألف ألف مثقال من الوَرِق. وأمر أبرويز فحُول إلى بيت مال بنى بمدينة طيسبون من ضرب فيروز بن يزدجرد وقباذ بن فيروز اثنتي عشرة ألف بدرة في أنواع من الجواهر والكُسَى وغير ذلك. فعتا واستهان بالناس والأحرار. وبلغ من جرأته أنه أمر رجلا كان على حَرَس بابه الخاصة يقال له زاذان فروخ أن يقتل كل مقيد في سجن من سجونه. فأحصوا فبلغوا ستة وثلاثين ألف إنسان. فلم يقدم زاذان فروخ على قتلهم وتقدم بالتوقف عما أمر به كسرى وأعد عللا له فيما أمر به فيهم. فكان هذا أحد ما كسب به أبرويز عداوة مملكته. 183a

§ 224[٢] والثاني احتقاره إياهم واستخفافه بعظمائهم. والثالث أنه سلط علجا يقال له الفرخان فزاد عليهم حتى استخرج بقايا الخراج بعنف وعذاب. وكان ضمن من ذلك مالا عظيما فسلطه على الناس. والرابع إجماعه على قتل الفَلّ الذين انصرفوا إليه من قبَل هرقل ملك الروم. فمضى قوم من العظماء إلى عقر بابل وشيرويه بن أبرويز مع إخوته بها. وقد وكل بهم مؤدبون وأساورة يحولون بينهم وبين براح ذلك الموضع. فأقبلوا به ودخلوا مدينة نهرشير ليْلا نخلى عمن كان في سجونها وأخرج

١ بغل: وضع المقريزي فوق هذه الكلمة رمز "٢" وكررها في الهامش ولكن لا توجد أي حاشية فيه.
١٠ حَرَس: وضع المقريزي رمز "ح" تحت الحرف الأول إشارة إلى تلفظه بالحاء. ١١ ألف إنسان: الزيادة بخط المقريزي في الهامش الأيمن من الأعلى إلى الأسفل + صح، ويشير إليها رمز ⌐ بعد "وثلاثين".

١ من تجارب الأمم لمسكويه ١: ١٦٤–١٦٥.
٢ من تجارب الأمم لمسكويه ١: ١٦٥.

mules, 20,000 Bactrian camels, and quantities of jewels, vessels, and tools to match. He gave orders to count how much tax he received from his country and his other sorts of income in his eighteenth regnal year, and it was reported to him that that year it was 600,000,000 dirhams.

§ 223[550] According to another manuscript, Abarwīz had under his power the Sawād and the country of the Persians (*al-ʿAǧam*), but not the districts of the Arabs. The border of his kingdom reached to Hīt, but the area beyond that, Mosul, the Ǧazīrah, and Syria, was under the Byzantines. The tax income from his kingdom in his eighteenth regnal year was 420,000,000 *miṯqāls* of silver. Abarwīz gave orders to take this into a treasury he had built in the city of Ṭaysabūn. The coins were from the mints of Fīrūz b. Yazdaǧird and Qubād b. Fīrūz, in 12,000 purses, together with various jewels, clothes, etc. He despised and slighted both common people and free men. His insolence reached such a level that he gave orders to the commander of the guards at his private door, called Zādān-Farrūḫ, to kill every prisoner chained in his prisons. Their number was counted and it came up to 36,000 people. Zādān-Farrūḫ did not kill them, but ordered men to abstain from fulfilling Kisrá's order and made excuses concerning the orders. This was one of the reasons Kisrá earned the hatred of his own kingdom.

§ 224[551] The second reason was that Abarwīz despised them (his people) and belittled their noblemen. The third was that he appointed a brute called al-Farruḫān over them, and the latter was overbearing,[552] extorting the remainder of the tax by brutality and torture. He had vouched a great sum of money to Kisrá, who then appointed him over people. The fourth was his decision to execute the remains of the army that returned to him after the defeat against the Byzantine king Heraclius. Some of the noblemen went to ʿAqar Bābil, where Šīrūyah b. Abarwīz and his brothers were. They had been given to the care of tutors and cavalrymen, who prevented them from leaving the place. Now they brought Šīrūyah out and went to the city of Nahrašīr by night. He released those who were in prison there and let them

550 Miskawayh, *Taǧārib al-umam*, 1:164–165 = C262–263; cf. al-Ṭabarī, *Taʾrīḫ*, 1:1042–1043 = trans., 5:377–379. Al-Ṭabarī probably provides the sentence on the 420,000,000 *miṯqāls*, not found in Miskawayh. The source of the first sentence remains unidentified.

551 Miskawayh, *Taǧārib al-umam*, 1:165 = C263; cf. al-Ṭabarī, *Taʾrīḫ*, 1:1043–1044 = trans., 5:378–379.

552 Al-Maqrīzī reads *sallaṭa* (…) *al-Farruḫān fa-zāda ʿalayhim*, misreading Miskawayh's *sallaṭa* (…) *al-Farruḫān-Zād ʿalayhim* "appointed (…) al-Farruḫān-Zād over them," following al-Ṭabarī.

من كان فيها واجتمع إليه الفَل الذين كانوا علموا بأمر أبرويز بقتلهم ونادوا: "قباذ شاه نشاه." وساروا حين أصبحوا إلى رحبة أبرويز. فهرب الحرس من قصر أبرويز وانحاز أبرويز بنفسه إلى باغ له قريب من قصره يدعى باغ الهندوان مارا مرعوبًا. فأُخِذ وحبس خارجا عن دار المملكة في دار رجل يقال له مارسفند إلى أن قتل بعد حديث طويل ومراسلات بينه وبين شيرويه بمواطأة العظماء وبعد تقريع كثير وتوبيخ على ما كان منه في أشياء عددها عليه فأجاب عن الكل بجوابات | مقنعة. 183b

§ 225[1] فمما كتب به شيرويه إلى أبيه أبرويز: "إنا لم نكن سببا لما أصبحت فيه ولكن الله قضاه عليك لسوء أعمالك. منها فتكك بأبيك وسملك عينيه ومنها سوء صنيعك واستخلاصك النساء وتركك العطف على أولادك وما آتيت إلى الرعية وما جَمَّرْتَ من البعوث واستخفافك بملك الروم وترك أَطْلَابه في خشبة الصليب ولم يك إليها حاجة." فأجاب: "إن الأمر إذا أقبل أعيت الحيل في الإدبار وإذا أدبر أعيت الحيل في الإقبال. أبلغ شيرويه القصير العُمر أنه لا ينبغي لذي عقل أن يبُثَّ الصغير من الذنب إلا بعد تحققه فضلا عن عظيم ما بثَثت. فإن كنت جاهلا بعيوبك فأستثبت. وإن كان لنا ذنب يوجب القتل فقضاة ملتك ينفون ولد المستوجب القتل عن أبيه."

§ 226[2] "وأما ما ذكرت من أمر أبينا فالجواب أن البغاة أغروه بنا حتى أتهمنا. فاعتزلنا بابَه فانتهك منه ما انتهك ولحقنا به فهجم علينا المنافق بهرام فلحقنا بالروم وأقبلنا بالجنود فهرب بهرام وقتلنا

---

١ شاه نشاه : كذا في الأصل و"شاه" في آخر السطر السابق. ٢ وانحاز : وضع المقريزي رمز "ح" تحت الحرف الثالث إشارة إلى تلفظه بالحاء.

---

٢ باغ : أضاف المقريزي الحاشية التالية في الهامش الأيمن من الأعلى إلى الأسفل: "الباغ البستان" ووضع تحت السين ثلاث نقط إشارة إلى تلفظها بالسين.

---

١ من تأريخ الطبري ١: ١٠٤٦–١٠٥٠.

٢ من تأريخ الطبري ١: ١٠٥١–١٠٥٣.

out. The remnants of the army, who knew that Abarwīz had given orders to kill them, joined Šīrūyah. They all cried: “Qubād is the King of Kings!” (*Qubād šāhanšāh*)[553] Next morning they marched to the square of Abarwīz. The guards of Abarwīz’s castle fled, and Abarwīz himself withdrew into a garden (*bāġ*) close by the castle, called Bāġ al-Hinduwān, fleeing in terror,[554] but he was captured and imprisoned outside of the royal palace in the house of a man called Mārasfand and later killed by the agreement of the noblemen after a long story and exchange of letters between him and Šīrūyah and after much censure and blame of various things he had done and which Šīrūyah listed to him, even though Abarwīz answered them in a satisfactory way.

§ 225[555] One thing Šīrūyah wrote to his father Abarwīz was the following: “I am not the reason for your present situation. God has condemned you because of your bad deeds, like killing your father and blinding his eyes, and of your bad way in devoting all your time to women and not caring about your own children and of what you did to people and of how you detained army expeditions in enemy territory and of how you thought lightly of the king of the Byzantines and ignored his requests of the wooden cross, even though we had no need for it.” Abarwīz answered (the messenger): “When matters are to advance, no trick will make them retreat, and when they are to retreat, no trick will make them advance. Tell Šīrūyah, who will not live long, that a wise man does not spread around (tales of) minor misdeeds without verifying them, let alone major ones, like you are doing. If you are ignorant of your own faults, then try to learn them. Even if I had done something to deserve death, the judges of your religion forbid a son from killing his father.”

§ 226[556] “The answer to what you said about my father is that unjust people incited him against me so that he grew suspicious of me. I withdrew from his court, and he violated the things you know. I then joined him, but the hypocrite Bahrām attacked me, so I went to Byzantium and returned from there

---

5 garden : *Bāġ* means garden (marginal gloss in al-Maqrīzī’s hand).

---

553 I.e., “Qubād is the King of Kings!” Qubād is the regnal name of Šīrūyah, cf. below.

554 The next word in the holograph is clearly *mārran* for al-Ṭabarī’s and Miskawayh’s much more natural *fārran*, although it should be noted that the word in Miskawayh (ed. Caetani) could equally well be *mārran*. I have translated following al-Ṭabarī and Miskawayh. Note also that both editions of Miskawayh, by Emāmī (1: 247–248) and Ḥasan, drop the word *marʿūban*.

555 Al-Ṭabarī, *Taʾrīḫ*, 1:1046–1050 = trans., 5:382–387.

556 Al-Ṭabarī, *Taʾrīḫ*, 1:1051–1053 = trans., 5:387–390.

من شرك في قتل أبينا. وأما أمر أبنائنا فوكلنا بهم من يمنعهم من الفساد ووسعنا عليهم في كل ما أرادوه. وأما أنت فإن المنجمين قضوا في مولدك أنك مترب علينا ووجدنا ملك الهند قد كتب إليك في ست وثلاثين من ملكنا: أبشر فإنك مُتَوج سنة ثمان وثلاثين من ملك كسرى. فوثقنا أنك لا تملك إلا بهلاكنا. وكتاب قَرْمِيْسِنَا وقصة مولدك عند شيرين فقف عليهما تكسبك قراءتهما ندما.»

§ 227[1] «وأما من حبَسْنا فلم نحبس إلا من استوجب القتل. وبلغني أنك أجمعت على إطلاقهم وهدم حبسهم. فإن فعلت أثمت مع أن أعداء الملك لا يحبون الملك أبدا. وأما جمعنا الأموال فاعلم أيها الجاهل إنما يقيم ملك الملوك بعد الله تعالى الأموال ولا سيما ملك فارس الذي قد اكتنفته الأعداء ولا يُقدَر على كفهم إلا بالجنود. ولا سبيل إلى الاستكثار من الجنود إلا بالأموال ولا تجمع الأموال إلا بالجد والتشمير.»

§ 228[2] ثم ألح العظماء على شيرويه في قتل أبيه فأمر بقتله. فضرب ضربات فلم تحك فيه. فوجد في | عضده خرزة لا يحيك السيف فيمن تعلقها. فنزعت من عضده ثم قتل {فبكى} شيرويه لقتله. 184a وكان هلاك أبرويز بعد ثمان وثلاثين سنة من ملكه. وعلى مضي اثنتين وثلاثين سنة وخمسة أشهر وخمسة عشر يوما من ملكه هاجر النبي صلى الله عليه وسلم من مكة إلى المدينة وخلف في بيت المال يوم قتل من الورق أربع مائة ألف بدرة سوى الكنوز والذخائر والجواهر وآلات الملك.

---

١١ فبكى: «فبكا» في الأصل. ١٢ من ملكه: الزيادة بخط المقريزي في الهامش الأيمن من الأعلى إلى الأسفل + صح، ويشير إليها رمز ˥ بعد «سنة». ١٤ ألف: كتب المقريزي «صح» فوق الكلمة.

---

١ من تأريخ الطبري ١: ١٠٥٣، ١٠٥٥.

٢ من تجارب الأمم لمسكويه ١: ١٦٥.

with an army. Bahrām fled, and I killed those who had taken part in killing my father. As to my sons, I appointed people to take care of them, so that they would protect them from corruption. I gave them amply whatever they wanted. As to you, astrologers decreed at your birth that you would find fault with me.[557] I have also found out that the king of India has written to you on my 36th regnal year: 'Rejoice, for you shall be crowned in the 38th regnal year of king Kisrá.' I was certain that you would not reign except through my death. The letter of Qarmīsinā[558] and the story of your birth is with Šīrīn:[559] peruse them. Reading them will make you regret what you are doing."

§ 227[560] "As to those I had imprisoned, I only imprisoned people who deserved to die. I have heard that you decided to let them loose and to destroy their prison. If you really have done so, you have sinned, because the enemies of the king will always hate the king. As to hoarding money, know, o ignorant one, that the next thing after God, He is Exalted, to keep the kingship of a king is money. This is especially true for the king of Fārs, who is surrounded by enemies, and these can only be held off by armies. Yet, the only way to have numerous armies is to have money, and money can only be gathered by earnest effort."

§ 228[561] The noblemen insisted on Šīrūyah that he should kill his father, and he gave orders to do so. Abarwīz was hit (by sword) several times, but this had no effect on him. Tied to his arm they found a bead (*ḫarazah*), and swords could not affect anyone who carried that bead. It was taken from him, and then he was killed. Šīrūyah cried for his death. Abarwīz died after 38 years of rule. When 32 years, 5 months, and 15 days had passed of his reign, the Prophet, may God honour him and grant him peace, emigrated from Mecca to Medina. The day Abarwīz was killed, he left 400,000 purses of silver, in addition to the treasures and stores, jewels and royal equipment.

557 I follow al-Ṭabarī, who reads *muṯarrib*. Al-Maqrīzī reads MTRB, which would lead to a somewhat forced translation "you would sprinkle dust upon me," i.e., cause sorrow.

558 Al-Ṭabarī reads FRMYŠʾ, which Bosworth (1999): 389 reads Furumīšā, mentioning in note 959 two attempts to identify this king.

559 For Šīrīn, see "Ḵosrow o Šīrīn," in *EIr*.

560 Al-Ṭabarī, *Taʾrīḫ*, 1:1053, 1055 = trans., 5:390–392.

561 Miskawayh, *Taǧārib al-umam*, 1:165 = C264 (end); cf. al-Ṭabarī, *Taʾrīḫ*, 1:1045 = trans., 5:381.

§229[1] وكان شعاره مورد مُوَشى وسراويله على لون السماء وتاجه أحمر وبيده رمح. ونصب بيت نار بقرية من رستاق كروان ووقف عليها قرى تقرب منها. وقيل: بعث النبي صلى الله عليه وسلم لاثنتين وعشرين سنة من ملكه وبقي بعد المبعث ست عشرة سنة. وكاتبه صلى الله عليه وسلم عند ما مضى من ملكه ثمان وثلاثون سنة فهلك من سنته. وقيل: كانت الهجرة لتسع وعشرين سنة من ملكه. وقيل: لثلاث وثلاثين. وقيل إنه أخرج خشبة الصليب من القدس لأربع وعشرين سنة من ملكه ثم كانت الهجرة بعد ذلك بتسع سنين. ثم أقام بعد الهجرة حتى خلع وقتل أربع سنين وأربعة أشهر واثنين وعشرين يوما.

§230[2] وقد رأى كسرى أبرويز عدة آيات بسبب رسول الله صلى الله عليه وسلم منها ما رواه محمد ابن إسحٰق قال: كان من حديث كسرى كما حدثني بعض أصحابي عن وهب بن منبه قبل أن يأتيه كتاب رسول الله صلى الله عليه وسلم فيما بلغني أنه كان سَكّر دجلة العوراء وأنفق عليها من الأموال ما لا يدرى ما هو. وكانت طاق مجلسه قد بنيت بنيانا لم ير مثله. وكان يعلق منها تاجه فيجلس فيها إذا جلس للناس. وكان عنده ستون وثلٰثمائة رجل من الحُزاة والحُزاة العلماء من بين كاهن وساحر ومنجم. وكان فيهم رجل من العرب اسمه السائب يعتاف اعتياف العرب قل ما يخطئ. بعث به باذان من اليمن. فكان أبرويز إذا حزنه أمر جمعهم فقال: "انظروا في هذا الأمر ما هو."

---

٦ خلع وقتل : كشط المقريزي عبارة أخرى قبل أن يصححها كما هي الآن. ٨-١٠ ما ... أنه : الزيادة بخط المقريزي في الهامش الأيمن من الأعلى إلى الأسفل إلا آخرها وهي من الأسفل إلى الأعلى + صح، ويشير إليها رمز ⌝ بعد "منها". ١١ يعلق : كشط المقريزي كلمة أخرى قبل أن يصححها كما هي الآن. ١١-١٢ فيجلس ... وثلٰثمائة : كشط المقريزي عبارة أخرى قبل أن يصححها كما هي الآن. ١٢-١٣ رجل ... ومنجم : الزيادة بخط المقريزي في الهامش الأيسر من الأسفل إلى الأعلى + صح، ويشير إليها رمز ⌐ بعد "وثلٰثمائة". ١٢ الحُزاة : وضع المقريزي رمز "ح" تحت الحرف الثالث إشارة إلى تلفظه بالحاء. ١٣ السائب : كشط المقريزي كلمة أخرى قبل أن يصححها كما هي الآن. ‖ يعتاف ... يخطئ : الزيادة بخط المقريزي في الهامش الأيسر + صح، ويشير إليها رمز ⌐ بعد "السائب". ‖ بعث به : كشط المقريزي عبارة أخرى قبل أن يصححها كما هي الآن وكتب "به" فوق السطر.

---

١ من تأريخ سني الملوك لحمزة ص ٤٧.

٢ من تأريخ الطبري ١: ١٠٠٩-١٠١٠.

§ 229[562] Abarwīz's vest was rose-coloured and embroidered, his trousers were sky-blue, and his crown red. In his hand, he had a spear. He established a fire temple in a village in the *rustāq* of Karwān and endowed it with some villages close by. It is said that the Prophet, may God honour him and grant him peace, was sent in the 22nd year of his reign and Abarwīz reigned 16 years after that. The Prophet, may God honour him and grant him peace, sent him a letter when 38 years of his reign had passed, and he died the same year. It is also said that the *hiğrah* took place in the 29th year of his reign or, according to others, 33rd. It is said that he took the wooden cross from Jerusalem in the 24th year of his reign and that the *hiğrah* took place 9 years later. After the *hiğrah*, he reigned for 4 years, 4 months, and 20 days until he was deposed and killed.

§ 230[563] Kisrá Abarwīz saw several signs concerning the Messenger of God, may God honour him and grant him peace. Muḥammad b. Isḥāq has transmitted one of these, saying: Some of my companions have transmitted from Wahb b. Munabbih, according to what I have heard, that before the letter of the Messenger of God, may God honour him and grant him peace, came to him, Kisrá had constructed a dam for the One-Eyed Tigris and spent huge sums of money on it, more than can be known.[564] The arch of his palace had been built in a way never seen before, and his crown was hanging from it. He used to sit there when he received people. He had 360 seers[565]—seers are learned men including soothsayers, magicians, and astrologers. Among them was an Arab, called al-Sā'ib, who practiced zoomancy (*ʿiyāfah*) in the Arab way. He was rarely wrong. Bādān[566] had sent him from Yemen. When some matter worried him, Abarwīz used to call them all and say: "Look into this matter and tell me what it is."

562 Ḥamzah, *Ta'rīḫ* 47 = trans. 74 (beginning).

563 Al-Ṭabarī, *Ta'rīḫ*, 1:1009–1010 = trans., 5:331–332.

564 For this dam, see Christensen (1936): 486–487.

565 For *ḥāzī*, see Fahd (1966): 112–113.

566 Later, § 240, also in the form Bādām, Persian governor of Yemen. For the name, see Justi (1895): 56.

§ 231[١] فلما بعث رسول الله صلى الله عليه وسلم أصبح كسرى غداة وقد انفصم طاق ملكه من وسطه وانخرقت دجلة العوراء. فلما رأى ذلك أحزنه وقال: "انفصم طاق مُلكي من غير ثقل وانخرقت علي دجلة. شاه بشكست." يعني انكسر الملك. "انظروا في هذا الأمر ما هو." فخرجوا من عنده فنظروا في أمره. فأخذ عليهم بأقطار السماء وأظلمت عليهم الأرض وتسكعوا في علمهم فلا يمضي لساحر سحره ولا لكاهن كهانته | 184b ولا يستقيم لمنجم علم نجومه. وبات السائب في ليلة ظلماء على ربوة من الأرض يرمق برقا نشأ من قبل الحجاز ثم استطار حتى بلغ المشرق. فلما أصبح ذهب ينظر إلى ما تحت قدميه فإذا روضة خضراء فقال فيما يعتاف: "لئن صدق ما أرى ليخرجن من الحجاز سلطان يبلغ المشرق تخصب عنه الأرض كأفضل ما أخصبت عن ملك كان قبله." فلما خلص الكهان والمنجمون بعضهم إلى بعض ورأوا ما قد أصابهم ورأى السائب ما قد رأى قال بعضهم لبعض: "تعلمون والله ما حيل بينكم وبين علمكم إلا لأمر جاء من السماء. وأنه لنبي قد بعث أو هو مبعوث يثلم هذا الملك ويكسره. ولئن نعيتم لكسرى ملكه ليقتلنكم. فأقيموا بينكم أمرا تقولونه وتؤخرونه عنكم إلى أمد ما."

§ 232[٢] {فجاؤوا} كسرى أبرويز فقالوا له: "إنا قد نظرنا في هذا الأمر فوجدنا حُسَّابَك الذين وضعتَ على حسابهم طاقَ ملكك وسِكرك دجلة العوراء وضعوه على النحوس. فلما اختلف عليه الليل والنهار وقعت النحوس على مواقعها فزال كل ما وضع عليها. وإنا سَنَحْسُب حسابا تضع عليه بنيانك فلا يزول." قال: "فاحسبوا لي." فحسبوا له ثم قالوا: "ابْنِه." {فبنى} وعمل في دجلة ثمانية أشهر

١ كسرى ... انفصم : كشط المقريزي عبارة أخرى قبل أن يصححها كما هي الآن. ٢ فلما ... طاق : كشط المقريزي عبارة أخرى قبل أن يصححها كما هي الآن. ٣-٤ انظروا ... أمره : كشط المقريزي عبارة أخرى قبل أن يصححها كما هي الآن. ١٣ فجاؤوا : "فجاوا" في الأصل. ١٦ فبنى : "فبنا" في الأصل. ‖ أشهر : كشط المقريزي كلمة أخرى قبل أن يصححها كما هي الآن.

١ من تأريخ الطبري ١: ١٠١٠–١٠١١.

٢ من تأريخ الطبري ١: ١٠١١–١٠١٢.

§ 231[567] When the Messenger of God, may God honour him and grant him peace, was sent, Kisrá woke up one morning. The royal arch had been cracked from the middle and (the dam of) the One-Eyed Tigris had been broken. When he saw this, he became sad and thought: "My royal arch has been cracked although nothing heavy was bearing on it and the (dam of the) Tigris has been broken against me. *Šāh be-šikast*"—this means 'the king has been broken'—"Look into this matter and see what it is." The seers left him and looked into the matter, but the regions of heaven had been closed to them and the earth had become dark to them. They had lost the way in their sciences. The magic of the magicians failed them, as did the soothsaying of the soothsayers, and astrology did not appear right to any of the astrologers. Al-Sāʾib spent the dark night on a hill in the open air watching a thunderbolt that originated from the direction of Ḥiǧāz and flew until it reached the East. Next morning, he went to see what was beneath his feet and found a verdant meadow. He said in his prognostication: "If what I see is true, there will indeed be a power coming from Ḥiǧāz and reaching the East, and it will make the earth prosper like it never did under a king before." When the soothsayers and the astrologers came together and compared their notes and al-Sāʾib related[568] what he had seen, they said to each other: "By God, you know that you were blocked from your knowledge only because of an order issued from heaven. A prophet must have been sent or will soon be sent. He will blunt and break this kingdom. But if we tell Kisrá the bad news about his kingdom he will surely have us killed. Let us agree to say something else to buy some time."

§ 232[569] The seers went to Kisrá Abarwīz and said: "We have now looked into this matter and have found out that those who made the calculations according to which you had the foundations of the royal arch laid and the (dam of the) One-Eyed Tigris constructed based them on the Malefic Ones. With days and nights going by, the Malefic Ones reached their positions and everything that had been based on them fell apart. We will now make new calculations, based on which you can lay the foundations of your building so that it will not fall apart." Kisrá gave them orders to do so. They made the calculations and then told him to start building. Kisrá started building and worked on the Tigris for eight months, spending huge sums of money.

567 Al-Ṭabarī, *Taʾrīḫ*, 1:1010–1011 = trans., 5:332–333.

568 The text has *raʾaw* and *raʾá*, but *rawaw* and *rawá* would make better sense.

569 Al-Ṭabarī, *Taʾrīḫ*, 1:1011–1012 = trans., 5:333–334.

فأنفق من الأموال ما لا يدرى ما هو حتى إذا فرغ قال لهم: "أَجْلِسُ على سورها؟" قالوا: "نعم." فأمر بالبسط والفرش والرياحين فوضعت عليها. وأمر بالمرازبة فجمعوا له واجتمع اللعابون. ثم [ثم] خرج حتى جلس عليها. فبينا هم هنالك انتسفت دجلة البنيان من تحته فلم يُسْتَخرج إلا بآخر رمق. فلما أخرجوه جمع كهانه وسُحَّارَه ومنجميه فقتل منهم قريبا من المائة وقال: "قربتكم وأدْنَيتكم دون الناس وأجريت عليكم أرزاقي. ثم تلعبون بي." قالوا: "أيها الملك أخطأنا ولكنا سنَحْسُب لك حسابا يثبت حتى نضعه على الوثاق من السعود." قال: "انظروا ما تقولون." قالوا: "فإنا نفعل." قال: "فاحسبوا." فحسبوا له ثم قالوا: "ابنه." {فبنى} وأنفق من الأموال ما لا يدرى ما هو في ثمانية أشهر من ذي قبل ثم قالوا: "قد فرغنا. فاخرج فاقعد عليها."

§233[1] فهاب الجلوس عليها | وركب برذونه وخرج يسير عليها. فبينا هو يسير فوقها إذ انتسفت 185a
دجلة البنيان فلم يدرك إلا بآخر رمق. فدعاهم فقال: "والله لآمرن بقتلكم أجمعين ولأنزعن أكتافكم أو لأطرحنكم تحت أيدي الفيلة أو لتَصدقُني ما هذا الأمر الذي تلفقون علي." قالوا: "لا نكذبك أيها الملك. أمرتنا حين انخرقت دجلة وانفصم عليك طاق مجلسك من غير ثقل أن ننظر في علمنا لم ذلك. فنظرنا فأظلمت علينا الأرض وأخذ علينا في أقطار السماء فتردد علمنا في أيدينا فلا ينفذ لساحر سحر ولا لكاهن كهانة ولا لمنجم علم نجومه. فعرفنا أن هذا الأمر حدث من السماء وأنه قد بعث نبي أو هو مبعوث ولذلك حيل بيننا وبين علمنا. فخشينا أن نعينا لك ملكك أن تقتلنا فكرهنا من الموت ما كره الناس فعللنا عن أنفسنا بما رأيت."

٧ فبنى: "فبنا" في الأصل.

١ من تأريخ الطبري ١: ١٠١٢–١٠١٣.

When he had finished, he said to them: "Shall I sit on its wall?" They told him to do so, and Kisrá gave orders to prepare carpets and rugs and flowers, which were then laid on the wall. Then he gave orders for the *marzubāns* to be called together, and they all came, as did musicians. Kisrá sat on the mats, but when they were sitting there, the Tigris demolished the building from below, and Kisrá was pulled out (of the rubble) half dead. When he had been pulled out, he gathered his soothsayers, magicians, and astrologers and killed almost a hundred of them, saying: "I admitted you close to myself and brought you nearer to me than other people and I have given you your wages, but now you play your games with me!" They replied: "O King, we have done wrong, but we will make you new calculations which will hold true. We will base[570] them on the Benefic Ones." Kisrá said: "Take care of what you say." They promised to do what they had said, and he told them to make their calculations. They did so and later advised him to start building, which he did, again spending huge sums of money during the following eight months. Then they said: "Now, we have finished. Go and sit on it."

§ 233[571] Kisrá was afraid of sitting on it, so he rode a pony and went for a ride on it, but while he was there, the Tigris demolished the building, and Kisrá was again only rescued half dead. He called his seers and said to them: "By God, I will have you all killed and your shoulders dislocated or I will have you trampled by elephants, if you do not tell me the truth of this matter in which you have been lying to me!" They answered: "We will not lie to you, o King. When the (dam of the) Tigris was broken and the arch of your palace was cracked without having been burdened by any weight, you gave us orders to use our knowledge to see why that had happened. We did so, but the earth had been darkened to us and the regions of heaven had been withdrawn from us, and our knowledge was of no use. The magic of the magician could not penetrate this, nor the soothsaying of the soothsayer, nor the astrologer's knowledge of the heavenly bodies. So we knew that this matter came from heaven and a prophet had been sent or would be sent, and this was why we were blocked from our knowledge. We were afraid that if we told you the bad news about your kingship, you would have had us killed, and we disliked death, like all people do. This is why we invented various excuses, as you have seen."

570 The text of al-Ṭabarī is slightly different: *fa-taṯabbat ḥattá taḍaʿahā* "make sure to base it." Bosworth (1999): 334, seems to have read the text differently from how it is vocalised in the edition.

571 Al-Ṭabarī, *Taʾrīḫ*, 1:1012–1013 = trans., 5:334.

§ 234[1] قال: "ويحكم أفلا تكونوا بينتم لي هذا فأرى فيه رأيي." قالوا: "منعنا ذلك ما تخوفنا منك." فتركهم ولهى عن دجلة حين {غلبته}. فكان انخراق دجلة سبب البطائح ولم تكن قبل ذلك بل كانت الأرض كلها عامرة. ثم في سنة ست من الهجرة زادت دجلة والفرات زيادة عظيمة جدا فانبثقت البثوق وطما الماء على الزرع وغرق عدة بلاد. ثم اتسع الخرق بدخول العرب العراق وتفجرت بثوق في أيام الحجاج بن يوسف فلم تَسَد فبقيت كذلك إلى الآن.

§ 235[2] قال الحافظ أبو نعيم: ورواه الواقدي قال: حدثني صالح بن جعفر قال: سمعت محمد بن كعب القرظي يقول: دخلت مدائن كسرى في سنة ثمانين عام الجحاف فنظرت إلى بناء كسرى فتعجبت فإذا شيخهم قائم يهدج فسألت عن بعض أمره فقال: "إن كسرى أول ما أنكر من ملكه أنه أصبح في الليلة التي أوحي إلى رسول الله صلى الله عليه وسلم ودجلة انثلمت وطاق ملكه متصدعا." فذكر نحوه. وقال محمد بن إسحق عن الفضل بن عيسى الرقاشي عن الحسن البصري أن أصحاب رسول الله صلى الله عليه وسلم قالوا: "يرسول الله ما حجة الله على كسرى فيك؟" قال: "بعث

٢ غلبته : في الأصل "غليته" خطأ. ٢–٥ فكان ... الآن : الزيادة بخط المقريزي في الهامش الأيمن من الأعلى إلى الأسفل وآخرها في الهامش الأسفل من الأسفل إلى الأعلى، ويشير إليها رمز ⌐ بعد "غلبته".
٧ الجحاف : وضع المقريزي رمز "ح" تحت الحرف الرابع إشارة إلى تلفظه بالحاء.

١ من تأريخ الطبري ١: ١٠١٣ ومن الكامل لابن الأثير ١: ٤٨١–٤٨٢.
٢ من تأريخ الطبري ١: ١٠١٣ وراجع دلائل النبوة لأبي نُعيم ص ١٤١.

§ 234[572] Kisrá replied: "Woe to you! Why did you not tell me this, so that I could have made my own decision!" They answered: "We were hindered from that because we were afraid of you." Kisrá left them and turned his attention away from the Tigris after it had got the better of him. The breaking loose of the Tigris was the reason for the existence of the swamps, which had not existed earlier. Instead the whole area had been cultivated. Then, in the year six of the *hiǧrah*, the Tigris and the Euphrates swelled greatly indeed, flood gates were broken, and water rose to the fields and flooded many areas. Afterwards, the breach grew even wider when the Arabs came to Iraq, and new breaches appeared during the time of al-Ḥaǧǧāǧ b. Yūsuf. These were not repaired, and they have remained so until today.

§ 235[573] Al-Ḥāfiẓ Abū Nuʿaym[574] has said: al-Wāqidī[575] has transmitted: We have been narrated by Ṣāliḥ b. Ǧaʿfar, who said: I heard Muḥammad b. Kaʿb al-Quraẓī[576] say: I entered Madāʾin Kisrá in the year 80, the Year of Sweeping Away,[577] and looked at the building of Kisrá, admiring it. An old Persian man was standing there, tottering. I asked him to tell me something about it, and he said: "The first omen Kisrá saw about his kingdom('s end) was when he woke up the morning the Messenger of God, may God honour him and grant him peace, was given his first revelation, and the Tigris had broken free and the royal arch was coming apart." Then the man mentioned something like what we have just narrated. Muḥammad b. Isḥāq has said, transmitting from al-Faḍl b. ʿĪsá l-Raqāšī from al-Ḥasan al-Baṣrī[578] that the companions of the Messenger of God, may God honour him and grant him peace, said: "O Messenger of God, what is God's argument against Kisrá concerning you(r

572 Al-Ṭabarī, *Taʾrīḫ*, 1:1013 = trans., 5:334–335; Ibn al-Aṯīr, *Kāmil*, 1:481–482.

573 Al-Ṭabarī, *Taʾrīḫ*, 1:1013 = trans., 5:335 (the end only); cf. Abū Nuʿaym, *Dalāʾil* 141 (no. 83).

574 Biographer of Sufis, who also wrote a book on the Prophet Muḥammad, d. 430/1038, see "Abū Nuʿaym," in *EI*², 1:142–143.

575 Historian, d. 207/822, see "al-Wāḳidī," in *EI*², 11:101–103.

576 Early *aḫbārī*, d. 118/736, see *GAS*, 1:32.

577 Year 80/699 was known as the Year of Sweeping Away because of a flood in Mecca, see al-Ṭabarī, *Taʾrīḫ*, 2:1040 = trans., 22:187.

578 Al-Ḥasan al-Baṣrī (d. 110/728), *ḥadīṯ* scholar and ascetic. See *GAS*, 1:591–594.

إليه ملكا فأخرج يده من سور جدار بيته الذي هو فيه تلألأ نورا. فلما رآها فزع فقال: لم تُرَع يا كسرى؟ أن الله تعالى قد بعث رسولا وأنزل عليه كتابا. فاتبعه تسلم دنياك وآخرتك. قال: سأنظر.“

§236[1] وقال محمد بن إسحٰق عن عبد الله بن أبي بكر عن الزهري عن أبي سلمة بن عبد الرحمٰن قال: بعث الله تعالى إلى كسرى ملكا وهو في بيت إيوانه الذي لا يدخل عليه فيه أحد. | فلم يرعه 185b إلا به قائما على رأسه وفي يده عصا بالهاجرة في ساعته التي كان يقيل فيها. فقال: ”يا كسرى أسلم أو أكْسِرُ هذه العصا.“ قال: ”بِهِلْ بِهِلْ.“ نخرج عنه. فدعا كسرى حراسه وحجابه وبوابيه فتغيظ عليهم وقال: ”من أدخل هذا الرجل علي؟“ فقالوا: ”ما دخل عليك أحد وما رأيناه.“ حتى إذا كان العام القابل أتاه في الساعة التي أتاه فيها وقال له كما قال له. ثم قال له: ”أسلم أو أكسر العصا.“ فقال: ”بهل بهل.“ نخرج عنه. فدعا كسرى حراسه وحجابه وبوابيه فتغيظ عليهم وقال لهم كما قال أول مرة. فقالوا: ”ما رأينا أحدا دخل عليك.“ حتى إذا كان العام الثالث أتاه في الساعة التي جاء فيها فقال له كما قال. ثم قال: ”أتسلم أو أكسر العصا؟“ فقال: ”بهل بهل.“ فكسر العصا. ثم خرج فلم يكن إلا تَهَوُّر ملكه وانبعاث ابنه والفُرس حتى قتلوه. قال الحافظ أبو نعيم: وقال عبد الله بن أبي بكر: فقال الزهري: حَدَّثْتُ عمر بن عبد العزيز بهذا الحديث عن أبي سلمة بن عبد الرحمٰن فقال: ذكر

١٢-١٣ الحافظ ... فقال: الزيادة بخط المقريزي في الهامش الأيسر من الأسفل إلى الأعلى + صح، ويشير إليها رمز ˥ بعد ”قال“.

١ من تأريخ الطبري ١: ١٠١٣-١٠١٤.

prophethood)?" He replied: "God sent him an angel, who put out a hand from the wall of the house he was in, resplendent with light. When Kisrá saw this, he was frightened, but the angel said: 'Do not fear,[579] o Kisrá. God, He is Exalted, has sent a Messenger and He has sent down to him a Book. Follow him[580] and you will be saved in this world and the next.' Kisrá replied: 'I'll see about that'."

§ 236[581] Muḥammad b. Isḥāq has said, transmitting from ʿAbd Allāh b. Abī Bakr from al-Zuhrī from Abū Salamah b. ʿAbd al-Raḥmān,[582] who said: God, He is Exalted, sent an angel to Kisrá when he was in a room of his *īwān*, into which no one but he had entrance. Suddenly, the angel was standing by his head with a staff in his hand, in midday at the time Kisrá used to take his rest. The angel said: "Kisrá, submit or I will break this staff!" Kisrá replied: "*Be-hil, be-hil*!"[583] The angel left, and Kisrá called his guards and chamberlains and door keepers and asked them, enraged: "Who let this man come to me?" They replied: "No one came to you! We did not see anyone!" Next year, at the same time as the previous year, the angel came to him and said the same thing to him and added: "Submit or I will break this staff!"[584] Kisrá replied: "*Be-hil, be-hil*!" The angel left, and Kisrá called his guards and chamberlains and door keepers and asked them, enraged like he had been the first time, and they replied: "We did not see anyone coming to you!" The third year, at the same time as earlier, the angel came to him and said the same thing to him and added: "Do you submit or will I break this staff?" Kisrá replied: "*Be-hil, be-hil*!" The angel broke the staff and left. Soon thereafter, his kingship collapsed and his son and the Persians revolted and killed him. Al-Ḥāfiẓ Abū Nuʿaym has said: ʿAbd Allāh b. Abī Bakr said: al-Zuhrī[585] said: I narrated to ʿUmar b. ʿAbd al-ʿAzīz[586] this *ḥadīṯ* from Abū Salamah b. ʿAbd al-Raḥman, and ʿUmar said:

579 The text, following al-Ṭabarī, reads *lam turaʿ*, but one would expect either *lima tarūʿu* or *lā taruʿ*.

580 Or: it.

581 Al-Ṭabarī, *Taʾrīḫ*, 1:1013–1014 = trans., 5:335–336. Even though the second story is quoted on the authority of Abū Nuʿaym, it is clearly taken from al-Ṭabarī, as it follows the sequence of al-Ṭabarī's material.

582 Abū Salamah b. ʿAbd al-Raḥmān al-Zuhrī, traditionist, see Rosenthal (1989): 189, note 177.

583 Persian: Let go, let go!

584 The text is not quite logical.

585 Muḥammad b. Muslim Ibn Šihāb al-Zuhrī (d. 124/742), *ḥadīṯ* scholar. See GAS, 1:280–283.

586 Caliph, r. 99–101/717–720.

لي أن الملك إنما دخل عليه بقارورتين في يده. ثم قال له: "أسلم." فلم يفعل. فضرب {إحداهما} على الأخرى فرضضهما ثم خرج فكان من هلاكه ما كان.

§ 237[١] قال الحافظ أبو نعيم: ورواه صالح بن كيسان عن الزهري عن أبي سلمة: أن كسرى بينا هو في دسكرة ملكه بعث إليه وقبض له عارض يعرض عليه الحق. فلم يفجأ كسرى إلا رجل يمشي وفي يده عصا. فقال: "يا كسرى هل لك في الإسلام قبل أن أكسر هذه العصا؟" قال: "نعم ولا تكسرها." فذكر نحو حديث عبد الله بن أبي بكر عن الزهري عن أبي سلمة. ورواه محمد بن عمر الواقدي عن محمد بن عبد الله عن الزهري عن أبي سلمة بن عبد الرحمٰن عن أبي هريرة. قال: "بينا كسرى مغلق بيته الذي يخلو فيه إذ دخله رجل في يده عصًا." وذكر الحديث بطوله نحوه.

§ 238[٢] وقيل: كان لكسرى أَبَرْويز ثمانية عشر ولدا وكان أكبرهم شهريار وكانت شيرين قد تبنته. فقال المنجمون لكسرى: "إنه سيولد لبعض ولدك غلام يكون خراب هذا المجلس وذهاب الملك على يده وعلامته نقص في بعض بدنه." فمنع ولده النساء حتى شكا شهريار إلى شيرين الشبق فأرسلت إليه جارية فعلقت منه | بيزدجرد فكتمه خمس سنين. ثم إنها رأت من كسرى رقة للصبيان حين كبر فقالت: "أيسرك أن ترى لبعض بنيك ولدا؟" قال: "نعم." فأتته بيزدجرد فأحبه وقربه فبينما هو يلعب ذات يوم ذكر ما قيل له. فأمر به فجرد من ثيابه فرأى النقص في أحد وركيه فأراد قتله فمنعته شيرين وقالت له: "إن كان الأمر في الملك قد حضر فلا مرد له." وأمرت بيزدجرد فحمل إلى سجستان وقيل: بل تركته بالسواد في قرية يقال لها حمانية. 186a

١ إحداهما: "احدهما" في الأصل. ٨ يخلو: "خلوا" في الأصل. ‖ الحديث: الزيادة بخط المقريزي في الهامش الأيسر من الأسفل إلى الأعلى + صح، ويشير إليها رمز ˥ بعد "وذكر".

١ راجع الكامل لابن الأثير ١: ٤٨٢.

٢ من تأريخ الطبري ١: ١٠٤٤–١٠٤٥.

I have been told that the angel came to him with two bottles in his hand and said: "Submit!" When Kisrá did not do so, the angel hit the one bottle against the other and broke them both. Then he left, and Kisrá died as he died.

§ 237[587] Al-Ḥāfiẓ Abū Nuʿaym has said: Ṣāliḥ b. Kaysān transmitted from al-Zuhrī from Abū Salamah that while Kisrá was in the Daskarah of his kingship an apparition was sent to him, which showed him the truth. All of a sudden, a man was there, walking with a staff in his hand, and said: "O Kisrá, would you like to submit before I break this staff?" Kisrá answered: "Yes, just do not break it!" A similar *ḥadīṯ* was told by ʿAbd Allāh b. Abī Bakr from al-Zuhrī from Abū Salamah. It was also narrated by Muḥammad b. ʿUmar al-Wāqidī from Muḥammad b. ʿAbd Allāh from al-Zuhrī from Abū Salamah b. ʿAbd al-Raḥmān from Abū Hurayrah,[588] who said: While Kisrá was behind a locked door in his room in which he used to withdraw, a man entered to him with a staff in his hand. Then Abū Hurayrah narrated a long *ḥadīṯ* in a similar way.

§ 238[589] It is said that Kisrá Abarwīz had eighteen sons, the oldest of them Šahriyār, whom Šīrīn had adopted. The astrologers said to Kisrá: "One of your sons will beget a boy that will cause the destruction of this assembly hall and the loss of your kingdom. His sign will be a bodily defect in him." Kisrá forbade women to his sons, until Šahriyār complained his lust to Šīrīn. She sent him a slave girl, who became pregnant of him with Yazdaǧird. Šahriyār[590] concealed him for five years. Then Šīrīn saw how Kisrá, who had become old, had a tenderness for little boys, and asked him: "Would it gladden you if you saw that one of your sons has a child?" Kisrá answered it would, and Šīrīn brought Yazdaǧird to him. Kisrá loved him and brought him near to himself. One day, when Yazdaǧird was playing, Kisrá remembered what had been said to him and gave orders for the boy to be brought and stripped him of his clothes, finding a defect in one of his hips. Kisrá would have killed him, but Šīrīn stopped him and said: "If the order has gone concerning the kingdom, there will be no stopping it." Šīrīn gave orders for Yazdaǧird to be sent to Siǧistān. Others say that she left him in the Sawād in a village called Ḥumāniyah.

587 Cf. Ibn al-Aṯīr, *Kāmil*, 1:482.

588 Abū Hurayrah (d. 57/678 or soon after), companion of the Prophet Muḥammad. See "Abū Hurayra," in *EI*³.

589 Al-Ṭabarī, *Taʾrīḫ*, 1:1044–1045 = trans., 5:379–380.

590 Al-Ṭabarī has a feminine verb (*wa-katamat*), which suits the context better, referring to Šīrīn. Al-Maqrīzī's masculine is probably a mere slip of pen.

§239[1] وكانت الفرس في عُظْم أمرها واحدة حتى ملك أبرويز فاستأثر بالمال والأعمال وخالف سير أولهم وأخرب الذي للناس وعمر الذي له واستخف بالناس. فأوغر نفوس فارس حتى ثاروا إليه وقتلوه فآمت نساءه ويتمت أولاده. وأَبْرَوِيْز هذا هو الذي كتب إليه رسول الله صلى الله عليه وسلم يدعوه إلى الإسلام فمزق الكتاب وبعث إلى باذان عامله على اليمن يأمره أن يبعث برجلين جلدين ليأتياه بخبره. فلما قدما على رسول الله صلى الله عليه وسلم بكتاب باذان أخبرهما أن الله عز وجل قد قتل كسرى في ليلة كذا بيد ابنه شيرويه. فرجعا إلى باذان فإذا الأمر كما قال رسول الله صلى الله عليه وسلم. وكان رسول الله صلى الله عليه وسلم لما بلغه أن أبرويز مزق كتابه دعا عليهم أن يمزقوا كل ممزق. فاستجاب الله تعالى دعاءه ومزق ملك فارس فلم يبق لهم ملك.

§240[2] قال أبو بكر بن أبي شيبة: حدثنا محمد بن فضيل عن حصين بن عبد الله بن شداد قال: كتب كسرى إلى باذام: "إني نبئت أن رجلا يقول شيئا لا أدري ما هو. فأرسل إليه فليقعد في بيته ولا يكن من الناس في شيء وإلا فليواعدني موعدا ألقاه به." فأرسل باذام إلى رسول الله صلى الله عليه وسلم رجلين حالقي لحاهما مرسلي شواربهما. فقال رسول الله صلى الله عليه وسلم: "ما يحملكما على هذا؟" فقالا: "يأمرنا به الذين يزعمون أنه ربهم." فقال: "لكنا نخالف سنتكم. نجز هذا ونرسل هذا." قال: فتركهما بضعا وعشرين يوما. ثم قال: "اذهبا إلى الذين تزعمون أنه ربكما فأخبراه أن ربي قتل الذي يزعم أنه ربه." قالا: "متى هو؟" قال: "اليوم." فذهبا إلى باذام فأخبراه الخبر.

١-٣ وكانت ... أولاده: الزيادة بخط المقريزي في الهامش الأيمن من الأسفل إلى الأعلى وآخرها في الهامش الأعلى من الأسفل إلى الأعلى + صح. ١٢ حالقي: وضع المقريزي رمز "ح" تحت الحرف الأول إشارة إلى تلفظه بالحاء. ١٥ هو: كتب المقريزي هذه الكلمة تحت السطر.

١ راجع دلائل النبوة لأبي نُعيم ص ٣٤٨-٣٤٩.

٢ راجع دلائل النبوة لأبي نُعيم ص ٣٥٠-٣٥١.

§ 239[591] In the days of their greatness, the Persians were unanimous until the reign of Abarwīz, who appropriated all money and the districts for himself and diverged from the ways of the earlier kings, let fall in ruins what people had, and made flourish what he himself had, belittling people. He aroused the anger of the Persians until they rose against him and killed him, so that his women were widowed and his children orphaned. This Abarwīz was the one to whom the Messenger of God, may God honour him and grant him peace, wrote, calling him to Islam, but Kisrá tore the letter and sent a word to his governor in Yemen, Bādān, giving him orders to send two valiant men to bring him information about the Prophet. When the two men brought the letter of Bādān to the Messenger of God, may God honour him and grant him peace, he told them that God, He is Mighty and Majestic, had killed Kisrá on such-and-such night through the hand of his son Šīrūyah. The men returned to Bādān, and the matter was as the Messenger of God, may God honour him and grant him peace, had said. When the Messenger of God, may God honour him and grant him peace, heard that Abarwīz had torn his letter, he prayed against the Persians that they would be torn most forcibly. God, He is Exalted, answered to his prayer and tore the kingdom of Fārs so that they had no kingdom anymore.

§ 240[592] Abū Bakr b. Abī Šaybah has said: We have been narrated by Muḥammad b. Fuḍayl[593] from Ḥuṣayn b. ʿAbd Allāh b. Šaddād, who said: Kisrá wrote to Bādām: "I have been told that a man is saying something but I do not know what. Send a word to him and let him sit in his house and let him have no plans concerning people. Otherwise, let him be prepared to meet me." Bādām sent to the Messenger of God, may God honour him and grant him peace, two men, who had shaven their beard but let their moustache grow long. The Messenger of God, may God honour him and grant him peace, said to them: "What has made you do this?" One of them answered: "We are told to do so by those who claim that he is their Lord."[594] He replied: "But we disagree with your *sunnah*. We cut this and let that grow." Then he left them for twenty-odd days. Then he said: "Go back to those who you claim that he is your Lord and tell him that my Lord has killed him who claims to be his Lord." They asked him when that had happened, and he said: "Today." The two men went back to Bādām and told him what had happened. Bādām

591 Cf. Abū Nuʿaym, *Dalāʾil* 348–349 (no. 241).

592 Cf. Abū Nuʿaym, *Dalāʾil* 350–351 (no. 241).

593 Traditionist, d. 194/809, see Rosenthal (1989): 200, note 239.

594 Sic. One would expect "by him who claims that he is our Lord." Likewise, one would expect "to him who you claim" a few sentences later.

فكتب إلى كسرى فوجدوا اليوم الذي قتل فيه كسرى. وأبرويز هو صاحب شيرين. نظر إليها وهي قُعَدَة للناكحين متبذلة مع الرجال فهويها وأرادها لنفسه فقالت له: "أيها الملك مَن قاده الهوى إلى من ليس له عنه غنى جدير أن يُتَصفَح مِن حاله ما | يخشاه أن يَسوءَه ويُفسد عليه صالح عيشه 185b ويُنغص عليه طِيْبَ حياته " فلم يلتفت إلى ذميم فعالها واتخذها لنفسه فعفت وكان من خبره معها (...).

§241[1] | شيرويه واسمه قباذ بن كسرى أَبْروِيْز بن هرمز بن كسرى أنوشروان. أمه مريم بنت 186b موريق قيصر ملك الروم. لما ملك دخل عليه العظماء والأشراف فقالوا: "لا يستقيم لنا أمر ولنا ملِكان. فإما أن تقتل كسرى ونحن عبيدك وإما أن نخلعك ونعطيه الملك ونطيعه." فانكسر عند ذلك شيرويه ونقل أباه من دار الملك إلى موضع آخر حبسه فيه ثم جمع العظماء وقال: "قد رأينا الإرسال إلى كسرى بما كان من إساءته ونوقفه على أشياء منها." فأرسل إليه أسباذ جسنس وكان على تدبير المملكة يعدد عليه ذنوبه فأجاب عنها. فعاد عظماء الفرس إلى شيرويه وقالوا: "إما أن تأمر بقتل أبيك وإما أن نطيعه ونخلعك." فأمر بقتله على كره فانتدب لقتله رجال ممن

---

٢ الهوى: كتب المقريزي هذه كلمة تحت السطر. ٣–٤ يخشاه ... معها: كتب المقريزي هذين السطرين منكسين في ورقة صغيرة. ٤ حياته: وضع المقريزي رمز "ح" تحت الحرف الأول إشارة إلى تلفظه بالحاء. || معها: بعد هذه الكلمة بياض بقدر ثمانية عشر سطرا في الأصل.

---

١ من تأريخ الطبري ١: ١٠٦٠ و١٠٥٨ و١٠٤٥–١٠٤٦.

wrote to Kisrá, but it was found out that that was the day when Kisrá had been killed. Abarwīz was the partner of Šīrīn. He had seen her when she was sitting, waiting for those who wanted intercourse with her, prostituting herself to men. He lusted for her and wanted her for himself, but she said: "O King, if desire leads one to someone without whom he cannot do, then he should examine his state for what he fears might harm him and spoil his good life and disturb his pleasurable life." Abarwīz, however, did not mind her reproachable deeds and took her for himself. She was chaste (thereafter). His story with her was (what it was).[595]

§ 241[596] Šīrūyah,[597] whose name was Qubād b. Kisrá Abarwīz b. Hurmuz b. Kisrá Anūširwān. His mother was Maryam, daughter of Mauricius the Caesar, the king of the Byzantines. When he became king, the noblemen and nobility came to him and said: "Our affairs will not be right as long as we have two kings. Either you must kill Kisrá and then we will be your servants, or we have to depose you and give the kingship back to him." Šīrūyah was broken by this. He moved his father from the royal palace to another place where he imprisoned him. Then he assembled the noblemen and said to them: "I have decided to send a messenger to Kisrá about his bad deeds and I will point out some of these to him." He sent to him Asbād-Ǧušnas,[598] who was in charge of the governance of the kingdom, and he enumerated his sins to him. Kisrá replied to these, but the noblemen came back to Šīrūyah to say: "Either you give us orders to kill your father or we will obey him and depose you." Unwillingly, Šīrūyah gave orders to have him killed. This task

595 § 240 ends abruptly (*wa-kāna min ḫabarihi maʿahā*), which would either need a telling of the story or at least the addition of *mā kāna*, on which the translation is based (cf. § 18 for al-Maqrīzī's use of this construction). The last lines have been written upside down on a separate slip of paper, and plenty of free space has been left after them. Al-Maqrīzī has obviously left the sentence incomplete in order later to add some information on Šīrīn. For the controversial marriage of Kisrā and Šīrīn, see, e.g., al-Ṯaʿālibī, *al-Ġurar* 691–694.

596 Al-Ṭabarī, *Taʾrīḫ*, 1:1045–1046, 1058, 1060 = trans., 5:381–382, 395, 398. Al-Ṭabarī relates the extensive exchange of messages between Kisrá and Šīrūyah, which al-Maqrīzī has omitted. This paragraph partly overlaps with §§ 224–228.

597 Cf. al-Bīrūnī, *al-Āṯār al-bāqiyah* 138.

598 Written by al-Maqrīzī consistently with S, not Š.

وترهم أبرويز. فباشر قتله منهم شاب اسمه مهرهرمز بن مردان شاه. فلما قتل أبرويز شق شيرويه ثيابه {وبكى} ولطم وجهه وحملت جنازته وتبعها العظماء وأشراف الناس.

§ 242[1] ثم أمر شيرويه بقتل مهرهرمز قاتل أبيه فقتل. ثم قتل إخوته وكانوا سبعة عشر رجلا ذوي آداب وشجاعة بمشورة من وزرائه. فجزع بعد قتلهم جزعا شديدا ودخلت عليه أختاه بوران وآزرميذخت فى اليوم الثاني من قتلهم فأغلظتا عليه وقالتا: "حملك الحرص على الملك الذي لا يتم لك على قتل أبيك وإخوتك." {فبكى} بكاء شديدا ورمى التاج عن رأسه ولم يزل مهموما حزينا مدنفا وابتلي بالاسقام فانتقض عليه بدنه فلم يلتذ بشيء من لذات الدنيا. ويقال إنه أباد من قدر عليه من أهل بيته وكان الطاعون فشا في أيامه فأهلك الفرس ثم هلك فيه فكان ملكه ثمانية أشهر.

§ 243[2] وكان شعاره وشي أحمر وسراويله على لون السماء موشحة وتاجه أخضر بيمناه سيف مخروط. وقيل إنه أحس من [من] إخوته نفورا منه فقتل منهم ثمانية عشر. وهم شهريار ومردانشاه وكورانشاه وفيروزانشاه وابْزُوذَشاه وزَرَابَرُوذ وشاذمان وشاذزيل وأَرْوَنْدزيل وأَرْوَنْددشت

---

٢ وبكى : "وبكا" في الأصل. ٦ فبكى : "فبكا" في الأصل.

---

١ من تأريخ الطبري ١: ١٠٦٠-١٠٦١ ومن تجارب الأمم لمسكويه ١: ١٦٥-١٦٦.

٢ من تأريخ سني الملوك لحمزة ص ٤٧-٤٨.

was assigned to men whom Abarwīz had wronged, and a young man among them, called Mihr-Hurmuz b. Mardānšāh took it to himself to do the deed. When Abarwīz was killed, Šīrūyah tore his clothes, cried, and struck his face. When his bier was carried, the noblemen and nobility followed it.

§ 242[599] Then Šīrūyah gave orders to kill Mihr-Hurmuz, the killer of his father, and he was killed. On the suggestion of his viziers, he then killed his brothers, seventeen well-educated and brave men, but having killed them he was devastated. His two sisters, Būrān and Āzarmīduḫt,[600] came to him the day after they had been killed, saying that he had been wrong in doing so: "Your desire of kingship, which you do not as yet completely possess, incited you to kill your father and your brothers." Šīrūyah cried bitterly and threw the crown from his head. He remained depressed by worries and sorrows, sick and inflicted, so that his body pained him and he could not enjoy any of the pleasures of this world. It is said that he killed all of his family as far as he could. During his reign, plague spread and decimated the Persians. Then Šīrūyah died of plague. He reigned for 8 months.

§ 243[601] Šīrūyah's vest was red and his trousers sky-blue with a belt. His crown was green, and in his right hand, he had an unsheathed sword. It is said that he sensed that his brothers were adverse[602] to him and killed eighteen[603] of them: Šahriyār, Mardānšāh, Kūrānšāh,[604] Fīrūzānšāh, Abzūdšāh,[605] Zarābrūd,[606] Šādmān, Šādazīl,[607] Arwandzīl,[608] Arwanddašt,[609]

599 Al-Ṭabarī, *Ta'rīḫ*, 1:1060–1061 = trans., 5:398–399; Miskawayh, *Taǧārib al-umam*, 1:165–166 = C264–265.

600 Consistently written by al-Maqrīzī with a Ḏ (*ḏuḫt*).

601 Ḥamzah, *Ta'rīḫ* 47–48 = trans. 74–75.

602 Ḥamzah has *nubū'an*.

603 Al-Maqrīzī only lists 16 names, while Ḥamzah, who also speaks of 18 brothers, gives 17 names (in addition to those of al-Maqrīzī, he gives Šādādḫurrah). *Nihāyat al-arab* 438–439, gives a list of 17 names. The number 18 may be a mistake and include Šīrūyah himself. Cf. § 242.

604 Cf. Justi (1895): 420 (Gūrānšāh).

605 Cf. Justi (1895): 420, and Ḥamzah (Afrūdšāh).

606 Cf. Justi (1895): 420, and Ḥamzah (Zadābzūdšāh).

607 Cf. Justi (1895): 420 (Šādrang).

608 Cf. Justi (1895): 420 (Arwandrang). Ḥamzah reads the end of both this name and Šādrang as *-zīk*.

609 Cf. Justi (1895): 420 (Arwanddast).

وفُس به وفُس دَل وخُرُه مرد | وخَرُه وزاذان خره وجَوَان شير وشِيْرزَاد وجهاربخت. ويقال: 187a
كان مهلك شيرويه في الطاعون لخمس سنين وأشهر من مقدم رسول الله صلى الله عليه وسلم إلى المدينة.

§244[1] وملك بعده ابنه أردشير كوجك بن شيرويه بن أبرويز بن هرمز بن أنوشروان وهو طفل ابن سَبْع سِنين لأنه لم يوجد غيره من أهل بيت المملكة. وحضنه رجل يقال له مَهَاذرخَشْنَس فأحسن سياسة الملك. فبلغ من إحكامه ذلك أنه لم يحس أحد بحداثة سن أردشير سوى أنه غلط في أمر شهرابراز المقيم بثغر الروم واستهان بأمره فكان ذلك سبب هلاكه. وذلك أن شهرابراز كان في جند ضمهم إليه كسرى أبرويز وكان قد صلح له بعد ما فعل ما فعل بالروم كما تقدم ذكره. وكان ينفذ إليه الهدايا والخلع. وكان أبرويز وابنه شيرويه من بعده لا يزالان يكتبان إلى شهرابراز في الأمر يهمهما ويستشيرانه. فلما لم يشاوره عظماء الفرس في تمليك أردشير ولم يكاتبه أيضا مهاذرجشنس اتخذ ذلك سببا وتعنت على الفرس وبسط يده وجعله ذريعة للطمع في الملك واستطال واحتقر أردشير لحداثة سنه ودعا الناس للتشاور في الملك. ثم أقبل بجنده يريد المدائن فحصن مهاذرجشنس سور مدينة طيسبون وأبوابها وحول أردشير ومن بقي من الملوك ونسائهم وما كان في بيت مال

١ من تجارب الأمم لمسكويه ١: ١٦٦ ومن تأريخ سني الملوك لحمزة ص ٤٨، ١٥.

Fus-Bih, Fus-Dil,[610] Ḫurramard, Ḫa(s)ruh,[611] Ǧawānšīr,[612] Šīrzād, and Ǧahārbaḫt.[613] It is said that Šīrūyah died of plague 5 years and some months after the Messenger of God, may God honour him and grant him peace, came to Medina.

§ 244[614] After him, there reigned his son Ardašīr Kūǧak[615] b. Šīrūyah b. Abarwīz b. Hurmuz b. Anūširwān. He was a seven-year-old child, but he was the only one of the royal family that could be found. He was taken care of by a man called Mih-Ādur-Ǧušnas,[616] who took good care of governing the kingdom. He did it with such a firm grip that no one really felt Ardašīr's young age. He did make a mistake, though, in the case of Šahrbarāz who stayed at the Byzantine frontier. He belittled him, and that was the cause of his perishing. Šahrbarāz still retained the army Kisrá Abarwīz had given him, and Kisrá had been reconciliated with him after he had done to the Byzantines what he had done, as we have already mentioned,[617] and had sent him presents and robes of honour. Abarwīz and, after him, his son Šīrūyah had kept writing to Šahrbarāz about matters that were of concern to them and asking his advice. When the Persian noblemen had not consulted him about proclaiming Ardašīr king and Mih-Ādur-Ǧušnas had not written to him, either, he took that as a reason to start causing troubles to the Persians. He put out his hand and used this as an excuse for desiring kingship. He became overbearing and despised Ardašīr because of his young age. He called people to a negotiation concerning kingship, and then approached al-Madā'in with his army. Mih-Ādur-Ǧušnas fortified the walls and gates of the city of Ṭaysabūn and moved Ardašīr and the remaining royal family[618] and their women there,

610 For the last two names, cf. Justi (1895): 420 (Pusbeh, Pusdil). Ḥamzah reads both as Qus-.

611 Cf. Justi (1895): 420, and Ḥamzah (Ḫurrah and Mardḫurrah). The latter ḪRH almost looks like ḪSRH in al-Maqrīzī, and it is vocalised as Ḫa(s)ruh. This could stand for Ḫusraw, which is occasionally found in Arabic sources as Ḫusrah.

612 Missing from Ḥamzah and Justi (1895): 420, but cf. Justi (1895): 123.

613 Cf. Justi (1895): 420, and Ḥamzah (Ǧahānbaḫt).

614 Miskawayh, *Taǧārib al-umam*, 1:166 = C265–266; cf. al-Ṭabarī, *Ta'rīḫ*, 1:1061–1062 = trans., 5:400–401; Ḥamzah, *Ta'rīḫ* 48, 15 = trans. 75, 34; Ḥamzah, *Ta'rīḫ* 20 = trans. 38, also gives one year.

615 Cf. al-Bīrūnī, *al-Āṯār al-bāqiyah* 138. Kūǧak stands for Persian *kūčak* "little."

616 Here the end is written Ḫašnas, but later we also find the correct form.

617 See §§ 211–221.

618 Miskawayh reads *min nasl al-mulūk*, and it would seem that al-Maqrīzī has accidentally dropped the word *nasl*.

أردشير من مال وخزائن وكراع إليها. فنزل شهرابراز عليها وحصر من فيها ونصب المجانيق عليها فلم يصل إلى شيء. فلما رأى عجزه عن إفتتاحها أتاها من قبل المكيدة فلم يزل يخدع رجلين حتى فتحا له باب المدينة. فدخلها وقتل جماعة من الرؤساء {واستصفى} أموالهم وقتل أردشير بن شيرويه. فكان ملكه سنة وستة اشهر. وكان شعاره موشحا على لون السماء وتاجه أحمر بيده رمح يعتمد بيسراه على سيفه. ولأربعة أشهر من ملكه استخلف أبو بكر الصديق رضي الله عنه وفيه نظر.

§245[1] فملك بعد أردشير بن شيرويه المتغلب | شهربراز واسمه فرخان ولقبه خُرَّهان ولم يكن من 187b
أهل بيت الملك ودعا نفسه ملكا. فإن أردشير بن شيرويه مات وقد هلك العظماء. ولما جلس على سرير الملك ضرب عليه بطنه وبلغ من شدة ذلك عليه أنه لم يقدر على إتيان الخلاء فوضع الطست أمام السرير ومد في وجهه بما ستره فتبرز في الطست. ثم امتعض رجل يقال له بسفروخ وأخوين له من قتل شهربراز أردشير بن شيرويه وغلبته على الملك فتحالفوا على قتله. وكان من العادة إذا ركب الملك أن يقف له حرسه سماطين عليهم الذروع والبيض والتِرَسة والسيوف وبأيديهم الرماح. فإذا حاذاهم الملك وضع كل رجل منهم ترسه على قربوس سرجه ثم وضع جبهته عليه كهيئة السجود. فركب شهربراز بعد أن ملك بأيام لما عوفي وقد وقف له بسفروخ وأخواه وكانوا من جملة حرسه. فلما حاذاهم طعنه بسفراخ ثم طعنه أخواه فسقط عن فرسه. فشدوا في رجله حبلا وجروه إقبالا وإدبارا ساعة وساعدهم قوم من العظماء وقتلوا عدة من أعوانه. فكانت مدة ملكه أربعين يوما. وملكوا بوران. وقيل إن الذي ملك بعد أردشير بن شيرويه إنما هو خرهان ولم يكن من بيت

---

٣ واستصفى: "واستصفا" في الأصل. ٥ وفيه نظر: الزيادة بخط المقريزي في الهامش الأيسر. ٦ ولقبه خُرَّهان: الزيادة بخط المقريزي في الهامش الأيسر من الأعلى إلى الأسفل + صح، ويشير إليها رمز ˥ بعد "فرخان". ٧ فإن ... العظماء: الزيادة بخط المقريزي في الهامش الأيمن منكسة + صح، ويشير إليها رمز ˥ بعد "ملكا". ١٣ لما عوفي: الزيادة بخط المقريزي في الهامش الأيسر من الأسفل إلى الأعلى + صح، ويشير إليها رمز ˥ بعد "بأيام". ‖ وكانوا ... حرسه: الزيادة بخط المقريزي في الهامش الأيسر من الأعلى إلى الأسفل + صح، ويشير إليها رمز ˥ بعد "وأخواه".

---

١ من تجارب الأمم لمسكويه ١: ١٦٦–١٦٧.

together with what was in Ardašīr's treasury of money and treasures, as well as his horses. Šahrbarāz encamped outside of the city and laid siege to those in it. He erected mangonels against it, but they were of no use. When he saw that he could not conquer the city, he took recourse to cunning. He kept deceiving two men until they opened the city gate to him, and he entered from there. He killed many of the leading men and confiscated their property and killed Ardašīr b. Šīrūyah, whose reign lasted for a year and six months. His vest had stripes, and it was sky-blue and his crown was red. In his hand, he had a spear, and with his left hand he leaned on his sword. In the fourth month of his reign, Abū Bakr al-Ṣiddīq,[619] may God be pleased with him, became Caliph, although there is some unclarity there.

§ 245[620] After Ardašīr b. Šīrūyah, there ruled the usurper Šahrbarāz, whose name was Farruḫān and cognomen Ḫurrahān.[621] He did not belong to the royal family but proclaimed himself king when Ardašīr b. Šīrūyah had died and the noblemen perished. When he ascended the royal throne, his stomach was infected so badly that he was not able to get to the toilet, but a pot was put in front of the throne and a curtain was drawn when he emptied his bowels there. A man called Bus-Farrūḫ and his two brothers resented Šahrbarāz having killed Ardašīr b. Šīrūyah and usurped the kingship and swore to each other to kill him. When the king rode by, his guards used to line up in two lines in their armour, with helmets, shields, and swords, holding a spear in their hand. When the king came opposite them, each man put his shield against his saddlebow and lowered his forehead against it as if they were making a prostration. A few days after he had become king and had recovered from his illness, Šahrbarāz rode by, and Bus-Farrūḫ and his brothers, who belonged to the guard, were in attendance. When Šahrbarāz was opposite them, Bus-Farrūḫ hit him with his spear and his brothers joined him. Šahrbarāz fell from his horse. They tied a rope around his foot and dragged him for a while to and fro, with some of the noblemen helping them. They also killed a number of his aids. The length of his reign was 40 days, and they appointed Būrān as queen. It is also said that after Ardašīr b. Šīrūyah there reigned Ḫurrahān, who did not belong to the royal family and that it

619 Abū Bakr al-Ṣiddīq, the first Caliph (r. 11–13/632–634).

620 Miskawayh, *Taǧārib al-umam*, 1:166–167 = C267–268; cf. al-Ṭabarī, *Taʾrīḫ*, 1:1062–1063 = trans. 5:402–403.

621 Cf. al-Bīrūnī, *al-Āṯār al-bāqiyah* 138.

المملكة فقتلته بوران بحيلة بعد اثنين وعشرين يوما من ملكه. فملك بعده كسرى بن قباذ ثلاثة أشهر وقتله ملك خراسان. فملك بعده بوران والقول الأول أشهر.

§246[1] وكانت الفرس قد قرب انصرام مدتهم وانقضاء ملكهم نخذلهم الله ونصر الله العرب عليهم. وذلك أن خالد بن الوليد رضي الله عنه لما فرغ من حروب أهل الردة أمره أبو بكر الصديق رضي الله عنه بالمسير إلى العراق. فسار في سنة اثنتي عشرة من الهجرة حتى نزل الحيرة وعليها قبيصة بن إياس الطائي. وقَدِم أيضا المثنى بن حارثة الشيباني قبل قدوم خالد في سنة إحدى عشرة. فوجه شهربراز إلى المثنى جندا عظيما عليهم هرمز المعروف بجاذُويه في عشرة آلاف ومعه فيل. فكتبت المسالح إلى المثنى بإقباله نخرج من الحيرة نحوه وضم إليه المسالح. وكتب شهربراز إلى المثنى: "إني قد بعثت إليك جندا من وَخَش أهل. إنما هم رعاة الدجاج والخنازير. ولست أقاتلك إلا بهم." فأجابه: "من المثنى إلى شهربراز. إنما أنت أحد رجلين: إما | باغ فذلك شر لك وخير لنا وإما كاذب 188a

٣ نخذلهم الله : الزيادة بخط المقريزي في الهامش الأيسر من الأسفل إلى الأعلى + صح، ويشير إليها رمز ⌐ بعد "ملكهم". ٤ الصديق : الزيادة بخط المقريزي في الهامش الأيسر من الأعلى إلى الأسفل + صح، ويشير إليها رمز ⌐ بعد "أبو بكر". ٩ وَخَش : وضع المقريزي فوق الكلمة رمز "ك" (لـ "كذا") إشارة إلى شكه في صحة قراءتها.

١ من تجارب الأمم لمسكويه ١: ١٩٢–١٩٣.

was Būrān who killed him by a stratagem after 22 days of his reign. After him, there reigned Kisrá b. Qubād for 3 months and he was killed by the king of Ḫurāsān and it was only after him that Būrān was appointed queen. But the first version is more commonly known.

§ 246[622] The end of the Persians' time and their kingship was drawing nigh. God brought them to shame and helped the Arabs against them. This happened so that when Ḫālid b. al-Walīd,[623] may God be pleased with him, was done with the *riddah*[624] wars, Abū Bakr al-Ṣiddīq, may God be pleased with him, gave him an order to march to Iraq. He marched there in the year 12[/633] and encamped in al-Ḥīrah, which was in the hands of Qabīṣah b. Iyās al-Ṭāʾī.[625] Al-Muṯanná b. Ḥāriṯah al-Šaybānī[626] had also come there in the year 11, even before Ḫālid's arrival. Šahrbarāz sent an army led by Hurmuz, known as Ǧādūyah, against al-Muṯanná with ten thousand men and an elephant. The frontier vanguards wrote to al-Muṯanná informing him of his approach. Al-Muṯanná left al-Ḥīrah and marched towards him, adding the frontier vanguards to his troops. Šahrbarāz wrote to al-Muṯanná: "I have sent against you an army of the lowliest of people. They are chicken keepers and swineherds.[627] I will not condescend to fight you with any people other than them." Al-Muṯanná replied: "From al-Muṯanná to Šahrbarāz. You are one of two men. Either you are an oppressor, and that is bad for you but

622 Miskawayh, *Taǧārib al-umam*, 1:192–193 = C320–321; cf. al-Ṭabarī, *Taʾrīḫ*, 1:2116–2117 = trans., 11:117–118.

623 One of the generals of the wars of conquest, d. 21/642, see "Khālid b. al-Walīd," in *EI*², 4:928–929.

624 "Wars of apostasy" after the death of the Prophet Muḥammad when certain tribes are said to have apostatised, see "al-Ridda," in *EI*², 12:692–695.

625 See al-Ṭabarī, *Taʾrīḫ*, 1:2017, and Blankinship (1993): 4, note 30.

626 Tribal chief, d. 14/635 or 15/636, see *EI*², s.v., 7:796–797.

627 There seems to be a wordplay involved that has evaded not only Miskawayh and al-Maqrīzī, but also the editors and translators of al-Ṭabarī. In al-Ṭabarī, Šahrbarāz says that the flanks of his army are commanded by al-KWKBD and al-ḪWKBD. The editors compare the first to Syriac *krūkbad* in *Addenda et emendanda* (al-Ṭabarī, *Taʾrīḫ*, 14:dcxiii), and, accepting this, Blankinship (1993): 118, suggests the emendation of the latter to **al-ḫarukbad* (already hesitatingly suggested by the editors in al-Ṭabarī, *Taʾrīḫ*, 14:dcxiii), adding that "the two names or titles" only appear in material coming from Sayf. The emendation is manifestly wrong, as the title seems to be *ḫūkbad* "chief swineherd," from Middle Persian *ḫūg* (MacKenzie 1971, s.v.)—the title seems unattested, though. The other title clearly derives from *kark* "chicken, hen" (MacKenzie 1971, s.v.), i.e., "chief chickenherd." I am unable to say whether these titles were in real use in the Sasanian court or whether they were just coined for this story, but, in any case, here they are used for the wordplay.

فأعظم الكاذبين عقوبة وفضيحة عند الله والناس الملوك. وأما الذي يدلنا عليه الرأي فإنكم إنما اضطررتم إليه. فالحمد لله الذي رد كيدكم إلى رعاة الدجاج والخنازير.“

§247[١] فلما وقف الفرس على كتابه جزعوا وقالوا: ”إنما أتي شهربراز من لؤم منشائه.“ وقالوا له: ”جرأت علينا عدونا بما كتبت إليه. فإذا كتبت فاستشر.“ ثم التقوا ببابل فاقتتلوا بعدوة الصراة الدنيا قتالا شديدا. ثم إن المثنى وعدة من المسلمين أعتوروا الفيل وكان يُفَرِق بين الصفوف والكراديس. فأصابوا مقتله فقتلوه وهزموا أهل فارس واتبعوهم يقتلونهم حتى جازوا بهم مسالحهم وطلبوا الفَل حتى بلغوا المدائن. ومات شهربراز منهزم هرمز جاذويه.

§248[٢] واختلف أهل فارس وتشاغلوا عن إزالة المسلمين عن السواد بما بينهم من الاختلاف حتى مات أبو بكر وقام من بعده أمير المؤمنين عمر بن الخطاب رضي الله عنهما. وكان المثنى قد سار نحو المدينة ليخبر أبا بكر رضي الله عنه خبر المسلمين ويستأذنه في أشياء يعملها واستخلف على عسكره بُشَير بن الخصاصية. فرد عمر بن الخطاب رضي الله عنه المثنى بن حارثة مع أبي عبيد بن مسعود بن عمرو الثقفي إلى العراق. وكان جمهور جند العراق من المسلمين بالحِيْرة والمسالح بالسِيْب والغارات تُنتهى بهم إلى شاطئ دجلةَ ودجلةُ بين المسلمين وفارس.

٨ عن السواد: الزيادة بخط المقريزي في الهامش الأيمن من الأعلى إلى الأسفل + صح، ويشير إليها رمز ⌐ بعد ”المسلمين“. ١٠ المسلمين: وضع المقريزي تحت الحرف الرابع ثلاث نقط إشارة إلى تلفظه بالسين. ١٢ بن ... الثقفي: الزيادة بخط المقريزي في آخر السطر في الهامش الأيسر. || والمسالح: وضع المقريزي تحت الحرف الرابع ثلاث نقط إشارة إلى تلفظه بالسين.

١ من تجارب الأمم لمسكويه ١: ١٩٣.

٢ من تجارب الأمم لمسكويه ١: ١٩٣–١٩٤.

good for us, or a liar. And no liar will be punished and put to shame more strongly in the eyes of God and people than a (lying) king. But reason tells us that you have been forced to this. Praise be to God, who has reduced your means to chicken keepers and swineherds!"

§ 247[628] When the Persians learned about his letter, they were frightened and said: "Šahrbarāz will be ruined by his ignoble origin!" To him they said: "You have emboldened our enemy against us by what you wrote! When you write, ask advice!" The armies met in Babel and fought fiercely on the nearer bank of al-Ṣarāt. Al-Muṯanná and a number of other Muslims attacked by turns the elephant, which had separated the lines and cavalry units, and managed to kill it, putting the Persian troops to flight and then following and killing them until they were beyond their frontier posts. They continued pursuing the remnants of the army until al-Madāʾin. Šahrbarāz died at about the time Hurmuz Ǧādūyah was put to flight.

§ 248[629] The people of Fārs quarrelled among themselves and were too busy with their internal schisms to drive the Muslims away from the Sawād until Abū Bakr died. After him ʿUmar b. al-Ḫaṭṭāb,[630] may God be pleased with them both, became the Commander of the Believers. Al-Muṯanná had gone towards Medina to inform Abū Bakr, may God be pleased with him, about the situation of the Muslims and ask his permission to do certain things. He had left Bušayr[631] b. al-Ḫaṣāṣiyyah in command of his army. ʿUmar b. al-Ḫaṭṭāb, may God be pleased with him, sent al-Muṯanná b. Ḥāriṯah back to Iraq with Abū ʿUbayd b. Masʿūd b. ʿAmr al-Ṯaqafī.[632] The majority of the Muslim army in Iraq was in al-Ḥīrah and the frontier vanguards in al-Sīb and their raids brought them to the banks of the Tigris, so that the Tigris was the boundary between the Muslims and the Persians.

628 Miskawayh, *Taǧārib al-umam*, 1:193 = C321; cf. al-Ṭabarī, *Taʾrīḫ*, 1:2117–2118, 2119 = trans., 11:118–119, 120.

629 Miskawayh, *Taǧārib al-umam*, 1:193–194 = C321–323; cf. al-Ṭabarī, *Taʾrīḫ*, 1:2119–2120 = trans., 11:120–122.

630 ʿUmar b. al-Ḫaṭṭāb, the second Caliph (r. 13–23/634–644).

631 Al-Ṭabarī reads Bašīr, see Blankinship (1993): 24, note 144.

632 On Abū ʿUbayd, see Blankinship (1993): 122, note 655. Again, al-Maqrīzī has first copied Miskawayh's text and then come back to add a longer genealogy of Abū ʿUbayd in the margin.

§ 249[1] ثم ملكت بُوْرَان دُخْت وتلقب السعيدة بنت كسرى أبرويز بن هرمز بن أنوشروان. أمها مريم بنت قيصر ملك الروم. وذلك أنه لما قتل شهربراز لم يجد الفرس رجلا من بيت المملكة ليملكوه عليهم فاضطروا إلى تمليك بوران. فأحسنت السيرة وبسطت العدل وأمرت برم القناطر والجسور وأعادت العمارات ووضعت بقايا الخراج عن الناس. وكتبت إلى الناس عامة كتبا تعلمهم ما هي عليه من الإحسان. وأنها ترجو أن يريهم الله تعالى من الرفاهة والاستقامة بمكانها ومن العدل وحفظ الثغور ما يعلمون به أنه ليس ببطش الرجال تدوخ البلاد ولا ببأسهم تستباح العساكر ولا بمكائدهم ينال الظفر وتطفأ النوائر | ولكن ذلك كله يكون بالله تعالى وحسن 188b
النية واستقامة التدبير. وأمرت بالمناصحة وحسن الطاعة وردت خشبة الصليب على ملك الروم. وكان شعارها موشى أخضر وسراويلها على لون السماء وتاجها كذلك وتجلس على السرير وبيدها طبرزين وكانت مدتها سنة وأربعة أشهر.

§ 250[2] قال ابن مسكويه: فقدم أبو عبيد بن مسعود الثقفي ومعه المثنى بن حارثة وقد استخرج الفرس يزدجرد وكانت بوران عَدْلا فيما بينهم لَمَّا افتتنت الفُرس وقتل الفُرُّخزاذ بن البندوان وكان سياوخش قدم فقتل آزَرْمي ذخت وذلك في غيبة المثنى. وكان شغل الفرس طول غيبته فيما بينهم. وكانت بوران دعت رُسْتم وشكتْ إليه تضعضع فارس ودعته إلى القيام بأمرهم وتَوَّجَتْه فقال رستم: "أنا عبد سامع مطيع." فولته أمر فارس وحربها وأمرت فارس أن يسمعوا له ويطيعوا.

١ ثم ملكت : الزيادة بخط المقريزي في آخر السطر في الهامش الأيسر. ٤ عن الناس : الزيادة بخط المقريزي في الهامش الأيمن من الأعلى إلى الأسفل + صح، ويشير إليها رمز ⌐ بعد "الخراج". ٥ ترجو : "ترجوا" في الأصل.

١ من تجارب الأمم لمسكويه ١: ١٦٧ ومن تأريخ سني الملوك لحمزة ص ٤٨، ١٥.

٢ من تجارب الأمم لمسكويه ١: ١٩٨–١٩٩.

§ 249[633] Then there reigned Būrānduḫt, whose cognomen was the Happy,[634] bt. Kisrá Abarwīz b. Hurmuz b. Anūširwān. Her mother was Maryam, daughter of the Caesar, the king of the Byzantines. When Šahrbarāz was killed the Persians could not find a male belonging to the royal family to appoint him as king over themselves so they had to appoint Būrān. She, however, ruled well and spread justice, ordered stone bridges and boat bridges to be repaired and restituted cultivated areas (as they had been). She forgave people the tax arrears and wrote to all of them letters, in which she told them what good she was going to do them and that she wished that God, He is Exalted, would give them abundance and uprightness through her position, as well as justice and safety of frontiers, so that they would know that it is not by the force of men that countries are conquered nor is it by their strength that camps are plundered nor is it by their cunning that victory is reached and flames of war extinguished, but that all this comes from God, He is Exalted, good intention, and proper government. She gave orders to people to be sincere and to obey nicely. She also returned the wooden cross to the king of the Byzantines. Her vest was embroidered and green and her trousers sky-blue, as was also her crown. She was sitting on the throne with an axe in her hand. Her reign was 1 year and 4 months.

§ 250[635] Ibn Miskawayh has said: Abū ʿUbayd b. Masʿūd al-Ṯaqafī approached, together with al-Muṯanná b. Ḥāriṯah. The Persians had brought forth Yazdağird. Būrān was an honest arbiter between them when the Persians suffered from internal unrest and al-Farruḫzād b. al-Binduwān was killed. Siyāwuḫš had gone forth and killed Āzarmīduḫt while al-Muṯanná was absent. During the whole time of his absence, the Persians were occupied with internal matters. Būrān had called Rustam to her and complained to him of the precarious situation of Fārs and asked him to manage their affairs. She was also ready to crown him,[636] but Rustam said: "I am an obedient slave." She appointed him over Fārs and the battle for it and told the

633 Miskawayh, *Tağārib al-umam*, 1:167 = C268; Ḥamzah, *Taʾrīḫ* 48, 15 = trans. 75, 34; cf. al-Ṭabarī, *Taʾrīḫ*, 1:1064 = trans., 5:403–405. Ḥamzah, *Taʾrīḫ* 20 = trans. 39, adds a variant length of her rule, one year and some days.

634 Cf. al-Bīrūnī, *al-Āṯār al-bāqiyah* 138.

635 Miskawayh, *Tağārib al-umam*, 1:198–199 = C330–332; cf. al-Ṭabarī, *Taʾrīḫ*, 1:2162–2168 = trans., 11:176–181.

636 While Miskawayh and al-Maqrīzī simply speak of crowning him (*wa-tawwağathu*), al-Ṭabarī refers to an offer by Būrān to let Rustam rule for ten years, after which the kingship would return to the family of Kisrá.

فقتل رستم سياوخش ودانت له الفرس وذلك بعد قدوم أبي عبيد. وكتب إلى دهاقين السواد أن يثوروا بالمسلمين ودس في كل رستاق رجلا ليثور بأهله. وبلغ ذلك المثنى وعَجِل جابان وكان اجتمع إليه بشر كثير بالنمارق ولحق أبو عبيد فأجم الناس. ثم تعبّى فجعل المثنى على الخيل وعنى الميمنة والميسرة. فنزلوا على جابان بالنمارق فقاتلهم قتالا شديدا ثم انهزم فأُسِر ثم خلي عنه لأنه أُمِّن وقسمت الغنائم وبعث بالأخماس إلى عمر رضي الله عنه.

§ 251[1] وثار نَرْسي بكسكر وكان رستم أمره بذلك. ونرسي هذا ابن خالة كسرى وكانت كسكر قطيعة له وكان النَرْسِيَان له يحميه لا يأكله ولا يشربه ولا يغرسه غير آل كسرى إلا من أكرموه بشيء منه. فلما انهزمت الفرس يوم النمارق اجتمعت الفَالّة إلى نرسي وهو في عسكره ونادى أبو عبيد بالرحيل وقال للمُجَرَدة: "اتبعوا الفالّة حتى تدخلوهم عسكر نرسي أو تبيدوهم." ومضى أبو عبيد حين ارتحل من النمارق حتى نزل على نرسي بكسكر والمثنى بن حارثة معه ومع نرسي ابنا خاله وهما ابنا خال كسرى بندويه وبيرويه ابنا بسطام. وكان قد أتى الخبر بوران ورستم بهزيمة جابان فبعثوا الجالنوس. | وبلغ ذلك نرسي ومن معه فرجوا أن يلحق بهم قبل الوقعة. فعاجلهم أبو عبيد 189a
وقاتلهم قتالا شديدا فانهزم نرسي وقتل أصحابه. وغلب أبو عبيد على عسكره وأرضه وجمع الغنائم.

٣ وعنى: كذا في الأصل لـ "عبأ"؟ ٧–٨ وكان ... منه: الزيادة بخط المقريزي في آخر السطر في الهامش الأيسر من الأعلى إلى الأسفل + صح.

١ من تجارب الأمم لمسكويه ١: ١٩٩–٢٠٠.

people of Fārs to listen to him and to obey him. Rustam killed Siyāwuḫš, and the Persians submitted themselves to him. This was after the arrival of Abū ʿUbayd. Rustam wrote to the *dihqāns* of the Sawād that they should rise against the Muslims. He sent a man to every *rustāq* to raise its people. Al-Muṯanná heard about this. Ǧābān, whom a lot of people had joined at al-Namāriq, made haste. Abū ʿUbayd joined (al-Muṯanná) and had the troops rest before preparing for battle. He put al-Muṯanná in charge of the cavalry and arranged[637] the right and the left flanks. They attacked Ǧābān at al-Namāriq. The latter fought fiercely against them, but was forced to flee and was taken prisoner. He was then let go, because he had been given indemnity, and the booty was divided and one fifth was sent to ʿUmar, may God be pleased with him.

§ 251[638] Narsī revolted in Kaskar after Rustam had given him orders to do so. This Narsī was the son of the maternal aunt of Kisrá, and Kaskar was an estate of his. Al-Narsiyān belonged to him, and he protected it: only the family of Kisrá could enjoy its products and cultivate it, in addition to those they wanted to honour with some of it. When the Persians fled on the Day of al-Namāriq, the fleeing army regrouped around Narsī, who was in his camp. Abū ʿUbayd called his army to set moving and said to the light cavalry: “Pursue the fugitives until you have made them enter the camp of Narsī or killed them.” Abū ʿUbayd left al-Namāriq and marched until he camped against Narsī in Kaskar. Al-Muṯanná b. Ḥāriṯah was with him, and with Narsī there were his maternal cousins, who were the sons of Kisrá’s maternal uncle, Bindūyah and Bīrūyah,[639] sons of Bisṭām. Būrān and Rustam had heard of the defeat of Ǧābān, and they sent al-Ǧālnūs. Narsī and those with him heard about this and hoped that he should be able to join them before the battle, but Abū ʿUbayd hurried and fought fiercely against them. Narsī fled, his companions were killed, and Abū ʿUbayd conquered his camp and his lands.

637 In the holograph, this looks more like ʿNY, which is also how MS T reads it, but *ʿabbá*, following Miskawayh, makes better sense. In any case, Miskawayh, whom al-Maqrīzī follows, messed up the text of al-Ṭabarī, who gave the reader the names of the commanders of the two flanks. These were dropped by Miskawayh, and the whole sentence lost its relevance.

638 Miskawayh, *Taǧārib al-umam*, 1:199–200 = C332–333; cf. al-Ṭabarī, *Taʾrīḫ*, 1:2168 = trans., 11:182–184.

639 Al-Ṭabarī reads Tīrūyah. Miskawayh (ed. Caetani) is not very clear, but seems to read the first letter as B.

فرأى المسلمون هناك من الأطعمة ما لم يروا مثله وأخذت خزائن نرسي واقتسم المسلمون النرسيان وكان حِمى فجعلوا يطعمونه الفلاحين وبعثوا بالخمس إلى عمر رضي الله عنه.

§ 252[1] وسار المثنى يُخرِّب ويَسْبي. فقدم الجالنوس فقاتله أبو عبيد بمن معه فانهزم منهم وغلب أبو عبيد على البلاد. فلما قدم الجالنوس على رستم بمن أفلت معه وجه بهمن جاذويه وهو ذو الحاجب ومعه فيلة ورد معه الجالنوس ودفع إليه درفش كابيان. وكانت راية من جلود النمر عرض ثماني أذرع في طول اثني عشر ذراعا. فعبر أبو عبيد بالمسلمين إليهم وقاتلوهم يوما فأصيب من الفرس يومئذ في المعركة ستة آلاف ولم يبق إلا الهزيمة. فحمل أبو عبيد على الفيل وضربه فخبط الفيل أبا عبيد وقام عليه فمات رحمه الله فجال المسلمون جولة. ثم تموا عليها فركبهم أهل فارس فبادر رجل من ثقيف الجسر فقطعه فانتهى الناس إليه والسيوف تأخذهم من خلفهم فتهافتوا في الفرات فأصابوا يومئذ من المسلمين أربعة آلاف بين غريق وقتيل وهرب ألفان.

§ 253[2] فحمى المثنى بن حارثة الناس بمن معه من الفرسان ونادى: "أيها الناس أنا دونكم فاعبروا." وعقد لهم الجسر فعبروا إلى ذلك الجانب وبقي المثنى في ثلاثة آلاف وقد جرح. والفرس في تسعين ألفا وهم يريدون العبور إلى المسلمين. فبينا هم كذلك إذ ورد الخبر باضطراب الفرس فرجع ذو

٨ فمات ... الله : الزيادة بخط المقريزي في الهامش الأيمن من الأعلى إلى الأسفل + صح، ويشير إليها رمز ⌝ بعد "عليه". ١٠ وهرب ألفان : الزيادة بخط المقريزي في الهامش الأيسر + صح، ويشير إليها رمز ⌝ بعد "وقتيل".

١ من تجارب الأمم لمسكويه ١: ٢٠٠-٢٠١.

٢ من تجارب الأمم لمسكويه ١: ٢٠٢-٢٠٤.

When he gathered the spoils, the Muslims saw dishes they had never seen before. The treasuries of Narsī were also taken, and the Muslims divided al-Narsiyān, which had been a reserved area, and started feeding the peasants from it. They sent a fifth to ʿUmar, may God be pleased with him.

§ 252[640] Al-Muṯanná marched on, destroying places and taking prisoners, and al-Ǧālnūs set himself against him. Abū ʿUbayd and his men fought against al-Ǧālnūs, who fled. Abū ʿUbayd conquered the area, and when al-Ǧālnūs came to Rustam with the remnants of the army, Rustam sent Bahman Ǧādūyah, who is known as Ḏū l-Ḥāǧib, with elephants, and he sent al-Ǧālnūs back to fight with him. Rustam gave Bahman the Kayanid banner,[641] which was a banner made of leopard skins, eight cubits wide and twelve long. Abū ʿUbayd and the Muslims crossed the river to their side, and they fought the whole day. On that day, 6,000 Persians died on the battleground. They were almost put to flight, but then Abū ʿUbayd attacked the elephant and hit it, and the elephant stroke him down and trampled him, so that he died, may God have mercy on him. The Muslims fled, but then turned around before finally completely losing their ground, the Persians pursuing them closely. A man from Ṯaqīf hastened to the bridge and cut it. When people reached the bridge, swords were striking them from behind, and they fell into the Euphrates. On that day, 4,000 Muslims were killed or drowned and 2,000 fled.[642]

§ 253[643] Al-Muṯanná b. Ḥāriṯah and his cavalrymen protected people, and he cried: "O people, I will protect you! Cross the river!" He repaired the bridge for them, and they passed onto the other side of the river. Al-Muṯanná, who had been wounded, remained (on the other side) with his 3,000 men. There were 90,000 Persians, and they wanted to cross over to the side of the Muslims. When they were in this situation, news reached them that there was unrest among the Persians. Ḏū l-Ḥāǧib turned back after his men had

640 Miskawayh, *Taǧārib al-umam*, 1:200–201 = C333–334; cf. al-Ṭabarī, *Taʾrīḫ*, 1:2172, 2174–2175 – trans., 11:186, 188–189.

641 For the *drafš ī kāviyān*, see al-Maqrīzī, *Ḫabar/Persia*, I § 73.

642 The words *wa-hariba alfān* are taken from Miskawayh some pages later (1:202 = C338), if not from al-Ṭabarī, *Taʾrīḫ*, 1:2180 = trans., 11:193.

643 Miskawayh, *Taǧārib al-umam*, 1:202–204 = C337–341; cf. al-Ṭabarī, *Taʾrīḫ*, 1:2175–2176, 2184, 2189–2190 (and cf. also 1:2179) = trans., 11:189, 195, 203–204 (and cf. also 11:192).

الحاجب وقد انفض عنه جنده لأنه بلغهم أن الناس بالمدائن ثاروا برستم. وصاروا فرقتين فرقة مع الفهلوج على رستم وفرقة مع الفيروزان. ثم إن جابان ومردانشاه خرجا حتى أخذا بالطريق وقد فروا ولا علم لهم بما ورد على ذي الحاجب من فُرقةِ أهل فارس. فخرج المثنى يريد جابان ومردانشاه جريدة فأخذهما أسيرين فضرب أعناقهما وعقد لأصحابهما ذمة ثم رجع إلى عسكره. وأتت المثنى الأمداد من | عمر رضي الله عنه. 189b فندب رستمُ والفيروزانُ لحرب المسلمين مهرانَ الهَمذاني. ثم اجتمع رستم والفيروزان معا واستأذنا بوران. وكذلك كانا يعملان إذا أرادا شيئا استأذنا من حُجابها. فكلماها به فأخبراها بعدد الجيش الذي ينفذ مع مهران فقالت: "ما بال فارس لا يخرجون إلى العرب كما كانوا يخرجون قبل اليوم؟" قالا: "إن الهيبة كانت قبل اليوم مع عدونا وإنها اليوم فينا." فعرفت رأيهم واستصوبتهم.

§ 254[1] ونزل مهران في جنده وراء الفرات والمثنى في جنده على الفرات والفرات بينهما. فعبر المثنى إليهم وقاتلهم قتالا طويلا حتى هزمهم وسبقهم إلى الجسر فأخذتهم سيوف المسلمين من كل جانب حتى حُزِرَتْ قتلاهم مائة ألف. وسرح في طلب المنهزمين فأصابوا غنائم كثيرة وأغاروا حتى بلغوا ساباط. ومضى المثنى إلى الأنبار غارة فتزود منها وطرق قرية يقال لها بغداد يجتمع فيها تجار المدائن والسواد. فوضع فيهم السيف وأخذ ما شاء من ذهب وفضة ورجع فقال أهل فارس

٧ الذي ... مهران : كشط المقريزي عبارة أخرى قبل أن يصححها كما هي الآن. ١٢ حُزِرَتْ : وضع المقريزي رمز "ح" تحت الحرف الأول إشارة إلى تلفظه بالحاء. ١٣ يقال ... فيها : كشط المقريزي عبارة أخرى قبل أن يصححها كما هي الآن وتابع الجملة في الهامش. ١٤ تجار ... والسواد : الزيادة بخط المقريزي في آخر السطر في الهامش الأيسر من الأسفل إلى الأعلى + صح.

١٣ بغداد : أضاف المقريزي الحاشية التالية في الهامش الأيمن منكسة: "حـ (لـ "حاشية") باغ هو البستان بالفارسية. وقد قيل إنه أهدي إلى كسرى خصي من عُباد الأصنام فأقطعه هذا البستان (وضع المقريزي ثلاث نقط تحت الحرف الرابع إشارة إلى تلفظه بالسين). وقال: "بَغْ دَاذِيْ." أي هذا الصنم أعطاني."

١ من تجارب الأمم لمسكويه ١: ٢٠٤، ٢٠٧-٢٠٨.

dispersed when they had heard that people in al-Madāʾin had risen against Rustam and were divided into two, one party lead by al-Fahlūǧ[644] against Rustam and the other by al-Fīrūzān. Then Ǧābān and Mardānšāh went forth and took to the road. They had escaped without knowing the news that had come to Ḏū l-Ḥāǧib concerning the disunion of the Persians. Al-Muṯanná left for Ǧābān and Mardānšāh with light cavalry and took the two prisoners. Al-Muṯanná cut their heads off, but gave a *ḏimmah* agreement to their troops. Then he returned to his camp. Help sent by ʿUmar, may God be pleased with him, came to al-Muṯanná. Rustam and al-Fīrūzān sent together Mihrān al-Hamaḏānī to fight the Muslims. Then they decided to ask for an audience with Būrān: when they wanted to do something, they used to ask for an audience from her chamberlains. They told her about this and informed her about the size of the army that went with Mihrān, and she said: "Why don't the Persians go out against the Arabs like they used to do before this day?" They replied: "In earlier days, the enemy used to fear us, but today it is we who are afraid." Būrān understood their point and thought they were right.

§ 254[645] Mihrān and his troops settled on the one side of the Euphrates and al-Muṯanná and his troops on the other, so that the Euphrates was between them. Al-Muṯanná crossed the river to them, and they fought long until he put them to flight. He reached the bridge first, and the Muslims' swords took them from every direction until the number of their dead was estimated at 100,000, and the fleeing remnants were freely chased. The Muslims got a lot of booty and invaded until Sābāṭ. Al-Muṯanná made a raid to al-Anbār and took provisions from there, coming also to a village called Baġdād, where the merchants of al-Madāʾin and the Sawād used to come together. He put the people there to sword and took what he wanted of gold and silver. Then he returned, and the people of Fārs said to Rustam and al-Fīrūzān: "You have

---

24 Baġdād : *Bāġ* means "garden" in Persian. It has been said: A eunuch from among the servants of idols was given as a present to Kisrá, who gave him this village. The eunuch said: "*Baġ dāḏī*," i.e., "This idol gave me." (marginal gloss in al-Maqrīzī's hand). Here, al-Maqrīzī confuses things. Elsewhere (see notes to §§ 140a and 224), he explains *bāġ* as "garden" and here he tries the same explanation for *baġ*, but his own example actually contradicts the explanation. For *baġ* "lord" (< *bhaga*), see MacKenzie (1971): 17.

---

644 Pourshariati (2008): 215–216, reads the word as *Fahlawaj* and takes it to refer to people of Parthian background.

645 Miskawayh, *Taǧārib al-umam*, 1:204, 207–208 = C341–342, 348; cf. al-Ṭabarī, *Taʾrīḫ*, 1:2190, 2209–2210 = trans., 11:204, 221–222.

لرستم والفيروزان: "إنه لم يبرح منكما الاختلاف حتى أوهنتما أهل فارس وأطمعتما فيهم عدوهم. وما نحن بتاركيكما على هذا فإنكما عرضتما فارس للهلكة. ما بعد بغداد وساباط وتكريت إلا المدائن. والله لتجتمعان أو لنبدأن بكما قبل أن يشمت شامت." فاجتمع رستم والفيروزان عند بوران وقالا لها: "اكتبي لنا نساء كسرى وسراريه." ففعلت فأرسلوا في طلبهن حتى جمعوهن وعاقبوهن ليدلوهم على ذَكَرٍ من أبناء كسرى. فلم يوجد عندهن أحد حتى دلتهم امرأة على يزدجرد. هكذا أورد هذه الحروب بأبسط من هذا أبو علي ابن مسكويه وأنها في أيام بوران وفيه نظر.

§255 فإن المشهور عند علماء السير أن رسول الله صلى الله عليه وسلم بعث إلى أبرويز رسوله بكتابه في سنة ست وأنه سار في محرم سنة سبع فهلك أبرويز من عامه. وعند ابن مسكويه أن شيرويه ابن أبرويز أقام ثمانية أشهر وأقام أردشير بن شيرويه سَنةً وستة أشهر وأقام شهربراز أربعين يوما. ثم ملكت بوران سَنةً وأربعة أشهر. فيكون على هذا من هلاك أبرويز إلى آخر مدة بوران ثلاث سنين وسبعة أشهر وعشرة | أيام. فإذا حملنا هذه المدة على هلاك أبرويز في السنة السابعة من الهجرة كان 190a انقضاء مدة بوران في آخر السنة العاشرة من الهجرة أو في أوائل الحادية عشر. فكيف يصح مع هذا أن تكون هذه الحروب المذكورة لفارس مع أبي عبيد بن مسعود الثقفي والمثنى بن حارثة في أيام بوران؟ وهذه الحروب إنما كانت في خلافة عمر بن الخطاب رضي الله عنه وفي سنة اثنتي عشرة وما بعدها.

---

٦ بأبسط ... هذا : الزيادة بخط المقريزي في آخر السطر في الهامش الأيسر من الأسفل إلى الأعلى + صح.

٧ إلى أبرويز : الزيادة بخط المقريزي في الهامش الأيسر من الأعلى إلى الأسفل + صح، ويشير إليها رمز ⌐ بعد "بعث".

not given up your disagreement and you have weakened the people of Fārs and made its enemies covetous of them. We will not allow you to do so. You have laid Fārs open to destruction. After Baġdād and Sābāṭ and Takrīt, there will only be al-Madā'in. By God, you must come to an agreement or else we will begin with you before the malicious gloater has occasion to gloat." Rustam and al-Fīrūzān met with Būrān and said to her: "Write down for us the names of the wives and concubines of Kisrá." She did so, and they sent for them and gathered them together. They tortured them to make them reveal a male descendant of Kisrá, but none could be found until a woman pointed Yazdaǧird to them. Abū 'Ali b. Miskawayh has narrated these wars thus, only in a more extensive manner, and he claims that they took place during the reign of Būrān, but this may be doubted.

§ 255 What is known among scholars of the *siyar*[646] is that the Messenger of God, may God honour him and grant him peace, sent his messenger with a letter to Abarwīz in the year 6 AH[/627–628], and the messenger travelled in Muḥarram[647] year 7[/May-June 628]. Abarwīz died in that year. According to Ibn Miskawayh, Šīrūyah b. Abarwīz reigned for 8 months and Ardašīr b. Šīrūyah for a year and 6 months. Šahrbarāz reigned for 40 days and Būrān for a year and 4 months. This would mean that from the death of Abarwīz to the end of Būrān's reign was 3 years, 7 months, and 10 days. Now, if we add this amount of time to the death of Abarwīz in year 7 AH[/628], the end of Būrān's reign would fall on the end of year 10 AH[/beg. 632] or the beginning of year 11[/March 632]. How could it then be true that these wars between Fārs and Abū 'Ubayd b. Mas'ūd al-Ṯaqafī and al-Muṯanná b. Ḥāriṯah we have been speaking about could have taken place during Būrān's reign when they took place during the Caliphate of 'Umar b. al-Ḫaṭṭāb, may God be pleased with him, and in year 12[/633–634] and thereafter?

646 *Siyar* (sg. *sīrah*) probably refers here to pre-Islamic Persian history, rather than the Life of the Prophet and early Islamic history.

647 I.e., the first month of the year.

§ 256 لا سيما وفي **الصحيح** ما يدل على أن بوران وَلِيَتْ في حياة رسول الله صلى الله عليه وسلم. فقد خرج البخاري من حديث الحسن عن أبي بَكْرَة رضي الله عنه قال: نفعني الله تعالى بكلمة سمعتها من رسول الله صلى الله عليه وسلم أيام الجمل بعد ما كدت أن ألحق بأصحاب الجمل فأقاتل معهم. قال: لما بلغ رسول الله صلى الله عليه وسلم أن أهل فارس ملكوا عليهم بنت كسرى قال: "لن يفلح قوم ولوا أمرهم امرأة." لكن يمكن أن يقال كانت فترات بين ولايات من قام بأمر الملك بعد أبرويز فإنه كان بين فارس اختلاف وتنازع كثير ولذلك لم يذكَر في سِيَرهم سوى مدة كل واحد منهم من غير تعيين وقت ابتداء المدة وانقضائها. ويؤيد هذا الاحتمال ما ذكر بعضهم أن قدوم خالد بن الوليد رضي الله عنه الحِيْرَةَ في زمن بوران لاثنتي عشرة مضت من الهجرة وأن بوران ملكت بعد قدوم خالد مدة سبعة أشهر منها ثلاثة أشهر في خلافة أبي بكر الصديق رضي الله عنه وأربعة أشهر في خلافة أمير المؤمنين عمر رضي الله عنه.

§ 257[1] وذكر أبو علي ابن مسكويه أن الذي ملك بعد بوران رجل من بني عم أبرويز يقال له جِشْنَسْبَنْدَه. وكان ملكه أقل من شهر ولم يظهر له أثر يستفاد منه تجربة. وذكر علي بن حمزة الإصفهاني أنه لم يكن من بيت الملك وأنه أقام شهرين. وقيل: أقام أياما وإن اسمه فيروز وحكي أيضا أن الذي ولي بعد بوران آزرمِيْدَخْت. وقال غيره: بل أقيم بعد بوران كسرى بن قباذ بن

٦ وتنازع: كتب المقريزي رمز "٢" في آخر السطر في الهامش ولا توجد أي حاشية فيه. ١١ ملك ... أبرويز: كشط المقريزي عبارة أخرى قبل أن يصححها كما هي الآن.

١ من تجارب الأمم لمسكويه ١: ١٦٧ ومن تأريخ سني الملوك لحمزة ص ١٥، ٢٥.

§ 256[648] Especially, as there is in the *Ṣaḥīḥ* [Sound *ḥadīṯs*] what indicates that Būrān ruled (already) during the lifetime of the Messenger of God, may God honour him and grant him peace. Al-Buḫārī [649]has transmitted a *ḥadīṯ* of al-Ḥasan from Abū Bakrah,[650] may God be pleased with him. He said: God, He is Exalted, has benefitted me with something I heard transmitted from the Messenger of God, may God honour him and grant him peace, during the days of the Camel, after I had almost joined the people of the Camel to fight on their side.[651] He said: When the Messenger of God, may God honour him and grant him peace, heard that the Persians had appointed as queen over themselves the daughter of Kisrá, he said: "People who give their matters into the hands of a woman will not flourish." Yet it might be possible that there were interregnums between the reigns of those who took the kingship over after Abarwīz, as the Persians had a lot of disagreements and disputes. This is why in their histories only the length of each reign is given, without specification of when the reign started and ended. This possibility would be supported by what some have related about the arrival of Ḫālid b. al-Walīd, may God be pleased with him, to al-Ḥīrah at the time of Būrān when 12 years had passed from the *hiǧrah* and said that Būrān ruled 7 months after the arrival of Ḫālid, 3 months during the Caliphate of Abū Bakr al-Ṣiddīq, may God be pleased with him, and 4 months during the Caliphate of the Commander of the Believers ʿUmar, may God be pleased with him.

§ 257[652] Abū ʿAlī b. Miskawayh has mentioned that after Būrān, there reigned a paternal cousin of Abarwīz called Ǧušnas-Bandah,[653] but he ruled less than a month and did nothing remarkable from which one could benefit any experience. ʿAlī b. Ḥamzah al-Iṣfahānī[654] has mentioned that he was not of the royal family and that he ruled for 2 months, but it is also said that he ruled only a few days and that his name was Fīrūz. He also transmitted that after Būrān there ruled Āzarmīduḫt, but others have denied this and said that after Būrān they appointed as king Kisrá b. Qubād b. Hurmuz b. Kisrá

648 Al-Buḫārī, *Ṣaḥīḥ* no. 7099 (*Kitāb al-fitan, bāb* 18).

649 Famous traditionist, d. 256/870, see "al-Bukhārī," in *EI*², 1:1296–1297.

650 For Nufayʿ b. Masrūḥ Abū Bakrah, see Poonawala (1990): 147, note 973.

651 For the Battle of the Camel 36/656, see "al-Djamal," in *EI*², 2:414 416.

652 Miskawayh, *Taǧārib al-umam*, 1:167 = C269; Ḥamzah, *Taʾrīḫ* 15, 25 = trans. 34, 44; cf. Ḥamzah, *Taʾrīḫ* 20, 25 = trans. 39, 44; al-Ṭabarī, *Taʾrīḫ*, 1:1064 = trans., 5:405.

653 Cf. al-Bīrūnī, *al-Āṯār al-bāqiyah* 138.

654 Suddenly, here and § 259 al-Maqrīzī calls Ḥamzah ʿAlī b. Ḥamzah, a mistake that is also occasionally found elsewhere, e.g., al-Nuwayrī, *Nihāya*, 1:185.

هرمز بن كسرى أبرويز ولقبه كوتاه وأنه | أقام عشرة أشهر وولي فيروز بن بهرام بن مذان جشر 190b ابن منوزاذ خَسْرو بن نَرْسي بن بهرام بن سابور بن يزدجرد الأثيم وهو الملقب جِشْنَسْبَنْدَه وأنه أقام شهرا وعشرين يوما.

§ 258[1] ثم ملكت آزَرْميدُخْت بنت كسرى أبرويز ولقبها العادلة. قال ابن مسكويه: كانت آزرمي ذخت من أجمل نساء دهرها وكان عظيم فارس يومئذ فرخ هرمز إصبهبذ خراسان فأرسل إليها {يسألها} أن تزوجه نفسها فأرسلت إليه: "إن التزويج للملكة غير جائز وقد علمتُ أن أَرَبك فيما ذهبت إليه قضاء حاجتك مني. فصر إلي ليلة كذا وكذا." ففعل فرخ هرمز وركب إليها في تلك الليلة وتقدمت آزرمي ذخت إلى صاحب حرسها أن يترصده في تلك الليلة التي تواعدا الالتقاء فيها حتى يقتله. فنفذ صاحب حرسها لأمرها وأمر به فجر برجله وطرح فى رحبة دار المملكة. فلما أصبح الناس ورأوه علموا أنه لم يقتل إلا لعظيمة فأمرت بجثته فغيبت.

§ 259[2] وكان رستم بن فرخ هرمز هذا عظيم البأس قويا في نفسه وهو رستم صاحب القادسية الذي تولى قتال العرب من قبل يزدجرد فيما بعد وسيحكى خبره هناك إن شاء الله. فلما بلغه ما صنع بأبيه أقبل في جند عظيم حتى نزل المدائن وسمل عيني آزرمي ذخت وقتلها وكان ملكها ستة أشهر. وقال علي بن حمزة: وشعارها أحمر موشى وسراويلها موشحة وتاجها أخضر تقعد على السرير وبيمناها طبرزين معتمدة بيسراها على السيف. وكانت جليدة ونصبت بيت نار وملك بعدها خُرْدَاذ خُسره وبعضهم يقول: فرخزاذ خسرو بن كسرى أبرويز وهو طفل. فأقام شهراً واحدا ثم ملك يزدجرد.

---

٦ يسألها: في الأصل "يسلها".

---

١ من تجارب الأمم لمسكويه ١: ١٦٧.

٢ من تجارب الأمم لمسكويه ١: ١٦٧ ومن تأريخ سني الملوك لحمزة ص ٤٨، ٢٠، ١٥، ٢٥ ومن تأريخ الطبري ١: ١٠٦٥–١٠٦٦.

Abarwīz. His cognomen was Kūtāh[655] and he ruled for 10 months. Then there ruled Fīrūz b. Bahrām b. Madān-Ǧašr b. Manūrād-Ḫusraw b. Narsī b. Bahrām b. Sābūr b. Yazdaǧird the Sinner, and his cognomen was Ǧušnas-Bandah and he ruled for 1 month and 20 days.

§ 258[656] Then there ruled Āzarmīduḫt bt. Kisrá Abarwīz. Her cognomen was the Just.[657] Ibn Miskawayh says that Āzarmīduḫt was one of the most beautiful women of her time. At the time, the mightiest man in Fārs was Farruḫ-Hurmuz, the *iṣbahbad* of Ḫurāsān. He sent a word to her suggesting marriage, but she replied: "It is not allowed for the queen to marry. I know that your motif in what you suggest is to satisfy your desire with me. So come to me on such-and-such night." Farruḫ-Hurmuz did so and rode to her on that night. Āzarmīduḫt had told the commander of her guard to ambush and kill him that night in which they had agreed to meet. The commander of the guard did so and gave orders to drag him by his foot and to throw him on the courtyard of the royal palace. Next morning, people saw him and knew that he had been killed for some major offence. Then Āzarmīduḫt gave orders for his body to be taken away.

§ 259[658] Rustam, the son of this Farruḫ-Hurmuz, was very strong and powerful by himself. He was the Rustam of the Battle of al-Qādisiyyah, who led the army against the Arabs on behalf of Yazdaǧird, and his story will be told in that part, God willing. When he heard what had been done to his father, he came with a strong army and encamped outside al-Madā'in, blinded Āzarmīduḫt, and killed her. Her reign lasted for 6 months. ʿAlī b. Ḥamzah has said: Her vest was red and embroidered, her trousers had stripes, and her crown was green. She was sitting on the throne with an axe in her right hand, leaning with her left on a sword. She was strong and established a fire temple. After her, there ruled Ḫurdād-Ḫusraw,[659] but some say Farruḫzād-Ḫusraw b. Kisrá Abarwīz, who was still a child. He ruled for a single month, and then there ruled Yazdaǧird.

---

655 For the Persian cognomen, meaning "Short," see al-Ḫwārizmī, *Mafātīḥ* 104, and Bosworth (1999): 403, note 995.

656 Miskawayh, *Taǧārib al-umam*, 1:167 = C269; cf. al-Ṭabarī, *Ta'rīḫ*, 1:1064–1065 = trans., 5:406.

657 Cf. al-Bīrūnī, *al-Āṯār al-bāqiyah* 139.

658 Miskawayh, *Taǧārib al-umam*, 1:167 = C269–270; Ḥamzah, *Ta'rīḫ* 48, 20, 15, 25 = trans. 75, 39, 34, 44; al-Ṭabarī, *Ta'rīḫ*, 1:1065–1066 = trans., 5:406–409. Ḥamzah, *Ta'rīḫ* 20, 25 = trans., 39, 44, also give one month and some days or one year.

659 Al-Ṭabarī reads Ḫurrazād-Ḫusraw.

§ 260[١] وقال ابن مسكويه: واختلف فيمن ملك بعد آزرمي ذخت فقيل: أتي برجل من عقب أردشير بن بابك كان ينزل الأهواز يقال له كسرى بن مهرجسنس. فلبس التاج وقتل بعد أيام ويقال: بل كان رجلا يسكن ميسان يقال له فيروز | فملكوه كرها. وكان ضخم الرأس فلما تُوِج 191a قال: "ما أضيق هذا التاج." فتطير له العظماء من افتتاح كلامه بالضيق وقتلوه. ثم أتي برجل من أولاد كسرى كان لجأ إلى موضع قريب من نصيبين يقال له حصن الحجارة حين قتل شيرويه بني كسرى يقال له فرخزاذ خَسْرو. فانقاد له الناس زمانا يسيرا ثم استعصوا عليه وخالفوه وكان ملكه ستة أشهر. وكان أهل إصطخر ظفروا بيزدجرد بن شهريار بن أبرويز بإصطخر قد هرب إليها حين قتل شيرويه إخوته. فلما بلغ عظماء إصطخر أن من بالمدائن خالفوا فرخ زاذ بن خَسْرُوْ أتوا بيزدجرد بيت نار يدعى بيت نار أردشير فتوجوه هناك وملكوه وكان حَدثا. ثم أقبلوا به إلى المدائن وقتلوا فرخ زاد خسرو بحِيَل احتالوها له وساغ الملك ليزدجرد.

§ 261[٢] يزدجرد بن شهريار بن كسرى أبرويز. قد تقدم أنه فر إلى إصطخر وأن أهل إصطخر ظفروا به وتوجوه ثم أتوا به المدائن. وروي أيضا أن رستم والفيروزان لما عاقبوا نساء كسرى أبرويز ليدلوهم على ذكر من أبناء كسرى قالت {إحداهن}: "لم يبق إلا غلام يدعى يزدجرد من ولد شهريار بن أبرويز وأمه من أهل بادوريا." فأرسلوا إليها فأخذوها به وكانت قد أنزلته حين جمعهن شيرويه في القصر الأبيض وقتل الذكور إلى أخواله وكانت واعدتهم ثم دلته إليهم في زنبيل. فلما أُخِذَتْ أمه به دلتهم عليه فأرسلوا. فجاؤوا به فملكوه وهو ابن إحدى وعشرين سنة

---

٦ يسيرا : وضع المقريزي ثلاث نقط تحت الحرف الثاني إشارة إلى تلفظه بالسين. ١٢ أن : الزيادة بخط المقريزي في الهامش الأيمن من الأعلى إلى الأسفل + صح، ويشير إليها رمز ⌝ بعد "أيضا". ١٣ إحداهن : "احدىهن" في الأصل.

---

١ من تجارب الأمم لمسكويه ١: ١٦٧–١٦٨.

٢ من تجارب الأمم لمسكويه ١: ٢٠٨ ومن تأريخ الطبري ١: ١٠٦٧، ٢٢١٠.

§ 260[660] Ibn Miskawayh has said: There is disagreement as to who reigned after Āzarmīduḫt. Some say that they brought a man from among the descendants of Ardašīr b. Bābak, who lived in al-Ahwāz and was called Kisrá b. Mihr-Ǧušnas. He assumed the crown but was killed after a couple of days. But it is also said that the next to rule was a man living in Maysān, called Fīrūz, whom they appointed king against his will. He had a big head, and when he was crowned, he said: "How tight this crown is!" The noblemen took the mention of tightness for his opening words as a bad omen and killed him. Then they brought a descendant of Kisrá, who had taken refuge in a place close to Nisibis, called The Stone Fortress, when Šīrūyah killed the sons of Kisrá. His name was Farruḫzād-Ḫusraw. People obeyed him for a short while, but then revolted and disobeyed. His reign lasted for six months. The people of Iṣṭaḫr got hold of Yazdağird b. Šahriyār b. Abarwīz in Iṣṭaḫr, whereto he had escaped when Šīrūyah had killed his brothers. When the noblemen of Iṣṭaḫr heard that people in al-Madā'in were disobeying Farruḫzād b. Ḫusraw they brought Yazdağird into a fire temple called the fire temple of Ardašīr, crowned him there and proclaimed him king. He was a youth. Then they took him to al-Madā'in and killed Farruḫzād-Ḫusraw by some stratagem, and the way was open for Yazdağird's kingship.

§ 261[661] Yazdağird b. Šahriyār b. Kisrá Abarwīz. We have already mentioned that he fled to Iṣṭaḫr and that the people of Iṣṭaḫr got hold of him and crowned him. Then they brought him to al-Madā'in. It is also narrated that when Rustam and al-Fīrūzān tortured the women of Kisrá Abarwīz to make them indicate some male from among the children of Kisrá, one of them said: "There only remains one boy, called Yazdağird, from the children of Šahriyār b. Abarwīz. His mother is from Bādūryā." They sent for her and tortured her because of her son. When Šīrūyah had gathered the women in the White Castle and killed the males, she had given him to the care of his maternal uncles, to whom she had sent a word. She lowered him to them in a basket. When his mother was now tortured, she indicated him to them. They sent for him and brought him and made him king. He was 21 years of age,

660 Miskawayh, *Tağārib al-umam*, 1:167–168 = C270–271; cf. al-Ṭabarī, *Ta'rīḫ*, 1:1066–1067 = trans., 5:408–410.

661 Miskawayh, *Tağārib al-umam, 1:208* = C348–349; al-Ṭabarī, *Ta'rīḫ*, 1:1067 = trans., 5:409–411, and 1:2210 = trans., 11:222–223.

لإحدى عشرة سنة من الهجرة واجتمعوا عليه واطمأنت فارس واستوسقوا. ودخل رؤساؤهم في طاعته ومعونته. فسمى الجنود لكل مسلحة كانت لكسرى أو موضع ثغر. فسمى جند الحِيْرة وجند الأنبار والأبلة والمسالح وأظهروا الجد والنصيحة غير أن ملكه كان عند ملك آبائه كالخيال وكالحلُم. وكانت العظماء والوزراء يدبرون ملكه لحداثة سنه. وكان أشدهم نباهة في وُزَرائه وأذكاهم رئيس الخول. وضعف أمر مملكة فارس واجترأ عليه أعداؤه من كل وجه | وتطرقوا بلاده وأخربوا منها. 191b وغَزَت العرب بلاده بعد أن مضى من ملكه ثلاث أو أربع سنين وله أحاديث.

§ 262[1] وذلك أن المثنى بن حارثة لما بلغه اجتماع فارس كتب إلى عمر رضي الله عنه بذلك. فكفر أهل السواد كلهم من كان له عهد ومن لم يكن له عهد. فكتب إليه عمر رضي الله عنه أن يتفرقوا في المياه التي على حدود أرضيهم. فنزل المثنى بذي قار ونزل الناس في المياه وأقاموا مسالح ينظر بعضهم إلى بعض وذلك في ذي القعدة من سنة ثلاث عشرة. وعزم عمر على المسير إليهم. ثم بعث سعد بن أبي وقاص رضي الله عنه أميرا على حرب العراق. ومات المثنى بن حارثة من جراحته وقدم سعد فأغار فيما يليه إلى أن ألح يزدجرد على رستم حتى خرج في العدة والعديد والخيول والفيول. فراسله سَعْد بالمغيرة بن شعبة وغيره فجرت بينهم مخاطبات إلى أن صافهم رستم

١ لإحدى ... الهجرة : الزيادة بخط المقريزي في الهامش الأيمن من الأعلى إلى الأسفل + صح، ويشير إليها رمز ˥ بعد "سنة". ٨ عمر ... عنه : الزيادة بخط المقريزي في الهامش الأيسر من الأسفل إلى الأعلى + صح، ويشير إليها رمز ˥ بعد "إليه". ١٠ المسير : وضع المقريزي ثلاث نقط تحت الحرف الرابع إشارة إلى تلفظه بالسين.

١ من تجارب الأمم لمسكويه ١: ٢٠٨–٢١٠.

and this happened 11 years after the *hiǧrah*. The Persians were united behind him, and Fārs became quiet and well-ordered. The leaders were obedient to him and helped him. Yazdaǧird appointed an army to each frontier vanguard of Kisrá or fortress. Thus, he appointed armies for al-Ḥīrah, al-Anbār, al-Ubullah, and the garrisons. They showed all earnestness and sincerity, but his reign was still just a shadow or a dream of that of his fathers. The noblemen and Viziers governed the kingdom because of his young age. The most intelligent and brightest of his Viziers was the Chief of Servants. The affairs of the kingdom of Fārs were weakened, and its enemies from every direction became bold, penetrating his country and laying parts of it waste. When three or four years had passed of his reign, the Arabs raided his country, and there are stories about him.

§262[662] When al-Muṯanná b. Ḥāriṯah heard that the Persians had become united, he wrote about this to ʿUmar, may God be pleased with him. The people of the Sawād rebelled, both those who had an agreement and those who had not. ʿUmar, may God be pleased with him, wrote back to him,[663] saying that they should disperse to various watering places on the borders of their country. Al-Muṯanná encamped at Ḏū Qār, and others encamped at other watering places and put up fortified posts, each at a sight of the previous. This happened in Ḏū l-Qaʿdah, year 13[/December 634–January 635]. ʿUmar first decided to march against them himself but then sent Saʿd b. Abī Waqqāṣ,[664] may God be pleased with him, to lead the war in Iraq. Al-Muṯanná b. Ḥāriṯah died of his wounds, and Saʿd arrived and raided the areas around him, until Yazdaǧird urgently asked Rustam to set out with numerous well-equipped men, horses, and elephants. Saʿd exchanged letters with al-Muġīrah b. Šuʿbah[665] and others, and they had discussions between each other until Rustam lined up against them and crossed the river to

662 Miskawayh, *Taǧārib al-umam*, 1:208–210 = C349–352; cf. al-Ṭabarī, *Taʾrīḫ*, 1:2210–2211 = trans., 11:223–224.

663 The formula *raḍiya llāh ʿanhu* has been added in the margin and the place indicated for it in the text is after *ilayhi* in *kataba ilayhi*. However, both al-Ṭabarī and Miskawayh show that it should be added after *kataba* and translated as above. Al-Maqrīzī's reading would translate as "he (= al-Muṯanná) wrote to him (= ʿUmar)."

664 One of the generals of the wars of conquest, d. in the 50s/670s, see "Saʿd b. Abī Waḳḳāṣ," in *EI*^{2}, 8:696–697.

665 Companion of the Prophet, who served in several high positions under the Umayyads, d. ca. 50/670, see "al-Mughīra b. Shuʿba," in *EI*^{2}, 7:347.

وعبر إليهم. وكان في القلب ثمانية عشر فيلا عليها الصناديق والرجال وفي المُجَنَّبَتين ثمانية وسبعة. وأقام الجالنوس بينه وبين ميمنته والفيروزان بينه وبين ميسرته. وبقيت القنطرة بين خيلين من خيول المسلمين والفرس.

§263[1] وكان يزدجرد وضع بينه وبين رستم رجالا فأولهم على باب إيوانه والآخر على دَعْوَة منه بحيث يسمعه والآخر كذلك حتى انتظم بينه وبين رستم بالرجال. فلما نزل رستم بساباط قال الرجل الذي بساباط: "نزل." وقال الذي يليه كذلك ثم الذي يليه حتى يقوله من يلي الإيوان ويسمعه يزدجرد. فكان كلما ارتحل أو نزل أو حدث أمر جرى الأمر فيه على ما شرحته وتَرَك البُرْدَ وكان ذلك شأنه إلى أن انقضى الحرب. وتعاهد الفرس وتواصوا واقترنوا بالسلاسل فكان المقترنون ثلاثين ألفا وجملتهم مائة وعشرون ألفا وثلاثون فيلا عليها المقاتلة وفيلة عليها الملوك وقوف لا تقاتل ونشب القتال فاعتور الضرب والطعن.

§264[2] وخرج هرمز إلى غالب بن عبد الله وكان هرمز من ملوك الباب متوجا. فأسره غالب وأتى به إلى سَعْد بن أبي وقاص. وخرج آخر | فانتدب له عمرو بن معدي كرب وحمل عليه فاعتنقه ثم 192a أخذ بمنطقته فاحتمله فوضعه بين يديه وجاء به حتى دنا من أصحابه فكسر عنق الرجل ثم ذبحه وألقاه. وخرج إلى طليحة عظيم منهم فبرز إليه فما لبث طليحة أن قتله. وندب الأشعثُ بن قيس كِنْدَةَ حتى أزالوا الفيلة عنهم. فحمل ذو الحاجب والجالنوس حملة منكرة فدارت رحى الحرب والفيلة تحمل على الميمنة والميسرة فكانت الخيول تحجم عنها وتحيد. فأقبل أصحاب عاصم بن عمرو

١٦ والميسرة: وضع المقريزي ثلاث نقط تحت الحرف الخامس إشارة إلى تلفظه بالسين.

١ من تجارب الأمم لمسكويه ١: ٢١١.

٢ من تجارب الأمم لمسكويه ١: ٢١١–٢١٣.

them. In the centre of his army, there were eighteen elephants, carrying palanquins and men on their backs, and on the flanks eight and seven elephants, respectively. Al-Ǧālnūs stood between him and the right flank and al-Fīrūzān between him and the left flank. The bridge was between the cavalry of the Muslims and the Persians.

§ 263[666] Yazdağird had arranged men between himself and Rustam, so that the first was at the door of his *īwān*, the next at a shouting distance from him, and so on, until he was linked to Rustam through these men. When Rustam encamped in Sābāṭ, the man in Sābāṭ shouted: "He has encamped!" The next man did the same and so on, until the one closest to the *īwān* repeated it for Yazdağird to hear. Every time Rustam set moving or encamped or something happened, they did as I have explained, instead of using the mail. This was done until the end of the war. The Persians swore mutual oaths and gave mutual promises. They chained themselves together. The chained men were 30,000 in number, and their total number was 120,000. They had 30 elephants carrying soldiers and others that stood at their places, carrying the kings and not taking part in the battle. The war broke out, and swords and spears started their work.

§ 264[667] Hurmuz came forth to Ġālib b. ʿAbd Allāh. Hurmuz was one of the crowned kings in the court, and Ġālib took him prisoner and brought him to Saʿd b. Abī Waqqāṣ. Then another came forth, and ʿAmr b. Maʿdīkarib[668] took him to himself and attacked him. ʿAmr took a grip of his opponent and grasped him by his belt and carried him away in front of himself until he was close to his companions and there broke his neck, killed him, and threw him down. One of the Persian noblemen came forth to Ṭulayḥah to challenge him. Ṭulayḥah killed him quickly. Al-Ašʿaṯ b. Qays[669] urged the Kindah to take the elephants out of the game. Ḏū l-Ḥāǧib and al-Ǧālnūs attacked a vicious attack, and the mill of war kept grinding. The elephants attacked on both flanks, and horses shrank from them and avoided them. The companions of ʿĀṣim b. ʿAmr[670] came forward and took them by their tails and cut off

666 Miskawayh, *Taǧārib al-umam*, 1:211 = C352–354; cf. al-Ṭabarī, *Taʾrīḫ*, 1:2258 = trans., 12:53.
667 Miskawayh, *Taǧārib al-umam*, 1:211–213 = C354–357; cf. al-Ṭabarī, *Taʾrīḫ*, 1:2296–2300 = trans., 12:91–95.
668 One of the generals of the conquest, d. probably in 16/637 or 21/641, see *EI*², s.v., 1:453.
669 Tribal leader, d. 40/661, see "al-Ashʿath b. Ḳays," in *EI*², 1:696–697.
670 For ʿĀṣim b. ʿAmr al-Tamīmī, see Blankinship (1993): 11, note 69.

فأخذوا بأذنابها وقطعوا وُضُنَها فألقت ما على ظهورها حتى ما بقي لهم فيل إلا عُرْي وقُتِل أصحابها. ولم يزل القتال حتى غربت الشمس ثم حتى إذا ذهبت هدأة من الليل. ثم رجع الفريقان وقد أصيب من بني أسد خمس مائة وكانوا رِدْءا للناس. وكان عاصم بن عمرو عَادِيَةَ الناس. فهذا يومهم الأول وهو يوم أرماث.

§ 265[1] وأصبحوا يوم أغواث فوافت المسلمين نجدة ستة آلاف بعث بهم أبو عبيدة بن الجراح رضي الله عنه بعد فتح دمشق. عليهم هاشم بن عتبة بن أبي وقاص وعلى مقدمته القعقاع بن عمرو. فبرز إليه ذو الحاجب بهمن جاذويه فاجتلدا فقتله القعقاع فانكسرت الفرس لذلك. ثم خرج الفيرزان والبندوان فبادر القعقاع الفيرزان وقتله وبادر الحرث بن ظبيان البندوان فقتله. واجتلد الفريقان حتى المساء وقد كثر القتل في الفرس. ولم يقاتلوا في هذا اليوم على فيل لأن توابيتها تكسرت بالأمس لجددوها. وكانت للقعقاع يومئذ ثلاثون حملة يصيب فيها فقتل ثلاثين فارسا آخرهم بزرجمهر الهمَذاني. ولم يزل القتال يوم أغواث حتى انتصف الليل وقد قتل عامة أعلام فارس. وكان لأبي محجن الثقفي في تلك الليلة بلاء عظيم. ثم تحاجز الناس لما انتصف الليل.

§ 266[2] وأصبحوا اليوم الثالث على مواقفهم وقد قتل من المسلمين ألفان ومن فارس عشرة آلاف. فكان القتال يوم عِمَاس وقد أصلح الفرس توابيت الفيلة من أول النهار إلى آخره. والعرب والعجم

---

١٤ النهار: الزيادة بخط المقريزي في الهامش الأيمن من الأعلى إلى الأسفل + صح، ويشير إليها رمز ⌐ بعد "أول".

---

١ من تجارب الأمم لمسكويه ١: ٢١٣-٢١٥.

٢ من تجارب الأمم لمسكويه ١: ٢١٦-٢١٩.

their girths, so that they threw down what was on their back, until all their elephants were naked and the elephant drivers had been killed. The fighting went on until the sun set and even until a part of the night had passed. Only then did the two sides go back to their camps. Banū Asad had lost 500 men, as they had been the support of others. ʿĀṣim b. ʿAmr had been the misfortune of the Persians. This was the first day, which is called the Day of Armāṯ.

§ 265[671] The following day was the Day of Aġwāṯ. The Muslims received an aid of 6,000 men, which Abū ʿUbaydah b. al-Ǧarrāḥ,[672] may God be pleased with him, had sent after the conquest of Damascus. They were led by Hāšim b. ʿUtbah b. Abī Waqqāṣ.[673] Their vanguard was led by al-Qaʿqāʿ b. ʿAmr.[674] Ḏū l-Ḥāǧib Bahman Ǧādūyah challenged him, and they fought until al-Qaʿqāʿ killed him. Persians were devastated because of this. Then al-Fīrzān and al-Binduwān came forth and al-Qaʿqāʿ hastened to take on al-Fīrzān and killed him, and al-Ḥāriṯ b. Ẓabyān hastened to take on al-Binduwān and killed him. Then the two groups fought until evening. The Persians lost many men. This day they did not fight on elephants, because their palanquins had been broken the day before and they were repairing them. That day al-Qaʿqāʿ fought 30 duels, in which he killed 30 cavalrymen, the last one being Buzurǧmihr al-Hamaḏānī. In the Day of Aġwāṯ the fighting continued until midnight and all the famous warriors of the Persians were killed. Abū Miḥǧan al-Ṯaqafī[675] suffered greatly that night. At midnight, the armies finally separated.

§ 266[676] On the morning of the third day both sides were in their positions. The Muslims had lost 2,000 men and the Persians 10,000. The Persians had repaired the palanquins of the elephants, and the fighting in the Day of ʿImās continued from early morning until evening. The Arabs and the Persians

671 Miskawayh, *Taǧārib al-umam*, 1:213–215 = C358–363; cf. al-Ṭabarī, *Taʾrīḫ*, 1:2304–2316 = trans., 12:96–106.

672 One of the generals of the wars of conquest, d. 18/639, see "Abū ʿUbayda ʿĀmir b. ʿAbdallāh b. al-Djarrāḥ," in *EI*², 1:158–159.

673 One of the generals of the wars of conquest, d. 37/657, see "Hāshim b. ʿUtba," in *EI*², 3:260.

674 One of the generals of the wars of conquest, see "al-Ḳaʿḳāʿ b. ʿAmr," in *EI*², 4:464.

675 Warrior and poet, see *GAS*, 2:300–302.

676 Miskawayh, *Taǧārib al-umam*, 1:216–219 = C366–372; cf. al-Ṭabarī, *Taʾrīḫ*, 1:2316–2326 = trans., 12:106–115.

فيه سواء ولا يكون بينهم لفظة إلا تعاورها الرجال بالأصوات حتى تبلغ يزدجرد. | وكان يبعث 192b إليهم بالنجدات ممن بقي عنده. وما كان عامة جُنَن المسلمين إلا براذع الرِحال قد أعرضوا فيها الجَريد ومن لم يكن له وقاية لرأسه عصَّبوا {رؤوسهم} بالأنْسَاع. وأبلي يومئذ قيس بن ميسرة بن المكشوح. وكان في قتل الفيلة أهوال حتى هلك من كان عليها. ثم تزاحفوا واجتلدوا بالسيوف حتى أمسوا واشتد القتال في الليل فسميت ليلة الهَرير. ثم لم يكن بعدها قتال بليل بالقادسية.

§267[١] وأصبحوا في اليوم الرابع وقد عبأ الفرس للزحف ثلاثة عشر صفا والناس حَسْرَى لم يغمضوا ليلتهم كلها. فصمد المسلمون لرستم فأزالوا لهرمزان والفيرزان فتأخرا وثبتا حيث انتهيا وقد انفرج القلب وركد عليهم النقع. ثم هبت ريح عاصف وهي دبور فقلعت طيارة رستم عن سريره فهرب ومال الغبار عليهم. فانتهى القعقاع إلى السرير وقد قام رستم حين طارت الريح بالطيارة إلى بغال قدمت عليه بمال فاستظل في ظل بغل وحِمْله. فقصده هلال بن عُلَّفة فولي رستم فاتبعه فرماه رستم فشك قدمه في الركاب فحمل عليه هلال فضربه ضربة نفحت مِسْكا. ومضى رستم فرمى بنفسه في العَتِيْق فاقتحمه هلال عليه فتناوله وقد عام وهلال قائم فأخذ برجله ثم خرج به وضرب

٢ الرِحال: وضع المقريزي رمز "ح" تحت الحرف الرابع إشارة إلى تلفظه بالحاء. ٣ رؤوسهم: "روسهم" في الأصل. ٨ وهي دبور: الزيادة بخط المقريزي في الهامش الأيسر من الأسفل إلى الأعلى + صح، ويشير إليها رمز ⌐ بعد "عاصف". ١٠ وحِمْله: وضع المقريزي فتحة فوق الحاء وكسرة تحتها. ١١ نفحت: وضع المقريزي رمز "ح" تحت الحرف الثالث إشارة إلى تلفظه بالحاء.

١ من تجارب الأمم لمسكويه ١: ٢٢١.

were equal, and whatever was said was carried on by the men from one to the other until it reached Yazdağird, who sent them reinforcements from the men he still had. Most Muslims were only shielding themselves with saddle cloths, on which they had put palm branches to protect themselves, and those who had no helmet wound around their head leather straps. Qays b. Hubayrah[677] b. al-Makšūḥ was afflicted on that day. Killing elephants was full of dangers until those who rode them had died. Then they marched against each other and fought with swords until evening. During the night the battle was fierce, and it was termed the Night of al-Harīr. After that, there was no nocturnal fighting at al-Qādisiyyah.

§ 267[678] On the morning of the fourth day the Persians had prepared thirteen battle lines. Men were exhausted, not having slept a wink during the whole night. The Muslims stood up against Rustam and forced Hurmuzān and al-Fīrzān[679] to retreat, and they fell behind but made a stand where they had retreated. The centre had been laid open, and dust covered them (the Persians). Then a strong westerly wind started blowing and tore down Rustam's sunshade (*ṭayyārah*) from his throne, and he fled. The dust turned to blow on their face. Al-Qaʿqāʿ reached the throne, from which Rustam had fled when the wind carried away his sunshade. Rustam had gone to the mules, which carried some property, and sought shade behind one of them and its litter. Hilāl b. ʿUllafah[680] came towards him, and Rustam fled, but Hilāl followed him. Rustam shot an arrow at him, and it broke his foot in the stirrup, but Hilāl then attacked him and struck a stroke that smelled of musk.[681] Rustam went on and threw himself in al-ʿAtīq, but Hilāl jumped in the river and caught him while he was swimming and Hilāl standing in the water. Hilāl took him by his foot and dragged him out and then hit his flanks

677 Both manuscripts have Maysarah, but Miskawayh and al-Ṭabarī read Hubayrah. For Qays b. Hubayrah, also called Qays b. al-Makšūḥ, see Friedmann (1992): 55, note 212.

678 Miskawayh, *Tağārib al-umam*, 1:221 = C375–376; cf. al-Ṭabarī, *Taʾrīḫ*, 1:2329, 2335–2337 = trans., 12:118, 122–124.

679 Miskawayh (ed. Caetani) has al-Binduwān, but the script is not quite clear.

680 See Blankinship (1993): 201, note 985.

681 This detail is somewhat odd in Miskawayh and al-Maqrīzī, who copies him. Usually, the scent of musk is associated with martyrs. The passage is somewhat difficult already in al-Ṭabarī (see Friedmann 1992: 124, note 414), but there musk may be something that gives away Rustam, who was hiding under the litter and had hitherto gone unnoticed by Hilāl, who stroke the ropes of the litter. A similar motif is found in § 291 about how Yazdağird was found.

جنبيه بالسيف حتى قتله. وجاء به حتى رمى به بين يدي رحله وأرجل البغال وأخذ سلبه. ثم صعد السرير ونادى: "قتلت رستم ورب الكعبة. إليَّ إلي." فأطافوا به وكبروا فانهزم الفرس.

§268[١] وقام الجالنوس ونادى أهل فارس إلى العبور وقد أسْفَر الغبار وذل المقترنُوْن فتوافوا العتيق فوخزهم المسلمون برماحهم. فما أفلت منهم أحد وهم ثلاثون ألفا. وأخذ ضرار بن الخطاب درفش كابيان فعوض منها ثلاثون ألفا وكانت قيمتها ألفي ألف ومائتي ألف. وجمعت الأسلاب والأموال فكان شيئا عظيما وخرج زُهْرة بن حَوِيَّة بن عبد الله بن قتادة بن مرثد بن معٰوية بن قَطَن بن مالك بن أرقم بن جُشَم بن الحٰرث الأعرج بن كعب بن سعد بن زيد مناة بن تميم في طلب الجالنوس حتى قتله.

§269[٢] وخرج القعقاع وشرحبيل في طلب من انهزم فقتلوهم في كل قرية وأَجَمةٍ وشاطئ نهر. ورجعوا فتوافوا عند صلاة الظهر وهنأ المسلمون بعضهم بعضا. وتدرع زهرة ما كان على | الجالنوس 193a فبلغ بضعة وسبعين ألفا. وأصاب الفرس من الذل بعدما انهزموا ما لم يصب أحدا قبلهم. لقد كان الرجل من المسلمين يدعو الفارس منهم وعليه السلاح التام فيأتيه حتى يقوم بين يديه فيضرب

١ رحله: وضع المقريزي رمز "ح" تحت الحرف الثاني إشارة إلى تلفظه بالحاء. ٦–٧ بن[٢] ... مناة: الزيادة بخط المقريزي في الهامش الأيسر من الأسفل إلى الأعلى، ويشير إليها رمز ⌐ بعد "حَوِيَّة". ١٠ المسلمون: وضع المقريزي ثلاث نقط تحت الحرف الرابع إشارة إلى تلفظه بالسين. ١٢ يدعو: "يدعوا" في الأصل.

٦ زُهْرة: أضاف المقريزي الحاشية التالية في الهامش الأيمن منكسة: "حـ (لـ "حاشية") زهرة بن حَوية (وضع المقريزي رمز "ح" تحت الحرف الأول إشارة إلى تلفظه بالحاء) بفتح الحاء المهملة وعِند ابن إسحٰق بجيم مضمومة. وفد على النبي صلى الله عليه وسلم وفده ملك هجر وشهد القادسية وقتل الجالنوس وبقي إلى أن قتله شبيب بن يزيد الخارجي وقيل قتل بالقادسية والأول أكثر."

١ من تجارب الأمم لمسكويه ١: ٢٢٢.

٢ القرآن، سورة إبراهيم، الآية ٤٤.

with his sword until he had killed him. Hilāl brought him out of the water and threw him between his saddle and the mules' feet and took his booty. Then he ascended the throne and shouted: "I have killed Rustam. To me, to me, by the Lord of the Kaaba!" The Muslims came around him and shouted "God is most great" and the Persians fled.

§ 268[682] Al-Ǧālnūs rose and called upon the Persians to cross the river. The dust had settled, and those chained together had been humbled. They all headed for al-ʿAtīq, the Muslims pricking them with their spears. None of them got away, and they had been 30,000! Ḍirār b. al-Ḫaṭṭāb[683] took the Kayanid banner and was given 30,000 for it, while its real value was 2,200,000. The booty and the money were collected, and amounted to enormous sums. Zuhrah b. Ḥawiyyah b. ʿAbd Allāh b. Qatādah b. Marṯad b. Muʿāwiyah b. Qaṭan b. Mālik b. Arqam b. Ǧušam b. al-Ḥāriṯ al-Aʿraǧ b. Kaʿb b. Saʿd b. Zayd-Manāt b. Tamīm went after al-Ǧālnūs and killed him.

§ 269[684] Al-Qaʿqāʿ and Šuraḥbīl went after those who had fled and killed them in villages, thickets, and river banks, coming back for midday prayers. The Muslims congratulated each other. Zuhrah put on what had been on al-Ǧālnūs, and the price reached over 70,000. After they fled, the Persians were so humiliated as no one before them had ever been. A Muslim might call one of their fully-armoured cavalrymen, and he would come to him and stand in front of him, and the Muslim would strike his head off and take his weapons, sometimes killing him with his own weapons. Among

---

12 Zuhrah … Ḥawiyyah : Zuhrah b. Ḥawiyyah—with an A after an Ḥ, but Ibn Isḥāq reads this with a U after a J. He went in an embassy sent by the king of Haǧar to the Prophet, may God honour him and grant him peace. He fought in the battle of al-Qādisiyyah, killed al-Ǧālnūs, and lived until he was killed by Šabīb b. Yazīd al-Ḫāriǧī or, according to others, he was killed at al-Qādisiyyah (marginal gloss in al-Maqrīzī's hand). This has been copied as a similar marginal note into MS T. Al-Maqrīzī uses such marginal notes rather sparingly, and the present may have been triggered by Miskawayh, *Taǧārib al-umam*, 1:225 = C383, who questions the identity of Zuhrah and his death at al-Qādisiyyah.

---

682 Miskawayh, *Taǧārib al-umam*, 1:222 = C377–378; cf. al-Ṭabarī, *Taʾrīḫ* 1:2337–2338, 2341 = trans., 12:124–125, 127–128.

683 Poet and chief of the clan of Muḥārib b. Fihr, see "Ḍirār b. al-Khaṭṭāb," *EI*², 2:317.

684 Miskawayh, *Taǧārib al-umam*, 1:222–225 = C378–382; cf. al-Ṭabarī, *Taʾrīḫ*, 1:2341, 2344–2346, 2358 = trans., 12:127, 130–132, 142.

عنقه ويأخذ سلاحه وربما قتله بسلاحه. وكان ممن هرب الهرمزان وقادن وأهوذ وكان ممن استقتل شهريار بن كنارا وابن الهربذ والفرخان وحسر سنوم. وباع هلال بن علفة سَلَب رستم وكان تخفف لما وقع في الماء بسبعين ألفا .وكانت قيمة قلنسوته مائة ألف لو ظفر بها. ثم بعث سَعْد بزُهرةَ بن حَويَّة إلى نهرشير فتلقاه شيرزاد بساباط بالصلح وتأدية الجزية. فبعث به إلى سَعْد وخرج هاشم. ثم خرج سعد في أثره وقد فَلّ زهرةُ كتيبةَ كسرى. وانتهى هاشم إلى مظلم ساباط فأتاه سعد وكانت به كتائب كسرى التي تدعى الأُسُوْد يحلفون بالله كل يوم: "لا يزول ملك فارس ما عشنا." ورئيسهم المُقَرَّط. فقتله هاشم وقرأ: "﴿أَوَلَمْ تَكُونُوا أَقْسَمْتُمْ مِّن قَبْلُ مَا لَكُم مِّن زَوَالٍ.﴾[١]"

§ 270[٢] ثم نزل نهرشير فأقاموا شهرين يقاتلون من هناك حتى غلبوهم. وقد رُمي زُهرةُ بن حَوية بسهم فمضى به وقتل بسيفه شهربراز من أهل إصطخر. ولما دخل المسلمون نهرشير وهي المدينة التي كان فيها منزل كسرى غربي المدائن وذلك بخمس سنين من ملك يزدجرد في صفر سنة ست عشرة من الهجرة لاح لهم الأبيض. فقال ضرار بن الخطاب: "الله أكبر. هذا ما وعد الله ورسوله أبيض كسرى والله." فتتابعوا بالتكبير حتى أصبحوا فوجدوا من المال في الخزائن مائة ألف ألف. ثم عبر سَعْد بالمسلمين دجلة بخيولهم عوما وهم يتحدثون في عومهم. وقد اقترنوا ما يكترثون كما يتحدثون في مسيرهم على الأرض فأعجلوا الفرس عن جمهور أموالهم.

---

٧ وقرأ ... زَوَالٍ: الزيادة بخط المقريزي في آخر السطر في الهامش الأيسر + صح. ٨-٩ رُمي ... به: كشط المقريزي عبارة أخرى قبل أن يصححها كما هي الآن. ٩-١١ وهي ... الهجرة: الزيادة بخط المقريزي في الهامش الأيمن من الأعلى إلى الأسفل وآخرها في الهامش الأسفل من الأسفل إلى الأعلى، ويشير إليها رمز ˺ بعد "نهرشير". ١٢ فوجدوا ... ألف ٢: الزيادة بخط المقريزي في الهامش الأيسر + صح، ويشير إليها رمز ˹ بعد "أصبحوا".

---

١ من تجارب الأمم لمسكويه ١: ٢٢٢-٢٢٥.

٢ من تجارب الأمم لمسكويه ١: ٢٢٥-٢٢٧.

those who ran away were al-Hurmuzān, Qāran,[685] and Ahwad, and among those who defied death were Šahriyār b. Kanārā, Ibn al-Hirbad, al-Farruḫān, and Ḫusraw-Šunūm.[686] Hilāl b. ʿUllafah sold for 70,000 what he had taken from Rustam, who had been lightly dressed when he fell into water, but the value of his headgear, had he got it, would have been 100,000. Then Saʿd sent Zuhrah b. Ḥawiyyah to Nahrašīr, and Šīrzād met him in Sābāṭ to agree on peaceful surrender and the paying of *ǧizyah*. He sent him to Saʿd. Hāšim set forth and then Saʿd after him. Zuhrah had vanquished a detachment of Kisrá, and Hāšim ended up in Muẓlim Sābāṭ, where Saʿd came to him. There was the detachment of Kisrá called the Lions, who swore every day by God: "The reign of the Persians will not end as long as we are alive." Their leader wore earrings, and Hāšim killed him and recited: "Did you not earlier swear that you would not cease"?[687]

§ 270[688] Then Saʿd[689] encamped at Nahrašīr, and they stayed there for two months, fighting from that base until they had vanquished their enemies. Zuhrah b. Ḥawiyyah was shot with an arrow, but he went on, killing with his sword Šahrbarāz from the people of Iṣṭaḫr. The Muslims entered Nahrašīr, which is the city in which Kisrá's abode was in the western al-Madāʾin, and this happened in the year 5 of Yazdağird's reign in Ṣafar, year 16 AH[/March 637], and the White Palace shone to them. Ḍirār b. al-Ḫaṭṭāb exclained: "God is most great! This is what God and His Messenger have promised us, Kisrá's White Palace, by God!" They joined him in shouting "God is most great!" until morning. They found property in the treasury worth 100,000,000. Then Saʿd crossed the Tigris with the Muslims and their horses by swimming,[690] talking while they were swimming, having yoked together what they considered important, just like they would have talked with each other travelling on dry land. They drove the Persians in haste from all their property.

---

685 In both manuscripts clearly Qādan.

686 Written ḪSR-SNWM, as in Miskawayh (ed. Caetani), but cf. al-Ṭabarī. The name is briefly discussed in Pourshariati (2008): 174, note 943.

687 Qurʾān (*Ibrāhīm*), 14:44.

688 Miskawayh, *Taǧārib al-umam*, 1:225–227 = C382–387.

689 Al-Maqrīzī does not mention Saʿd's name, but Miskawayh shows that this refers to him.

690 Miskawayh explains that they swam as they had not been able to procure a sufficient number of boats.

§ 271[1] وكان يزدجرد قدم عياله وما خف من ذخائره حين نزل المسلمون نهرشير إلى حلوان. فسَلِمَ المسلمون جميعهم في عبورهم الماء. فخرج يزدجرد إلى حلوان وأخرج ما قدر عليه من جوهر وآنية ذهب وفضة مع ولده ونسائه وحشمه. فكان مما خرج معه ألف طباخ وألف جوسان وألف فهاد وبازيار. وخلف مهرَان الرازي والنخيرجان بالنهروان. وخرجت الفرس بما قدرت عليه من أموالها ونسائها وذراريها. وتركوا من الثياب والأمتعة والآنية والعِطْر وما أعدوا للحصار من الأطعمة وغيرها ومن الحيوانات ما لا يدرى ما قيمته. فدخل المسلمون المدائن بغير مانع فأحاطوا | بالقصر 193b الأبيض حتى أخذوه وحَوَوا الغنائم. فوجد في بيوت الأموال ثلاثة آلاف ألف ألف.

§ 272[2] ونزل سَعْد القصر الأبيض واتخذ إيوان كسرى مصلى وقدم جيشا إلى النهروان. فتراجع أهل المدائن إليها بالأمان والرضا بالجزية. وأخذت خرزات كسرى ووشائحه التي كان يجلس فيها يوم المباهات وعليها من الجوهر ما لا تعرف قيمته. وأخذ تاج كسرى وفيه من الجوهر شيء عظيم وأخذت ثياب كسرى منسوجة بالذهب المنظوم بالجوهر. وأخذت أذراع كسرى ومغافره وساقاه وساعده وذرع هرقل وذرع سياوخش وذرع خاقان وذرع داهر وذرع بهرام شوبين وذرع النعمٰن بن المنذر. وأخذ سَفَط فيه فرس من ذهب مسرج بسرج من فضة على ثفره الياقوت والزمرد منظوما على الفضة ولجامه كذلك. وفارس من فضة مكلل بالجوهر. وناقة من فضة عليها شليل من ذهب وبطان من ذهب وزمام من ذهب كل ذلك منظوم بالجوهر. وعليها رجل من ذهب مكلل بالياقوت. كان كسرى يضعهما إلى أصطوانتي التاج. فإن تاجه لا يحمله إلا أصطوانتان.

٢–٤ وأخرج ... وبازيار: الزيادة بخط المقريزي في الهامش الأيسر وآخرها من الأسفل إلى الأعلى، ويشير إليها رمز ⌐ بعد "حلوان". ١٧ أصطوانتان: كتب المقريزي أول الكلمة فوق السطر وآخرها في الهامش الأيسر.

---

١ من تجارب الأمم لمسكويه ١: ٢٢٧–٢٢٨ ومن تأريخ سني الملوك لحمزة ص ٤٩.

٢ من تجارب الأمم لمسكويه ١: ٢٢٨–٢٢٩.

§ 271[691] When the Muslims encamped in Nahrašīr, Yazdağird had already sent to Ḥulwān his family and those of his treasures that were lightly carried. All Muslims got safely across the river, and Yazdağird went to Ḥulwān, taking with him all that he could of his jewels and gold and silver vessels, together with his children, women, and servants. Together with him, there went 1,000 cooks, 1,000 musicians (*gōsān*), and 1,000 cheetah and falcon masters. He left Mihrān al-Rāzī and al-Naḫīrğān in al-Nahrawān. The Persians fled with whatever they could take along of their property, women, and family, leaving behind clothes, wares, vessels, perfumes, and whatever food and provisions they had reserved for a siege, as well as animals, of an enormous value. The Muslims entered al-Madā'in without hindrance and laid siege on the White Palace until they seized it and got its booty. In the treasury, there was found 3,000,000,000 (dirhams).

§ 272[692] Saʿd encamped in the White Palace and made the *īwān* of Kisrá his praying place. He sent an army to al-Nahrawān. The people of al-Madā'in came there, asking indemnity and declaring their willingness to pay the *ğizyah*. He took Kisrá's beads and belts, which Kisrá had used to wear on days of pride. They had invaluable jewels. He also took Kisrá's crown, which had a great number of jewels, and Kisrá's clothes, woven with gold and embellished with jewels. He took Kisrá's armours and helmets, as well as his leg and arm armours, and the armours of Heraclius, Siyāwuḫš, the Ḫāqān, Dāhir, Bahrām Čūbīn, and al-Nuʿmān b. al-Munḏir.[693] Someone took a basket in which there was a golden horse with a silver saddle on the crupper of which there were rubies and emeralds, set in silver, with a similar bridle. Its rider was made of silver and crowned with jewels. They also found a silver camel with a golden saddle cloth and a golden girth and a golden nose rope, all encrusted with jewels. Riding on it there was a golden man, crowned with rubies, all used by Kisrá as props for his crown, since his crown could not be worn without props.

691 Miskawayh, *Tağārib al-umam*, 1:227–228 = C387–389; Ḥamzah, *Ta'rīḫ* 49 = trans. 76; cf. al-Ṭabarī, *Ta'rīḫ*, 1:2439 = trans., 13:20.

692 Miskawayh, *Tağārib al-umam*, 1:228–229 = C389–392; cf. al-Ṭabarī, *Ta'rīḫ*, 1:2446–2448 = trans., 13:26–28.

693 Dāhir, king of Sind (or Mukrān), later defeated by Muslims as narrated in the *Čač-nāmah*, see "*Čač-Nāma*," in *EI*², 13:162–163, and Juynboll (1989): 26, note 81. The others have already been mentioned by al- Maqrīzī. See also Christensen (1936): 499.

§ 273[1] وأخذوا بساط كسرى وهو ستون ذراعا في ستين ذراعا فيه طرُق كالصُوَر وفصوص كالأنهار وفي حافاته كالأرض المزروعة وعليه ما كانوا يُعِدُونَه في الشتاء إذا ذهبت الرياحين. فكانوا إذا أرادوا الشرب شربوا عليه فكأنهم في رياض لأن أرض البساط مُذهب ووشيه فصوص وعليه قضبان الذهب عليها الأنوار من ذهب وفضة وأوراق كذلك من حرير أجْري فيه ماء الذهب. فكانت العرب تسميه القُطْف. حمل إلى عمر رضي الله عنه فقطعه وقسمه. فأصاب علي بن أبي طالب رضي الله عنه قطعة باعها بعشرين ألفا وما هي بأجود تلك القطع. وحُمل إليه تاج كسرى وبزته وزَبْرَجه ومنطقته وسلاحه.

§ 274[2] ثم خرج هاشم إلى جلولا في اثني عشر ألفا وعلى مقدمته القعقاع وقد اجتمع الفرس هناك وخندقوا عليهم وقام بأمرهم مهران. ومضى يزدجرد إلى | حلوان ورماهم بالرجال وخلف فيهم 194a الأموال. فأحاط بهم هاشم وزاحفهم ثمانين زحفا كل ذلك يُنصر المسلمون فيه. ثم خرجوا واقتتلوا قتالا شديدا لم يقتتلوا مثله حتى أنفذوا النبل وقصفوا الرماح وصاروا إلى السيوف والطبرزينات. وصلى المسلمون إيماء وأتت النجدات لفارس. فحمل عليهم القعقاع بمن معه حملة منكرة فانهزموا.

١ من تجارب الأمم لمسكويه ١: ٢٣١.

٢ من تجارب الأمم لمسكويه ١: ٢٣٢-٢٣٣.

§ 273[694] They also took Kisrá's carpet, which was 60 cubits by 60. It had patterns like pictures and ring stones like rivers, and its fringes were like sown soil, and on it it had what they prepared for winter when the flowers were gone.[695] When they wanted to drink, they drank on it, as if they had been in a garden, as the ground of the carpet was golden and its embroidery ring stones, with golden branches with flowers of gold and silver and leaves alike of silk embellished with gold water. The Arabs used to call it *al-quṭf*.[696] It was carried to ʿUmar, may God be pleased with him, who cut it in pieces and distributed it (to the Muslims). ʿAlī b. Abī Ṭālib, may God be pleased with him, received a piece, which he sold for 20,000, and that was not even the best piece. The crown of Kisrá, his clothes, ornaments, belt, and weapons were all brought to ʿUmar.

§ 274[697] Then Hāšim went to Ǧalūlā[698] with 12,000 men, with al-Qaʿqāʿ leading the vanguard. The Persians had gathered there and dug trenches around them. They were led by Mihrān. Yazdaǧird went to Ḥulwān and provided them with men and left them money. Hāšim laid siege on them and attacked them eighty times, and in each the Muslims were victorious. Then the Persians came forth and fought fiercely, like they never had before, until they had used their arrows and broken their spears and started wielding their swords and axes. The Muslims prayed by signs (*īmāʾan*).[699] The Persians got reinforcements. Al-Qaʿqāʿ attacked them fiercely with the men he had,

694 Miskawayh, *Taǧārib al-umam*, 1:231 = C394–395; cf. al-Ṭabarī, *Taʾrīḫ*, 1:2452–2454 = trans., 13:32–34.

695 Here al-Maqrīzī follows Miskawayh, who actually combines two separate passages of al-Ṭabarī, *Taʾrīḫ*, 1:2452 and 1:2453. The description of the carpet ends in al-Ṭabarī with "its fringes were like sown soil." In al-Ṭabarī, the rest of al-Maqrīzī's and Miskawayh's sentence is no more related to the patterns of the carpet but refers to the carpet having been kept for winter when the flowers were gone.

696 Following the *Glossarium* to al-Ṭabarī (*Taʾrīḫ*, 14:cdxxix), Juynboll (1989): 32–33, vocalises this as *qiṭf*. The *Glossarium* explains this as "flores fructusque decerpti," from *qiṭf* "bunch of grapes," for which see Lane (1863–1893), 8:2991, s.v.

697 Miskawayh, *Taǧārib al-umam*, 1:232–233 = C396–399; cf. al-Ṭabarī, *Taʾrīḫ*, 1:2456–2463 = trans., 13:36–42.

698 The word is not very clear in the holograph, and the copyist of MS T seems first to have written XLWʾ (X = Ǧ, Ḥ, or Ḫ) and then added N above the *alif* to make it Ḥulwān.

699 I.e., they did not make the body movements usually required, but only indicated them by signs, which is permissible when for some reason, here the impending danger, normal prayer is not possible or safe to perform.

وتبعهم المسلمون فلم يفلت إلا من لا يُعد. وقتل منهم يومئذ زيادة على مائة ألف. فسار يزدجرد من حلوان نحو الجبل ومعه ألف بغل تحمل المال وألف باز وألف صناجة وثماني مائة فهد. فسيبت الفهود ثم البزاة وخلف الصناجات بمرو.

§275[1] وفي سنة سبع عشرة عبر العلاء بن الحضرمي البحر من البحرَيْن إلى فارس بغير إذن عمر رضي الله عنه ومعه الجارود بن المعلى وسوار بن همام وخليد بن المنذر بن ساوي في جنود كثيرة. فخرجوا في إصطخر وبإزائهم أهل فارس عليهم الهربذ. فحالوا بين المسلمين وبين سفنهم فقاتلهم المسلمون فقتل سوار والمنذر بن الجارود في جماعة وقتل من الفرس مقتلة لم يقتلوا مثلها وهزم باقيهم. وسار المسلمون يريدون البصرة فغرقت سفنهم ولم يجدوا إلى الرجوع سبيلا ووجدوا شهرك قد أخذ على المسلمين الطرق فعسكروا وأقاموا كذلك مع خليد بن المنذر. وبلغ عمر رضي الله ⟨عنه⟩ ما صنع العلاء بن الحضرمي فاشتد غضبه عليه وعزله وتوعده وأمره أن يلحق بسَعْد بن أبي وقاص ممن معه. فسار بهم إليه وندب عتبة بن غزوان الناس بأمر عمر رضي الله عنه.

٢-٣ ومعه ... بمرو: الزيادة بخط المقريزي في الهامش الأيمن من الأعلى إلى الأسفل + صح، ويشير إليها رمز ˥ بعد "الجبل". ٤ البحرَيْن: وضع المقريزي رمز "ح" تحت الحرف الرابع إشارة إلى تلفظه بالحاء. ٦ فحالوا: وضع المقريزي رمز "ح" تحت الحرف الثاني إشارة إلى تلفظه بالحاء. ٩ مع ... المنذر: الزيادة بخط المقريزي في الهامش الأيسر + صح، ويشير إليها رمز ˥ بعد "كذلك".

---

١١ عتبة ... غزوان: أضاف المقريزي الحاشية التالية على جزازة كانت ملصقة في الهامش الأيمن وهي موجودة الآن بين 193b و194a: "(193*a) عتبة بن غزوان بن جابر بن نُسَيب بن وهيب بن زيد بن مالك بن عبد بن عوف بن الحٰرث بن مازن بن منصور بن عكرمة بن خَصَفة (وضع المقريزي رمز "٢" بعد هذه الكلمة وكرره في الهامش ولكن لا توجد أي حاشية فيه) بن قيس بن عيلان بن مضر بن نزار بن معد بن عدنان المازني حليف بني نوفل بن عبد مناف بن قصي أبو عبد الله. وقيل: أبو غزوان أسلم سابع سبعة وهاجر إلى الحبشة ثم إلى المدينة. وهو الذي اختط البصرة في خلافة عمر سنة أربع عشرة بعد فتحه الأبلة. مات سنة سبع عشرة منصرفه من مكة إلى البصرة وهو بالربذة وقيل غير ذلك."

---

١ من تجارب الأمم لمسكويه ١: ٢٣٥-٢٣٦.

and they fled. The Muslims pursued them. Only an insignificant number of them escaped. That day more than 100,000 of them were killed. Yazdağird went from Ḥulwān towards al-Ǧabal with 1,000 mules carrying money, 1,000 falcons, 1,000 lute players, and 800 cheetahs. First the cheetahs and then the falcons were left behind, and finally the lute players were left behind in Marw.

§ 275[700] In the year 17, al-ʿAlāʾ b. al-Ḥaḍramī crossed the sea from Bahrain to Fārs without permission from ʿUmar, may God be pleased with him, with al-Ǧārūd b. al-Muʿallá,[701] Sawwār b. Hammām, Ḫulayd b. al-Munḏir b. Sāwī, and numerous armies. They headed for Iṣṭaḫr, coming face to face with Persians led by the *hērbad*. The Persians moved in between the Muslims and their ships, and the Muslims fought against them. Sawwār and al-Munḏir b. al-Ǧārūd and many others were killed. Of the Persians, more were killed than ever before. The rest of them were put to flight, and the Muslims marched towards Basra, but their ships had been sunk, so that they could not return. They found that Šahrak had occupied the roads against the Muslims, so they encamped and remained there with Ḫulayd b. al-Munḏir. ʿUmar, may God be pleased with him, heard what al-ʿAlāʾ b. al-Ḥaḍramī had done and grew furious and dismissed him, threatening him and telling him to join Saʿd b. Abī Waqqāṣ with the rest of his troops, so he marched to them. ʿUtbah b. Ġazwān sent some people by the order of ʿUmar, may God be pleased with him.[702]

20 ʿUtbah … Ġazwān : ʿUtbah b. Ġazwān b. Ǧābir b. Nusayb b. Wuhayb b. Zayd b. Mālik b. ʿAbd b. ʿAwf b. al-Ḥāriṯ b. Māzin b. Manṣūr b. ʿIkrimah b. Ḫaṣafah b. Qays b. ʿAylān b. Muḍar b. Nizār b. Maʿadd b. ʿAdnān al-Māzinī, the *ḥalīf* of Banū Nawfal b. ʿAbd Manāf b. Quṣayy Abū ʿAbd Allāh. It is also said Abū Ġazwān. He became a Muslim as the seventh of seven and made the *hiǧrah* first to Ethiopia and then to Medina. He is the one who designed Basra during the Caliphate of ʿUmar in the year 14 after having conquered al-Ubullah. He died in the year 17 in al-Rabḏah when returning from Mecca to Basra, but it is also told otherwise (marginal gloss in al-Maqrīzī's hand).

700 Miskawayh, *Taǧārib al-umam*, 1:235–236 = C403–405; cf. al-Ṭabarī, *Taʾrīḫ*, 1:2546–2548 = trans., 13:127–129.

701 For Ǧārūd b. ʿAmr b. Ḥanaš b. al-Muʿallá, see al-Ṭabarī, *Taʾrīḫ*, 1:1736 = trans., 9:94.

702 For ʿUtbah, see al-Ṣafadī, *Wāfī*, 20:8–9.

§276[1] فسار عاصم بن عمرو وعرفجة والأحنف بن قيس وسعد بن أبي العرجاء وصعصعة بن معْوية في اثني عشر ألفا على البغال يجنبون الخيل. وعليهم أبو سَبْرة بن أبي رُهم حتى التقى مع خليد بن المنذر بن ساوي وهو ومن معه حيث أخذ عليهم الطريق. وقد أتاهم الفرس من كل وجه وكورة فالتقوا هم وأبو سبرة واقتتلوا. فقتل الفرسُ وعليهم شهرك وغنم المسلمون ما معهم وعادوا إلى عتبة بالبصرة. وكان عتبة بن غزوان قد فتح الأهواز وقاتل فيها الهرمزان حتى ظفر بتستر بعد وقعات أسر في آخرها الهرمزان ملك الأهواز. وأعطى بيده على الرضا بحكم عمر بعدما قتل الهرمزان بيده البراء بن مالك ومجزأة بن ثور.

§277[2] | فسار به أنس بن مالك والأحنف بن قيس إلى المدينة. فلما دخلوها هيؤوا الهرمزان في 194b {هيئته} وعليه كسوته وتاجه فأسلم. وفرض له عمر في ألفين وأنزله بالمدينة وله معه حديث مذكور في السِيَر. ومضى يزدجرد بمشورة المؤْبذ إلى إصطخر فنزلها لأنها دار المملكة. وقدم سياه فانتخب من كل بلدة مقاتلة ومضى إلى السوس. فلما قدم عمار بن ياسر وأبو موسى الأشعري رضي الله عنهما يومئذ بتستر دعا سياه الرؤساء الذين خرجوا معه من إصبهان فقال لهم: "قد علمتم أنا كنا نتحدث أن هؤلاء القوم أهل الشقاء والبؤس سيغلبون على هذه المملكة وتروث دوابهم في أبواب إصطخر ومصانع الملوك ويشدون خيلهم بشجرها. وقد غلبوا على ما رأيتم وليس يلقون جندا إلا

٤ ما معهم : كشط المقريزي كلمة أخرى قبل أن يصحح العبارة كما هي الآن. ٥ وعادوا ... بالبصرة : الزيادة بخط المقريزي في الهامش الأيمن من الأعلى إلى الأسفل + صح، ويشير إليها رمز ⌝ بعد "معهم". ٦ ملك الأهواز : الزيادة بخط المقريزي في الهامش الأيسر + صح، ويشير إليها رمز ⌐ بعد "الهرمزان". ٩ هيئته : "هيته" في الأصل. ١١-١٢ الأشعري ... عنهما : الزيادة بخط المقريزي في آخر السطر في الهامش الأيسر من الأسفل إلى الأعلى + صح.

١ من تجارب الأمم لمسكويه ١: ٢٣٧.

٢ من تجارب الأمم لمسكويه ١: ٢٣٧، ٢٤٠-٢٤٢.

§ 276[703] ʿĀṣim b. ʿAmr, ʿArfağah,[704] al-Aḥnaf b. Qays,[705] Saʿd b. Abī l-ʿArğāʾ, and Ṣaʿṣaʿah b. Muʿāwiyah rode with 12,000 men on mules leading the horses on side, led by Abū Sabrah b. Abī Ruhm, until they met with Ḫulayd b. al-Munḏir b. Sāwī, who had been stuck with his men where the road had been closed to them. The Persians had come to them from every side and district, meeting Abū Sabrah in battle. The Muslims killed the Persians, led by Šahrak, and took as booty what they had, returning to ʿUtbah in Basra. ʿUtbah b. Ġazwān had conquered al-Ahwāz, fighting there against al-Hurmuzān, and he won in Tustar after several battles, in the last of which he took al-Hurmuzān, the king of al-Ahwāz, as prisoner. Following ʿUmar's instructions, he accepted his surrender, after al-Hurmuzān had killed with his hand al-Barāʾ b. Mālik and Mağzaʾah b. Ṯawr.

§ 277[706] Anas b. Mālik[707] and al-Aḥnaf b. Qays took al-Hurmuzān to Medina. When they arrived there, they clothed al-Hurmuzān in his own fashion, with his own clothes and his crown, and he converted to Islam. ʿUmar ordered for him (a stipend of) 2,000 and settled him in Medina. There is a story about them related in the books of *siyar*.[708] Yazdağird went to Iṣṭaḫr on the advice of the *mōbad* and stayed there, because it was his capital. Siyāh came and selected from every region soldiers and went to al-Sūs. When ʿAmmār b. Yāsir[709] and Abū Mūsá l-Ašʿarī,[710] may God be pleased with them both, arrived that day to Tustar, Siyāh called the chiefs, who had come forth from Isfahan with him, and said to them: "You know how we have been saying that these people, wretched and miserable though they are, will one day vanquish this kingdom, their mounts will drop dung at the gates of Iṣṭaḫr and the villages (*maṣāniʿ*) of the kings, and they will tie their horses at their trees. Now you can see what they have already conquered, and whenever they meet with an army, they vanquish it, and whenever they set against a

703 Miskawayh, *Tağārib al-umam*, 1:237 = C406–407; cf. al-Ṭabarī, *Taʾrīḫ*, 1:2548–2556 = trans., 13:129–136.
704 For ʿArfağah b. Harṯamah, see see Blankinship (1993): 199, note 974.
705 General and tribal leader, d. 67/686, see *EI*², s.v., 1:303–304.
706 Miskawayh, *Tağārib al umam*, 1:237, 240–242 = C407, 411–415; cf. al-Ṭabarī, *Taʾrīḫ*, 1:2557, 2561–2564 = trans., 13:137, 142–145.
707 Famous traditionist, d. between 91–93/709–711, see *EI*², s.v., 1:482.
708 Related, e.g., by Miskawayh and al-Ṭabarī, but omitted by al-Maqrīzī.
709 Companion of the Prophet and one-time governor of Kufa, d. 37/657, see *EI*², s.v., 1:448.
710 Companion of the Prophet, d. 42/662, see *EI*², s.v., 1:695–696.

فلوه ولا ينزلون بحصن إلا فتحوه. فانظروا لأنفسكم.“ قالوا: ”رأينا رأيك.“ قال: ”فليكفني كل منكم حشمه والمنقطعين إليه. فإني أرى أن ندخل في دينهم.“ ووجهوا شيرويه في عشرة من الأساورة إلى أبي موسى الأشعري رضي الله عنه فأخذوا لهم شروطا وقدموا عليه فأسلموا. ففرض لمائة منهم في ألفين ألفين ولستة منهم في ألفين وخمس مائة وهم سياه وخَسْرو وسماه مقلاص وشهريار وشيرويه وساروه وأفريذون. فمضى سياه وفتح حصنا بحيلة وفتح خَسرو حصنا. ونزل أبو سبرة بعد فراغه من السوس على جندي سابور حتى أخذها بعد أيام بأمان.

§ 278[1] ثم عقد عمر رضي الله عنه الألوية للأمراء والجنود من أهل الكوفة وأهل البصرة. فعقد للأحنف بن قيس على خراسان. وكان يزدجرد قد خرج من الجبل وصار إلى مرو. وكاتب الجيوش بالأطراف ممن بين الباب والسِنْد وخراسان وحلوان. فتحركوا وتكاتبوا وركِب بعضهم إلى بعض فأجمعوا أن يوافوا نهاوند ليبرموا فيها أمورهم. فتوافى إليها من بين حلوان ⟨وخراسان ومن بين الباب وحلوان ومن بين سجستان إلى حلوان⟩. فاجتمعت حَلَبة فارس والفهلوج وأهل الجبال وهم مائة وخمسون ألفا. ثم {تآمر} الرؤساء عند الفيرزان وكان عليهم وتعاهدوا وتعاقدوا على حرب المسلمين وكتبوا بذلك كتابا. فسار إليهم النعمٰن بن مقرن بالمسلمين واقتتلوا يومين. وفي الثالث حصرهم

---

٧ عنه: كتب المقريزي هذه الكلمة فوق السطر. ٩ وركِب: كشط المقريزي ما يلي الراء ثم صحح الكلمة كما هي الآن. ١٠-١١ وخراسان ... حلوان: الزيادة من تجارب الأمم لمسكويه ويقتضيها السياق. ١١ حَلَبة: وضع المقريزي رمز ”ح“ تحت الحرف الأول إشارة إلى تلفظه بالحاء. ١٢ تآمر: ”توامر“ في الأصل.

---

١٣ النعمٰن ... مقرن: أضاف المقريزي الحاشية التالية في الهامش الأعلى من الأسفل إلى الأعلى: ”النعمٰن ابن عمرو بن مُقَرّن بن عامر بن مِيْجا بن هجين بن نصر حُبْشِيَّة بن كعب بن عبد بن ثور بن عبد مناة بن أد بن طابخة بن إلياس بن مضر بن نزار بن معد بن عدنان أبو عمرو صاحب لواء مُزينة يوم فتح مكة. استشهد على نهاوند.“

---

١ من تجارب الأمم لمسكويه ١: ٢٤٢-٢٥١.

fortress, they conquer it. Now look after yourselves!" They replied: "We will follow your opinion." He said: "Let each of you protect me with his retinue and dependents. I think we should enter their religion." They sent Šīrūyah with ten of the cavalrymen to Abū Mūsá l-Aš'arī, may God be pleased with him. They made certain conditions, and then they came to him and converted to Islam. Abū Mūsā decreed (as stipends) for one hundred of them each 2,000 and for six of them 2,500. These six were Siyāh, Ḫusraw—whom Abū Mūsā renamed Miqlāṣ[711]—Šahriyār, Šīrūyah, Sārūh,[712] and Afrīdūn. Siyāh went and conquered a fortress by cunning, and Ḫusraw conquered another. After he was done with al-Sūs, Abū Sabrah encamped against Gundīsābūr and took it by indemnity after a few days.

§ 278[713] Then 'Umar, may God be pleased with him, tied flags[714] for commanders and troops from Kufa and Basra. He tied one for al-Aḥnaf b. Qays for Ḫurasan. Yazdağird had come forth from al-Ğabal and marched to Marw, writing letters to troops in different regions from al-Bāb, Sind, Ḫurāsān, and Ḥulwān, and these set on moving and exchanged further letters. Some rode to meet others, and they decided to gather at Nihāwand to set their affairs right there. People came there from between Ḥulwān (and Ḫurāsān, al-Bāb and Ḥulwān, and Siğistān and Ḥulwān).[715] The cavalry of the Persians, al-Fahlūğ, and the people of al-Ğibāl came there, altogether 150,000 men. The chiefs negotiated in the presence of al-Fīrzān, who led them, and they made mutual promises and oaths to fight against the Muslims, writing this down in a document. Al-Nu'mān b. Muqarrin led the Muslims against them, and they fought for two days. On the third day, the Muslims besieged them behind

---

23 Al-Nu'mān … Muqarrin : Al-Nu'mān b. 'Amr b. Muqarrin b. 'Āmir b. Mibğā b. Huğayn b. Naṣr b. Ḥubšiyyah b. Ka'b b. 'Abd b. Ṯawr b. 'Abd Manāt b. Udd b. Ṭābiḫah b. Ilyās b. Muḍar b. Nizār b. Ma'add b. 'Adnān Abū 'Amr, the flag carrier of Muzaynah on the day of the conquest of Mecca, who was martyred at Nihāwand (marginal gloss in al-Maqrīzī's hand).

---

711 Cf. above p. 14.

712 Miskawayh reads Sārūyah and al-Ṭabarī Šahrawayh.

713 Miskawayh, *Tağārib al-umam*, 1:242–251 = C415–431; cf. al-Ṭabarī, *Ta'rīḫ*, 1:2608–2626 = trans., 13:192–209.

714 I.e., sent them on expeditions.

715 The end of the sentence has accidentally been dropped by al-Maqrīzī and is here translated on the basis of Miskawayh.

المسلمون في | خنادقهم أياما ثم اقتتلوا قتالا شديدا لم يسمع بوقعة قط كانت أشد منها. قتلوا فيها 195a من الفرس فيما بين الزوال والعتمة ما طبق الأرض وزلق الناس في الدماء. وزلق بالنعمٰن بن مقرن فرسه فصُرع وأصيب رضي الله عنه. فأخذ الراية أخوه نعيم بن مقرن وأتى حذيفة بن اليمان بها وكان عهد إليه بعده فأخذ اللواء واقتتلوا. فلما أظلم الليل انكشف الفرس وأخذوا نحو اللهب فوقعوا فيه. فمات منهم فيه نحو مائة ألف وقتل في المعركة أعدادهم ولم يفلت إلا الشريد. ونجا الفيرزان نحو همذان فاتبعه نعيم بن مقرن والقعقاع قدامه فأخذه القعقاع أسِيْرا.

§279[1] ودخل المسلمون نهاوند واحتووا ما فيها وظفروا بذخيرة كسرى وهي سفطان فيهما اليواقيت واللؤلؤ. فأبيعت بأربعة آلاف ألف درهم وجاء دينار فصالح حذيفة عن ماه وفتح نعيم ابن مقرن همذان وسار إلى الري وبها سياوخش بن مهران بن بهرام شوبين. وقد استمد أهل دنباوند وطبرستان وقومس وجرجان فقاتلهم نعيم وقتل منهم مقتلة عظيمة وهزمهم وملك المدينة وما فيها وهو شيء عظيم جدا. وأخذ بكير بن عبد الله آذربيجان ودخل أهل دنباوند والخزر في الطاعة صلحا. وأخذ سويد بن مقرن قومس سلما وصالح رزبان صول ملك جرجان عما بيده وصالح أيضا الإصبهبذ. ومضى بكير بن عبد الله إلى الباب وعليه شهربراز الذي غزا الشام فدخل صلحا. وأخذت الجبال المطيفة بأرمينية وأخذت موقان وتفليس بغير مؤنة.

٦ أسِيْرا: الزيادة بخط المقريزي في آخر السطر في الهامش الأيسر. ١٠ نعيم: الزيادة بخط المقريزي في الهامش الأيسر + صح، ويشير إليها رمز ˥ بعد "فقاتلهم". ١١ الطاعة: الزيادة بخط المقريزي في آخر السطر في الهامش الأيسر.

١ من تجارب الأمم لمسكويه ١: ٢٥١-٢٥٦.

their trenches, and this continued for several days. They fought fiercely: one had never heard of a battle fiercer than this. Between sunset and the first third of the night, the Muslims killed so many Persians that their bodies covered the soil and people slipped in the blood. The horse of al-Nuʿmān b. Muqarrin slipped and fell down with him, and he died, may God be pleased with him. His brother, Nuʿaym b. Muqarrin[716] took the flag and brought it to Ḥuḏayfah b. al-Yamān,[717] who had been nominated to lead the army after al-Nuʿmān. Ḥuḏayfah took the flag, and they fought. When the night darkened, the Persians were uncovered and they started towards al-Lahab but fell into it, and about 100,000 of them died. A number of them were also killed on the battle field, and only a few managed to escape. Al-Fīrzān escaped towards Hamaḏān, and Nuʿaym b. Muqarrin and before him al-Qaʿqāʿ followed him. Al-Qaʿqāʿ took him prisoner.

§ 279[718] The Muslims entered Nihāwand and took possession of what was there. They seized the treasury of Kisrá, which consisted of two baskets of rubies and pearls, which were sold for 4,000,000 dirhams. Dīnār came and made a peace agreement with Ḥuḏayfah concerning Māh. Nuʿaym b. Muqarrin conquered Hamaḏān and marched to Rayy, where there was Siyāwuḫš b. Mihrān b. Bahrām Čūbīn, who had asked help from the people of Demavend, Tabaristan, Qūmis, and Ǧurǧān. Nuʿaym fought against them and killed a great number of them, putting them to flight and taking over the city and what was in there, which was a very great amount indeed. Bukayr b. ʿAbd Allāh[719] conquered Azerbaijan, and the people of Demavend and the Ḫazars submitted themselves to him by agreement. Suwayd b. Muqarrin[720] took Qūmis peacefully. Rūzbān Ṣūl, the king of Ǧurǧān made a peace agreement for the areas governed by him, as did also the *iṣbahbad*. Bukayr b. ʿAbd Allāh went on to al-Bāb, which was in the hands of Šahrbarāz, who had raided Syria, and entered there by agreement. Al-Ǧibāl, surrounding Armenia, was taken, as were Mūqān and Taflīs, without efforts.

716 For the brothers al-Nuʿmān, Nuʿaym, and Suwayd (§ 279), sons of Muqarrin, see Smith (1994): 3, note 14, and 5, note 26.

717 See Smith (1994): 6, note 30.

718 Miskawayh, *Taǧārib al-umam*, 1:251–256 = C432–442; cf. al-Ṭabarī, *Taʾrīḫ*, 1:2631–2632, 2654–2666 = trans., 13:215–217, 14:24–37.

719 Bukayr b. ʿAbd Allāh al-Layṯī, military commander, see Smith (1994): 3, note 17.

720 See § 278, note 716.

§280[1] وخرج عبد الرحمٰن بن ربيعة لغزو الترك حتى قطع الباب فغزا بلنجر وتعداها بمائتي فرسخ. ولما انتهى يزدجرد بعد جلولا إلى الري وعليها آبان جاذويه وثب عليه آبان فقال: "يآبان جاذويه تغدر بي." قال: "لا ولكنك تركت ملكك وصار في يد غيرك وأريد أن أكتتب على ما كان لي من شيء. وما أردت مِنْ غير ذلك." وأخذ خاتم يزدجرد وكتب الصكاك على الأدم وسجل السجلات بكل ما أعجبه ثم ختم عليها ورد الخاتم. فاستوحش منه يزدجرد وكرهه وخرج هاربا إلى إصبهان ومعه النار وأراد كِرْمان. ثم عزم على خراسان ليستمد الترك والصين. | فأتى مرو فنزلها {وبنى} 195b للنار بيتا واطمأن في نفسه. فلما فتح عبد الله بن عامر نيسابور وطوس ونسا وبلغ سرخس وعلى مقدمته الأحنف بن قيس لقيه الهياطلة وهم أهل هراة. فهزمهم الأحنف ومضى إلى طخارستان. فلما دنا من مرو الشاهجان خرج منها يزدجرد نحو مرو ونزل الأحنف مرو الشاهجان. كتب يزدجرد إلى خاقان من مرو الروذ يستمده وكتب إلى ملك الصُغْد يستمده فخرج رسولاه إليهما وكتب إلى ملك الصين يستعينه.

§281[2] وخرج الأحنف من مرو الشاهجان واستخلف عليها بعد ما أتته الأمداد يريد مرو الروذ. فخرج يزدجرد إلى بَلْخ ونزل الأحنف مرو الروذ. فسارت أمداد البصرة والكوفة إلى بلخ وتبعهم الأحنف فالتقى أهل الكوفة ويزدجرد ببلخ. فانهزم يزدجرد وتوجه في أهل فارس إلى النهر فعبر

---

٦ وبنى: "وبنا" في الأصل. ٧ عبد الله: وضع المقريزي فوق هذا الاسم رمز "ك" (ل "كذا") إشارة إلى شكه في صحة قراءته. || نيسابور: كشط المقريزي ما يلي السين ثم صحح الكلمة كما هي الآن بإطالة السين لملء البياض. ١٠ يستمده: وضع المقريزي ثلاث نقط تحت الحرف الثاني إشارة إلى تلفظه بالسين.

---

١ من تجارب الأمم لمسكويه ١: ٢٥٦–٢٥٧.

٢ من تجارب الأمم لمسكويه ١: ٢٥٧–٢٥٨.

§ 280[721] ʿAbd al-Raḥmān b. Rabīʿah[722] set out to raid the Turks until he was beyond al-Bāb. He raided Balanǧar and went beyond it for further 200 *farsaḫs*. After Ǧalūlā, when Yazdaǧird came to Rayy, which was governed by Ābān Ǧādūyah, Ābān rushed to him, and he asked: "O Ābān Ǧādūyah, do you betray me?" Ābān replied: "No, but you have abandoned your kingship, which is now in the hands of others. I only want to register what is mine. It is all I want." He took Yazdaǧird's signet ring and wrote documents on parchment, recorded records, and wrote there what he wanted, sealed the documents, and then returned the ring to Yazdaǧird.[723] Yazdaǧird was alienated from him, disliked him, and escaped to Isfahan with the sacred fire, wanting first to go to Kirmān, but then deciding on Ḫurāsān to ask help from the Turks and the Chinese. He came to Marw, settled there, and built a temple for the fire, and felt more relaxed. When ʿAbd Allāh b. ʿĀmir conquered Nīsābūr, Ṭūs, and Nasā and reached Saraḫs, with al-Aḥnaf b. Qays leading the vanguard, the Hephthalites met him. They were the people of Herat. Al-Aḥnaf put them to flight and marched to Tuḫāristān. When he was approaching Marw al-Šāhiǧān, Yazdaǧird left it and went towards Marw. Al-Aḥnaf encamped in Marw al-Šāhiǧān, and Yazdaǧird wrote from Marw al-Rūd to the Ḫāqān, asking for help. He also wrote to the king of the Sogdians, asking for his help, too. The two messengers went their ways, and Yazdaǧird also wrote to the king of China asking for his help.

§ 281[724] After he had received reinforcements al-Aḥnaf set out from Marw al-Šāhiǧān and left someone to govern it and headed for Marw al-Rūd. Yazdaǧird went to Balḫ, while al-Aḥnaf encamped in Marw al-Rūd. Reinforcements from Basra and Kufa arrived to Balḫ, and al-Aḥnaf followed them. The troops from Kufa and Yazdaǧird met in battle in Balḫ, and Yazdaǧird was put to flight. He and the Persians took themselves to the river and

721 Miskawayh, *Taǧārib al-umam*, 1:256–257 = C442–444; al-Ṭabarī, *Taʾrīḫ*, 1:2667, 2682–2683 = trans., 14:39, 51–54.

722 See Smith (1994): 5, note 24.

723 This is prone to remain rather unclear for a reader not familiar with the story. Al-Ṭabarī, *Taʾrīḫ*, 1:2681 = trans., 14:52, explains that Ābān later showed the list to Saʿd, who returned to him everything that belonged to him.

724 Miskawayh, *Taǧārib al-umam*, 1:257–258 = C444–447; cf. al-Ṭabarī, *Taʾrīḫ*, 1:2683–2688 = trans., 14:54–58.

وأخذ المسلمون بلخ. وبلغ رسولا يزدجرد خاقان وعارك ملك الصغد ولم يتهيأ لهما إنجاده حتى عبر إليهما النهر مهزوما. فأنجده خاقان وأقبل في الترك وحشر أهل فرغانة والصغد حتى خرج بهم إلى خراسان فعبر إلى بلخ ومعه يزدجرد. فتراجع المسلمون إلى الأحنف بمرو الروذ وخرج المشركون من بلخ حتى نزلوا على الأحنف مرو الروذ. فارتحل الأحنف بمن معه وأسندوا إلى الجبل فجعلوه في ظهورهم. وصار النهر بينهم وبين العدو وهم في عشرة آلاف فقاتلوهم ما شاء الله فكانوا يغادونهم ويراوحونهم ويتنحون عنهم بالليل.

§ 282[1] فلما طال مقامهم قال خاقان: "قد طال مقامنا وأصيب قومنا. ما لنا في قتال هؤلاء القوم من خير. انصرفوا بنا." ورحل ليلا يريد بلخ. وقد كان يزدجرد خرج إلى مرو الشاهجان وحصر حارثة بن النعمن[1] خليفة الأحنف واستخرج خزائنه من موضعها وخاقان ببلخ ينتظره مقيم له. ولما جمع يزدجرد ما وضع بمرو وكان أمرا عظيما من خزائن أهل فارس ليلحق بخاقان قال له أهل فارس: "ما تريد أن تصنع؟" قال: "أريد اللحاق بخاقان فأكون معه أو بالصين." فقالوا له: "هذا رأي سَوء. إنك إنما تأتي قوما في مملكتهم وتدع أرضك وقومك. ولكن ارجع بنا إلى هؤلاء القوم فتصالحهم فإنهم أوفياء وأهل دين | وهم يلون بلادنا. وإن عدوا يلينا في بلادنا أحب إلينا من عدو 196a
يلينا في بلاده لا دين لهم ولا ندري ما وفاؤهم." فأبَى عليهم وأبوا عليه. قالوا: "فدع خزائننا نردها إلى بلادنا ومن يليها. لا تخرجها من بلادنا إلى غيرها." فأبى فقالوا: "فإنا لا ندعك." واعتزلوا عنه وتركوه في حاشيته.

١ المسلمون: وضع المقريزي ثلاث نقط تحت الحرف الرابع إشارة إلى تلفظه بالسين.

١ من تجارب الأمم لمسكويه ١: ٢٥٩-٢٦٠.

crossed it, and the Muslims captured Balḫ. Meanwhile, Yazdağird's messengers had reached the Ḫāqān and ʿĀrik,[725] the king of the Sogdians, but these were unable to help him before he had crossed the river to them, fleeing. The Ḫāqān then helped him, approaching with the Turks and collecting people from Farġānah and Sogdiana. With these troops he came to Ḫurāsān and crossed the river to Balḫ with Yazdağird. The Muslims retreated to al-Aḥnaf in Marw al-Rūd. The polytheists marched from Balḫ and encamped against al-Aḥnaf at Marw al-Rūd. Al-Aḥnaf took his troops and put the mountain behind their backs so that the river was between them and their enemies. They were 10,000 men and they fought against the enemy God knows how long. They attacked them in the morning and the evening and only retreated by night.

§ 282[726] When the Turks had stayed there long, the Ḫāqān said: "We have stayed here long, and our people have suffered losses. There is no good fighting these people. Withdraw with us." He left by night towards Balḫ. Yazdağird had gone to Marw al-Šāhiğān and besieged Ḥāriṯah b. al-Nuʿmān,[727] the second in command to al-Aḥnaf. Yazdağird took out his treasuries from where they were, while the Ḫāqān was staying in Balḫ, waiting for him. When Yazdağird had collected what he had left in Marw, which was a large part of the treasures of the people of Fārs, and was prepared to join the Ḫāqān, the people of Fārs asked him: "What are you doing?" He replied: "I want to join the Ḫāqān to be either with him or in China." They said to him: "This is a bad plan! You go to a people in their kingdom and leave your own country and your own people. Return instead with us to these people and we will make a peace agreement with them. They are reliable and religious. Even though they govern our country, we like it better being governed by an enemy in our own country than by an enemy in his country, an enemy that has no religion and about whom we do not know whether they are reliable or not." Yazdağird refused to do so, but they also refused to let him go and said: "Leave then our treasures for us to take back to our country and those who govern it and do not carry it from our country to another country." When Yazdağird refused to do so, they said that they would not allow this, retreated from him and left him with only his retinue.

725 So also in Miskawayh, but read Ġūrak, cf. Smith (1994): 56, note 271.

726 Miskawayh, *Tağārib al-umam*, 1:259–260 = C448–450; cf. al-Ṭabarī, *Taʾrīḫ*, 1:2688–2689 = trans., 14:58–59.

727 Al-Maqrīzī follows Miskawayh, but in al-Ṭabarī, *Taʾrīḫ*, 1:2684 = trans., 14:54, this person is called Ḥātim b. al-Nuʿmān, on whom see Smith (1994): 54, note 260.

§283[١] ثم قاتلوه وهزموه وأخذوا الخزائن وكتبوا إلى الأحنف بالخبر. فاعترض المسلمون وأهل فارس يزدجرد بمرو فقاتلوه وأعجلوه عن الأثقال. فمضى حتى قطع النهر إلى فرغانة والترك فلم يزل مقيما زمان عمر كله يكاتبهم ويكاتبونه إلى زمان عثمٰن. وأقبل أهل فارس إلى الأحنف فصالحوه وعاقدوه ودفعوا إليه تلك الخزائن والأموال. وتراجعوا إلى بلدانهم وأموالهم على أفضل ما كانوا في زمان الأكاسرة. فكانوا كأنما هم في ملكهم إلا أن المسلمين أوفى لهم وأعدل عليهم. فلما سمع خاقان بما لقي يزدجرد عبر من بلخ النهر. فدخل الأحنف بلخ وعبر مع خاقان النهر حاشية آل كسرى الذين مع يزدجرد. فلقوا رسول يزدجرد الذي بعث به إلى ملك الصين ومعه هدية وجواب كتابه من ملك الصين. فسألوه عما وراءه فقال: "لما قدمت عليه بالكتاب والهدايا كافأنا بما ترون." وأراهم هديته وجوابه عن كتاب يزدجرد إليه.

§284[٢] وقال: وكان قال لي: "قد علمتُ أن حقا على الملوك إنجاد الملوك على من غلبهم. فصف لي صفة هؤلاء القوم الذين أخرجوكم من بلادكم. فإني أراك تذكر قلة منهم وكثرة منكم ولا يبلغ أمثال هؤلاء القليل الذين تصف معكم معما أسمع من كثرتكم إلا بخير عندهم وشر عندكم." فقلت: "سلني عما أحببت أخبرك." قال: "أيوفون بالعهد؟" قلت: "نعم." قال: "وما يقولون لكم قبل أن

٧ الذين مع: الزيادة بخط المقريزي في الهامش الأيسر من الأعلى إلى الأسفل + صح، ويشير إليها رمز ⌐ بعد "كسرى".

١ من تجارب الأمم لمسكويه ١: ٢٦٠.

٢ من تجارب الأمم لمسكويه ١: ٢٦٠–٢٦١.

§ 283[728] Then they (the Persians) fought against him (Yazdağird) and put him to flight, taking the treasuries and writing to al-Aḥnaf about what had happened. The Muslims and the people of Fārs offered battle to Yazdağird in Marw. They fought against him and forced him to retreat quickly, leaving the heavy baggage behind. Yazdağird crossed the river over to Farġānah and the Turks. For the rest of the reign of ʿUmar he remained there, writing letters to them (the Persians) and receiving their answers until the time of ʿUṯmān.[729] The people of Fārs came to al-Aḥnaf and made peace with him and made an agreement with him. They gave him the treasuries and the money and returned to their countries and their own properties, enjoying better conditions than they had had during the time of the Kisrás. They felt as if they were still living in their own kingdom, except that the Muslims were more trustworthy and just to them (than their earlier rulers). When the Ḫāqān heard what had happened to Yazdağird, he crossed the river from Balḫ, and al-Aḥnaf entered Balḫ. Together with the Ḫāqān the retinue of Kisrá's family, who were with Yazdağird, crossed the river, too. There they met with Yazdağird's messenger whom he had sent to the king of China. He had with him presents and an answer to Yazdağird's letter by the king of China. They asked him about his trip, and he said: "When I brought him the letter and the presents, he reciprocated by what you see." He showed them the presents and the reply to Yazdağird's letter.

§ 284[730] The messenger told them that the king had said to him: "I know that it is the responsibility of kings to help other kings against those who have vanquished them. Now describe to me this people, who have driven you from your country. I notice that you mention that they are few while you are many. Such few people, as you describe them to be, would not get the better of you with what I hear from your numbers except by some good they have and some bad you have." I said: "Ask me what you want, and I will tell you." He asked: "Do they hold their pact?" I said they do, and he continued: "What do they say to you before they start fighting against you?" I replied: "They call

728 Miskawayh, *Tağārib al-umam*, 1:260 = C450–451; cf. al-Ṭabarī, *Taʾrīḫ*, 1:2689–2691 = trans., 14:59–61.

729 Al-Ṭabarī also implies that the people of Ḫurasan rebelled during the time of ʿUṯmān due to this correspondence.

730 Miskawayh, *Tağārib al-umam*, 1:260–261 = C451–452; cf. al-Ṭabarī, *Taʾrīḫ*, 1:2691 = trans., 14:61. For a similar discussion between Abū Sufyān and Heraclius, see El Cheikh (2004): 48–50.

يقاتلوكم؟" قلت: "يدعوننا إلى واحدة من ثلاث. إما دينهم فإن أجبناهم أجرونا مجراهم أو الجزية والمنعة والمنابذة." قال: "فكيف طاعتهم أمراءهم؟" قلت: "أطوع قوم لمرشدهم." قال: "فما يحلون وما يحرمون؟" فأخبرته. قال: "أفيحلون ما حرم عليهم أو يحرمون ما حلل لهم؟" قلت: "لا." قال: "فإن هؤلاء القوم لا يهلكون أبدا حتى يبدِّلوا."

[1]285 § ثم قال: "أخبرني عن لباسهم." فأخبرته. "وعن مطاياهم؟" فقلت: "الخيل العِراب." | 196b ووصفتها فقال: "نعْمت الحصون هذه." ووصفت له الإبل وبروكها وانبعاثها بحملها فقال: "هذه صفة دواب طوال الأعناق." وكتب معه إلى يزدجرد: "إنه لم يمنعني أن أبعث إليك بجيش أوله بمرو وآخره بالصين الجهالة بما يحق علي ولكن هؤلاء القوم الذين وصف لي رسولك صفتهم لو يحاولون الجبال لهدوها ولو خُلي سِرْبُهم أزالوني ما داموا على ما وصف. فسالمهم وارض منهم بالمساكنة ولا تهجهم ما لم يهيِّجوك."

[2]286 § وأقام يزدجرد وآل كسرى بفرغانة معهم عهد من خاقان. ثم كان مقتل يزدجرد. وذلك أنه لما وقع إلى أرض فارس بقي سنين. ثم أتى كرمان فأقام بها مثل ذلك. فطلب دهقان كرمان شيئا فلم يجبه فطرده عن بلاده. ثم أجمع أن ينزل خراسان. فأتى سجستان فأقام بها ثم سار إلى

١ من تجارب الأمم لمسكويه ١: ٢٦١.

٢ من تجارب الأمم لمسكويه ١: ٢٦١، ٢٦٩.

us to one of three: either to join them in their religion, in which case they will treat us like they do themselves, or to pay the *ǧizyah* and be protected, or to fight." Then he asked how obedient they are to their commanders, and I said: "They are the most obedient people towards their master." He asked: "What do they proclaim licit and what do they forbid?" I told him, and he asked: "Do they proclaim licit what has been forbidden to them and do they forbid what has been proclaimed licit to them?" I told him that they do not do so. Then he said: "Such people will never perish until they change!"

§ 285[731] Then the king said: "Tell me how they dress themselves." I told him. "And their mounts?"[732] I told him they rode thoroughbred horses and described these to him. He said that they were excellent fortresses.[733] Then I described camels to him, how they kneel down and how they set out with their burdens, and he said: "This describes long-necked mounts." The king of China sent with him a letter to Yazdaǧird: "I am hindered from sending you an army, the first part of which would be in Marw while the last was still in China, not because I were ignorant of my responsibility, but because these people, who your messenger has described to me, would be able to demolish mountains if they tried, and if their way were left open they could destroy me, as long as they remain like I have been informed. Make peace with them and be satisfied with living side by side with them. Do not stir them up as long as they don't stir you up."

§ 286[734] Yazdaǧird and the family of Kisrá stayed in Farġānah, in agreement with the Ḫāqān. Then Yazdaǧird was killed. This happened as follows: When he came to the land of Fārs, he remained there for years. Then he went to Kirmān and stayed there for years, too. The *dihqān* of Kirmān asked for something, but Yazdaǧird did not acquiesce, so the *dihqān* drove him out of his country. Then Yazdaǧird decided to settle in Ḫurāsān. He came to Siǧistān and stayed there for a while. Then he went to Marw, taking with

731 Miskawayh, *Taǧārib al-umam*, 1:261 = C452; cf. al-Ṭabarī, *Taʾrīḫ*, 1:2691–2692 = trans., 14:61–62.

732 Already in al-Ṭabarī and Miskawayh this comes without any introductory formula, such as "and he asked me."

733 Smith (1994): 61, translates *al-ḥuṣūn* as horses, but the usual plural of *ḥiṣān* "stallion" is *ḥuṣun* or *aḥṣina*. Even though *ḥuṣūn* is a rare plural of *ḥiṣān*, I take it here in its usual sense as the plural of *ḥiṣn* "fortress." Metaphorically, of course, the king is speaking of horses, not fortresses.

734 Miskawayh, *Taǧārib al-umam*, 1:261, 269 = C453, 465–466; cf. al-Ṭabarī, *Taʾrīḫ*, 1:2692, 2876–2877 = trans., 14:68; 15:82–83.

مرو ومعه الرهن من أولاد الدهاقين ومعه من رؤسائهم فرُّخْزاذ بن خرهرمز أخو رستم صاحب القادسية ومعه أيضا ماهُويه. فلما قدم مرو واستغاث منها بالملوك وكتب إليهم يستمدهم مثل ملك الصين وملك فرغانة وملك كابل وملك الخزَر. وكان الدهقان بمرو ماهويه وكان له ابن يسمى ترار. فوكل ماهويه ابنه ترار بمدينة مرو وتقدم إليه وإلى أهل المدينة ألا يفتحوا الباب ليزدجرد. وقال لهم: "ليس هذا لكم بملك لأنه قد سلم بلاده وجاء كم مفلولا مجروحا. ومرو لا تحتمل ما تحتمل غيرها من الكور. فإذا جئتكم غدا مع يزدجرد فلا تفتحوا الباب."

§ 287[1] فلما أتاهم فعلوا ذلك وانصرف فرخزاذ فجثا بين يدي يزدجرد وقال: "اسْتَعْصَت عليك مرو وهذه العرب قد أتتك." قال: "فما الرأي؟" قال: "أن تلحق ببلاد الترك فتقيم بها حتى يتبين لنا أمر العرب. فإنهم لا يَدعُون بلدة إلا دخلوها." قال: "لست أفعل ولكن أرجع عودي على بدئي." فعصاه ولم يقبل رأيه. فساريزدجرد وأجمع على صرف الدهقنة عن ابنه ترار إلى صنحان ابن أخيه. فبلغ ذلك ماهويه وهو أبو ترار فعمل في هلاك يزدجرد. وكتب إلى نيزك طرخان يخبره أن يزدجرد وقع إليه مفلولا. ودعاه إلى القدوم عليه لتكون أيديهما معا في أخذه | والاستيثاق منه فيقتلوه أو 197a يصالحوا عليه العرب.

١ فرُّخْزاذ : كشط المقريزي "و" بعد هذه الكلمة وزاد النص الذي يلي في الهامش. ١–٢ بن ... أيضا : الزيادة بخط المقريزي في الهامش الأيسر من الأسفل إلى الأعلى + صح، ويشير إليها رمز ¬ بعد "فرُّخْزاذ".

١ من تجارب الأمم لمسكويه ١: ٢٦٩.

him the hostages from among the children of the *dihqāns*. Of their leaders, he had with him Farruḫzād b. Ḫar-Hurmuz, brother of Rustam, the general at al-Qādisiyyah. Māhūyah was also with him.[735] When he came to Marw, he asked for help from other kings and sent to them asking for support, like the king of China, the king of Farġānah, the king of Kābul, and the king of the Ḫazars. The *dihqān* of Marw was Māhūyah, and he had a son called Barāz.[736] Māhūyah had given the city of Marw in his son's custody and told him and the people of the city not to open the gate to Yazdağird, saying to them: "This one is no more your king because he has given his country away and comes to you fleeing and wounded. Let not Marw suffer what some other districts have suffered. When I bring you tomorrow Yazdağird, do not open the gate!"

§ 287[737] When he came to them they did so. Farruḫzād turned away, knelt in front of Yazdağird and said: "Marw has become insubordinate[738] to you, and these Arabs are closing by." Yazdağird asked him what should be done, and he replied: "You should go to the land of the Turks and stay there until we know what happens to the Arabs. They do not let any country in peace, but invade them all." Yazdağird said: "I will not do so, but I will return to the beginning." Yazdağird did not obey him nor did he accept his opinion. He went and decided to move the *dihqānate* from Māhūyah's son Barāz to his nephew Sanğān.[739] Māhūyah, the father of Barāz, heard about this and plotted to bring Yazdağird down. He wrote to Nīzak Ṭarḫān, telling him that Yazdağird had come to him defeated and asking him to come to him, so that their hands would be united in capturing and securing him and they could either kill him or use him to negotiate a peace agreement with the Arabs.

735 There is a *wa-* before Māhūyah that has been scratched off, and *ibn Ḫar-Hurmuz* (…) *maʿahu ayḍan* has been written in the margin. Thus, al-Maqrīzī had originally written *wa-maʿahu min ruʾasāʾihim Farruḫzād wa-Māhūyah*. The latter is also implicitly given as accompanying Yazdağird in al-Ṭabarī, who tells the details of the story. This is not quite clear in Miskawayh, so it is possible that al-Maqrīzī has, after a long break, actually used al-Ṭabari here.

736 Al-Maqrīzī consistently writes TR'R, but cf. al-Ṭabarī. Miskawayh (ed. Caetani) leaves the name consistently without diacritics, obviously being at a loss as to how to read it.

737 Miskawayh, *Tağārib al-umam*, 1:269 = C466–467; cf. al-Ṭabarī, *Taʾrīḫ*, 1:2877–2878 = trans., 15:83–84.

738 Al-Ṭabarī reads *iṣtaṣʿabat*, which al-Maqrīzī has misread as *istaʿṣat*, probably due to the unclear writing in Miskawayh (ed. Caetani), where the B of *iṣtaṣʿabat* is almost illegible. *Istaʿṣat* is the only word in the sentence that has been vocalised, which shows that al-Maqrīzī did give it some attention.

739 Al-Maqrīzī consistently writes Ṣanḥān or Sanḥān.

§288[1] وجعل له في كل يوم ألف درهم وسأله أن يكتب إلى يزدجرد مما كرا له لينحي عامة جنده ويحصل في طائفة من خواصه فيكون أضعف لركنه وأهون لشوكته. وقال: "تعلمه في كتابك إليه الذي عزمت عليه من مناصحته ومعونته على العرب وأن يشتق لك اسْما من أسماء أهل الدرجات بكتاب مختوم بالذهب. وتعلمه أنك لست قادما عليه حتى ينحِي عنه فرخزاذ." فكتب نيزك بذلك إلى يزدجرد. فلما ورد عليه كتابه بعث إلى عظماء مرو فاستشارهم. فقال له صنحان: "لست أرى أن تنحي عنك جندك ولا فرخزاذ." وقال أبو ترار: "بلى أرى أن تبالغه نيزك وتجيبه إلى ما سأل." فقبل رأيه وفرق جنده وأمر فرخزاذ أن يأتي أجمة سرخس. فصرخ فرخزاذ وشق جيبه وتناول عمودا بين يديه يريد ضرب ترار به وقال: "يا قتلة الملوك. قتلتم ملكين وأظنكم قاتلي هذا." ولم يبرح فرخزاذ حتى كتب له يزدجرد كتابا بخطه نسخته:

§289[2] "هذا كتاب لفرخزاذ. إنك قد أسلمت يزدجرد وأهله وولده وحاشيته وما معه إلى ماهويه دهقان مرو وأشهد عليه بذلك." فأقبل نيزك إلى موضع من مرو يقال له جُلَنْبذان. فلما أجمع يزدجرد

١ من تجارب الأمم لمسكويه ١: ٢٦٩-٢٧٠ ومن تأريخ الطبري ١: ٢٨٧٨-٢٨٧٩.

٢ من تجارب الأمم لمسكويه ١: ٢٧٠.

§ 288[740] Māhūyah settled for Nīzak 1,000 dirhams a day and asked him to write to Yazdağird, deceiving him so as to make him send away the main part of his army and to retain only a small number of men of his special entourage. So he would be weaker and less dangerous. Māhūyah also said: "You should let him know in your letter that you have decided to help him against the Arabs and that he should give you a title suitable to men of rank in a letter sealed with gold. Let him also know that you will not come to him until he has sent Farruḫzād away." Nīzak wrote so to Yazdağird. When the letter arrived, Yazdağird sent for the noblemen of Marw and asked for their advice. Ṣanğān said to him: "I don't think you should send away either your army or Farruḫzād." The father of Barāz said: "Nay, I think that you should make a contract with Nīzak[741] and consent to what he asks." Yazdağird followed this opinion, dispersed his army, and told Farruḫzād[742] to go to the thickets of Saraḫs. Farruḫzād cried out loud and tore his shirt, reaching for a mace in front of him to smash Barāz with it, saying: "You killers of kings, you have already killed two kings, and I believe you are now going to kill this one, too!" Farruḫzād did not stop until Yazdağird wrote him a letter in his own hand. This is its text:

§ 289[743] "This is a letter to Farruḫzād. You have now handed over Yazdağird with his family, children, entourage, and what he had with him, to Māhūyah, the *dihqān* of Marw. I bear witness to this." Nīzak went to a place in Marw called Ğulanbadān.[744] When Yazdağird decided to meet him there, the fa-

740 Miskawayh, *Tağārib al-umam*, 1:269–270 = C467–468; al-Ṭabarī, *Ta'rīḫ*, 1:2878–2879 = trans., 15:84.

741 Reading *tubāyi'ahu ya'nī Nīzak*. The holograph is somewhat unclear, but seems to read *tubāliğahu Nīzak*. In Miskawayh (ed. Caetani), the word is half erased.

742 In Miskawayh (ed. Caetani) (C468) the first line begins with a blank before *atá ağamat Saraḫs*. Al-Maqrīzī has either added the name by guesswork or has used al-Ṭabarī to check it.

743 Miskawayh, *Tağārib al-umam*, 1:270 = C468–469; cf. al-Ṭabarī, *Ta'rīḫ*, 1:2879 = trans., 15:85–86.

744 The real form of the name evades me, as it did Humphreys (1990): 85, and the editors of Miskawayh (ed. Ḥasan, 1:270, ed. Imāmī, 1:424, note 3), who print the word with an initial Ḥ.

على لقائه والمسير إليه أشار عليه أبو ترار ألا يلقاه في السلاح فيرتاب به وينفر عنه ولكن يلقاه بالملاهي والمزامير. ففعل وسار إليه كذلك وتأخر عنه أبو ترار وكردس نيزك أصحابه كراديس. فلما تدانيا استقبله نيزك ماشيا ويزدجرد على فرس له. فأمر لنيزك بجنيبة من جنائبه فركبها. فلما توسط عسكره قال له نيزك: "زوجني إحدى بناتك لأناصحك فأقاتل معك عدوك." فقال له يزدجرد: "أعلي تجترئ يا كلب." فعلاه نيزك بمخفقته فصاح يزدجرد: "غدر الغادر." وركض منهزما. ووضع أصحاب نيزك سيوفهم فيهم فأكثروا القتل.

§290[1] وانتهى يزدجرد في هزيمته إلى مكان من أرض مرو. فنزل عن فرسه ودخل بيت طحان فمكث فيه ثلاثة أيام. فقال له الطحان: "أيها الشقي اخرج فاطعم شيئا فإنك جائع منذ ثلاث." قال: "لست أصل إلى ذلك إلا بزمزمة." وكان رجل من زمازمة مرو قريبا منه. | فأتاه الطحان وسأله 197b
أن يزمزم عليه ليأكل ففعل ذلك. فلما انصرف إلى مرو سمع أبا ترار يذكر يزدجرد ويطلبه فأتاه فسأله وأصحابه عن حليته فوصفوه. فأخبرهم أنه رآه في بيت طحان وهو رجل جعد مقرون حسن الثنايا مُقَرط مُسَوَّر.

---

١ من تجارب الأمم لمسكويه ١: ٢٧٠–٢٧١.

ther of Barāz suggested that he[745] should not meet him armed, so as not to make him suspicious and cause him to shy away, but that he should meet him with musical instruments and pipes, and he did so. He came to him like this, and the father of Barāz lagged a bit behind. Nīzak divided his companions to squadrons. When they drew near to each other, Nīzak came on foot while Yazdağird was riding a horse. Yazdağird gave orders to give a spare horse to Nīzak, and Nīzak mounted it. When they were in the middle of his camp, Nīzak said to Yazdağird: "Give a daughter of yours to me in marriage and I will fight by your side against your enemy." Yazdağird replied to him: "You dog, are you becoming bold with me!" Nīzak attacked him with his whip. Yazdağird shouted: "He has deceived me!" Yazdağird rode fleeing away, and the companions of Nīzak laid their swords on them (the companions of Yazdağird) and killed many of them.

§ 290[746] Yazdağird's flight ended at a certain place in the land of Marw. He dismounted and went into a miller's house where he stayed for three days. The miller said to him: "You poor man, come and have something to eat! You haven't eaten anything for three days!" Yazdağird answered: "I will not do that without prayers." One of the *zamāzimah* of Marw[747] lived close by, and the miller went to him and asked him to read the prayers for him, so that he could eat. The man did this, but when he returned to Marw and heard the father of Barāz speaking about Yazdağird and looking for him, he went to him and his companions and asked them about what jewelry Yazdağird was wearing. When they had described him, he told them that he had seen him in the house of a miller, and that he was a man with curly hair, joined eye-brows, and beautiful teeth, wearing earrings and bracelets.

---

745 Syntactically, the most natural way to read this scene is that the father of Barāz suggests that Yazdağird should go unarmed to meet Nīzak, and this is also how Humphreys (1990): 85, understands it. This can be supported by the earlier demand, § 288, that Yazdağird should disperse his armies. On the other hand, one cannot exclude the reading that the father of Barāz gives a clandestine suggestion to Nīzak, as it is Nīzak who is going to deceive Yazdağird and has to be careful not to frighten him away. In order not to force either reading on the text, I have left the ambiguous pronouns stand as they are, without interpreting them as to their reference.

746 Miskawayh, *Tağārib al umam*, 1:270–271 = C469; cf. al-Ṭabarī, *Taʾrīḫ*, 1:2879–2880 = trans., 15:85–86.

747 *Zamāzimah* is not a Zoroastrian term, but a vague Islamic designation of Zoroastrian priests. *Zamzamah* refers to the "mumbled" prayer that opens and closes a meal eaten in silence, see, e.g., Ḥamzah's comments in Abū Nuwās, *Dīwān*, 2:145, and *zamāzimah* are the ones to read this prayer.

§291[1] فوجه إليه رجلا من الأساورة وأمره أن يخنقه بوتر ويطرحه في نهر مرو. فلقوا الطحان فضربوه ليدل عليه فلم يفعل وجحدهم أن يعرف أين توجه. فلما أرادوا الانصراف عنه قال رجل منهم: "إني أجد ريح المسك فلو تتبعته." فنظر إلى طرف ثوب من ديباج في الماء فاجتذبه إليه فإذا هو يزدجرد. فسأله ألا يقتله ولا يدل عليه ويجعل له خاتمه وسواره ومنطقته. فقال: "أعطني أربعة دراهم وأخلي عنك." قال: "ويحك خاتمي لك وثمنه لا {يُحصى}." فأبى عليه فقال يزدجرد: "قد كنت أخبرت أني سأحتاج إلى أربعة دراهم وأضطر إلى أن يكون أكلي أكل الهر فقد عاينته." ثم انتزع أحد قرطيه وأعطاه الطحان مكافأة لكتمانه عليه ودنا منه كأنه يكلمه بشيء. فأنذر الرجل أصحابه فأتوه فطلب إليهم يزدجرد أن لا يقتلوه وخوفهم ما عليهم في دينهم من ذاك وقال: "آتوا بي الدهقان أو سرحوني إلى العرب فإنهم يستحيون مثلي من الملوك." فأخذوا ما كان عليه من الحلي فجعلوه في جراب وختموا عليه. ثم خنقوه بوتر وطرحوه في نهر مرو. فجرى به الماء حتى انتهى إلى الفُوْهَة تعلق بعود فأخذ من هناك. ثم تفقد أبو تَرار قرطيه فأخذ الذي دل عليه فضربه حتى أتي على نفسه وبعث بما أصيب له إلى الخليفة يومئذ. فأغرم الخليفة الدهقان قيمة القرط المفقود.

---

٥ يُحصى: "يُحصا" في الأصل.

---

١ من تجارب الأمم لمسكويه ١: ٢٧١.

§ 291[748] The father of Barāz sent a cavalryman and gave him orders to strangle Yazdağird with a string and to throw the body into the river of Marw. They found the miller and beat him to make him show the way to Yazdağird, but the man refused and denied knowing where he had gone. When they were about to return, one of them said to himself: "I detect the scent of musk. Perhaps I should follow it." Then he saw a part of silk brocade robe in the water and started pulling it up, and there was Yazdağird! Yazdağird asked him not to kill him and not to give him up. He offered him his ring and bracelet and belt, but the man said: "Give me four dirhams, and I will let you go." Yazdağird said: "Woe to you, I will give you my ring, the price of which is beyond counting." The man refused, and Yazdağird said: "I was told that one day I would need four dirhams and that I would be reduced to eating what a cat eats. Now I have seen this happen." He took off one of his earrings and gave it to the miller[749] as a reward for having hid him and drew closer to him as if he were to say something to him, but the other man shouted to his companions, and these came to them. Yazdağird asked them not to kill him and tried to scare them by telling them what the reward for regicide was according to their religion. He also said: "Take me to the *dihqān* or send me to the Arabs. They will leave a king like me alive." They took the jewelry he was wearing and put it[750] in a sack and sealed it. Then they strangled him with a string and threw his body into the river of Marw. The river carried the body to a gulf where it stuck to a tree, and it was from there that it was taken out of water. The father of Barāz noticed that the earrings were missing and took the man who had shown the way to him and beat him half dead. Then he sent what had been found of his (jewelry) to the Caliph the same day, and the Caliph fined the *dihqān* for the price of the lost earring.

748 Miskawayh, *Tağārib al-umam*, 1:271 = C469–470; cf. al-Ṭabarī, *Taʾrīḫ*, 1:2880–2881 = trans., 15:86–87.

749 The narration is very dense here, and the passage may be slightly confused already in al-Ṭabarī, who has an additional sentence (*fa-waṣafa lahu mawḍiʿahu*) after *ka-annahu yukallimuhu bi-šayʾ*. In al-Ṭabarī, the scenario seems to be as follows: 1) the cavalryman notices Yazdağird; 2) Yazdağird gives the miller an earring by whispering to him where it is to be found; 3) meanwhile, the cavalryman calls his companions. In Miskawayh and al-Maqrīzī, the reader is not told why Yazdağird approached the miller "as if he were to say something to him," and it would bc natural to understand this as a way of giving him the earring without the others noticing it.

750 Humphreys (1990): 87, translates "put him in a sack," which confuses the scene (how does one strangle a man who has already been put in a sealed sack? Why should the sack be sealed?). Unfortunately, while Bosworth (1999) is an excellent translation, Smith (1994) and Humphreys (1990) would need some revision.

§ 292[١] وقد حكي في رواية أخرى أن ترار وسنحان كانا متباغضين متحاسدين وخُص به تَرار. فحسده سنحان وظهر ذلك لترار فجعل يوغر صدر يزدجرد ويسعى في قتله حتى عزم على ذلك. وأفشى ما عزم عليه من ذلك إلى امرأة من نسائه كان ترار واطأها. فأرسلت إلى ترار تبشره بإجماع يزدجرد على قتل سنحان. وفشا الحديث حتى بلغ سنحان. فجمع جموعا وتوجه نحو القصر الذي فيه يزدجرد وبلغ ذلك ترار فنكص عن ترار لكثرة جمعه. وأرعب ذلك | يزدجرد فخرج 198a
ذاهبا على وجهه راجلا لينجو بنفسه. فمشى نحوا من فرسخين حتى وقع إلى رحى من ماء فدخل بيت {الرحى} فجلس فيه كالّا لَغِبا. فرآه صاحب {الرحى} ذا {هَيْئة} وطُرة وبزة كريمة. ففرش له وأتاه بطعام فطعم ومكث عنده يوما وليلة. فسأله صاحب الرَحَى أن يأمر له بشيء فبذل له منطقته وكانت مكللة بجوهر. فأبى أن يقبلها وقال: "إنه ليرضيني من هذه المنطقة أربعة دراهم آكل بها وأشرب." فأخبره ألا وَرِق معه فتملقه صاحب الرحى حتى إذا أغفى قام إليه بفأس فضرب بها هامته فقتله. وأخذ ما كان عليه من ثياب وحلي وألقى جيفته فى النهر وبقر بطنه وأدخل فيه من أصول طرفاء كانت نابتة على ذلك النهر لتحبس جثته في الموضع الذي ألقاها فيه فلا ينتقل فيعرف ويطلب قائله وما أخذ من سلبه. وهرب على وجهه.

٧ الرحى١: "الرحا" في الأصل. ‖ الرحى٢: "الرحا" في الأصل. ‖ هَيْئة: "هَية" في الأصل.

١ من تجارب الأمم لمسكويه ١: ٢٧١–٢٧٢.

§ 292[751] There is also another version of the events. According to it, Barāz and Sanǧān hated and envied each other. When Yazdaǧird favoured Barāz, Sanǧān became envious of him. This was noticed by Barāz, who started to incite Yazdaǧird urging him to have Sanǧān killed. Finally, Yazdaǧird decided to do so and revealed his intention to one of his women with whom Barāz had an understanding. She sent a word to Barāz, giving him the news that Yazdaǧird had decided to kill Sanǧān. The story spread until Sanǧān heard it and collected a group of men, heading towards the castle in which Yazdaǧird was. Barāz heard about this and shied away from Sanǧān[752] because of the many men he had with him. This frightened Yazdaǧird, who fled on foot to save himself. He walked about two *farsaḫs* until he came to a water mill. He entered the mill house and sat there, tired and exhausted. The miller saw him to be of impressive form, with a noble face[753] and attire, so he spread the table for him and brought him some food. Yazdaǧird ate and stayed with him for the day and the night. The miller asked him to give him something, and he offered him his belt, which was encrusted with jewels. The man refused to take it and said: "Instead of the belt, I will be satisfied with four dirhams I can use for eating and drinking." When Yazdaǧird explained to him that he did not have any money on him, the miller played friendly with him until he fell asleep. Then he took an axe and hit him on the head, killing him and taking his clothes and jewels and throwing his body into the river. He ripped his belly open and stuck there some tamarisk roots from the trees growing by the river to keep the corpse from floating away, so that it would not be recognised and the killer and what he had robbed sought after. Then he fled away.

751 Miskawayh, *Taǧārib al-umam*, 1:271–272 = C470–472; cf. al-Ṭabarī, *Ta'rīḫ*, 1:2881–2883 = trans., 15:87–89.

752 The text has here Tarār/Barāz, which does not make sense. The translation follows al-Ṭabarī and Miskawayh.

753 Humphreys (1990): 88, translated *ṭurrah* as "knotted scarf," which is possible, but would be a surprisingly detailed description. I take the three words to describe Yazdaǧird's impressive stature (*hay'ah*), the handsomeness of his face (*ṭurrah, pars pro toto* for face), and attire (*bizzah*).

§ 293[1] وبلغ قتل يزدجرد رجلا من أهل الأهواز كان مطرانا على مرو ويقال له إيليا. فجمع من كان قبله من النصارى وقال لهم: "إن ملك الفرس قتل وهو ابن شهريار بن كسرى. وإنما شهريار ولد شيرين المؤمنة التي عرفتم حقها وإحسانها إلى أهل ملتها وكانت بنت قيصر. ثم لهذا الملك عنصر في النصرانية مع ما نال النصارى في ملك جده من الشرف حتى بنى لهم البيع وشد ملتهم. فينبغي أن نَجْزِي هذا الملك بقدر طاقتنا من الكرامة وقد رأيت أن أبني له ناووسا وأحمل جثته في كرامة حتى أجعلها فيه." فقال {النصارى}: "أمرنا لأمرك تبع." فأمر المطران فبنى له في جوف بستانه بمرو ناووس. ومضى بنفسه ومعه نصارى مرو حتى استخرج جثة يزدجرد وكفنها وحملها ومن كان معه على عواتقهم في تابوت حتى أتوا به الناووس وواروه فيه. وقيل: بل حمله إلى إصطخر فوضع في الناووس هناك. وذلك في سنة إحدى وثلاثين من الهجرة.

§ 294[2] وكان ملك يزدجرد عشرين سنة. منها أربع سنين بالمدائن في دعة وست عشرة في تعب من محاربة العرب إياه ومحنته بهم وغلظتهم عليه. وكان شعاره أخضر موشى وسراويله لون السماء موشى وتاجه أحمر وكانت خفافهم | كلهم حمر وبيده رمح ويعتمد على سيفه. وكان يزدجرد هذا 198b
آخر ملكٍ ملَكَ من آل أردشير بن بابك. فجميع ما ملك ملوك الفرس أربعة آلاف سنة وإحدى وسبعين سنة وعشرة أشهر وتسعة عشر يوما فيها ستون ملكا. وفي نسخة: جملة الطبقة الرابعة. وكانوا ثمانية وعشرين ملكا سِوى ثلاثين سنة تحارب فيها أردشير بن بابك مع ملوك الطوائف أربع مائة سنة وست وخمسون سنة وشهر واحد واثنان وعشرون يوما. وجميع ذلك من ابتداء التناسل إلى آخر

٥ وقد رأيت: كشط المقريزي عبارة أخرى قبل أن يصححها كما هي الآن. ٦ النصارى: "النصارا" في الأصل. ٨ تابوت: الزيادة بخط المقريزي في آخر السطر في الهامش الأيسر. ١٠ بالمدائن: الزيادة بخط المقريزي في الهامش الأيمن من الأعلى إلى الأسفل + صح، ويشير إليها رمز ⌐ بعد "سنين".

١ من تجارب الأمم لمسكويه ١: ٢٧٢.

٢ من تجارب الأمم لمسكويه ١: ٢٧٢–٢٧٣ ومن تأريخ سني الملوك لحمزة ص ٤٨–٤٩، ١٥، ٢٥.

§ 293[754] The news of Yazdağird's death reached a man from al-Ahwāz, who was the metropolitan of Marw, called Īliyā. He called together the Christians under his authority and said to them: "The king of the Persians has been killed. He was the son of Šahriyār b. Kisrá, and Šahriyār was the son of Šīrīn the Believer, and you know what right she has on us and what good deeds she did to the people of her religion. She was the daughter of the Caesar. Thus, this king had his roots in Christianity. Add to that the respect the Christians enjoyed during the time of his grandfather, so that he even had churches built for them and strengthened their religion. Now we must pay back to this king his generosity as far as we are able to. I think I should build a tomb for him and carry his body to it in honour." The Christians replied: "We will follow you." The metropolitan gave orders for a tomb to be built within his own garden in Marw. He himself and the other Christians of Marw went to take the body of Yazdağird out (of the river) and to wrap it in shrouds. They carried it on their shoulders in a coffin until they came to the tomb and placed it there. According to others, the metropolitan carried it to Iṣṭaḫr and put it into a tomb there. This happened in the year 31 AH[/651–652].

§ 294[755] The reign of Yazdağird lasted for 20 years, of which 4 were in peace in al-Madāʾin and 16 in toil with the Arabs fighting against him and his tribulations with them and their roughness towards him. His vest was green and embroidered, his trousers sky-blue and embroidered, and his crown red. The shoes of them all were red. In his hand, he held a spear, and he leaned on his sword. This Yazdağird was the last king of the house of Ardašīr b. Bābak to reign. In all, the Persian kings reigned for 4,071 years, 10 months, and 19 days. They were 60 kings, and, according to one manuscript, the total number of the kings of the fourth class was 28 kings, (and the total length of their reign), excluding the 30 years during which Ardašīr b. Bābak fought against the Petty kings, was 456 years, 1 month, and 22 days. All this, from the beginning of generation until the end of the days of the Persians, who

754 Miskawayh, *Taǧārib al-umam*, 1:272 = C472–473; cf. al-Ṭabarī, *Taʾrīḫ*, 1:2883–2884 = trans., 15:89.

755 Miskawayh, *Taǧārib al-umam*, 1:272–273 = C473; Ḥamzah, *Taʾrīḫ* 48–49, 15, 25 = trans. 75–76, 30, 44; cf. al-Ṭabarī, *Taʾrīḫ*, 1:2884 = trans., 15:89–90. Cf. also § 3.

أيام الفرس وكانوا ستة وستين ملكا أربعة آلاف وأربع مائة وتسع سنين وتسعة أشهر وعشرون يوما. وفي نسخة: جملة مدة الطبقة الرابعة أربعمائة وإحدى وثلاثون سنة. وقيل: أربع مائة وتسع وسبعون سنة. وقيل: أربع مائة وأربع وخمسون سنة. وقيل: أربع مائة وثلاث وأربعون سنة. وقيل: ستمائة وست وتسعون سنة وليس بصحيح.

§295[1] وقال الطبري: لا تدافع بين علماء الأمم أن جيومرت هو أبو الفرس وإنما اختلفوا فيه هل هو آدم أبو البشر أم هو غيره. ثم مع ذلك فملكه وملك أولاده لم يزل منتظما على سياق متسقا بأرض المشرق وجبالها إلى أن قتل يزدجرد بن شهريار من ولد ولده بمَرْو أيام عثمٰن بن عفان رضي الله عنه. فتاريخ سني العالَم على أعمارهم أسهل بيانا وأوضح منارا منه على أعمار ملوك غيرهم من الأمم إذ لا نعلم أمة من الأمم الذين ينسبون إلى آدم دامت لها المملكة واتصل لها الملك وكان لهم ملوك تجمعهم {ورؤوس} تحامي عنهم من ناوأهم ويغالب بهم من عاداهم ويدفع ظالمهم عن مظلومهم ويحملهم من الأمور على ما فيه حظهم على اتصال ودوام ونظام يأخذ ذلك آخرهم عن أولهم وعابرهم عن سالفهم سواهم. فالتاريخ على أعمار ملوكهم أصح مخرجا وأحسن وضوحا. (...)

---

١٠ ورؤوس: "وروس" في الأصل. || تحامي: وضع المقريزي رمز "ح" تحت الحرف الثاني إشارة إلى تلفظه بالحاء. ١٢ وضوحا: بعد هذه الكلمة بياض بقدر ثلاثة أسطر في الأصل.

---

١ من تأريخ الطبري ١: ١٤٨.

were 66 kings, was 4,409 years, 9 months, and 20 days.[756] According to one manuscript,[757] the total length of the period of the fourth class was 431 years or, according to others, 479 years, but it is also said 454 years, or 443 years, or 696 years,[758] but this (last) is not correct.

§ 295[759] Al-Ṭabarī has said: Scholars of different nations agree that Gayōmart was the father of the Persians. What they disagree about is whether he was Adam, the father of the humankind, or someone else. In addition to this, his and his offspring's kingship was continuous and orderly in the East and the mountains there until Yazdaǧird b. Šahriyār, one of his descendants, was killed in Marw at the time of ʿUṯmān b. ʿAffān, may God be pleased with him. Universal chronology based on their lives is easier and clearer than one based on the lives of other kings, because we know of no people descending from Adam, whose kingdom would have continued and whose rule would have been continuous and who would have had kings to unite them and leaders to protect them from their enemies and to fight with them against those who attacked them, defending the wronged against the wrong doer and who would have continuously, on long duration, and orderly brought them things in which they were fortunate. The later of them followed in this the earlier and the bygone their predecessors in a like manner. A chronology based on the lives of their kings is more reliable and clearer than others.[760]

756 According to Ḥamzah, *Taʾrīḫ* 25, from where this seems to have been taken, they ruled for 4,409 years, 9 months, and 22 days.

757 I.e., al-Bīrūnī. Note that the expression does not necessarily refer to another manuscript of the text which is being quoted but may well, as here, refer to another text.

758 The tens are written somewhat unclearly in the holograph. The copyist of MS T has read the word as *sabʿūn*. In the holograph, there are two dots on the first letter, but otherwise the word does look more like *sabʿūn*.

759 Al-Ṭabarī, *Taʾrīḫ*, 1:148 = trans., 1:319.

760 Last three lines of fol. 198[b] have been left blank.

199a فَصْلٌ في ذِكْرِ دِيَانَةِ الفُرْسِ وعِبَادَتِهِمْ ورُسُوْم دَولتهم وعَوائدهم في سياسَتِهِم

§ 296 أما ديانة الفرس التي كانت تتقرب بها إلى الله تعالى فيقال: إنها كانت أولا تعتقد توحيد الله عز وجل إلى أن ظهر فيهم بيوداسف المشرقي. وأتى إلى طهمورث ثالث ملوك الطبقة الأولى من الفرس بمذهب الصابئة في أول سنة من ملكه. ودعاه إليها فأجابه طمهورث إلى ذلك وحمل الرعية عليه فدانوا بملة الصابئين نحو ألف سنة وثماني مائة سنة.

§ 297 ثم ظهر زَرْذُشت الفارسي في سنة ثلاثين من ملك كيبشتاسف. ودعا إلى دين المجوسية من تعظيم النار وسائر الأنوار والقول بتركيب العالم من النور والظلام واعتقاد القدماء الخمسة التي هي عندهم الباري تعالى وإبليس والهيولى والزمان والمكان وغير ذلك من شريعة المجوس. فقبله كيبشتاسف منه وألزم الفرس اعتقاده فدانوا به ورجعوا عن ملة الصابئين. وجعلوا حينئذ الهيا كل بيوتا للنيران ولم تقنع الفرس في تعظيم النار بما كانت أهل الديانة الأولى تفعله. بل استكثروا منها واتخذوا لها بيوتا وسَدَنَة ووقفوا عليها الضياع والأملاك. ثم غلبهم الغلو فيها حتى عبدوها من دون الله تعالى. وكيفية عبادتهم لها أن حفروا لها أخدودا مربعا في الأرض وأججوا فيه النار. ثم كانوا لا يدَعون طعاما شهيا ولا شرابا لذيذا ولا ثوبا فاخرا ولا نباتا عطرا إلا طرحوه فيها تقربا إليها وتبركا بها. وكانوا يأمرون بإحيائها وينهون عن إطفائها ويمنعون الحُيض من مسها والدنو منها وما زالوا متمسكين بدين زراذشت وشريعته إلى أن انقضت دولتهم.

---

٤ من الفرس: الزيادة بخط المقريزي في الهامش الأيمن من الأعلى إلى الأسفل + صح، ويشير إليها رمز ˥ بعد "الأولى". ١٠ الفرس: الزيادة بخط المقريزي في الهامش الأيمن من الأعلى إلى الأسفل + صح، ويشير إليها رمز ˥ بعد "تقنع".

Chapter concerning the Religion and Rites of the Persians and the Traces of Their Empire and the Advantages of Their Government

§ 296 As to the religion of the Persians through which they sought the favour of God, He is Exalted, it is said that they first used to believe in the unity of God, He is Great and Majestic, until there appeared among them Būdāsf[761] the Eastern. He brought to Ṭahmūraṯ, the third of the Persian kings of the first class, the doctrine of the Sabians in the first year of his reign and summoned him to it. Ṭahmūraṯ accepted it and brought his subjects to it. They continued professing the Sabian religion for about 1,800 years.

§ 297 Then there appeared Zarathustra the Persian in the year 30 of the reign of Kay-Bištāsf. He summoned (the king) to the religion of Magianism, including the veneration of fire and the other lights and the doctrine of the world consisting of light and darkness and the belief in the five eternals, which according to them are the Creator, He is Exalted, Iblīs, prime matter, time, and place, as well as in other things according to the Magian law. Kay-Bištāsf accepted this from him and made the Persians adopt these beliefs. They converted to this religion from the religion of Sabianism. At that time, they made temples into fire temples. The Persians were no more satisfied with venerating fire than those of the first religion, but they exaggerated and assigned temples and custodians for it and assigned villages and properties as endowments for it. Finally, excess took them over, and they started worshiping it instead of God, He is Exalted. They worshiped it by digging a quadrangular hole in the soil and kindling a fire there. When they had some desirable food, delicious drink, precious clothes, or aromatic herbs, they threw (some of) it into the fire as an offering, seeking blessing from it. They ordered the fire to be kept alive and forbade extinguishing it. They also prevented menstruating women from touching it or drawing close to it. They continued to keep fast to the religion of Zarathustra and his law until their empire ended.

---

761 In both manuscripts, the name is written BYWD'SF.

§298 وقد كانت للفرس محنة يمتحنون بها الأشياء العظيمة بالنار. فيجمعون الحطب الجزل الكثير ويشعلون فيه نارا حتى إذا تأججت واستعرت أتي {بالمُدعَى} عليه فاحشة أو عظيمة في دِيْن أو دُنْيا والمدعِي معه ثم يتكلم متكلم بكلام لهم كان هو المحنة التي تفرق بين الأمرين وتفصل بين | الخَصْمين. فإذا فرغ من كلامه أمر المدعي {والمدعى} عليه باقتحامها وخوضها والمرور فيها 199b إلى الناحية الأخرى. وهي تشب وتستعر والناس وقوف على أقدامهم رافعو أيديهم إلى الله بتضرع ورنين وبكاء. فمن كان مبطلا أخذته النار فاحترق حتى يصير رمادا ومن كان بريئا محقا خاضها ونفذ فيها حتى يجوزها لا تتعلق منه بثوب ولا شعَر ولا بَشَر. وكان الموكل بالكلام الذي يمتحن به من أهل بيت معروفين بالدين يتوارثونه خلف عن سلف يرثه العقب بعد العقب فلا يجح إلا على أيديهم وفيهم. فكانت هذه المحنة من أعظم سياساتهم التي يرتدعون بها عن الفواحش ويكفون أنفسهم عن الظلم ونحوه من العظائم. وكان يقال لدينهم الدين الأكبر ويقال لهم الأمة الكبرى والملة العظمى والحنفاء. وكانت الرعية من الفرس تدين بدين ملوكها وهم يعترفون بمتوسط من البشر بين الحق تعالى وبين الخلق تكون درجته في الطهارة ومرتبته في الطاعة فوق درجة الملائكة ومرتبتهم فيهما.

§299 وكان يقال لعظيمهم مُوبذ مُوْبذان أي عالم العلماء ومكانه من الملوك مكانة الخلفاء من المسلمين فيرجعون إليه ويصدرون عن رأيه. وكانت الفرس فرقا وهم الكيومرتية والزروانية والزرادشتية وغيرهم وآراؤهم متقاربة. ويجمعهم القول بالنور والظلمة وإنهما أصلان قديمان.

---

١ محنة : وضع المقريزي رمز "ح" تحت الحرف الثاني إشارة إلى تلفظه بالحاء. ٢ بالمُدعَى : "بالمُدعَا" في الأصل. ٣ المحنة : وضع المقريزي رمز "ح" تحت الحرف الرابع إشارة إلى تلفظه بالحاء. ٤ الخَصْمين: كشط المقريزي ما يلي الخاء ثم صحح الكلمة كما هي الآن وزاد نصا فوق السطر كما يلي. ‖ فإذا ... كلامه : الزيادة بخط المقريزي في الهامش الأعلى منكسة. ‖ والمدعى : "والمدعا" في الأصل. ٥ رافعو : "رافعوا" في الأصل. ١١ والحنفاء : وضع المقريزي رمز "ح" تحت الحرف الرابع إشارة إلى تلفظه بالحاء. ١٢ الطهارة ... في : الزيادة بخط المقريزي في الهامش الأيسر من الأسفل إلى الأعلى + صح، ويشير إليها رمز ˥ بعد "في".

§ 298 The Persians used to have an ordeal, according to which they examined important cases through fire.[762] They would collect an enormous amount of firewood and light it until it was ablaze and burning. Then they would bring the person accused of an indecency or a major offence in a religious or a secular matter, together with the accuser. A speaker would speak aloud some words of theirs, and these were the ordeal that would separate between the two matters and distinguish between the contestants. When he finished, he would give orders for the accused and the accuser to plunge and delve into the fire and to walk through it to the other side, while it was ablaze and burning and people were standing around it and raising their hands towards God, imploring Him, crying and wailing. The one who was wrong would be consumed by the fire and burned to ashes, while the other who was innocent and right would delve into it and pass through it without the fire catching his clothes, or hair, or skin. The one entrusted with reading the words through which they were examined in the ordeal belonged to a family well-known for their religiosity, and they inherited this role, the offspring from their forefathers, from generation to generation, and the ordeal was successful only through them. Among the Persians, this ordeal was one of their greatest governing mechanisms that kept them from committing indecencies and detained them from doing injustice and committing other major sins. Their religion used to be called "the greatest religion," and they "the greatest nation" and "the grandest religious community," as well as *ḥunafāʾ*. The Persian subjects used to follow the religion of their kings. They acknowledged the existence of a human mediator between the creation and God, He is Exalted, whose level in purity and rank in obedience was above those of the angels.

§ 299 Their greatest (religious authority) was called *mōbad mōbadān* or the greatest of scholars. He had the same position vis-à-vis kings[763] as the Caliphs have vis-à-vis Muslims. They resorted to his opinion and followed it. The Persians were divided into several sects: Kayūmartiyyah, Zurwāniyyah, Zarādustiyyah, and others, but their doctrines were close to each other and they were united in the belief in light and darkness, which (for them) are

762 For the importance of fire (and molten metal) ordeals, *var ī garm*, see Christensen (1936): 299–300.

763 Sic. One would here expect a reference to Zoroastrian believers. For a comparison between the Byzantine Emperor and the Caliph, see al-Maqrīzī, *Ḫabar/Greeks* § 81.

وبعضهم يرى أن الظلمة حادثة ويُسْندون إليهما سائر الحوادث ولذلك يقال لهم الثنوية. فيرون أن النور والظلمة هما الفاعلان في عالم الكون والفساد يستند أشرف المتقابلين من الحوادث إلى أشرف المتقابلَيْن من المحْدِثين.

§300 ومنهم من يرى أن فوق النور والظلمة غيرهما هو إلاههما وإلاه كل شيء لا يشبه شيئا ولا يشبهه شيء. ودينهم عبادته وطاعته إلا أنهم يتزهونه من إسناد الحوادث إليه ويسندونها إلى النور والظلمة كما تسند الفلاسفة إلى الحركة الدورية. وهؤلاء أصلح فرق المجوس وأقرب طوائفهم إلى المعقول وهم الزرادشتية. والنبي الأول بجميعهم كيومرت الذي يَزعمون أنه آدم والنبي الثاني زرادشت. ومباحثهم تدور على أصلين أحدهما امتزاج النور بالظلمة والآخر خلاص النور من | 200a الظلمة. والأول هو المبدأ والثاني هو المعاد. وخرج أبو داود من حديث عمران القطان عن أبي حمزة عن ابن عباس رضي الله عنه قال: "إن أهل فارس لما مات نبيهم كتب لهم إبليس المجُوسِيَّة." (...)

١٠ المجُوسِيَّة: بعد هذه الكلمة بياض بقدر اثنين وعشرين سطرا في الأصل.

two eternal principles. Some of them considered darkness to have been created in time. They derived from these two all other beings created in time. Because of this they are called Dualists, as they consider light and darkness to be the two (pre-eternal) agents in the world of generation and decay, with the most noble beings created in time deriving from the most noble creator.[764]

§300 Some of them considered that above light and darkness there was something else, which was the God of light and darkness and the God of everything: nothing resembled it and it resembled nothing.[765] Their religion was to worship it and to obey it, but they declared it free from the creation of beings created in time. These they linked to light and darkness, like the philosophers linked them to circular movement. They were the best of Magian sects and their closest group to reasonable thinking, and they were the Zarāduštiyyah. According to all of their sects, the first prophet was Gayōmart, whom they claim to have been Adam, and the second prophet was Zarathustra. Their doctrines revolve around two principles. One is the mixture of light and darkness and the other the liberation of light from darkness. The first is creation (*mabdaʾ*), the second eschatology (*maʿād*). Abū Dāʾūd[766] has quoted from the *ḥadīṯ* of ʿImrān al-Qaṭṭān from Abū Ḥamzah from Ibn ʿAbbās,[767] may God be pleased with him: "When the prophet of the Persians died, Iblīs wrote for them Magianism."[768]

764 Respectively, the ignoble principle is the cause of the creation of ignoble beings.

765 This refers to Zurvanism, where the existence of the good and the bad principle, Ohrmazd and Ahriman, is derived from "Unlimited Time," *Zurvān akanārag*, who is beyond good and evil and unrelated to the material creation.

766 Abū Dāʾūd al-Siǧistānī (d. 275/889), traditionist, see "Abū Dāʾūd al-Sidjistānī," in *EI*², 1:114.

767 ʿAbd Allāh b. ʿAbbās (d. 68/687 or soon after), *ḥadīṯ* scholar. See *GAS*, 1:25–28.

768 The last 22 lines of fol. 200ᵃ have been left blank.

Bibliography

Primary Sources

Abū Nuʿaym, *Dalāʾil*

Abū Nuʿaym al-Iṣbahānī (d. 430/1038), *Dalāʾil al-nubuwwah*, ed. M.R. Qalʿah-ǧī and ʿA. ʿAbbās, 2nd edition (Beirut: Dār al-Nafāʾis, 1406/1986), 2 vols. in one.

Abū Nuwās, *Dīwān*

Abū Nuwās (d. ca. 198/813), *Dīwān*, ed. E. Wagner and G. Schoeler (*Bibliotheca Islamica* 20a–e) (Wiesbaden–Stuttgart: Franz Steiner, for vol. 5: Berlin: Klaus Schwarz, 1958–2003), 5 vols.

ʿAhd Ardašīr

ʿAhd Ardašīr (8th century?), ed. I. ʿAbbās (Beirut: Dār Ṣādir, 1387/1967).

Al-Aʿšā Maymūn (d. 5/625 or later), *Dīwān*

R. Geyer, *Gedichte von (…) al-ʾAʿshā* (*E.J.W. Gibb Memorial, New Series* VI) (London: E.J.W. Gibb Memorial, 1928).

Asadī Ṭūsī, *Garšāspnāmah*

Asadī Ṭūsī (d. ca. 465/1072), *Garšāspnāmah*, ed. Ḥ. Yaġmāʾī, 2nd ed. (Tehran: Dunyā-ye kitāb, 1389 AHŠ/[2011]).

Al-Bīrūnī, *al-Āṯār al-bāqiyah*

Abū Rayḥān Muḥammad b. Aḥmad al-Bīrūnī (d. ca. 442/1050), *al-Āṯār al-bāqiyah ʿan al-qurūn al-ḫāliyah*, ed. P. Aḏkāʾī (*Mīrāṯ-e maktūb* 91) (Tehran: Mīrāṯ-e Maktūb, 1380 AHŠ/2001).

Al-Buḫārī, *Ṣaḥīḥ*

Muḥammad b. Ismāʿīl al-Buḫārī (d. 256/870), *Ṣaḥīḥ*, ed. M. Nizār Tamīm and H. Nizār Tamīm (Beirut: Dār al-Arqam, n.d.).

Al-Dīnawarī, *al-Aḫbār al-ṭiwāl*

Abū Ḥanīfah Aḥmad b. Dāʾūd al-Dīnawarī (d. not later than 290/902–903), *al-Aḫbār al-ṭiwāl*, ed. V. Guirgass (Leiden: Brill, 1888).

Ps.-al-Ǧāḥiẓ, *Kitāb al-Tāǧ*

Ps.-al-Ǧāḥiẓ (mid-3rd/9th century), *Kitāb al-Tāǧ*, ed. F. ʿAṭawī (Beirut: al-Šarika al-lubnāniyyah li-l-kitāb, 1970).

Ḥamzah al-Iṣfahānī, *Taʾrīḫ*

Ḥamzah b. al-Ḥasan al-Iṣfahānī (d. 350/961 or 360/971), *Taʾrīḫ sinī mulūk al-arḍ wa-l-anbiyāʾ* (Beirut: Manšūrāt Dār Maktabat al-Ḥayāt, n.d.).

Ḥamzah al-Iṣfahānī, *Taʾrīḫ* (ed. Gottwaldt)

Hamzae Ispahanensis annalium libri X, ed. J.M.E. Gottwaldt (Leipzig, 1844–1848), 2 vols.

Al-Ḫaṭīb al-Baġdādī, *Taʾrīḫ Baġdād*

Al-Ḫaṭīb al-Baġdādī (d. 463/1071), *Taʾrīḫ Baġdād*, ed. M.ʿA. ʿAṭā (Beirut: Dār al-kutub al-ʿilmiyyah, 2011), 24 vols.

Al-Ḫwārizmī, *Mafātīḥ*

Al-Ḫwārizmī (d. 387/997), *Mafātīḥ al-ʿulūm*, ed. G. van Vloten (Leiden: Brill, 1895).

Ibn al-Aṯīr, *al-Kāmil*

ʿAlī b. Muḥammad b. al-Aṯīr (d. 637/1239), *al-Kāmil fī l-taʾrīḫ* (Beirut: Dār Ṣādir, n.d.), 13 vols.

Ibn al-Balḫī, *Fārsnāmeh*

Ibn al-Balḫī (d. after 510/1116), *Fārsnāmeh*, ed. G. Le Strange and R.A. Nicholson (*E.J.W. Gibb Memorial Publications. New Series* 1) (London: Luzac, 1921).

Ibn al-ʿIbrī, *Muḫtaṣar*

Ibn al-ʿIbrī (Bar Hebraeus) (d. 685/1286), *Taʾrīḫ muḫtaṣar al-duwal* (n.d., n.p.).

Ibn Isfandiyār, *Tārīḫ-e Ṭabaristān*

Ibn Isfandiyār (d. after 613/1216), *Tārīḫ-e Ṭabaristān*, ed. ʿA.I. Āštiyānī (*Intišārāt-e Asāṭīr* 524) (Tehran: Asāṭīr, 1389 AHŠ/[2011]).

Ibn Manẓūr, *Lisān*

Ibn Manẓūr (d. 711/1311), *Lisān al-ʿarab*, ed. (and reorganised according to the first radical) ʿA. Šīrī (Beirut: Dār Iḥyāʾ al-turāṯ al-ʿarabī, 1408/1988), 18 vols.

Ibn al-Nadīm, *al-Fihrist*

Muḥammad b. Isḥāq b. al-Nadīm (d. in the 380s/990s), *al-Fihrist*, ed. R. Taǧaddud (*Intišārāt-e Asāṭīr* 348) (Tehran: Asāṭīr, 1381 AHŠ/[2003]).

Al-Iṣfahānī, *Aġānī*

Al-Iṣfahānī (Abū l-Faraǧ) (d. 356/967), *Kitāb al-Aġānī* (Būlāq 1285, repr. Beirut: Dār Ṣaʿb, n.d.), 20 vols.

Kay Kāʾūs, *Qābūsnāmah*

The Naṣīḥat-nāma known as Qābūs-nāma of Kai Kāʾūs b. Iskandar b. Qābūs b. Washmgīr (d. after 475/1082), ed. R. Levy (*E.J.W. Gibb Memorial Series, New Series* XVIII) (London: Luzac, 1951).

Kitāb Hurūšiyūš

Kitāb Hurūšiyūš (4th/10th c.) = Traducción árabe de las Historiae adversus paganos de Orosio. Edición y estudio Mayte Penelas (*Fuentes arábico-hispanas* 26) (Madrid: Consejo superior de investigaciones científicas, 2001).

Al-Maqdisī, *al-Badʾ*

al-Muṭahhar b. Ṭāhir al-Maqdisī (d. after 355/966), *Kitāb al-Badʾ wa-l-taʾrīḫ*, ed. C. Huart (Paris 1899–1907, repr. [of the Arabic text only] Beirut: Dār Ṣādir, n.d.), 6 vols.

Al-Maqrīzī, *al-Ḫabar*

Aḥmad b. ʿAlī l-Maqrīzī, (d. 845/1442), *Kitāb al-Ḫabar ʿan al-bašar. Vol. V, Section 4: Persia and Its Kings, Part I*, ed. J. Hämeen-Anttila (*Bibliotheca Maqriziana. Opera maiora* 5) (Leiden–Boston: Brill, 2018).

Al-Maqrīzī, *Kitāb al-Ḫabar ʿan al-bašar. Vol. V, Sections 1–2: The Arab Thieves*, ed. P. Webb (*Bibliotheca Maqriziana. Opera maiora* 6) (Leiden–Boston: Brill, 2019).

Al-Maqrīzī, *Kitāb al-Ḫabar ʿan al-bašar. Vol. V, Section 6: The Greeks, Romans, Byzantines, Franks, and Goths*, ed. M. Penelas (*Bibliotheca Maqriziana. Opera maiora* 7) (Leiden–Boston: Brill, 2021).

Al-Maqrīzī, *Kitāb al-Ḫabar ʿan al-bašar*, ed. Ḫ.A. al-Mullā l-Suwaydī and ʿĀ. ʿAbd al-Ġanī (Beirut: al-Dār al-ʿArabiyyah li-l-Mawsūʿāt, 2013), 8 vols.

Al-Masʿūdī, *Murūǧ al-ḏahab*

ʿAlī b. al-Ḥusayn al-Masʿūdī (d. 345/956), *Murūǧ al-ḏahab*, ed. B. de Meynard and P. de Courteille, revised by C. Pellat (*Publications de l'Université Libanaise. Section des études historiques* XI) (Beirut: Librairie orientale, 1966–1979), 8 vols.

Miskawayh, *Taǧārib al-umam*

Aḥmad b. Muḥammad Miskawayh (d. 421/1030), *Taǧārib al-umam wa-taʿāqub al-himam*, ed. S. Kisrawī Ḥasan (Beirut: Dār al-Kutub al-ʿIlmiyyah, 1424/2003), 7 vols.[1]

Taǧārib al-umam wa-taʿāqub al-himam, ed. Abū l-Q. Emāmī (Tehran: Soruš, 1379 AHŠ/[2001]), 8 vols.

Leone Caetani (ed.), *The Tajârib al-Umam or History of Ibn Miskawayh*, vol. 1 (*E.J.W. Gibb Memorial Series, Series* VII) (Leiden–London: Brill–Luzac, 1909).

Nihāyat al-arab

Nihāyat al-arab fī taʾrīḫ al-Furs wa-l-ʿArab (4th/10th c.?), ed. M.T. Dānišpažūh (Teheran: Anǧuman-e Āṯār o-Mafāḫir-e Farhangī, 1374 AHŠ/[1976]).

Al-Nuwayrī, *Nihāyat al-arab*

Muḥammad b. al-Qāsim al-Nuwayrī (d. 733/1333), *Nihāyat al-arab* (Cairo: Wizārat al-Ṯaqāfah, n.d.), 31 vols.

Procopius. *History*

Procopius (d. ca. 570), *History of the Wars*, vol. I (Books 1–2), ed. H.B. Dewing (*Loeb Classical Library* 48/1) (Cambridge, Mass.—London, 1914).

Al-Ṣafadī, *Wāfī*

Ḫalīl b. Aybak al-Ṣafadī (d. 764/1363), *Kitāb al-Wāfī bi-l-wafayāt*, vol. 20, ed. A. Ḥuṭaiṭ (*Bibliotheca Islamica* 6t) (Wiesbaden–Beyrut: Klaus Schwarz, 2007).

Al-Suhaylī, *al-Rawḍ*

al-Suhaylī (d. 581/1185), *al-Rawḍ al-unuf fī šarḥ al-sīrah al-nabawiyyah*, ed. ʿA. al-Wakīl (n.p., n.d.), 7 vols.

Al-Ṯaʿālibī, *al-Ġurar*

al-Ṯaʿālibī, *al-Ġurar* (written ca. 412/1022) = H. Zotenberg, *Histoire des Rois des Perses* (Paris, 1900, repr. Amsterdam: Oriental Press, n.d.).

1 If not otherwise indicated, this edition is used throughout the text.

Al-Ṭabarī, *Taʾrīḫ*
Muḥammad b. Ǧarīr al-Ṭabarī (d. 310/923), *Taʾrīḫ al-rusul wa-l-mulūk = Annales quod scripsit (…) al-Ṭabarî*, ed. M.J. de Goeje et al. (Leiden: Brill, 1879–1901), 15 vols. Trans. vol. I, see Rosenthal (1989); vol. V, see Bosworth (1999); vol. XI, see Blankinship (1993); vol. XII, see Friedmann (1992); vol. XIII, see Juynboll (1989); vol. XIV, see Smith (1994); vol. XV, see Humphreys (1990); vol. XXII, see Rowson (1989).
Tansarnāmah, see Mīnuwī (1932).

Secondary Sources

Arkoun (1970)
Arkoun, M., *Contribution à l'étude de l'humanisme arabe au IVe/Xe siècle* (Paris: J. Vrin, 1970).
Bauden (2014)
Bauden, F., "Taqī al-Dīn Aḥmad ibn ʿAlī al-Maqrīzī", in *Medieval Muslim Historians and the Franks in the Levant*, ed. A. Mallett (Leiden–Boston: Brill, 2014): 161–200.
Bauden (forthcoming)
"Maqriziana XIV: Al-Maqrīzī's last opus (*al-Ḫabar ʿan al-bašar*) and its significance for the historiography of the pre-modern Islamicate world."
BeDuhn (2011)
BeDuhn, J., "The New Marcion. Rethinking the "Arch-Heretic"," *Forum*. Third Series 4 (2015): 163–179.
Blankinship (1993)
Blankinship, Kh.Y. (trans.), *The History of al-Ṭabarī. XI: The Challenge to the Empires* (*Bibliotheca Persica*) (Albany: State University of New York Press, 1993).
Bosworth (1999)
Bosworth, C.E. (trans.), *The History of al-Ṭabarī. V: The Sāsānids, the Byzantines, the Lakhmids, and Yemen* (*Bibliotheca Persica*) (Albany: State University of New York Press, 1999).
Boyce (1957)
Boyce, M., "The Parthian gosan and Iranian minstrel tradition," *JRAS* N.S. 89 (1957): 10–45.
Boyce (1968)
Boyce, M. (1968), *The Letter of Tansar* (*Serie Orientale Roma* 38) (Roma: Istituto italiano per il medio ed estremo Oriente, 1968).
Christensen (1936)
Christensen, A., *L'Iran sous les sassanides* (Copenhagen: Levin&Munksgaard–Ejnar Munksgaard, 1936).

Crone (1991)

Crone, P., "Kavād's heresy and Mazdak's revolt," [Iran 29, 1991: 1–49], repr. in P. Crone, *From Kavād to al-Ghazālī. Religion, Law and Political Thought in the Near East, c. 600–c. 1100* (Aldershot: Ashgate Variorum, 2005), no. I.

Daryaee (2009)

Daryaee, T., *Sāsānian Persia. The Rise and Fall of an Empire* (London: I.B. Tauris, 2009).

Durkin-Meisterernst (2004)

Durkin-Meisterernst, D., *Dictionary of Manichaean Middle Persian and Parthian* (*Dictionary of Manichaean Texts* III/1, *Corpus Fontium Manichaeorum*) (Turnhout: Brepols, 2004).

El Cheikh (2004)

El Cheikh, N.M., *Byzantium Viewed by the Arabs* (*Harvard Middle Eastern Monographs* 36) (Cambridge, Ma.—London: Harvard University Press, 2004).

Fagnan (1893)

Fagnan, E., *Catalogue général des manuscrits des bibliothèques publiques de France*, vol. 18: Alger (Paris: E. Plon, Nourrit et Cie, 1893).

Fahd (1966)

Fahd, T., *La divination arabe. Études religieuses, sociologiques et folkloriques sur le milieu natif de l'Islam* (Leiden: Brill, 1966).

Fihris al-kutub

Fihris al-kutub al-ʿarabiyyah al-mawǧūdah bi-l-Dār (Cairo: Dār al-kutub al-Miṣriyyah, 1924–1963), 10 vols.

Friedmann (1992)

Friedmann, Y. (trans.), *The History of al-Ṭabarī. XII: The Battle of al-Qādisiyyah and the Conquest of Syria and Palestine* (*Bibliotheca Persica*) (Albany: State University of New York Press, 1992).

Grenet (2003)

Grenet, F., *La geste d'Ardashir fils de Pâbag Kārnāmag ī Ardaxshēr ī Pābagān* (Die: Éditions A Die, 2003).

Grignaschi (1966)

Grignaschi, M., "Quelques spécimens de la littérature sassanide conservés dans les bibliothèques d'Istanbul," *JA* (1966): 1–142.

Hämeen-Anttila (2006)

Hämeen-Anttila, J., *The Last Pagans of Iraq. Ibn Waḥshiyya and his Nabatean Agriculture* (*Islamic History and Civilization. Studies and Texts* 63) (Leiden–Boston–Köln: Brill, 2006).

Hämeen-Anttila (2018a)

See al-Maqrīzī, *al-Ḫabar*.

Hämeen-Anttila (2018b)
Khwadāynāmag. The Middle Persian Book of Kings (*Studies in Persian Cultural History* 14) (Leiden–Boston: Brill, 2018).

Hämeen-Anttila (2022a)
"Sharwīn of Dastabay: Reconstructing an early Persian tale," *JRAS*, 32 (2022): 671–684.

Hämeen-Anttila (2022b)
"The letters of Shahrbarāz and Middle Persian historiography on the Last Great War of Late Antiquity," *Journal of Late Antique, Islamic and Byzantine Studies*, 1 (2022): 65–93.

Harb (2019)
Harb, L., "Persian in Arabic poetry: Identity politics and Abbasid macaronics," *JAOS*, 139 (2019): 7–21.

Hoyland (2018)
Hoyland, R.G., *The 'History of the Kings of the Persians' in Three Arabic Chronicles. The Transmission of the Iranian Past from Late Antiquity to Early Islam* (*Translated Texts for Historians* 69) (Liverpool: Liverpool University Press, 2018).

Humphreys (1990)
Humphreys, R.St. (trans.), *The History of al-Ṭabarī. XV: The Crisis of the Early Caliphate* (*Bibliotheca Persica*) (Albany: State University of New York Press, 1990).

Justi (1895)
Justi, F., *Iranisches Namenbuch* (Marburg, 1895).

Juynboll (1989)
Juynboll, G.T.A. (trans.), *The History of al-Ṭabarī. XIII: The Conquest of Iraq, Southwestern Persia, and Egypt* (*Bibliotheca Persica*) (Albany: State University of New York Press, 1989).

Khalidi (1975)
Khalidi, T., *Islamic Historiography. The Histories of Masʿūdī* (Albany: State University of New York Press, 1975).

Kilpatrick (2003)
Kilpatrick, H., *Making the Great Book of Songs. Compilation and the Author's Craft in Abū l-Faraj al-Iṣbahānī's Kitāb al-Aghānī* (*Routledge Studies in Arabian and Middle Eastern Literature*) (London–New York: RoutledgeCurzon, 2003).

Lane (1863–1893)
Lane, E.W., *An Arabic–English Lexicon* (London, 1863–1893, repr. Cambridge: The Islamic Texts Society, 1984), 8 vols. in 2.

MacKenzie (1971)
MacKenzie, D.N., *A Concise Pahlavi Dictionary* (Oxford–New York–Toronto: Oxford University Press, 1971).

Macuch (2009)

Macuch, M., "Pahlavi literature," in R.E. Emmerick–M. Macuch (eds.), *The Literature of Pre-Islamic Persia. Companion Volume I to A History of Persian Literature* (*A History of Persian Literature* XVII) (London–New York: I.B. Tauris, 2009): 116–196.

Mīnuwī (1932)
Mīnuwī, M., *Nāme-ye Tansar* (Maṭbaʿ-e Mağlis, 1311 AHŠ/1932).

Mittwoch (1909)
Mittwoch, E., "Die literarische Tätigkeit Ḥamza al-Iṣbahānīs. Ein Beitrag zur älteren arabischen Literaturgeschichte," (*Mitteilungen des Seminars für Orientalische Sprachen an der Königlichen Friedrich-Wilhelms-Universität zu Berlin*. Jahrgang XII, Zweite Abteilung: Westasiatische Studien, 1909): 109–169.

Nöldeke (1879)
Nöldeke, Th., *Geschichte der Perser und Araber zur Zeit der Sāsāniden aus der arabischen Chronik des Tabari* (Leiden: Brill, 1879).

Nyberg (1974)
Nyberg, H.S., *A Manual of Pahlavi. II: Glossary* (Wiesbaden: Harrassowitz, 1974).

Penelas (2021)
See al-Maqrīzī, *al-Ḫabar*.

Poonawala (1990)
Poonawala, I.K. (trans.), *The History of al-Ṭabarī. IX: The Last Years of the Prophet* (*Bibliotheca Persica*) (Albany: State University of New York Press, 1990).

Pourshariati (2008)
Pourshariati, P., *Decline and Fall of the Sasanian Empire. The Sasanian-Parthian Confederacy and the Arab Conquest of Iran* (London–New York: I.B. Tauris, 2008).

Reeves (2011)
Reeves, J.C., *Prolegomena to a History of Islamicate Manichaeism* (*Comparative Islamic Studies*) (Sheffield–Bristol: Equinox, 2011).

Rosenthal (1989)
Rosenthal, F. (trans.), *The History of al-Ṭabarī. I: General Introduction and From the Creation to the Flood* (*Bibliotheca Persica*) (Albany: State University of New York Press, 1989).

Rowson (1989)
Rowson, E.K. (trans.), *The History of al-Ṭabarī. XXII: The Marwānid Restoration* (*Bibliotheca Persica*) (Albany: State University of New York Press, 1989).

Saadi-nejad (2021)
Saadi-nejad, M., *Anahita: A History and Reception of the Iranian Water Goddess* (London–New York–Oxford–New Delhi–Sydney: I.B. Tauris, 2021).

Schindel (2013)
Schindel, N., "Sasanian coinage," in D.T. Potts (ed.), *The Oxford Handbook of Ancient Iran* (Oxford: Oxford University Press, 2013), 814–839.

Shaked (1984)
Shaked, S., "From Iran to Islam: notes on some themes in transmission," *JSAI* 4 (1984): 31–67.
Shboul (1979)
Shboul, A.M.H., *al-Masʿūdī & His World. A Muslim humanist and his interest in non-Muslims* (London: Ithaca Press, 1979).
Smith (1994)
Smith, G.R. (trans.), *The History of al-Ṭabarī. XIV: The Conquest of Iran* (*Bibliotheca Persica*) (Albany: State University of New York Press, 1994).
Toral-Niehoff (2014)
Toral-Niehoff, I., *Al-Ḥīra. Eine arabische Kulturmetropole im spätantiken Kontext* (*Islamic History and Civilization. Studies and Texts* 104) (Leiden–Boston: Brill, 2014).
Vacca (2017)
Vacca, A., *Non-Muslim Provinces under Early Islam: Islamic rule and Iranian legitimacy in Armenia and Caucasian Albania* (*Cambridge Studies in Islamic Civilization*) (Cambridge: Cambridge University Press, 2017).
Webb (2019)
See al-Maqrīzī, *al-Ḫabar*.
Zakeri (2008)
Zakeri, M., "al-Ṭabarī on Sāsānian History: a Study in Sources," in *al-Ṭabarī. A Medieval Muslim Historian and His Work*, ed. H. Kennedy (*Studies in Late Antiquity and Early Islam* 15) (Princeton, New Jersey: The Darwin Press, 2008), 27–40.

List of Quoted Manuscripts

Algiers, Bibliothèque nationale, MS 1059a

Cairo, Dār al-Kutub, MS 5251, *Taʾrīḫ*

Istanbul, Süleymaniye Kütüphanesi, MS Aya Sofya 3365
Istanbul, Süleymaniye Kütüphanesi, MS Fatih 4340
Istanbul, Topkapı Sarayı Müzesi Kütüphanesi, MS2926/5

Index of Qurʾānic Verses

Page and line numbers between parentheses refer to the translation.

إبرٰهيم [14]
أَوَلَمْ تَكُونُوٓا أَقْسَمْتُم مِّن قَبْلُ مَا لَكُم مِّن زَوَالٍ [44]
348:7 (349:12–13)

الروم [30]
الم غُلِبَتِ ٱلرُّومُ فِي أَدْنَى ٱلْأَرْضِ [1–3]
288:7 (289:13–14)

Index of Verses

ص/p.	بحره/meter	قافيته/rhyme	صدر البيت/beg. of 1st hemistich
102	wāfir/الوافر	الجُنودِ	أتاهم
96	mutaqārib/المتقارب	القُدُم	أقام
102	khafīf/الخفيف	الثرثارِ	أقفرَ
96	mutaqārib/المتقارب	نَعْمِ	ألم ترَ
102	wāfir/الوافر	العَبِيد	ألم يُخْبِرك
96	sarīʿ/السريع	كالسَّعِيْرِ	دلفنا
92	khafīf/الخفيف	وُكُورُ	شَادَه
94	khafīf/الخفيف	مَكْنونِ	صرعته
96	sarīʿ/السريع	شَهْرَزُورِ	فلاقَتْ
96	mutaqārib/المتقارب	جَشَم	فموتوا
102	wāfir/الوافر	الحديد	فهدَّم
96	mutaqārib/المتقارب	لم يُقَمْ	فهل زادَه
96	sarīʿ/السريع	الذُكورِ	لقيناهم
92	khafīf/الخفيف	مهْجورُ	لم يهبْه
38	sarīʿ/السريع	التين	نشربها
92, 10	khafīf/الخفيف	والخابورُ	وأخو الحَضْر
94	khafīf/الخفيف	السَّاطِرُوْن	وأرى
96	mutaqārib/المتقارب	صَرِم	وكان
102	wāfir/الوافر	تَزِيد	ومَصْرعُ
96	sarīʿ/السريع	شروين	يا أيها السائل

Index of Names (People and Places)

Place names, tribes, families, and ethnic groups are to be searched respectively under Places and Tribes, dynasties, families and other groups.

Ābān Ǧādūyah 363
Abarwīz (Kisrá) 9–10, 20, 253–255, 259–261, 265–315, 319, 325, 331–333, 337, 349–353, 361, 367–369
ʿAbd Allāh b. ʿAbd al-Muṭṭalib 211
ʿAbd Allāh b. Abī Bakr 305–307
ʿAbd Allāh b. ʿĀmir 363
ʿAbd al-Raḥmān b. Rabīʿah 363
Abraham the Friend 131, 187
Abū Bakr b. Abī Šaybah 309
Abū Bakr al-Ṣiddīq 317–321, 333
Abū Bakrah 333
Abū Dāʾūd 389
Abū Duʾād al-Iyādī 95
Abū Ḥamzah 389
Abū Hurayrah 307
Abū Miḥǧan al-Ṯaqafī 343
Abū Mūsá l-Ašʿarī 357–359
Abū Nuʿaym 2, 6, 303–307
Abū Sabrah b. Abī Ruhm 357–359
Abū Salamah b. ʿAbd al-Raḥmān 305–307
Abū ʿUbayd b. Masʿūd b. ʿAmr al-Ṯaqafī 321–327, 331
Abū ʿUbaydah b. al-Ǧarrāḥ 343
Abzūdšāh 313
Adam 383, 389
ʿAdī b. Zayd 93, 105
Ādīn-Ǧusnas 259
ʿAḍud al-Dawlah 51
Ādurbād 141
Afrīdūn 359
Ahasverus 41n27
al-Aḥnaf b. Qays 357–359, 363–367
Aḫšawīruš 41
Aḫšunwār 175–183
Aḫšunwāz *see* Aḫšunwār
Ahwad 349
al-ʿAlāʾ b. al-Ḥaḍramī 355
Alexander 37, 43, 49, 61, 105, 115, 249
ʿAlī b. Abī Ṭālib 353
ʿAlī b. Būyah, ʿImād al-Dawlah 51n57
ʿAlī b. Ḥamzah *see* Ḥamzah al-Iṣfahānī
al-Āmidī 1, 7, 95
ʿAmmār b. Yāsir 357
ʿAmr b. ʿAdī b. Naṣr b. Rabīʿah 119
ʿAmr b. Alah 97, 101
ʿAmr b. Fahm 49
ʿAmr b. Imriʾ al-Qays 141, 151
ʿAmr b. Maʿdīkarib 341
Anāhīd 49
Anas b. Mālik 357
Anūširwān (Kisrá) 4, 10, 19, 71n105, 121, 173, 183, 187, 191–231, 235, 239, 243–245, 253
Ardašīr b. Bābak 3, 8, 19, 35, 39–55, 87–91, 105–109, 113, 153, 197, 203, 253, 337, 381
Ardašīr b. Hurmuz (Ardašīr) 19, 141–143
Ardašīr b. Šīrūyah (Ardašīr) 20, 315–317, 331
Ardawān 47, 53–55, 111
ʿArfaǧah 37
ʿĀrik 365
Artaxerxes 41n27
Arwanddašt 313
Arwandzīl 313
al-Aʿšā Maymūn 10n28, 97–99
al-Ašʿaṯ b. Qays 341
Asbād-Ǧušnas 311
ʿĀṣim b. ʿAmr 341–343, 357
Ašk ibn Ḫurrah 89
Aws b. Qalām 151
Āzarmīduḫt bt. Kisrá (Ādarmīgduḫt) 20, 313, 323, 333–337
Azdašīr *see* Ardašīr

Bābak b. Sāsān the Younger 6, 19, 41–45
Baʿbūr (generic) 221
Bādām *see* Bādān
Bādān 297, 309
Bahman Ǧādūyah, Ḏū l-Ḥāǧib 327–329, 341–343
Bahman b. Isfandiyād b. Yustāsf 19, 35, 165, 219, 253
Bahrām b. Bahrām (Warahrān) 19, 99, 121, 147
Bahrām b. Bahrām b. Bahrām (Warahrān) 19, 41, 99, 121, 147

Bahrām b. Hurmuz (Warahrān) 19, 99, 111, 115–119
Bahrām b. Sābūr (Warahrān) 3, 19, 145, 151
Bahrām b. Siyāwuš 269
Bahrām b. Yazdağird b. Bahrām Ğūr 41
Bahrām Ğūbīn (Čūbīn) b. Bahrām-Ğusnas (Warahrān) 20, 257–261, 265–273, 295, 351
Bahrām Ğūr b. Yazdağird (Warahrān) 2, 19, 39, 151–169, 177
Balāš b. Fīrūz (Walāẖš) 19, 181–183
al-Barāʾ b. Mālik 357
Barāz 20, 371–379
Bardaisan 113
Barmūdah b. Šābah 257
al-Binduwān 343
Bindūyah 261, 267–271
Bindūyah (son of Bisṭām) 325
al-Bīrūnī 2
Bīrūyah (son of Bisṭām) 325
Bisṭām 261, 267, 271
Bistāsf 243
Būdāsf 385
al-Buẖārī 333
Bukayr b. ʿAbd Allāh 361
Būrān bt. Kisrá (Bōrānduẖt) 20, 313, 317–319, 323–325, 331–333
Bus-Farrūẖ 317
Bušayr b. al-Ḫaṣāṣiyyah 321
Buṭrā 273
Buzurğmihr al-Hamaḏānī 343

Caesar (generic) 137–139, 203–205, 221, 225, 235–239, 271, 323, 381
Constantine 131–133
Cyrus 253

Dāhir 351
Dakwā 113
Dārā the Elder 35
Dārā the Younger b. Dārā 49, 61
Darius 249
al-Ḍayzan b. Muʿāwiyah 95–99, 103–105
Dīnār 361
Ḍirār b. al-Ḫaṭṭāb 347–349
Ḏū l-Ḥāğib *see* Bahman Ğādūyah
al-Ḍubayb 269

al-Faḍl b. ʿĪsá l-Raqāšī 303
al-Fahlūğ 329, 359
Farīd b. Sāsān b. Bahman b. Isfandiyād 219
Farruẖ-Hurmuz 335
al-Farruẖān 275, 281, 317, 349
al-Farruẖzād b. al-Binduwān 323
Farruẖzād b. Ḫar-Hurmuz 371–373
Farruẖzād-Ḫusraw b. Kisrá Abarwīz 20, 335–337
Fattiq 111n203
Fīrūz 20, 333, 337
Fīrūz b. Ardašīr 113
Fīrūz b. Bahrām Ğušnas-Banda 20, 335
Fīrūz b. Yazdağird (Pērōz) 19, 41, 171–183, 207, 291
al-Fīrūzān 329–331, 337, 341
Fīrūzānšāh 313
Fīrūzduẖt bt. Fīrūz 179
al-Fīrzān 343–345, 349–351
Fūqāṣ 275
Fus-Bih 315
Fus-Dil 315

Ğābān 325, 329
Ğādūyah *see* Hurmuz Ğādūyah
Ğahārbaẖt 315
Ğaẖğabā b. ʿAtīk 151
Ġālib b. ʿAbd Allāh 341
al-Ğālnūs 325–327, 341, 347
Ğāmāsf b. Fīrūz (Ğāmāsp) 19, 187–191
al-Ğārūd b. al-Muʿallá 355
Ğawānšīr 315
Gayōmart 383, 389
Ğayhalah 95
Ġūrak 365n725
Ğušnas-Bandah 333–335

al-Ḥağğāğ b. Yūsuf 303
Ḫalaf al-Aḥmar 95
Ḫālid b. ʿAbd Allāh al-Qasrī 1, 17
Ḫālid b. Ğabalah 205n403
Ḫālid b. al-Walīd 319, 333
al-Hamdānī 2, 5, 53–55
Ḥammād al-Rāwiyah 95
Ḥamzah al-Iṣfahānī 1–2, 5–7, 9, 18, 37, 41, 49, 105, 121n232, 143–147, 169, 333–335
Ḥanẓalah b. Šarqī 95
Ḫāqān (generic) 161–167, 183, 201, 209, 221, 227, 237–239, 253, 273, 351, 363–369

al-Ḥāriṯ b. Abī Šamr 205
al-Ḥāriṯ b. ʿAmr b. Ḥuǧr al-Kindī 191–197, 211–213
al-Ḥāriṯ b. Ẓabyān 343
Ḥāriṯah b. ʿImrān b. al-Ḥaǧǧāǧ 95
Ḥāriṯah b. al-Nuʿmān 365
al-Ḥasan al-Baṣrī 303, 333
Hāšim b.ʿUtbah b. Abī Waqqāṣ 343, 353
Ḫa(s)ruh 315
Ḥassān b. Ḥanẓalah b. Abī Ruhm 269
Ḥātim b. al-Nuʿmān 365n727
Ḫātūn 273
Ḥawānī 155
Ḥawṯarah b. al-Ḥaǧǧāǧ 95
Heraclius 14, 277–283, 291, 351
Hilāl b. ʿUllafah 345–349
Hišām b. Muḥammad al-Kalbī 2, 95–97, 119, 145
Ḥuḏayfah b. al-Yamān 361
Ḫulayd b. al-Munḏir b. Sāwī 355–357
Ḫumānī 35
Ḫurdāḏ-Ḫusraw 20, 335
Hurmuz (man sent to the Turks) 273
Hurmuz b. Kisrá (Ohrmazd) 19, 253–267, 277
Hurmuz b. Narsī (Ohrmazd) 19, 123–125
Hurmuz b. Sābūr (Ohrmazd) 19, 99, 107–111, 119
Hurmuz b. Yazdaǧird (Ohrmazd) 19, 171
Hurmuz Ǧādūyah 319–321, 341
al-Hurmuzān 345, 349, 357
Ḫurrahān 317
Ḫurramard 315
Ḫurrīn 39n21
Ḫuršīdān 267
Ḥuṣayn b. ʿAbd Allāh b. Šaddād 309
Ḫusraw Miqlāṣ 14, 359
Ḫusraw-Šunūm 349
Ḫwarrīn 39n21

Iblīs 389
Ibn ʿAbbās 389
Ibn al-Aṯīr 2, 6
Ibn Dayṣān *see* Bardaisan
Ibn Ǧayhalah *see* al-Ḍayzan b. Muʿāwiyah
Ibn al-Hirbad 349
Ibn Hišām 1, 7, 97
Ibn Isḥāq 1, 7, 97–101, 297, 303–305
Ibn Miskawayh *see* Miskawayh
Ibn al-Muqaffaʿ 43n35
Ibn al-Nadīm 2, 6
Īliyā 381
ʿImrān b. al-Qaṭṭān 389
Imruʾ al-Qays al-Badʾ b. ʿAmr 119, 141
al-Iṣfahānī 2
Ishmael 131

Jesus 113
Jovian (Yūsānūs) 135–137
Julian 131–135
Justinian 205n403

Kābulšāh 237
Kay Bahman *see* Bahman b. Isfandiyād
Kay Bištāsf 385
Kay Qubād 197
Kisrá (generic) 19, 367
Kisrá (descendant of Ardašīr) 19, 153–159
Kisrá b. Hurmuz (Ḫosrow) 20
Kisrá b. Mihr-Ǧušnas 337
Kisrá b. Qubāḏ (Ḫosrow) *see* Anūširwān
Kūrānšāh 313
Kurdī 267, 271–273
Kurdiyyah 273

Māʾ al-Samāʾ 211
Maǧzaʾah b. Ṯawr 357
Māhūyah 371–373
Mālik b. Fahm 49
al-Maʾmūn 117
Mani 2, 6, 105, 111–117
al-Maqrīzī 1–21
Mār Maryam 111
Mārasfand 293
Marbūd 177
Mardbūd 177n346
Marcion 113
Mardānšāh 313, 329
Maryam, daughter of Mauricius 271–273, 311, 323
al-Marzubānī 1, 7, 95
Masrūq the Ethiopian 207
al-Masʿūdī 101
Mauricius 269–275
Mawrīǧiyuš Qayṣar 269
Mays 111
Mazdak b. Bāmdādān/Bāmārd 185–189, 197–199, 211–213

Messenger of God *see* Muḥammad
Mih-Ādur-Ǧušnas 315
Mihr-Hurmuz b. Mardānšāh 313
Mihr-Narsī 149, 165–171
Mihrak 107–109
Mihrān al-Hamaḏānī 329
Mihrān al-Rāzī 351–353
Miqlāṣ *see* Ḫusraw Miqlāṣ
Miskawayh 1–9, 11–14, 18, 55, 133, 145–147, 169, 221, 323, 331–337
al-Muġīrah b. Šuʿbah 339
Muḥammad (the Prophet) 131, 197, 295–299, 303–305, 309, 315, 331–333
Muḥammad b. ʿAbd Allāh 307
Muḥammad b. Fuḍayl 309
Muḥammad b. Kaʿb al-Quraẓī 303
Muʿizz al-Dawlah b. Būyah 117
al-Munḏir b. al-Ǧārūd 355
al-Munḏir b. al-Nuʿmān 151–155, 191, 197, 205, 211–213
al-Muqtadir 117
Mūrān 275
Mušel (Mamikonean) 271
al-Muʿtaṣim 117
al-Muṯanná b. Ḥāriṯah al-Šaybānī 319–331, 339
Muzdbuqad 177n346

al-Naḍīrah bt. al-Ḍayzan 99, 103
Naḫǧīrakān *see* Narsī b. Bahrām
al-Naḫīrǧān 351
Narsī (son of Kisrá's maternal aunt) 325–327
Narsī (Vizier of Yazdaǧird the Sinner) *see* Mihr-Narsī
Narsī b. Bahrām (Narseh) 19, 121–123, 161, 165
Naṣr b. Rabīʿah 119
Nīzak Ṭarḫān 371–375
Nuʿaym b. Muqarrin 361
al-Nuʿmān b. Imriʾ al-Qays al-Badʾ 151
al-Nuʿmān b. al-Munḏir 153, 191, 207, 283, 351
al-Nuʿmān b. Muqarrin 359–361

Orosius 2, 6, 133

Paracletus 113
Phocas 275

Places
Abaršahr 47n49, 189
Aden 207
al-Ahwāz 47, 129, 137, 183, 205, 337, 357, 381
Aleppo 205
Alexandria 203, 275
Āmid 191
ʿĀnāt 213
al-Anbār 105, 129, 213, 329, 339
Anšaʾa-Ardašīr 51n60
Antioch 93, 105, 203–205, 269
Apamea 205
ʿAqar Bābil 291
Ardašīr-ḫurrah 47, 51, 125, 173
Ariš 191
Armenia 47, 161, 201, 207, 211, 277, 361
Arraǧān 183
Arrān 191
Ašaʾ-Ardašīr 51n60
Astābād-Ardašīr 51n60
Aštād-Ardašīr 51
al-ʿAtīq 345–347
ʿAyn al-Tamr 103
Azerbaijan 47, 161–163, 173, 227, 237, 259, 265–267, 269–271, 361
Bā Ǧarmā 97n159
Bāʾišrawān 147
Bāb (wa)-al-Abwāb 191, 207–209, 235–237, 359–363
Bāb (Allān) 191
Bāb Ṣūl 173, 227
Babel 43, 111, 117, 321
Bādġīs 257
Bādūryā 337
Bāġ al-Hinduwān 293
Bāǧarwān 147
Baġdād 15, 117, 329–331
Bahman-Ardašīr 51
Bahmanšīr 51
Bahrain 49, 125, 129, 137, 355
Balanǧar 227, 363
Balḫ 47, 165, 207, 363–367
Bardaʿah 191
Bardašīr 51
Basra 355, 363
al-Baylaqān 191
Bī-Šābūr 105n189
Bih-Ardašīr 51

Bih-az-Andīw-Sābūr 105
Bihrasīr 51
al-Burǧān 207, 237
Buzurǧ-Sābūr 129
Byzantium 93, 131, 137–139, 147, 165, 171, 203, 207, 213, 225, 275, 279–281
China 12, 115–117, 363–371
Constantinople 131–133, 245, 275–277, 289
Damascus 343
al-Danaq 271
Dārā 205
Dārābǧird 45
al-Darb 283
Darband 209
Dardistān 199
Dārīn 129
Darwistān 199n393
al-Daskarah 221, 279, 307
Dastabá 147
Dastmaysān 111
al-Dāwar 237
al-Daybul 165, 169
Dayṣān 113
Demavend 361
al-Dīnawar 191
Ḏū Qār 283, 339
Dūristān 191n393
Egypt 205, 213, 275
Ethiopia 355
Euphrates 93, 193–195, 257, 267, 303, 327–329
Farġānah 207, 365–371
Fārs 41, 47–51, 98, 91, 105, 111, 115–117, 125, 129–133, 137–139, 155, 167–169, 173, 183, 191–195, 273, 277, 281, 285, 289, 295, 321–325, 329–331, 335, 339, 355, 365–369
Fasā 197
Fīrūz-Bahrām 167
Fīrūz-Ḫusrah 227
Fīrūz-Šābūr 105
Fīrūzābād 51
Furāt-Maysān 51
al-Ǧabal 9, 47, 173, 355, 359
Ǧabal al-Qabaq 163
Ǧalūlā 17, 353, 363
Ǧarwā'ān 141
Ǧay 173
Ǧazīrah 97, 119, 205, 285, 289–291
al-Ǧibāl 359–361
Ǧūbānān 45
Ǧulanbadān 373
Ǧundī-Sābūr 105
Gundīsābūr 93, 115, 139–141, 359
Ǧurǧan 47, 149, 173, 201, 361
Ǧustān 51
Ḫabur 93, 105
al-Ḥadīṯah 17, 139
Haǧar 129
Hamadan 47, 111, 221, 227, 361
al-Ḥaskāniyyah 111n204
Hatra 93–115
al-Ḫaṭṭ 129
Heraclea 203
Herat 257, 263
Hiǧaz 119, 229
Ḥimṣ 205
al-Ḥīrah 49, 105, 195, 207, 211, 319–321, 333, 339
Ḫīr 41n30
Hīt 213
al-Ḥudaybiyah 17, 139n274
Hūǧistān Wāǧār 41n61
Ḥulwān 9, 17, 181–183, 351–355, 359
Ḥumāniyah 307
Ḫurasan 93, 97, 109, 115–117, 131, 165, 171, 177–181, 271–273, 319, 335, 359, 363–365, 369
Ḫūristān 51n61
Hurmuz-Ardašīr 51n61
al-Ḫusrakāniyyah 111
Ḫuzistan 51–53, 105, 123
Ḫwarizm 47, 163, 237
Ifrīqiyah 289
India 115, 161–163, 167, 207, 237, 295
Iran 1
Īrānšahr 51, 139
Īrānšahr-Sābūr 139n273
Iraq 47, 51, 105, 117–119, 205, 217, 285, 289, 303, 321, 339
Isfahan 53, 137, 173, 271, 357, 363
Iṣṭaḫr 35, 41–49, 55, 137, 337, 349, 357, 381
Jerusalem 275
Kaaba 347
Kābul 371
Kalah 237

al-Karḫ 129, 141
Karḫ-Maysān 51
Karwān 297
Kaskar 325
Kāẓimah 125, 213
Kirmān 45, 51, 129, 137, 145, 363, 369
Kufa 363
Kūṯā 131
al-Lahab 361
al-Madāʾin 49–53, 111, 125, 139–141, 147, 171, 183, 203, 207, 261, 265–273, 279, 303, 315, 321, 329–331, 335–337, 351, 381
Māh 169, 253, 361
Makrān 165, 169
Manbiǧ 205
Maʾrib 197
Marw 47, 355, 359, 363, 367–377, 381–383
Marw al-Rūd 363–365
Marw al-Šāhiǧān 363–365
Maysān 51, 337
Mecca 295, 355
Medina 129, 295, 315, 321, 355–357
al-Mirbāʿ 103
Mosul 47, 93, 279, 291
Mūqān 361
Muẓlim Sābāṭ 349
al-Naǧaf 195
Nahr Šīr 51n60, 97n162
Nahrašīr 51n60, 153, 291, 349–351
Nahrawān 265, 351
al-Namāriq 325
al-Narsiyān 325–327
Nasā 363
Nī-Šābūr 105
Nihāwand 359–361
Nineveh 279
Nišapur 47, 131, 183, 363
Nisibis 93, 137, 277–279, 337
Nubia 275
Persia 121, 125, 133
Persian Sea 45
al-Qādisiyyah 11, 335, 345, 371
Qālīqalā 269
Qirqīsiyā 285
Qūmis 361
al-Rabḏah 355
Rām-Ardašīr 51n61
Rām-Hurmuz 51, 109, 123
Rām-Hurmuz-Ardašīr 51n61
Rāšahr 125
Rayy 13, 165, 172–173, 195, 223, 361–363
al-Ruhā 205
al-Ruḫḫaǧ 199
al-Rumaylah 129
al-Rūmiyyah 203
Sābāṭ al-Madāʾin 181, 255, 329–331, 341
Šahrazūr 97
Samarqand 117
Saraḫs 363, 373
al-Ṣarāt 321
Sawād 47, 53, 95–97, 131, 137, 193–195, 205, 213, 217, 291, 307, 321, 325, 339
Serendip 207, 237
al-Sīb 321
Siǧistan 47, 121, 141, 171, 181, 307, 359, 369
al-Sind 141, 165, 199, 359
Širwān 191
Sogdiana 365
Ṣūl 201
Sumaysāṭ 269
Sūq al-Ahwāz 51
Surūš-Ādurān (Fire of) 141, 173
al-Sūs 105, 129, 141, 357–359
Syria 49, 53, 93, 97, 137, 205, 213, 275, 283–285, 289–291, 361
Ṭabaristān 121, 361
Taflis 361
al-Ṭālaqān 171, 181
al-Ṭarṯār 103
Tawwaǧ 137
Ṭaysabūn 125, 135, 141, 155, 291, 315
Tigris 51, 125, 171, 261–263, 279, 297, 301–303, 321
Tikrit 93, 331
Ṭīrūdih 41
Transoxania 163, 173
Tuḫaristan 171, 181, 199, 363
Ṭūs 363
Tustar 93, 105, 357
al-Ubullah 339, 355
ʿUkbarā 129
Wahišt-Hurmuz 123n240
al-Yamāmah 129, 137
Yemen 165, 195–197, 207, 211, 219, 297, 309
Zābulistān 199
Prophet *see* Muḥammad

Qabīṣah b. Iyās al-Ṭāʾī 319
al-Qaʿqāʿ b. ʿAmr 343–347, 353, 361
Qāran 349
Qarmīsinā 295
Qays b. Hubayrah b. al-Makšūḥ 345
Qubād (one of the Petty Kings) 197
Qubāḏ b. Fīrūz (Kawād) 10, 15, 19, 121, 179–197, 207, 215, 219, 243, 291–293
Qubāḏ b. Kisrá *see* Šīrūyah
Qunnaq 111, 113

Rāḥab bt. Šālatyāyal 35
Rāhzād 279
Rāmbihišt 35n5, 41n31
Rustam 323–331, 335–341, 345–349, 371
Rūzbān Ṣūl 361

Šābah 257
Sābūr b. Ardašīr of the Armies (Šābuhr) 8, 19, 49, 87–93, 97–109, 113–115, 119
Sābūr b. Bābak 45n42
Sābūr b. Hurmuz of Shoulders (Šābuhr) 8, 19, 97–99, 123–143, 151
Sābūr b. Sābūr (Šābuhr) 19, 143–145
Sābūr al-Rāzī 185
Saʿd b. Abī l-ʿArǧāʾ 357
Saʿd b. Abī Waqqāṣ 339–341, 349–351, 355
Šādādḫurrah 313n603
Šādazīl 313
Šādmān 313
Šāhbūr *see* Sābūr
Šāhīn 275
Šahrak 357
Šahrbarāz Farruḫān Ḫurrahān 20, 275–285, 289, 315–323, 331, 349
Šahriyār (convert to Islam) 359
Šahriyār b. Abarwīz 307, 313, 337, 381
Šahriyār b. Kanārā 349
al-Sāʾib 297–299
Ṣāliḥ b. Ǧaʿfar 303
Ṣāliḥ b. Kaysān 307
Šamir, Ḏū l-Ǧanāḥ 195
Sanǧān 21, 371–373, 379
Sārūh 359
Šarwīn al-Dastabī 39, 147
Ṣaʿṣaʿah b. Muʿāwiyah 357
Sāsān the Elder 19, 35, 41, 87, 219
al-Sāṭirūn 95–97, 101
Sawwār b. Hammām 355
Sayf b. Ḏī Yazan 219
Sergius 271
Shealtiel 35n4
Šihrāzād 35
Simon 113
Sinḫibū 201
Šīrīn 10, 295, 307, 311, 381
Šīrūyah (convert to Islam) 359
Šīrūyah Qubāḏ b. Kisrá (Kawād) 10, 20, 291–295, 309–315, 331, 337, 359
Šīrzād 315, 349
Sīs 117
Sisinnios *see* Sīs
Siyāh 357, 359
Siyāwuḫ 351
Siyāwuḫš b. Mihrān b. Bahrām Čūbīn 323–325, 361
al-Suhaylī 17, 95, 99
Sūḫrā 181–185
Ṣūl (generic) 173
Šuraḥbīl 347
Suwayd b. Muqarrin 361

al-Ṭabarī 1–3, 5–9, 11–14, 18, 43, 97, 101, 133, 145–147, 169, 383
Ṭahmūraṯ 105, 385
Tansar 43
Ta(r)rār *see* Barāz
al-Tawm 113
Theodosius 271
Tīrī 43n33
Tribes, dynasties, families, and other groups
ʿAbd al-Qays 125, 129, 137
Abǧar 201
al-ʿadliyyah 185
Antiochians 203
Arabs 4, 11–12, 53, 95, 129–131, 135–137, 151–153, 157, 193, 205, 303, 319, 329, 335, 339, 343, 353, 371–373, 377, 381
Aramaeans 43, 53
Ardawānians 53
Ašǧānians 1, 37–39, 111
Aškānians 87
Assyrians 95n159
al-Bāfirz 199
Bahrā 213
Bakr Iyād 129
Bakr b. Wāʾil 129, 137
Balanǧar 201

Banǧar 201
Banū ʿAbīd b. al-Aǧrām 97, 103
Banū Asad 343
Banū Fārān 151
Banū Ḥanẓalah 129
Banū Ḥulwān 101
Banū ʿIlāf 97
Banū Taġlib 129, 137, 213
Barāhimah 113
al-Bāriz 199n394
Berbers 249
Byzantines 125, 129–131, 135, 139, 191, 207, 211, 235, 243, 247–251, 257, 267–293, 311, 315, 323
Christians 205, 287, 381
Daylamites 165–167, 207, 231
Dualists 389
Ethiopians 207, 219–221
Ḫazars 131, 135, 173, 191, 207–209, 213, 227, 235, 257, 371
Hephthalites 171, 175–177, 181–183, 201, 207, 221, 363
Ḥimyar 53
Ḥīrans 53
Indians 213, 243, 247–249
Iyād 213
Jews 41, 173
al-Kanǧ 227
Kangarāyē 227n443
Kayūmartiyyah 387
Kindah 341
Kūṯaeans 131
Laḫmids 12, 15, 151n300
Magians 43, 115, 273
Mandaeans 111n204
Manichaeans 105n188, 111, 115–117, 199
Mazdakites 185, 189, 201
Mihrān 185
Muḍar 119, 141
al-Muġtasilah 111
Muslims 277, 321, 325–329, 341–347, 351, 355–361, 365–367, 387
Nabateans 53, 97n159, 219
Persians 4, 11, 35–37, 41, 49, 53, 97, 109, 119, 125, 131, 135, 141, 151–157, 161, 177, 181–185, 195, 209, 217–221, 271, 281, 291, 309, 319–333, 339–363, 381–387
Petty Kings 35, 43, 49–51, 87, 97–99, 381
Quḍāʿah 49, 97, 101
Qurayš 131
Rabīʿah 119, 141
Sabians 111, 385
Sāsānians 4, 35–39
Sogdians 363–365
Ṣūl 199
Tamīm 129
Tanūḫ 49, 95
Ṯaqīf 327
Tazīd 95, 103
Turks 115, 125, 161–163, 167, 173, 177–179, 201, 211–213, 227–229, 235–239, 245–251, 257–259, 267, 273, 363–367, 371
Zanǧ 249
Zarāduštiyyah 387–389
Zurwāniyyah 387
al-Zuṭṭ 161
Tubbaʿ 53, 195–197
Ṭulayḥah 341

ʿUmar b. ʿAbd Allāh al-Manẓarāwī 16
ʿUmar b. ʿAbd al-ʿAzīz 305
ʿUmar b. al-Ḫaṭṭāb 18, 217, 253, 321, 325–333, 339, 353–359, 367
Ūtāḫīm 111
ʿUtbah b. Ġazwān 355–357
ʿUṯmān b. ʿAffān 367–383

Valentinian (Balansiyān) 133
Valerian 93n146

Wahb b. Munabbih 297
Wahriz 219–221
al-Wāqidī 303, 307
Warz 201

Yāḫīn 35
Yazdaǧird b. Bahrām (Yazdgerd) (the Sinner) 3, 19, 39, 147–155
Yazdaǧird b. Bahrām Ǧūr (Yazdgerd) 19, 39, 169–171
Yazdaǧird b. Sābūr (Yazdgerd) 19, 147
Yazdaǧird b. Šahriyār b. Kisrá (Yazdgerd) 12, 20, 37 39, 307, 323, 331, 335–341, 345, 349–359, 363–383
Yazdaǧird b. Yazdaǧird 39, 147

Zādān-Farrūḫ 291
Zakwā 113n211

Zarābrūd 313
Zarathustra 187, 385, 389
Zarathustra (second) 187n369, 197
Zarbābīl 35n4
Zarmihr b. Sūḫrā 189
Zuhrah b. Ḥawiyyah 347–349
al-Zuhrī 305–307

Index of Quoted Titles in *al-Ḫabar ʿan al-bašar*

ʿAhd Ardašīr 55, 197, 253

Kitāb Aḫbār al-Furs (Ḥamzah al-Iṣfahānī) 37

Kitāb al-Iklīl (al-Hamdānī) 53

Sīrat Anūširwān wa-siyāsatuhu 221

Taǧārib al-umam (Miskawayh) 169

Taʾrīḫ al-Rūm (Orosius) 133

Index of Sources in *al-Ḫabar ʿan al-bašar*

Kitāb Aḫbār al-Furs (Ḥamzah al-Iṣfahānī) 37
Kitāb al-Iklīl (al-Hamdānī) 53
Taǧārib al-umam (Miskawayh) 169
Taʾrīḫ al-Rūm (Orosius) 133
[*Taʾrīḫ al-rusul wa-l-mulūk*] (al-Ṭabarī) 43, 97, 101, 133, 145, 147, 169, 383

Index of Glosses

This index contains the words glossed by al-Maqrīzī (in the body of the text or in the margins)

Ardašīr 41

bāġ 195, 293
Baġdād 329
(Bih-az)-Andīw-Sābūr 105

faḏšaḫār 121

Hūyah-sunbā 123

kar 121

mil-Ǧazīrah 97

qudum 99

Šakān 121
al-Sāṭirūn 95

tafar 121
tanaḫū 95
al-Tawm 113

Index of Technical Terms

dīwān 183

ǧurmuqānī 97

hērbad 43

iṣbahbad 185

marzubān 235
mōbad mōbadān, mōbadān mōbad 45

Facsimile of MS *Fatih 4340 (Istanbul, Süleymaniye Kütüphanesi), Fols. 137[a]–200[a]*

∵

200

الظلمة والهدى هو المبدا والثاني هو المعاد وخرج ابو داود و[illegible]
عمران الغطان عن [illegible] حمزة عن ابن عباس رضي الله عنه قال ان
اهل فارس لما مات نبيهم كتب لهم ابليس المجوسية

200a

© JAAKKO HÄMEEN-ANTTILA, 2023 | DOI:10.1163/9789004528765_009

الخصمين امر المدعي والمدعا عليه باقتحامها وخوضها والمرور فيها الى
الناحية الاخرى وهي تلتهب وتستعر والناس وقوف على افواهها رافعوا
ايديهم الى الله بتضرع ورنين وبكا فمن كان مبطلا اخذته النار فاحترق
حتى يصير رمادا ومن كان برا بريا خاضها ونفذ فيها حتى يجوزها لا
تتعلق منه بثوب ولا شعر ولا بشر وكان الموكل بالكلام الذي يمتحن
به من اهل بيت معروفين بالدين يتوارثونه خلف عن سلف يرثه العقب
بعد العقب فلا يتجاوز الى غيرهم وكانت هذه المحنة من اعظم سياساتهم
التي يرتدعون بها عن الفواحش ويكفون انفسهم عن الظلم ونحوه من العظايم
وكان يقال لدينهم الدين الاكبر ويقال لهم الامة الكبرى والملة العظمى والحنفا
وكانت الرعية من الفرس ترى بان ملوكها وهم يعترفون بمتوسط من البشر
بين الحق تعالى وبين الخلق يكون درجته في الطاعة فوق درجة الملايكة
ومرتبتهم فيها وكان يقال لعظيمهم موبذ موبذان اي عالم العلما ومكانه
من الملوك مكانه الخلفا من المسلمين يرجعون اليه ويصدرون عن رايه
وكانت الفرس فرقا وهم الكيومرثية والزروانية والزرادشتية
وغيرهم واراوهم متقاربة ويجمعهم القول بالنور والظلمة وانهما اصلان
قديمان وبعضهم يرى ان الظلمة حادثة ويسندون اليها سائر الحوادث
ولذلك يقال لهم الثنوية فيرون ان النور والظلمة هما الفاعلان في عالم
الكون والفساد ويسندون اشرف المتقابلين من الحوادث الى اشرف
المتقابلين من المحدثين ومنهم من يرى ان فوق النور والظلمة غيرهما
هو الاله جهما والاله كل شي لا يشبه شيا ولا يشبهه شي وفيهم عبادته
وطاعته الا انهم ينزهونه من اسناد الحوادث اليه ويسندونها الى
النور والظلمة كما تسند الفلاسفة الى الحركة الدورية وهولا اصلح فرق
المجوس واقربهم الى المعقول وهم الزرادشتية والنبي الاول
بجميعهم كيومرث الذي يزعمون انه ادم والنبي الثاني زرادشت ومباحثهم
تدور على اصلين احدهما امتزاج النور بالظلمة والاخر خلاص النور من

الظلمة

199b

199

فصل في ذكر ديانة الفرس وعباداتهم ورسوم دولتهم وعوائدهم في سياستهم

اما ديانة الفرس التي كانت تتقرب بها الى الله تعالى فيقال
انها كانت اولاً تعتقد توحيد الله عز وجل الى ان ظهر فيهم بيوراسف
المشرقي واتى الى طهمورث الذي هو من ملوك الطبقة الاولى بمذهب الصابية في
اول سنة من ملكه ودعاه اليها فاجابه طهمورث الى ذلك وحمل الرعية
عليه فدانوا بملة الصابيين نحو الف سنة وثمانمائة سنة ثم ظهر
زردشت الغازي في سنة ثلاثين من ملك كيبشتاسف ودعا الى
دين المجوسية من تعظيم النار وساير الانوار والقول بتركيب العالم من
النور والظلمة واعتقاد القدماء الخمسة التي هي عندهم البارئ تعالى
وابليس والهيولى والزمان والمكان وغير ذلك من شريعة المجوس
فقبله كيبشتاسف منه والزم الفرس اعتقاده فدانوا به ورفضوا
ملة الصابيين وجعلوا حيث هياكلها بيوتاً للنيران ولم تتغير في
تعظيم النار كما كانت اهل الديانة الاولى تفعله بل استكثروا منها
واتخذوا لها بيوتاً وسدنة ووقفوا عليها الضياع والاملاك ثم غلبهم
الغلو فيها حتى عبدوها من دون الله تعالى وكيفية عبادتهم لها انهم حفروا
لها اخدوداً في بقاع الارض واججوا فيه النار ثم كانوا لا يدعون
طعاماً شهياً ولا شراباً لذيذاً ولا ثوباً فاخراً ولا نباتاً عطراً الا طرحوه
فيها تقرباً اليها وتبركاً بها وكانوا يأمرون باحيائها وينهون عن
اطفائها ويمنعون الحيض من مسها والدنو منها ولم يزالوا متمسكين
بدين زرادشت وشريعته الى ان انقضت دولتهم وقد كانت للفرس
محنة يمتحنون بها الاشياء العظيمة بالنار فيجمعون الحطب
الجزل الكثير ويشعلون فيه ناراً حتى اذا تأججت واستعرت اتي
بالمدعى عليه فاحشة او عظيمة في دين او دنيا والمدعي معه ثم يتكلم
متكلم بكلام لهم كان هو المحنة التي تفرق بين الامرين وتفصل بين

كلهم حسنو السيرة ويعتمد على سيفه وكان يزدجرد هذا آخر ملك ملك
من آل اردشير بابك فجميع ما ملك ملوك الفرس اربعة الاف سنة
واحدى وسبعين سنة وعشرة اشهر وتسعة عشر يوما فيها استوى
ملكا وفي نسخة جملة الطبقة الرابعة وكانوا ثمانية وعشرين ملكا سوى
ثلاثين سنة تحارب فيها اردشير بابك مع ملوك الطوايف اربع مائة
سنة وست وخمسون سنة وشهر واحد واثنان وعشرون يوما
وجميع ذلك من انتشاء النسل الى اخر ايام الفرس وكانوا ستة وستين
ملكا اربعة الاف واربع مائة وتسع سنين وتسعة اشهر وعشرون
يوما وفي نسخة جملة مدة الطبقة الرابعة اربعمائة واحد وثلاثون سنة
وقيل اربع مائة وتسع وسبعون سنة وقيل اربع مائة واربع وخمسون سنة
وقيل اربع مائة وثلث واربعون سنة وقيل سبعمائة وست وتسعون
سنة وليس بصحيح وقال الطبري لا تنازع بين علما الامم ان جيومرث
هو ابو الفرس وانما اختلفوا فيه هل هو ادم ابو البشر ام هو غيره
ثم مع ذلك فملكه وملك اولاده لم يزل منتظما على سياق متسقا بارض
المشرق وجبالها الى ان قتل يزدجرد بن شهريار [illegible] بمرو ايام
عثمان بن عفان رضي الله عنه فتاريخ سني العالم على اعمارهم اسهل بيانا
واوضح منارا منه على اعمار ملوك غيرهم من الامم اذ لا نعلم امة من الامم
الذين ينتسبون الى ادم دامت لها المملكة واتصل لها الملك وكان
لهم ملوك تجمعهم وروس تحامي عنهم من ناواهم وتغالب بهم من عاداهم
وتدفع ظالمهم عن مظلومهم وتحملهم من الامور على ما فيه حظهم على
اتصال ودوام ونظام ياخذ ذلك اخرهم عن اولهم وغابرهم عن سالفهم
سواهم فالتاريخ على اعمار ملوكهم اصح مخرجا واحسن وضوحا

198

سخين

يزدجرد فخرج ذاهبا على وجهه راجلا لينجو بنفسه فمشى نحوا من فر
حتى وقع الى رحى ماء فدخل بيت الرحا فجلس فيه كالا لغبا فرآه صاحب
الرحا ذا هيئة وطرة وبزة كريمة ففرش له واتاه بطعام فطعم ومكث
عنده يوما وليلة فسأله صاحب الرحى ان يأمر له بشيء فبذل له منطقته
وكانت مكللة بجوهر فأبى ان يقبلها وقال انه ليرضيني من هذه المنطقة
اربعة دراهم آكل بها واشرب فأخبره انه لا ورق معه فتملقه صاحب
الرحى حتى اذا اغفى قام اليه بفاس فضرب بها هامته فقتله واخذ ما
كان عليه من ثياب وحلي والقى جيفته في النهر وبقر بطنه وادخل فيه من
اصول طرفا كانت نابتة على حافة النهر لتحبس جثته في الموضع الذي
القاها فيه فلا ينتقل فيعرف ويطلب قاتله وما اخذ من سلبه وهرب
على وجهه وبلغ قتل يزدجرد رجلا من اهل الاهواز كان مطرانا على
مرو يقال له ايليا فجمع من كان قبله من النصارى وقال لهم ان ملك الفرس
قتل وهو ابن شهريار بن كسرى وانما شهريار ولد شيرين المؤمنة التي
عرفتم حقها واحسانها الى اهل ملتها وكانت بنت قيصر ثم لهذا الملك
عنصر في النصرانية مع ما نال النصارى في ملك جده من الشرف حتى
بني لهم البيع وشيد ملتهم فينبغي ان نحزن هذا الملك بقدر ما اقنا من
الكرامة وقد رأيت ان ابني له ناووسا واحمل جثته في كرامة حتى اجعلها
فيه فقال النصارى امرنا لامرك تبع فامر المطران فبني له في جوف
بستان بمرو ناووس ومضى بنفسه ومعه نصارى مرو حتى
استخرج جثة يزدجرد وكفنها وحملها ومن كان معه على عواتقهم حتى
اتوا به الناووس وواروه فيه وقيل بل حمل الى اصطخر فوضع
في الناووس هناك وذلك في سنة احدى وثلاثين من الهجرة وكان
ملك يزدجرد عشرين سنة منها اربع سنين في دعة وست عشرة في
تعب من محاربة العرب اياه ومحنتهم وغلظتهم عليه وكان شعاره
اخضر موشى وسراويله لون السماء موشى وتاجه احمر وكان خفافه

فاواه الطحان وساله ان يزمزم عليه لياكل ففعل ذلك فلما انصرف الى
مرو سمع ابا تراز يذكر يزدجرد ويطلبه فاواه فساله واصحابه عن حليته
فوصفوه فاخبرهم انه راه في بيت طحان وهو رجل جعد مقرون حسن
الثنايا مقرط مشنف فوجه اليه رجلا من الاساورة وامره ان يخنقه بوتر
ويطرحه في نهر مرو فلقوا الطحان فضربوه ليدل عليه فلم يفعل وجحدهم
ان يعرف اين توجه فلما ارادوا الانصراف عنه قال رجل منهم اني اجد ريح
المسك فلو تتبعته فنظر الى طرف ثوب من ديباج في الماء فاجتذبه اليه
فاذا هو يزدجرد فساله الا يقتله ولا يدل عليه ويجعل له خاتمه وسواره
ومنطقته فقال اعطني اربعة دراهم واخلي عنك قال ويحك خاتمي لك وثمنه لا
يحصى فابى عليه فقال يزدجرد قد كنت اخبرت اني ساحتاج الى اربعة
دراهم واضطر الى ان يكون اكلي اكل الهر فقد عاينته ثم انتزع احد قرطيه
واعطاه الطحان مكافاة لكتمانه عليه ودنا منه كانه يكلمه بشيء فانذر
الرجل اصحابه فاتوه فطلب اليهم يزدجرد الا يقتلوه وخوفهم ما عليهم في
دينهم من ذلك وقال انتو انيته الدهقان وسرحوه الى العرب فانهم
يستحيون شيئا من الملوك فاخذوا ما كان عليه من حلي فجعلوه في جراب
وختموا عليه ثم خنقوه بوتر وطرحوه في نهر مرو فجرى به الماء حتى
انتهى الى فوهة تعلق بعود فاخذه من هناك ثم بعث ابو تراز قرطيه
واخذ الذي دل عليه فضربه حتى اتى على نفسه وبعث بما اصيب له الى
الخليفة يومئذ فاغرم الخليفة الدهقان قيمة القرط المفقود وقد حكي
في رواية اخرى ان تراز وسنجان كانا متباغضين متحاسدين فخص به
تراز فحسده سنجان وطلب ذلك لتراز فجعل يوغر صدر يزدجرد ويسعى
في قتله حتى عزم على ذلك وافشى ما عزم عليه من ذلك الى امراة من نسائه
كان تراز واطاها فارسلت الى تراز تبشره باجماع يزدجرد على قتل
سنجان وفشا الخبر حتى بلغ سنجان فجمع جموعا وتوجه نحو القصر
الذي فيه يزدجرد وبلغ ذلك تراز فنكص عن تراز لكثرة جمعه وارعبه ذلك

يزدجرد

197b

197

الا استيثاق منه فيقتلوه او يصالحوا عليه العرب وجعل له في كل يوم الف
درهم وسأله ان يكتب الى يزدجرد بما يكون ليبقى عامة جنده ويحصل
في طايفة من خواصه فيكون اضعف لركنه واوهن لشوكته وقال
تعلم ان كتابك اليه الان عرفت عليه من هنا بحته ومعونته على العرب
وان يشتق ذلك اشتماما من اسما اهل الدرجات بكتاب يختم بالذهب ويعلمه
انك استقادا عليه حتى ينحي عنه فرخزاد فكتب نيزك بذلك الى يزدجرد
فلما ورد عليه كتابه بعث الى اعلام مرو فاستشارهم فقال له صاحبان لست
ارى ان تنحي عنك جندك ولا فرخزاد وقال ابو تراز بل ارى ان تبالغه بمرو خيس
وتجيبه الى ما سال فقبل رايه وفرق جنده وامر فرخزاد ان ياتي اجمة تيس
فصرخ فرخزاد وشق جيبه وتناول عمودا بين يديه يريد ضرب ابي تراز
به وقال يا قتلة الملوك قتلتم ملكين واظنكم قاتلي هذا ولم يبرح فرخزاد
حتى كتب له يزدجرد كتابا بخطه نسخته هذا الكتاب لفرخزاد انك قد اسلمت
يزدجرد واهله وولده وحاشيته وما معه الى ماهويه دهقان مرو
واشهد عليه بذلك فاقبل نيزك الى موضع من مرو يقال له جلنبذان
فلما اجمع يزدجرد على لقايه والمسير اليه اشار عليه ابو تراز الا يلقاه في
السلاح فيرتاب به وينفر عنه ولكن يلقاه بالملاهي والمزامير ففعل
وسار اليه كما هو وتاخر عنه ابو تراز وكردس نيزك اصحابه كراديس
فلما تدانيا استقبله نيزك ماشيا ويزدجرد على فرس له فامر لنيزك
بجنيبة من جنايبه فركبها فلما توسط عسكره قال له نيزك زوجني احدى
بناتك لاناصحك فاقاتل معك عدوك فقال له يزدجرد اعلي تجترئ يا كلب
فعلاه نيزك بمخفقة فصاح يزدجرد غدر الغادر وركض منهزما ووضع
اصحاب نيزك سيوفهم فيهم فاكثروا القتل وانتهى يزدجرد في هزيمته
الى مكان من ارض مرو فنزل عن فرسه ودخل بيت طحان فمكث فيه ثلاثة
ايام فقال له الطحان ايها الشقي اخرج فاطعم شيئا فانك جايع منذ ثلاث
قال لست اصل الى ذلك الا بزمزمة وكان رجل من زمازمة مرو قد باع منه

197a

ووصفتها فعال نعمت الحصون هذه ووصفت له الابل وبروكها
وانبعاثها بحملها فعال هذه صفة دواب طوال الاعناق وكتب
معه الى يزدجرد انه لم يمنعني ان ابعث اليك بجيش اوله بمرو واخره
بالصين الجهالة بما يحق علي ولكن هولاء القوم الذين وصف لي رسولك
صفتهم لو يحاولون الجبال لهدوها ولو خلي سربهم ازالوني ما داموا على
ما وصف فسالمهم وارض منهم بالمساكنة ولا تهجهم ما لم يهيجوك
واقام يزدجرد وال كسرى بفرغانة معهم عهد من خاقان ثم كان
مقتل يزدجرد وذلك انه لما وقع الى ارض فارس بقي سنين ثم اتى
كرمان فاقام بها مشتدا فطلب دهقان كرمان شيئا فلم يجبه فطرده
عن بلاده ثم اجمع ان ينزل خراسان فاتى سجستان فاقام بها ثم سار
الى مرو ومعه الرهن من اولاد الدهاقين ومعه من روسائهم
فرخزاد ... ماهويه فلما قدم مرو واستغاث منها بالملوك وكتب اليهم
يستمدهم فكتب الى ملك الصين وملك فرغانة وملك كابل وملك الخزر وكان
الدهقان بمرو ماهويه وكان له ابن يسمى براز فوكل ماهويه ابنه
براز بمدينة مرو وتقدم اليه والى اهل المدينة الا يفتحوا الباب ليزدجرد
وقال لهم ليس هذا لكم بملك لانه قد سلم بلاده وجاءكم مفلولا مجروحا
ومرو لا تحمله يحتمل غيرها من الكور فاذا جاءكم غدا مع يزدجرد
فلا تفتحوا الباب فلما اتاهم فعلوا ذلك وانصرف فرخزاد فجثا بين
يدي يزدجرد وقال استصعبت عليك مرو وهذه العرب قد اتتك
قال فما الراي قال ان تلحق ببلاد الترك فتقيم بها حتى تتبين لنا امر
العرب فانهم لا يدعون بلدة الا دخلوها قال لست افعل ولكني ارجع
عودي على بدي فعصاه ولم يقبل رايه فسار يزدجرد واجمع على صرف
الدهقنة عن ابنه براز الى سنجان ابن اخيه فبلغ ذلك ماهويه وهو ابو براز
فعمل في هلاك يزدجرد وكتب الى نيزك طرخان يخبره ان يزدجرد
وقع اليه مفلولا ودعاه الى القدوم عليه ليكونا يدا عليه معا فاخذه

وارا سيبتاق

ابن حرب هو من خراسان حصار الطالقان ومعه وبعضها

196

وهم يلونا بلادنا والعدو يلينا في بلادنا احب الينا من عدو يلينا في بلاده
لا دين لهم ولا ندري ما وفاوهم فابى عليهم وابوا عليه فقالوا فدع خزائننا
نردها الى بلادنا ومن يليها لا تخرجها من بلادنا الى غيرها فابى فقالوا
فانا لا ندعك فاعتزلوا عنه وتركوه في حاشيته ثم قاتلوه وهزموه
واخذوا الخزائن وكتبوا الى الاحنف بالخبر فاعترض المسلمون واهل
فارس يزدجرد بمرو فقاتلوه واعجلوه عن الاثقال فمضى حتى قطع النهر
الى فرغانه والترك فلم يزل مقيما زمان عمر كله يكاتبهم ويكاتبونه الى زمان
عثمن واقبل اهل فارس الى الاحنف فصالحوه وعاقدوه ودفعوا اليه
تلك الخزائن والاموال وتراجعوا الى بلدانهم واموالهم على افضل ما
كانوا في زمان الاكاسرة وكانوا كانما هم في ملكهم الا ان المسلمين اوفى لهم
واعدل عليهم فلما سمع خاقان بما لقي يزدجرد عبر من بلخ النهر فدخل
الاحنف بلخ وعبر مع خاقان النهر حاشية آل كسرى مع يزدجرد
فلقوا رسول يزدجرد الذي بعث به الى ملك الصين ومعه هدية وجواب
كتابه من ملك الصين فسالوه عما وراءه فقال لما قدمت عليه بالكتاب
والهدايا كافانا بما ترون واراكم هديته وجوابه عن كتاب يزدجرد
اليه وقال وكان قال لي قد علمت ان حقا على الملوك انجاد الملوك على من
غلبهم فصف لي صفة هولاء القوم الذين اخرجوكم من بلادكم فاني
اراك تذكر قلة منهم وكثرة منكم ولا يبلغ امثال هولاء القليل الذين تصف
معكم فيما اسمع من كثرتكم الا بخير عندهم وشر عندكم فقلت سلني عما
احببت اخبرك فقال ايوفون بالعهد قلت نعم قال وما يقولون لكم قبل ان
يقاتلوكم قلت يدعوننا الى واحدة من ثلاث اما دينهم فان اجبناهم اجرونا
مجراهم او الجزية والمنعة او المنابذة قال فكيف طاعتهم امراءهم قلت اطوع
قوم لمرشدهم قال فما يحلون وما يحرمون فاخبرته فقال فيحلون ما حرم
عليهم او يحرمون ما حلل لهم قلت لا قال فان هولاء القوم لا يهلكون ابدا حتى
يبدلوا قال اخبرني عن لباسهم فاخبرته وعن مطاياهم فقلت الخيل العراب

196a

فاتى مرو فنزلها وبنا النار بيتا واطمان في نفسه فلما فتح عبد الله بن عامر
نيسابور ابيورد طوس ونسا وبلغ سرخس وعلى مقدمته
الاحنف بن قيس لقيه الهياطلة وجمع اهل هراة فهزمهم الاحنف ومضى الى
طخارستان فلما دنا من مرو الشاهجان خرج منها يزدجرد نحو مرو ونزل
الاحنف مرو الشاهجان كتب يزدجرد الى خاقان من مرو الروذ يستمده
وكتب الى ملك الصغد يستمده فخرج رسولاه اليهما وكتب الى ملك الصين
يستعينه وخرج الاحنف من مرو الشاهجان واستخلف عليها بعد ما اتته
الامداد يريد مرو الروذ فخرج يزدجرد الى بلخ ونزل الاحنف مرو الروذ
فسار بنا امداد البصرة والكوفة الى بلخ وتبعهم الاحنف والتقى اهل
الكوفة ويزدجرد ببلخ فانهزم يزدجرد وتوجه في اهل فارس الى النهر
فعبروا واخذ المسلمون بلخ وبلغ رسولا يزدجرد خاقان وغارك ملك
الصغد فلم يتهيا لهما انجاده حتى عبر اليهما النهر مهزوما فانجده خاقان
واقبل في الترك وحشر اهل فرغانة والصغد حتى خرج بهم الى خراسان
فعبر الى بلخ ومعه يزدجرد فتراجع المسلمون الى الاحنف بمرو الروذ
وخرج المشركون من بلخ حتى نزلوا على الاحنف بمرو الروذ فارتحل الاحنف
بمن معه واسندوا الى الجبل فجعلوه في ظهورهم والنهر بينهم وبين العدو
وهم في عشرين الف فقاتلوهم ما شا الله وكانوا يغادونهم ويراوحونهم
ويتنحون عنهم بالليل فلما طال مقامهم قال خاقان قد طال مقامنا واصيب
قومنا المنا في قتال هولا القوم من خير انصرفوا بنا وارتحل ليلته من بلخ وقد
كان يزدجرد خرج الى مرو الشاهجان وحصر حارثة بن النعمان خليفة الاحنف
واستخرج خزاينه من موضعها وخاقان ببلخ ينتظره مقيم له ولما جمع
يزدجرد ما وضع بمرو وكان امرا عظيما من خزاين اهل فارس ليلحق بخاقان
قال له اهل فارس ما تريد ان تصنع قال اريد اللحاق بخاقان فاكون معه او
بالصين فقالوا له هذا راي سوء انك انما تاتي قوما في مملكتهم وتدع ارضك
وقومك ولكنا نرجع بنا الى هولا القوم فنصالحهم فانهم اوفيا واهل دين

195

فنادى بهم ايها الناس اقتلوا فقاتلوا شديدا لم يسمع بوقعة قط كانت اشد
منها قتلوا فيها من الفرس فيما بين الزوال والعتمة ما طبق الارض
وزلق الناس في الدما وزلق بالنعمان بن مقرن فرسه فصرع واصيب
رضي الله عنه فاخذ الراية اخوه نعيم بن مقرن ولف نعيم بعد النعمان
بها وكان عهد اليه بعده فاخذ اللوا واقتتلوا فلما اظلم الليل انكشف
الفرس واخذوا نحو اللهب فوقعوا فيه فمات منهم فيه نحو مائة الف
وقتل في المعركة اعداد هم لم يفلت الا الشريد ونجا الفيروزان وسير
نحو همذان فاتبعه نعيم بن مقرن والقعقاع فلامه فاخذه القعقاع
ودخل المسلمون نهاوند واحتووا ما فيها وظفروا بذخيرة كسرى
في سفطان فيها اليواقيت واللولو فبيعت باربعة الاف الف
درهم وجا دينار فصالح حذيفة عن ماه وفتح نعيم بن مقرن همذان
وسار الى الري وبها سياوخش بن مهران بن بهرام شوبين وقد
استمد اهل دنباوند وطبرستان وقومس وجرجان فقاتلهم وقتل نعيم و
منهم مقتلة عظيمة وهزمهم وملك المدينة وما فيها وهو شي عظيم جدا
وافتتح بكير بن عبد الله اذربيجان ودخل اهل دنباوند والخزر في
صلحا واخذ سويد بن مقرن قومس سلما وصالح زربان صول
ملك جرجان عما بيده وصالح ايضا الاصبهبذ ومضى بكير بن عبد الله
الى الباب وعليه شهربراز الذي غزا الشام فدخل صلحا واخذت
الجبال المطيفة بارمينية واخذت موقان وتفليس بغير مؤنة وخرج
عبد الرحمن بن ربيعة لغزو الترك حتى قطع الباب فغزا بلنجر وبعدها
مائتي فرسخ ولما انتهى يزدجرد بعد جلولا الى الري وعليها ابان
جاذويه وثب عليه ابان فقال يا ابان جاذويه تغدرنا قال لا
ولكنك تركت ملكك وصار في يد غيرك واردت ان اكتتب على ما كان
لي من شي وما اردت غير ذلك واخذ خاتم يزدجرد وكتب الصكاك
على الادم وسجل السجلات بكل ما اعجبه ثم ختم عليها ورد الخاتم
فاستوحش منه يزدجرد وكرهه وخرج هاربا الى اصبهان ومعه
النار واراد كرمان ثم عزم على خراسان ليستمد الترك والصين

فسار به انس بن مالك والاحنف بن قيس الى المدينة فلما دخلوها هيئوا
الهرمزان في هيئته وعليه كسوته وتاجه فاسلم وفرض له عمر في الفين
وانزله بالمدينة وله معه حديث من كور في البسيط ومضى يزدجرد بمشورة
الموبذ الى اصطخر فنزلها لانها دار المملكة وقدم سياه فانتخب من
كل بلدة مقاتلة ومضى الى السوس فلما قدم عمار بن ياسر وابو موسى
يوم فتح تستر دعا سياه الرؤساء الذين خرجوا معه من اصبهان فقال
لهم قد علمتم انا كنا نتحدث ان هؤلاء القوم اهل الشقاء والبؤس سيغلبون
على هذه المملكة وتروث دوابهم في ابواب اصطخر ومصانع الملوك
ويشدون خيلهم بشجرها وقد غلبوا على ما رأيتم وليس يلقون جندا الا
فلوه ولا ينزلون بحصن الا فتحوه فانظروا لانفسكم قالوا رأينا رأيك
قال فليكفني كل منكم حشمه والمنقطعين اليه فاني ارى ان ندخل في دينهم
ووجهوا شيرويه في عشرة من الاساورة الى ابي موسى الاشعري رضي
الله عنه فاخذ والهم شروطا وقدموا عليه فاسلموا ففرض لمائة منهم في
الفين الفين ولستة منهم في الفين وخمسمائة وهم سياه وخسرو وسماه
مقلاص وشهريار وشيرويه وسار وه وافريذون ففتح سياه وفتح
حصنا بحيلة وفتح خسرو حصنا ونزل ابو سبرة بعد فراغه من
السوس على جنديسابور حتى اخذها بعد ايام بالامان ثم عقد عمر
رضي الله عنه الالوية للامراء والجنود من اهل الكوفة واهل البصرة ؛
فعقد للاحنف بن قيس على خراسان وكان يزدجرد قد خرج من
الجبل وصار الى مرو وكاتب الجيوش بالاطراف فيما بين الباب
والسند وخراسان وحلوان فتحركوا وتكاتبوا وركب بعضهم الى
بعض فاجمعوا ان يوافوا نهاوند ليبرموا فيها امورهم فتوافى اليها
من بين حلوان فاجتمعت حلبة فارس والفهلوج واهل الجبال
وهم مائة وخمسون الفا فتوامروا الرؤساء عند الفيرزان وكان عليهم
وتعاهدوا وتعاقدوا على حرب المسلمين وكتبوا بذلك كتابا فسار اليهم النعمان
مقرن بالمسلمين واقتتلوا يومين وفي الثالث حصرهم المسلمون في

خنادقهم

194b

194

حلوان ووراهم الرجال وخافت فيهم الاموال فاحاط بهم هاشم وزاحفهم
ثمانين زحفا كل ذلك ينتصر المسلمون فيه ثم خرجوا واقتتلوا قتالا
شديدا لم يقتتلوا مثله حتى انفذوا النبل وقصفوا الرماح وصاروا الى
السيوف والطبرزينات وصلى المسلمون يومئذ ايماء واتت الخيول الفارس
فحمل عليهم القعقاع بمن معه حملة منكرة فانهزموا وتبعهم المسلمون
فلم يفلت الا من لا يعد وقتل منهم يومئذ زيادة على مائة الف فسار
يزدجرد من حلوان نحو الجبل وفي سنة سبع عشرة عبر العلاء بن
الحضرمي البحر من البحرين الى فارس بغير اذن عمر رضي الله عنه ومعه
الجارود بن المعلى وسوار بن همام وخليد بن المنذر بن ساوى في جنود
كثيرة فخرجوا في اصطخر وبازائهم اهل فارس عليهم الهربذ فحالوا بين
المسلمين وبين سفنهم فقاتلهم المسلمون فقتل سوار والمنذر بن الجارود
في جماعة وقتل من الفرس مقتلة لم يقتلوا مثلها وهزم باقيهم وسار
المسلمون يريدون البصرة فغرقت سفنهم ولم يجدوا الى الرجوع سبيلا
ووجدوا شهرك قد اخذ على المسلمين الطرق فعسكروا واقاموا
مكانهم وبلغ عمر رضي الله ما صنع العلاء الحضرمي فاشتد غضبه عليه
وعزله وتوعده وامره ان يلحق بسعد بن ابي وقاص بمن معه فسار بهم
اليه وندب عتبة بن غزوان الناس بامر عمر رضي الله عنه فسار عاصم
بن عمرو وعرفجة والاحنف بن قيس وسعد بن العرجاء وصعصعة بن
معوية في اثني عشر الفا على البغال يجنبون الخيل وعليهم ابو سبرة بن
ابي رهم حتى التقى مع خليد بن المنذر بن ساوى وهو ومن معه حيث
اخذ عليهم الطرق وقد ناهم الفرس من كل وجه وكورة فالتقوا
هم وابو سبرة واقتتلوا فقتل الفرس وعليهم شهرك وغنم المسلمون
اموالهم وكان عتبة بن غزوان قد فتح الاهواز وقاتل فيها الهرمزان حتى
ظفر بتستر بعد وقعات اسر في اخرها الهرمزان واعطى بيده على
الرضا بحكم عمر بعد ما قتل الهرمزان بيده البراء بن مالك ومجزاة بن ثور

مع خليد بن المنذر

ملك الاهواز

[illegible]

[illegible]

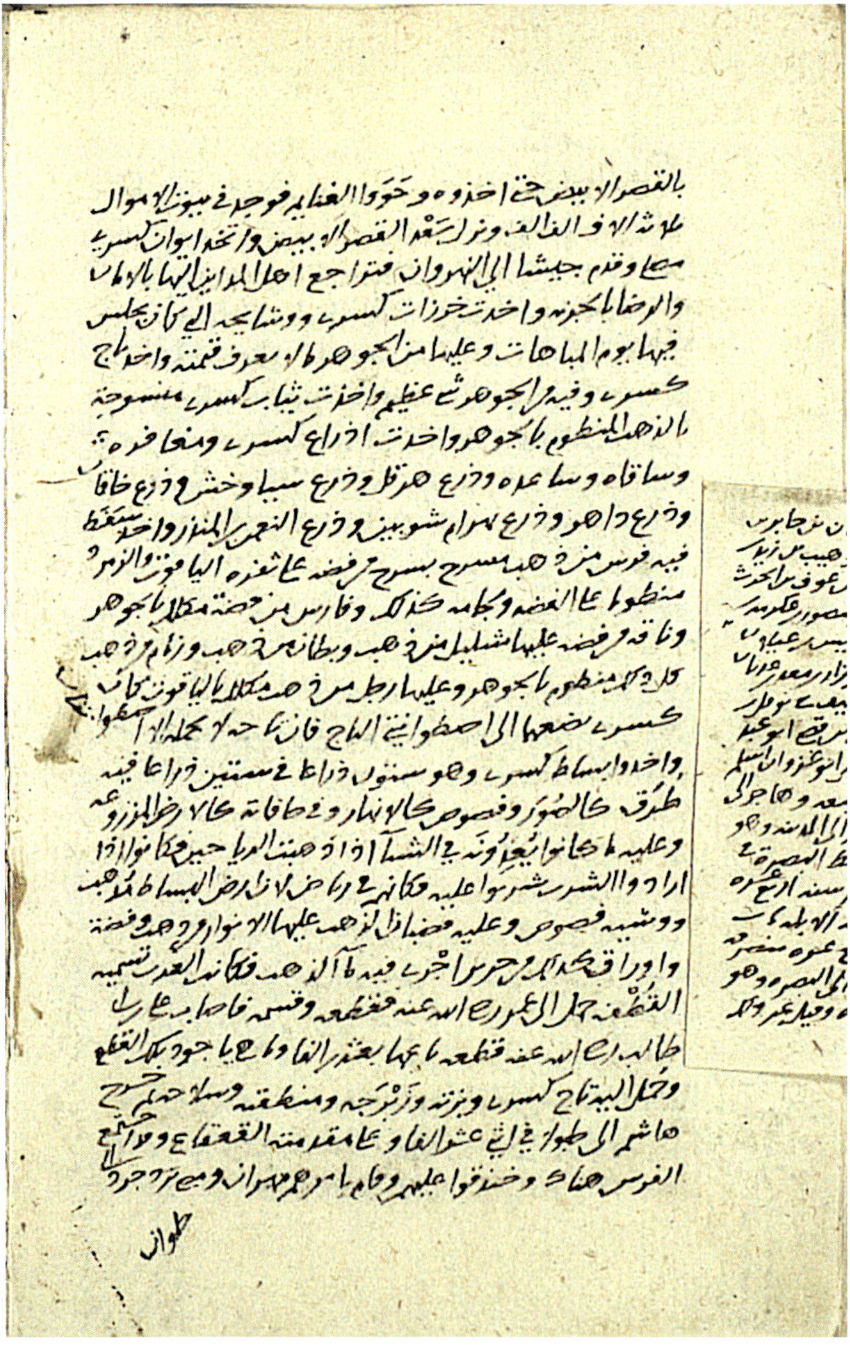

بالقصر الابيض حتى اخذوه وحووا الغنايم فوجد في بيوت الاموال
ثلاثة الاف الف الف ونزل سعد القصر الابيض واتخذ ايوان كسرى
مصلى وقدم جيشا الى النهروان فتراجع اهل المداين اليها بالامان
والرضا بالجزية واخذت خزانات كسرى ووشاحه التي كان يجلس
فيها يوم المباهات وعليها من الجوهر ما لا يعرف قيمته واخذ تاج
كسرى وفيه من الجوهر شي عظيم واخذت ثياب كسرى منسوجة
بالذهب المنظوم بالجوهر واخذت ادراع كسرى ومغافره
وساقاه وساعداه ودرع هرقل ودرع سياوخش ودرع خاقان
ودرع داهر ودرع بهرام شوبين ودرع النعمان بن المنذر واخذ سفط
فيه فرس من ذهب مسرج بسرج من فضة على ثفره الياقوت والزمرد
منظوم على الفضة ولجامه كذلك وفارس من فضة مكلل بالجوهر
وناقة من فضة عليها شليل من ذهب وبطان من ذهب وزمام من ذهب
كل ذلك منظوم بالجوهر وعليها رجل من ذهب مكلل بالياقوت كان
كسرى يضعهما الى اسطوانتي التاج فان ناحه لا يحمله الا اسطوانة
واخذوا بساط كسرى وهو ستون ذراعا في ستين ذراعا فيه
طرق كالصور وفصوص كالانهار وفي حافاته كالارض المزروعة
وعليه ما كانوا يعدونه في الشتا اذا ذهبت الريا حين فكانوا اذا
ارادوا الشرب شربوا عليه فكانهم في رياض لان ارض البساط مذهب
ووشيه فصوص وعليه قضبان الذهب عليها الانوار من ذهب وفضة
واوراق ... من حرير اجري فيه ما الذهب فكانت العرب تسميه
القطف حمل الى عمر رضي الله عنه فقطعه وقسمه فاصاب علي بن ابي
طالب رضي الله عنه قطعة باعها بعشرين الفا وما هي باجود تلك القطع
وحمل اليه تاج كسرى وبزته وزبرجه ومنطقته وسلاحه ...
هاشم الى حلوان في اثني عشر الفا وعلى مقدمته القعقاع و... اجتمع
الفرس هناك وخندقوا عليهم وقام بامرهم مهران ...

حلوان

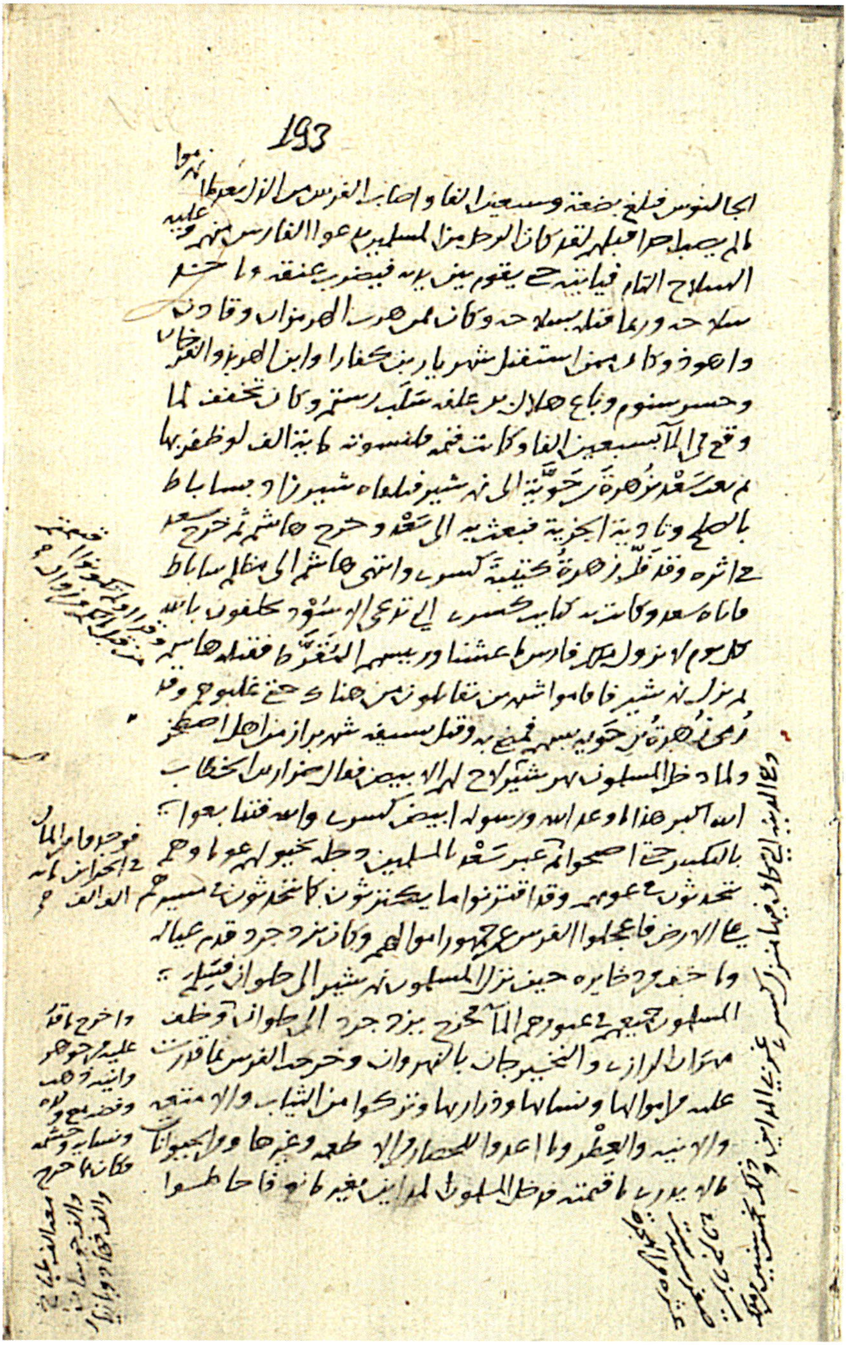
الى النوبس فبلغ بضعة وتسعين الفا واصاب الفرس من الزاد معوظا
ما لم يصبها احد قبلهم لقد كان الرجل من المسلمين يلقى الفارس منهم وعليه
السلاح التام فيأتيه حتى يقوم بين يديه فيضرب عنقه ويأخذ
سلاحه وربما قتله بسلاحه وكان ممن هرب الهرمزان ومهران
والهوذ وكان ممن استقتل شهريار بن كنارا وابن الهربذ والفرخان
وخسر شنوم وناس هلال بن علقمة سلب رستم وكان تخفف لما
وقع في الماء بسبعين الفا وكانت قيمته فيما يقومونه مائة الف لو ظفر بها
ثم بعث سعد زهرة بن حوية الى نهرشير فلقاه شيرزاذ بساباط
بالصلح وتأدية الجزية فبعث به الى سعد وخرج هاشم ثم خرج سعد
في اثره وقد فل زهرة كتيبة كسرى وانتهى هاشم الى مظلم ساباط
فأتاه سعد وكانت به كتائب كسرى التي تدعى بوران يحلفون بالله
كل يوم لا يزول ملك فارس ما عشنا ودونهم المقرّط فقتله هاشم
ثم نزل نهرشير فأقاموا شهرين يقاتلونهم هناك حتى غلبوهم وقد
رمى زهرة بن حوية بسهم فصخ به وقتل بسيفه شهربراز من اهل اصطخر
ولما دخل المسلمون نهرشير لاح لهم الابيض فقال ضرار بن الخطاب
الله اكبر هذا ما وعد الله ورسوله ابيض كسرى واتبعه فيما بعد وا
بالتكبير حتى اصبحوا ثم عبر سعد المسلمين دجلة يخبون فيها وهم
يتحدثون في عبورهم وقد اقترنوا ما يكترثون كما يتحدثون في مسيرهم
في الارض فاعجلوا الفرس عن جمهور اموالهم وكان يزدجرد قدم عياله
واخف ذخائره حين نزل المسلمون نهرشير الى حلوان فلما
المسلمون بجمعهم في عبورهم الماء خرج يزدجرد الى حلوان وخلف
مهران الرازي والنخيرجان بالنهروان وخرج الفرس بما قدرت
عليه من اموالها ونسائها وذراريها وتركوا من الثياب والامتعة
والآنية والعطر وما اعدوا للحصار الا طعمة وغيرها ومن الحيوانات
ما لا يدرى ما قيمته فدخل المسلمون المداين بغير مانع فاحاطوا

193a

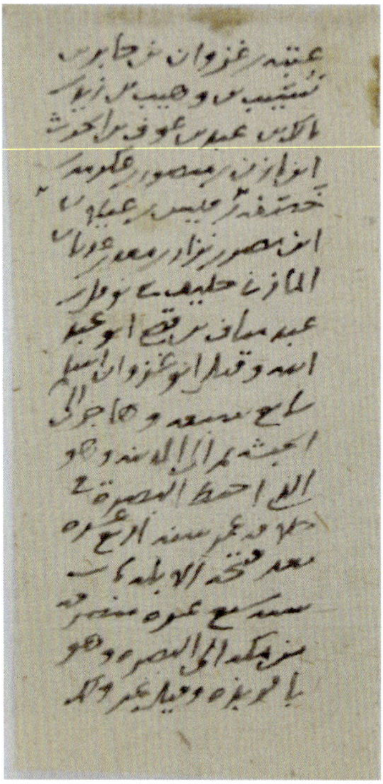
عتبة بن غزوان بن جابر بن
نسيب بن وهيب بن زيد بن
مالك بن عبد بن عوف بن الحرث
ابن مازن بن منصور بن عكرمة بن
خصفة بن قيس بن عيلان بن
ابن مضر بن نزار بن معد بن عدنان
المازني حليف بني نوفل بن
عبد مناف بن قصي ابو عبد
الله وقيل ابو غزوان اسلم
سابع سبعة وهاجر الى
الحبشة ثم الى المدينة وهو
الذي اختط البصرة في
خلافة عمر سنة اربع عشرة
بعد فتحه الابلة مات
سنة سبع عشرة منصرفه
من مكة الى البصرة وهو
بالربذة وقيل غير ذلك

193*b

193*a

وكان يبعث الليل بالنجدات الى من بين عنده وما كان علامة جند المسلمين الا
براذع الرحال قد اعترضوا فيها الجريد ومن لم يكن له وقاية لرأسه
عصب رأسه بالانساع وابلى يومئذ قيس بن هبيرة المكشوح
وكان في قتل الفيلة اهوال حتى هلك من كان عليها ثم تزاحفوا واجتلدوا
بالسيوف حتى امسوا واشتد القتال في الليل فسميت ليلة الهرير
ثم لم يكن بعدها قتال بليل بالقادسية واصبحوا في اليوم الرابع وقد
عبا الفرس للزحف ثلثة عشر صفا والناس حسرى لم يغمضوا ليلتهم
كلها فحمل المسلمون لرستم فازالوا الهرمزان والفيرزان فتأخرا
وثبتا حيث انتهيا وقد انفرج القلب وركد عليهم النقع ثم هبت ريح
عاصف فقلعت طيارة رستم عن سريره فهوت ومال الغبار عليهم فانتهى
القعقاع الى السرير وقد قام رستم حين طارت الريح بالطيارة الى
بغال قد قدمت عليه بمال فاستظل في ظل بغل وحمله فقصده هلال
ابن علفة فولى رستم فاتبعه فرماه رستم فنشبه قدمه في الركاب
فحمل عليه هلال فضربه ضربة نفحت مسكا ومضى رستم فرمى بنفسه
في العتيق فاقتحم هلال عليه فتناوله وقد عام وهلال قائم فاخذ
برجله ثم خرج به وضرب جبينه بالسيف حتى قتله وجاء به حتى رمى به
بين ارجل البغال واخذ سلبه ثم صعد السرير ونادى
قتلت رستم ورب الكعبة الي الي فاطافوا به وكبروا فانهزم الفرس
وقام الجالنوس ونادى اهل فارس الى العبور وقد اسفر الغبار وال
المقترنون فتواقفوا العتيق فوخزهم المسلمون برماحهم فما افلت
منهم احد وهم ثلثون الفا واخذ ضرار بن الخطاب درفش كابيان
فعوض منها ثلثون الفا وكانت قيمتها الفي الف ومائتي الف وجمعت
الاسلاب والاموال فكان شيئا عظيما وخرج زهرة بن حوية في
طلب الجالنوس حتى قتله وخرج القعقاع وشرحبيل في طلب من
انهزم فقتلوهم في كل قرية واجمة وشاطئ نهر ورجعوا فتوافوا
عند صلاة الظهر وهنأ المسلمون بعضهم بعضا وتورع زهرة ما كان على
الجالنوس

[illegible]

192

فانتدب له عمرو بن معدي كرب وحمل عليه فاعتنقه ثم احتمله
فوضعه بين يديه وجاء به حتى دنا من اصحابه وكسر عنق الرجل ثم ذبحه والقاه
وخرج الى طليحة عظيم منهم فبرز اليه فما لبث طليحة ان قتله وضرب
الاشعث بن قيس بكثرة حتى ازالوا الفيلة عنهم فحمل ذو الحاجب
والجالنوس حملة منكرة فدارت رحى الحرب والفيلة تحمل على الميمنة
والميسرة فكانت الخيول تحجم عنها وتحيد فاقبل اصحاب عاصم بن عمرو
فاخذوا باذنابها وقطعوا وضنها فالقت ما على ظهورها حتى ما بقي
لهم فيل الا عري وقتل اصحابها ولم يزل القتال حتى غربت الشمس ثم
ذهبت هداة من الليل ثم رجع الفريقان وقد اصيب من بني اسد خمس
مائة وكانوا ردءا للناس وكان عاصم بن عمرو عادية الناس فهذا يومهم
الاول وهو يوم ارماث واصبحوا يوم اغواث فوافت المسلمين تجارة
ستة الاف بعث بهم ابو عبيدة بن الجراح رضي الله عنه بعد فتح دمشق
عليهم هاشم بن عتبة بن ابي وقاص وعلى مقدمته القعقاع بن عمرو فبرز
اليه ذو الحاجب بهمن جاذويه فاجتلدا فقتله القعقاع فانكسرت
الفرس لذلك ثم خرج الفيرزان والبندوان فبادر القعقاع الفيرزان
فقتله وبادر الحرث بن ظبيان البندوان فقتله واجتلد الفريقان حتى
المساء وقد كثر القتل في الفرس ولم يقاتلوا في هذا اليوم على فيل لان
توابيتها انكسرت بالامس فجددوها وكانت للقعقاع يومئذ ثلثون
حملة يصيب فيها فقتل ثلاثين فارسا اخرهم بزرجمهر الهمذاني
ولم يزل القتال يوم اغواث حتى انتصف الليل وقد قتل عامة اعلام :.
فارس وكان لابي محجن الثقفي في تلك الليلة بلاء عظيم ثم تحاجز الناس
لما انتصف الليل واصبحوا اليوم الثالث على مواقفهم وقد قتل من المسلمين
الفان ومن فارس عشرة الاف وكان القتال يوم عماس وقد اصلح
الفرس توابيت الفيلة مرة اخرى والعرب والعجم فيه سواء ولا
يكون بينهم لغطة الا تغاورها الرجال بالاصوات حتى تبلغ يزدجرد

وتطرقوا بلاده واخربوا منها وغزت العرب بلاده بعد ان مضى من
ملكه ثلاث او اربع سنين وله احاديث وذلك ان المثنى بن حارثة
لما بلغه اجتماع فارس كتب الى عمر رضي الله عنه بذلك فنفر اهل
السواد كلهم من كان له عهد ومن لم يكن له عهد وكتب اليه ان
يتفرقوا في المياه التي على حدود ارضهم فنزل المثنى بذي قار ونزل
الناس في المياه واقاموا مسالح ينظر بعضهم الى بعض وذلك في
ذي القعدة من سنة ثلاث عشرة وعزم عمر على المسير بنفسه ثم بعث سعد
بن وقاص رضي الله عنه اميرا على حرب العراق ومات المثنى بن حارثة من
جراحته وقدم سعد فاغار فيما يليه الى ان الح يزدجرد على رستم حتى
خرج في العدة والعديد والخيول والفيول فراسله سعد بالمغيرة بن شعبة
وغيره فجرت بينهم مخاطبات الى ان صاف رستم وعبر النهر وكان في
القلب ثمانية عشر فيلا عليها الصناديق والرجال وفي المجنبتين
ثمانية وسبعة واقام الجالنوس بينه وبين ميمنته والفيرزان بينه
وبين ميسرته وبقيت القنطرة بين خيلين من خيول المسلمين والفرس
وكان يزدجرد وضع بينه وبين رستم رجالا فاولهم على باب ايوانه
والاخر على دعوة منه بحيث يسمعه والاخر كذلك حتى انتظم بينه
وبين رستم بالرجال فلما نزل رستم بساباط قال الرجل الذي بساباط
نزل وقال الذي يليه كذلك ثم الذي يليه حتى يقوله من على الايوان ويسمعه
يزدجرد وكان كلما ارتحل او نزل او حدث امر جرى الامر فيه على ما
شرحته وترك البريد وكان ذلك شانه الى ان تقع الحرب وتعاهد
الفرس وتواصوا واقترنوا بالسلاسل فكان المقترنون ثلاثين
الفا وجملتهم مائة وعشرون الفا وثلاثون فيلا عليها المقاتلة وفيلة
عليها الملوك وقوف لا تقاتل ونشب القتال فاعتوروا الضرب
والطعن وخرج هرمز الى غالب بن عبد الله وكان هرمز من ملوك
الابواب متوجا فاسره غالب واتى به الى سعد بن وقاص وخرج اخر

فاستدبر

191

فملكوه كرها وكان ضخم الراس فلما تُوّج قال ما اضيق هذا التاج فتطير
العظما من افتتاح كلامه بالضيق وقتلوه ثم اتي برجل من اولاد كسرى
كان لجا الى موضع قريب من نصيبين يقال له حصن الحجارة حين قتل
شيرويه من قتل من ولد كسرى يقال له فرخزاد خسرو فانقاد له الناس ولما
يلبث الا يسيرا حتى استعصوا عليه وخالفوه وكان ملكه ستة اشهر وكان اهل
اصطخر ظفروا بيزدجرد بن شهريار بن ابرويز باصطخر قد هرب اليها
حين قتل شيرويه اخوته فلما بلغ عظما اصطخر ان من بالمداين خالفوا
فرخزاد بن خسرو اتوا بيزدجرد بيت نار يدعى بيت نار اردشير
فتوجوه هناك وملكوه وكان حدثا ثم اقبلوا به الى المداين وقتلوا
فرخزاد خسرو بحيلة احتالوها له وساغ الملك ليزدجرد

يزدجرد بن شهريار بن كسرى ابرويز قد تقدم
انه فر الى اصطخر وان اهل اصطخر ظفروا به وتوجوه ثم اتوا به المداين
وروي ايضا ان رستم والفيروزان لما عاقبوا نسا كسرى ابرويز
ليدلوهم على ذكر من ابنا كسرى قالت لهم احداهن لم يبق الا غلام يدعى
يزدجرد من ولد شهريار بن ابرويز وامه من اهل بادوريا فارسلوا
اليها فاخذوه بها وكانت قد انولته حين جمعهم شيرويه في القصر
الابيض وقتل الذكور الى اخواله وكانت واعدتهم ردّه اليهم في
زنبيل فلما اخذت نساسه بدلتهم عليه فارسلوا اليه فجاوا به فملكوه وهو
ابن احدى وعشرين سنة واجتمعوا عليه واطمانت فارس واستوسقوا
ودخل روساوهم في طاعته ومعونته فسمى الجنود لكل مسلحة
كانت لكسرى او موضع ثغر فسمى جند الحيرة وجند الانبار والابلة
والمسالح واظهروا الجد والنصيحة غير ان مملكته كانت عند ملك
ابايه كالخيال وكالحلم وكانت العظما والوزرا يدبرون مملكته لحداثة
سنه وكان اشدهم نباهة في وزرايه واذكاهم رستم لخول
وضعف امر مملكة فارس واجترا عليه اعداوه من كل وجه

[illegible marginal note]

[illegible marginal note]

ايام عشرة اشهر وولي فيروز بن بهرام بن مهران جشنس منوزاذ
خشنوه بن نرسي بن بهرام بن سابور بن يزدجرد الاثيم وهو الملقب
جشنسبنده وانما اقام شهرا او عشرين يوما ثم ملكت

آزرميدخت بنت كسرى ابرويز ولقبها العادلة قال
ابن مسكويه كانت آزرمي دخت من اجمل نساء دهرها وكان
عظيم فارس يومئذ فرخ هرمز اصبهبذ خراسان فارسل اليها يسالها
ان تزوجه نفسها فارسلت اليه ان التزوج للملكة غير جائز وقد علمت
ان اربك فيما ذهبت اليه قضاء حاجتك مني فصر الي ليلة كذا وكذا
ففعل فرخ هرمز وركب اليها في تلك الليلة وتقدمت آزرمي دخت الى
صاحب حرسها ان يترصده في تلك الليلة التي تواعدوا الالتقاء فيها حتى
يقتله فنفذ صاحب حرسها لامرها وامر به فجر برجله وطرح في رحبة
دار المملكة فلما اصبح الناس ورأوه علموا انه لم يقتل الا لعظيمة
فامرت بجثته فغيبت وكان رستم بن فرخ هرمز هذا اعظم الناس
قويا في نفسه وهو رستم صاحب القادسية الذي تولى قتال العرب
من قبل يزدجرد فيما بعد وسيجيء خبره هناك ان شاء الله فلما بلغه ما صنع
بابيه اقبل في جند عظيم حتى نزل المداين وسمل عيني آزرمي دخت وقتلها
وكان ملكها ستة اشهر وكان ثيابها حمرة وشعارها احمر موشى وسراويلها
موشحة وتاجها اخضر تقعد على السرير وبيمناها طبرزين
معتمدة بيسراها على السيف وكانت جليلة ونصبت بيت
نار وملك بعدها خرداذ خسره وبعضهم يقول
فرخزاذ خسرو بن كسرى ابرويز وهو طفل فاقام شهرا
واحدا ثم ملك يزدجرد وقال ابن مسكويه ما خلف فيمن ملك
بعد آزرمي دخت فقيل اتي برجل من عقب اردشير بابك كان
ينزل الاهواز يقال له كسرى بن مهر جشنس فلبس التاج
وقتل بعد ايام وقيل بل كان رجلا يسكن ميسان يقال له فيروز

ملكو

190b

190

ايام فاذا احملنا هذه المدة على هلاك ابرويز في السنة السابعة من
الهجرة كان انقضاء مدة بوران في اخر السنة العاشرة من الهجرة او
في اوايل الحادية عشر فكيف يصح مع هذا ان تكون هذه الحروب
المذكورة لفارس مع ابي عبيد بن مسعود الثقفي والمثنى بن حارثة في
ايام بوران وهذه الحروب انما كانت في خلافة عمر بن الخطاب رضي
الله عنه وفي سنة اثني عشرة وما بعدها لا سيما وفي الصحيح ما يدل على
ان بوران وليت في حياة رسول الله صلى الله عليه وسلم فقد خرج
البخاري من حديث الحسن عن ابي بكرة رضي الله عنه قال نفعني الله
تعالى بكلمة سمعتها من رسول الله صلى الله عليه وسلم ايام الجمل بعد ما
كدت ان الحق باصحاب الجمل فاقاتل معهم قال لما بلغ رسول الله صلى
الله عليه وسلم ان اهل فارس ملكوا عليهم بنت كسرى قال لن يفلح
قوم ولوا امرهم امراة لكن يمكن ان يقال كانت فترات بين ولايات
من قام بامر الملك بعد ابرويز فانه كان بين فارس اختلاف وتنازع
كثير ولم يكن الكل يذكر في سيرهم سوى مدة كل واحد منهم من غير
تعيين وقت ابتداء المدة وانقضائها ويؤيد هذا الاحتمال ما
ذكر بعضهم ان قدوم خالد بن الوليد رضي الله عنه الحيرة في زمن بوران
لاثني عشرة مضت من الهجرة وان بوران ملكت بعد قدوم خالد مدة
سبعة اشهر منها ثلاثة اشهر في خلافة ابي بكر الصديق رضي الله
عنه واربعة اشهر في خلافة امير المومنين عمر رضي الله عنه وذكر
ابو علي ابن مسكويه ان الذي ملك بعد بوران رجل من بني عم ابرويز يقال له
جشنسبنده وكان ملكه اقل من شهر ولم يظهر له اثر يستفاد
منه تجربة وذكر علي بن حمزة الاصفهاني انه لم يكن من بيت الملك
وانه اقام شهرين وقيل اقام اياما وان اسمه فيروز وحكى ايضا ان
الذي ولي بعد بوران ازرميدخت وقال غيره بل اقيم بعد بوران
كسرى بن قباذ بن هرمز بن كسرى ابرويز ولقبه كوتاه وانه

190a

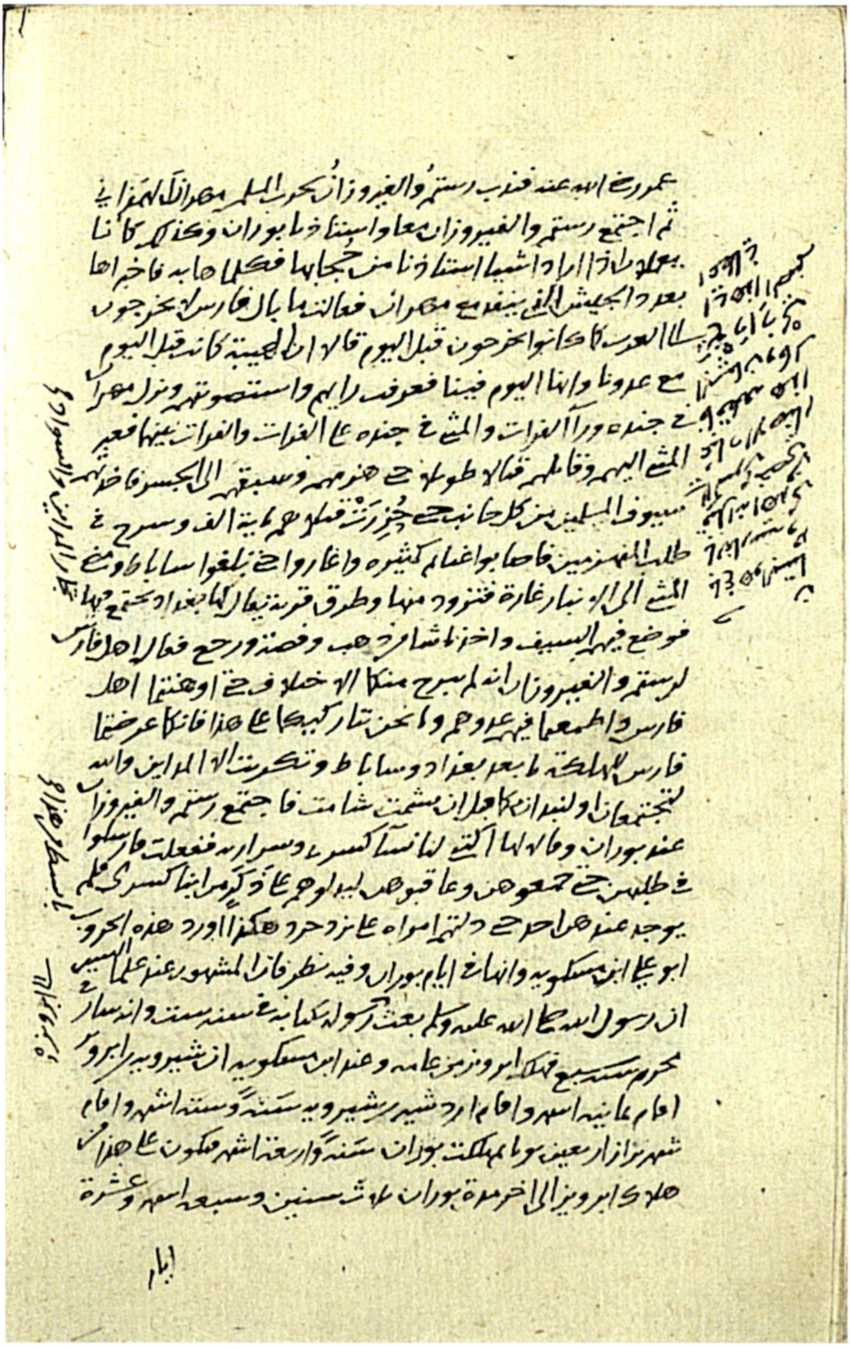
عمر رضي الله عنه فغضب رستم والفيروزان بحرب المسلمين مهران الهمذاني
ثم اجتمع رستم والفيروزان معا واتيا خدا بوران وتحاكما كانا
يعملون ما اراد اشيا استاذنا من حجابها فكملا هابة فاخبراها
بعدد الجيش الذي بيفدو مع مهران فعالنهما بال فارس لا يخرجون
الى العدو كما كانوا يخرجون قبل اليوم قالوا ان الجنبة كانت قبل اليوم
مع عدونا وانها اليوم فينا فعرفت رايهم واستصوبتهم ونزل مهران
في جنده وراء الفرات والمثنى في جنده على الفرات والفرات بينهما فعبر
المثنى اليهم وقاتلهم فقاتلوا طويلا حتى هزمهم وسبقهم الى الجسر فاخذتهم
سيوف المسلمين من كل جانب حتى جزرت فقتلوهم مائة الف وسرح في
طلب المنهزمين فاصابوا غنائم كثيرة واغاروا حتى بلغوا ساباط ومضى
المثنى الى الانبار غارة فتزود منها وطرق قرية يقال لها بغداد يجتمع فيها
موضع فيهم السيف واخذ ما شاء من ذهب وفضة ورجع فقال اهل فارس
لرستم والفيروزان انه لم يبرح منكما الا خلاف حتى اوهنتما اهل
فارس واطمعا فيهم عدوهم وانكن تتاركتكما على هذا فانكما عرضتما
فارس للهلكة ما بعد بغداد وساباط وتكريت الا المداين والله
لتجتمعان او لنبدان بكما قبل ان يشمت شامت فاجتمع رستم والفيروزان
عند بوران وقالا لها اكتبي لنا نساء كسرى وسراريه ففعلت فارسلوا
في طلبهن حتى جمعوهن وعاقبوهن ليدلوهم على ذكر من ابناء كسرى فلم
يوجد عندهن احد حتى دلتهم امراة على يزدجرد هكذا اورد هذه الحروف
ابو علي ابن مسكويه وانها في ايام بوران وفيه نظر فان المشهور عند علماء السير
ان رسول الله صلى الله عليه وسلم بعث رسوله بكتابه في سنة ست وانه سار
محرم سنة سبع فهلك ابرويز من عامه وعند ابن مسكويه ان شيرويه بن ابرويز
اقام ثمانية اشهر واقام اردشير بن شيرويه سنة وستة اشهر واقام
شهربراز اربعين يوما وملكت بوران سنة واربعة اشهر فيكون على هذا ان
هلاك ابرويز الى اخر مدة بوران ثلث سنين وسبعة اشهر وعشرة
ايام

189

وبلغ ذلك نرسي ومن معه فرجوا ان يلحق بهم قبل الوقعة فعاجلهم ابو عبيد
وقاتلهم قتالا شديدا فانهزم نرسي وقتل اصحابه وغلب ابو عبيد على
عسكره وارضه وجمع الغنائم فراى المسلمون هناك من الاطعمة
ما لم يروا مثله واخذ خزائن نرسي واقتسم المسلمون النرسيان وكانوا
حتى جعلوا يطعمونه الفلاحين وبعثوا الخمس الى عمر رضي الله عنه
وسار المثنى يخرب ويسبي فتقدم الجالنوس فقاتله ابو عبيد بمن معه
فانهزم منهم وغلب ابو عبيد على البلاد فلما قدم الجالنوس على رستم ممن
افلت معه وجه بهمن جاذويه وهو ذو الحاجب ومعه فيلة وورد
معه الجالنوس ودفع اليه درفش كابيان وكانت راية من جلود
النمر عرض ثمانية اذرع طول اثني عشر ذراعا فعبر ابو عبيد بالمسلمين
اليهم وقاتلوهم يوما فاصيب من الفرس يومئذ في المعركة ستة الاف
ولم يبق الا الهزيمة فحمل ابو عبيد على الفيل وضربه فخبط الفيل ابا عبيد وقام
عليه فجال المسلمون جولة ثم تموا عليها فركبهم اهل فارس فبادر رجل من
ثقيف الى الجسر فقطعه فانتهى الناس اليه والسيوف تاخذهم من خلفهم
فتهافتوا في الفرات فاصابوا يومئذ من المسلمين اربعة الاف بين
غريق وقتيل وحمى المثنى وجماعة من الفرسان الناس ونادى ايها
الناس انا دونكم فاعبروا واعقدوا لهم الجسر فعبروا الى ذلك الجانب وبقي
المثنى في ثلاثة الاف وقد جرح والفرس يستعدون للقاء وهم يريدون
العبور الى المسلمين فبيناهم كذلك اذ ورد الخبر باختلاف الفرس
فرجع ذو الحاجب ومن انفض عنه جنده لانه بلغهم ان الناس بالمدائن
ثاروا برستم وصاروا فرقتين فرقة مع الفهلوج على رستم وفرقة مع
الفيرزان ثم ان جابان ومردانشاه خرجا فاخذا بالطريق وقد
فروا لا علم لهم بما ورد على ذي الحاجب من فرقة اهل فارس فخرج المثنى
يريد جابان ومردانشاه جريدة فاخذهما اسيرين فضرب اعناقهما
وعفوا اصحابهما ثم رجع الى العسكر واتت المثنى الامداد من

ومن الفارس ج

189a

وليس ذلك كله يكون بالله تعالى وحسن النية واستقامة التدبير وامرت
بالمناصحة وحسن الطاعة وردت خشبة الصليب على ملك الروم وكان
شعارها موشى اخضر وسراويلها على لون السما وتاجها كذلك وتجلس
على السرير وبيدها طبرزين وكانت مدتها سنة واربعة اشهر قال
ابن مسكويه فقدم ابو عبيد بن مسعود الثقفي ومعه المثنى بن حارثة وقد
استخرج الفرس يزدجرد وكانت بوران عدلا فيما بينهم لما
اختلفت الفرس وقتل الفرخزاد بن البندوان وكان سياوخش
قدم فقتل ازرمي دخت وذلك في غيبة المثنى وكان شغل الفرس طول
غيبته فيما بينهم وكانت بوران دعت رستم وشكت اليه تضعضع
فارس ودعته الى القيام بامرهم وتوجته فقال رستم انا عبد سامع
مطيع فولته امر فارس وحربها وامرت فارس ان يسمعوا له
ويطيعوا فقتل رستم سياوخش ودانت له الفرس وذلك بعد قدوم
ابي عبيد وكتب الى دهاقين السواد ان يثوروا بالمسلمين ودس في كل
رستاق رجلا ليثور باهله وبلغ ذلك المثنى وعجل جابان وكان اجتمع
اليه بشر كثير بالنمارق وخرج ابو عبيد فاجم الناس ثم تعبى فجعل المثنى
على الخيل وعلى الميمنة والميسرة فنزلوا على جابان بالنمارق فاقتتلوا
قتالا شديدا ثم انهزم فاسر ثم خلا عنه لانه آمنه وقسمت الغنائم وبعث
بالاخماس الى عمر رضي الله عنه وثار نرسي بكسكر وكان رستم
امره بذلك ونرسي هذا ابن خالة كسرى وكانت كسكر قطيعة له
فلما انهزمت الفرس يوم النمارق اجتمعت الفالة الى نرسي وهو في
عسكره ونادى ابو عبيد بالرحيل وقال للمجردة اتبعوا الفالة حتى
تلطوهم عسكر نرسي او تبيدوهم ومضى ابو عبيد حين ارتحل
من النمارق حتى نزل على نرسي بكسكر والمثنى بن حارثة معه ومع نرسي
ابنا خاله وهما ابنا خال كسرى بندويه وبيرويه ابنا بسطام وكان
قد اتى الخبر بوران ورستم بهزيمة جابان فبعثوا الجالنوس

وبلغ

[illegible]

188

باع من ملكه شيرويه وخير لنا والكاذب فاعظم الكاذبين عقوبة وفضيحة عند
الله والناس الملوك واما الذي يدلنا عليه الراي فانكم انما اضطررتم اليه
فاحمد الله الذي رد كيدكم الى دعاة الدجاج والخنازير فلما وقع الفرس
على كتابه جزعوا وقالوا انما اتى شهربراز من لوم منشاه وقالوا الجرا
علينا عدونا ما كتبت اليه فاذا كتبت فاستشيروا التقوا ببابل فاقتتلوا
بعدوة الصراة الدنيا قتالا شديدا ثم ان المثنى دعوة من المسلمين عقروا
الفيل وكان يفرق بين الصفوف والكراديس فاصابوا مقتله فقتلوه
وهزموا اهل فارس واتبعوهم يقتلونهم حتى جازوا بهم مسالحهم
وطلبوا الفلال فبلغوا المداين ومات شهربراز منهزم هرمز جاذويه
واختلف اهل فارس وتشاغلوا عن ازالة المسلمين فيما بينهم الى خلوف (?)
حتى مات ابو بكر وقام بعده امير المؤمنين عمر بن الخطاب رضي الله عنهما
وكان المثنى قد سار نحو المدينة ليخبر ابا بكر رضي الله عنه خبر المسلمين
وبينا ذلك في اشياء يحملها واستخلف على عسكره بشير بن الخصاصية
فرد عمر بن الخطاب رضي الله عنه المثنى بن حارثة مع ابي عبيد بن مسعود بن عمرو الثقفي
الى العراق وكان جمهور جند العراق من المسلمين بالحيرة والمسالح بالسيب
والغارات تنتهي بهم الى شاطئ دجلة ودجلة بين المسلمين وفارس ثم ملكت
بوران دخت وتلقب السعيدة بنت كسرى
ابرويز بن هرمز بن انوشروان امها مريم بنت قيصر ملك الروم وذلك
انه لما قتل شهربراز لم يجد الفرس احدا من بيت المملكة يملكوه عليهم
فاضطروا الى تمليك بوران فاحسنت السيرة وبسطت العدل
وامرت برم القناطر والجسور واعادت العمارات ووضعت بقايا
الخراج وكتبت الى الناس عامة كتبا تعلمهم ما هي عليه من الاحسان
وانها ترجوا ان يريها الله تعالى من الرفاهة والاستقامة بمكانها من
العدل وحفظ الثغور يعلمون به انه ليس ببطش الرجال توطا البلاد
ولا بباسهم تستباح العساكر ولا بمكايدهم ينال الظفر وتطفا النوايب (?)

عن المسلمين (?)

عن الناس (?)

شهربراز واسمه فرخان ولم يكن من اهل بيت الملك ووثب على
نفسه ملكا ولما جلس على سرير الملك ضرب عليه بطنه وبلغ من شدة
ذلك عليه انه لم يقدر على اتيان الخلاء فوضع الطست امام السرير ومد
في وجهه بما ستره فتبرز في الطست ثم استعمل رجل يقال له بسفروخ
واخوين له من قبل شهربراز اردشير بن شيرويه وغلبته على الملك
فتحالفوا على قتله وكان من العادة اذا ركب الملك ان يقف له حرسه سماطين
عليهم الدروع والبيض والترسة والسيوف وبايديهم الرماح فاذا حاذاهم
الملك وضع كل رجل منهم ترسه على قربوس سرجه ثم وضع جبهته عليه
كهيئة السجود فركب شهربراز بعد ان ملك بايام وقد وقف له بسفروخ
واخواه فلما حاذاهم طعنه بسفروخ ثم طعنه اخواه فسقط عن
فرسه فشدوا في رجله حبلا وجروه اقبالا وادبارا ساعة وساعدهم
قوم من العظماء وقتلوا عدة من اعوانه فكانت مدة ملكه اربعين يوما وملكوا
بوران وقيل ان الذي ملك بعد اردشير بن شيرويه انما هو خرها
ولم يكن من بيت المملكة فقتلته بوران بحيلة بعد اشهر وعشرين يوما وملك
فملك بعده كسرى بن قباذ ثلاثة اشهر وقتله ملك خراسان فملك بعده
بوران والقول الاول اشهر وكانت الفرس قد قربت انصرام مدتهم وانقضاء
ملكهم فنصر الله العرب عليهم وذلك ان خالد بن الوليد رضي الله عنه لما
فرغ من حرب اهل الردة امره ابو بكر رضي الله عنه بالمسير الى
العراق فسار في سنة اثنتي عشرة من الهجرة حتى نزل الحيرة وعليها
قبيصة بن اياس الطائي وقدم ايضا المثنى بن حارثة الشيباني قبل قدوم خالد
في سنة احدى عشرة فوجه شهربراز الى المثنى جندا عظيما عليهم هرمز
المعروف بجاذويه في عشرة الاف ومعه فيل فكتبت المسالح الى المثنى
باقباله فخرج من الحيرة نحوه وضم اليه المسالح وكتب شهربراز الى المثنى
اني قد بعثت اليك جندا من وخش اهلا انما هم رعاة الدجاج والخنازير
ولست اقاتلك الا بهم فاجابه المثنى الى شهربراز انما انت احد رجلين اما

باغ

187b

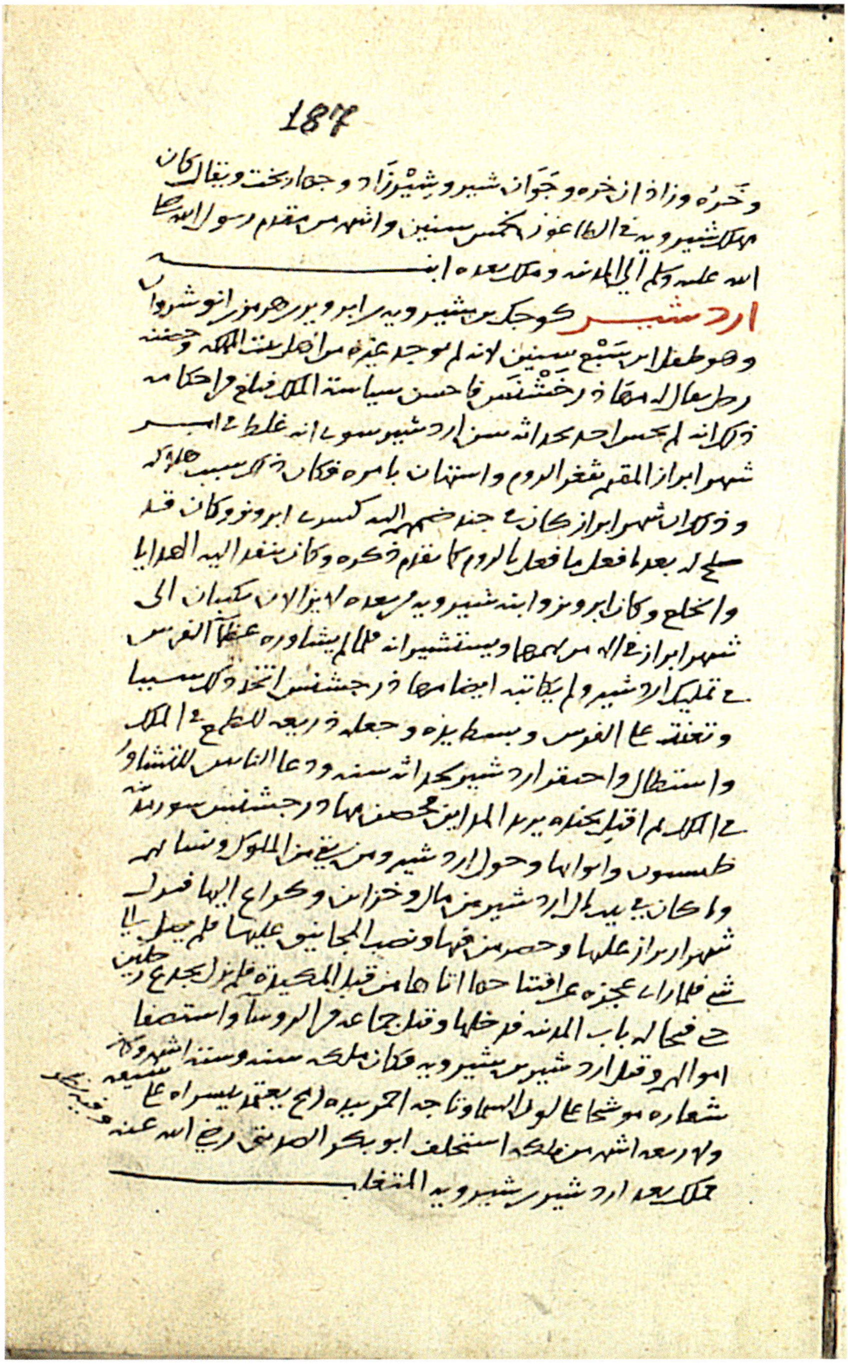
187

وخره وزاد ازخره وجوان شير وشيرزاد وجوانبخت وبغالك كان
مهلك شيرويه في الطاعون بخمس سنين واشهر من مقدم رسول الله صلى
الله عليه وسلم الى المدينة وملك بعده ابنه
اردشير كوجك بن شيرويه بن ابرويز بن هرمز بن انوشروان
وهو طفل ابن سبع سنين لانه لم يوجد غيره من اهل بيت المملكة وحضنه
رجل يقال له مهاذرخشنس فاحسن سياسة الملك فبلغ من احكامه
ذلك انه لم يحس احد بحداثة سن اردشير سوى انه غلط في امر
شهربراز المقيم بثغر الروم واستهان بامره فكان ذلك سبب هلاكه
وذلك ان شهربراز كان في جند ضمهم اليه كسرى ابرويز وكان قد
صلح له بعد ما فعل بالروم ما تقدم ذكره وكان ينفذ اليه الهدايا
والخلع وكان ابرويز وابنه شيرويه من بعده لا يزالان يكتبان الى
شهربراز في الامر يهمهما ويستشيرانه فلما لم يشاوره عظماء الفرس
في تمليك اردشير ولم يكاتبه ايضا مهاذرجشنس اتخذ ذلك سببا
وتعلقه على الفرس وبسط يده وجعله ذريعة للطمع في الملك
واستطال واحتقر اردشير بحداثة سنه ودعا الناس للتشاور
في الملك ثم اقبل بجنده يريد المدائن فحصن مهاذرجشنس سور مدينة
طيسفون وابوابها وحول اردشير ومن بقي من الملوك ونسائهم
وما كان في بيت مال اردشير من مال وخزائن وكراع اليها فنزل
شهربراز عليها وحصرهم فيها ونصب المجانيق عليها فلم يصل اليها
شيء فلما راى عجزه عن افتتاحها اتاها من قبل المكيدة فلم يزل يخدع رجلين
حتى فتحا له باب المدينة فدخلها وقتل جماعة من الرؤساء واستصفى
اموالهم وقتل اردشير بن شيرويه فكان ملكه سنة وستة اشهر وكان
شعاره موشحا على لون السماء وتاجه احمر بيده رمح يعتمد بيسراه على سيفه
ولاربعة اشهر من ملكه استخلف ابو بكر الصديق رضي الله عنه
وملك بعد اردشير بن شيرويه المتغلب

187a

شيرويه واسمه قباذ بن كسرى أبرويز بن هرمز بن كسرى
انوشروان امه مريم بنت موريق قيصر ملك الروم لما ملك دخل
عليه العظماء والاشراف فقالوا انه لا يستقيم لنا امر ولنا مليكان فاما
ان تقتل كسرى ونحن عبيدك واما ان نخلعك ونعطيه الطاعة ونطيعه
فانكسر عند ذلك شيرويه ونقل اباه من دار الملك الى موضع اخر
حبسه فيه ثم جمع العظماء وقال قد رأيت ان ارسل الى كسرى بما كان
من اساءته ونوقفه على اشياء منها فارسل اليه اسباذ جشنس وكان
على تدبير المملكة يعدد عليه ذنوبه فاجاب عنها فعاد عظماء الفرس الى
شيرويه وقالوا اما ان تامر بقتل ابيك واما ان نطيعه ونخلعك فامر
بقتله على كره فانتدب لقتله رجال ممن وترهم ابرويز فباشر قتله
منهم شاب اسمه مهرهرمز بن مردانشاه فلما قتل ابرويز شق شيرويه
ثيابه وبكى ولطم وجهه وحملت جنازته وتبعها العظماء واشراف
الناس ثم امر شيرويه بقتل مهرهرمز قاتل ابيه فقتل ثم قتل اخوته
وكانوا سبعة عشر رجلا ذوي اداب وشجاعة ومشورة ومروءة
فجزع بعد قتلهم جزعا شديدا ودخلت عليه اختاه بوران وازرميدخت
في اليوم الثاني من قتلهم فاغلظتا عليه وقالتا حملك الحرص على الملك
الذي لا يتم لك على قتل ابيك واخوتك فبكى بكاء شديدا ورمى التاج عن
راسه ولم يزل مهموما حزينا مدنفا وابتلي بالاسقام فانتقض
عليه بدنه فلم يلتذ بشيء من لذات الدنيا ويقال انه اباد من قدر عليه
من اهل بيته وكان الطاعون فشا في ايامه فاهلك الفرس ثم هلك فيه
وكان ملكه ثمانية اشهر وكان شعاره وشي احمر وسراويله على لون
السماء موشحة وتاجه اخضر بيمناه سيف مخروط وقيل انه احس من
من اخوته نفورا منه فقتل منهم ثمانية عشر وهم شهريار ومردانشاه
وكوانشاه وفيروزانشاه وابرويزشاه وزرابرود وشادمان
وشادزيله وازونوزيله وازونوردشت وفسبه وفسرداو خره

وخره

186b

186

يزدجرد فملكه خمس سنين ثم انهارت من كسرى رقة للصبيان حين كبر
فقال ابرويز اني ارى ان تروى لبعض بنيك ولا اكانهم فاتبه بيزدجرد واحبه
وقربه فبينما هو يلعب ذات يوم ذكر ما قيل له فامر به يحجر من شابه
فرأى النقص في احد وركيه فاراد قتله فمنعته شيرين وقالت له
ان كان الامر في الملك قد حضر فلا مرد له وامرت بيزدجرد فحمل
الى سجستان وقيل بل تركته بالسواد في قرية يقال لها جمانيه
وابرويز هذا هو الذي كتب اليه رسول الله صلى الله عليه وسلم يدعوه
الى الاسلام فمزق الكتاب وبعث الى باذان عامله على اليمن يامره ان
يبعث برجلين جلدين ليأتياه بخبره فلما قدما على رسول الله صلى الله عليه
وسلم بكتاب باذان اخبرهما ان الله عز وجل قد قتل كسرى في ليلة كذا
بيد ابنه شيرويه فرجعا الى باذان فاذا الامر كما قال رسول الله صلى الله
عليه وسلم وكان رسول الله صلى الله عليه وسلم لما بلغه ان ابرويز مزق
كتابه دعا عليهم ان يمزقوا كل ممزق فاستجاب الله تعالى دعاه ومزق
ملك فارس فلم يبق لهم ملك قال ابو بكر بن ابي شيبة حدثنا محمد بن فضيل عن
حصين عن عبد الله بن شداد قال كتب كسرى الى باذام اني نبئت ان رجلا
يقول شيئا لا ادري ما هو فارسل اليه فليقعد في بيته ولا يكن من الناس
في شيء والا فليواعدني موعدا القاه به فارسل باذام الى رسول الله صلى الله
عليه وسلم رجلين حالقي لحاهما مرسلي شواربهما فقال رسول الله صلى الله عليه
وسلم ما يحملكما على هذا فقالا يا مرنا به الذين يزعمون انه ربهم فقال لكنا نخالف
سنتكم نجز هذا ونرسل هذا قال فتركهما بضعا وعشرين يوما ثم قال اذهبا
الى الذين يزعمون انه ربكما فاخبراه ان ربي قتل الذي يزعم انه ربه قال في
هذا اليوم فذهبا الى باذام فاخبراه الخبر فكتبا الى كسرى فوجدوا اليوم
الذي قتل فيه كسرى وابرويز هو صاحب شيرين نظر اليها وهي معتزة
للناكحين متبرزة مع الرجال فهويها واراد ها لنفسه فقالت له انها
الملك من قادة الى من ليس له عندي جدير ان يتشفع من حاله ما

الهوى

فلم يرعه الا به قايما على راسه وفي يده عصا بالهاجرة في ساعته
التي كان يقيل فيها فقال يا كسرى اسلم او اكسر هذه العصا قال
بيل بيل ثم يخرج عنه فدعا كسرى حراسه وحجابه وبوابيه فتغيظ
عليهم وقال من ادخل هذا الرجل علي فقالوا ما دخل عليك احد وما رايناه حتى
اذا كان العام القابل اتاه في الساعة التي اتاه فيها وقال له كما قال له ثم
قال له اسلم او اكسر العصا فقال بيل بيل ثم يخرج عنه فدعا كسرى
حراسه وحجابه وبوابيه فتغيظ عليهم وقال لهم كما قال اول مرة
فقالوا ما راينا احدا دخل عليك حتى اذا كان العام الثالث اتاه في الساعة
التي جاءه فيها فقال له كما قال ثم قال اتسلم او اكسر العصا فقال بيل بيل
فكسر العصا ثم خرج فلم يكن الا تهور ملكه وانبعاث ابنه والفرس
حتى قتلوه قال الزهري حدثت عمر بن عبد العزيز بهذا الحديث عن ابي سلمة
ابن عبد الرحمن فقال ذكر لي ان الملك انما دخل عليه بقارورتين في يده ثم قال له
اسلم فلم يفعل فضرب احداهما على الاخرى فرضضهما ثم خرج فكان من
هلاكه ما كان قال الحافظ ابو نعيم ورواه صالح بن كيسان عن الزهري
عن ابي سلمة ان كسرى بينا هو في دسكرة ملكه بعث الله وقيض له
عارض يعرض عليه الحق فلم يفجا كسرى الا برجل يمشي وفي يده عصا فقال
يا كسرى هل لك في الاسلام قبل ان اكسر هذه العصا قال نعم فلا تكسرها
فذكر نحوه حدثنا عبد الله بن ابي بكر عن الزهري عن ابي سلمة ورواه محمد بن عمر
الواقدي عن محمد بن عبد الله عن الزهري عن ابي سلمة بن عبد الرحمن عن ابي هريرة
قال بينا كسرى مغلق بيته الذي يخلو فيه اذ دخله رجل في يده عصا
وذكر نحوه وقيل كان لكسرى ابرويز ثمانية عشر ولدا وكان
اكبرهم شهريار وكانت شيرين قد تبنته فقال المنجمون لكسرى
انه سيولد لبعض ولدك غلام يكون خراب هذا المجلس وذهاب
الملك على يده وعلامته نقص في بعض بدنه فمنع ولده النساء حتى
شكا شهريار الى شيرين الشبق فارسلت اليه جارية فعلقت منه

185

ورکب برذونه وخرج يسير عليها فبينا هو يسير فوقها اذ انتسفت دجلة
البنيان فلم يدرك الا باخر رمق فدعاهم فقال والله لانزعنكم اجمعين
ولانزعن اكتافكم اولاطرحنكم تحت ايدي الفيلة او لتصدقني ما هذا
الامر الذي تلفقون علي قالوا لا نكذبك ايها الملك امرتنا حين انخرقت
دجلة وانفصم عليك طاق مجلسك من غير ثقل ان ننظر في علمنا لم ذلك
فنظرنا فاظلمت علينا الارض واخذ علينا في اقطار السما فتردد
علمنا في ايدينا فلا ينفذ لساحر سحر ولا لكاهن كهانته ولا لمنجم علم
نجومه فعرفنا ان هذا الامر حدث من السما وانه قد بعث نبي او
هو مبعوث ولذلك حيل بيننا وبين علمنا فخشينا ان نعينا لك
ملكك ان يقتلنا فكرهنا من الموت ما يكره الناس فعللناك عن
انفسنا بما رايت قال ويحكم افلا تكونوا بينتم لي هذا فارى فيه
رايي قالوا منعنا ذلك ما تخوفنا منك فتركهم ولهى عن دجلة حين
غلبته قال الحافظ ابو نعيم ورواه الواقدي قال حدثني صالح بن
جعفر قال سمعت محمد بن كعب القرظي يقول دخلت مداين كسرى
سنة ثمانين عام الجحاف فنظرت الى بنا كسرى فصحبت فاذا
شيخ قائم يهاج فسالته عن بعض امره فقال ان كسرى اول ما انكر من
ملكه انه اصبح في الليلة التي اوحى الى رسول الله صلى الله عليه وسلم
ودجلة انثلمت وطاق ملكه منصدعا فذكر نحوه وقال محمد بن اسحق
عن الفضل بن عيسى الرقاشي عن الحسن البصري ان اصحاب رسول الله صلى
الله عليه وسلم قالوا يا رسول الله ما حجة الله على كسرى فيك قال بعث
اليه ملكا فاخرج يده من سور جدار بيته الذي هو فيه تلالا نورا فلما
رآها فزع فقال لم ترع يا كسرى ان الله تعالى قد بعث رسولا وانزل
عليه كتابا فاتبعه تسلم دنياك واخرتك قال سانظر وقال محمد بن اسحق
عن عبد الله بن ابي بكر عن الزهري عن ابي سلمة بن عبد الرحمن قال بعث الله تعالى
الى كسرى ملكا وهو في بيت ايوانه الذي لا يدخل عليه فيه احد

[illegible]

185*b

185*a

ولا يستقيم لمنجم علم نجومه وبات السائب في ليلة ظلما على ربوة من الارض يرمق
برقا نشا من قبل الحجاز ثم استطار حتى بلغ المشرق فلما اصبح ذهب ينظر
الى ما تحت قدميه فاذا روضة خضرا فقال فيما يعتاف لئن صدق ما ارى
ليخرجن من الحجاز سلطان يبلغ المشرق تخصب عنه الارض كافضل ما
اخصبت عن ملك كان قبله فلما خلص الكهان والمنجمون بعضهم الى بعض
وراوا ما قد اصابهم وراى السائب ما قد راى قال بعضهم لبعض تعلمون والله
ما حيل بينكم وبين علمكم الا لامر جاء من السما وانه لنبي قد بعث او هو مبعوث
يسلب هذا الملك ويكسره ولئن نعيتم لكسرى ملكه ليقتلنكم فاقيموا بينكم
امرا تقولونه وتوخرونه عنكم الى امد ما فجاوا كسرى ابرويز فقالوا
له انا قد نظرنا في هذا الامر فوجدنا حسابك الذين وضعت على
حسابهم طاق ملكك وسكرت دجلة العورا وضعوه على
النحوس فلما اختلف عليه الليل والنهار وقعت النحوس على مواقعها فزال
كل ما وضع عليها وانا سنحسب حسابا تضع عليه بنيانك فلا يزول
قال فاحسبوا فحسبوا له ثم قالوا ابنه فبنا وعمل في دجلة ثمانية
اشهر فانفق من الاموال ما لا يدرى ما هو حتى اذا فرغ قال لهم
اجلس على سورها قالوا نعم فامر بالبسط والفرش والرياحين
فوضعت عليها وامر بالمرازبة فجمعوا اليه واجتمع اللعابون ثم
خرج حتى جلس عليها فبينا هو هنالك انتسفت دجلة البنيان
من تحته فلم يستخرج الا بآخر رمق فلما اخرجوه جمع كهانه وسحاره
ومنجميه فقتل منهم قريبا من المائة وقال قربتكم وادنيتكم دون الناس
واجريت عليكم ارزاقي ثم تلعبون بي قالوا ايها الملك اخطانا ولكنا
سنحسب لك حسابا تثبت فتضعها على الوثاق من السعود قال
انظروا ما تقولون قالوا فانا نفعل قال فاحسبوا فحسبوا له ثم
قالوا ابنه فبنا وانفق من الاموال ما لا يدرى ما هو في ثمانية اشهر من
ذي قبل ثم قالوا قد فرغنا قال افاخرج فاقعد عليها فهاب الجلوس عليها

واركب

184b

184

عضده جرحه ولا يحيك السيف فيه فعلقها فقر عرق من عضده ثم قتل فبكا
شيرويه لقتله وكان هلاك ابرويز بعد ما ملك ثمانيا وثلاثين سنة وبقا
من ابنتين وثلاثين سنة وخمسة اشهر وخمسة عشر يوما من ملكه هاجر
النبي صلى الله عليه وسلم من مكة الى المدينة وخلف في بيت المال سوى فضل
من الورق اربع مائة الف بدرة سوى الكنوز والذخاير والجواهر
والالات الملوكية وكان شعاره موردا موشى وسراويله على لون السما
وتاجه احمر وبيده رمح ونصب بيت نار بقرية من رستاق جرجان
ووقف عليها قرى تعرف بها وقيل بعث النبي صلى الله عليه وسلم لاثنتين
وعشرين سنة من ملكه وبقي بعد البعث سبعة عشر سنة وكان بعده صلى الله
عليه وسلم عندما مضى من ملكه ثمان وثلاثون سنة فهلك من سنته
وقيل كانت الهجرة لتسع وعشرين سنة من ملكه وقيل لثلث وثلاثين و
انه اخرج خشبة الصليب من القدس لاربع وعشرين سنة من ملكه ثم كانت
الهجرة بعد ذلك بتسع سنين ثم اقام بعد الهجرة حتى خلع
وقتل اربع سنين واربعة اشهر واثني عشر يوما وقد راى
كسرى ابرويز عدة ايات بسبب رسول الله صلى الله عليه وسلم
منها انه كان سكر دجلة العوراء وانفق عليها من الاموال ما لا يدرى ما هو
وكان طاق مجلسه قد بني بنيانا لم ير مثله وكان يعلق فيها تاجه
فيجلس فيها اذا جلس للناس وكان عنده ستون ومائة رجل من
العرب اسمه الحساب تعرفه باذان عن الهم وكان ابرويز اذا حزبه امر
جمعهم فقال انظروا في هذا الامر ما هو فلما بعث رسول الله صلى الله عليه
وسلم اصبح كسرى غداة وقد انقصم طاق ملكه من وسطه وانخرقت دجلة
العوراء الى اي ذلك احزنه وقال انقصم طاق ملكي من غير ثقل وانخرقت على دجلة
شاه بشكست يقول انكسر الملك انظروا في هذا الامر ما هو فخرجوا من
عنده فنظروا في امره فاخذ عليهم باقطار السما واظلمت عليهم
الارض وتسكعوا في علمهم فلا يمضي لساحر سحره ولا لكاهن كهانته

مقنعة فمما كتب به شيرويه الى ابيه ابرويز ان الملك سبيلا اصبحت
فيه وكلنا الله قضاه عليك لسوء اعمالك منها فتكك بابيك وسملك عينيه
ومنها سوء صنيعك واستحلالك النسا وتركك العطف على اولاد
وما اتيت الى الرعية وما جمعت من البعوث واستخفافك بملك الروم
وتركك اطلاقه في خشبة الصليب ولم يكن اليها حاجة فاجاب
ان الامر اذا اقبل اعيت الحيل في الادبار واذا ادبر اعيتنا الحيل في
الاقبال ابلغ شيرويه القصير العمر انه لا ينبغي لذي عقل ان يبث
الصغير من الذنب الا بعد تحققه فضلا عن عظيم ما بثثت فان كنت
جاهلا بعيوبك فاستثبت وان كان لنا ذنب يوجب القتل فقضاه
ملكك ينفون ولد المستوجب القتل عن ابيه واما ما ذكرت من امر
ابينا فالجواب ان البغاة اغروه بنا حتى اتهمنا فاعتزلنا بابه
فانتهك منه ما انتهك ولحقنا به فهجم علينا المنافق بهرام فلحقنا
بالروم واقبلنا بالجنود فهرب بهرام وقتلنا من شرك في قتل
ابينا واما امر ابنائنا فوكلنا بهم من يمنعهم من الفساد ووسعنا
عليهم في كل ما ارادوه واما انت فان المنجمين قضوا في مولودك انك تعرب
علينا ووجدنا ملك الهند قد كتب اليك في سنة وكان شيء من ملكنا ابشر
فانك مشئوم سنة ثمان وثلاثين من ملك كسرى فوثقنا انك لا تملك
الا بهلاكنا وكتاب قرميسينا وقصة مولودك عند شيرين فخفف
عليها تكسيبك قراتها واما امر حبسنا فلم نحبس الا من استوجب
القتل وبلغ انك اجمعت على اطلاقهم وهدم حبسهم فان فعلت اثمت
مع ان اعداء الملك لا يحبون الملك ابدا واما جمعنا الاموال فاعلم ايها الجاهل
انما يقوم ملك الملوك بعد الله تعالى بالاموال ولا سيما ملك فارس الذي قد
اكتنفته الاعداء ولا يقدر على كفهم الا بالجنود ولا سبيل الى الاستكثار
من الجنود الا بالاموال ولا تجمع الاموال الا بالجد والتشمير ثم الح العقلاء
على شيرويه في قتل ابيه فامر بقتله فضرب ضربات فلم تحك فيه فوجد

عشره

183b

183

كان في يده السواد وارض العجم دون اعمال العرب وان حد مملكته بيسا
حيث وكان ما وراء ذلك من الموصل والجزيرة والشام بيد الروم فكانت
جباية مملكته في سنة ثماني عشرة من ملكه اربعمائة الف الف وعشرين
الف الف مثقال من الورق وامر ابرويز بتحويل المال الى بيت مال في مدينة
طيسفون من ضرب فيروز ويزدجرد وقباذ بن فيروز وانتخ حشو
الف بدرة في انواع من الجواهر والكسى وغير ذلك فعتا واستخف
بالناس في الاحرار وبلغ من جرأته انه امر رجلا كان على حرس بابه
الخاصة يقال له زاذان فروخ ان يقتل كل مقيد في سجونه
فاحصوا فبلغوا ستة وثلاثين الفا فلم يقدم زاذان فروخ على قتلهم
وتقدم بالتوقف على امره كسرى واعد عللا له فيما امره فيهم فكان
هذا احد ما كسبه ابرويز عداوة مملكته والثاني احتقاره اياهم
واستخفافه بعظمائهم والثالث انه سلط علجا يقال له الفرخان حزاد
عليهم حتى استخرج بقايا الخراج بعنف وعذاب وكان جمع من ذلك
مالا عظيما فسلطه على الناس والرابع اجماعه على قتل الغل الذين
انصرفوا اليه من قبل هرقل ملك الروم فمضى قوم من العظماء الى عقر بابل
وشيرويه بن ابرويز مع اخوته بها وقد وكل بهم مؤدبون واساورة
يحولون بينهم وبين البراح من ذلك الموضع فاقبلوا به ودخلوا مدينة
بهرسير ليلا فخلى عمن كان في سجونها واخرج من كان فيها واجتمع
اليه الغل الذين كانوا علموا بامر ابرويز بقتلهم ونادوا قباذ شاه
نشاه وساروا حين اصبحوا الى رحبة ابرويز فهرب الحرس من قصر
ابرويز وانحاز ابرويز بنفسه الى باغ له قريب من قصره يدعى
باغ الهندوان مارا مرعوبا فاخذ وحبس خارجا عن دار المملكة
في دار رجل يقال له مارسفند الى ان قتل بعد حديث طويل من مراسلات
بينه وبين شيرويه بمواطاة العظماء وبعد تقريع كثير وتوبيخ
على ما كان منه في اشياء عددها عليه فاجاب عن الكل بجوابات

183a

تعلم ما فيه فلما قراه ادخله في جيبه ثم مضى فلما صار في عسكر الروم نظر
الصلبان والقسيسين في حججهم بالتقديس والصلوات احترق
قلبه لهم واشفق لما خاف ان تقع بهم وكان في نفسه انا شر الناس
حملت بيدي حتف النصرانية وهلاك جل الخلق فصاح انا قد
حملني كسرى رسالة ومعي كتاب منه فاخذوه فوجدوا الكتاب
معه وقد كان ابرويز وجه رسولا قبل ذلك اختصر الطريق حتى مر
بعسكر الروم فكان رسول ابرويز من صاحبه الذي طابق ملك
الروم ومعه كتاب فيه ان الملك قد كان امرني بمقاربة ملك الروم وان
اخدعه واطاول الطريق فياخذه الملك من امامه وآخذه انا من خلفه
وقد فعلت ذلك فراى الملك في اعلاه في وقت خروجه اليه فاخذ ملك
الروم الرسول وقرا الكتاب وقال يجب ان يكون هذا الفارسي داهية
كسرى وبينا هو في ذلك اذ وافاه ابرويز فيمن امكنه من جنده فوجد
ملك الروم قد ولى هاربا فاتبعه يقتل وياسر من ادرك وبلغ صاحب
الجيش ببلاد الشام هزيمة الروم فاحب ان يحيا بنفسه ويستر
ذنبه لما فاته فادبر يخرج خلف الروم الهاربين فلم يسلم منهم الا
القليل ثم كان ابرويز بسبب هلاك نفسه وذلك انه تجبر واحتقر
العظماء وعتا واستخف بما لا يستخف به الملك الحازم وكان جمع
الاموال ما لم يجمعه احد من الملوك وبلغت خيله قسطنطينية
وافريقية وكان له اثنا عشر الف جارية والف فيل
الا فيلا واحدا وخمسون الف دابة ورتب في خزانته ستة الاف
رجل وكان في اصطبله ثمانية الاف وخمسمائة دابة لركابه خاصة
واثنا عشر الف بغل لاثقاله وعشرون الف تخت ومن الجواهر والاواني
والالات ما يليق بذلك وامر ان يحصى ما اجتبي من خراج بلاده وسائر
ابواب المال في سنة ثماني عشرة من ملكه فرفع اليه ان الذي اجتبي في تلك
السنة من الخراج وسائر الابواب ستمائة الف الف درهم وفي نسخة اثنا

كان

... هذه الحادثة انزل الله تعالى على نبينا ... الروم ... ادنى الارض الاية

182b

182

واسكت عليه اياما ثم اعلمه ان الكتاب الثاني ورد عليك واوصله اليه ليقيم
بموضعه فخرج رسول ابرويز حتى ورد على شهربراز صاحب الجيش ببلاد
الشام فاوصل الكتاب اليه فلما قراه قال ما ان يكون كسرى قد تغير
لي وكره موضعي او يكون قد اختلط عقله بصرف مثلي وانا في نحر
العدو فدعا اصحابه وقرا عليهم الكتاب فانكروه فلما كان بعد ثلثة
ايام اوصل الكتاب الثاني بالمقام واوهمه ان رسوله ورد به فلما قراه
قال هذا تخليط ولم تقع منه موقعا ودس الى ملك الروم من ناظره
في ايقاع صلح بينهما على ان يخلي الطريق لملك الروم حتى يوطيه
العراق على غرة من ابرويز وعلى ان لملك الروم ما يغلب عليه من دون
العراق وللفارسي ما وراء ذلك الى بلاد فارس فاجابه ملك الروم الى
ذلك وتنحى الفارسي عنه في ناحية من الجزيرة واخذ افواه الطرق فلم
يعلم ابرويز حتى ورد خبر ملك الروم عليه من ناحية قرقيسيا وهو غير
مستعد وجنده متفرقون في اعماله فوثب من سريره مع قراة
الخبر وقال هذا وقت حيلة لا وقت شدة وجعل ينكت في الارض
مليا ثم دعا برق وكتب فيه كتابا باصغر الخط دقيقا الى صاحبه
بالجزيرة يقول فيه قد علمت ما كنت امرتك به من مواصلة صاحب
الروم واطماعه في نفسك وتخلية الطريق له حتى اذا توسط في
بلادنا اخذته من امامه واخذته انت ومن معك من خلفه
فيكون ذلك بواره وقد تم في هذا الوقت ما دبرناه وميعاد ذلك في
الايقاع به يوم كذا ثم دعا راهبا كان في دير بجانب مدينته
وقال له اي جار كنت لك قال افضل جار قال فقد بدت لنا اليك حاجة
قال الراهب الملك اجل من ان يكون له حاجة الي مثلي ولكني ابذل نفسي
للذي يامر الملك به قال ابرويز تحمل لي كتابا الى فلان صاحبي قال نعم قال
ابرويز فانك تجتاز باصحابك النصارى فاخفه قال نعم فلما ولى عنه
الراهب قال له ابرويز اعلمت ما في الكتاب قال لا قال فلا تحمله حتى

ايتوني بشهربراز فقدموه ليضرب عنقه فقال لا تعجل حتى اكتب وصيتي
قال افعل فدعا بسفط واعطاه ثلاث صحايف وقال كل هذا راجعت
فيك كسرى وانت اردت ان تقتلني بكتاب واحد فرد فرخان الملك على
اخيه شهربراز فكتب شهربراز الى هرقل قيصر ملك الروم ان لي اليك
حاجة لا تحملها البرد ولا تبلغها الصحف فالقني ولا تلقني الا في خمسين
روميا فاني ايضا القاك في خمسين فارسيا فاقبل هرقل في خمسين الف
رومي وجعل يضع العيون بين يديه في الطريق وخاف ان يكون قد
مكر به حتى اتاه عيونه انه ليس معه الا خمسون رجلا ثم بسط لهما
والتقيا في قبة ديباج ضربت لهما واجتمعا ومع كل واحد منهما
سكين ودعوا ترجمانا بينهما فقال شهربراز ان الذين خربوا مدينتك
وبلغوا منك ومن جنودك ما بلغوا انا واخي بشجاعتنا وكيدنا وان
كسرى ابرويز حسدنا فاراد ان اقتل اخي فابيت ثم امر اخي ان
يقتلني فقد خلعناه جميعا فنحن نقاتله معك قال قد اصبتما ووفقتما
ثم اشار احدهما الى صاحبه ان السر انما يكون بين اثنين فاذا جاوز
اثنين فشا قال صاحبه اجل فقاما جميعا الى الترجمان بسكينيهما
فقتلاه واتفقا على قتال ابرويز ومات ابرويز كانت وقعة ذي قار
فانتصرت العرب فيها على فارس ومنها ذلت فارس ورق امرها
ثم كانت لابرويز حيلة على ملك الروم وذلك انه كان قد وجه رجلا
من جلة اصحابه في جيش جرار الى بلاد الروم فانكا فيهم وبلغ منهم
وفتح الشامات وبلغ الدرب في اثارهم فعظم امره وخافه ابرويز
فكاتبه بكتابين يامره في احدهما ان يستخلف على جيشه من يثق به
ويقبل اليه ويامره في الاخر ان يقيم بموضعه فانه لما تدبر امره واجال
الراي لم يجد من يسد مسده ولم يامن الخلل ان غاب عن موضعه
وارسل بالكتابين رسولا من ثقاته وقال له اوصل الكتاب الاول الامر
بالقدوم فان خف لذلك فهو ما اردت وان كره وتثاقل عن الطاعة

فاسكت

[illegible]

181

طاعته فلما تتابعت على زاهزاذ جوابات ابرويز بذلك عبا جنده وناهض
الروم بهم فقتلت الروم زاهزاذ وستة آلاف رجل وانهزمت بقيتهم
وهربوا على وجوههم وبلغ ابرويز ذلك فتهزم مصالحه وانحاز من
دستجرة الملك الى المداين وتحصن بها لعجزه عن محاربة هرقل وسار
هرقل حتى كان قريبا من المداين فلما استعد ابرويز لقتاله انصرف
راجعا الى بلاد الروم وكتب ابرويز الى قواد الجند الذين انهزموا
ان يدلوه على كل رجل منهم ومن اصحابه ممن فشل في تلك الحروب ولم
يرابط مركزه فيهابان يعاقب فاخرجهم هذا الى الخلاف عليه وطلب
الحيل للنجاة منه وكتب مع ذلك الى شهربراز يامره بالقدوم عليه
ويستعجله في ذلك ويصف له ما نال الروم منه ومن بلاده وحكي
ان ابرويز عرف امراة من فارس لم تلد الا الملوك الا بطال فدعاها
وقال لها انى اريد ان ابعث الى الروم جيشا واستعمل عليهم رجلا من بنيك
فاشيري على ايهم استعمل فوصفت اولادها فقالت هذا فرخان
انفذ من سنان وهذا شهربراز احكم من كذا وهذا فلان اروغ
من كذا فاستعمل ايهم شئت فاستعمل شهربراز فسار الى الروم
فظهر عليهم وهزمهم وخرب مدائنهم فلما ظهرت فارس على الروم
جلس فرخان يشرب فقال لاصحابه لقد رايت كاني جالس على سرير
كسرى فبلغت ابرويز فكتب الى شهربراز اذا اتاك كتابي هذا فابعث
الي براس فرخان فكتب اليه ايها الملك انك لن تجد مثل فرخان فان
له نكاية في العدو وصوتا فلا تفعل فكتب اليه ان في رجال فارس
خلفا منه فعجل على براسه فراجعه فغضب ابرويز ولم يجبه وبعث
بريدا الى اهل فارس اني قد نزعت عنكم شهربراز واستعملت فرخان
ثم دفع الى البريد صحيفة صغيرة وقال اذا ولي الفرخان الملك وانقاد
له اخوه فاعطه فلما قرا شهربراز الكتاب قال سمعا وطاعة
ونزل عن سريره وجلس فرخان ودفع الصحيفة اليه فقال

181a

فارس بلادهم وقتلهم مقاتلتهم وسبيهم ذراريهم واستباحتهم اموالهم
تضرع الى الله تعالى واكثر الدعاء والابتهال فبينا الا انه رأى في منامه
رجلا ضخما رفيع المجلس عليه فرط عليها داخل فاقلع ذلك الرجل
عن مجلسه وقال لهرقل اني قد سلمته في يديك فلم يقصص رؤياه تلك في
يقظته حتى توالت عليه امثاله فرأى في بعض لياليه كأن رجلا دخل
عليهما وبيده سلسلة طويلة فالقاها في عنق صاحبه اعني صاحب
المجلس الرفيع عليه ثم دفعه اليه وقال له ها قد دفعت اليك كسرى
برمته فلما تتابعت عليه هذه الاحلام قصها على عظماء الروم وذوي
العلم منهم فاشاروا عليه ان يغزوه فاستعد هرقل واستخلف ابنه
على مدينة قسطنطينية واخذ غير الطريق الذي فيه شهربراز وسار
حتى وغل في بلاد ارمينية ونزل نصيبين بسنة وقد كان صاحب
ذلك الثغر من قبل ابرويز قد استدعى هرقل لموجدة كانت من هرمز
واما شهربراز فكانت كتب كسرى ابرويز ترد عليه في الجثوم
على الموضع الذي هو به وترك البراح ثم بلغ ابرويز تساقط
هرقل في جنوده الى نصيبين فوجه لمحاربته رجلا من قواده
يقال له راهزاد في اثني عشر الف رجل من الانجاد وامره ان يقيم
بنينوى وهي التي تدعى الان الموصل على شاطئ دجلة ويمنع
الروم ان يجوزوها وكان ابرويز بلغه خبر هرقل وانه مغذ وهو
يومئذ مقيم بدسكرة الملك فنفذ راهزاد لامر ابرويز وعسكر
حيث امره فقطع هرقل دجلة في موضع اخر الى الناحية التي كان
فيها جند فارس فاذكى راهزاد العيون عليه فانصرفوا اليه واخبروه
انه في سبعين الف مقاتل فايقن راهزاد انه ومن معه من الجند
عاجزون عن مناهضته فكتب الى ابرويز غير مرة ان هرقل دهمه
بما لا طاقة له ولمن معه بهم لكثرتهم وحسن عدتهم كل ذلك يجيبه
ابرويز بانه ان يعجز عن الروم فلن يعجز عن استقبالهم وبذل دمائهم في

طاعته

180b

180

المداين بعد ان فرق في جنود الروم اموالا عظيمة وصرفهم الى ملك
الروم ولبث بهرام شوبين في الترك مكرما عند الملك حتى احتال
له ابرويز بتوجيه رجل يقال له هرمز الى الترك بجوهر نفيس وغيره حتى
احتال للخاتون امراة الملك واطمعها بذلك الجوهر وغيره من الهدايا حتى
دست لبهرام من قتله فاغتم الملك خاقان لموته وارسل الى اخته
كردية وامراته يعلمها بلوغ الحادث بهرام منه ويسالها ان يتزوجها
وطلق امراته خاتون بهذا السبب فاجابته كردية نحن اولى بالبنا وحملت
من كان مع اخيها شوبين من المقاتلة اليها وخرجت بهم من بلاد
الترك المحدود مملكة فارس فاتبعها ملك الترك اخاه بطراغا في
الف فارس فقاتلته كردية وقتلته بيدها ومضت حتى لحقت باخيها
الفرس وكتبت الى اخيها كردي فاخذ لها امانا من ابرويز فلما قدمت
عليه اغتبط بها وتزوج بها ابرويز ثم كانت من ابرويز سو سياسة في
جنده حتى طمع الروم عليه وذلك انه لم يزل على طاعة ملك الروم الذي كان نصره
وبها وبه الى ان وثب الروم عليه في شي انكروه منه فقتلوه وقد
فر احدهم الى ابرويز فانتصر من اخذ به الخليفة فاوى ابن الملك
المقتول وقد التجا اليه وتوجه وملكه على الروم ووجه معه جنودا
كثيفة مع شهربراز فدوخ بهم البلاد وملك بيت المقدس واخذ
خشبة الصليب وبعث بها الى ابرويز في اربع وعشرين سنة من ملكه
ثم احتوى على مصر والاسكندرية وبلاد نوبة وبعث بمفاتيح مدينة
الاسكندرية الى ابرويز في سنة ثمان وعشرين من ملكه وقصد قسطنطينية
فاناخ على ضفة الخليج القريب منها وخيم هنالك فامره ابرويز فخرب
بلاد الروم غضبا مما انتهكوا من ملكهم وانتقاما له ولم يخضع له احد من
ملكهم المقتول احد ولا منحوا الطاعة غير انهم قتلوا الملك الذي ملكوه
بعد ابيه المسمى فوقا لما ظهر من فجوره وسو تدبيره وملكوا عليهم
رجلا يقال له هرقل فلما راى هرقل عظيم ما فيه الروم من تخريب جنود

في ذكرهم ان ساقت الامور بالمقادير الى ان زوجه ابنته مريم وحملها
اليه وبعث اليه بثياذوس اخيه ومعه ستون الف مقاتل عليهم
رجل يقال له سرجيس يتولى تدبير امورهم ورجل اخر يقال له كان
يعد بالف رجل معظم في الروم وساله ترك الاتاوة التي كان اباوه
يسلمونها ملوك الروم اذا هو ملك فاغتبط بهم ابرويز وازاحهم
خمسة ايام ثم عرضهم وعرّف عليهم العرفا وفي القوم ثياذوس
وسرجيس والكمي الذي وصفناه وسار بهم حتى نزل صحرا اذربيجان
في صحرا تدعى الدنق فوافاه هناك بندويه ورجل من اصبهبذي الناحية
يقال له موشيل في اربعين الف مقاتل وانقض اليه الناس من خيل من
اصبهان وخراسان وفارس وانتهى الى شوبين مكانه فشخص نحوه
من المداين فجرت بينهما حروب شديدة قيل فيها الكمي الرومي بضربة
ضربه بها بعض الفرس على راسه فقد راسه ويده وعاد فرسه بنصف
بدنه الباقي الى معركة ابرويز ومعسكره فاستضحك ابرويز وعظم
ذلك على الروم وكثر الكلام فيه وعوتب وقيل هلا جراونا مثل هذا يقتل
كمينا وواحد عصره فيما عندك وبين يديك فتضحك فاعتذر بان قال
اني والله ما ضحكت لما تكرهون ولقد شق علي ان فقدت مثله اكثر
مما شق عليكم ولكني رايتكم تستصغرون شان بهرام شوبين وتنكرون
هربي منه فذكرت ذلك من قولكم الان وعلمت انكم ترونكم هذه
الضربة واثرها على هذا الكمي تعذروني وتعلمون يقينا ان هربي
انما كان من امثال هولا القوم الذين هذا مبلغ نكايتهم في الابطال ويقال
ان ابرويز بارز بهرام شوبين منفردا من العسكر باربعة عشر رجلا منهم
كردي اخو بهرام وبندويه وبسطام حربا شديدة ووصل فيها بعضهم
الى بعض والمجوس تحكي حكايات عظيمة لا فايدة في حكاياتها وجملتها
ان ابرويز استظهر استظهارا ليس معه بهرام شوبين وعلم انه لا حيلة
له فيه فانحاز عنه نحو خراسان ثم صار الى الترك وصار ابرويز الى

المداين

179b

179

الملك فابيه فلم يحر جوابا فانصرف بندويه وبسطام وطايفة معهما الى
هرمز في المطبق فخنقاه ثم رجعوا الى ابرويز وقالوا اسر على خير
طاير فحثوا دوابهم وصاروا الى الفرات فقطعوه واخذوا طريق
المفازة بدلالة رجل يقال له خرشيذان وصاروا الى بعض الديارات
التي في اطراف العمارة فلما اوطنوا الراحة لحقتهم خيل بهرام فلما نذروا
بهم انتبه بندويه ابرويز من نومه وقال له احتل لنفسك فان
القوم قد اظلوك فقال كسرى ابرويز ما عندي حيلة فقال بندويه
فاني ساحتال لك بان ابذل نفسي دونك قال وكيف ذلك قال تدفع
الي بزتك وزينتك لاعلو الدير وتنجو انت ومن معك من وراء الدير
فان القوم اذا وصلوا الي وراوا هيئتك علي اشتغلوا عن غيري
وطاولتهم حتى تفوتهم ففعلوا ذلك وبادروا حتى تواروا بالجبل
ثم وافاهم خيل بهرام وعليهم قايد يقال له بهرام بن سياوش فاطلع
عليه بندويه من فوق الدير وعليه بزة ابرويز فاوهمه انه هو
وساله ان ينظره الى غد ليصير اليه سلما ويصير الى بهرام
فامسك عنه وحفظ الدير بالحرس ليلته فلما اصبح اطلع عليه في
بزته وحليته وقال ان علي وعلى اصحابي بقية شغل من استعداد
لصلوات وعبادات فامهلنا ولم يزل يدافع حتى مضى عامة النهار
وامعن ابرويز وعلم انه قد فاتهم ففتح الباب حينيذ واعلم بهرام بامره
فانصرف به الى شوبين فحبسه في يد بهرام بن سياوش واما
بهرام شوبين فانه دخل المداين وجلس على سرير الملك وجمع
العظما فخطبهم وذم ابرويز ودار بينهم كلام فكان كلهم منصرفا عنه
الا انه تتوج وانقاد له الناس خوفا ثم ان بهرام بن سياوش
واطا بندويه على الفتك بشوبين فظهر شوبين على ذلك فقتله وافلت
بندويه ولحق باذربيجان وسار ابرويز حتى اتى انطاكية وكاتب ملك
الروم منها وارسل جماعة ممن كان معه وساله نصرته فاجابه

179a

شروان

كسرى أبرويز الملقب بالملك العزيز بن هرمز بن كسرى أنو
كان قد خرج خوفا من أبيه هرمز إلى أذربيجان واجتمعوا عليه كما تقدم فلما
بلغه خلع أبيه وسمل عينيه بادر إلى المدائن وتتوج وجمع إليه الوجوه
والأشراف وجلس لهم على سريره ومنّاهم ووعدهم وقال إن أبانا هرمز
كان لكم قاضيا عادلا ومن نيتنا لكم البر والإحسان فعليكم بالسمع والطاعة
فاستبشر به الناس ودعوا له فلما كان اليوم الثاني أتى أباه فسجد له وقال
له عمرك الله أيها الملك إنك تعلم أني بريء مما أتاه إليك المنافقون وإنما هربت
خوفا منك فصدقه هرمز وقال له يا بني لي إليك حاجتان فأسعفني بها إحداهما
أن تنتقم لي ممن عاون على خلعي والسمل لعيني ولا تأخذك بهم رأفة والأخرى
أن تؤنسني كل يوم بثلاثة نفر لهم أصالة رأي وتأذن لهم في الدخول علي
فتواضع له أبرويز وقال عمرك الله أيها الملك إن المارق بهرام قد أظلنا
ومعه الشجاعة والنجدة ولسنا نقدر أن نمد يدا إلى من أتى عليك ما أتى
فإنهم وجوه أصحابك ولكن إن أدالني الله تعالى من المنافق فأنا خليفتك
وطوع أمرك ثم إن أبرويز خرج إلى النهروان لما وردها بهرام شوبين
ووافقه وجعل النهر بينه وبينه ودار بينهما كلام كثير كان كله يدور على
استصلاح بهرام فلا يزيد عليه بهرام إلا يبسوه حتى يئس منه وأجمع على
حربه ولها أخبار كثيرة وأحاديث طويلة آخرها أن أبرويز ضعف عنه
بعد أن قتل بهرام ثلاثة نفر من الأتراك كانوا ضمنوا لبهرام قتل أبرويز
ووعدهم بمال عظيم وكان هؤلاء الثلاثة من أشد الأتراك وأعظمهم أجساما
وشجاعة فلما رأى أبرويز من أصحابه فتورا وحرض أصحابه فتبين منهم
فشلا فصار إلى أبيه وشاوره فرأى له المصير إلى ملك الروم فأحرز
نساءه وشخص في عدة يسيرة فيهم بندويه وبسطام وكردي أخو
بهرام شوبين فإنه كان شديد الطاعة لأبرويز فلما خرجوا من
المدائن خافوا القوم أن بهرام وأشفقوا أن يرد هرمز إلى الملك ويكاتب
ملك الروم عن هرمز في ردهم فيتلفوا فأعلموا ذلك أبرويز واستأذنوه

الاوف

178

ور

داره يلحقوهم قال ان يلحقوهم عرفوا جميعهم فجعلت في نفسي اني اذا جا
سلطانا هو اقوى مني واما عمل مجوا النسا في جهة الشمال فانا قصدنا به
ان الشمال ارق هوا واقل وخامة والنسا ايه زهر البيوت فعمل لهن ذلك واما
الغيرة فان الرجال لا يخلون بالنسا وكل من يدخل هذه الدار انما هو مملوك
وعبيد مقيم واما انت فما اخرج هذا منك الا بغض فيا تخبرنا سببه فقال
الرجل لي قرية ملك كنت انفق حاصلها على عيالي فغلبني فلان المرزبان
واخذها مني فقصدت اتظلم منذ سنين فلم اصل اليك فقصدت وزيرك
وتظلمت اليه فلم ينصفني وانا اودي خراج القرية حتى لا يزول اسمي عنها و ١١٥
غاية الظلم ان يكون غيري ياخذ دخلها وانا اودي خراجها فسال هرمز
وزيره فصدقه وقال خفت ان اعلمك فتود بي المرزبان فامر هرمز ان يحمل
من المرزبان ضعف ما اخذ وان يستخدمه صاحب الضيعة في اي شغل
شا سنتين وعزل وزيره وقال في نفسه اذا كان الوزير يراعي
الظالم فبالحري ان غيره يراعيه فامر باتخاذ صندوق وكان يقفله
ويختمه بخاتمه ويتركه على باب داره وفيه خرق فيلقى فيه رقاع
المظلومين وكان يفتحه كل اسبوع ويكشف المظالم ثم افكر وقال ان
اعرف ظلم الرعية ساعة بساعة فاتخذ سلسلة طرفها في مجلسه في
السقف والطرف الاخر خارج الدار في روزنة وفيها جرس فكان
المتظلم يحرك السلسلة فيتحرك الجرس فيحضره ويكشف ظلامته

178a

ابيه هرمز وكتبت اليه اخت له بجسنس وكانت تربته تخبره
بضعف ابيه هرمز واعلمته ان العظما والوجوه قد اجمعوا
على خلعه واعلمته ان جوبين ان سبقه الى المداين احتوى على
الملك ولم يلبث العظما بعد ذلك ان وثبوا على هرمز وفيهم بندويه
وبسطام خالا ابرويز فخلعوه وسملوا عينيه وتركوه محجوبا
من قبله فلما بلغ ذلك ابرويز بادر بمن معه وسبق بهرام الى
المداين وتتوج فكانت مدة هرمز احدى عشره سنه وسبعه
اشهر وعشره ايام وكان شعاره احمر موشى وسراويله على لون
السما موشى وتاجه اخضر ويعتمد اذا جلس على سريره بيسراه
على سيفه ويمناه جرز ولم يُشتمل من ملوك قبله ولا بعده غيره
ومن محاسن سيره انه لما فرغ من بنا داره الى بشرق دجلة
مقابل المداين عمل وليمة عظيمة واحضر الناس من الاطراف فاكلوا ثم قال
هل رايتم في هذه الدار عيبا فكلهم قال لا عيب فيها فقام رجل وقال فيها
ثلاثة عيوب فاحشة احدها ان الناس يجعلون دورهم في الدنيا
وانت جعلت الدنيا في دارك فقد افرطت في توسيع صحونها وبيوتها
فيتمكن الشمس منها في الصيف والسموم فيوذي ذلك اهلها ويكثر فيها
في الشتا البرد والثاني ان الملوك ينزلون في البنا على الانهار لتزول
همومهم وافكارهم بالنظر الى المياه ويترطب الهوا وتصح ابصارهم
وانت تركت دجلة وبنيتها في القفر والثالث انك جعلت حجرة
النسا اماما في الشمال من مساكن الرجال وهوا دوم هبوبا فلا يزال
الهوا يجي باصوات النسا وريح طيبهن وهذا مما تمنعه الغيرة والحمية
فقال هرمز اما سعة الصحون والمجالس فخير المساكن ما سافر فيه
البصر وشدة الحر والبرد يدفعان بالخيش والملابس والنيران واما
مجاورة الما فكنت عنراى وهو يشرف على دجلة فغرقت سفينة تحته
فاستغاث من فيها اليه واكثر تاسفه عليهم وصيح بالسفن الى تحت

٥١٢

177b

177

الشباب وكانت عدة من يشتمل عليها الديوان سبعين الف مقاتل فمضى بهرام
بجد واعداد حتى جاز هراة وباد غيس ولم يشعر شابه ببهرام حتى
نزل بالقرب منه معسكرا فجرت بينهما رسايل وحروب قتل فيها بهرام
شابه برمية رماه واستباح عسكره واقام موضعه فوافاه
برموده بن شابه وكان يعدل اباه فحاربه فهزمه وحصره في بعض
الحصون حتى استسلم له فوجهه اسيرا الى هرمز وغنم كنوزا
عظيمة فيقال انه حمل الى هرمز من الاموال والجواهر والانية
والامتعة مما غنمه وقر مايتي الف وخمسين الف بعير في مدة تلك
الايام فشكر هرمز على ذلك الا انه اراد منه ان يتقدم لمن بعد بيلا
بلاد الترك فكاتبه في ذلك فلم ير بهرام ذلك صوابا ثم خاف بهرام
سطوة هرمز وحكي له ان الملك يستقل ما حمله اليه من الغنايم في
جنب ما وصل اليه وانه يقول في مجالسه بهرام قد ترفه وا
الدعة وبلغ ذلك الجند فخافوا مثل خوفه فيقال ان بهرام جمع وجوه
عسكره فاجلسهم على مراتبهم ثم خرج عليهم في زي النسا وبيده
مغزل وقطن ثم جلس في موضعه وحمل لكل واحد من اوليك
مغزل وقطن موضع بين ايديهم فامتعضوا من ذلك وانكروه
فقال بهرام ان كتاب الملك ورد علي بذلك فلا بد من امتثال الامر
ان كنتم طايعين فاظهروا انفة وحمية وخلعوا هرمز واظهروا
ان ابنه ابرويز اصلح للملك منه وساعدهم على ذلك خلق ممن
كان بحضرة هرمز وانفذ هرمز جيشا كثيفا مع
اذين جشنس لمحاربة بهرام واشفق ابرويز من الحدث وخاف
سطوة ابيه فهرب الى اذربيجان فاجتمع اليه هناك عدة
من المرازبة والاصبهبذين فاعطوه بيعتهم ولم يظهر ابرويز
شيا واقام بمكانه الى ان بلغه ان اذين جشنس الموجه لمحاربة
بهرام شوبين قتل وانفض الجمع الذي معه واضطراب امر

177a

هذا الابان فاتاه حافظ ذلك الكرم فلزمه وصرخ فبلغ اشفاق
الرجل من عقوبة هرمز على تناوله من ثمر ذلك الكرم ان دفع الى حافظ
الكرم منطقة محلاة بذهب كانت عليه عوضا له من الحصرم الذي
رزاه من كرمه وافتدى بها نفسه وراى ان قبض الحافظ اياها
منه وتخليته عنه منة من بها عليه فهذه كانت سيرة هرمز في
العدل والضبط والهيبة وكان مظفرا لا يمد يده الى شي الا واتاه
وكان مع ذلك اديبا داهيا الا عرقا قد نزعه اخواله من الترك
وكان لذلك مقصيا للاشراف واهل البيوتات والعلما وقيل انه
قتل ثلثة عشر الف رجل وستماه رجل ولم يكن له راي الا في تالف السفله
واستصلاحهم عليه وحبس خلقا من العظما وحط مراتب خلق
وقصر بالاساوره ففسدت عليه نيات جنده من الكبرا واتصل
ذلك الى ما جناه على بهرام شوبين فكان ذلك سبب هلاكه وذلك
انه خرج على هرمز خوارج منهم شابه ملك الترك الى ان عظم وصار
بباذغيس وذلك بعد احدى عشرة سنة من ملكه وخرج
عليه ملك الروم في ثمانين الف مقاتل قاصدا له وخرج عليه ملك الخزر
حتى صار الى الباب والابواب وخرج عليه من العرب خلق نزلوا شاطي
الفرات وشنوا الغارة على اهل السواد واجترا عليه اعداوه وغزوا
بلاده فاما شابه ملك الترك فانه ارسل الى هرمز والى عظما الفرس
يوذنهم باقباله ويقول رموا قناطر انهاركم واوديه اجتاز عليها الى
بلادكم واعقدوا القناطر على كل نهر لا قنطرة له وافعلوا ذلك
في الانهار والاودية التي عليها مسلكي من بلادكم الى بلاد الروم فاني
مجمع على المسير اليها من بلادكم فاستفظع هرمز ما ورد عليه من ذلك
وشاور فيه فاجمع رايهم على قصد ملك الترك وصرف العناية اليه فوجه
اليه رجلا من اهل الري يقال له بهرام بن بهرام جشنس ويعرف
بشوبين فاختار بهرام من الجند اثنى عشر الف رجل من الكهول دون

الشبان

176

هرمز الملقب ترك زاذ بن كسرى انوشروان بن
قباذ امه ابنة خاقان الاكبر كان كثير الادب حسن النية في
الاحسان الى الضعفاء والمساكين الا انه كان يحمل على الاشراف فعادوه
وابغضوه فعلم بذلك منهم وكان في نفسه منهم مثل ما كان في انفسهم منه
وكان من سيرته المرتضاة انه تحرى الخير والعدل على الرعية وتشدد على
العظماء المستطيلين على الضعفاء وبلغ من عدله انه كان يسير الى الماه
ليصيف هناك فامر فنودي في مسيره ذلك في مواضع الحرث ان
يتحاموا ولا يسير فيها الراكب لئلا يضروا باحد ووكل بتعهد ما يجري في
عسكره ومعاقبة من تعدى امره وتغريمه عوضا لصاحب الحرث
وكان ابنه كسرى ابرويز في عسكره فعار مركب من مراكبه فوقع في محرثة
من المحارث التي كانت في طريقه فرتع فيها وافسد منها فاخذ ذلك المركب
ودفع الى الرجل الذي وكل بمعاقبة من افسد هو او دابته شيئا من المحارث
وتغريمه فلم يقدر الرجل على انفاذ امر هرمز في ابنه ولا احد من حشمه
فرفع ما راى من افساد ذلك المركب الى هرمز فامره ان يجدع اذنيه
ويبتر ذنبه ويغرم ابرويز فخرج الرجل لانفاذ الامر فدس له ابرويز
رهطا من العظماء ليسالوه التغبب في امره فلقوه وكلموه في
ذلك فلم يجب اليه فسالوه ان يؤخر ما امر به هرمز حتى يكلموه فامر
بالكف عنه فلقي اولئك الرهط هرمز واعلموه ان بذلك الدابة الذي
عار زعارة وانه اخذ الوقت وسالوه ان يامر بالكف عن جدع اذنه
وتبتيره لما فيه من سوء الطيرة فلم يجبهم وامر بالمركب فجدع اذناه
وبتر ذنبه وغرم ابرويز ما يغرم غيره في هذا الحد فامضى ما امر به
ثم ارتحل وركب ذات يوم في اوان ايناع الكروم الى ساباط المداين
وكان ممره على بساتين وكروم فاطلع بعض اساورته في كرم
فراى فيها حصرما فاصاب منه عناقيد ودفعها الى غلام معه وقال
اذهب بها الى المنزل واطبخها بلحم واتخذ منها مرقة فانها نافعة في

الخلوة بقوم من الفرس يقرؤون عليه سياسات الملوك ولا سيما ملوك
العجم الفضلاء وسيما انوشروان فانه كان معجبا بها كثير الاقتدا بها
وكان انوشروان يقتدي ما بسيرة اردشير اخذا نفسه بها وبعهده
الذي يتقدم في خبره مطالبا به غيره وكان اردشير متتبعا لبهمن
وكورش مقتديا بهما فعلى جملة الفرس فضلاء وعجم الذين ينبغي ان
يقتدى بافعالهم ويتعلم سياساتهم ويتشبه بهم

175

قهر هذه الاعدا احب الي وخير لكم من قهر اعدائكم من الترك والروم فاما
انا يا ايها الناس فقد طبت نفسا بترك هذه الامور ومحبتها وجمعها
ونفعها عني لا حاجة لي فيها ولا بالذي على منها فطيبوا انفسا بالذي
طبت به نفسا منكم يا ايها الناس فقد احببت ان انفي عنكم عدوكم الباطن
والظاهر فاما الظاهر منها فانا نحمد الله ونعمته قد نفيناه واعانا الله تعالى
عليه وخضدنا شوكته واحسنتم فيه واجملتم واتيتم واجتهدتم
فافعلوا في هذا العدو كما فعلتم في ذلك العدو واعملوا فيه كالذي عملتم في
ذلك واحفظوا على ما اوصيكم به فاني شفيق عليكم ناصح لكم يا ايها
الناس من احيا هذه الامور فينا فقد افسد طاعة عفرنا بقتاله من كان
بعاملنا من اعدائنا فان هذه اكثر مضرة واشد شوكة واعظم بلية واصعب
تبعة واعلموا ان خيرهم من جمع الى رايه السالف عقولنا المعونة لنا على
نفسه في هذا العابر واعلموا ان من غلبه هذا غلب عليه ذلك ومن غلب
هذا فقد قهر ذلك وذلك ان السلامة والمودة والالفة والاجماع
والتناصح منكم يكون العز والقدرة ومع التحاسد والبغي والنميمة
والتشتت يكون ذهاب العز وانقطاع القوة وهلاك الدنيا والاخرة
فعليكم على ما امرناكم به واحذروا ما نهيناكم عنه ولا قوة الا بالله عليكم
بمواساة اهل الفاقة وضيافة السابلة واكرموا جوار من جاوركم
واحسنوا صحبة من دخل من الامم فيكم فانهم في ذمتي لا تجبهوهم
ولا تظلموهم ولا تتسلطوا عليهم ولا تحرجوهم فان الاحراج يدعو الى
المعصية ولكن اصبروا الهم على بعض الاذى واحفظوا امانكم وعهودكم
واحفظوا ما عهدت اليكم من هذه الاخلاق فانا لم نر سلطانا قط ولا
امة هلكوا الا بترك هذه الاخلاق ولا صلحوا الا معها وبالله ثقتنا
في الامور كلها وكان شعاره ابيض ووشيه الوان مختلفة وسراويله
على لون السما وكان يعتمد على سيفه وكانت مدة ملكه الى ان هلك سبعا
واربعين سنة وسبعة اشهر وكان عمر بن الخطاب رضي الله عنه يكتب

الله تعالى ذكره وتم هذا العز والنصر وهذا الشرف والتمكين وهذه الثروة
والمنزلة يا ايها الناس اني فكرت بعد فراغي من كتابي هذا وما صنعت
من نعم الله تعالى علينا في الامر الذي لما غلب دارا الملوك والامم وقهرها
واستولى على بلادها ثم لما لم يحكم امر هذا العدو وهلاك وهلكت جنوده
بعد السلامة والظفر والنصر والغلبة وذلك انه لم يرض بالامر الذي تم
له به الملك واشتد به له السلطان وقوي به على الاعداء وتمت عليه به
النعمة وفاضت عليه من وجوه الدنيا كلها الكرامة حتى احتيل له
بوجوه النميمة البغي فدعا البغي الحسد فتقوى به وتمكن ودعا
الحسد بعض اهل الفقر لاهل الغنى واهل الخمول لاهل الشرف فتم اتاهم
الاسكندر على ذلك من تفرق الاهواء واختلاف الامور وظهور البغضاء
وقوة العداوة فيما بينهم والفساد منهم ثم ارتفع ذلك الى ان قتله حاجب
حرسه وابنه على دمه للذي شمل قلوب العامة من الشر والضغينة
وثبت فيها من العداوة والفرقة فكفى الاسكندر مؤونته بنفسه وقد
انقطعت بذلك اليوم وذكرته يا ايها الناس فلا اسمعن في هذه النعمة
تفرقا ولا بغيا ولا حسدا ظاهرا ولا سعاية ولا وشاية فان الله تعالى
قد طهر من ذلك اخلاقنا وملكنا واكرم عنه ولا بيننا وما نلت ما نلته
بنعمة ربنا وحمده بشيء من هذه الامور الخبيثة التي نفتها العلماء وعافتها
الحكماء ولكني نلت هذه الرتبة بالصحة والسلامة والحب للرعية والوفاء
والعدل والاستقامة والتودة وانما تركنا ان نأخذ عن هذه الامم
التي سميناها غير الترك والبربر والزنج واهل الجبال وغيرهم مثل ما
اخذنا عن الهند والروم لظهور هذه الاخلاق فيهم وغلبتها عليهم ولم تصلح
امة قط ولا تملكها التي ظهور هذه الاخلاق فيها واذا ولا انا في
وتاري من هذه الامور هذه الاخلاق فانك في اعدا عدائكم يا ايها الناس ان
في ما بسط الله تعالى علينا من السلامة والعافية والاستصلاح غنى لنا عما
نطلب بهذه الاخلاق الردية المشومة كالعفو في ذلك انفسكم فان

فقد

174b

174

فقد تم لكم الظفر والنصر وتمت فيكم القوة وتم بكم العز وتمت عليكم النعمة
وتم لكم الفضل وتم لكم الاجتماع والالفة والنصيحة والسلامة وان
انتم قصرتم ووهنتم وظفر هذا العدو بكم فان الظفر الذي كان منكم
على عدوكم بالمغرب والمشرق وفي الجنوب والشمال لم يكن ظفرا منكم
فاطلبوا ان تعملوا في هذا العدو الباقي مثل الذي فعلتم في ذلك العدو
الماضي وليكن جدكم في هذا واجتهادكم واحتشادكم اكبر واطول
واحزم واعزم واصح واسد فان احق الاعدا بالاستعداد له اعظمهم
مكيدة واشدهم شوكة وليس الذي كنتم تخافون من عدوكم الذي قاتلتم
بقريب من شوكة الذين امركم بقتالهم الان فاطلبوه وصلوا ظفرا بظفر
ونصرا بنصر وقوة بقوة وتاييدا بتاييد وحزما وعزما بعزم وحزم وجهدا
بجهد فان بذلك اجتماع صلاحكم وتمام النعمة عليكم والزيادة في الكرامة
من الله تعالى لكم والفوز برضوانه في الاخرة ثم اعلموا ان عدوكم من الترك
والروم والهند وساير الامم لم يكونوا ليبلغوا منكم ان ظهروا عليكم
وغلبوكم مثل الذي يبلغ هذا العدو منكم ان غلبكم فان باس هذا
العدو اشد وكيده اكبر وامره اخوف من ذلك العدو ايها الناس اني
قد نصبت لكم كاراتكم ولقيت ما قد علمتم بالسيف والرمح والمفاوز
والبحار والسهولة والجبال اقارع عدوا عدوا واكابد جندا جندا واكابر
ملكا ملكا لم اتضرع اليكم هذا التضرع في قتال اوليك الجنود والملوك
ولم اسالكم هذه المسالة في طلب الجد منكم والاجتهاد والاحتفال
والاحتشاد وانما فعلت هذا اليوم لعظم خطره وشدة شوكته
ومخافة صولته بكم واني انا ايها الناس لم اغلب هذا العدو وانفيه عنكم
فقد ابقيت فيكم اكبر الاعداء ونفيت عنكم اضعفها فاعينوني على
نفي هذا العدو المخوف عليكم القريب الدار منكم فانشدكم الله ايها الناس
لما اعنتموني عليه حتى انفيه عنكم واخرجه من بين اظهركم فيتم بلائي
عندكم ويتم الله تعالى فيكم عنايته وتتم النعمة بها وعليكم والكرامة من

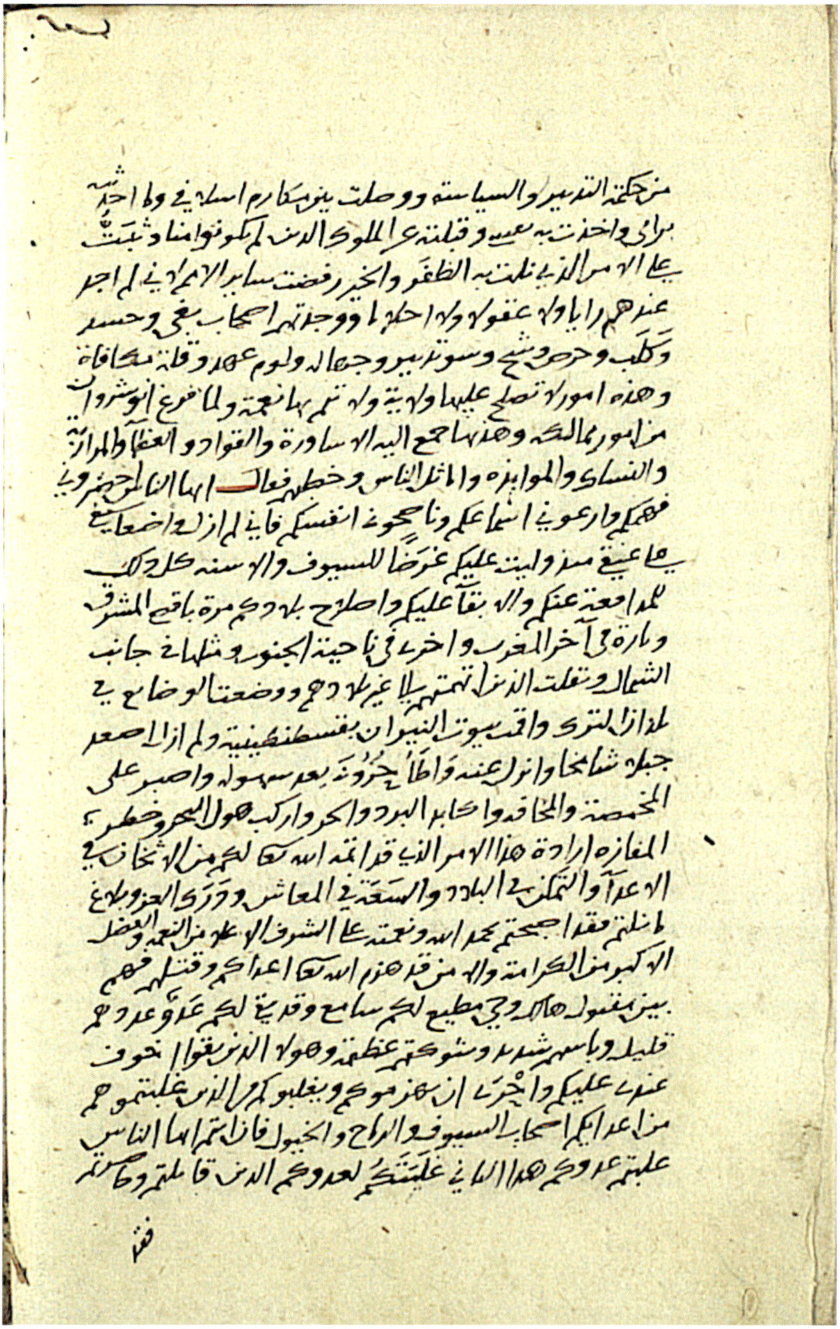

من حكمة التدبير والسياسة ووصلت بين مكارم اسلافي وما احدثته
برأيي واخذت به نفسي وقبلته عن الملوك الذين لم يكونوا امثالنا وثبتُّ
على الامر الذي نلت به الظفر والخير رفضت سائر الامم الذين لم اجد
عندهم رأيا ولا عقولا ولا احلاما ووجدتهم اصحاب بغي وحسد
وكذب وحرص وشح وسوء تدبير وجهالة ولؤم عهد وقلة مكافاة
وهذه امور لا تصلح عليها ولاية ولا تتم بها نعمة ولما فرغ انوشروان
من امور مملكته وهذبها جمع اليه الاساورة والقواد والعظماء والمرازبة
والنساك والموابذة واماثل الناس وخطبهم فقال ايها الناس احضروا لي
فهمكم وارعوني اسماعكم وناصحوني انفسكم فاني لم ازل اضع سيفي
فيما ... منذ وليت عليكم عرضا للسيوف والاسنة كل ذلك
للمدافعة عنكم والابقاء عليكم واصلاح بلادكم مرة باقصى المشرق
وتارة في آخر المغرب واخرى في ناحية الجنوب ومثلها في جانب
الشمال ونقلت الذين اتهمتهم الى غير بلادهم ووضعت الوضائع في
بلاد الترك واقمت بيوت النيران بقسطنطينية ولم ازل اصعد
جبلا شامخا وانزل عنه واطأ حزونة بعد سهولة واصبر على
المخمصة والمخافة واكابد البرد والحر واركب هول البحر وخطر
المفازة ارادة هذا الامر الذي قد اتمه الله تعالى لكم من الاثخان في
الاعداء والتمكن في البلاد والسعة في المعاش ودرك العز وبلوغ
ما نلتم فقد اصبحتم بحمد الله ونعمته على الشرف الاعلى من النعمة والفضل
الاكبر من الكرامة والامن قد هزم الله تعالى اعداءكم وقتلهم فهم
بين مقتول هالك وحي مطيع لكم سامع وقد بقي لكم عدو وعددهم
قليل وباسهم شديد وشوكتهم عظيمة وهؤلاء الذين تخوفوا اخوف
عندي عليكم واجدر ان يهزموكم ويغلبوكم من الذين غلبتموهم
من اعدائكم اصحاب السيوف والرماح والخيول فان انتم ايها الناس
غلبتم عدوكم هذا الثاني غلبتكم لعدوكم الذين قاتلتم وحاربتم

فقد

173b

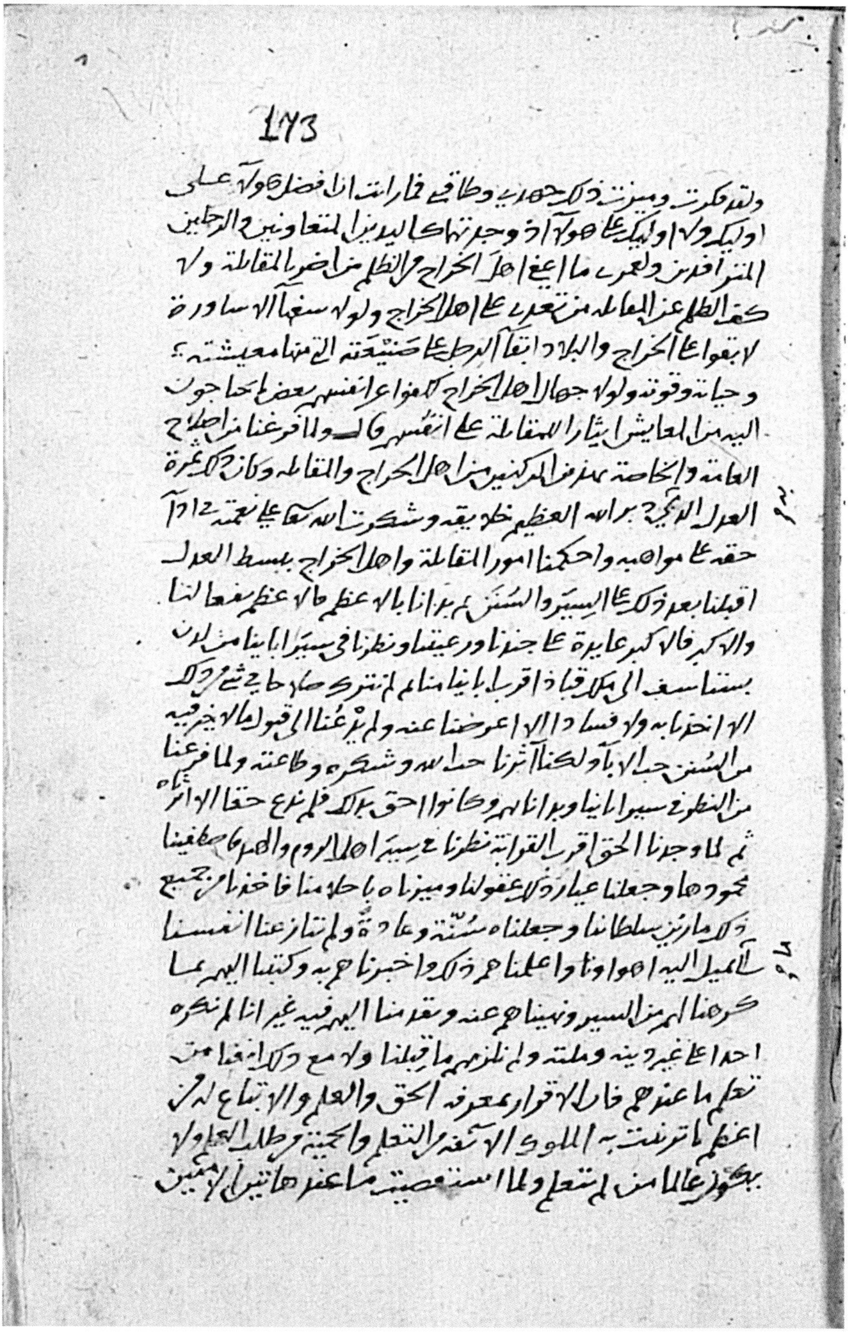

173

ولقد فكرت ومن شان ذلك جهدي وطاقتي فرايت ان افضل الوكلا على
اوليك والا اوليك على الولاة اذ وجدتهما كاليدين المتعاونتين والرجلين
المترافدتين ولعمري ما اغنى اهل الخراج من الظلم من اصناف المقاتلة ولا
كف الظلم عن المقاتلة من تعدي على اهل الخراج ولولا سعي الاساورة
لا بقوا على الخراج والبلاد ابقا الرجل على ضيعته التي منها معيشته
وحياته وقوته ولولا جهال اهل الخراج لا تعوا انفسهم بعض ما يحتاجون
اليه من المعايش ايثارا للمقاتلة على انفسهم [illegible] ولما فرغنا من اصلاح
العامة والخاصة بمن فيه المركتين من اهل الخراج والمقاتلة وكان ذلك ثمرة
العدل الذي جبر الله العظيم خلايقه وشكرت الله تعالى على نعمته الى آخر
حقه على مواهبه واحكمنا امور المقاتلة واهل الخراج ببسط العدل
اقبلنا بعد ذلك على السير والسنن ثم برانا بالاعظم فالاعظم نفعا لنا
والاكبر فالاكبر عايدة على جندنا ورعيتنا ونظرنا في سير ابائنا من لدن
بستاسف الى ملك قباذ اقرب ابائنا منا ثم لم نترك صالحا جايا شيء من ذلك
الا اخذنا به ولا فسادا الا اعرضنا عنه ولم يرغنا الى قبول ما لا خير فيه
من السنن حب الاباء ولكنا آثرنا حب الله وشكره وطاعته ولما فرغنا
من النظر في سير اباينا وبراباتهم وكانوا احق بذلك فلم ندع حقا الا اثرناه
ثم لما وجدنا الحق اقرب القرابة نظرنا في سير اهل الروم والهند فاصطفينا
محمودها وجعلنا عيار ذلك عقولنا وميزناه باحلامنا فاخذنا من جميع
ذلك ما زين سلطاننا وجعلناه سنة وعادة ولم تنازعنا انفسنا
الى الميل الى اهوائنا واعلمناهم ذلك واخبرناهم به وكتبنا اليهم بما
كرهنا لهم من السير ونهيناهم عنه وتقدمنا اليهم فيه غير انا لم نكره
احدا على غير دينه وملته ولم نلزمهم ما قبلنا ولا مع ذلك ابقينا من
تعلم ما عندهم فان الاقرار بمعرفة الحق والعلم والاتباع له من
اعظم ما تزينت به الملوك لان [illegible] التعلم والحمية من طلب العلم ولا
يجوز عالما من لم يتعلم ولما استقصيت ما عندها تبين لي [illegible]

173a

يكونوا على استعداد وحذر ولا يكون من غفلتهم ما كان في المرة الاولى وبا
ئل وكان شكري لله تعالى لما وهبني واعطاني متصلا بنعمه الاول
التي وجهها الي في اول خلقه اياي فايما الشكر والنعم عدلان كعدلي
الميزان لا يمارح بصاحبه احتاج الاخف الى ان يزاد فيه حتى يعادل
صاحبه فاذا كانت النعم كثيرة والشكر قليلا انقطع الحمل وهلك
ظهر الحامل واذا كان ذلك مستويا استمر الحامل فكثير النعم يحتاج
صاحبها الى كثير الشكر وكثير الشكر يجلب كثير النعم ولما وجدت
الشكر بعضه بالقول وبعضه بالعمل نظرت في احب الاعمال الى الله فوجدته
الشيء الذي اقام به السموات والارض واقام به الجبال واجرى به
الانهار وبرأ به البرية وذلك الحق والعدل فلزمته ورايت ثمرة الحق
عمارة البلدان التي بها معاش الناس والدواب والطير وسكان الارض
ولما نظرت في ذلك وجدت المقاتلة اجراء لاهل العمارة ووجدت ايضا
اهل العمارة اجراء للمقاتلة فاما المقاتلة فانهم يطلبون اجورهم من
اهل الخراج وسكان البلدان لمدافعتهم عنهم ومجاهدتهم من ورائهم فحق
على اهل العمارة ان يوفوهم اجورهم فان عمارتهم قيمهم وان ابطئوا
عليهم او حبسوهم فتقوى عدوهم فرايت من الحق على اهل الخراج الا
يكون لهم بعد عمارتهم الا ما اقام معايشهم وعمروا به بلدانهم ورايت
الا اجتاحهم واستفرغ ذات ايديهم للخراج على المقاتلة فاني اذا
فعلت ذلك ظلمت المقاتلة مع ظلم اهل الخراج وذلك انه اذا افسد
المعمور ذاك اهل الارض والارض فانه اذا لم يكن لاهل الخراج
ما يعيشهم ويعمرون به بلادهم هلكت المقاتلة الذين قوتهم بعمارة
الارض واهل العمارة فلا عمارة للارض الا بفضل ما في ايدي اهل الخراج
فمن الاحسان الى المقاتلة والاكرام لهم ان ارفق باهل الخراج
واعمر بلادهم وادع لهم فضلا في معايشهم فاهل الارض ذوو الخراج
ايدي المقاتلة والجند وقوتهم والمقاتلة ايضا ايدي اهل الخراج وقوتهم

ولعل

172b

172

الا قواد في اهل بيوتاتهم على تسع مراتب واثبت عليهم منهم
واقطعتهم وكسوت اصحابهم واجريت عليهم الارزاق وامرت لهم
بالمياه والارضين واسكنت بعضهم مع قايد ابن برجان وبعضهم
باذربيجان وقسمتهم في كل ما احتجنا اليه من الثغور وضممتهم الى
المرزبان لعلم ان الذي من مناصحتهم واجتهادهم فيما توجهوا
له ما يسرني في جميع المداين والثغور وغيرها قال وكتب الى
خاقان الاكبر يعتذر اليّ من بعض غدراته ويسال المراجعة
والتجاوز وذكر في كتابه ورسالته ان الذي حمله على عداوتي
وغدري ان من لم ينظر له وناشدني الله ان اتجاوز عنه وتوقف
سالا على الطمين اليه وذكر ان قيصر ارسل اليه وزعم انه بيننا في
في قبول رسله وانه لا يجاري في قبول رسول احد الا بما امرته لا يجاوز
امري ولا يرغب في الاموال ولا في المودات لاحد الا برضاي وكان
دسيبنبس ياني التركي كاتبني بندم خاقان وندم اصحابه على غدره
وعداوته اياي فاجبته اني لعمري لما ابالي بطبيعة نفسك وغريزتك
غدرت بنا ان اطعت غيرك في غدرك بنا واذنبك في طاعة من
اطعت في ذلك الا كذنبك فيما فعلته براي نفسك وانك قد
استحققت اشد العقوبة وكتبت اني لا اظن شيا مما وجب علي
وبينكم الا وقد صنعته ولا اظن شيا من الوثيقة بيني وبينكم الا وقد
وثقت لنا به قبل اليوم ثم غدرتم فكيف نطمين اليك ونثق بقولك
ولسنا نامنك على مثل ما فعلت من الغدر ونقض العهد والكذب في
اليمين وذكرت ان رسل قيصر عندك ووقفنا على استيذانك ايانا
فيهم ولست انهاك عن مودة احد وكرهت ان تري اني اتخوف
مصادقته واهابه لكم منه فاحببت ان اعلمك اني لا ابالي بشي مما
يجري بينهما ثم سرحت لمرمة المداين والحصون التي بخراسان
وجمع الاطعمة والاعلاف فيها وما يحتاج اليه الجند وامرتهم ان

اصناف من الترك من ناحية الخزر ولكل صنف منهم ملك يذكرون ما
دخل عليهم من الحاجة وما لهم من الحظ في عبوديتنا وسالونا ان
ناذن لهم في القدوم باصحابهم لخدمتنا والعمل بما نامرهم به والاجتماع
عليهم لما سلف منهم قبل تملكنا وان ننزلهم منزلة ساير عبيدنا فانا
سنفوض في كل ما نامرهم به من قتال وغيره كافضل ما نرى من اهل
نصيحتنا فرايت في قبولي اياهم عدة منافع منها جلدهم وباسهم
ومنها ان نخوف ان تحملهم الحاجة على اتيان قيصر او بعض الملوك
فيتقووا بهم علينا وقد كان فيما سلف يستاجر قيصر منهم لقتال
ملوكنا خيلنا ما علا الاجرة فكان لهم في ذلك الغنا لبعض الشوكة
بسبب اوليك الاتراك لان الترك ليس عندهم لذة الحياة فهو في
بحريهم مع شقا معيشتهم على الموت فكتبت اليهم انا نقبل من دخل في
طاعتنا ولا نبخل على احد بما عندنا وكتبت الى مرزبان الباب امره ان
يرخلهم اولا فاولا فكتب لي انه قد اتاه منهم خمسون الفا بنسايهم
واولادهم وعيالاتهم واتاه من رؤسايهم ثلاثة الاف واهل بيتهم ونسايهم
واولادهم وعيالاتهم ولما بلغني ذلك احببت ان اقربهم الي ليعرفوا
احساني اليهم فيما اكرمهم به واعطيهم وليطمينوا الى قوادنا حتى
اذا اردنا تسريحهم مع بعض قوادنا كان كل واحد بصاحبه
واثقا فشخصت الى اذربيجان فلما نزلت اذربيجان اذنت لهم في القدوم
وانا في عند ذلك طرايف من هدايا قيصر واتاني رسول خاقان الاكبر
ورسول خوارزم ورسول ملك الهند والاداور وكابلشاه وصاحب
سرنديب وصاحب كله وكثير من الرسل وتسعة وعشرون ملكا
في يوم واحد وانتهت الي اوليك الاتراك الثلاثة والخمسين الالف
فامرت ان يحتفلوا هناك وركبت لذلك فكان يوما من احسن ايامي
ومن قدم علي ومن دخل في طاعتي وعبوديتي من لم يبتغهم مرح كان
طوله نحو عشرة فراسخ فحمدت الله تعالى كثيرا وامرت بجمع اوليك

الاتراك

171b

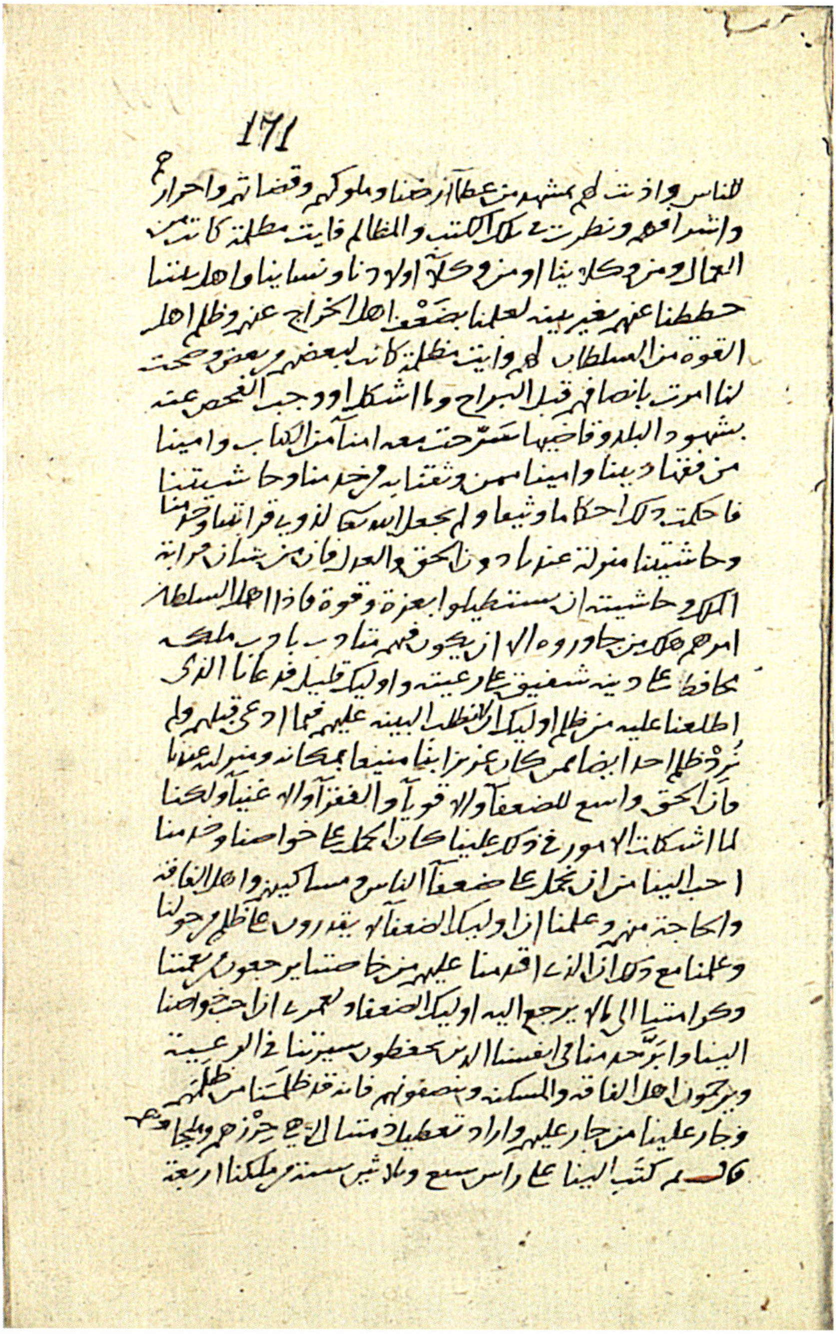

171

للناس واذنت لهم بشهود من عطا ارضنا وملوكهم وقضاتهم واحرارهم
واشرافهم ونظرت في تلك الكتب والمظالم فرايت مظلمة كانت من
العمال ومن كان قبلنا او من كان اولادنا ونسايبنا واهل بيتنا
حططنا عنهم بغير بينه لعلمنا بضعف اهل الخراج عنهم وظلم اهل
القوة من السلطان لهم ورايت مظلمة كانت لبعضهم من بعض وصحت
لنا امرت بانصافهم قبل البراح وما اشكل او وجب الفحص عنه
بشهود البلد وقاضيها فسرحت معه امينا من الكتاب وامينا
من فقها دينا وامينا ممن نثق به من خدمنا وحاشيتنا
فاحكمت ذلك احكاما وثيقا ولم يجعل الله تعالى لذوي قراباتنا وخدمنا
وحاشيتنا منزلة عندنا دون الحق والعدل فان من شان جرأة
الملك وحاشيته ان يستطيلوا بعزة وقوة فاذا اهمل السلطان
امرهم هلك من جاوروه الا ان يكون فيهم متادب بادب ملكه
يحافظ على دينه شفيق على رعيته واوليك قليل فمن علمنا الذي
اطلعنا عليه من ظلم اوليك الا نطلب البينه عليهم فيما ادعى قبلهم ولم
نر ظلم احد ابنا ممن كان عندنا منيعا بمكانه ومنزلته عندنا
فان الحق واسع للضعفا والاقويا والفقرا والاغنيا ولكنا
لما اشكلت الامور في ذلك علينا كان ان نحمل على خواصنا وخدمنا
احب الينا من ان نحمل على ضعفا الناس ومساكينهم واهل الفاقة
والحاجة منهم وعلمنا ان اوليك الضعفا لا يقدرون على ظلم من حولنا
وعلمنا مع ذلك ان الذي اقدمنا عليهم من خاصتنا يرجعون بحمتنا
وكرامتنا الى مال يرجع اليه اوليك الضعفا فيعمرون ان اجحفوا
الينا واثر احد منا الى انفسنا الذين يحفظون سيرتنا في الرعية
ويرحمون اهل الفاقة والمسكنة وينصفونهم فانه قد ظلمنا من ظلمهم
وجار علينا من جار عليهم واراد تعطيل ما منا الى جيع حزهم والجاهم
قال ثم كتب الينا على راس سبع وثلاثين سنة من ملكنا اربعة

171a

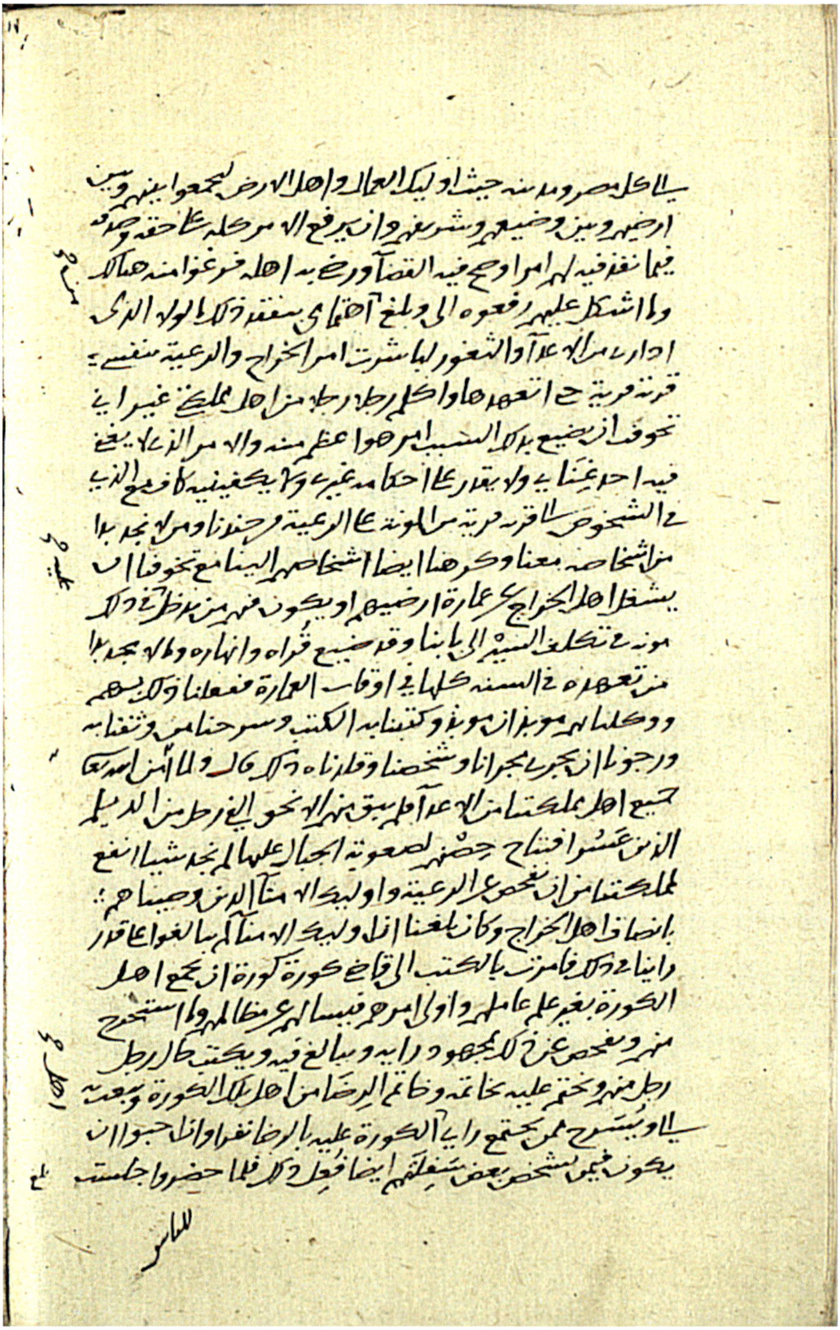
في كل مصر ومدينة حيث اولئك العمال واهل الارض ليجمعوا بينهم وبين
ارضيهم وبين ضيعهم وشربهم وان يرفع الامر كله على حقه وصدقه
فيما نعرفه لهم امرا وصح فيه القضاء ورضى به اهله فرغوا منه هنالك
وما اشكل عليهم رفعوه الي وبلغ اهتمامي بتفقد ذلك الحد الذي
ادار الامر الى عدا والثغور لباشرت امر الخراج والرعية بنفسي في
قرية قرية حتى اتعهدها واكلم رجلا رجلا من اهل مملكتي غير اني
تخوفت ان يضيع بذلك السبب امر هو اعظم منه والامر الذي لا ينبغي
فيه احد غنائي ولا يقدر على احكامه غيري ولا يكفينيه كاف في الذي
في الشخوص الى قرية قرية من المؤنة على الرعية وجنودا ومن لا نجد بدا
من اشخاصه معنا وكرهنا ايضا اشخاصهم الينا مع تخوفنا ان
يشغل اهل الخراج عن عمارة ارضيهم او يكون منهم من يلحقه في ذلك
مؤنة في تكلف المسير الى بابنا وقد ضيع قراه وانهاره ولا بد
من تعهده في السنة كلها في اوقات العمارة ففعلنا ذلك بسعيهم
وكلما هم موسرون وكتبنا به الكتب وسرحنا وثقاته
ورجونا ان يجري مجرانا وشخصنا وطلبناه في ذلك قال والاكثر اشد ما
جميع اهل مملكتنا من الاعداء لم يبق منهم الا نحو الفرط من الديلم
الذين عسر افتتاح حصونهم لصعوبة الجبال عليها لم نجد شيئا انفع
لمملكتنا من ان نحض على الرعية واولياء الله منا الدين وصباهم
بانصاف اهل الخراج وكان بلغنا انا ولينا اليه منا امر بالغوا على قدر
وانباء في ذلك فامرت بالكتب الى قاضي كورة كورة ان يجمع اهل
الكورة بغير علم عاملهم ووالي امرهم فيسالهم عن مظالمهم وما استحق
منهم ويفحص عن ذلك بمجهود رايه ويبالغ فيه ويكتب كل رجل
رجل منهم ويختم عليه بخاتمه وخاتم الرضا من اهل تلك الكورة ويبعثه
الي ويسرح ممن يجتمع راي الكورة عليه بالرضا نفرا وانا احب ان
يكون فيمن يشخص بعض شغلهم ايضا فعل ذلك فلما حضروا جلست
للناس

170b

170

هم احتاجوا اليه واحببنا مسيرنا ان نجري لهم على ايدينا الجوائز والحملان
والقرب من المجلس واللطف في الكلام ولنزيدهم بذلك مودة لنا ورغبة
فينا وحرصا على قتال اعدائنا واحببنا ايضا التعهد لحصونهم وان
نسال اهل الخراج عن امورهم في مسيرنا فسرت في طريق جرجان
واذربيجان فلما بلغنا باب الصول ومدينة فيروز خسرو رممت
تلك المداين العتيقة والحدود وامرت ببناء حصون من حجارة على خاقان
الخزر من ولنا هناك تخوفا ان نغزوه فكتب انه لم يزل منذ ملكت
تحت مواد عتي وانه يرى الدخول في طاعتي سعادة وراى بعض
قواده الا شاهد حاله تركه فاتانا في الفين من اصحابه فقبلناه
وانزلناه مع اساورتنا في تلك الناحية واجرينا عليه وعلى اصحابه
الرزق وامرت لهم بحصن كان هناك وامرت بعمارته لهم حتى بنينا
وجعلت فيه مونا وقوتا نسائهم وامرتهم ان يعلموا من دخل في
طاعتنا من الترك ما في طاعة الولاة من المنفعة العاجلة في الدنيا
والثواب الاجل في الاخرة وان يحثوهم على المودة والعدل والنصيحة
ومجاهدة العدو وان يعلموا احداثهم راينا ومذهبنا واحسنت لهم في
تلك التخوم الاسواق واصلحت طرقهم وقومت السكك ونظرنا
فيما اجتمع لنا هناك من الخيل والرجال فاذا هو بحيث لو كان في
وسط فارس لكان مبلغنا بها فاحمد الله ولما اتى لملكنا ثمان
وعشرون سنة جددت النظر في امر المملكة والعدل على الرعية
والنظر في امرهم واحصاء مظالمهم وانصافهم وامرت موبذ كل بلد ومدينة
وثغر وجند ان ينهى ذلك الي وامرت بعرض الجند من كان منهم بالباب
بمشهد مني ومن غاب في الثغور والاطراف بمشهد القايد وباذوسبان
والعامل وامين من قبلنا وامرت بجمع اهل كور الخراج في كل ناحية
من مملكتي الى مصرها مع العامل وقاضي البلد والكاتب والامين ومن حضر
من قبلنا ممن عرف نصيحته وامانته ونسكه وعلمه ومن جربت ذلك منه

170a

وكورة كورة ورستاق رستاق وقرية قرية ورجل رجلا واستعملت
عليهم اهل الثقة والامانة في نفسي وجعلت في كل بلد مع كل عامل
امناء يحفظون عليه ووليت قاضيا في كل كورة النظر في اهل كورته
وامرت اهل الخراج ان يرفعوا ما يحتاجون الى رفعه الينا الى القاضي
الذي وليته امر كورتهم حتى لا يقدر العامل ان يزيد شيا وان يؤدوا
الخراج بمشهد من القاضي وان يعطي به البراة وان يرفع خراج من هلك
منهم ولا يزاد الخراج ممن لم يدرك منا له حراثة وان يرفع القاضي
وكاتب الكورة وامين اهل البلد والعامل بمحاسبتهم الى ديواننا وتوقيع
الكتب بذلك وقال رفع الينا موبذان موبذ ان قوما سماهم من ذوي
الشرف بعضهم بالباب كان شاهدا وبعضهم ببلاد اخرى دينهم يخالف
لما ورثنا عن نبينا وعلمائنا وانهم يتكلمون بينهم سرا ويدعون اليه
الناس وان ذلك مفسدة للملك حيث لا تقوم الرعية على هوى واحد
فيجوزون جميعهم ما يحرم الملك ويستحلون ما يستحل الملك في دينه فان
ذلك اذا اجتمع للملك قوي في جنده لاجل الموافقة بينهم وبين الملك
فاستظهرت على قول الداعي فامرت باحضار اولئك المختلفين في الاهوا
وان يناظروا حتى يقفوا على الحق ويقرروا به وامرت ان ينفوا من
مدينتي وبلادي ومملكتي وتتبع كل من هو على هواهم ففعل ذلك
وقال ان الترك الذين في ناحية الشمال كتبوا الينا ما قد اصابهم من
الحاجة وانهم لا يجدون بدا ان لم نعطهم شيا من ان يغزونا في
وسالونا خصالا احدها ان نجعلهم جندا ونجري عليهم ما يعيشون به
وان نعطيهم من ارض الجبل وبلنجر وتلك الناحية ما يعيشون منه
فرايت ان اسير في ذلك الطريق الى باب صول واحببت ان تعرف الملوك
من قبلنا هناك نشاطنا للاسفار وقوتنا عليها في همتنا وان
يروا ما رأوا من هيبة الملوك وكثرة الجنود وتمام العدة وكمال
السلاح وما يقوون به على اعدائهم ويعرفون به قوة من خلفهم وان

169b

169

يستبين الامر فلم اجبهم الى ذلك ليلتي ثم رد الرسل حين جننا فخرجت لشربي
فلما فرغنا هددت الرازي بقطع اليمين والعقوبات وسالته ان
يصدقني عن الذي حمله على ذلك وانه ان صدقني لم تنله عقوبة بعد ذلك
فذكر ان قوما وضعوا من قبل انفسهم كتابا وكلاما وذكروا انه من
عند الله تعالى اشاروا عليه بذلك واخبروه ان قتله اياي يدخله الجنة
فلما فحصت عن ذلك وجدته حقا فامرت بتخلية الرازي وبرد ما اخذ
منه من المال وتقدمت بضرب اولئك الذين تحلوا الدين واشاروا
به عليه حتى لم ادع منهم احدا وقال انوشروان اني لما حضرت
القوم الذين اختلفوا في الدين وجمعتهم للمناظرة فيما يقولونه بلغ من جراتهم
وخبثهم وقوة شياطينهم ان لم يبالوا بالقتل والموت في اظهار دينهم
الخبيث حتى اني سالت افضلهم رجلا على رؤوس الناس عن استحلاله قتلي
فقال نعم استحل قتلك وقتل من لم يطاوعنا على ديننا فلم امر بقتله حتى
اذا حضر وقت الغدا امرت ان يحتبس للغدا وارسلت اليه بطرف من
الطعام وامرت الرسول ان يبلغه عني ان يتقاضى انفع له مما ذكر فاجاب
رسولي انه كله حق ولكن ساله الملك ان اضاعه ذات نفسي ولا اكتمه
شيئا مما ادين به وانما ادين بما اخذته من موبذي وقال انوشروان
لما غزونا قيصر وغزوته فذل وطلب الصلح وانقاد الى ما لزمه وافرغ الخراج
والفدية بصدقة على مساكين الروم وضعفا من اربعها مما بعث الى
قيصر بعشرة الاف دينار وذلك فيما وطيته من بلاد الروم دون
غيرها قال ولما هممت بتصفح امر الرعية بنفسي ورفع البلايا والظلم
عنهم وما ينوبهم من ثقل الخراج فان فيه مع الاجر تزيين المملكة وغناهم
وقوة الوالي على ما يجب ان يستخرج منهم ان هو احتاج الى ذلك وقد كان
في ابائنا من يرى ان وضع الخراج عنهم السنة والسنتين والتخفيف
احيانا مما يقويهم على عمارة ارضيهم فجمعت العمال ومن يؤدي الخراج
فرايت من تخليطهم ما لم ار له حيلة الا التعديل والمقاطعة على ملاة بلاد

169a

المحبّسين فبلغ عددهم ثمانمائه وتسعة رجال اكثرهم من ولد ساسان
وولد بهمن بن اسفندياذ وولى عليهم وهرز وهو من ولد وهرز
ابن فريد بن ساسان بن بهمن بن اسفندياذ فقال له سيف بن ذي يزن
يا ملك الملوك اين تقع هولاء ممن خلفت ورائي فقال كسرى اخبرك
ان كثير الحطب يكفيه قليل النار فسار وراح بهم في ثماني سفن غرق منها
اثنتان ونجت ست فخرجوا من السفن فامر وهرز اصحابه ان
ياكلوا فاكلوا ثم عمد الى ما في المطعوم فغرقه في البحر فقال اصحابه عمدت
الى زادنا فاطعمته السمك فقال ان عشتم اكلتم السمك وان لم تعيشوا
فلا تاسفوا على عدم الطعام مع تلف الارواح ثم عمد الى السفينة فاحرقها
ثم قال لاصحابه يجب ان تختاروا لانفسكم الفوز لمجاهدة هولاء فان
الهلاك في استعمال التقصير ثم حمل في الستماية الذين نجوا معه من الفرس
على الحبشة وجعل شعاره اسم الله ثم اسم الملك فهزموهم باذن الله
وولج القتل عليهم في خمس ساعات من نهار ذلك اليوم واشتهر هذا الظفر
عند ملوك الامم قال ابن مسكويه ذكر قطعة من سيرة انوشروان
وسياساته كتبتها على ما حكاه انوشروان نفسه في كتاب عمله في
سيرته وسياسته مملكته قال ابن مسكويه وقرات فيما كتبه انو
شروان من سيرة نفسه قال كنت يوما جالسا بالدسكرة وانا
سائر الى همذان لنصيف هناك وقد اعد طعام الرسل الذين بالباب
من قبل خاقان والهياطلة والصين وقيصر وبعبور اذ دخل رجل من
الاساورة مخترطا سيفه حتى وصل الى الستر وقطع الستر في ثلثة
اماكن واراد الدخول حيث نحن والوثوب علينا فاشار علي بعض حاشيتي
ان اخرج اليه بسيفي فعلمت انه لو كان انما هو رجل واحد فسوف يحال بيننا
وبينه وان كانوا جماعة فان سيفي لا يغني شيئا فلم اخف ولم اتحرك عن مكاني
فاخذه بعض الحرس فاذا ارطبراز من حشمنا وخاصتنا فلم يشكوا ان
من هو على رايه كثير فسالوني ان لا اجلس ولا احضر الشرب في جماعة

سنتين

168b

168

والعطا والمقابلة والهرابذة والكتاب ومن كان في خدمة الملك
وصيروها على طبقات اثنا عشر درهما وثمانية وستة واربعة على
قدر اكثار الرجل واقلاله ولم يلزموا الجزية من كان اتا له من السنين
دون العشرين او فوق الخمسين ورفعوا هذه الوضايع الى كسرى
فرضيها وامر بامضائها والاجتبا عليها في ثلثة انجم كل سنة وسماها
ابراسبار وتاويله الامر المتراضى به وهي الوضايع التي اقتدى بها
امير المومنين عمر بن الخطاب رضي الله عنه حين افتتح بلاد الفرس وامر
باجتباء الناس من اهل الذمة عليها الا انه وضع على كل جريب عامر على
قدر احتماله مثل الذي وضع على الارض المزروعة وزاد على جريب
ارض مزارع حنطة او شعير قفيزا من حنطة الى القفيزين ورزق
منه الجند ولم يخالف بالعراق خاصة وضايع كسرى على جربان
الارض وعلى النخل والزيتون والجماجم والغى ما كان كسرى الغاه في
معايش الناس ولم يزل السواد في مملكة النبط والفرس مقاسمة الى
ايام قباذ بن فيروز فانه فرض على كل جريب درهمين والزم الناس
المساحة واطلقوا في املاكهم وكانوا ممنوعين منها الى وقت
القسمة فهلك قباذ قبل اتمام ذلك فلما ملك انوشروان تممه واخذ
الناس به على ما تقدم ذكره فارتفع اول سنة بمائة الف الف وخمسين
الف الف درهم من الدراهم التي وزن الدرهم منها مثقال ومن عجيب صنع
الله تعالى لكسرى ان الحبشة لما اخذت اليمن واخرجت رجالها واستعبدت
النساء قام سيف بن ذي يزن الى كسرى فاقام ببابه سبع سنين
حتى وصل اليه ورفع اليه خبر الحبشة وما ظهر منهم بالحرم وكان كسرى
غيورا فرحمه وقال سانظر في امرك فاكرمه وقال لا يجوز لي في ديني ان
اغرر بجيشي فاحملهم في البحر الى بعوثة من ليس على ديني ولكن في سجوني
من قد استحق القتل والصواب ان ارمي بهم في نحر هذا العدو فان
ظفروا جعلت لهم البلاد طعمة وان هلكوا لم آثم فيهم فامر بجمع

وقاموا بنجامها في السنة في ثلاثة انجم ونجمع في بيوت اموالنا من الاموال
ما لو اتانا عن ثغر من ثغورنا او طرف من اطرافنا فتق او شي نكرهه
واحتجنا الى تداركه او حسمه ببذلنا فيه مالا كانت الاموال عندنا
معدة موجودة ولم نرد استينافا فاجتبايها على تلك الحال فما ترون
فيما رايناه واجمعنا عليه فلم يشر عليه احد منهم بمشورة ولم ينبس
بكلمة فكرر كسرى هذا القول عليهم ثلاث مرات فقام رجل من عرضهم
وقال لكسرى اتضع ايها الملك عمرك الله الخالد من هذا الخراج على
الفاني من كرم يموت وزرع يهيج ونهر يغيض وعين او قناة ينقطع ماوها
فقال له كسرى يا ذا الكلفة المشوم من اي طبقات الناس انت قال
انا رجل من الكتاب فقال كسرى اضربوه بالدوي حتى يموت فضربوه
بها الكتاب خاصة تبريا منهم الى كسرى من رايه وما جا منه حتى قتلوه
وقال الناس نحن راضون ايها الملك بما انت ملزمنا من خراج فاختار
كسرى رجالا من اهل الراي والنصيحة فامرهم بالنظر في اصناف
ما ارتفع اليه من المساحة وعدد النخل والزيتون ورووس الجزية
ووضع الوضايع على ذلك بقدر ما يرون ان فيه صلاح رعيته ورفاهة
عيشهم ورفع ذلك اليه فتكلم كل امري منهم بمبلغ رايه في ذلك وفي
قدر الوضايع وادار والامر بينهم فاجتمعت كلمتهم على وضع الخراج
على ما يعصم الناس والبهايم وهو الحنطة والشعير والارز والكرم
والرطاب والنخل والزيتون وكان الذي وضعوا على جريب ارض
من مزارع الحنطة والشعير درهما وعلى كل جريب كرم ثمانية دراهم
وعلى كل جريب ارض رطاب سبعة دراهم وعلى كل اربع نخلات
فارسية درهما وعلى كل ست نخلات دقل مثل ذلك وعلى كل ستة
اصول زيتون مثل ذلك ولم يضعوا الا على كل نخل في حديقة او مجتمع
غير شاذ وتركوا ما سوى ذلك من الغلات السبع فقوي
الناس في معايشهم والزموا الناس الجزية ما خلا اهل البيوتات

والعظما

167

في اتباع مزدك فجلس انوشروان واذن للناس اذنا عاما فدخل
عليه مزدك ثم دخل عليه المنذر فقال انوشروان اني كنت تمنيت امنيتين
ارجو ان يكون الله عز وجل جمعهما لي فقال مزدك وما هما ايها الملك
قال تمنيت ان املك فاستعمل هذا الرجل الشريف يعني المنذر وان اقتل
هذه الزنادقة فقال له مزدك او تستطيع ان تقتل الناس كلهم فقال
وانك ها هنا يا ابن الزانية والله ما ذهب نتن ريح جوربك من انفي
منذ قبلت رجليك الى يومي هذا وامر به فقتل وصلب وولى المنذر
وطلب الحرث بن عمرو بن حجر وكان بالانبار فخرج هاربا في صحابته
وماله وولده فتبعه المنذر بالخيل من تغلب وبهرا واياد وكان
من احسن ما دبره انوشروان في استغزار الاموال وتثميرها
انه بعد فراغه من الثغور وملوك الاطراف وتوظيفه الوظايف
على اقاصي الملوك من الترك والخزر والهند وغيرهم وسبيه مدن
الشام ومصر والروم على ملك الروم باموال عظيمة والزامه جزية يحملها
في كل سنة على ان لا يغزو بلاده نظر في الخراج وابواب الاموال التي
كان يستاديها الملوك قبله من بلاده فاذا رسوم الناس كانت جارية على
الثلث من الارتفاع خراجا ومن بعض الكور الربع ومن بعضها الخمس
ومن بعضها السدس على حسب شربها وعمارتها ومن جزية الجماجم
شيا معلوما وكان الملك قباذ بن فيروز تقدم في اخر ملكه بمسح الارض
سهلها وجبلها ليصح الخراج عليها فمسحت غير ان قباذ هلك قبل
ان يستحكم له امر تلك المساحة فلما ملك انوشروان امر باستتمامها
واحصا النخل والزيتون والجماجم ثم امر الكتاب فاخرجوا جمل ذلك
غير مفصلة واذن للناس اذنا عاما وامر كاتب خراجه ان يقرا عليهم
الجمل المستخرجة من اصناف الغلات وعدد النخل والزيتون
والجماجم فقرا ذلك عليهم ثم قال لهم كسرى انا قد راينا ان نضع على ما
احصي من جربان هذه المساحة ومن النخل والزيتون والجماجم وضايع

[illegible]

167a

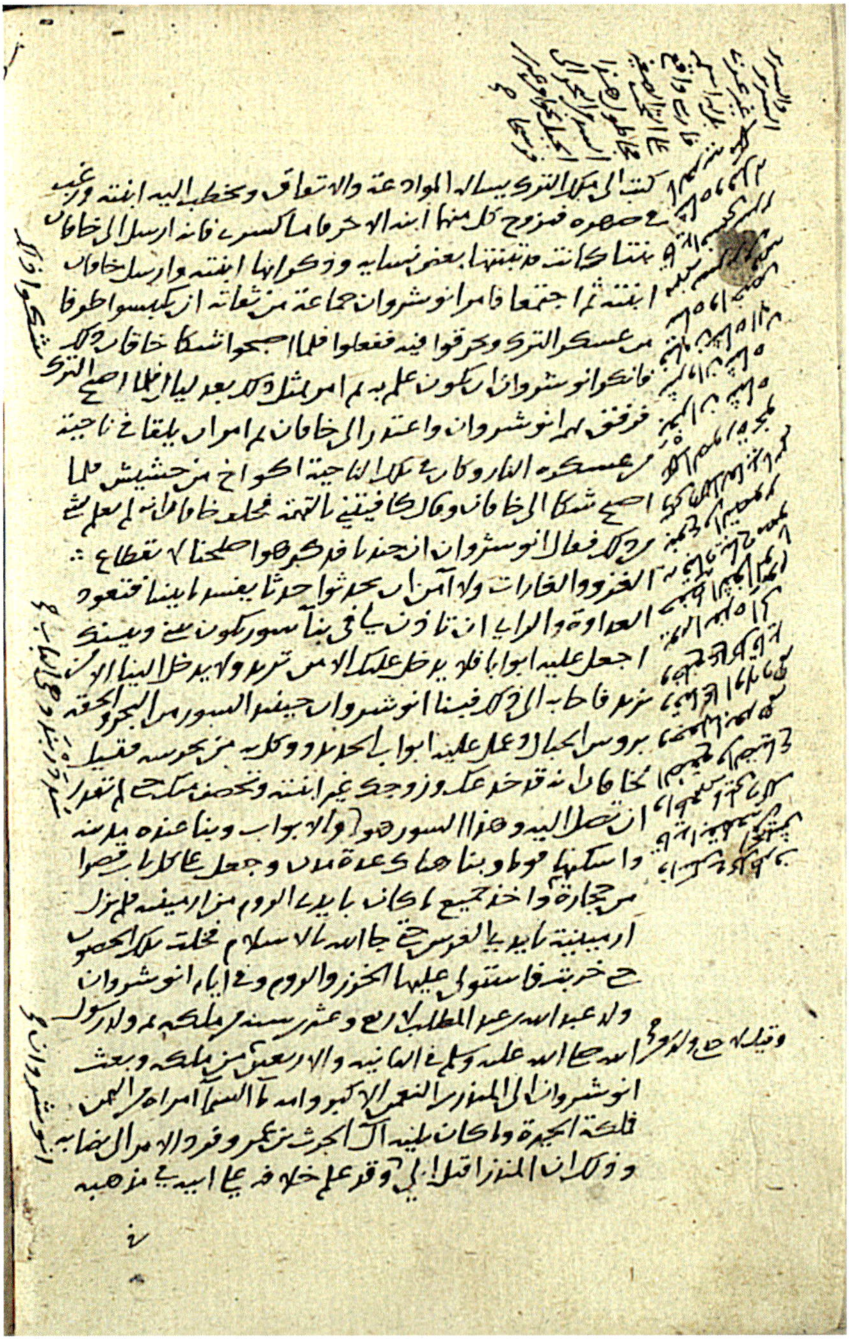
كتب الى ملك الترك يسأله الموادعة والاتفاق ويخطب اليه ابنته ورغب
في صهره فيزوج كل منهما ابنه الآخر فاما كسرى فانه ارسل الى خاقان
بنتا كانت قد تبنتها بعض نسائه وذكر انها ابنته وارسل خاقان
ابنته ثم اجتمعا فامر انوشروان جماعة من ثقاته ان يكبسوا طرفا
من عسكر الترك ويحرقوا فيه ففعلوا فلما اصبحوا شكا خاقان ذلك
فانكر انوشروان ان يكون علم به ثم امر بمثل ذلك بعد ليال فلما اصبح الترك
ضجوا فتبرأ انوشروان واعتذر الى خاقان ثم امر ان يلقى في ناحية
من عسكره النار وكان في تلك الناحية اكواخ من حشيش فلما
اصبح شكا الى خاقان وقال كافيتني بالتهمة فحلف خاقان انه لم يعلم شيء
من ذلك فقال انوشروان ان جندنا قد كرهوا صلحنا لانقطاع
الغزو والغارات ولا آمن ان يحدثوا حدثا يفسد ما بيننا فتعود
العداوة والراي ان تاذن لي في بناء سور يكون بيني وبينك
اجعل عليه ابوابا فلا يدخل عليك الا من تريد ولا يدخل الينا الا من
نريد فاجاب الى ذلك فبنا انوشروان حينئذ السور من البحر والحقه
برؤوس الجبال وعمل عليه ابواب الحديد ووكل به من يحرسه فقيل
لخاقان انه قد خدعك وزوجك غير ابنته وتحصن منك ثم لم تقدر
ان تصل اليه وهذا السور هو باب الابواب وبنا عنده مدينة
واسكنها قوما وبنا هناك عدة مدن وجعل على كل باب قصرا
من حجارة واخذ جميع ما كان بايدي الروم من ارمينية ولم يزل
ارمينية بايدي الفرس حتى جاء الله بالاسلام فخلت تلك الحصون
حتى خربت فاستولى عليها الخزر والروم وفي ايام انوشروان
ولد عبد الله بن عبد المطلب لاربع وعشرين سنة من ملكه ثم ولد رسول
الله صلى الله عليه وسلم في الثانية والاربعين من ملكه وبعث
انوشروان الى المنذر بن النعمان الاكبر وامه ماء السماء امراة من النمر
فملكه الحيرة وما كان يليه آل الحرث بن عمرو ورد الامر الى نصابه
وذلك ان المنذر اقبل الى [illegible] وقد علم خلافه [illegible] ابيه في مذهبه

166b

166

يفعل انتقض الصلح وولى الكتب فلما لم يفعل سار كسرى في بضعة وتسعين
الف او مر على الجزيرة فاخذ مدينة دارا والرها وعبر الى الشام فاخذ
مدينة منبج وحلب وانطاكية وكانت افضل مداين الشام ومدينة
افامية ومدينة حمص ومدنا كثيرة متاخمة لهذه البلاد عنوة واحتوى
على ما فيها من الاموال وغيرها وسبى اهل انطاكية ونقلهم الى ارض السواد
وانزلهم المدينة التي بناها لها على ما تقدم ذكره وتكون هذه المدينة خمسة
طساسيج واجرى على من انزلهم بها الارزاق واقام عليهم رجلا من نصارى
الاهواز ليانسوا به لانهم كانوا نصارى فابتاع منه قيصر مدن الشام
ومصر باموال عظيمة حملها اليه وضمن له مالا يحمله كل سنة على ان لا
يغزو بلاده وصار يحملها كل عام فسار كسرى انوشروان من الروم
واخذ نحو الخزر فقتل منهم وغنم واخذ منهم بثار رعيته ثم عطف نحو اليمن جبا
بلغها فعسكر نحو عدن ناحية من البحرين بين جبلين بالصخور وعمد الحديد
بعد ما قتل وغنم وسار الى الهياطلة مطالبا لهم بدم فيروز جده وذلك بعد
ان صاهره خاقان واستعان به فاتاهم فقتل ملكهم واستاصل
اهل بيته وتجاوز بلخ وما وراها وانزل جنوده فرغانة ثم انصرف الى
المداين وغزا البرجان ثم رجع وبعث قوما الى اليمن لقتل الحبشة الذين
بها في جند من الديلم فقتلوا مسروقا الحبشي باليمن ودانت له بلاد
اليمن ووجه منها الى سرنديب من بلاد الهند قايدا من قواده في جند كثيف
فقاتل ملكها فقتله واستولى عليها وحمل الى كسرى منها اموالا
عظيمة وجواهر كثيرة واقام كسرى انوشروان مظفرا منصورا
تهابه جميع الامم وتحضر بابه وفود الترك والصين والخزر ونظرائهم
وكان مكرما للعلماء وكان لما غزا برجان ثم رجع بنى الباب
والابواب وذلك ان ارمينية واذربيجان كان بعضها للروم
وبعضها للخزر فبناها قباذ بن فيروز وسورا مما يلي بعض الناحية ثم
هلك كسرى انوشروان وقوي امره وغزا فرغانة وبرجان

ووجه الى كور اليمن
واستغلوا لكسرى
في ذكر …
عجيبة فان اصغر
سلاحه رجل …
لا شيء الا …
فقتلوهم كلهم
على … منهم …
… البحر …

وعاد الى المداين … واتسع ملكه … الى … على الجزيرة

166a

اهلها، تخيير المرأة بين الاقامة عنده وبين التزوج بغيره الا ان يكون
لها زوج اول فترد اليه وامر بقتل من كان اضرّ برجل في ماله او
ركب احدا بمظلمة ان يؤخذ منه الحق ثم يعاقب الظالم بعد ذلك بمقدار
جُرْمه وامر بعيالات ذوي الاحساب الذين مات قيّمهم فكتبوا له فانكح
بناتهم الاكفاء وجعل جهازهم من بيت المال وانكح بنيهم من بيوتات
الاشراف واغناهم وامرهم بملازمة بابه ليستعان بهم في اعماله
وخيّر نساء والده ان يقمن مع نسائه فيواسَيْن ويُصيَّرن في
الاجر امثالهن او يبتغي لهن اكفاءهن من البعولة وامر بكري
الانهار وحفر القُنيّ واسلاف العُمّار وتقويتهم وامر باعادة كل
جسر قُطع وكل قنطرة كُسرت وكل قرية خربت وان ترد الى احسن
ما كانت عليه وامر بتسهيل سُبُل الناس وبناء الطرق القصور
والحصون وتخيّر الحكام والعمال وتقدم الى من ولى منهم ابلغ التقدم
وتقدم بكتب سير اردشير ووصاياه فاقتدى بها وحمل الناس عليها
فلما انتظمت له هذه الامور واستوسق ملكه ووثق بجنده وقوته
سار نحو انطاكية فافتتحها وامر ان تصوّر له المدينة على ذرعها وطرقها
وعدة منازلها وان يُبنى على صورتها له مدينة الى جانب المداين
فبنيت المدينة المعروفة بالرومية ثم حمل اهل انطاكية حتى اسكنهم
اياها فلما دخلوا باب المدينة مضى اهل كل بيت منهم الى ما يشبه منازلهم
التي كانوا فيها بانطاكية ثم قصد لمدينة هرقل فافتتحها ثم الاسكندرية
واذعن له قيصر وحمل اليه الفدية وسبب ذلك ان كسرى انو
شروان كان بينه وبين قيصر ملك الروم هدنة فوقع بين الحرث بن ابي
شمر ملك عرب الشام من قبل قيصر وبين المنذر بن النعمان ملك العرب
بالعراق من قبل كسرى فاغار على النعمان وقتل من اصحابه مقتلة عظيمة
وغنم امواله فكتب كسرى الى قيصر يذكر ما بينهما من العهد والصلح
ويعلمه ما لقي المنذر من الحرث ويسأله ان يامر برد ما اخذ المنذر وان
يدفع اليه ديات من قتل من اصحابه وينصف المنذر منه وان لم

يفعل

المنذر بن [illegible]

165b

165

الاطراف التي غلب عليها الامم بعلل واسباب شتى منها السند والرخج
وزابلستان وطخارستان ودردستان وغيرها وقتل امة
يقال لها البارز واستبقى منهم بقية واستعبدهم واستعان
بهم في حروبه واسر امة اخرى يقال لها صول وقدم بهم عليه
فقتلهم واستبقى ثمانين رجلا من كماتهم وعمل اعمالا عظيمة منها
بنيانه الحصون والآطام والمعاقل لاهل بلاده لتكون حرزا لهم
يلجؤن اليها من عدو ان دهمهم فكان من ثمرة هذه الاعمال
ان خاقان واسمه سنجبوا كان في ذلك الوقت امنع الترك
واشجعهم وهو الذي قاتل وزر ملك الهياطلة غير هايب كثرة الهياطلة
ومنعتهم وباسهم فقتل وزر وعامة جنده وغنم اموالهم واحتوى
على بلادهم الا ما كان كسرى غلب منها واقبل في جموع عدة مع امم
استمالهم وهم ابخر وبنجر وبلنجر وبلغ عدة الجميع ماية الف وعشر
الاف مقاتل انجاد فارسل الى كسرى يتوعده ويطلب منه اموالا
وانه ان لم يعجل بالبعثة اليه بما ساله وطئ بلاده وناجزه فلم يحفل
كسرى به ولم يجبه الى ما سال لتحصينه نواحيه لا سيما ناحية
صول التي اقبل منها خاقان ولمناعة السبل والفجاج ولمعرفته
بمقدرته على ضبط ثغر ارمينية فاقام خاقان على ناحية صول
من نواحي جرجان فراى من الحصون والرجال الذين اعدهم كسرى
بها ما لا حيلة له فيه فانصرف خائبا واما تدبيره للمزدكية
فانه ضرب اعناق رؤسائهم وقسم اموالهم في اهل الحاجة وقتل
جماعة كثيرة ممن دخل على الناس في اموالهم واهاليهم ممن عرف
ورد الاموال الى اربابها وامر بكل مولود اختلف فيه ان يلحق
بمن هو منهم اذا لم يعرف ابوه وان يعطى نصيبا من
مال الرجل الذي يسند اليه ان قبله الرجل وبكل امراة غلبت
على نفسها ان يؤخذ الغالب لها حتى يغرم لها مهرها ويرضي

165a

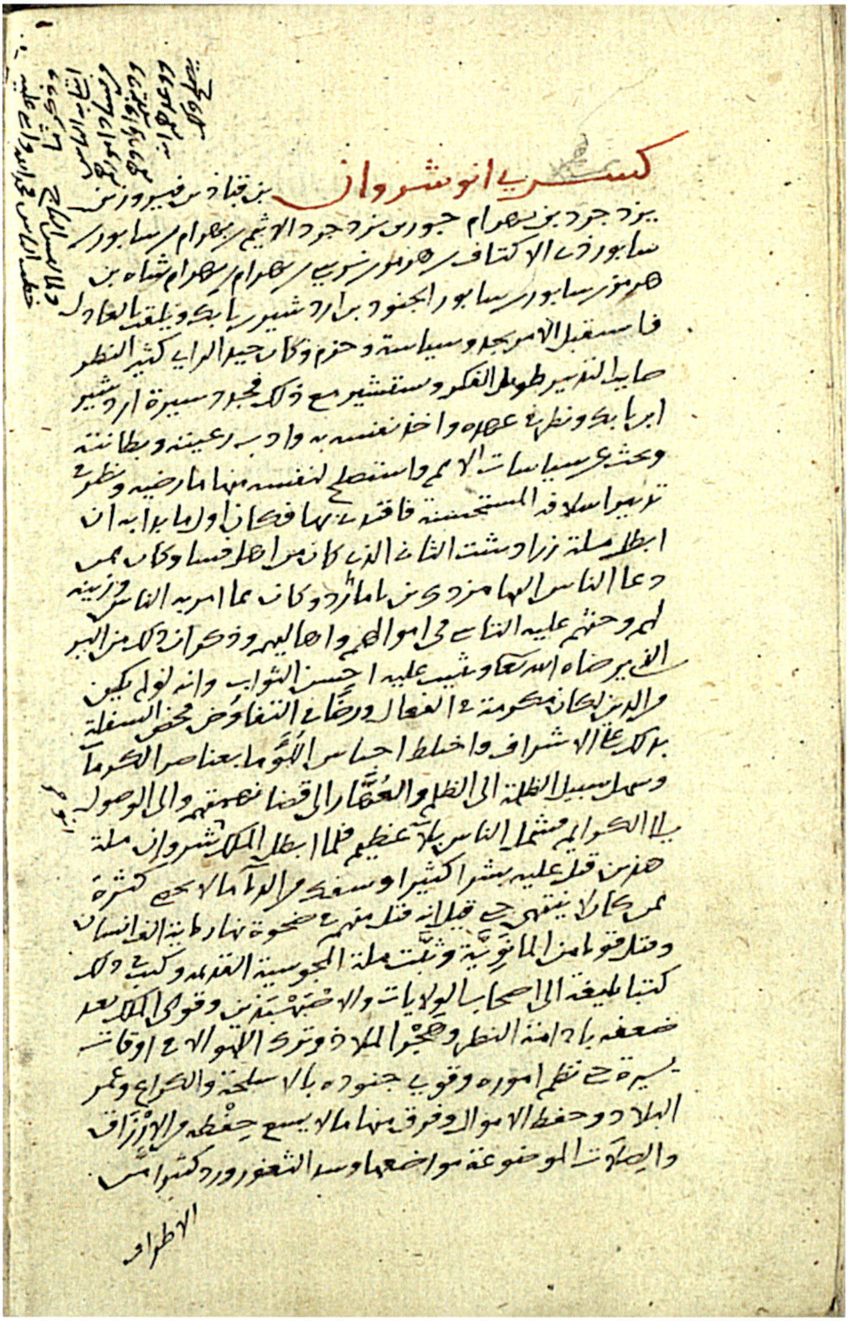
كسرى انوشروان بن قباذ بن فيروز بن
يزدجرد بن بهرام جور بن يزدجرد الاثيم بن بهرام بن سابور
سابور ذي الاكتاف بن هرمز بن نرسي بن بهرام بن بهرام شاه بن
هرمز بن سابور بن سابور الجنود بن اردشير بن بابك ويلقب بالعادل
فاستقبل الامر بجد وسياسة وحزم وكان جيد الراي كثير النظر
صايب التدبير طويل الفكر ويستشير مع ذلك فجدد سيرة اردشير
ابن بابك ونظر في عهده واخذ نفسه به وادب رعيته وبطانته
وبحث عن سياسات الامم واستصلح لنفسه منها ما رضيه ونظر في
تدبير اسلافه المستحسنة فاقتدى بها فكان اول ما بدا به ان
ابطل ملة زرادشت الثاني الذي كان من اهل فسا وكان ممن
دعا الناس اليها مزدك بن بامادد وكان مما امر به الناس وزينه
لهم وحثهم عليه التاسي في اموالهم واهاليهم وذكر ان ذلك من البر
الذي يرضاه الله تعالى ويثيب عليه احسن الثواب وانه لو لم يكن
من الدين لكان مكرمة في الفعال ورضا في التفاوض فحض السفلة
بذلك على الاشراف واختلط اجناس اللوما بعناصر الكرما
وسهل سبيل الظلمة الى الظلم والعهار الى قضا نهمتهم والى الوصول
بالكرايم فشمل الناس بلا عظيم فلما ابطل الملك انوشروان ملة
هذين قتل عليه بشرا كثيرا وسفك من الدما ما لا يحصى كثرة
مما كان لا ينتهي حتى قيل انه قتل منهم في ضحوة نهار مايه الف انسان
وقتل قوما من المانوية وثبت ملة المجوسية القديمة وكتب في ذلك
كتبا بليغة الى اصحاب الولايات والاصبهبذين وقوي الملك بعد
ضعفه بادامة النظر وهجر الملاذ وترك الملاهي اوقات
يسيرة حتى نظم اموره وقوي جنوده بالاسلحة والكراع وعمر
البلاد وحفظ الاموال وفرق منها ما لا يسع حفظه من الارزاق
والصلات الموضوعة مواضعها وسد الثغور ورد كثيرا من
الاطراف

164b

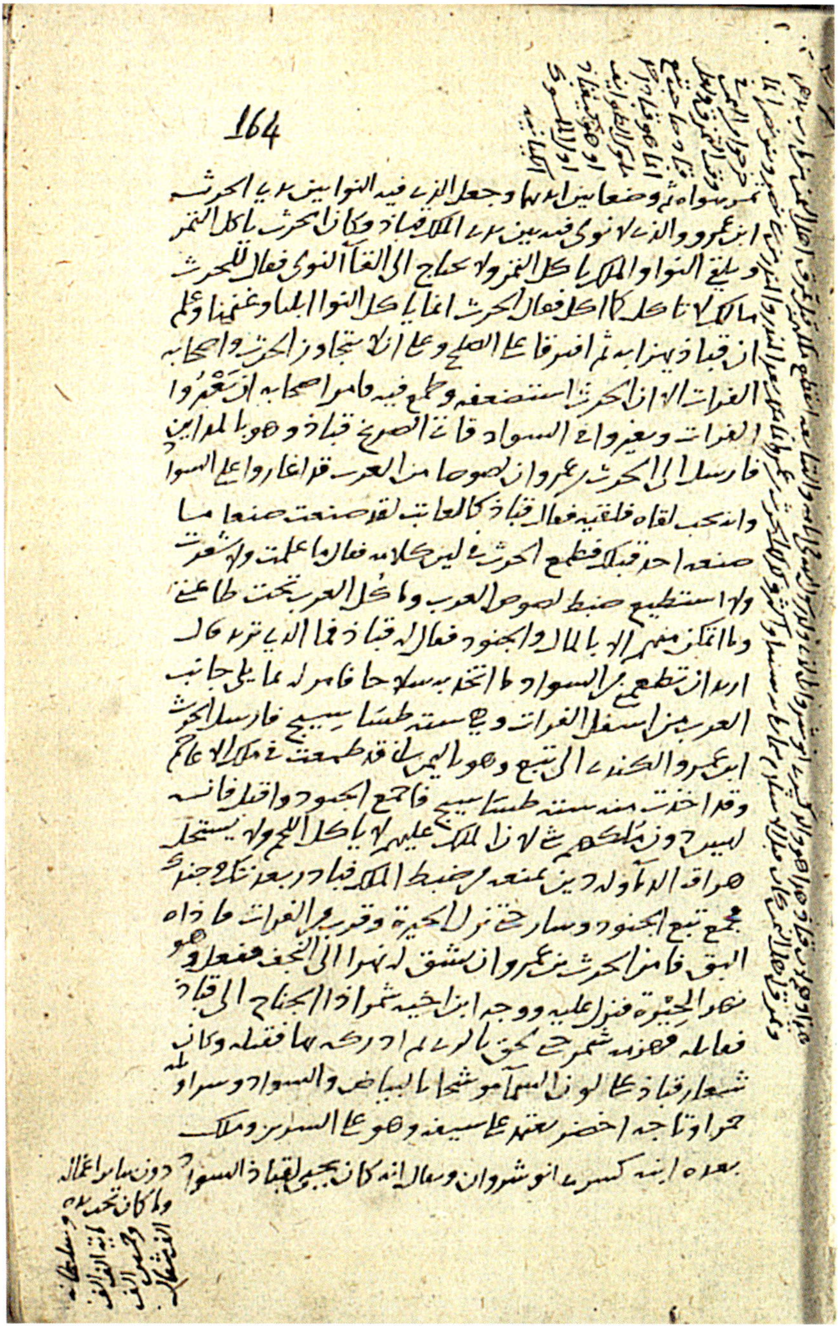
164

تمر سواء ثم وضعا بين ايديهما وجعل الذي فيه النوا بين يدي الحرث
ابن عمرو والذي لا نوى فيه بين يدي الملك قباذ وكان الحرث ياكل التمر
ويلقي النوا والملك ياكل التمر ولا يحتاج الى القا النوى فقال للحرث
ما لك لا تاكل كما اكل فقال الحرث انما ياكل النوا الابل والغنم وعلم
ان قباذ يهزا به ثم افترقا على الصلح وعلى ان لا يتجاوز الحرث واصحابه
الفرات الا ان الحرث استضعفه وطمع فيه وامر اصحابه ان يعبروا
الفرات ويغيروا على السواد فاتى الصريخ قباذ وهو بالمداين
فارسل الى الحرث ان عمروا لصوصا من العرب قد اغاروا على السوا
وانه يحب لقاه فلقيه فقال قباذ كالعاتب لقد صنعت صنعا ما
صنعه احد قبلك فقطع الحرث في لين كلامه فقال ما علمت ولا شعرت
ولا استطيع ضبط لصوص العرب وما كل العرب تحت طاعتي
وما اتمكن منهم الا بالمال والجنود فقال له قباذ فما الذي تريد قال
اريد ان تطعمني من السواد ما اتخذ به سلاحا فامر له بما يلي جانب
العرب من اسفل الفرات وهي ستة طساسيج فارسل الحرث
ابن عمرو الكندي الى تبع وهو باليمن قد طمعت في ملك الاعاجم
وقد اخذت منه ستة طساسيج فاجمع الجنود واقبل فانه
ليس دون ملكهم شي لان الملك عليهم لا ياكل اللحم ولا يستحل
هراقة الدما وله دين يمنعه من ضبط الملك قباذ وبعد ذلك جمع
فجمع تبع الجنود وسار حتى نزل الحيرة وقرب من الفرات فاذاه
البق فامر الحرث بن عمرو ان يشق له نهرا الى النجف ففعل وهو
نهر الحيرة فنزل عليه ووجه ابن اخيه شمر ذا الجناح الى قباذ
فقاتله فهزمه شمر حتى لحق بالري ثم ادركه بها فقتله وكان
شعار قباذ على لون السما موشحا بالبياض والسواد وسراويله
حمرا وتاجه اخضر يعقد على سيفه وهو على السرير وملك
بعده ابنه كسرى انوشروان وسماله انه كان يجبي لقباذ السواد

164a

الحبس فلما مر الغلام بوالي الحبس سأله عما حمله فاضطرب فلحقته
قباذ وأخبرته أنه فراش حيضها وأنها إنما خرجت لتتطهر وتنصرف
فصدقها ولم يمس البساط ولم يدن منه استقذاراً له على مذهبهم وجاز
الغلام الحامل لقباذ فمضى به وخرجت في أثره وهرب قباذ فلحق
بأرض الهياطلة يستمد ملكها فجار من خالفه فيقال إنه في مسيره
هذا نزل بأبرشهر على رجل من عظمائها فتزوج بابنة له فعلقت وأنها
أم كسرى أنوشروان وأن نكاحه أم أنوشروان في سفره هذا
كان ثم إن قباذ رجع في سفره هذا بابنه أنوشروان وغلب على
أخيه جاماسف بعد أن ملك أخوه ست سنين ثم غزا الروم وافتتح
آمد وبنا مدناً وملّك ابنه كسرى أنوشروان وأعطاه خاتمه ثم
هلك فكان ملكه بين ملك أخيه جاماسف نحواً وأربعين سنة وقيل
إن الخزر خرجت في أيامه وأغارت على بلاده فبلغوا الدينور فوجه
قايد من عظماء قواده في اثني عشر ألفاً فوطئ بلادهم وأراد وفتح ما بين
النهر المعروف بارس إلى شروان ثم إن قباذ لحق به وبنى في مدينة
البيلقان ومدينة بردعة ونفا الخزر ثم بنا سوراً فيما بين أرض
شروان وباب وبنا على السور مدناً كثيرة خربت بعد بناء
باب الأبواب وكان سبب هلاكه سوء رأيه وفساد عقيدته
وضعف ملكه وذلك أنه لما التقى الحرث بن عمرو بن حجر الكندي
والنعمن بن المنذر ابن امرئ القيس قتله وأفلت المنذر بن النعمن
الأكبر وملك الحرث بن عمرو ما ملك النعمن فبعث قباذ بن فيروز
إلى الحرث بن عمرو الكندي أنه قد كان بيننا وبين الملك الذي كان
قبلك عهد وإني أحب لقاك وكان قباذ زنديقاً يظهر الخير ويكره
سفك الدما ويداري أعداه فيما يكره وكثرت الأهواء في زمانه
واستضعفه الناس فخرج إليه الحرث بن عمرو في عدد وعدة حتى
التقيا فأمر قباذ بطبق من تمر فنزع نواه وأمر بطبق آخر فجعل فيه

ثم

163b

163

زاد شيئا في بعض ما جاء به وزاد ونقص واستحل المحارم والمنكرات

وسوى بين الناس في الاموال والاملاك والنساء والعبيد والاماء

حتى لا يكون لاحد على احد فضل في شي البتة فكثر اتباعه من السفلة والاغنياء

حتى صاروا عشرات الوف وكان مزدك ياخذ امراة هذا فيسلمها

لهذا وكذا في الاموال والالات والعقار والضياع فاستولى على الامر

وعظم شانه حتى قال يوما للملك قباذ اليوم نوبتي من امراتك ام انوشروا

فاجابه الى ذلك فقام انوشروان اليه ونزع خفيه بيديه وقبل رجليه

وشفع اليه حتى لا يتعرض لامه وله حكمة في سائر ملكه فتركها وحرم

ذبح الحيوان وقال يكفي في طعام الانسان ما تنبته الارض وما يتولد

من الحيوان كالبيض واللبن والجبن والسمن فلما عظمت البلية به على الناس

اجمعت الفرس حين راوا افساد الملك قباذ على تمليك اخيه جاماسف

ابن فيروز وقد كان ايضا اول المزدكية هم الذين اجلسوا جاماسف

ليكون الملك من قبلهم لا منة لغيرهم عليه الا ان الحكاية الاولى اشبه

بالحق وذلك انه لما مضى عشر سنين من ملك قباذ اجتمع موبذا

موبذ والعظماء فخلعوه وقالوا له انك قد اثمت باتباعك مزدك

وما عمله اصحابه بالناس وليس يخلصك الا اباحة نفسك وازواجك

واراده على ان يسلم نفسه اليهم ليذبحوه ويقربوه للنار فامتنع من

ذلك فحبسوه وتركوه لا يصل اليه احد وخرج زرمهر بن سوخرا

فقتل من المزدكية خلقا واعاد قباذ الى ملكه وازال اخاه

جاماسف وقيل بل تحيلت اخت قباذ فتمت لها الحيلة في اخراجها

قباذ من الحبس وذلك انها اتت الحبس الذي فيه قباذ وحاولت

الدخول اليه فمنعها الموكل به وطمع ان يفضحها بذلك السبب واعلمها

بذلك وراودها عن نفسها فاطمعته بانها غير مخالفة له في شي مما

يهواه منها فاذن لها حتى دخلت واقامت عند قباذ يوما ثم امرت

فلف قباذ في بساط وحمل على عاتق غلام قوي ضابط كان يعد لـ

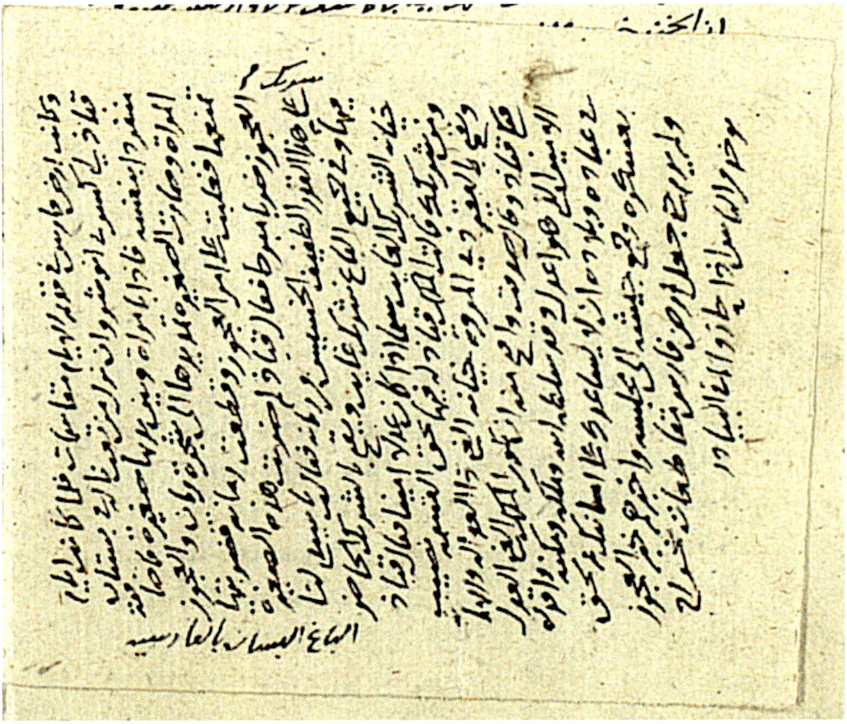

163*b

163*a

اعني بلاش وقباذ فعظموه ورفعوا منزلته الى حيث ليس بينه
وبين الملك الا مرتبة واحدة فتولى سياسة الامر بحنكته وتجربته
واستولى على الامر ومال اليه الناس واستخفوا بقباذ وتهاونوا
به فلم يحتمل قباذ ذلك وكتب الى سابور الرازي الذي يقال للبيت
الذي هو منه مهران وكان اصبهبذ البلاد في القدوم عليه فقدم في قبيلة
من الجند فقدم اليه سابور فواضعه قباذ حالة سوخرا وامره فيه
بامره في القبض عليه وكتمان شديد حتى قعد سابور عند قباذ فوجد
عنده سوخرا جالسا فمشى نحو قباذ مجاوزا له وتغفل سوخرا
فلم يأبه سوخرا الا وسابور حط الوهق في عنقه وهقا كان معه ثم
اجتذبه فاخرجه فاوثقه واستودعه السجن فحينئذ ضربت الفرس
المثل بان قالوا انطفأت ريح سوخرا وهبت ريح مهران ثم قتل
قباذ سوخرا وكان هزار ايامه على سكون ولم يضطرب فيه امر
وكان مما اساء فيه التدبير والراي حتى اجتمعت كلمة موبذان موبذ
وجماعة الفرس على حبسه وازالة ملكه عنه انه اشتمل على رجل يقال له
مزدك مع اصحاب له يقال لهم العدلية فقالوا ان الله تعالى انما
جعل الارزاق في الارض مبسوطة ليقسمها عباده بينهم بالتاسي
ولكن الناس تظالموا فيها وزعموا انهم آخذون للفقراء من الاغنياء ورادون
من المكثرين على المقلين وانه من كان عنده فضل في المال والقوت
او النساء والامتعة فليس هو اولى به من غيره فاغتنم السفلة ذلك
وكانفوا مزدك واصحابه حتى قوي امره وكانوا يهجمون على الرجل
في داره فيغلبونه على ماله ونسائه فلا يستطيعون الامتناع منهم
ودعواهم قبول الملك رايهم ودخوله معهم فلم يلبثوا الا قليلا حتى
صار الرجل لا يعرف اباه ولا الاب ولده ولا يملك احد شيئا مما
يتسع به وصيروا قباذ في مكان لا يصل اليه غيرهم فيه وكان
مزدك يزعم انه يدعو الى شريعة ابرهيم عليه السلام وتوافق

قباذ ج

بن بامداد ... موبذ موبذان

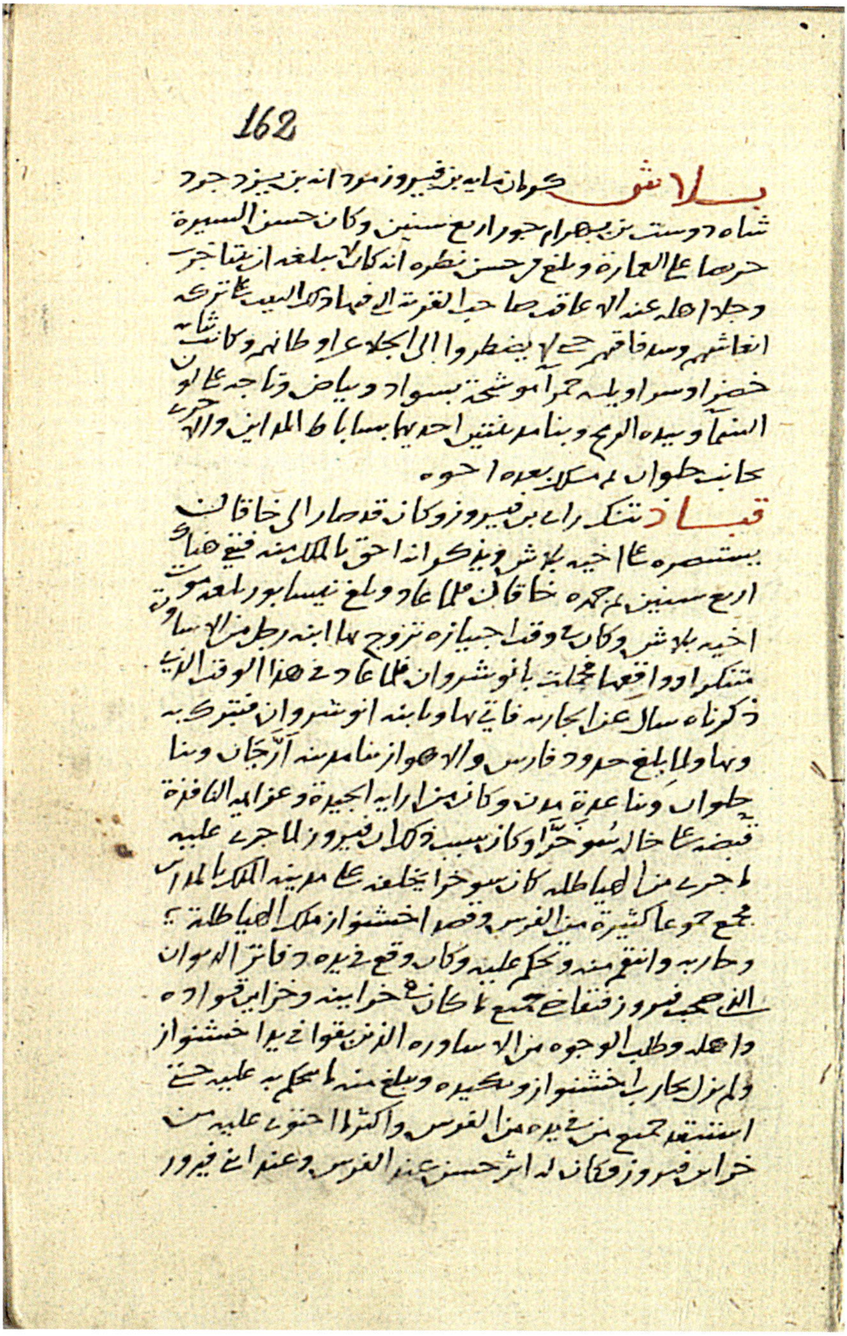

162

بلاش كرمانشاه بن فيروز ملكه انه بن يزدجرد
شاه دوست بن بهرام جور اربع سنين وكان حسن السيرة
حريصا على العمارة وبلغ من حسن نظره انه كان لا يبلغه ان بيتا خرب
وجلا اهله عنه الا عاقب صاحب القرية التى فيها ذلك البيت على تركه
انعاشهم وسد فاقتهم حتى لا يضطروا الى الجلاء عن اوطانهم وكانت ثيابه
خضرا او سودا وسراويله حمرا موشحة بسواد وبياض وتاجه على لون
السما وبيده الرمح وبنا مدينتين احديهما بساباط المداين والاخرى
بجانب حلوان ثم هلك فملك بعده اخوه
قباذ شنكراى بن فيروز وكان قد صار الى خاقان
يستنصره على اخيه بلاش ويذكر انه احق بالملك منه فبقى هناك
اربع سنين ثم جهزه خاقان فلما عاد وبلغ نيسابور بلغه موت
اخيه بلاش وكان فى وقت اجتيازه تزوج بها ابنة رجل من الاساورة
متنكرا فواقعها فحملت بانوشروان فلما عاد فى هذا الوقت الذى
ذكرناه سال عن الجارية فاتى بها وبابنه انوشروان فتبرك به
وبها ولما بلغ حدود فارس والاهواز بنا مدينة ارجان وبنا
حلوان وبنا عدة مدن وكان من ارايه الجيدة وعزايمه النافذة
قبضه على خاله سوخرا وكان بسبب هلاك فيروز لما جرى عليه
ما جرى من الهياطلة كان سوخرا يخلفه على مدينة الملك بالمداين
فجمع جموعا كثيرة من الفرس وقصد اخشنواز ملك الهياطلة
وحاربه وانتقم منه وتحكم عليه وكان وقع فى يده دفاتر الديوان
التى صحبت فيروز فتناول جميع ما كان فى خزاينه وخزاين قواده
واهله وطلب الوجوه من الاساورة الذين بقوا فى يد اخشنواز
ولم يزل يحارب اخشنواز ويكيده ويبلغ منه ما يحكم به عليه حتى
استنقذ جميع من فى يده من الفرس واكثر ما احتوى عليه من
خزاين فيروز فكان له اثر حسن عند الفرس وعند ابنا فيروز

162a

طلبا اخشنواز واصحابه واغذوا السير وكان مسلكهم على ذلك
الخندق فلما بلغوه اقتحموه على عماية فتردى فيه فيروز وعامة
جنده فهلكوا عن آخرهم وعطف اخشنواز على عسكر فيروز
واحتوى على كل شي فيه واسر موبذان موبذ وصارت فيروزدخت
بنت فيروز فيمن صار في يده من نسا فيروز ثم استخرج جثة فيروز
ومن سقط معه فجعلها في النواويس وقيل ان فيروز لما انتهى
الى الخندق الذي حفره اخشنواز ولم يكن مغطا عقد عليه قناطر
وجعل عليها اعلاما له ولاصحابه يعبرون بها في عودهم وجاز الى
القوم فلما التقى العسكران احتج عليه اخشنواز بالعهود التي بينهما
وحذره عاقبة الامر فلم يرجع فناشده اصحابه فلم يرجع وضعفت
نياتهم في القتال فلما ابا الا القتال رفع اخشنواز نسخة العهد على
رمح وقال اللهم خذ بما في هذا الكتاب وقلده بغيه ثم قاتله فانهزم
فيروز وعسكره وضلوا عن مواضع القناطر فسقطوا في الخندق
فهلك فيروز واصحابه وغنم اخشنواز اموالهم ودوابهم وجميع
ما معهم وغلب على عامة خراسان فسار اليه رجل من اهل فارس
يقال له سوخرا في زي محتسب وقيل بل كان فيروز استخلفه على
ملكه لما سار وكان له سجستان فلقي اخشنواز ملك الهياطلة
واخرجه من خراسان واستعاد منه كل ما وجده مما كان في
عسكر فيروز من سبي وغيره وعاد فعظمته الفرس حتى لم يكن
احد فوقه الا الملك فقط وكانت مملكة الهياطلة طخارستان
وكان فيروز قد اعطى الملك منهم لما عاهده على حرب اخيه الطالقان
وكان ملك فيروز من لدن ان مات يزدجرد سبعا وعشرين سنة وقيل سبع
عشرة سنة وفي نسخة ستا وعشرين سنة وقيل احدى وعشرين سنة وكان
شعاره احمر وسراويله على لون السما موشاة بالذهب وتاجه
على لون السما وسيره رمح وهو على سريره ثم ملك بعد فيروز ابنه

بلاش

161

له فيروز عهد الله وميثاقه الا يغزوه ولا يروم ارضه ولا يبعث اليهم
جيشا يقاتلهم وجعل بين المملكتين حدا لا يجوزه فرضي اخشنواز
بذلك وكتب له به كتابا مختوما واشهد له على نفسه شهودا ثم خلى
سبيله فانصرف فلما صار الى مملكته حمله الانف على معاودة
اخشنواز فكان من عاقبة غزاته اياه هلاكه وهلاك جنوده وذلك انه غزاه
بعد ان نهاه وزراوه وخاصته عن ذلك لما فيه من نقض العهد فلم يقبل
منهم وابى الا ركوب رايه وكان ممن نهاه عن ذلك رجل كان يخصه
ويتقدم برايه يقال له مزبوذ فلما راى لجاجته كتب ما دار بينهما في
صحيفة وساله ان يختم عليها ومضى فيروز لوجهه نحو بلاد اخشنواز
فلما بلغ منارة كان بناها بهرام جور فيما بين تخوم بلاد خراسان
وبلاد الترك لئلا يجوزها الترك الى خراسان لميثاق كان بين
الترك والفرس على ترك الفريقين التعدي لها وكان فيروز عاهد
اخشنواز الا يجاوزها الى بلاد الهياطلة امر فيروز فصير فيها
خمسون فيلا وثلاثمائة رجل فجرت امامه جرا واتبعها وزعم
انه يريد بذلك الوفاء وترك مجاوزة ما عاهد عليه فلما بلغ اخشنواز
ذلك من فعل فيروز بعث اليه يقول ان الله عز وجل بما جرى ولا
تخادع فانته عما انتهى عنه اسلافك ولا تقدم على ما لم يقدموا
عليه فلم يحفل فيروز بقوله ولم يكترث لرسالته وجعل يتحرش
بمحاربة اخشنواز ويدعوه اليها وجعل اخشنواز يمتنع من
محاربته ويتنكرها لان جل محاربة الترك انما هو بالخداع والمكر
والمكايد ثم ان اخشنواز امر فحفر خلف عسكره خندق عرضه
عشرة اذرع وعمقه عشرون ذراعا وغمي بخشب ضعاف
والقى عليه تراب ثم ارتحل في جنده ومضى غير بعيد فبلغ فيروز
رحلة اخشنواز بجنده من معسكره فلم يشك ان ذلك هزيمة منهم
وانه قد انكشف وهرب فامر بضرب الطبول وركب في جنده

ثم جوا جلد ظهر رجلين منا لهرابذة في الصغو احد الجلادين
الا حروف بغو هما وسار بجنوده نحو خراسان يريد حرب اخشنوار
ملك الهياطلة لاشيا كانت في نفسه ولان الهياطلة كانوا ياتون
الذكران ويرتكبون الفواحش مخافة اخشنوار لعلمه انه لا
طاقة له به فحيل عليه حتى قهره وقتله وعامة من كان معه وذلك
ان رجلا من اصحاب اخشنوار تنصح اليه وقال له اني رجل كبير السن
قريب الاجل وقد فديت الملك واهل مملكته بنفسي فاقطع يدي
ورجلي واظهر في جسمي وجنبي اثار السياط والعقوبات والقني
في طريق فيروز واحسن الى ولدي وعيالي بعدي فاني اكفيك
امر فيروز ففعل ذلك اخشنوار بذلك الرجل والقاه على طريق
فيروز فلما مر به انكر حاله وراى شيئا فظيعا فسأله عن امره
فاخبره ان اخشنوار فعل به ذلك لانه قال له لا قوام لك بالملك فيروز
وجنوده واشار عليه بالاستقبال له والعبودية فرق له فيروز ورحمه
وامر بحمله معه فاعلمه على وجه النصح له فيما زعم انه يدله على طريق
قريب مختصر لم يسلك احد منه قط الى اخشنوار على طريق المفازة
وسأله ان يتبع له منه فاغتر فيروز بذلك منه واخذ الاقطع
بالقوم في الطريق التي ذكره له ولم يزل يقطع بهم مفازة بعد مفازة
وكلما شكوا عطشا اعلمهم انهم قد قربوا من الماء ومن قطع المفازة
حتى اذا بلغ بهم موضعا اعلمهم انهم لا يقدرون فيه على تقدم ولا
تاخر وبين لهم امره فقال اصحاب فيروز لفيروز قد كنا حذرناك
هذا ايها الملك فلم تحذر فاما الان فلا بد من المضي فانه لا سبيل الى
الرجوع فلعلك توافي القوم على الحالات كلها فمضوا لوجوههم
وقتل العطش اكثرهم وصار فيروز بمن معه الى عدوهم فلما
اشرفوا عليهم وهم باسوا حال من الضر والضعف دعوا اخشنوار
الى الصلح على ان يخلي سبيلهم حتى ينصرفوا الى بلادهم على ان يجعل

له

160b

160

فيروز بن يزدجرد بن بهرام جور بعد ان قتل اخاه
هرمز وملك ثم نفر من اهل بيته وتفال الفيروز هذا فيروز مبرد انه
ما ظهر العدل وحسن السيرة وكان يتدين الا انه كان مجدودا مشؤوما
على رعيته قحط الناس في زمانه سبع سنين متواليه فغارت فيها جميع
الانهار والقنى والعيون وقحلت الاشجار والغياض وتماوتت
الوحوش والطيور وجاعت الانعام والدواب حتى كانت لا تطيق ان
تحمل حمولة وعم اهل البلاد الجهد والمجاعة فاحسن فيروز الى الناس
وقسم ما في بيوت الاموال وكف عن الجباية وساسهم احسن سياسة
وكتب الى جميع عماله انه لا خراج عليكم ولا جزية ولا سخرة وانه
قد ملككم انفسكم وامرهم بالسعي فيما يقوتهم ويصلحهم ثم كتب اليهم في
اخراج الحب والطعام من المطامير لكل من كان عنده شيء مما
يقوت الناس والتاسي فيه وترك الاستيثار به وان يكون حال
اهل الفقر والغنا واهل الشرف والضعة في التاسي واحدة وانه
ان بلغه ان انسانا مات جوعا عاقب اهل تلك المدينة
او القرية او الموضع الذي مات فيه ونكل بهم اشد النكال فلم يعرف
انه هلك في تلك المجاعة احد من رعيته جوعا الا رجل واحد من رستاق
كورة اردشير خره فلما حييت بلاده واغاثه الله وعادت المياه
وصلحت الاشجار واستوسق له الملك اثخن في الاعداء وقهرهم وبنا
مدنا احدها بالري واخرى بين جرجان وصول واخرى بناحية
اذربيجان وسماها باسما مشتقة من اسمه وابتنا حايطا وراء النهر
بين مملكة فارس وارض الترك وهو حايط ممتد والجبل طول اربعة
فراسخ يدخل مع بحر الخزر ليحول بين ناحية صول الترك وبينه محا
طوله اربعة وعشرين فرسخا تممه انوشروان بعد ذلك واستتم بنا
سور مدينة جي وامر بقتل نصف يهود اصبهان واسلام صبيانهم
في بيت نار سروشاذران ليكونوا عبيدا وسبب ذلك انهم

160a

وقيل تسع عشرة سنة وذكر ابو جعفر محمد بن جرير الطبري انه ملك ثماني
عشرة سنة وعشرة اشهر وعشرين يوما وقيل كان ملكه ثلاثا وعشرين
سنة وعشرة اشهر وعشرين يوما ثم ملك بعده ابنه
يزدجرد بن بهرام جور ويقال له يزدجرد
شاه دوست اي اللين ولما لبس التاج جلس للناس ووعظهم
وذكر اباه ومناقبه واعلمهم انه ان كانوا فقدوا منه طول جلوسهم
لهم فان خلوته انما كانت في مصالحهم وكيد اعدائهم وانه قد استوزر
نرسي صاحب ابيه وعدل في رعيته وقمع اعداءه واحسن الى
جنده ورافق برعيته وكان له ابنان احدهما يسمى هرمز والاخر
فيروز وكان هرمز بسجستان فتغلب على الملك بعد هلاك ابيه يزدجرد
ففر منه اخوه فيروز ولحق ببلاد الهياطلة واخبر ملكها بقصته
مع اخيه هرمز وانه اولى بالملك منه وساله ان يمده بجيش يقاتل
به اخاه فابى عليه ملك الهياطلة وقال سا علم علمه ثم انصرك
ان كنت صادقا فلما عرف ملك الهياطلة ان هرمز ملك ظلوم غشوم
قال ان الجور لا يرضاه الله ولا يصلح عليه الملك ولا يقوم عليه سياسة
ولا يحترف الناس في ملك الملك الجائر الا بالجور وفي هذا هلاك الناس
وخراب الارض فامد فيروز ودفع اليه الطالقان فاقبل فيروز بمن
معه بجيش طخارستان وطوائف خراسان وسار الى اخيه
هرمز وهو بالري وكانت امهما واحدة وكانت بالمداين تدبر ما
يليهما من الملك فظفر فيروز باخيه فحبسه وقيل قتله وكان ملك
الروم قد منع حمل الخراج الى يزدجرد فوجه اليه نرسي في العدة
التي انفذه ابوه بهرام فيها فبلغ ارادته وكان ملك يزدجرد ثماني عشرة
سنة واربعة اشهر وثمانية عشر يوما وقيل اربع عشرة سنة واربعة اشهر
وثمانية عشر يوما وكان شعاره احمر موشى وسراويله موشاة سوداء
وشيها ذهب وتاجه بلون السماء وانه قاعد على سريره اعتمد على سيفه

فيروز

159b

159

انه استوزر نرسي واعلمه انه ماض الى الهند في خفية وسار من غير ان
يعرفه احد حتى دخل بلاد الهند غير ان الهند سروا بشجاعته وقتله
السباع فيحبون له الى ان ظهر فيل فقطع السبيل وقتل خلقا كثيرا
فخرج اليه بهرام ومعه ترجمة الملك من يدله عليه حتى وقف على الاجمة
التي فيها الفيل فصعد ترجمان الملك شجرة ومضى بهرام منفردا الى الاجمة
الى ان قرب منه فرماه بسهم وقع بين عينيه وتابع الرمي بالنشاب حتى
اثخنه وللفيل صياح عظيم ثم حمل على الفيل واخذ بمشفره ولم يزل
يطعنه حتى صرعه واحتز راسه وخرج به وعاد فاكرمه عند
ذلك ملك الهند واحسن اليه وساله عن حاله فذكر ان ملك فارس
سخط عليه فهرب منه وكان لملك الهند عدو فقصده فاذعن لذلك
العدو وسال الملك في العفو عنه فنهاه بهرام عن ذلك واشار بمحاربته
فلما التقى الجمعان قال بهرام لاساورة الهند احفظوا ظهري
ثم حمل بنفسه حملة منكرة وجعل يضربهم ويرميهم بالنشاب حتى
هزمهم فغنم ملك الهند ما كان معهم وحينئذ اعطى بهرام الديبل ومكران
وانكحه ابنته فعاد بهرام الى مملكته وضم ذلك الى ارض فارس
ثم خرج في اخر ملكه الى ماه يريد الصيد فشد على عير وامعن في
طلبه فارتطم في جب ماء وغرق هناك فسارت والدته الى
ذلك الموضع باموال عظيمة واقامت قريبا منه وامرت بانفاق
تلك الاموال على من يخرجه فنقلوا طينا كثيرا وحماة كثيرة وجمعوا
منه اكاما عظاما فلم يقدروا على جثة بهرام هكذا ذكر ابو علي ابن
مسكويه في تجارب الامم وذكر حمزة الاصفهاني ان بهرام كتب على
ناووسه انه بعد ان يمكن لنا في الارض فتيقنا بها اثارا محمودة
اقتصرنا على هذه المحلة وقد كنا من سكوننا اياه على يقين وكان
شعاره على لون السماء وسراويله خضر موشاة قال ابن مسكويه
وكان ملكه ثماني عشرة سنة وقال حمزة ملك ثلاثا وعشرين سنة

159a

منطعر اقصا الهند فيحكى له حكايات عظيمة وامور كبار تنوه بها وغلب
عليها وزوجه ملك الهند ابنته ونحله الديبل ومكران وما يليها فضمها
بهرام الى ارض فارس وحمل خراجها اليه ثم اغزى بهرام مهر نرسى
الى بلاد الروم في اربعين الف مقاتل وامره ان يقصد عظيمها ويناظره
في امر الاتاوة وغيرها فتوجه مهر نرسى في تلك العدة ودخل الى
قسطنطينية فهادنه ملك الروم وانصرف بجميع ما اراد بهرام
وبلغ مبلغا عظيما بهيبة بهرام وبما تمكن له في قلوب الملوك واهل
الاطراف والجند من جودة الراي وحسن التدبير والشجاعة
ونفاذ العزيمة وقلة الاتكال على غيره وذكر ان بهرام بعد فراغه
من امر خاقان وامر ملك الروم والسند مضى الى بلاد السودان
من ناحية اليمن فاوقع بهم وقتل منهم مقتلة عظيمة وسبى منهم خلقا
وانصرف الى مملكته وولى نرسى خراسان وامره ان ينزل مدينة
بلخ فبلغه ان بعض رؤسا الديلم جمع جمعا كبيرا واغار على الري
واعمالها فغنم وسبا وخرب البلاد وقرر على اهل البلاد اتاوة تحمل
اليه فبعث مرزبانا على عسكر كثيف الى الري وامره ان يضع
على الديلمي من يطمعه في البلاد ويغريه بقصدها ففعل ذلك وجمع
الديلمي جموعه وقصد الري فلما بلغ بهرام ذلك كتب الى نرسى يامره
بالمسير الى الديلمي وعين له موضعا يقيم به ثم سار جريدة في نفر
من خواصه الى عسكره المقيم بالموضع الذي عينه والديلمي لا يعلم
بوصوله وقد قوي طمعه في البلاد فعبى بهرام اصحابه وسار نحو
الديلمي حتى لقيه وباشر القتال بنفسه فاخذ الديلمي اسيرا وانهزم
الديلم فامر فنودي فيهم بالامان فعادوا باجمعهم فامنهم ولم يقتل
منهم احدا واحسن اليهم وافرج عن الديلمي وجعله من خواصه و
وقيل ان هذه الحادثة كانت قبل محاربة خاقان ملك الترك
ولما ظفر بهرام بالديلم امر ببناء مدينة سماها فيروز بهرام وقبله

انه

158b

158

حين بلغهم مسير بهرام فيمن سار بهم واستخلافه اخاه في ادراك حرب
عدوه واستسلام للملك وتوامروا في انفاذ وفد الى خاقان والاقرار
له بالخراج مخافة منه ان يستبيح بلادهم ويصطلم مقاتلتهم ووجوههم
ان هم لم يفعلوا ذلك وبادروا اليه فبلغ خاقان الذي اجتمع عليه الفرس
من الانقياد والخضوع له فامنهم وترك كثيرا من الحذر والاستعداد
وان بهرام عين له من جهة خاقان فاخبره بحاله وحال جنده وفتورهم
عن الجد الذي كانوا عليه فسار في العدة الذين كانوا معه فبيت خاقان
وقتله بيده وانهزم من سلم من القتل منهم وخلفوا عسكرهم واثقالهم
فامعن بهرام في طلبهم يقتلهم ويحوي الغنائم ويسبي الذراري وانصرف
هو وجنده سالمين وظفر بتاج خاقان واكليله وغلب على بلاد
الترك وخضع له اهل البلاد المتاخمة لما غلب عليه بالطاعة وسالوه
ان يحد لهم حدا بينه وبينهم فلا يتعدوه ثم بعث قايدا الى ما وراء النهر
فاثخنهم واقروا بالعبودية واداء الجزية وانصرف بهرام بالغنائم
العظيمة والتاج والاكليل وما فيهما من اليواقيت الحمر وسائر
الجواهر فجعلها في بيت النار باذربيجان ورفع الخراج عن الناس ثلاث
سنين وقسم في الفقرا مالا عظيما وفي البيوتات واهل الاحساب
عشرين الف الف درهم وكتب كتبا الى الافاق يذكر فيها ان الخبر كان
ورد عليه بورود خاقان بلاده وانه بحمد الله تعالى وتوكل عليه
وسار في سبعة رهط من اهل البيوتات وثلاثمائة فارس من نخبة
رابطة على طريق اذربيجان وجبل القبق حتى نفذ الى برار ب
خوارزم ومفاوزها فابلاه الله احسن بلا وذكر في الكتاب ما
وضع عن الناس من الخراج وهذا الكتاب كان بليغا والفرس تحفظه
ويقال ان بهرام ترك من حق بيت المال من الخراج سبعين الف الف
درهم بقسط تلك السنة وكان هذا مقدار ما بقي منه لم امر بترك
الخراج كله ثلاث سنين اخر ثم لما انصرف بهرام من غزوة خاقان

جلس بهرام وهو ابن عشرين سنة سبعة ايام متوالية للجند والرعية
يعدهم الخير من نفسه ويحضهم على تقوى الله عز وجل وطاعته وعبر زمانا
بحسن السيرة ومنع الظلم وبعمر البلاد ويدر الارزاق ثم آثر
اللهو على ذلك وكثرت خلواته باصحاب الملاهي والجواري واخذ
الناس بان يعملوا من كل يوم نصفه ثم يستريحوا ويتوفروا على الاكل
والشرب واللهو وان يشربوا بالخواشنة والاكاليل فعز المغنون
في ايامه حتى بلغ رسم كل دستة من الخواشنة مائة درهم ومر يوما
بقوم يشربون على غير ملهين فقال الستم قد نهيتكم عن اغفال
الملاهي فقاموا اليه وسجدوا وقالوا طلبناه بزيادة على مائة درهم
فلم نقدر عليه فدعا بالدواة والمصراف وكتب الى ملك الهند يستوهب
ملهين فانفذ اليه اثني عشر الف رجل منهم ففرقهم على بلدان مملكته
فتناسلوا بها وهم نسلهم الزط فلما امعن في اللهو كثرت ملامة
رعيته اياه على ذلك وطمع من حوله من الملوك في استباحة حريمه
والغلبة على ملكه وكان اول من سبق الى مغالبته خاقان ملك
الترك فانه غزاه في مائتين وخمسين الفا من الاتراك فبلغ العجم
اقبال خاقان في هذا الجمع فهالهم ذلك ودخل اليه من عظمائهم قوم
من اهل الراي فقالوا ايها الملك قد ازفت من بائقة هذا العدو ما
يشغلك عما انت فيه من اللهو والتلذذ فتاهب له كيما يلحقك منه
امر يلزمك فيه مسبة وعار وكان بهرام لثقته بنفسه ورايه
يجيب القوم بان الله ربنا قوي ونحن اولياؤه ثم يقبل على المثابرة
واللزوم لما هو فيه من اللهو والصيد الى ان اظهر ذات يوم التجهز
الى اذربيجان لينسك في بيت نارها ويتوجه منها الى ارمينية
ويطلب الصيد في آجامها ويلهو في مسيره في سبعة رهط من العظماء
واهل البيوتات وثلثمائة رجل من رابطته ذوي باس ونجدة
واستخلف اخاه نرسي على ما كان يليه من ملكه فلم يشك الناس

في

157

رضينا بحكمه وان يوضع التاج والزينة بين اسدين كما ذكرت
بحيث رسمت وتنازعا هما اشد وكسرى فاتى بالتاج والزينة ووضعا
موبذان موبذ الذي كان يعقد التاج على راس كل ملك منهم ووضعها
ناحية وجا اصبهبذ مع شعار القوم باسدين ضاريين مجوعين
مشبلين فوقفا احدهما عن جانب الموضع الذي وضع فيه التاج
والزينة والاخر بحذايه وارخى وثاقهما ثم قال بهرام لكسرى
دونك التاج والزينة فقال كسرى انت اولى به لانك تطلبه الملك
بوراثة وانا فيه دخيل فلم يكره بهرام قوله لثقته بنفسه وحمل
جرزا وتوجه نحو التاج والزينة فقال له موبذان موبذ استماتتك في
هذا الامر الذي تعزم عليه تطوع منك لا عن راي منا ولا عن راي
احد من الفرس ونحن برآء الى الله من اتلافك نفسك فقال بهرام نعم انتم
برآء ولا وزر عليكم ثم اسرع نحو الاسدين فلما راى موبذان موبذ
جده هتف به وقال بح بذنوبك وتب منها ثم اقدم ان كنت لا محالة
مقدما فباح بهرام بما سلف من ذنوبه ثم مشى نحو الاسدين فبادر
احدهما فلما دنا من بهرام وثب وثبة فاذا هو على ظهر الاسد
وعصر جنبي الاسد بفخذيه حتى اثخنه وجعل يضرب راسه بالجرز
ثم قرب من الاسد الاخر فلما تمكن منه قبض على اذنيه وعركهما بكلتا
يديه ولم يزل يضرب راسه براس الاسد الذي ركب ظهره حتى دمغهما
ثم قتلهما ضربا على راسيهما بالجرز وكان ذلك كله بمشهد من جميع من حضر
ذلك المحفل ومرأى من كسرى فتناول بهرام التاج والزينة فكان
كسرى اول من هتف به وقال عمر الله بهرام الذي يسمع له من حوله
ويطيع ورزقه الله ملك اقاليم الارض السبعة ثم هتف جميع من حضر
ذلك المجلس وقالوا قد خضعنا للملك بهرام ورضينا به ملكا واكثروا
الدعاء والضجيج ودخل الروسا المنذر بعد ذلك وسالوه ان يكلم بهرام
في التغمد لمساويهم والصفح عنهم فساله في ذلك فشفعه الملك بطلبته ثم

ان يغشيكم قربا منها وبعث جلاوبعه الينا وان يتغالى من قابله
ويغير على البلاد ففعل ذلك فبعث عظما فارس الى المنذر بجواب صاحب
رسايل يزدجرد ليعلم خبره فادخله على بهرام فلم يستجز له فكلمه
بهرام ووعده احسن وعد ورده الى المنذر وامره ان يجيبه فقال
انا الملك بهرام ارسل النعمن الى ناحيتكم وقد ملكه الله بعد ابيه فاشار
بان يسير المنذر وبهرام الى مدينة الملك ليجتمع اليه الاشراف والعظما
ويتشاوروا في ذلك فقبل رايه واعاده ثم سار بعد عوده بيومين
في ثلاثين الف من فرسان العرب ومعه بهرام حتى وافى المدينة
فصعد بهرام منبرا من ذهب مكللا بالجواهر وحضر عظما الفرس
فذكروا فظاظة يزدجرد والد بهرام وسو سيرته وكثرة قتله
واخرابه البلاد وانهم من اجل هذا صرفوا الملك عن ولده فقال بهرام
لست اكذبكم ومازلت زاريا عليه ولم ازل اسال الله تعالى ان يملكني
لاصلح ما افسد واسد الثغور وانفي اهل الفساد فاذا اتت لملكي
سنة ولم اف لكم بهذه الامور تبرات من الملك طايعا واشهد
الله تعالى وملايكته وموبذان موبذ بذلك فرضي اكثر الناس الا
طايفة كان رايها مع كسرى فانها تكلمت فقال بهرام فاني مع
ما ضمنته لكم واستحقاقي للملك وانه حق ابائي قد رضيت ان
يوضع التاج والزينة بين اسدين ضاريين فمن تناوله فهو
الملك فاظهروا الرضا وقالوا ان تمادينا على صرفنا الملك عن
بهرام لم نامن هلاك الفرس على يده بما نرى من رايه وكثرة من استجاش
من العرب وقد عرض علينا ما لم يدع اليه احد ولولا ثقته ببطشه
وجراته ما عرض نفسه لذلك فان فعل ما وصف فما الراي الا
تسليم الملك اليه والسمع والطاعة له وان هلك عجزا وضعفا نحن
براآ منه آمنون لشره وغايلته وافترقوا على ذلك وجلس بهرام
من الغد وحضر من كان ينازعه فقال اما ان تجيبوني عما تكلمت
به امس واما ان تسكتوا باخعين لي بالطاعة فقال القوم

احسنا

156

بهرام جور ويقال جور بن يزدجرد الخشن ويقال
له المجرم والاثيم والغشوم بن بهرام كرمان شاه بن شابور بن
شابور ذي الاكتاف بن هرمز بن نرسي بن بهرام بن بهرام بن بهرام شاه
ابن هرمز بن شابور بن شابور الجنود بن اردشير بن بابك اسلمه
ابوه يزدجرد الاثيم الى المنذر بن النعمن وكفله اياه رغبة في ان
تحضنه العرب وتتولى تربيته فسار به المنذر الى الحيرة واختار
لرضاعه ثلث نسوة ذوات اجسام صحيحة واذهان ذكية
واداب حسنة من بنات الاشراف منهن عربيتان وعجمية فارضعنه
ثلث سنين فلما بلغ خمس سنين احضر له مؤدبين فعلموه الكتابة
والفقه والرمي بطلب من بهرام لذلك واحضر حكيما من حكما الفرس
فتعلم ووعى كلما علمه بادنى تعليم فلما بلغ اثنى عشرة سنة تعلم كلما
افيد وفاق معلميه فامرهم المنذر بالانصراف واحضر معلمي الفروسية
فاخذ بهرام عنهم كلما ينبغي له ثم صرفهم المنذر واحضر خيل العرب
للسباق فسبقها فرس اشقر للمنذر فقربه لبهرام بيده فقبله ثم
ركبه يوما للصيد فراى عانة حمر وحش فرمى عليها وقصدها فاذا
هو باسد قد اخذ عيرا منها فرماه واظهره بغمه فرماه بهرام بسهم
فنفذ فيه وفي العير ووصل الى الارض فساخ السهم الى ثلثه
فتعجب من كان معه من ذلك واقبل على الصيد واللهو حتى مات ابوه
يزدجرد فاتفق عظما الدولة على ان لا يملكوا احدا من ذرية يزدجرد
لسوء سيرته فيهم وعلى ان لا يملكوا بهرام لنشوه في العرب وتخلقه
باخلاقهم وملكوا رجلا من عقب اردشير بن بابك يقال له
كسرى فجمع بهرام المنذر وابنه النعمن بن المنذر واشراف العرب
وذكرهم احسان ابيه اليهم وشدته على الفرس فوعدوه من
انفسهم النصر والمعونة وتكفل له المنذر بالامر وجهز ابنه النعمن
على عشرة الاف فارس الى طيسفون وبهرشير مدينتي الملك وامره

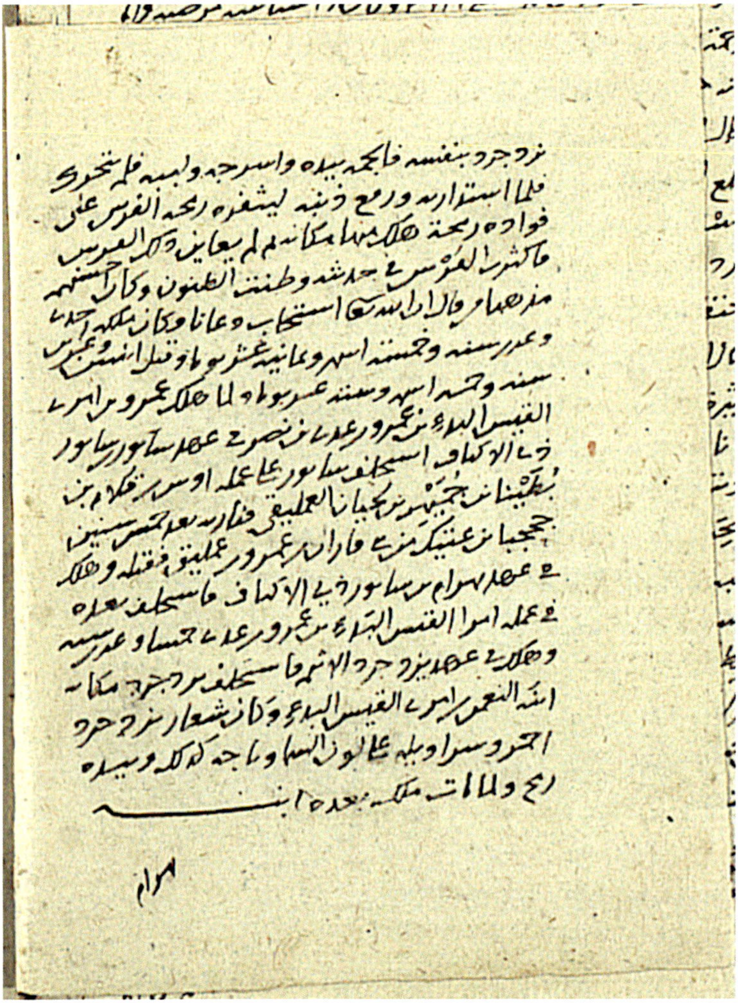

يزدجرد بنفسه فالجمه بيده واسرجه ولببه فلم يتحرك
فلما استدار به ورفع ذنبه ليثفره رمحه الفرس على
فؤاده رمحة هلك منها مكانه ثم لم يعاين ذلك الفرس
فاكثرت العجم في حديثه وظنت الظنون وكان احسنهم
منطقا من قال ان الله تعالى استجاب دعانا وكان ملكه احدا
وعشرين سنة وخمسة اشهر وثمانية عشر يوما وقيل اثنتين وعشرين
سنة وخمسة اشهر وستة عشر يوما ولما هلك عمرو بن امرئ
القيس البدء بن عمرو بن عدي في نصرح عهد سابور بن سابور
ذي الاكتاف استخلف سابور على عمله اوس بن قلام بن
بطينا بن جميهير بن الحيان العمليقي فثار به بعد خمس سنين
جحجبا بن عتيك من بني فاران بن عمرو بن عمليق فقتله وهلك
في عهد بهرام بن سابور ذي الاكتاف فاستخلف بعده
في عمله امرأ القيس البدء بن عمرو بن عدي خمسا وعشرين سنة
وهلك في عهد يزدجرد الاثيم فاستخلف يزدجرد مكانه
ابنه النعمان بن امرئ القيس البدء وكان شعار يزدجرد
احمر وسراويله على لون السما وتاجه كذلك وبيده
رمح ولما ات ملكه بعده ابنه

بهرام

155?b

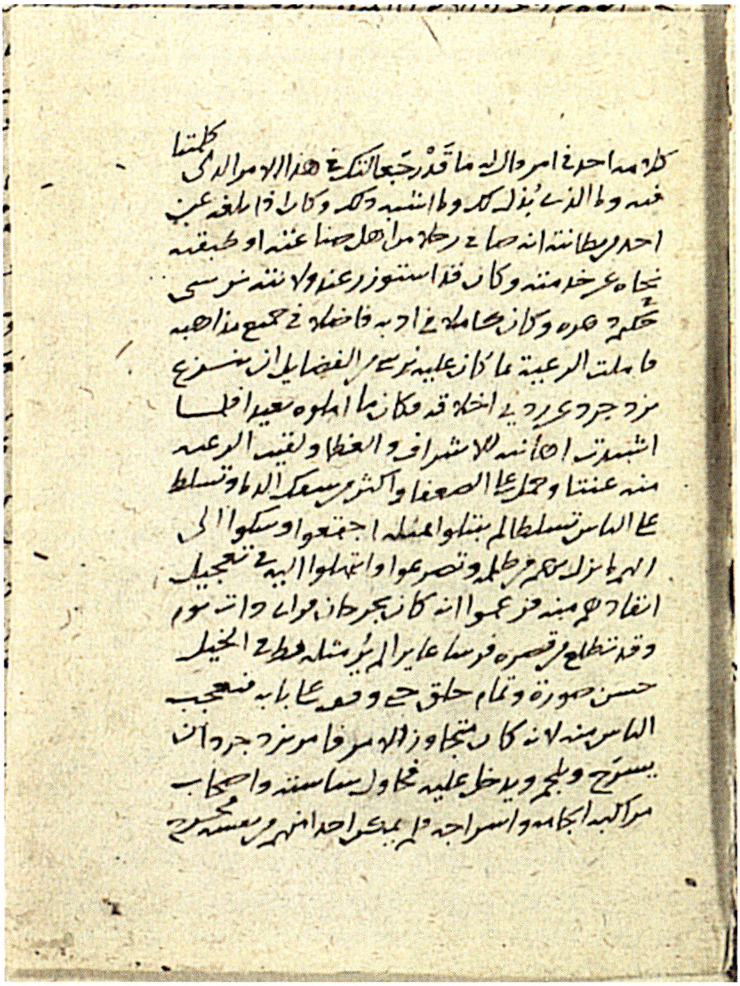
كان مما حدث في امر الله ما قد رجعنا النكتة في هذا اليوم الذي كلمتنا
عنه وهو الذي يذكر كلمة وما اشبه ذلك وكان اذا بلغه عن
احد من بطانته انه صافى رجلا من اهل صناعته او طبقته
نحاه عن خدمته وكان قد استوزر عنوا لا يشبه نرسي
حكمه في عمره وكان حسن الملكة في ادبه فاختلف في جميع مذاهبه
فاملت الرعية بما كان عليه من سرير الفضائل ان يخرج
يزدجرد عن رد في اخلاقه فكان ما املوه بعيد فلما
اشتدت اذاته للاشراف والعظماء ولقيت الرعية
منه عنتا وحمل على الضعفاء واكثر من سفك الدماء وتسلط
على الناس تسلطا لم يتبلوا بمثله اجتمعوا وشكوا الى
الله ما نزل بهم من ظلمه وتضرعوا وابتهلوا اليه في تعجيل
انقاذهم منه فزعموا انه كان بجرجان عن اوان ذات يوم
وقد نطلع من قصره فرسا عائرا لم ير مثله في الخيل
حسن صورة وتمام خلق حتى وقف على بابه فتعجب
الناس منه لانه كان متجاوز الحد فامر يزدجرد ان
يسرج ويلجم ويدخل عليه فحاول سياسته واصحاب
مراكبه الجامه واسراجه فلم يمكن احدا منهم من مسه

155?a

والقفط ويقال له بالفارسية دفز وتباه كرد ابن بهرام كرمان شاه
سابور ذي الاكتاف وقال آخرون ان يزدجرد الاثيم هو اخو بهرام كرمان شاه
وليس بابنه وانه يزدجرد بن سابور ذي الاكتاف وقال حمزة في
نسخة ان يزدجرد الاثيم والد بهرام جور هو يزدجرد بن يزدجرد الاثيم
وهو صاحب شروين الدستبي لا الاثيم وكان ذا سياسة مرضية واناة
ورحمة وعطف بخلاف ابنه وبلغ من رواية ان ملكا من ملوك الروم كان في
زمانه حضرته الوفاة وله ابن صغير فاوصى الى يزدجرد هذا ان ينفذ من
رجال مملكته خليفة له الى بلاد الروم يضبط على ابنه عمله الى ان يبلغ
مبلغ الرجال فانفذ اليها شروين بن برزينيان رئيس كورة
دستبي وملكه على بلاد الروم فضبطها له عشرين سنة ثم ادى الامانة
في رده مملكة الروم على ابنه واسترداده شروين منها بعد ان
اختط مدينة بها وسماها باشروان ان لم تعرف معقيل باجروان
وقال الطبري وابو مسكويه ان يزدجرد الاثيم كان فظا غليظا ذا عيوب
كثيرة وكان من اشد عيوبه وضعه ذكاء ذهنه وحسن ادبه
كان فيه وصنوف من العلم قد مهرها وعلمها غير موضعها وكثرة
رويته في الضار من الامور واستعماله كل ما عنده من ذلك في الدهاء
والحيل والمكايد والمخاتلة مع فطنة كانت له بجهات الشرور وشدة
عجبه بما عنده من ذلك واستخفه بكل علم وادب واحتقر ذلك
واستطال على الناس بما عنده وكان مع ذلك غلقا سيء الخلق رديء
الطعمة حتى بلغ من شدة غلقه وحدته ان كان يستعظم صغير
الزلات ويكبر السقطات ولا يرضى في عقوبتها الا بما لا يستطاع
ان يبلغ مثله ثم لم يتجرأ احد من بطانته وان كان لطيف المنزلة منه ان
يشفع لمن ابتلي به وان كان ذنب المبتلى به يسيرا ولم يكن يأتمن
احدا على شيء من الاشياء ولم يكن يكافئ على حسن البلاء وكان يعتد
بالخسيس من العرف اذا اولاه ويستجزل ذلك فاذا جسر على

كلامه بهرام

155

اللقا وكتب الى عماله يامرهم بحسن السيرة والرفق بالرعية وامر وزراه وكتابه
بذلك وخطبهم خطبة بليغة ولم يزل عادلا في رعيته متحننا عليهم لما يبين
له من مودتهم ومحبتهم وطاعتهم وخضع له عمه اردشير المخلوع وتحقق
الطاعة ولم يزل على ذلك الى ان قطع العظما واهل البيوتات اطناب
فسطاط كان قد ضرب عليه في حجرة من حجره فسقط عليه فقتله وكانت
مدة ملكه خمس سنين وذكر حمزة انه ملك اثنتين وثمانين سنة وقيل
خمسين سنة واربعة اشهر قال وفي نسخة انه ملك خمس سنين وفي اخرى
انه هو الذي عقد على بطن امه التاج وفيه نظر قال وكان شعاره احمر
موشى وسراويله لون السما وتحت شعاره شعار اصفر وتاجه اخضر
في حمرة بين شرفتين من ذهب وهلال من ذهب بيده قضيب على
طرفه راس طاير معتمد بيسراه على مقبض سيفه وملك بعده اخوه
بهرام بن سابور ذي الاكتاف وكان يلقب بكرمان شاه
لان سابور ولاه كرمان فكتب الى قواده كتابا يحثهم فيه على الطاعة
ويامرهم بتقوى الله تعالى والنصيحة للملك وبنى بكرمان مدينة قال
الطبري وكان حسن السياسة لرعيته محمودا في اموره وقال ابن مسكويه
قضيته محموده وكان جميل السياسة محببا وقال حمزة وكان فظا ذاهبا
بنفسه لم يقرا طول ايامه قصة ولم ينظر في مظلمة فلما مات وجدوا الكتب
الواردة عليه مختومة ما فكها بعد وملك اثنتي عشرة سنة وقيل
احدى عشرة سنة وامر ان يكتب على ناووسه قد علمنا ان فنا الجسد
سيعود في هذه البنية فلا ينفعه راي شفيق ولا يضره نبو عدو
وكان شعاره لون السما موشى وسراويله حمرا موشاة وتاجه اخضر
بين ثلاث شرفات ذهب وبيده اليمنى رمح وهو باليسرى معتمد على
سيفه قال الطبري وكان ملكه احدى عشرة سنة وان ناسا من
الفتاك ثاروا اليه فقتله رجل منهم برمية رماه بها اباه نشاب وملك
يزدجرد الخشن ويقال المجرم والاثيم

بناحية السوس سماها ايران شهر وكان كلما ظفر بملك الروم او بعيد كلأ جره
واسكنوا على عادته لما كان بالتبن والطين بالاجر والجص فسوّر مدينة
جندي سابور نصفه باللبن ونصفه بالاجر وبنا على مرو بسجستان
والسند ونصب بغزنية جرو آتش نارا سماها تناوشروس آذران ووقف
عليها قرية ونقل اطباء الهند واسكنه الكرخ والسوس فلما مات
ورث طبه اهل السوس فصاروا اعلم العجم بالطب واقام سابور منذ وكد بالا
تمام ثلاثين سنة بجندي سابور ثم تحول الى المداين فاقام بها باقي عمره حتى
مات عن اثنتين وسبعين سنة كان ملكها جميعها وكان شعاره موردا
موشى وسراويله حمراء موشاة وتاجه على لون السماء حواليه ملون بالذهب
من شرفة ذهب وهلال ذهب وسطه وكان يقعد على السرير وبيده
طبرزين وفي زمانه كان آذرباد الزراذيب الصغر على صراره وهلك
عمرو عامله على ناحية مضر وربيعة امرو القيس البدء بن عمرو بن
عدي بن ربيعة بن نصر فاستعمل على عمله ابنه عمرو بن امرى القيس فبقي
في عمله بقية ملك سابور وجميع ايام اخيه اردشير وهرمز بن نرسي وبعض ايام
سابور بن سابور ذي الاكتاف ولما احتضر سابور ذو الاكتاف عهد الى اخيه

اردشير الجميل بن هرمز بن نرسي بن بهرام بن بهرام بن هرمز
ابن سابور الجنود بن اردشير بن بابك فلما عقد التاج على راسه دخل
عليه العظماء ودعوا له بالنصر وشكروا اخاه سابور ذا الاكتاف
فاحسن جوابهم واعلمهم موقع ما كان من شكرهم لاخيه فلما استقر
به الملك قراره عطف على العظماء وذوي الرياسة فقتل منهم خلقا
كثيرا فخلعه الناس بعد اربع سنين من ملكه وكان شعاره وشي
مدنر على لون السماء وسراويله موشاة بحمرة وبيمناه رمح وبيسراه
معتمدا بها على سيفه وتاجه اخضر وملك بعده ابن اخيه

سابور بن سابور ذي الاكتاف وقد ادرك وخرج عن
الطفولية فاستبشرت الرعية برجوع الملك اليه وتلقاهم هو اجمل

اللقا

154

ومات وضرب سابور على العرب فقتلهم ونزع اكتافهم وسماهم زمانا طولا
فسمته العرب ذا الاكتاف ثم انه استصلح العرب واسكن بعض تغلب
وعبد القيس وبكر بن وائل كرمان وتوج والاهواز وذكروا ان سابور بعد
ان اثخن في العرب واجلاهم عن النواحي التي كانوا صاروا اليها مما قرب
من نواحي فارس والبحرين واليمامة ثم هبط الى الشام وصار الى حد الروم
اعلم اصحابه انه عزم على دخول بلاد الروم حتى يبحث عن اسرارهم ويعرف
اخبار مدنهم وعدد جنودهم فدخل الى الروم فجال فيها حينا وبلغه ان
قيصر اولم وليمة وامر بجمع الناس ليحضروا طعامه فانطلق سابور
بهيئة السؤال حتى شهد ذلك الجمع لينظر الى قيصر ويعرف هيئته وحاله
في طعامه ففطن له فاخذ وامر به قيصر فادرج في جلد ثور ثم سار
بجنوده الى ارض فارس ومعه سابور على تلك من حاله فاكثر من القتل
وخراب المدائن والقرى وقطع النخل والاشجار حتى انتهى الى مدينة
جندي سابور وقد تحصن اهلها فنصب عليها المجانيق وهدم بعضها فبينا هم
كذلك ذات ليلة اذ غفل الروم الموكلون بحراسة سابور وكان بقربه
قوم من سبي الاهواز فامرهم ان يلقوا على القد الذي كان عليه زيتا من زقاق
كانت بقربهم ففعلوا ذلك فلان الجلد فانسل منه ولم يزل يدب حتى دنا
من باب المدينة واخبر حراسها باسمه فادخلوه المدينة فاجتمع اليه
اهلها وسروا به سرورا كثيرا وارتفعت اصواتهم بالحمد والتسبيح
فانتبه اصحاب قيصر باصواتهم وجمع سابور من كان في المدينة وخرج
سحرا من ليلته فقتل الروم واخذ قيصر اسيرا وغنم امواله ونساءه
ثم اثقله بالحديد وامره بعمارة ما اخرب والزمه بنقل التراب من ارض
الروم الى المدائن وجندي سابور حتى يرم به ما هدم منها والزمه ان يغرس
الزيتون مكان النخل والشجر الذي عقره ثم قطع عقبه وبعث به الى
بلاد الروم على حمار وقال هذا جزاؤك ببغيك علينا ثم اقام سابور حينا
وغزا الروم فقتل من اهلها وسبى سبيا كثيرا واسكنهم مدينة بناها

مدينة طيسبون محلة سابور وظفر ببيوت امواله وخزاينه التي فيها
واجتمع الى سابور من آفاق بلاده جنوده وحارب لليانوس حتى استنقذ
منه مدينة طيسبون واختلفت الرسل بينه وبين لليانوس فاتفق
في اثناء ذلك ان لليانوس بينا هو جالس في فسطاطه والرسل يختلف بينهما
اذ جاءه سهم غرب في فواده فسقط ومات فتهال جنده لما اصابه وجمعوا
الى العابد يوسانوس وملكوه عليهم فاظهر دين النصرانية فاجابه
جنده على التدين بها وبلغ سابور الخبر كله فبعث الى قواد الروم يقول
ان الله تعالى قد امكننا منكم واذالنا عليكم بظلمكم ايانا وتخطيكم الى
بلادنا وانا نرجوا ان تهلكوا ببلادنا جوعا من غير ان نهز لقتالكم
سيفا او نشرع لكم رمحا فسرحوا الينا رئيسا ان كنتم رايتموه
عليكم فعزم يوسانوس على اتيان سابور بنفسه لما كان بينه وبينه
من اذاره والمن عليه ما لم يوافقه احد من قواده على ذلك فاستبد برايه
وجاء الى سابور في ثمانين رجلا من اشراف من في عسكره وعليه تاجه
فتلقاه سابور بنفسه وسجد كل منهما لصاحبه وتعانقا ثم اكلا ونعما
وانصرفا فكتب سابور الى قواد جند الروم ورؤساهم يعلمهم انهم لو
ملكوا غير يوسانوس لجرى هلاككم في بلاد فارس ولكن تمليككم
اياه ينجيكم من سطوتنا ثم قوى يوسانوس بكل جهده وقال له عند
منصرفه ان الروم قد شنوا الغارة على بلادنا وقتلوا بشرا كثيرا
وقطعوا بارض السواد من الشجر والنخل ما كان بها وخربوا عمرانها
فاما ان يدفعوا الينا قيمة ما افسدوا وخربوا واما ان يعوضونا من
ذلك نصيبين وحيزها فاجاب يوسانوس واشراف جنده الى ذلك
ودفعوا الى سابور مدينة نصيبين فلما بلغ ذلك اهلها جلوا عنها الى
مدن الروم خوفا على انفسهم من سابور لمخالفته ملتهم فنقل سابور اثني
عشر الف اهل بيت من اهل اصطخر واصبهان وكور اخر من بلاده الى
نصيبين فاسكنهم اياها وانصرف يوسانوس الى الروم وملكها قليلا

ومات

153b

153

كثيره من مع لليانوس من الجنود وشدة بصايرهم وحنق العرب و عدد
الروم والخزر هاله ذلك ووجه عيونا ياتيه باخبارهم وبلغ عدتهم
وشجاعتهم وعدتهم فاختلفت عليه اقاويل اوليك العيون مما اتوه به
من الاخبار عن لليانوس وجنده فتنكر سابور وسار في ثقاته
ليعاين عسكرهم قلت هكذا ذكر الطبري وابن مسكويه ان اسم ملك
الروم الذي قصد محاربة سابور لليانوس وذكر هروشيوش في تاريخ
الروم وهو اقعد باخبارهم من العراقيين ان قسطنطين باني قسطنطينية
واول من تنصر من ملوك الروم لما مات استخلف على الملك ابنه قسطنطين
فاقام اربعا وعشرين سنة ومات فولي الامر بعده يليان قيصر بن
قسطنطيش وكان يعبد الاوثان فعبا لمحاربة الفرس فسار وقتل في
مسيرة وكانت ولايته سنة واحدة وولي بعده يليان بن قسطنطين
قيصر سنة واحدة وغزا ارض الفرس فاحيط بعسكره فاضطر الى
مصالحة سابور ملك الفرس وانصرف فمات وولي بعده بلنتينيان بن
ابن قسطنطين قيصر فظهر ان صاحب حرب سابور انما هو يليان بن
قسطنطش وهو الثالث من ملوك الروم بعد قسطنطين المومن باني
قسطنطينية وكان مما خص سابور على نفسه وتخلص منه بحسن
الاتفاق انه لما اقترب من عسكر البطريق الذي كان على المقدمة وكان
اسمه يوسانوس ومعه العرب والخزر وجه قوما يتجسسوا له
الاخبار وياتوه بحقايقها فنذرت بهم الروم فاخذوهم ودفعوهم
الى يوسانوس فاقر جملتهم رجل واحد واخبر بالقصة على وجهها
وبمكان سابور وساله ان يوجه معه جندا فيدفع اليهم سابور فارسل
يوسانوس رجلا من بطانته الى سابور يعلمه ما القي اليه من امره وينذره
فارتحل سابور من الموضع الذي كان فيه وصار الى عسكره ثم رجع
لليانوس بمسالة العرب له فعاجل سابور وفض جموعه وقتل منهم
مقتلة عظيمة وهرب سابور فيمن بقي معه واحتوى لليانوس على

من وجد هنالك من العرب واسر ثم عطف نحو بلاد بكر وتغلب فيما بين
مملكة فارس ومناظر الروم بارض الشام فقتل من وجد بها من العرب
وسبى وطم مياههم ثم اسكن قوما من بني تغلب ومن سكن منهم البحرين
دارين والخط ومن كان من عبد القيس وطوايف بني تميم هجر ومن كان
من بكر بن وائل بكرمان وهم الذين يدعون بكر اباذ ومن كان منهم
من بني حنظلة بالرميلة من بلاد الاهواز وبنى بالسواد مدينة بزرج
سابور وهي عكبرا وبنى الانبار وبنى السوس والكرخ ثم غزا
بعد ذلك ارض الروم فسبى منها سبيا كثيرا وبنى بخراسان نيسابور ثم
هادن قسطنطين ملك الروم الذي بنى قسطنطينية وهو اول من
تنصر من ملوك الروم فلما هلك تفرق ملكه حتى قام لليانوس ملك الروم
وكان لا يدين بدين النصرانية فهدم الكنايس وقتل الاساقفة وجمع
جموعا من الروم والخزر ومن كان في مملكته من العرب ليقاتل سابور
فانتهزت العرب الفرصة في الانتقام من سابور بما كان من قتله العرب
واجتمعوا الى ليانوس وهم مايه وسبعون الف مقاتل من العرب فبعث
بهم مع بطريق له في مقدمته فساروا الى فارس حنقين موتورين
وذكر ان سابور لم يقتصر في اسرافه في قتل العرب على الانتقام ممن
اذنب وتجاوز حده بل قتل البري وسفك دما لا اثما لا يحل سفكه
وسبب ذلك ان الفرس لم تزل تتحدث ان الملك ينتقل عنهم الى قبيل من
نسل اهل كوثا وهي المدينة التي ولد بها ابرهيم الخليل عليه السلام ولذلك
اسقطوا اكثر من اهل السواد من كوثا ونهرها في ازمنة طويلة فلما كانت
غلبة العرب على اطراف فارس اوقع بهم سابور يريد استيصالهم خوفا من
انتقال الملك اليهم لانهم من ولد ابرهيم عليه السلام ولم يعلم البايس ان الله
جعل زوال ملك فارس على ايدي اصحاب محمد رسول الله صلى الله عليه وسلم
الذين هم قريش اولاد اسمعيل بن ابرهيم عليهما السلام ليقضي الله امرا
كان مفعولا واذا اراد الله بقوم سوءا فلا مرد له فلما انتهى الى سابور

كثره

طمع العرب في بلاد فارس

152b

152

اهله فلينصرف مأذونا له في ذلك ومن احب ان يستكمل الفضل بالصبر في موضعه
عرف له ذلك وتقدم الى من اختار الانصراف في لزوم اهله وبلاده الى
وقت الحاجة اليه فلما سمع الوزراء ذلك من قوله ورأيه استحسنوه وقالوا
لو كان قد اطال تجربة الامور وسياسة الجنود ما زاد رأيه على ما
سمعنا منه ثم تتابعت آراؤه في ثغور اصحابه وقمع اعدائه حتى تمت
له ست عشرة سنة واطاق حمل السلاح وركوب الخيل واشتد عظمه
جمع اليه رؤساء اصحابه واجناده ثم قام فيهم خطيبا فذكر الله تعالى
وذكر ما انعم به عليه وعليهم بآبائه وما اقاموا من آثارهم ونفوا من اعدائهم
وما اختل من امورهم في الايام التي مضت من ايام صباه واعلمهم انه
يستأنف العمل في الذب عن البيضة وانه عزم على الشخوص الى بعض
الاعداء لمحاربته في الف رجل من المقاتلة فنهضوا باجمعهم داعين شاكرين
وسألوه ان يقيم بموضعه ويوجه القواد والجنود ليكفوه ما قدر من
الشخوص فيه فأبى ان يجيبهم الى المقام فسألوه الازدياد على العدة
التي ذكرها فأبى ثم انتخب الف فارس من صناديد جنده وابطالهم واغنيائهم
وتقدم اليهم في المضي لامره ونهاهم عن الابقاء على العرب وعلى من لقوا منهم
ووصاهم الا يعرجوا على مال ولا غنيمة ولا يلتفتوا اليه ثم سار بهم حتى
اوقع بمن انتجع بلاد فارس من العرب وهم غارّون فقتل منهم اسرع
القتل واسر اعنف الاسر وهرب بقيتهم ثم قطع البحر في اصحابه
فورد الخطّ واستقرى بلاد البحرين يقتل اهلها ولا يقبل فداء ولا يعرج
على غنيمة ثم مضى على وجهه فورد هجر وبها ناس من تميم وبكر بن وائل
وعبد القيس فسفك فيهم من الدماء سفكا سالت كسيل المطر حتى
كان الهارب منهم يرى انه لن ينجيه غار ولا جبل ولا بحر ولا جزيرة
ثم عطف الى بلاد عبد القيس فأباد اهلها الا من هرب منهم فلحق بالرمال
ثم اتى اليمامة فقتل بها مثل تلك المقتلة ولم يمر بماء من مياه العرب الا
عوّره ولا جبّ من جبابهم الا طمّه ثم اتى قرب المدينة فقتل من وجد

قصص وانبآء وكان من امره انه لما ولد استبشر الناس بولادته وبثوا
خبره في الآفاق وكتبوا الكتب بوصية ابيه هرمز له بالملك من بعده
ووجهوا البرد بها الى الاطراف وتقلد الوزرآء والكتاب والعمال الاعمال
التي كانوا يعملونها في ايام ابيه فشاع الخبر وفشا في اطراف المملكة ان ملك
الفرس صبي يدبر ولا يدرى ما يكون منه فطمع فيهم وفي مملكتهم الروم
والترك والعرب وكانت العرب اقرب بلاد الى اعمالهم وكانوا من احوج
الامم الى تناول شيء من المعاش لسوء حالهم وشظف عيشهم فسار جمع عظيم
منهم في البحر من ناحية بلاد عبد القيس والبحرين وكاظمة حتى اناخوا
بابرشهر وسواحل اردشير خره واسياف فارس وغلبوا اهلها على
مواشيهم وحروثهم ومعايشهم واكثروا الفساد في تلك البلاد ومكثوا
بذلك حينا لا يغزوهم احد من الفرس لقلة الهيبة وانتشار الامور وكثرة
المدبرين ولان الملك طفل حتى ترعرع سابور وكان اول ما عرف من
حسن تدبيره انه استيقظ ليلة من الليالي وهو في قصر المملكة بمدينة
بطيسبون فسمع في السحر ضوضآء الناس فسال عن ذلك فقيل له هذه
ضجة الناس عند ازدحامهم على الجسر بدجلة في وقت اقبالهم وادبارهم
منه فامر باتخاذ جسر اخر حتى يكون احدهما معبرا للمقبلين والاخر معبرا
للمدبرين فلا يزدحم الناس في المرور عليهما فعقد الجسر الذي امر به قبل
غروب الشمس من يومه بحذآء الجسر القديم فاستراح الناس بعد ذلك
من المخاطرة بانفسهم في الجواز على الجسر واستبشر العظمآء بما ظهر من
فطنته على صغر سنه وكانت النجابة تتبين فيه كل يوم اضعاف ما تتبين
في غيره وجعل الوزرآء يعرضون عليه امر الدولة شيئا بعد شيء فكان مما
عرضوا عليه امر الجنود الذين في الثغور وان اكثرهم قد اختل وعظموا عليه
الامر بعد الامر فقال لهم لا يكبرن عليكم هذا فان الحيلة فيه يسيرة وامر
بالكتاب الى اولئك الجنود جميعا بانه انتهى الي طول مكثكم في النواحي التي انتم
فيها وعظم غنائكم عن اخوانكم واوليائكم فمن احب منكم الانصراف الى

اهله

151b

151

لون السما موشى وسراويله حمرا وتقعده على السرير معتمدا بيديه على سيفه
وتاجه اخضر بين شرفتي ذهب وملك ـــــ بعده اخوه
نرسي ولقبه نخجيركان بن بهرام شاه بن بهرام بن بهرام بن هرمز
بن سابور بن اردشير بن بابك فلما عقد التاج على راسه وحضر الاشراف
وعدهم خيرا وامرهم بمعاونته على امره ثم سار فيهم احسن سيرة وقال
يوم ملك انا لن نضيع شكر الله على ما انعم به علينا فاقام تسع سنين
وكان شعاره وشي احمر وسراويله موشاة على لون السما وهو معتمد
على سيفه بيديه جميعا وتاجه اخضر ثم ملك ـــــ بعده ابنه
هرمز الملقب كونده بن نرسي بن بهرام شاه بن بهرام
بن بهرام بن هرمز بن سابور الجنود بن اردشير بن بابك وكان فظا فوجل
الناس منه وخشوا غلظته وشدته فلما جلس على السرير اعلمهم انه
علم تخوفهم من شدته وقال لهم انه قد بدلت ما كان في خلقي من الفظاظة
والغلظة بالرقة والرافة ووفى بما قال ورفق بالرعية وسار فيهم
احسن سيرة وحرص على العمارة وانتعاش الضعفا واقام ملكه عشرة
سنة وقيل سبع سنين وقيل تسع سنين وخمسة اشهر وقيل ست
سنين وخمسة وانشا بلد خوزستان في كورة رامهرمز وكان شعاره
وشي احمر وسراويله موشاة بلون السما وتقعده معتمدا على سيفه
وتاجه اخضر ومات عن غير ولد فشق على الناس خروج الملك عن ذريته
وفحصوا عن نسائه فوجدوا بامراة منهن حملا فعقدوا التاج على بطنها
وقيل انه اوصى بالملك لما في بطن امه فولدت تلك المراة
سابور وهو ذو الاكتاف بن هرمز بن نرسي بن
بن بهرام بن بهرام بن سابور الجنود بن اردشير بن بابك وكان
لقب شابور هويه سنبا ومعنى هويه الكتف ومعنى سنبا نقاب
فقالت العرب ذو الاكتاف وذكر انه غزا العرب وكان ينقب اكتافهم
فيجمع بين كتفي الرجلين منهم بحلقة ويخلي عنهما ولسابور هذا

وابنه هرمز بن بهرام بن هرمز بعد مهلك عمرو بن عدي بن نصر بن ربيعة على ربيعة
ومضر وسائر بادية العراق والجزيرة والحجاز امرؤ القيس البدء بن عمرو
ابن عدي وهو اول من تنصر من ملوك آل نصر بن ربيعة وعمال الفرس وكان
في قول هشام بن محمد الكلبي في عمله مائة واربع عشرة سنة منها في زمن
سابور ارذشير ثلثا وعشرين سنه وشهرا وفي زمان سابور ارذشير
سنه وعشرة ايام وفي زمن بهرام بن هرمز بن سابور ثلث سنين وثلثة
اشهر وثلثة ايام وفي زمان بهرام بن بهرام بن هرمز ثماني عشرة سنة

بهرام شاه بن بهرام بن هرمز بن ارذشير بابك
ولي بعد ابيه بهرام بن هرمز فلما عقد التاج على راسه دعا العظما له بمثل ما كانوا
يدعون لابائه فرد عليهم ردا حسنا واحسن فيهم السيرة وكان ذا علم
بالامور وقال ان ساعدنا الدهر نقبل ذلك بالشكر وان يكن غير ذلك
نرض بالقسم فاقام ملكا ثلثا وعشرين سنه وقيل سبع عشرة سنه وقيل
ثماني عشرة سنه وكان شعاره احمر موشى وسراويله خضرا وتاجه على
لون السما بين شرفتي ذهب وهلال ذهب يقعد على سريره وفي يمينه
قوس موترة وفي يسراه ثلث نشابات وملك بعده ابنه

بهرام ويقال له بهرامان شكانشاه بن بهرام شاه بن
ابن بهرام بن هرمز بن سابور بن ارذشير بن بابك وانما قيل له شكانشاه
لان الفرس كان ملكهم اذا جعل ابنه او اخاه ولي عهده لقبه
بشاهية بلد فيدعى بذلك الملقب طول حياة ابيه او اخيه فاذا استقل
بالملك الملقب سمي شاهنشاه وعلى هذا اجرى امر بهرام الملقب كرمانشاه
وكان انوشروان يلقب في حياة ابيه قباذ تغز شخوار كرشاه وهو
الملك على طبرستان لان تغز اسم الجبل وفذشخوار اسم السهل والسيخ
وكر اسم التلال والهضاب وشكان اسم لسجستان ولما عقد التاج على
راسه واجتمع العظما دعوا له بالبركة في الولاية وطول العمر فرد عليهم احسن
الرد وكان قبل ان يفضي الملك اليه ملكا على سجستان وكان شعاره في

لون

150b

150

صلوات في كل يوم وليلة واوجب عليهم ان يستقبلوا في صلاتهم الشمس بعد مسح
الاعضا بالما وحرم عليهم عبادة الاصنام واكل اللحوم باسرها وتحريم
شرب الخمر والاعراض عن الكذب وتحريمه وتحريم الزنا والقتل والسرقة
والسحر واوجب تعظيم يوم الاحد على العامة وتعظيم يوم الاثنين على الخاصة وله زيادة على ما
فلما كانت ايام بهرام بن هرمز جمع له العلما فناظروه لانه قام عليه ودعاه
الى دينه فاجابه وطلب منه ان يجمع له اصحابه المانوية ليعرفهم فجمعهم له وعند
ما ناظره علما المجوس من فارس حجوه والزموه الحجة على روس الملا فامر به
بهرام فقتل وسلخ جلده وحشي تبنا وعلق على باب مدينة جندي سابور و
وتتبع المانوية فقتلوا حيث وجدوا وكان قتله بعد مضي [illegible] من سنة اربع
وستين وخمسماية من سني الاسكندر فلبث المجوس وتزعم المانوية انه
قبل ما ان ارتفع الى جنان النور فخلفه من بعده سيس الامام وتوارثت
خلفه من بعد سيس جماعة وكانت امامتهم لا تتم الا ببابل ولا يجوز ان يكون
الامام بغيرها فلما كانت الملة الاسلامية وتمزق ملك فارس قويت المانوية
وبلاد الترك الى العراق وكثروا في ايام خالد بن عبد الله القسري ايام ملك
امية فكان خالد الكاتب يعني بهم ولم يزالوا الى ايام المامون والمعتصم واخرجوا
من العراق غير مرة اخرها في ايام المقتدر فلحقوا بخراسان واستتر من بقي
منهم واجتمع من المانوية بسمرقند نحو الخمسمائة فاراد صاحب خراسان
قتلهم فبعث ملك الصين فيهم وهدد انه ان قتل منهم احد قتل من في مملكته
الصين من المسلمين فكف عنهم واخر ما عرف من المانوية ببغداد في ايام
معز الدولة ابن بويه نحو ثلثمائة نفس ثم تفانوا حتى لم يبق منهم قبل الاربعمائة
من سني الهجرة الا خمسة نفر ولا اعلم اليوم احدا ينتحل مذهبهم [illegible]
وكان شعار بهرام احمر وسراويله حمرا وتاجه على لون السما وعليه
شرف فيه ذهب وفي يده اليمنى رمح وفي اليسرى سيف وهو معتمد
عليه وملك بعده ابنه بهرام الثاني فكان ملكه تسع سنين وفي نسخة ثلث
ثلث سنين وثلثة اشهر وثلثة ايام وكان عامل سابور على اردشير بابكان

من جهته وكانت امرأته حاملة بماني فلما ولدته كانت ترى له المنامات الحسنة
وكانت ترى كأنه اخذ منها وصعد به الى السماء ثم يرد فربما بقي مع ابيه
فتق على ملته وصار يتكلم في صغره بالحكمة فلما بلغ تمام اثني عشر سنة
زعم انه اتاه الوحي من ملك جنان النور وهو الله تعالى وكان الملك الذي اتاه
بالوحي يسمى التوم ومعناه القرين بالعربية فقال له التوم مما جاء به من
الوحي اعتزل هذه الملة فلست من اهلها وعليك بالنزاهة وترك الشهوات
ولم يأن لك ان تظهر لحداثة سنك فلما تم له اربع وعشرون سنة اتاه التوم
فقال قد حان لك ان تخرج فتنادي بامرك فخرج في اليوم الذي ملك فيه سابور
ابن اردشير بابك وهو يوم الاحد اول نيسان والشمس في برج الحمل
وخرج معه رجلان قد تبعاه على دينه وهما شمعون وزكوا وخرج
معه ابوه فتق وكان قد ظهر قبله بنحو مائة سنة مرقيون ثم ظهر
ابن ديصان بعد مرقيون بنحو ثلاثين سنة وقيل له ابن ديصان لانه ولد
على نهر يقال له ديصان وادعى ماني انه الفارقليط الذي بشر به المسيح عيسى
ابن مريم عليه السلام واستخرج ملته من المجوسية والنصرانية وجال في
البلاد اربعين سنة يدعو الناس فكان ممن دعاه فاستجاب له على يد
فيروز اخو سابور بن اردشير بابك فاوصله الى اخيه سابور الجنود
فلما دخل عليه كبر في عينه وبالغ في تعظيمه بعدما كان قد عزم على قتله
بعدما وقعت عينه عليه داخلته له هيبة وسر به فسأله سابور عن
مذهبه ووعده ان يعود اليه بعدما سأله ان يعز اصحابه في جميع مملكته
وان يسيروا حيث شاؤوا فاجابه سابور الى ذلك وكان ماني قد دعا
اهل الهند والصين وخراسان فاستجاب له خلق كثير وخلف على كل
ناحية رجلا من ثقات اصحابه يقوم بامر شريعته وكان من شريعته ان
مبدأ العالم من اصلين هما النور والظلمة فالنور هو الله تعالى والظلمة هي
الشيطان وله في صفة الاله تعالى وفي كيفية بدو التناسل ووجود
المخلوقات وكيف تسلك طريقته كلام طويل وعرض على قوم ممتنع

صلوات

149

ابنه اردشير وولى ابنه هرمز خراسان وبعثه اليها فاستقل عمله بقوة
وجمع من كان يليه من ملوك الامم وزاد في التجبر فوشي به الى سابور انه يريد
الامر لنفسه وانه ان دعاه للحضور لم يحضر فبلغ ذلك هرمز فخلا بنفسه
وقطع يده وحسمها والقى عليها ما يحفظها وادرجها في ثوب نفيس وبعث
بها في سفط الى سابور وكتب اليه يعلمه بما نقل اليه عنه وانه فعل بيده
ما فعل ليزيل عنه التهمة وذلك انه كان من رسم الفرس الا يملكوا ذا عاهة
فلما وصل ذلك الى سابور تقطع اسفا وحسرة وكتب الى هرمز بما اصابه
من الغم واعتذر اليه واعلمه انه لو قطع بدنه عضوا عضوا لم يقدم عليه احدا
فلما مات سابور وعقد التاج على راس هرمز دعاه العقلاء فاحسن جوابهم
ووعدهم بالخير وكانوا يعرفون منه صدق الحديث فاحسن السيرة فيهم
وعدل في رعيته وسلك سبيل ابائه وكور كورة رام هرمز وكان شعاره
احمر موشى وسراويله اخضر وتاجه ايضا اخضر في ذهب وبيده اليمنى
رمح وفي يساره ترس وكانت مدة ملكه سنة وعشرة اشهر وفي نسخة سنتين
بهرام بن هرمز البطل بن سابور الجنود بن اردشير بابكان
وكان يلقب بيرد خارحام ملك فارس بعد موت ابيه هرمز البطل فظهر عن حلم
وتؤدة فاستبشر الناس بولايته فاحسن السيرة واتبع في سياسة
الناس اثار ابائه وقتل ماني الزنديق وداعيتهم بعدما هرب سنين وكان
ماني بن فتق بن بيتك من الحسكانية وامه ميس ويقال
اوتاخيم ويقال مارمريم من الاشغانية كان اسقفا وكان احنف الرجل
اليمنى واصله من همذان ونزل المداين في بيت الاصنام فكان
يحضرها كما يحضر الناس فهتف به ذات يوم هاتف يا فتق لا تاكل
لحما ولا تشرب خمرا ولا تنكح بشرا وكرر ذلك عليه دفعات في ثلثة
ايام فسار حتى نزل بقوم في نواحي دستميسان يعرفون بالمغتسلة
وهم من فرق الصابية يغسلون جميع ما ياكلونه ولهم اراء شنيعة
وهم ممن يقول بالاصلين كما يقول المانوية ويعظمون النجوم فاقام فيهم وتبع

المدن على تصوير اشيا وكانت مدينة السوس على صورة باز ومدينة تستر على صورة
فرس وكان شعار سابور اسمانجون وسراويله وشي احمر وتاجه احمر
في خضرة وهو قائم بيده رمح وهو اول من سكن الحيرة
هرمز البطل الجري بن سابور الجنود بن اردشير
ابن بابك عهد اليه ابوه عند ما حضره الموت وكان يشبه في عظم خلقه و
جزالته باردشير جده الا انه غير لاحق به في رايه وتدبيره وله اخبار
عظيمة وكانت امه من بنات مهرك الملك الذي قتله اردشير بن بابك وتتبع
نسله فقتلهم لان المنجمين اخبروه انه يكون من نسله من يملك فهربت ام هرمز
الى البادية وكانت ذات عقل وجمال وكمال فوقعت عند بعض الرعاة حتى
خرج سابور يوما متصيدا فامعن في طلب الصيد واشتد به العطش فراى
اخبية فقصدها وقد غاب الرعاة عنها فطلب الماء فناولته امراة ماء
فراى جمالا فائقا وقواما حسنا وبيانا فهو يتاملها اذ حضر الرعاة
فسالهم عنها فادعى بعضهم انها ابنته فساله ان يزوجه بها فاجابه
الى ذلك فصار بها الى منزله وامر بها فاصلح شانها وخلا بها فامتنعت
عليه مرارا حتى عجب من قوتها فلما طال عليه امرها وفحص عنها اخبرته
انها انما هي ابنة مهرك وانها انما فعلت ما فعلت خوفا عليه من اردشير
فعاهدها على ستر امرها عن ابيه ووطئها فولدت له هرمز في ستر
وخفية حتى اتت له سنون فاتفق ان اردشير ركب يوما وعاد من طريقه على
ابنه سابور منزله على حين غفلة فراى هرمز وقد ترعرع وبيده صولجان
يلعب به وهو يصيح في اثر الكرة فانكره واخذ يتامله فراى المشابه
فيه وكانت صفات آل اردشير لا تخفى بعلامات فيهم من حسن الوجوه
وعبالة الخلق فاستدناه وسال سابور عنه فخر له ساجدا واعترف
بالخطا وحدثه بما كان منه فسر اردشير وقال الان تحقق ما ذكره
المنجمون من تملك ولد مهرك وان الذي يملك منهم انما هو هرمز اذ كانت امه
من نسل مهرك والان قد زال ما كان في نفسي من ذلك فلما مات سابور بعد
ابيه

148

ومصرع ضيزن وبني ابيه واجلوا من الكتايب من تزيد
اتاه بالفيول مجللات وبالابطال سابور الجنود
فهدم من اواسي الحضر صخرا كان ثقاله زبر الحديد

واخرب سابور المدينة واحتمل النضيرة فاعرس بها بعين التمر فذكر انها
لم تزل ليلتها تتضور من خشونة فرشها وكانت الفرش من حرير حشوه القز
وقيل كان حشوه زغب الطير فالتمس ما كان يوذيها فاذا ورقة
آس ملتزقة بعكنة من عكنها قد اثرت فيها ويقال كان ينظر الى مخها
في ساقها من لين بشرتها فقال لها سابور ويحك باي شي كان يغذوك
ابوك قالت بالزبد والمخ وشهد الابكار من النحل وصفو الخمر قال وابيك
لانا احدث عهدا بك واوتر لك من ابيك الذي غذاك بما تذكرين ثم اركب
رجلا فرسا جموحا وربط غدايرها بذنبه ثم استركضها فقطعها
قطعا فذلك قول الشاعر

اقفر الحضر من نضيرة فالمرباع منها فجانب الثرثار

وقد اكثر الشعرا من ذكر الضيزن هذا في اشعارهم واياه عنا عدي
ابن زيد العبادي في قصيدة

واخو الحضر اذ بناه واذ دجلة تجبى اليه والخابور

وذكر حمزة ان سابور الجنود ملك بعد اردشير بابكان اثنتين وثلثين
سنة واربعة اشهر وفي نسخة ثلثين سنة وخمسة عشر يوما وفي اخرى
ثلثين سنة وشهرا الا يومين وفي ايامه ظهر ماني الزنديق وسابور
هو الذي بنى شادروان تستر احد عجايب الدنيا وانشا مدنا منها نيشابور
من مدن فارس وعربت فقيل نيسابور وكانت مدينة من انشا طهمورث
خربها الاسكندر فبنى اسمها ومنها فيروز شابور وتسمى بالعربية
الانبار من مدن العراق ومنها انديو شابور من مدن خورستان وعربت
فقيل جندي سابور واشتقه بالفارسية الخير من انديو اسم انطاكية
وبه اسم الخير فكون المعنى خير من انطاكية وبناها على صورة رقعة
الشطرنج تخترقها في وسطها ثمانية طرق في ثمانية طرق وكانوا يلقبون

وجعله غيره سابور بن اردشير بن بابك وهو اول من جمع ملك فارس وازال
ملوك الطوائف حتى دان الكل له والضيزن كان من ملوك الطوائف فيبعد
ان يكون هذه القصة لسابور ذي الاكتاف وهو سابور بن هرمز لانه
كان بعد سابور الاكبر بدهر طويل وبينهما ملوك وهم هرمز بن سابور
وبهرام بن هرمز وبهرام بن بهرام وبهرام الثالث ونرسي بن بهرام وبعده
كان ابنه سابور ذو الاكتاف وقول الاعشى شاهبور الجنود فخفض
الدال يدل على انه ليس بشاهبور ذي الاكتاف ثم ان النضيرة بنت
الضيزن عركت اي حاضت فاخرجت الى ربض المدينة وكانت من اجمل نساء
زمانها وكانت سنتهم في الجارية اذا حاضت اخرجوها الى الربض وكان
سابور من اجمل رجال زمانه فرأى كل واحد منهما صاحبه فعشقته
وعشقها فارسلت اليه ما تجعل لي ان دللتك على ما تهدم به سور هذه
المدينة وتقتل ابي فقال حكمك وارفعك على نسائي واخصك بنفسي دونهن
فاختلف في السبب الذي دلته عليه فقال ابن اسحق فلما امسى ساطرون
شرب حتى سكر فاخذت مفاتيح باب الحضر من تحت راسه فبعثت بها مع
مولى لها ففتح الباب فدخل سابور فقتل ساطرون واستباح الحضر وخربه
وسار بها معه فتزوجها وقال المسعودي دلته على نهر واسع كان يدخل
منه الماء الى الحضر فقطع لهم الماء ودخلوا منه وقال الطبري قالت له
بحمامة ورقاء مطوقة فاخضب رجليها بحيض جارية بكر زرقاء ثم ارسلها
فانها تقع على حائط المدينة فتقع المدينة وكان ذلك طلسم المدينة لا
يهدمها غيره ووعدته النضيرة ان تسقي
الحرس الخمر فاذا صرعوا قتلهم ودخل المدينة ففعل سابور ذلك
فسقطت الاسوار ودخلها عنوة وقتل الضيزن فابيدت قضاعة الذين
كانوا مع الضيزن حتى لم يبق منهم باق واصيبت قبائل من حلوان
فانقرضوا وقال عمرو بن الة (?) وفي نسخة ابن آلة يذكر من هلك (?) في تلك الوقعة
الم تخبرك والانباء تنمى بما لاقت سراة بني العبيد (?)

147

الاهدي حوثره بن الحجاج وعند السهيلي حنظلة بن شرقي وفي كلامه قوله من ابيات

وارى الموت قد تدلى من الحضر على رب اهله الساطرون

صرعته الايام من بعد ملك ونعيم وجوهر مكنون

والساطرون بالسريانية هو الملك واسمه الضيزن بن معاوية بن العبيد بن

الاجرام بن عمرو بن النخع بن سليح بن حلوان بن الحاف بن قضاعة قال ابن

الكلبي هو قضاعي من العرب الذين تنخوا بالسواد فسموا تنوخ اي

اقاموا بها وهم قبايل شتى وام الضيزن جيهلة وبها كان يعرف وهي

ايضا قضاعية من بني تزيد بالتاء المثناة من تحت وقال ابو جعفر الطبري ان

الضيزن جرمقاني وكان من ملوك الطوايف يقدمهم اذا اجتمعوا لحرب عدو

من غيرهم وملك ارض الجزيرة وكان معه من بني عبيد بن الاجرام وقبايل قضاعة

ما لا يحصى وبلغ ملكه الشام وتطرف بعض السواد في غيبة سابور بخراسان

وفي ذلك يقول عمرو بن الة بن الرهاب بن عنم بن حلوان بن عمران بن الحاف بن قضاعة

لقيناهم بجمع من علاف وبالخيل الصلادم الذكور

فلاقت فارس منا نكالا وقتلنا هرابذ شهرزور

دلفنا للاعاجم من بعيد بجمع من الجزيرة كالسعير

وقوله من الجزيرة يريد من الجزيرة فلما اخبر سابور بما كان من الضيزن

شخص اليه حتى اناخ على الحضر وقد تحصن به فزعم ابن الكلبي ان سابور اقام

عليه اربع سنين لا يقدر على هدمه ولا الوصول الى الضيزن وذكر ابن هشام

ان الذي غزا ساطرون ملك الحضر سابور ذو الاكتاف وحصره سنتين قال

السهيلي وذكر الاعشى في شعره حولين لا يقدر على فتح الحضر حيث

يشير الى قول الاعشى اي بصير ميمون بن قيس بن جندل بن شراحيل بن عوف

ابن سعد بن ضبيعة بن قيس بن ثعلبة وهو الحصن بن عكابة بن صعب بن علي

ابن بكر بن وايل الملقب الصناجة الم تر للحضر اذ اهله بنعمى وهل خالد من نعم

اقام به شاهبور الجنود حولين تضرب فيه القدم

قال السهيلي غير ان ابن اسحق قال ان المستبيح للحضر سابور ذو الا

وعقد له التاج من بعده قبلا منه اهل فارس في حياة ابيه عقلا وفضلا
وعلما وشدة بطش وبلاغة منطق ورافة بالرعية على ان سابور شبير
وعقد التاج على راسه اجتمع اليه العظماء فدعوا له بطول البقاء واطنبوا
في ذكر والده وبثوا فضايله فقال لهم انهم لم يكونوا يستدعون احسانه
بشيء يعدل عندي ذكرهم اياه بخير ووعدهم الخير ثم امر بما في الخزائن من
الاموال فوسع بها على الناس من الجنود والوجوه واهل الحاجة وكتب
الى عماله بالكور والنواحي فيفعلوا مثل ذلك في الاموال التي كانت بها فعم
احسانه البعيد والقريب والخاص والعام والشريف والوضيع ثم
تخير العمال واستقصى النظر في امورهم وامور الرعية فبان لكل احد فضله
وحسن سيرته فانتشر ذكره في الافاق حتى فاق جميع الملوك ثم سار
الى مدينة نصيبين وهي احدى عشرة مدينة من مملكته وبها جنود الروم فحاصرهم
مدة ثم رحل عنها لحادث اتاه خبره بخراسان حتى احكم امره ثم عاد اليها
نصيبين فنزل عليها فاتفق ان سور المدينة تصدع وانفرجت منه فرجة
فدخل منها وقتل المقاتلة وسبى واخذ الاموال وكانت عظمته ثم سار الى
الشام وبلاد الروم ففتح مدنا كثيرة واخذ ملك انطاكية بعد ما حاصرها
مدة حتى ملكها وساقه مع من ساق من الاسرى حتى اسكنه جندي سابور
وجعل ملك انطاكية يبني شاذروان تستر بنفسه على ان يجعل عرضه
الف ذراع فبناه الرومي بقوم اشخصهم اليه من الروم فلما تم بناؤه جدع انفه
واطلقه وقيل قتله وكان بجبال تكريت بين الموصل والفرات مدينة
يقال لها الحضر والحضر حصن عظيم كالمدينة على شاطئ الفرات وهو
الذي ذكره عدي بن زيد العبادي في قوله من قصيدة

واخو الحضر اذ بناه واذ دجلة تجبى اليه والخابور
شاده مرمرا وجلله كلسا فللطير في ذراه وكور
لم يهبه ريب المنون فباد الملك عنه فبابه مهجور

وذكره ابو دواد الايادي واسمه عند المرزباني حارثة بن عمران من الحجاج وعنى

146b

146

وكانت ابنة الملك المقتول فاخفت نسبها وذكرت انها كانت خادم لبعض نسا
الملك وانها بكر فاتخذها لنفسه فعلقت منه فلما امنته اخبرته انها
من نسل اشك فنفر منها ودعا شيخا مسنا من اصحابه واخبره خبرها وامره
بقتلها فمضى بها ليقتلها فاخبرته انها حبلى فاودعها سربا في الارض وقطع
مذاكيره وجعلها في حق وختم عليه وعاد الى اردشير فاخبره انه
اودع المراة الارض ودفع اليه الحق وساله ان يختم عليه بخاتمه ويودعه
بعض خزائنه ففعل واقامت الجارية عند الشيخ حتى وضعت غلاما فسماه
شاه بور بعد ان عرف في طالعه وانه يدل على انه سيملك وغبر اردشير
دهرا لا يولد له حتى دخل اليه الشيخ الامين الذي عنده الصبي فوجده محزونا
فقال ما يحزنك ايها الملك فقال كيف لا احزن وقد ضربت بسيفي ما بين
المشرق والمغرب حتى ظفرت بحاجتي وصفا لي ملك ابائي ثم اهلك ولا
يعقبني فيه عقب ولا يكون لي فيه بقية فقال له الشيخ سرك الله ايها الملك
وعمرك لك عندي ولد طيب نفيس فادع بالحق الذي استودعتك وختمته
بخاتمك اريك برهان ذلك فدعا اردشير بالحق ثم فض خاتمه فوجد فيه
مذاكير الشيخ وكتابا فيه انا لما اختبرت فلانة التي علقت من ملك الملوك
اردشير حين امر بقتلها لم استحل اتلاف زرع الملك الطيب فاودعتها
بطن الارض كما امر ملكنا وتبرات اليه من نفسي لئلا يجد عائب الى عيبها سبيلا
فامر اردشير ان يجعل الغلام مع مائة غلام وقيل مع الف غلام من اترابه واشباهه
في الهيئة والقامة ثم يدخلهم عليه جميعا حتى لا يفرق بينهم زي ففعل الشيخ
ذلك فعندما نظر اليهم اردشير قبلت نفسه ابنه من بينهم فامر ان
يعطوا صوالجة ويخرجوا تجاه الايوان فلعبوا جميعا بالكرة وهو
في الايوان على سريره فدخلت الكرة الايوان فلم يجسر احد من الغلمان
اليه واقدم سابور من بينهم فدخل الايوان فاستدل اردشير بدخوله عليه
واقدامه وجراته مع ما كان من قبول نفسه له حين راه ورقته له دون
اصحابه انه ابنه فقال له ما اسمك فقال شاه بور فعند ذلك شهر امره

المعروف بالغش قد خلفت لكم رأيا اذ لم استطيع تخليفه بدنا وقد حبوتكم
بما حبوت به نفسي وقضيت حقكم فيما آتيتكم به من رأيي فاقتصوا حقي
بالتشفيع لي في صلاح انفسكم والتمسك بعهدي اليكم فانه قد عهدت اليكم
عهدا وفيه صلاح جميع ملوككم وعامتكم وخاصتكم ولن تضيعوا ما
احتفظتم بما رسمت لكم ما لم تضيعوا غيره فاذا تمسكتم به كان علامة في
بقائكم ما بقي الدهر ولولا اليقين بالبوار النازل على رأس الالف من السنين
لظننت اني قد خلفت فيكم ما ان تمسكتم به كان علامة في بقائكم ما بقي الدهر ولكن
القضاء اذا جاءت ايامه اطعتم اهواءكم واستعملتم ولاتكم وامنتم وتنقلتم
عن مراتبكم وعصيتم خياركم وكان اصغر ما تخطون فيه سلما الى اكبر منه
حتى تنقضوا ما رتقنا وتضيعوا ما حفظنا والحق علينا وعليكم الا
تكونوا للبوار اغراضا وفي الشرع اعلاما فان الدهر اذا اتى بالآلاء تنظرون
الكيف من حرمته ونحن ندعوا الله لكم بنما المنزلة وبقا الدولة دعوة لا يغيبها
فما قابلها من المنقلب ونسال الله الذي يجعل بنا وخلفتكم ان يرعاكم رعاية
يرعى بها ما تحت يد اكرم ويحوطكم حياطة يحفظ بها منزلتكم وانتم تستودعكم
الله وديعة يكفيكم بها الدهر الذي يبتليكم الى زواله وتغيره وعليه
والسلام على اهل الموافقة ممن يات عليه العهد من الامم الكاينة بعدي ۝

سابور الجنود بن اردشير بن بابك كان يلقب نبرده
فلما اكثر من الغزو قيل له سابور الجنود قام بملك فارس بعد ابيه اردشير
وله قصص وانبا منها ان اردشير بن بابك لما افضى اليه الملك اسرف في قتل
الاشكانية من ملوك الطوائف حتى افناهم بسبب ان ساسان الاكبر بن
بهمن كان آلى الية انه ان ملك يوما من الدهر لم يبق من نسل اشك بن
احدا واوجب ذلك على عقبه واوصاهم الا يبقوا منهم احدا ان هم ملكوا منهم
احد ملكا وان ملك من نسل ساسان اردشير فقتلهم جميعا رجالهم ونساءهم
بحيث لم يبق منهم احدا غير جارية وجدها في دار المملكة فاعجبه حسنها

وكانت

145b

145

الملك واخاه وعمه وابن عمه كلهم يقول حدثت ان اكون ملكا وبالحرى الا اموت حتى
اكون ملكا فاذا قال ذلك قائل قال ما لا يسر الملك فان كتمه فالداء في كل مكتوم وان
اظهره كلم في قلب الملك كلما يكون لقاحا للتباين والتعادي وستجد القائل
ذلك من المتابعين والمحتملين والمتمنين ما تمنى لنفسه ما يريه انه الى مسا
اشتاق اليه شوقا فاذا تمكن في صدره الامل لم يرج النيل له الا في
اضطراب الحبل وزعزعة تخطي الملك واهل المملكة فاذا تمنى ذلك فقد جعل
الفساد سلما الى الصلاح ولم يكن الفساد سلما الى صلاح قط وقد رسمت
لكم في ذلك مثالا لا مخرج لكم منه الا به اجعلوا اولاد الملك من بنات
عمومتهم ثم لا يصلح من اولاد بنات الاعمام الا كامل غير سخيف العقل ولا
عازب الراي ولا ناقص الجوارح ولا معيوب عليه في دين فانكم اذا فعلتم
ذلك قل طلاب الملك واذا قل طلابه استراح كل امرء الى ما يليه وعرف
حاله وغض بصره ورضي معيشته واستطاب زمانه واعلموا انه سيقول
قائل من عرض رعيتكم او من ذوي قرابتكم ما لاحد علي فضل ولو كان
لي ملك فاذا قال ذلك فانه قد تمنى الملك وهو لا يشعر ويوشك ان يتمناه بعد
ذلك وهو يشعر فلا يرى ذلك من رايه خطلا ولا من فعله زللا وانما يستخرج
ذلك فراغ القلب واللسان مما يكلف اهل الدين والكتاب والحساب
او فراغ اليد مما يكلف الاساورة او فراغ البدن مما يكلف التجار والمهنة
والخدم واعلموا ان الملك ورعيته جميعا يحق عليهم الا يكون للفراغ عندهم
موضع فان التضييع في فراغ الملك وفساد المملكة في فراغ الرعية
واعلموا انا على فضل قوتنا واجابة الامور ايانا وجدة دولتنا وشدة
باس انصارنا وحسن نية وزرائنا لم نستطع احكام تفتيش الناس
حتى بلغنا من الرعية مكروهها ومن انفسنا مجهودها واعلموا انه لا بد
من سخط سيحدث منكم على بعض اعوانكم المعروفين بالنصيحة لكم ولا بد من
رضى سيحدث لكم من بعض اعدائكم المعروفين بالغش لكم فلا تحدثوا
عند ما يكون من ذلك انقباضا عن المعروف بالنصيحة ولا استرسالا الى

ذلك وكثير ممن معه تحرّيا للدين فان اراد الملك هوانهم لم يعرف لهم ذنبا
يهانون عليه وان اراد اكرامهم فهي منزلة حبوا بها انفسهم على رغم
الملوك وان اراد اسكاتهم كان السماع في ذلك انه استثقل ما عندهم من
حفظ الدين وان امروا بالكلام قالوا انما يفسد ولا يصلح فاولئك اعداء
الدول وآفات الملوك فالراي للملوك تقريبهم من الدنيا فانهم اليها اجروا وفيها عملوا
ولها سعوا واياها ارادوا فاذا تلوثوا فيها بدت فضائحهم والآفات فيما يحرس
ما يجعل للملوك سبيلا الى سفك دمائهم وكان بعض الملوك يقول القتل اقل
للقتل وفي الرعية صنف اتوا الملوك من قبل النصائح لهم والتمسوا اصلاح
منازلهم بافساد منازل الناس فاولئك اعداء الناس واعداء الملوك ومن عادى
الملوك وجميع الناس الرعية فقد عادى نفسه واعلموا ان الدهر حاملكم على
طبقات فمنهن حال السخاء حتى تدنوا من السرف ومنهن حال التقتير حتى تقرب
من البخل ومنهن حال الاناة حتى تصير الى البلادة ومنهن حال المناهزة حتى
تدنوا من الخفة ومنهن حال الطلاقة في اللسان حتى تدنوا من الهذر ومنهن
حال الاخذ بحكم الصمت حتى تدنوا من العي فالملك منكم جدير ان يبلغ من كل طبقة في
محاسنها حدّها فاذا وقف على الحدود التي ما وراها سرف الجم نفسه عما
وراها واعلموا ان الملك منكم ستعرض له شهوات في غير ساعاتها والملك
اذا قدّر ساعة العمل وساعة الفراغ وساعة المطعم وساعة المشرب
وساعة الفضيلة وساعة اللهو كان جديرا الا يعرف منه الاستقدام
بالامور ولا الاستيخار عن ساعاتها فان اختلاف ذلك يورث مضرتين
احداها السخف وهي اشد الامرين والاخرى نقص الجسد بنقص اقواته
وحركاته واعلموا ان من ملوككم من سيقول لي الفضل على من كان قبلي من
ابائي وعمومتي ومن ورثت عنه هذا الامر لبعض الاحسان يكون منه فاذا
قال ذلك شنوعي عليه بالمتابعة له فليعلم ذلك الملك ان المتابعين انما صنعوا
ايديهم والسنتهم في قصب ابائه من الملوك وهم لا يشعرون وكيا يحوي ان
يشعر بعض المتابعين له فيغمض على ما يجزيه من ذلك واعلموا ان اب

الملك

144

العضب والحرص والزهو فلا تكونوا الى شي من ساعات الدهر اشد قناة منكم
عند هن حتى يتقشعن وكان يقال اتق مقارنة الحريص الغادر فانه ان راك في
الغرب راي منك اخبث حالاتك وان راك في الفضول لم يدع عليك فضولك
اشبعه والراي على الهوى فان ذلك تمليك للراي واعلموا انه من شان الراي
الاستخذا للهوى اذا جرى الهوى على عادته وقد عرفنا رجالا كان الرجل
منهم يونس من قوة طباعه ونباله رايه ما يثربه نفسه انه على ازاحة الهوى
عنه وان جرى على عادته ومعاودته الراي وان طال به عهده قادر لثقته
بجدها بقوة الراي فاذا تمكن الهوى منه فسخ عزم رايه حتى تسميه كثير من
الناس ناقصا في العقل فاما البصرا فيستبينون من عقله عند غلبة الهوى
عليه ما يستبان من الارض الطيبة الموات واعلموا ان في الرعية صنفا
من الناس هم باساءة الوالي افرح منهم باحسانه وان كان الوالي لم يترهم
وكان الزمان لم ينكبهم وذلك لاستطراف حادثات الاخبار فان استطراف
الاخبار معروف من اخلاق حشو الناس ثم لا طرفة عندهم فيما يجمعوا في ذلك
سرور لكل عدو لهم ولعامتهم معا وتروا به لنفسهم ولا تهم فلا دوا لاوليك
الا بالاشغال وفي الرعية صنف وتروا الناس كلهم وهم الذين قووا
على جفوة الولاة ومن قوي على جفوتكم فهو غير ساد ثغرا ولا مناصح
اماما ومن غش الامام فقد غش العامة وان ظن انه للعامة مناصح وكان
يقال لم ينصح عملا من غش عامله وفي الرعية صنف تركوا اتيان الملوك
من قبل ابوابهم واتوهم من قبل وزرايهم فليعلم الملك ان من اتاه من
قبل بابه فقد اثره بنصيحته اذ كانت عنده ومن اتاه من قبل وزرايه
فهو موثر للوزير على الملك في جميع ما يقول ويفعل وفي الرعية صنف دعوا
الى انفسهم الجاه بالاباء ووجدوا ذلك عند المغفلين نافقا وعلى قرب الملك
الرجل من اوليك لغير نبل في راي ولا اجزا في العمل ولكن الا باعزوه به وفي
الرعية صنف اظهروا التواضع واستشعروا الكبر فالرجل منهم يعظ
الملوك زاريا عليهم بالموعظة يجد ذلك اسهل طرق في طعنه عليهم ويسمي و

ان يكون فرحها بما نالا من ذلك واحدا وليس فضل الملك على السوقة الا بقدرته

على اقتناء المحامد واستفادة المكارم فان الملك اذا اشتغل حسن وليس

السوقة بحذر ذلك واعلموا انه يحق على الملك منكم ان يكون الطف ما يكون نظرا

اعظم ما يكون خطرا والا يذهب حسن اثره في الرعية خوفه لها

والا يستغني بتدبير اليوم عن تدبير غد وان يكون حذره للملا قبل اشره من

حذره للمباعدين وان يتقي بطانة السوء اشد من اتقائه عامة السوء

ولا يطمعن ملك في اصلاح العامة اذا لم يبدا بتقويم الخاصة واعلموا ان

لكل ملك بطانة وان لكل رجل من بطانته بطانة ثم لكل امرئ من بطانة البطانة

بطانة حتى يجتمع في ذلك اهل المملكة فاذا اقام الملك بطانته على حال الصواب

اقام كل امرئ منهم بطانته على مثل ذلك حتى يجتمع على الصلاح عامة الرعية

اعلموا ان الملك منكم قد تكون عليه العيوب لانه لا يستقبل بها وان علمها

حتى يرى ان الناس يتكاتمونها بينهم كما تكتمه اياه تلك العيوب و منها

من الابواب الداعية الى طاعة الهوى وطاعة الهوى داعية الى غلبته فاذا

غلب الهوى اشتد علاجه من السوقة المغلوب فضلا عن الملك الغالب

اتقوا بابا واحدا طالما امنته فضرني وحذرته فنفعني احذروا افشا

السر عند الصغار من اهليكم وخدمكم فانه لا يصغر احد منهم عن حمل

ذلك السر كاملا لا يفوته منه شيا حتى يضعه حيث تكرهون اما

سقطا واما غشا والسقط اكثر ذلك اجعلوا حديثكم لاهل المراتب

وحباءكم لاهل الجهاد وبشركم لاهل الدين وسركم عند من يلزمه

خير ذلك وشره وزينه وشينه اعلموا ان صحة الظنون مفاتيح اليقين

وانكم ستستيقنون بعض غيبكم بخير وشر وستظنون ببعضهم خيرا

او شرا فمهما استيقنتم منه بالخير والشر فليستيقن منكم بهما ومن ظننتموه

به فليظنها بكم في امره فعند ذلك يبدو امر المحسن احسانه مخالف

الظن فيغتبط ومن المسيء اساءته فيصدق الظن به فيندم واعلموا ان

للشيطان في ساعات من الدهر طمعا في السلطان عليكم منها ساعة

الغضب

143b

143

الامور الاخر وهو حنق على جيل من الناس يرى انه موتور ان لم يحرمهم ويضعهم
ويشنا بهم الى كانوا يرجون ابن البابه لو ولوا كان او وضع بعض الرعية
واسخط بعضا على هذه الجهة تولد من ذلك ضغن وسخط من الرعية
ثم ترامى ذلك الى بعض ما احذر عليكم بعدي ولكن ليتخير الوالي منكم لله ثم
للرعية ثم لنفسه وليا للعهد من بعده ثم يكتب اسمه في اربع صحايف
فيختمها بخاتمه فيضعها عند اربعة نفر من خيار اهل مملكته ثم لا يكون
منه في سر ولا علن امر يستدل به على ولي العهد لا في ادناء ولا تقريب يعرف
به ولا في اقصا وتنحيه يستراب له وليتق ذلك في اللحظة والكلمة
فاذا هلك جمعت تلك الكتب التي عند الرهط الاربعة الى النسخة التي عند
الملك فيفضض جميعا ثم نوه بالذي وضع اسمه في جميعهن فيلقى الملك
اذا لقيه بحداثة عهده بحال السوقة فيلبس ذلك الملك اذا لبسه بتبصر
السوقة وسمعها ورايها فان في سكر السلطان الذي يسناله ما يكتفي به
له من سكر ولاية العهد مع سكر الملك فيعم ويعمى قبل لقا الملك حكم الملوك
وعلمهم ثم يلقى الملك فيزيده صمما وعمى مع ما يلقى من ولاية العهد من بطر
السلطان وحيلة الغواة وبغي الكذابين وتمنية الباغين وتحميل
الوشاة بينه وبين من فوقه ثم اعلموا انه ليس للملك ان يكذب لانه
لا يقدر احد على استكراهه وليس له ان يغضب لان الغضب والعداوة
لقاح الشر والندامة وليس له ان يلعب ولا يعبث لان العبث واللعب
من عمل الفراغ وليس له ان يفرغ لان الفراغ من امر السوقة وليس له
ان يحسد الا الملوك الامم على حسن التدبير وليس له ان يخاف لان الخوف
من المعوز وليس له ان يتسلط اذ هو معوز واعلموا ان زين الملوك
في استقامة الحال ان لا تختلف منه ساعات العمل والمباشرة
وساعات الفراغ والدعة وساعات الركوب والنزهة فان اختلافها
منه خفة وليس للملك ان يخف اعلموا انكم لن تقدروا على ختم افواه
الناس من الطعن والازرا عليكم ولا قدرة بكم على ان تجعلوا القبيح حسنا
واعلموا ان لباس الملك ومطعمه مقارب للباس السوقة ومطعمهم وبالحرى

143a

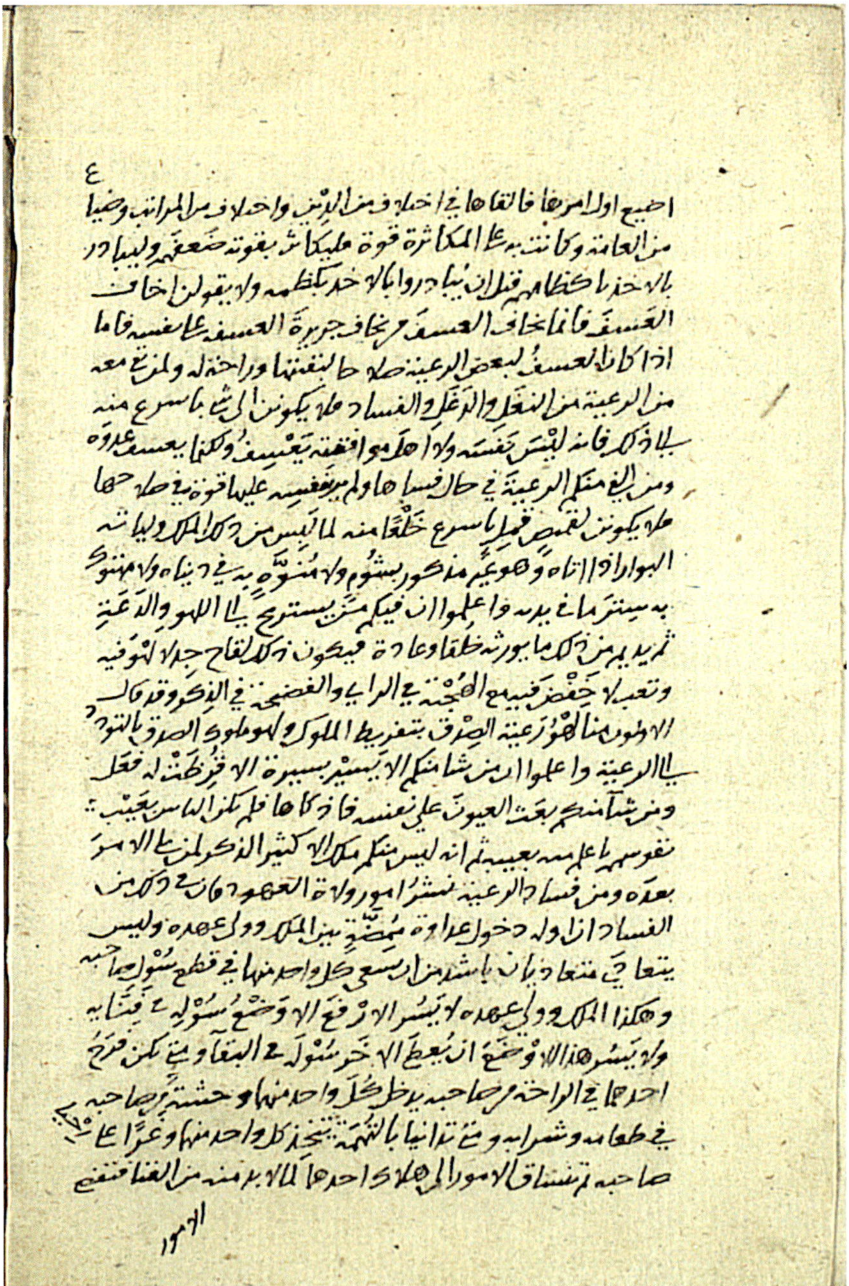

٤

أصبح أول أمرها فالتقاها في اختلاف من الزي واختلاف من المراتب وضيا
من العامة وكانت به على المكاثرة قوة عليكم اشد بقوته ضعفهم وليبادر
بالأخذ بأكظامهم قبل أن يبادروا بالأخذ بكظمه ولا يقولن إنما أخاف
التعسف فإنما يخاف التعسف من يخاف جريرة التعسف على نفسه فأما
إذا كان التعسف لبعض الرعية صلاحا لبقيتها وراحة له ولمن معه
من الرعية من النغل والدغل والفساد فلا يكونن لشيء بأسرع منه
إلى ذلك فإنه ليس بعسف ولا هو من موافقة تعسيف ولكنما يعسف عدوه
ومن البغي منكم الرعية في حال فسادها ولم يعتقد عليها قوة في صلاحها
فلا يكونن لقميص قمل بأسرع خلعا منه لما لبس من ذلك الملك ولباسه
البوار إذا أتاه وهو غير مذكور بشؤم ولا منوه به في دنياه ولا مهتوك
به ستر مما في يديه واعلموا أن فيكم من يستريح إلى اللهو والدعة
ثم يزيد من ذلك ما يورثه خلقا وعادة فيكون ذلك لقاح جدا لا توفيه
وتعبا لا خفض فيه مع العجز في الرأي والفضيحة في الذكر وقد قال
الأولون منا الهوى زعيمة الصدق بتفريط الملوك والهو ملوك الصدق بالتودد
في الرعية واعلموا أن من شأن منكم الا يبصر بسيرة الأخرى خطة له فعل
ومن شأنه منكم بعث العيون على نفسه فإذا كان ها فلم تكن الناس بعيب
نفوسهم أعلم منه بعيبه ثم إنه ليس منكم ملك إلا كثير الذكر لمن في الأمر
بعده ومن فساد الرعية نشر أمور ولاة العهود فإن في ذلك من
الفساد أن أوله دخول عداوة ممضة بين الملك وولي عهده وليس
يتعادى متعاديان بأشد من أن يسعى كل واحد منهما في قطع سؤل صاحبه
وهكذا الملك وولي عهده لا يسر الأرفع إلا وضع سؤله في بقائه
ولا يسر هذا الأوضع أن يعطي الآخر سؤله في البقاء وبين تكن فرح
أحدهما في الراحة من صاحبه يحظى كل واحد منهما وحشة من صاحبه
في طعامه وشرابه ومتى تدانيا بالتهمة يتخذ كل واحد منهما وعوا على [illegible]
صاحبه ثم تنساق الأمور إلى هلاك أحدهما لما لا بد منه من الفناء فيعفي

الأمور

142b

142

بقيتهم ثم يتولد من عداوتهم كثرتهم فان من شان العامة الاجتماع على استثقا
الولاة والنفاسة عليهم لان في الرعية المحروم والمضروب والمقام
عليه وفيه وفي حميمه الحدود والداخل عليه بعز الملك الذل في نفسه
وخاصته فكل هولا يجري الى متابعة اعدا الملك ثم يتولد من كثرتهم
ان يجبن الملك عن الاقدام عليهم فان اقدام الملك على جميع الرعية تغرير
بملكه ونفسه ويتولد من جبن الولاة عن ذا دبيب العامة تضييع الثغور
التي فيها الامم من ذوي الدين وذوي الباس لان الملك اذا سد الثغور
بخاصته المناصحين له وخلت به العامة الحاسدة المعادية لم يعد
بذلك بلايلهم في الحرس وتعوقهم في السلاح وتعليمهم المكيدة مع البغضة
فيهم عند ذلك اقوى عدو واحضره واخلقه بالظفر ولا بد من استنظار
هذا كله اذا ضيع اوله فمن الغي منكم الرعية بعدي وهي على حال
اقسامها الاربعة التي هي اصحاب الدين والحرب والتدبير والخدمة
من ذلك الاساورة صنف والعباد والنساك وسدنة النيران صنف
والكتاب والمنجمون والاطبا صنف والزراع والمهان والتجار صنف
فلا يكونن باصلاح عبيده اشد اهتماما منه باحيا تلك الحال وتفتيش ما
يحدث فيها من الاخلات ولا يكونن لانتقاله عن الملك باجزع منه من انتقال
صنف من هذه الاصناف الى غير مرتبته لان تنقل الناس عن مراتبهم
سريع في نقل الملك عن ملكه اما الى الخلع واما الى القتل فلا يكونن من شي من الاشيا
اوحش بتة من راس صار ذنبا او ذنب صار راسا او يد مشغولة
احدثت فراغا او كريم ضر او لئيم مرح فانه يتولد من تنقل الناس عن
حالاتهم ان يلتمس كل امرئ منهم اشيا فوق مرتبته فاذا انتقل اوشك
ان يرى اشيا ارفع مما انتقل اليه فيغبط وينافس وقد علمتم ان من الرعية
اقواما هم اقرب الناس من الملوك حالا وفي تنقل الناس عن حالاتهم
مطمعة للذين يلون الملوك في الملك ومطمعة للذين دون الذين يلون
الملوك في تلك الحال وهذا الفساح بوار الملك وعمن الغي منكم الرعيه وقد

الا بالاصابة في السياسة وراس اصابة السياسة ان يفتح الوالي لمن قبله من
الرعية بابين احدهما باب رقة ورحمة وبشر وتهلل وانبساط وانشراح
والاخر باب غلظة وخشنة وتعنف وتشدد وامساك ومباعدة
واقصا ومخالفة ومنع وقطوب وانقباض وتجهم الى ان يبلغ
القتل واعلموا اني لم اسم هذا الباب باب رفق وباب عنف ولكني سميتهما
جميعا باب رفق لان فتح باب المكروه مع باب الشرور هو اوشك لغلقه
حتى لا يبتلى به احد في الرعية من الا هو الغالبة للراي والفجور المستقل
للدين والسفلة الخبيثة على الوجوه بالنفاسة والحسد ما لا بد معه
ان يقرن بباب الرافة باب الغلظة وبباب الاستبقا باب القتل وقد يفسد
الوالي بعض الرعية من حرصه على صلاحها ويغلظ عليها من رقته لها
ويقتل فيها من حرصه على حياتها واعلموا ان قبلكم الاعدام الامم
قبلنا وما لكم الادب من انفسكم عيبكم ليس بحفظ ولكنه اضاعة وكيف
يجاهد العدو بقلوب مختلفة وايد متعادية وقد علمتم ان الذي بني عليه
الناس وجبلت عليه الطباع حب الحياة وبغض الموت فلا دفع ولا
منع ولا صبر ولا محاماة مع هذا الا باحد وجهين اما بنية والنية ما
لم يغدر عليه الوالي عند الناس بعد النية التي تكون في اول الدولة واما
بحسن الادب واصابة السياسة واعلموا ان بدء ذهاب الدول من
قبل اهمال الرعية بغير اشغال معروفة ولا اعمال معلومة فاذا فشا
الفراغ تولد منه النظر في الامور والفكر في الاصول فاذا نظروا
في ذلك نظروا فيه بطبائع مختلفة فتختلف بهم المذاهب وتتولد من
اختلاف مذاهبهم تعاديهم وتضاغنهم وتطاعنهم وهم في ذلك يجتمعون
في اختلافهم على بغض الملوك لان كل صنف منهم انما يجري الى فجيعة
الملك بملكه ولكنهم لا يجدون سلما الى ذلك اوثق من الدين ولا اكثر اتباعا
ولا اعز امتناعا ولا اشمل على الناس صبرا ثم تتولد من تعاديهم ان
الملك لا يستطيع جمعهم على هوى واحد فاذا انفرد ببعضهم فهو عدو

بقيتهم

141

ودولتنا احسابنا كان من ابتعاثه ايانا ما كان وبالاعتبار تتبع الغير و
تخلفنا اوجد الاعتبار منا لما استدبروا من عاجيب ما اتى علينا
اعلموا ان سلطانكم انما هو على اجساد الرعية وانه لا سلطان للملوك
على القلوب واعلموا انكم ان غلبتم الناس على ذات ايديهم فلن تغلبوهم
على عقولهم واعلموا ان العاقل سال عليكم لسانه وهو اقطع سيفيه
وان اشد ما يضر بكم من لسانه ما صرف الحيلة فيه الى الدين فكان بالدين
يحتج وللدين فيما يظهر يغضب فيكون للدين بكاؤه واليه دعاؤه وهو
اوجد للتابعين والمصدقين والمناصحين والموازرين منكم لان بغضة
الناس موكلة بالملوك ومحبتهم ورحمتهم موكلة بالضعفا المغلوبين
وقد كان من قبلنا من الملوك يحتالون لعقول من يحذرون تخريبها فان
العاقل لا تنفعه تجربته اذا اصيب عقله خرابا وكانوا يحتالون للطاعنين
بالدين على الملوك فيسمونهم المبتدعين فيكون الدين هو الذي يقتلهم ويريح
الملوك منهم ولا ينبغي للملك ان يعترف للعباد والنساك ان يكونوا اولى
بالدين ولا احدب عليه ولا اغضب له منه ولا ينبغي للملك ان يدع
النساك بغير الامر والنهي لهم في نسكهم فان خروج النساك وغير النساك
من الامر والنهي عيب على الملوك وعيب على المملكة وثلمة يتسنمها الناس
بينة الضرر للملك ولمن بعده واعلموا ان تصيير الوالي الى غير اخذانه
وبتقريبه غير وزرائه فتح لابواب المحجوب عنه علمها وقد قيل اذا
استوحش الوالي ممن لم يوطن نفسه عليه اطبقت عليه ظلم الجهالة
ومن الخوف ما تكون العامة امن ما تكون للوزرا اعلموا ان دولكم
توتى من مكانين احدهما غلبة بعض الامم المخالفة لكم والاخر فساد
ادبكم ولن يزال حريمكم من الامم محروسا ودينكم من غلبة الاديان
محفوظا ما عظمت فيكم الولاة وليس تعظيمهم بترك كلامهم ولا
الاجلال لهم بالتنحي عنهم ولا المحبة لهم بالمحبة لكل ما يحبون ولكن تعظيمهم
تعظيم اديانهم وعقولهم والاجلال لهم اجلال منزلتهم من الله ومحبتهم محبة
اصابتهم وحكايتها الصواب عنهم واعلموا انه لا سبيل الى ان يعظم الوالي

والاستعانة من الملوك ولم يختص منه الا بما يرضيه سمي تلك النعمة نعمة
خاصة ثم اكثر شيخية الدهر ومزمنة الامور نقم للسلطان يسوق المودة
ما اقام له سوق الارباح ولا يعلم ذلك الوزير والقرين انه في التماس الربح
على السلطان فساد جميع الامور وقد قال الاولون منا ان رشاد الوالي خير
للرعية من خصب الزمان واعلموا ان الملك والدين اخوان لا قوام
لاحدهما الا بصاحبه لان الدين اس الملك وعماده وصار الملك بعد
حارس الدين فلا بد للملك من اسه ولا بد للدين من حارسه فان ما لا
حارس له ضايع وان ما لا اس له مهدوم وان راس ما اخاف عليكم
مبادرة السفلة اياكم الى دراسة الدين على التهاون بهم فتحدث في الدين
رياسات مستسرات فيمن قد وترتم وجفوتم وحرمتم واخفتم وصغرتم
من سفلة الناس والرعية وحشو العامة ولم يجتمع رئيس في الدين
مسر ورئيس في الملك معلن في مملكة واحدة قط الا انتزع الرئيس في
الدين ما في يد الرئيس في الملك لان الدين اس والملك عماد وصاحب
الاس اولى بجميع البنيان من صاحب العماد وقد مضى قبلنا ملوك كان الملك
منهم يتعهد الجملة بالتفسير والجماعات بالتفصيل والفراغ بالاشغال
كتعهده جسده بقص فضول الشعر والظفر وغسل الدرن والغمر
ومداواة ما ظهر من الادواء وما بطن وقد كان من اولئك الملوك من صحة
ملكه احب اليه من صحة جسده وكان بما يخلفه من الذكر المحمود
افرح وابهج منه بما يستمتع به في حياته فتتابعت تلك الاملاك
بذلك كانهم ملك واحد وكان ارواحهم روح واحدة يمكن اولهم لاخرهم
ويصدق اخرهم اولهم يجتمع انباء اسلافهم ومواريث ارائهم وحبا
عقولهم عند الباقي منهم بعدهم فكانهم جلوس معه يحدثونه ويشاورونه
حتى كان على راس دارا بن دارا ما كان وغلبة الاسكندر على ما غلب
من ملكه وكان افساده امرنا وتفريقه جماعتنا وتخريبه عمران
مملكتنا ابلغ له فيما اراد من سفك دمائنا فلما اذن الله في جمع مملكتنا

ودوله

140

وفي بعدي واردة عليكم فيما بينكم السرور والاذى في الملك من حيث
اتيانه وانكم من يسير حب الملك صعبا فيتمنى من شماسه
وجماحه وخبطه واعتراضه بمثل الذي ينبته ومنكم من يبرث
الملك عن الجفاة المتذللين له مركبه ويجري على لسانه ويلقي
في قلبه ان قد فرغ له وجمع واكتفى وفرغ للسعي في العبث
والملاهي وان من قبله من الملوك الى التوطيد له اجروا وفي
التمكين له سعوا وان قد خص بما حرموا واعطي ما منعوا فيكثر
ان يقول مسرا ومعلنا خصوا بالعناء وخصصت بالدعة وقدموا
قبلي الى الغرر وخلفت في الثقة وهذا الباب من الابواب الى تكثير
سكون الفساد وتهاج بما فتوا باثار البلاد ويغني البصير اللطيف
ما ينهنك من الامور في ذلك فانا قد راينا الملك الرشيد السعيد
المنصور المكفي المظفر الحازم في الفرصة البصير بالعورة
اللطيف المبسوط له في العلم والعمر يجتهد فلا يعدو اصلاح ملكه
حياته الا ان تشبه به متشبه ورأينا الملك القصير عمره القريبة
مدته اذا كان سعيه بارسال اللسان بما قال واليد بما عملت بغير
تدبير يتدارك افسد جميع ما قدم له من الصلاح قبله ويخلف المملكة
خرابا على من بعده وقد علمت انكم ستبتلون مع الملك بالازواج
والاولاد والقرباء والوزراء والاخوان والانصار والاصحاب
والاعوان والمتنصحين والمتقربين والمضحكين والمزينين لكل
هوى الا قليلا اذ ياخذ لنفسه احب اليه من ان يعطي منها وانما
عمله ليسوق يومه وحياة غده فنصيحة الملوك فضل نصيحته لنفسه
وغاية الصلاح عنده صلاح نفسه وغاية الفساد عنده فسادها
يجعل نفسه في العامة والعامة في الخاصة فان خص بنعمة دون
الناس فهي عنده نعمة عامة واذا عم الناس بالنصر على العدو والعدل
في البيضة والامن على الحرم والحفظ للاطراف والرافة والمسكنة

أردوان مع مداراته لهم خائفا منهم هائبا لهم متقيا لشرهم ويجمع فيهم إحسانه
ومداراته فكف بعضهم عن بعض وكان يخدم أردوان غلام من أبناء أشراف
فارس يقال له أردشير بن بابك حتى إذا كان ليلة من الليالي وكان أردوان
رجلا عالما بصيرا بالنجوم فأبصر نجم ملك قد طلع يريد رأي دولة لمن يسلبه
ملكه ففزع أردوان لذلك وقال الشدة داخله وهو يحدث نفسه ولا
يرى أن أحدا يسمعه أي عبد من عبيدي قام الساعة فركب دابة من دوابي
بسرجي ولجامي وخرج يطلب الملك فإنه يظفر به ويسلبني ملكي وملك
أصحابي وإن جارية لأردوان سمعت منه ذلك الحديث وهو يحدث به نفسه
ولا يحسب أن أحدا يسمعه وكانت مصادقة لأردشير فانطلقت من فورها
فأخبرته بالذي سمعت من أردوان فقام من ساعته فركب الدابة التي كان يركبها
أردوان بسرجها ولجامها وسار حتى لحق باصطخر فأقام بها يدعو إلى
نفسه فاجتمع إليه أربعون رجلا من أشراف أبناء فارس فوثبوا على
صاحب اصطخر فقتلوه وذكر الهمداني خبر أردشير كله وقال ابن مسكويه
فمن أحسن ما حفظ له عهده إلى الملوك بعده وهذه نسخته

باسم ولي الرحمة من ملك الملوك أردشير بن بابك إلى من يخلفه بعقبه
من ملوك فارس السلام والعافية أما بعد فإن صنيع الملوك
على غير صنيع الرعية فالملك يطبعه العز والأمن والسرور
والقدرة على طباع الأنفة والجرأة والعبث والبطر ثم كلما
ازداد في العمر تنفسا وفي الملك سلامة زاده في هذه الطبائع
الأربعة حتى تسلمه إلى سكر السلطان الذي هو أشد من سكر
الشراب فينسى النكبات والعثرات والغير والدوائر وفحش
تسلط الأيام ولؤم غلبة الدهر فيرسل يده ولسانه
بالفعل والقول وقد قال الأولون منا عند حسن الظن بالأيام
تحدث الغير وقد كان من الملوك من يذكره بعزه الذل وأمنه
الخوف وسروره الكآبة وبطره بالسوقة ولا حزم إلا في
جميعها اعلموا أن الذي أنتم لاقون بعدي هو الذي لقيني من الأمور

وبه

139b

139

زال بذلك الامور حتى قتل تسعين ملكا من ملوك الطوائف بمملكة ايران شهر في مدة
ثلاثين سنة واقام ملكا بعدها اربع عشرة سنة وعشرة اشهر وقيل وستة
اشهر وفي نسخة تسع عشرة سنة وعشرة اشهر وبنى عدة مدن منها
اردشير خرّه وهي مدينة فيروزاباد من ارض فارس وكانت تسمى بكور
وكور وكان اسمان للوهدة والحفرة لا للقبور والحجر فان الفرس لا تعرف
القبور انما كانت تغيب الموتى في النواويس الذي سماها فيروزاباد الامير
عضد الدولة وفي اردشير ايضا مدينة به اردشير وهي من نيابات اجلها
بالعراق وهي احدى مدن المداين السبع قيل لها لما عربت بهرسير وهي
بكرمان يقال لها بردشير وفي ايضا بهمن اردشير وهي على دجلة بارض
ميسان تعرف بهمن شير وبفرات ميسان وفي مدينة استاذا اردشير
وتعرف بكرخ ميسان وفي رام هرمز احدى مدن خوزستان وفي
جستان وعربت فقيل سوق الاهواز وفي ايضا عدة مدن منها مدينة
بناسورها على جثث اهلها لانهم فارقوا طاعته وعصوه فجعل بها في
السور لبنا وبها قاجث القنا وقسم مياه واح اصبهان ومياه
واح خوزستان وكان شعاره مدثّر وسرا وبله اسمانجون وتاجه
اخضر في ذهب وبيده رمح قائم وحكى لي حمزة ان ابو محمد الحسن بن
احمد بن يعقوب في كتابه الاكليل ان اردوانيس نبط الشام والاردوانيس
نبط السواد كان ولما انقطع ملوك اليونانيس وباختت نايرة
حمير حدث اردوان وكان رجلا عاقلا ذا حنكة ودهاء ونجدة
وعلم وحسن تدبير وروية فجمع الجموع وهيا العدة فلما تمت
اليه جموع الفرس واستبد امره اقبل في جموعه حتى نزل دار مملكة
الفرس بالمداين فلما نزل اردوان المداين احسن السيرة واستعمل
على كل كورة رجلا من اشراف الفرس ولم يعرض لاطراف العرب
ولم يتناول شيئا من بلادهم وحاسن اهل الحيرة وهم اعقاب الجند
الذين خلفهم تبع هناك وكانوا اهل ثروة ونجدة وباس وكان

139a

ملكها وعاد الى فارس وسار من ثم الى الاهواز فملكها في مسيره عدة مدائن
وقتل جماعة من الملوك وغنم غنائم كثيرة وحارب اردوان وملك الاردوانيين
فكان يحارب هذا يوما وهذا يوما فاذا كان يوم ملك الاردوانيين لم يقم له اردشير
واذا كان يوم اردوان لم يقم لاردشير فصالح عند ذلك اردشير ملك
الاردوانيين على ان يكف عنه واقبل هو بعد على اردوان على محاربته فلم يلبث
ان قتله واستولى على ما كان له ودخل ملك الاردوانيين في طاعته فسمي حينئذ
ودعي اردشير شاهنشاه ثم مضى في فتح همذان والجبل واذربيجان وارمينية
والموصل وملك سواد العراق وعاد الى اصطخر ثم سار منها فملك سجستان
وجرجان ونيسابور ومرو وبلخ وخوارزم وعاد الى فارس فاتاه رسل
الملوك بالطاعة له ثم سار فملك البحرين وعاد فنزل المداين وتوج ابنه
سابور بتاجه ولم يزل محمود السيرة مظفرا في حروبه منصورا على اعاديه
لا ترد له راية ولا يهزم له جيش وبنى المداين وكور الكور ورتب المراتب
وعمر البلاد وهو الذي جمع كلمة فارس على واحد بعد ما كانوا طوايف لا يدين
منهم ملك لاخر ولما استبد اردشير بالامر وملك العراق كره كثير من تنوخ
المقام في مملكته فخرج من كان منهم من قضاعة الى الشام واذعن له اهل الحيرة
بالطاعة وذكر حمزة ان اردشير لما ظهر تغلب اولا على مدينة اصطخر
وتقوى باهلها فتغلب بهم على من في كور فارس من ملوك الطوائف فلما
استوثق عليها عقد التاج على راسه ثم نظر في امور الناس فراى عدد من
حوله من الملوك كثيرا وحوزة كل ملك منهم قليلة الخطر ضيقة الرقعة ومؤونتهم
على رعيتهم عظيمة فانكر الخلاف العارض في ممالكهم مع اتفاقهم في اصل
دينهم وعلم انه لم يجمعهم على الدين الا الغلبة عليهم فاستخبر من بحضرته
من العلماء عن ذلك فعرفوه ان اوائل ملوكهم ما زال امرهم منتظما لا يتجاوز
المملكة واحد ويجتمع الرعية على طاعته الى ان ملك دارا بن دارا وكان
قتله وتملك الاسكندر ما كان فعلم اردشير انه لا يوصل الى نيل العدل في
ملكهم واحد فانتصب لارسال الكتب الى من بحضرته من ملوك الطوايف وما

138b

138

وكان جده ساسان شجاعا مغرى بالصيد وتزوج امراة من نسل ملوك فارس
وصار قيما على بيت نار باصطخر فلما كبر بابك قام بامره بعد ابيه وولد له ابنه
اردشير فلما بلغ من العمر سبع سنين قدمه ابوه الى ملك اصطخر فنشا عنده
وحسن قيامه بما فوض اليه وحدثه المنجمون بانه يملك وراى في منامه ذلك
فقويت نفسه وكان حازما اريبا كثير الاستشارة طويل الفكر معتمدا في
تدبيره على رجل فاضل من الفرس يعرف بتنسر كان هربذا فلم يزل يدبر امره
ويجمع معه على سياسة الملك الى الطاعة من جاوره من ملوك الطوائف
وعرفوا فضله ودخلوا تحت رايته فحارب من امتنع منهم عليه وكانت له
مكايد وحروب وكان اول ما فعل انه سار من دارابجرد الى موضع يسمى
جوبانان فقتل ملكها ومضى الى موضع اخر فقتل ملكه ثم الى موضع اخر
فقتل ملكه واقام في كل موضع منها قوما من قبله وكتب الى ابيه بابك بامره
ان يثب بملك اصطخر فثار عليه وقتله واخذ تاجه فقام من بعده ابنه وجمع
لحرب اردشير بن بابك فغلبه اردشير وتتوج وجلس على السرير وابتدا
امره بجد وقوة وجعل له وزيرا ورتب موبذ موبذان وقتل عدة من اخوته
وجماعة من اصحابه توهم منهم الفتك به واوقع باهل دارابجرد وقتل جماعة
منهم لعصيانهم عليه ومضى الى كرمان وقاتل ملكها قتالا شديدا حتى غلب عليه
عليها واقام فيها ولدا له وسار الى سواحل بحر فارس وملكها وقتل ملكها
واستخرج اموالا عظيمة وكاتب بقية الملوك يدعوهم الى الطاعة فلم يجيبوه
فسار اليهم وقتلهم وبينا هو كذلك اذ ورد عليه كتاب اردوان فيه انك
عدوت طورك واجتلبت حتفك وانكر عليه لبسه التاج ومحاربته اهل
البلاد وانه قد بعث الى ملك الاهواز ان يحمله اليه في وثاق فكتب اليه ان
الله تعالى قد حباني بالتاج وملكني البلاد وانا ارجو ان يمكنني الله منك
حتى ابعث براسك الى بيت النار الذي اسسته ثم سار نحو اصطخر وخلف
وزيره باردشير خره فلم يلبث الا قليلا حتى اتاه كتاب وزيره بمسير ملك
الاهواز وعوده منكوبا ثم ان اردشير مضى الى اصبهان وملكها وقتل

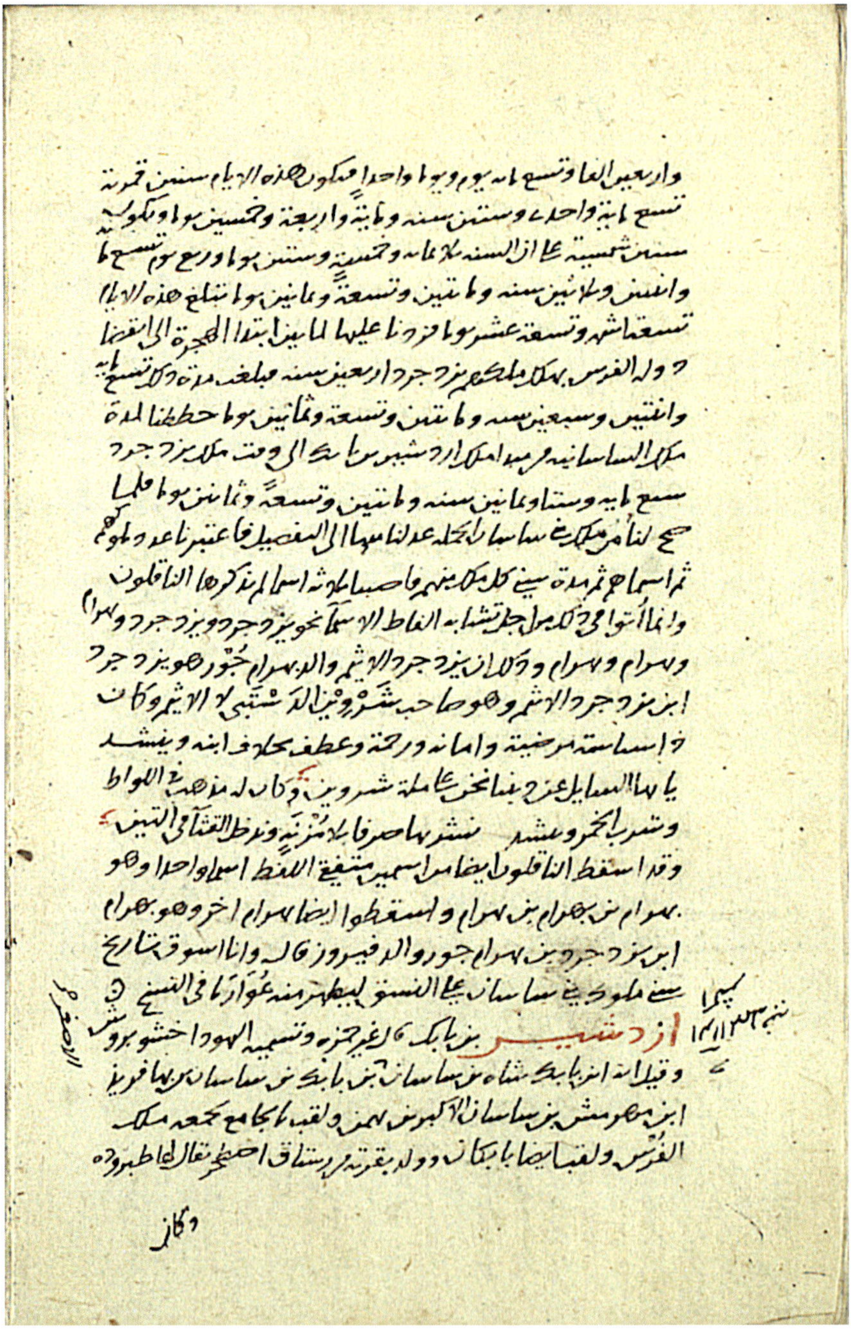

واربعين الفا وتسع مائة يوم ويوما واحدا فيكون هذه الايام سنين قمرية
تسع مائة واحدى وستين سنة ومائة واربعة وخمسين يوما ويكون
سنين شمسية على ان السنة ثلث مائة وخمسة وستين يوما وربع يوم تسع مائة
واثنين وثلاثين سنة ومائتين وتسعة وثمانين يوما فتبلغ هذه الايام
تسعة اشهر وتسعة عشر يوما فزدنا عليها ما بين ابتداء الهجرة الى انقضا
دولة الفرس بهلاك ملكهم يزدجرد اربعين سنة فبلغ مدة ذلك تسع مائة
واثنين وسبعين سنة ومائتين وتسعة وثمانين يوما حططنا المدة
ملك الساسانية من مبدا ملك اردشير بن بابك الى وقت ملك يزدجرد
سبع مائة وستا وثمانين سنة ومائتين وتسعة وثمانين يوما فلما
صح لنا من ملك بني ساسان الجملة عدلنا منها الى التفصيل فاعتبرنا عدد ملوكهم
ثم اسماءهم ثم مدة ملك كل ملك منهم فاصبنا ملوكه اسماء لم يذكرها الناقلون
وانما اتوا في ذلك من جهة تشابه الفاظ الاسماء نحو يزدجرد ويزدجرد وبهرام
وبهرام وبهرام وذلك ان يزدجرد الاثيم والد بهرام جور هو يزدجرد
ابن يزدجرد الاثيم وهو صاحب شروين الدستبى الاثيم وكان
في سياسته مرضية وامانة ورحمة وعطف يخلف فيه ابنه وينشد
يا ايها السائل عن حبينا نحن في ملة شروين وكان له مذهب في اللواط
وشرب الخمر وينشد نشربها صرفا لا مزية ونرط التقامي التيف
وقد اسقط الناقلون ايضا من اسمين متفقي اللفظ اسما واحدا وهو
بهرام بن بهرام بن بهرام واسقطوا ايضا بهرام اخر وهو بهرام
ابن يزدجرد بن بهرام جور والد فيروز فاما الاسوق في تاريخ
ملوك بني ساسان على النسق ليظهر منه عوارها في النسخ
اردشير بن بابك في غير جزء وتسميه الهود اخشو بروش
وقيل انه ابن بابك شاه بن ساسان بن بابك بن ساسان بن بابا فريد
ابن مهرمش بن ساسان الاكبر بن بهمن ولقبه الجامع لجمعه ملك
الفرس ولقبه ايضا بابكان وولد بقرية من رستاق اصطخر يقال لها طيروده

الاصغر

وكان

137

ذكر الطبقة الرابعة من الفرس ويقال لها الساسانية

وهم يرجعون في انسابهم الى ساسان الراعي بن الملك بهمن وكان من
خبره ان اباه بهمن اتخذ ابنته خماني لفراشه كما في ديانة الفرس وكانت
تدعى شهرازاد فولدت منه ولدا اسماه دارا وهو دارا الاكبر بن بهمن
وكانت لما حملت به سالت اباها التزمته حتى عقد له في بطنها التاج وكان ابنه
ساسان بن بهمن رجلا قد تاهل للملك فغضب من عقد ابيه التاج على
بطن خماني لابنها ولحق بمدينة اصطخر وبرهود فر الى رؤوس الجبال
يتعبد فيها واتخذ له غنيمة وتولى امرها بنفسه فشنع الفرس عليه
وقالوا قد صار ساسان راعيا وكانت ام ساسان من بني اسرائيل وهي
راحب بنت شالتيال من الملك ياخين وكان

وعدة ملوك هذه الطبقة الساسانية اربعة وعشرون
ومدة زمان ملوكهم اربع مائة وتسع وسبعون سنة وعشرة اشهر
وثمانية عشر يوما وفي كتاب جملة مدة الطبقة الرابعة وكانوا ثمانية
وعشرين ملكا سوى ثلاثين سنة كانت مدة زمان حروب اردشير بن بابك
مع ملوك الطوائف اربع مائة سنة وست وخمسون سنة وشهر واحد
واثنان وعشرون يوما فجميع ذلك من ابتداء التناسل الى اخر ايام ملك
الفرس وكانوا مائة وستين ملكا اربعة الاف واربع مائة وتسع
سنين وتسعة اشهر وعشرون يوما قال حمزة الاصفهاني في كتاب
اخبار الفرس وفي كتاب قابلنا سني مملكة مملكة الطبقة الثالثة
والطبقة الرابعة من ملوك الفرس الذين ملكوا بعد الاسكندر وهم الاشغانية
والساسانية بتاريخ الاسكندر الذي هو مضبوط فطلبنا ما بين ابتداء
سني الاسكندر الى ابتداء سني الهجرة لنجعله اصلا فوجدنا بين سني
الاسكندر وبين سني الهجرة وذلك من نصف نهار يوم الاثنين اول يوم
من تشرين الاول الى نصف نهار يوم الخميس كذا من المحرم ثلاثمائة الف
اول يوم